A History of Muslims, Christians, and Jews in the Middle East

Across centuries, the Islamic Middle East hosted large populations of Christians and Jews in addition to Muslims. Today, this diversity is mostly absent. In this book, Heather J. Sharkey examines the history that Muslims, Christians, and Jews once shared against the shifting backdrop of state policies. Focusing on the Ottoman Middle East before World War I, Sharkey offers a vivid and lively analysis of everyday social contacts, dress, music, food, bathing, and more, as they brought people together or pushed them apart. Historically, Islamic traditions of statecraft and law, which the Ottoman Empire maintained and adapted, treated Christians and Jews as protected subordinates to Muslims while prescribing limits to social mixing. Sharkey shows how, amid the pivotal changes of the modern era, efforts to simultaneously preserve and dismantle these hierarchies heightened tensions along religious lines and set the stage for the twentieth-century Middle East.

Heather J. Sharkey is an associate professor in the Department of Near Eastern Languages and Civilizations at the University of Pennsylvania. She is the author of *Living with Colonialism: Nationalism and Culture in the Anglo-Egyptian Sudan* (2003) and *American Evangelicals in Egypt: Missionary Encounters in an Age of Empire* (2008).

T0371366

The Contemporary Middle East

Series editor
Beth Baron, *The Graduate Center, The City University of New York*

Books published in **The Contemporary Middle East** series address the major political, economic, and social debates facing the region today. Each title comprises a survey of the available literature against the background of the author's own critical interpretation, designed to challenge and encourage independent analysis. While the focus of the series is the Middle East and North Africa, books are presented as aspects of a rounded treatment, which cut across disciplinary and geographic boundaries. They are intended to initiate debate in the classroom and to foster understanding amongst professionals and policy-makers.

Books in this Series:

1 Clement Moore Henry and Robert Springborg, *Globalization and the Politics of Development in the Middle East* (First Edition, 2001: Second Edition, 2010)
2 Joel Beinin, *Workers and Peasants in the Modern Middle East*
3 Zachary Lockman, *Contending Visions of the Middle East: The History and Politics of Orientalism* (First Edition, 2004: Second Edition, 2009)
4 Fred Halliday, *The Middle East in International Relations: Power, Politics and Ideology*
5 Dawn Chatty, *Displacement and Dispossession in the Modern Middle East*
6 Heather J. Sharkey, *A History of Muslims, Christians, and Jews in the Middle East*

A History of Muslims, Christians, and Jews in the Middle East

Heather J. Sharkey
University of Pennsylvania

CAMBRIDGE
UNIVERSITY PRESS

CAMBRIDGE
UNIVERSITY PRESS

University Printing House, Cambridge CB2 8BS, United Kingdom

One Liberty Plaza, 20th Floor, New York, NY 10006, USA

477 Williamstown Road, Port Melbourne, VIC 3207, Australia

314–321, 3rd Floor, Plot 3, Splendor Forum, Jasola District Centre, New Delhi – 110025, India

79 Anson Road, #06-04/06, Singapore 079906

Cambridge University Press is part of the University of Cambridge.

It furthers the University's mission by disseminating knowledge in the pursuit of education, learning, and research at the highest international levels of excellence.

www.cambridge.org
Information on this title: www.cambridge.org/9780521186872
DOI: 10.1017/9781139028455

First published 2017
3rd printing 2018

Printed and bound in Great Britain by Clays Ltd, Elcograf S.p.A.

A catalogue record for this publication is available from the British Library.

ISBN 978-0-521-76937-2 Hardback
ISBN 978-0-521-18687-2 Paperback

For Ravi, Aruna, and Vijay

Contents

Illustrations		*page* x
Acknowledgments		xiii
1	Muslims, Christians, and Jews in the Middle East	1
2	The Islamic Foundations of Intercommunal Relations	27
3	The Ottoman Experience	64
4	The Ottoman Empire in an Age of Reform: From Sultan Mahmud II to the End of the Tanzimat Era, 1808–1876	115
5	The Pivotal Era of Abdulhamid II, 1876–1909	179
6	Coming Together, Moving Apart: Ottoman Muslims, Christians, and Jews at the Turn of the Century	243
	Epilogue	301
	Bibliography	325
	Index	361

Illustrations

Cover image "Intérieur de la porte de Jaffa," by Felix Bonfils, albumen photograph, post-1898. Courtesy of the Library at the Herbert D. Katz Center for Advanced Judaic Studies, University of Pennsylvania. The Lenkin Family Collection of Photography.

1 *Massacres d'Arménie: Arméniens égorgés à Ak-Hissar*, c. 1895–96, by Chocolaterie d'Aiguebelle (Drôme, France). Chromolithographic chocolate card. Kislak Center for Special Collections, Rare Books and Manuscripts, University of Pennsylvania Libraries. Caption on reverse states that the image depicts Armenians massacred by Circassians in the market at Ak-Hissar, in the Vilayet of Ismidt, on October 3, 1895   *page* 5

2 "Guard turc à la porte de St. Sepulchre" (Turkish Guard at the Gate of the Church of the Holy Sepulchre, Jerusalem), c. 1885–1901, Bonfils Collection, Image Number 165914. Courtesy of the Penn Museum   9

3 *Napoleon in Egypt*, 1867–68. Oil on wood panel, 35.8 × 25.0 cm. Princeton University Art Museum. Museum purchase, John Maclean Magie, Class of 1892, and Gertrude Magie Fund, 1953–78   13

4 The Palmer Cup, wine goblet with Arabic inscription, Islamic, c. 1200–1250. Museum Number WB.53. ©The Trustees of the British Museum   43

5 *Marriage Contract of Zein, Daughter of R. Aaron Ha-Mumheh (The Expert)*, Fustat, Egypt, c. 1080–1114. Judeo-Arabic manuscript on parchment. Courtesy of the Library at the Herbert D. Katz Center for Advanced Judaic Studies, University of Pennsylvania. Cairo Genizah Collection, Halper 333   45

6 "Chorbadgi en cérémonie" (Janissary colonel in
   ceremonial dress), watercolor painting on paper, 1790.
   Museum Number 1974,0617,0.12.1.85. ©The Trustees of
   the British Museum   68
7 Vermeer, Johannes (1632–75). *A Maid Asleep.* 1656–57.
   Oil on canvas, 34 1/2 × 30 1/8 in. (87.6 × 76.5 cm).
   Bequest of Benjamin Altman, 1913 (14.40.611). The
   Metropolitan Museum of Art. Image copyright
   ©The Metropolitan Museum of Art. Image source:
   Art Resource, NY   71
8 Opaque watercolor and ink on paper showing a Bekci, or
   Ottoman night watchman, carrying a club and a lantern,
   including pink and yellow tulip cut-outs on either side.
   Folio from an album titled "A briefe relation of the
   Turckes, their kings, Emperors, or Grandsigneurs, their
   conquests, religion, customes, habbits, etc," Istanbul,
   1618. Museum Number 1974,0617,0.13.32.
   ©The Trustees of the British Museum   90
9 Nineteenth-century bath clogs, wood with leather strap
   covered in metallic thread, Ottoman Empire. Museum
   Number 2013,6008.1.a-b. ©The Trustees of the British
   Museum   92
10 Excavations of the Nippur Temple Court, photograph
    by John Henry Haynes, 1893. Image Number 185157.
    Courtesy of the Penn Museum   120
11 "Femmes juives en costume de sortie" (Jewish women in
    outdoor clothes), c. 1876–85, Bonfils Collection, Image
    Number 165856. Courtesy of the Penn Museum   133
12 *At the Mosque Door*, oil painting by Osman Hamdi Bey,
    1891, Image Number 184892. Courtesy of the Penn
    Museum   195
13 "Cawas et employé du consulat de France" (Guard and
    employee at the French consulate), c. 1885–1901, Bonfils
    Collection, Image Number 165926. Courtesy of the Penn
    Museum   214
14 *Students, imperial military middle school*, Halep [Aleppo],
    c. 1890–93. Albumen photographic print by Abdullah
    Frères. Library of Congress, Washington, DC. Abdul
    Hamid II Collection   226
15 *Interior of the Imperial Fez Factory*, c. 1890–1983.
    Albumen photographic print by Abdullah Frères.

Library of Congress, Washington, DC. Abdul Hamid II
Collection   244

16 "Jeune arménienne" (Young Armenian woman),
c. 1876–85, Zangaki Brothers Collection, Image Number
291176. Courtesy of the Penn Museum   275

17 *Armenian Widows, with Children, Turkey*, near Adana, April
or May 1909. Glass negative by Bain News Service.
Library of Congress, Washington, DC. George Grantham
Bain Collection   280

18 Oud, North African, twentieth century (signed
Casablanca, 1944, Hassan Ben Bou Chaïb), Yale
University Collection of Musical Instruments, Gift of
Theodore Woolsey Heermance. Accession No. 4550.
Photography credit: Alex Contreras   309

19 Bath clogs, wood with velvet and silver
metal, nineteenth century. Museum Number
2013,6033.2.a-b. © The Trustees of the British Museum.
The curator's comments in the British Museum's online
catalogue trace these clogs to an Armenian woman whose
family settled in Aleppo, Syria, after 1915 and whose
grandmother had received them for her wedding trousseau   312

20 "Ferblantier juif à Jerusalem" (Jewish tinsmith in
Jerusalem), c. 1876–85, Bonfils Collection, Image
Number 165858. Courtesy of the Penn Museum   315

21 Glazed ceramic dish fragment, Islamic, Egypt,
c. 700–1299 AD. Object Number 29-140-11.
Courtesy of the Penn Museum   320

Acknowledgments

Writing this book has entailed a process of "un-learning" that has been nearly as significant as the process of learning anew. When I was an undergraduate in a history class at Yale, I read Bernard Lewis's book *The Emergence of Modern Turkey*. Naïve, I came away convinced that the Ottoman Tanzimat decrees of 1839 and 1856 had "declared" religious equality – that the sultan had made equality happen by fiat. By the time I was a PhD student at Princeton, I realized that the changes of the nineteenth century had been much more protracted, partial, and complicated. And yet, there was no book that described this process. By writing this book, now with my students at the University of Pennsylvania in mind, I have tried to explain how religious communities worked in practice in the Ottoman Empire, while tracing the relationship between official state policies, popular attitudes, and daily life as it unfolded among people on the ground. I have also tried to write in clear language, while approaching a delicate subject with sympathy. I hope that this volume, which covers up to World War I, will enable a broad range of readers to appreciate more fully the cultural foundations for twentieth and early twenty-first-century Middle Eastern states and societies.

I have many thanks to convey. Thanks, first, to my students at the University of Pennsylvania, who in 2004 inspired me to offer the mixed undergraduate and graduate-student seminar, "Muslim, Christian, and Jewish Relations in the Modern Middle East," which launched this book. In Fall 2014 and Spring 2015, students read draft chapters in two seminars, and their enthusiastic reactions propelled me into the final stretches of writing.

Just as decisive was a collaborative project that began in 2004 with three colleagues from the Penn Libraries: Arthur Kiron (curator of Judaica collections), William Kopycki (then Middle East Studies librarian), and Debra Bucher (then Religious Studies librarian). They helped me to develop a research portal on the web for students conducting independent research on the history of Muslim, Christian, and Jewish relations.

A small grant from a program at Penn called PRRUCS – the Program for Research on Religion and Urban Civil Society (which was supported, in turn, by the Pew Charitable Trusts) – boosted this effort. William Kopycki subsequently left Penn to head the Library of Congress's field office in Cairo, Debra Bucher left for Vassar College, but Arthur Kiron (thankfully!) stayed. Arthur offered unstinting support in my efforts to connect Muslim, Christian, and Jewish histories via scholarship and teaching.

Marigold Acland, former Middle East acquisitions editor of Cambridge University Press, saw the website for my seminar and invited me to write this book. Shortly afterward, Eugene Rogan read my proposal and helped me to strengthen it. Eugene also gave encouragement and sage advice chapter by chapter – and for this, I remain profoundly grateful. Maria Marsh at Cambridge offered upbeat support and de facto "pep talks" by email. The anonymous referees offered valuable insights, both for the initial proposal and for the final clearance review. John O. Voll, who later identified himself as one of these referees, has been an informal behind-the-scenes mentor since my graduate school days, and I am very grateful.

Bernard Heyberger welcomed me as a visiting professor at the Institut d'études de l'Islam et des sociétés du monde musulman (IISMM) of the École des Hautes Études en Sciences Sociales (EHESS) in Paris during the 2012–13 year. I therefore had the pleasure and privilege of writing a large part of this book in Paris. The talk that I gave in Bernard's seminar, which he offers annually on "the historical anthropology of Christians in the Islamic world," proved critical to sharpening the ideas in this book. Critical, too, were multiple conversations with Bernard, who has become a friend. I am indebted, more broadly, to the government of France, which provided the funds that enabled my Parisian sojourn, and to other scholars in France who made my stay congenial, especially Chantal Verdeil, Elena Vezzadini, Iris Seri-Hersch, and Barbara Casciarri.

The Penn Humanities Forum (PHF) also gave me a boost. I presented the first chapter of the book at the forum in Spring 2010, during the theme year on "Connections" led by Wendy Steiner and Peter Conn. As a discussant of my first draft chapter, Jeffrey Green offered insights and suggestions that helped to clear my path moving forward. At the University of Pennsylvania, another major turning point came in Summer 2015, when I joined the Faculty Writing Retreat jointly sponsored by Penn's School of Arts and Sciences and Graduate School of Education. From nine to five for one week in June, the retreat glued me to a chair in a rooftop lounge with a view of Philadelphia's skyline, and enabled me to focus with colleagues who were similarly grappling with writing. In Spring 2016, Penn's School of Arts and Sciences awarded me a teaching leave to finish the manuscript along with a small grant from the Dean's Weiler Fund.

Many others read and gave critical feedback on portions of the draft. Those who read chapters include Kathleen Cann, Ellen Fleischmann, Betty S. Anderson, T. R. and Jaya Balasubramanian, Richard Sharkey, Mina Khalil, and Daniel Cheely. Alon Tam gave especially detailed and helpful feedback on the entire manuscript. Alessandro ("Alex") Pezzati in the Penn Museum archives, David Giovacchini (Penn's late Middle East studies librarian), Bruce Nielsen (Judaica Public Services Librarian at the Katz Center for Advanced Judaic Studies), and John Pollack (Library Specialist in the Kislak Center, Rare Books and Manuscripts division) helped me to gain access to Penn's special collections. Colleagues at the City University of New York (CUNY) Graduate Center, Vanderbilt Divinity School, and Yale invited me to give guest lectures on the book – opportunities that elicited constructive feedback from audiences. Friends and relatives motivated me by asking at regular intervals about the book's progress. Debi Hoffman and the Hoffman family of Aspen, Antoine Chambaz and *la famille* Chambaz of Paris, and Phil Nelson (who was in the throes of writing his own book, on biological physics) fall into this category. So do my parents-in-law, T. R. and Jaya Balasubramanian, who cheered me along the way.

I have never met Helen Sword of the University of Auckland, but want to thank her, anyway. Her book *Stylish Academic Writing* (Harvard University Press, 2012) and her online tool called "The Writer's Diet" pushed me to prune my drafts. "The Writer's Diet" made me compete against myself, to shrink my verbiage from the occasionally "flabby" to "fit and thin," or even – joy! – to "lean."

Others helped me in the final stages of the manuscript's preparation. I am grateful to Claire Sissen and James Gregory at Cambridge University Press; Siva Prakash Chandrasekaran at Newgen in Madras; and Kathleen Paparchontis. Others helped me to secure illustrations for this book: Beatriz Waters, at British Museum Images; Susan E. Thompson, curator of the Yale University Collection of Musical Instruments; Cathryn L. Goodwin at Princeton University Art Museum; and Robbi Siegel at Art Resource, Inc. Alex Pezzati, again, was especially helpful in providing me with access to archived photographic collections in the Penn Museum.

I owe thanks, too, to many places – especially libraries and cafés – which gave me room to think, read, write, and most of all rewrite, with the reassuring hum of other people doing stuff in the background. Congenial libraries included those of the Aspen Center for Physics in Bethe Hall, with its view of aspen leaves swaying in the breeze; Pitkin County Library, also in Aspen, with its tempting collection of novels on the second floor; the Kavli Institute for Theoretical Physics in Kohn Hall, with its views of the sunny Santa Barbara coastline; and the Fondation Maison des sciences de l'homme, overlooking the Quai de la Gare and the drizzle of Paris. The congeniality of certain cafés was equally critical. Thanks to several Philadelphia venues, above all, Good Karma (both the 10th Street and Walnut Bridge locations); Lovers and Madmen, later the Green Line Café (36th Street); Volo (Manayunk), and Starbucks (Manayunk). Ink! (Aspen) was a site of revision and inspiration. I feel the greatest café debt, however, to Coffee Cat on Anacapa Street in Santa Barbara, which is where I had my final epiphany: the moment when the end of the book appeared before me. Finally, among places that hosted me, I have especially warm memories of the second floor of Rotonde 12 of the Résidence Jussieu, and to the desk that gave me a bird's-eye view of the Institut du Monde Arabe and the Seine.

My children, Ravi and Aruna, grew from toddlers to teens during the time that it took me to conceive, write, and finish the book. They made life dash, with every day a privilege.

Throughout this time my husband, Vijay, remained my steady side-kick, sounding board, valued critic, cheerleader, and cajoler extraordinaire. I dedicate the book to the three of them, with boundless love and thanks.

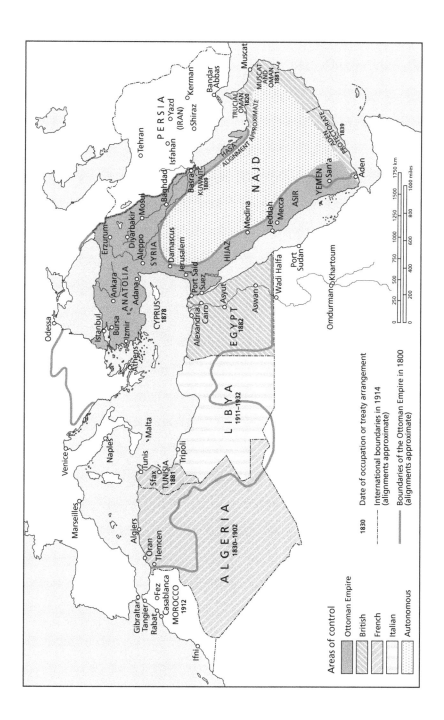

Areas of control

Ottoman Empire

British

French

Italian

Autonomous

1830   Date of occupation or treaty arrangement

---   International boundaries in 1914 (alignments approximate)

———   Boundaries of the Ottoman Empire in 1800 (alignments approximate)

PERSIA (IRAN)

NAJD

ANATOLIA

SYRIA

HIJAZ

YEMEN

ASIR

EGYPT 1882

LIBYA 1911–1932

ALGERIA 1830–1902

TUNISIA 1881

MOROCCO 1912

CYPRUS 1878

MUSCAT AND OMAN 1881

TRUCIAL OMAN 1820

ADEN PROTECTORATE 1839

HASA

KUWAIT 1809

ALIGNMENT APPROXIMATE

Muscat
Bandar Abbas
Kerman
Yazd
Shiraz
Isfahan
Tehran
Baghdad
Mosul
Basra
Erzurum
Diyarbakir
Aleppo
Damascus
Jerusalem
Ankara
Bursa
Izmir
Istanbul
Athens
Adana
Port Said
Suez
Alexandria
Cairo
Asyut
Aswan
Wadi Halfa
Port Sudan
Omdurman
Khartoum
Medina
Jeddah
Mecca
San'a
Aden
Odessa
Venice
Naples
Marseilles
Malta
Tunis
Sfax
Tripoli
Algiers
Oran
Tlemcen
Fez
Casablanca
Rabat
Tangier
Gibraltar
Ifni

0   250   500   750   1000   1250   1500   1750 km
0   200   400   600   800   1000 miles

1   Muslims, Christians, and Jews in the Middle East

Overview

When the twentieth century opened, Muslims, Christians, and Jews inhabited shared worlds in the region that stretches across North Africa and through western Asia. They held in common daily experiences, attitudes, and languages – even foods that they cooked and ate.[1] They rubbed shoulders in villages, city neighborhoods, and apartment buildings, and crossed paths in shops and markets.[2] In the history that this book examines – a history that goes roughly up to the start of World War I in 1914 – these contacts were on wide display.

The richness and depth of this shared history was no longer apparent as the twentieth century ended and the twenty-first century began. Indigenous or permanent resident communities of Jews and Christians had dwindled, following the impact of wars, decolonization movements, and the politics of the Arab-Israeli conflict, all of which propelled waves of migration. The Islamic societies of the Middle East were more solidly Muslim than ever before in history.

During the twentieth century, Jews dispersed almost completely from Arabic-speaking domains. By 2014, for example, the Jewish population of Egypt numbered just forty or so people[3] – a steep drop for a community that, at its peak during the 1920s and 1930s, had included some 75,000–85,000 members, many with deep roots in the land of the Nile.[4] In Libya, not a single Jew remained by 2000.[5] In Turkey, whose territory was once a haven for Jews fleeing the Iberian peninsula in the wake of the Reconquista, just eighteen thousand remained in 2012.[6] At the beginning of the twenty-first century, the largest Jewish population living within an Islamic polity may have been in Iran, a theocratic republic that justified its official tolerance for non-Muslims on readings of the Qur'an. Iranian government census data from 2012 only counted about nine thousand Jews, but outside observers estimated that Iran may have actually hosted a Jewish population that was closer to twenty-five thousand.[7] The striking exception to this pattern of Jewish diminution was Israel, whose mid-twentieth-century creation provided a haven for Jews around the world but at the same time uprooted several hundred thousands of Arabic-speaking Muslims, together with a proportionally smaller number of Christians, who became known as Palestinians.[8]

During the twentieth century, Middle Eastern Christian populations also diminished. In Egypt, Lebanon, Jordan, and Syria, historic Christian communities persisted but dwindled as a proportion of the population.[9] A dramatic version of this shrinkage occurred in the territory that became the British mandate of Palestine, where in 1900 Christians had comprised perhaps 16 percent of the population. A century later they accounted for less than 2 percent in Israel, the West Bank, and Gaza – a demographic shift that resulted from voluntary migration, displacement, and probably also lower birthrates.[10] Twentieth-century change was even more extreme in Anatolia, a territory that belonged to the Ottoman Empire until the empire's demise after World War I, but then became the heart of the Republic of Turkey. Approximately two million Christian Armenians were living in Anatolia in 1915, when Muslim Turks, Kurds, and *muhajirs* (the latter Muslim refugees from Russian imperial expansion in the Caucasus) carried out a series of massacres and forced marches that nearly annihilated them.[11] Today, only about sixty thousand Armenians remain in Turkey as citizens, while the Turkish population as a whole is 99 percent Muslim.[12]

As the twenty-first century opened, many Christian churches, monasteries, and other landmarks – in Israel, the West Bank of Palestine, Turkey, and parts of Jordan – had lost the local Christian populations that once sustained them. One scholar remarked that these Christian sites ran the risk of becoming theme parks for Western tourists, and thereby cash cows for Middle Eastern governments eager to boost their tourist revenues.[13] In Syria and Iraq, meanwhile, civil wars prompted Christians to flee abroad disproportionately even as one-third of Syrians – Muslims and Christians alike – became refugees by 2016.[14] And while economically motivated migration from Asia and Africa added diversity to Middle Eastern populations (with workers from Muslim, Christian, Hindu, Buddhist, and other backgrounds arriving in countries such as Saudi Arabia, the United Arab Emirates, and Israel), migrants tended to be short-term guest workers.[15] Throughout the Middle East, permanent resident and citizen populations had become more homogeneous in religion.

Locally rooted Jewish populations have vanished throughout most of the Middle East, vast numbers of Muslim Palestinians have lost their place in the "Holy Land," and Christians in the region have experienced an attrition that one observer called a "never-ending exodus."[16] So then why bother to tell a history of contact among Muslims, Christians, and Jews as this book does, by studying the Middle East before World War I? Why focus on community – even comity – rather than on conflict, rupture, and trauma?

Looking back on the expanse of Islamic history, many historians have argued that Islamic states, with few exceptions across the centuries, tolerated cultural diversity and promoted stability so that Muslims, Christians, and Jews were able to persist, coexist, and often flourish together. Islamic civilization, thus understood, was a collaborative and amicable enterprise. Other historians, however, have emphasized violence and tyranny as leitmotifs of Islamic statehood, arguing that non-Muslims fared especially badly during long periods of political decline, however one dates them. In interpretations of the twentieth century, an emphasis on repression persisted, with critics pointing to cases such as the Armenian massacres (1915), the Arab-Israeli conflict (1948–present), and the Lebanese Civil War (1975–c. 1990) to emphasize a Middle Eastern propensity for a kind of political violence that drew on religious antipathies.

The long history of intercommunal relations in the Islamic Middle East may never have seen a "golden age," but neither was it a saga of perpetual crisis. A sober look at history suggests that, in most times and places, relations between communities were, as one might say in colloquial Egyptian Arabic, *kwayyis* ("pretty good" or "okay"); Muslims, Christians, and Jews simply persisted in proximity. Daily lives were the sum of getting by – the quotidian with an admixture of tension and rapport. When the twenty-first century started, this picture of the unsensational in Middle Eastern intercommunal relations did not prevail in Europe and North America. Instead, the more common notion was that the history of intercommunal relations in the Middle East reflected what one may call a "banality of violence," with routine, even absentminded, religious conflict assumed as the normal way of life.[17]

In an essay collection titled *Imaginary Homelands*, the novelist Salman Rushdie (b. 1947) suggested not only that "description is itself a political act" but also that "redescribing a world is the necessary first step towards changing it."[18] Certainly redescribing a lapsed world may offer a way of living with the past, in the sense of putting up with it, recovering from it, and coming to terms through a *modus vivendi*. This redescribing involves choice and selection – what the philosopher Paul Ricoeur characterized as an active searching for the past, a going out and doing something, in the perpetual sifting of history for meaning.[19]

In sifting through the past, this book offers an alternative to the "banal violence" interpretation of the Middle East by reclaiming the history of the mundane in social contacts that wove the fabric of everyday life. It analyzes the complex roles of religion within Middle Eastern societies. And it studies the tension between individuals and collectives vis-à-vis religious identity. There are two reasons for focusing on this tension. First, people are quirky, so that what one Muslim, Christian, or Jewish person did in a particular place or time may not have typified Muslim, Christian, or Jewish behavior collectively. Second, and increasingly in the modern era, Islamic states in the region struggled to classify and treat people as members of religious collectives, in accordance with Islamic law and tradition, while respecting the needs, responsibilities, and aspirations of people when they were thinking, speaking, and acting on their own, as individuals.

I will now elaborate on the idea of the history of the mundane and consider the spatial scope and timescale for this study. After explaining the book's approaches and assumptions, I will present the book's arguments in a nutshell.

Picturing the Mundane

Sometime around 1900, a chocolate company called D'Aiguebelle, operated by Trappist monks in Drôme (southern France), published a series of chromolithographic cards with explanatory texts on their backs. These purported to show and tell the story of Turkish, Kurdish, and Circassian atrocities perpetrated against Greeks and Armenians in the 1890s.[20] If the images alone failed to convey the story of Muslim-Christian conflict, then the captions on the reverse were explicit. One card shows the "Pillage of the Monastery of Hassankale and the Murder of the Patriarch": there in the picture rests the patriarch, at that moment still living but fallen and bloodied near the altar, as Muslims carry off loot. The caption on the reverse explains that on November 28, 1895, "Musulman" marauders burned, pillaged, and murdered their way through the district where the monastery was located; the marauders spared only three villages out of forty, and forced survivors to convert to Islam. Equally evocative from D'Aiguebelle's chocolate cards are those illustrating the decapitation of Greek insurgents in Crete, the dragging of Armenian corpses through the streets of Galata in Istanbul, and the sale of Armenian captives as slaves. The last two cards presented atrocities against Armenians twenty years before the events of 1915, which survivors and their heirs later remembered as the Armenian Genocide.

How did these particular images shape public opinion among French chocolate lovers in the late 1890s – people who came to possess chocolate cards depicting bucolic scenes, masterpieces of medieval Christian

Image 1 *Massacres d'Arménie: Arméniens égorgés à Ak-Hissar,* c. 1895–96, by Chocolaterie d'Aiguebelle (Drôme, France). Chromolithographic chocolate card. Kislak Center for Special Collections, Rare Books and Manuscripts, University of Pennsylvania Libraries. Caption on the reverse states that the image depicts Armenians massacred by Circassians in the market at Ak-Hissar, in the Vilayet of Ismidt, on October 3, 1895.

art, French monarchs and their castles, maps of the French Empire, and so forth?[21] For the person nibbling on chocolate, and considering the cards that came in its wrappers, the images may have reinforced the notion that in the Ottoman Islamic world, outrageous sectarian violence between Muslims and Christians was common to the point of mundane. These cards, which as a "democratic art" were items that many schoolchildren collected and traded,[22] broadcast news in western Europe about grim conditions for Christian Greeks and Armenians farther east. (Certainly the D'Aiguebelle monks regarded them as vehicles for promoting a "Christian conscience" and social "catechism," particularly among children, who were their target audience.[23]) Like the French picture postcards of the same period, which presented studio-staged fantasy portraits of seminaked (but still head-veiled) Algerian Muslim women, these D'Aiguebelle chocolate cards advanced fantasies and stereotypes about the peoples of the "Orient."[24] As humble as they were, the chocolate cards wielded power and contributed to the waging of discursive wars that recall the social critic Susan Sontag's famous essay on photography, the "ethics of seeing," and the role of the shooting camera as a weapon.[25]

If anything, popular European and North American associations of the Middle East with banal religious violence have become stronger than they were a century ago, as a quick survey can show. In 1993, the political scientist Samuel T. Huntington (1927–2008) published an article in the journal *Foreign Affairs*, in which he speculated on global trends in the post–Cold War era. "World politics is entering a new phase," he claimed. Henceforth, among humankind, "the dominating source of conflict will be cultural ... [and] will occur between nations and groups of different civilizations." Huntington foresaw a "clash of civilizations" in which some would be more prone to violence than others. He predicted special problems "along the boundaries of the crescent-shaped Islamic bloc of nations from the bulge of Africa to central Asia," and concluded, "Islam has bloody borders."[26] Huntington was not the first to describe a "clash of civilizations" between a "Christian West" and "Islamic East."[27] Certainly his portrayal of Islam's "bloody borders" tapped into a deep discursive history that stretched at least as far back as 1095, when the Roman Catholic pope, Urban II (1042–99), issued his call for a crusade. Nevertheless, the "clash of civilizations" became Huntington's trademark, while ensuing events led many observers in news outlets and blogs to describe his prognosis as "prophetic" (as even the most casual internet search makes abundantly clear).

In the 1990s, around the time that Huntington published his article, Sunni Muslim extremist groups were becoming increasingly strident in their endorsement and pursuit of violent jihad. Some of these groups, consisting of Bosnian Muslim fighters and Arab Muslim volunteers, had begun to prove their mettle in the Balkan or Yugoslav Wars (1991–c. 2001), which sharpened regional, ethnic, and religious lines of distinction.[28] In 1998, Osama bin Laden (1957–2011) tried to stake out a leadership position at the forefront of international jihadists, by declaring a "World Islamic Front" dedicated to "jihad against Jews and Crusaders." It was the duty of every Muslim everywhere, bin Laden asserted, "to kill the Americans and their allies – civilians and military – ... in any country in which it is possible to do it."[29] The goal, he declared, was to liberate Jerusalem's al-Aqsa mosque (and by extension, the land of Palestine from Israeli Jewish control) and the Great Mosque of Mecca. The latter goal contained an oblique reference either to American troops, who had arrived in Saudi territory in the wake of Iraq's invasion of Kuwait in 1990, or to the ruling house of Sa'ud, which controlled the holy sites of early Islam in western Arabia.

The subsequent terrorist attacks of September 11, 2001, exceeded the worst expectations of the most pessimistic political analysts. In the wake of this tragedy, American scholars produced a vast literature on the themes of "what we did wrong" (entailing a critique of Western imperialism and cultural hegemony in the Middle East), "where they went wrong" (suggesting a generalized Muslim failure to construct stable and progressive Islamic societies in the modern age), and "what Islam really is" (attempting to dismantle popular stereotypes among non-Muslims that have associated Islam with terrorism and violence).[30] Meanwhile, bin Laden's "world front" expanded but atomized, and developed "franchises," to use the commonly invoked marketing term that made Al-Qaeda sound like a fast-food chain. Al-Qaeda's ostensible affiliates went on to stage attacks on civilians in a variety of places and venues: a synagogue in Tunisia (2002), a nightclub in Bali (2002), subways in Madrid (2004), and London (2005), and more.

In the aftermath of the September 11 attacks, the US government and some of its allies launched wars in Afghanistan (Al-Qaeda's training ground) and Iraq (where 9/11 offered a pretext for unseating a brutal dictator who had played no role in the attacks). The US invasion of Iraq triggered, in turn, an Iraqi civil war, as ethnic and sectarian groups and factions jockeyed for power. In the seven years following the US invasion, many Iraqi civilians died amidst violence – perhaps one hundred thousand people[31] – the vast majority of them Muslims (representing both the Sunni and Shi'i sects of Islam). Unknown numbers died or led diminished lives as a result of the auxiliary phenomena of war, such as damaged medical infrastructures and psychological traumas.

During the first decade of the twenty-first century, western Europe witnessed a rising tide of Islamophobia and anti-Muslim-immigrant sentiment as some politicians and pundits questioned the ability of immigrants to assimilate into liberal host societies. Among questions asked were these: Could a woman wear a *burka* or *niqab*, thus covering her face, and still be French? What about a girl in a French government school? And if such a female was not French-born, was she worthy of receiving citizenship in France? (In a case that received considerable attention in 2008, the French government answered this last question with a *"non."*[32]) An even more sensational episode occurred in Denmark in 2005, when a newspaper published a set of editorial cartoons lampooning the Prophet Muhammad. Many Muslims around the world took grave offense and staged protests. But many Danes, non-Muslims, and liberal Muslims took offense, too, resenting efforts to curb free expression, and viewing protests as another iteration of banal violence by Muslim conservatives.[33] In early 2015, local militants claiming an affiliation with a Yemeni branch of Al-Qaeda staged an attack in Paris on the French newspaper *Charlie Hebdo*, which had also published satirical portrayals of the Prophet Muhammad and Islam, and in a coordinated attack, slaughtered shoppers at a kosher grocery in the city. These events confirmed popular fears in the West about Muslim anti-Jewish sentiment and suppression of free speech, while seeding anti-Muslim xenophobia.

Other crises that appeared to have some religious dimension – for example, between the Israeli government and the Palestinians, between the Russian government and Chechens in Chechnya – persisted in the background, riveting Muslim viewers throughout the world via satellite television.[34] Meanwhile, amidst the Syrian Civil War which erupted in 2011, a jihadist insurgency group, which had already established a foothold in Iraq after the US invasion of 2003, seized control over parts of Syria after that country's descent into chaos. Outsiders tended to call this entity by various acronyms, such as ISIS (Islamic State of Iraq and Syria) and *Da'ish* (based on the acronym of the group's name in Arabic). Claiming to lead a revived caliphate in the parts of Syria and Iraq that it controlled, supporters of this group engaged in egregious acts of violence against Muslim opponents, Christians, Jews, Yezidis, and others, and spawned copycat affiliates in places like Libya. Meanwhile, Da'ish sympathizers in western Europe perpetrated outrageous acts of mass murder, killing scores in Paris and Brussels during attacks in 2015 and 2016 that targeted people in cafés, a music hall, an airport and metro station, and other venues of everyday life.

New violence, meanwhile, begat memories of old violence. In 2013, as one of his first deeds as pope of the Roman Catholic Church, Francis (born 1936 as Jorge Mario Bergoglio) canonized the 813 "martyrs of Otranto" who had reportedly died at the hands of Ottoman forces in 1480 when they refused to convert to Islam. In doing so, he completed the canonization process that his immediate predecessor, Benedict XIV, had started, building, in turn, upon an initiative that Pope Clement XIV had opened in 1771.[35] The canonization of the Otranto martyrs suggested the importance of persistent memories of jihads, crusades, and mutual martyrdom in imagined, and continually reconfigured, histories of Muslim-Christian relations.

Conflict between communities in the Middle East is easy to imagine when stories and images of animosity abound in books, on the news, and in other popular media. But what does it look like for communities to share history, and to spend decades in a state of proximity characterized by relative quiet? What method can one use to gain access to the un-sensational, the un-newsworthy, and the day-to-day familiar, before capturing it in words?

Image 2 "Guard turc à la porte de St. Sepulchre" (Turkish Guard at the Gate of the Church of the Holy Sepulchre, Jerusalem), c. 1885–1901, Bonfils Collection, Image Number 165914. Courtesy of the Penn Museum.

The method used here is to draw not only on history books, but also memoirs, cookbooks, novels, anthologies, ethnographies, films, and musical recordings, which can offer insights into cultures of contact. However impressionistically, such sources can yield insights into the history and anthropology of the senses – the sounds, tastes, touches, and smells that have added up to shared experience.[36] One can find evidence for contact and affinity, for example, in shared Arabic songs and stories, sung or recounted by Muslims, Christians, and Jews;[37] in the remembered smell of jasmine blossoms, threaded and sold on strings after dusk; in "recollections of food" that "have been wedged into the emotional landscape,"[38] like a particular bread sold on street carts during

Ramadan;[39] even affection for the same bumps in the road (a sentiment that one young Jewish woman expressed to a documentary filmmaker, as she moved through Tehran in a car).[40] Then, too, there are common sights, spaces, and places – rivers, monuments, landmarks, humble abodes, cafés. From the nineteenth century, photographs and film media appear as well to "thicken the environment we recognize as modern."[41] Photographs can remind us of what we may otherwise forget: for example, the long history of Muslim custodianship in caring for and protecting the Church of the Holy Sepulchre (built on the site in Jerusalem where Jesus was reportedly crucified). Indeed, a photograph from the well-known, late nineteenth-century French firm, Maison Bonfils, captured such an image for posterity, by showing three Muslim men and a boy resting in a niche at this church's entrance.[42]

The Middle East: Pinning Down a Slippery "Where"

This book seeks to tell the history of intercommunal relations in the Middle East during the modern period up to World War I. But in fact, the terms "Middle East" and "modern" are both very slippery, so that scholars over the years have been debating – and changing their minds about – what they mean.

Among English speakers, the "Middle East" has been more of an idea than a fixed place, and the region associated with the term has shifted. In 1902, an American naval historian and evangelical Christian named Alfred Thayer Mahan (1840–1914) – a man who believed in the "divinely imposed duties of governments"[43] – coined the term "Middle East" to suggest the area stretching from the Arabian Peninsula and the Persian Gulf eastward to the fringes of Pakistan. Mahan intended the "Middle East" to complement rather than replace the extant term "Near East," which in his day suggested the region from the Balkans and Asia Minor to the eastern Mediterranean. After World War I, however, the term "Middle East" gained momentum, until by World War II it was displacing "Near East" for current affairs.[44]

Reflecting larger geopolitical trends, some places that English speakers had once deemed "Near Eastern" did not make the transition to "Middle Eastern" in the mid-twentieth century. Thus during the Cold War era of the early 1950s, the US government's Central Intelligence Agency (CIA) reclassified Greece and Turkey (which had joined the Council of Europe a few years earlier) as "European" rather than "Near Eastern" for purposes of its analysis.[45] (Their reclassification points, of course, to the fact that "Europe" has also been notoriously slippery as an idea.[46]) At the same time, other areas – notably the Arabic-speaking countries of North Africa as far west as Morocco – became more closely associated with the "Middle East" for purposes of the CIA's intelligence gathering. The foundation of the Arab League in 1945, and its subsequent development and expansion in membership, also strengthened the links between *al-Maghrib* and *al-Mashriq*, meaning the western and eastern halves of the Arabic-speaking world.

Bearing this somewhat complicated history of regional naming in mind, readers should understand that when this book uses the term "Middle East" to refer to an area stretching from Morocco to Iran, and from Turkey to Yemen, it does so for convenience. There is, of course, some historical rationale for identifying a region along these lines. Except for Turkey and Iran, all of the countries thus covered have had significant Arabic-speaking communities; except for Morocco and Iran, all were once claimed by the Ottoman Empire (even if the extent of Ottoman control varied greatly in practice). Except for Turkey, all were among the early heartlands of Islamic civilization, having become part of the Islamic empire that emerged within a century of the death of the Prophet Muhammad (c. 570–632 CE). Two centuries ago, moreover, this "Middle Eastern" region had small but significant Jewish communities dotting its landscapes (and particularly its urban landscapes), while outside the Maghreb and Arabia, the region hosted substantial indigenous Christian communities as well.

By the early seventeenth century, one empire claimed most of the territory that constitutes the Middle East of the present-day imagination: this, again, was the Ottoman Empire. Having originated around the year 1300 in what is now western Turkey, the Ottoman Empire claimed its oldest and most populous territories in southeastern Europe. The Ottoman Empire therefore began as more of a European empire than a Middle Eastern one, at least until the nineteenth century, when territorial losses in the Balkans tilted the empire's focus toward the Arab world. After its conquest of Constantinople in 1453, the Ottoman Empire devised distinctive and fairly consistent policies for administering the Muslim, Christian, and Jewish communities in its domains, and these policies left their marks on the countries that emerged in the wake of the collapse of the Ottoman Empire after World War I.[47] To repeat a point worth emphasizing, the Ottoman Empire never managed to conquer either Iran or Morocco, two places that were not only countries but, in many periods, empires and even ideas (just as the Middle East is an "idea") in their own right. In the course of their histories, Iran and Morocco evinced their own distinctive policies and practices toward Muslims, Christians, and Jews.

In this book, I focus on the Ottoman Empire, while mentioning Morocco and Iran only occasionally, in a comparative context. There are two reasons for this choice. First, the relative coherence of Ottoman policies toward Muslim, Christian, and Jewish peoples makes the Ottoman Middle East a practical unit for study. Second, I am writing this book under constraints of length. Although there would be enough material on the subject at hand to fill a multi-volume encyclopedia, the goal here is to examine the contours and sweep of a rich history within a single readable volume.

The Modern Era: Pinning Down a Slippery "When"

The timeframe of this book requires explanation. I begin my survey in the seventh century, at the moment when Islam and Muslims appear on the world stage, although I focus primarily on the modern period after approximately 1700. Readers should know that deciding when to start the history of the "modern" Middle East is a tricky business. A generation ago, most historians of the Middle East hailed 1800 as a rough starting point for the modern period, but scholars today are more inclined to look deeper into the past. These debates over the timing of the "modern" Middle East arise from questions that are relevant to world history at large. If we assume that modernity "happened" in different places at different times, then what was it exactly: a state of mind; a set of accomplishments; a condition? How did it begin; that is, what or who started it? Did it emerge at definable moments, or did it just creep up? And what did modernity look or feel like both from the outside and to those who were living it?

Some scholars see modernity as an economic phenomenon: the product of an accelerating global trade in raw and finished materials, of capitalist accumulation, and of new patterns of mass consumption. But modernity's humanistic and cultural manifestations are just as striking. Notably, modernity entailed a new kind of individualism relative to extended families and larger communities, expressed, for example, through the *individual* accumulation of wealth, the *individual* use of new technologies and its products (such as printed books, used for silent, solo reading[48]), and the *individual* consumption of goods (such as coffee – particularly when bought as personal, brewed cups in a coffeehouse, as opposed to as beans for the family coffeepot). The shift to this kind of individualistic behavior, which one can trace in Ottoman domains from at least 1700, if not earlier, allowed for new forms of social mobility and thereby challenged or overturned established social conventions and hierarchies. By the nineteenth century this shift was also leading to contradictions in government policies. For, on the one hand, the Ottoman state was beginning to conceive of its subjects sometimes as individuals (e.g., theoretically endowed with a freedom of conscience, or individually liable for taxation or military conscription). But, on the other hand, it was continuing to classify and treat them as members of older collectives, and above all, as members of religious communities of Muslims, Christians, and Jews. This tension between older state policies toward people as

Image 3 *Napoleon in Egypt*, 1867–68. Oil on wood panel, 35.8 x 25.0 cm. Princeton University Art Museum. Museum purchase, John Maclean Magie, Class of 1892, and Gertrude Magie Fund. Year 1953–78.

members of collectives and the newer, albeit uneven, recognition of peo-ple as individuals was a part and parcel of modernity.

A generation ago, many historians and literary scholars in Europe and North America pointed to 1798 as a particularly significant "moment" for the advent of modernity in the Arabic-speaking world. This was when French troops, led by Napoleon Bonaparte (1769–1821), invaded Egypt and held the country for a rocky three years – just long enough to over-turn local power structures and to introduce new ideas, practices, and technologies in ways that had substantial long-term consequences.[49] Leading scholars no longer regard the Napoleonic conquest of Egypt as the trigger for modern Middle Eastern history,[50] but in retrospect the conquest retains symbolic import anyway – if only because it so vividly points to dramatic changes that were afoot.

Consider, for example, how Napoleon brought Egypt its first Arabic moveable-type printing press, which he had stolen from the Vatican. Partly because of the introduction of this press, which in turn seeded the development of a local Arabic periodical culture and later of a government-sponsored translation enterprise from European languages into Arabic, historians of an earlier generation celebrated 1798 as the starting point for "modern" Arabic literature, as well as for a "liberal age" of Arab social, cultural, and political thought that eventually seeded forms of nationalism.[51] Napoleon's printing press definitely helped to stimulate the expansion of Arabic reading, writing, and literacy – just as Johannes Gutenberg's moveable-type press, which made its debut in Mainz, in what is now Germany, in 1454, had done in Western Europe three centuries before.[52]

Even while acknowledging the tremendous significance of printing for modern cultures and politics, it would still be too much to say that Napoleon inaugurated modernity by introducing the Arabic printing press. For, indeed, Arabic printed works were known long before Napoleon – as early as 1633 – when the Propaganda Fide (the missionary wing of the Roman Catholic Church) first published an Arabic grammar amidst new efforts to appeal to Middle Eastern Christians. Soon other Catholic printed works appeared in Arabic, too. And while this literature appealed to a small Christian, educated, church-centered elite, its readership was growing, as attested by the brisk trade in printed Arabic books that monks from Shuwayr, in Mount Lebanon, began exporting to cities like Beirut, Damascus, and Cairo, during the second half of the eighteenth century – decades before Napoleon appeared on the scene.[53]

The same "Napoleon effect," as one may call this attribution of impact, also obscured the Arabic literary production of Muslims. Until a generation ago, many scholars of Arabic literature (both within and outside the Arab world) celebrated 1798 as the start of a new literary era, while ignoring much of what came before it. Many scholars, indeed, shunted the Arabic literary production of 550 years – the period from the Mongol conquest of Baghdad in 1258 until the Napoleonic conquest of Egypt – into a black hole that they called the "Age of Decadence" (*'asr al-inhitat*), implying an era of decline and torpor when nothing much happened. The work of rediscovering and reappraising the Arabic literary output of the eighteenth century (and indeed, of the seventeenth century) is only just beginning.[54]

What Napoleon's conquest of Egypt *did* do, however, was to exemplify the stronger assertion of European imperial might that was occurring within the lands of the Ottoman Empire as the eighteenth century turned to the nineteenth. Napoleon's conquest of Egypt proved to be one among many more military incursions to come – such as the British, French, and Russian entry into the Greek war for independence from the Ottomans during the 1820s, and the French invasion of Algeria in 1830. There were European economic incursions as well, though these became more manifest during the latter half of nineteenth century, when European countries or individuals gained monopoly concessions over raw materials, services, and transit routes – such as the Suez Canal. In different parts of the Middle East, the Western imperial push into the heartlands of the Islamic world facilitated, accompanied, or followed the arrival of European and American Christian missionaries, Jewish activists (representing organizations like the French Alliance Israélite Universelle), and eventually, in Jerusalem and its "Holy Land" environs, Christian and (much more significantly in the long run) Jewish settlers. Ideas about restoration to, and of, the lands of the Bible inspired these settlers and seeded the ideas and ideology that became known as Zionism.

The encroachment of foreign European imperialism (as opposed to domestic Ottoman imperialism in places like Greece and Bulgaria) put Ottoman authorities on the defensive, and prompted nineteenth-century Ottoman sultans to declare reforms in educational, military, and legal affairs. As the nineteenth century ended, too, Muslim thinkers began to formulate new ideologies of Muslim unity, Islamic revival, and nationalism. All of these developments, which had major consequences for the history of Middle Eastern communities, added strains to the mutual relations between local Muslims, Christians, and Jews, particularly as Christians and Jews began to more closely identify with – or to be perceived as identifying with – the languages, economies, values, and interests of foreign powers.

The bottom line is simple: Napoleon did not inaugurate Middle Eastern modernity, which helps to explain why this study looks to 1700, rather than 1800, as a rough starting point for "modern" Middle Eastern history. Nevertheless, because of his conquest of Egypt, Napoleon manages even now, almost two centuries after his death, to embody the kind of foreign influence and intervention that simultaneously alienated and enchanted people in Ottoman lands.

End dates are just as important as start dates to the construction of a story. This book wraps up its story in the decade after the Young Turks Revolution of 1908, when the Ottoman Empire still appeared to have the potential for durability in the twentieth century, and when World War I was just beginning.

The pre–World War I history covered in this book remains very relevant to our world today. The post-Ottoman states of the Middle East and

North Africa – that is, states that emerged in territories that the Ottoman Empire had once controlled – did *not* break sharply from inherited traditions of Islamic and Ottoman statecraft. Nor were mid- to late-twentieth-century states such as Egypt, Syria, Iraq, and Algeria ever as secular as some of their proponents and critics once claimed – or as their own socialist or "nonaligned" (Cold War–era) rhetoric once made them seem on the international stage. In many respects, on the contrary, Islamic state traditions (which include laws of personal status) have carried on to today. Many old attitudes and expectations have also persisted, and these have continued to influence behaviors.

Approach and Assumptions

Traditional approaches to the history of intercommunal relations in the Middle East have either posited primordial, large-scale corporate identities (Muslims, Christians, Jews) or have emphasized the heterogeneity within communities. In both approaches, interconnectedness and overlap between the units of analysis have figured prominently. However, the usefulness of these approaches depends on the issue one is trying to understand. At a certain scale of analysis, there is such a thing as a "Muslim," a "Christian," and a "Jew," and it makes sense to employ these as key concepts. But if one looks closely for fine details, then the categories become much fuzzier. One sees, for example, myriad distinctions among Muslims, Christians, and Jews with regard to ethnicity, sect, economic stature, and the like, and these often have a more important function on the ground than ostensible membership in a religious community. Likewise, there are vagaries of time and circumstance. Thus, a social category that is relevant to either a long-duration or abstract analysis may not be so relevant in analyzing relations among neighbors, in practice, during a particular historical moment.

In narrating history, this book starts from five main assumptions. First, Islamic civilization in the Middle East was not produced only by and for Muslims. Islamic civilization was a big house. Muslims, Christians, Jews, and others built it and took shelter, even as they created distinct Muslim, Christian, and Jewish cultures within it.[55] Yet while Muslims, Christians, and Jews had distinctive cultures, they did not live in social oases. The challenge for the historian is to examine where their cultures intersected, and where they did not.

Second, Muslim, Christian, and Jewish populations in the Middle East historically exhibited considerable internal diversity in religious doctrines and practices. Although Muslims, Christians, and Jews sometimes embraced the idea of religious solidarity – with Muslims imagining an *"umma,"* Christians "Christendom," and Jews common "Jewry" – divisions within each of these three groups were often pronounced and fraught with tensions. Among Muslims, for example, there were those we now call Sunnis and Shi'is, while diversity in custom and belief prevailed *among* Sunnis and *among* Shi'is as well. Among Christians, there were divisions between various Eastern or Orthodox churches and newer Catholic and Protestant churches. Among Jews, there were differences among Sephardic, Mizrahi, and Karaite Jews, and later among immigrant Ashkenazis.[56] These "cultures of sectarianism"[57] shaped perceptions and affected relations both among and between Muslims, Christians, and Jews.

Third, just as Middle Eastern societies were never monolithic, so intercommunal and intersectarian relations were never static. On the contrary, communities and individuals responded to ever-changing circumstances that reflected broader local, regional, and global trends. Population movements, shifting trade routes, new technologies, and wars – these developments and others affected how communities lived and how different groups in society fared and related to each other. Beirut in 1860 differed substantially from Beirut in 1900; Cairo differed from Fez or Algiers; life in remote villages was unlike life in big cities; the list goes on. For scholars of the modern Middle East, recognition of such variability is essential for dealing with the baggage of Orientalism, a series of "Western" discourses about the "East" that have emphasized the monolithically exotic and tyrannical nature of Islamic societies, along with their need for rescue or uplift.[58]

Fourth, religious affinity intersected with other variables – including language, ethnicity, gender, profession, social status, and affinity to place – to make individual and communal identities. Religion was only one variable – and not necessarily the most important – in determining how groups and individuals behaved. This last point presents the historian with looming questions for which there are no easy answers. When does it make sense, for example, to describe someone as a "Muslim" rather than as a "Kurd" or a "peasant," as a "Jew" rather than a "merchant" or man of Damascus, or as a "Christian" rather than a poor widow? The question becomes more complicated and more pressing still when violence assumes a "religious idiom."[59] For example, to what extent is it accurate and fair to describe the Armenian massacres of the late nineteenth and early twentieth centuries as "religious" conflicts, given that the Armenians happened to be Christians while their attackers, who spoke Turkish, Kurdish, and other languages, happened to be Muslims? Territorially rooted ideas about nationalism and citizenship, which grew more important as the twentieth century opened and advanced, add yet another factor to the equation of communal identities, by challenging the historian to consider, for example, the possibility of "Turkish" and "Syrian" collectives.

Fifth and finally, "religion" itself is a murky concept, more like a fog than like a fixed and sturdy box. The same is true of the adjective "religious." As one historian of the ancient Mediterranean world observed in an analytical critique of these concepts, "The very idea of 'being religious' requires a companion notion of what it would mean to be 'not religious'," while the concept of religion, as it developed in modern European history, has often rested on the premise of its relative distinction from other spheres like science, politics, and economics.[60] The reality is that ordinary people in the Middle East – like ordinary people everywhere, Europe included – were (and still are!) likely to fold invocations of the divine or concerns about life, death, destiny, and so on into the most ordinary everyday matters. To take one small example from early Islamic history, consider a letter that a Jewish merchant in Sicily wrote in Arabic in 1094, griping to his partner in Egypt about the latter's decision to buy low-quality peppercorns without consulting him.[61] If this spice merchant dropped God's name into the argument, to dignify the exchange or signal honorable intentions, would that have made the document automatically "religious"? If we answer yes, then we are likely to find religion everywhere and nowhere. (Note that the guardians of the synagogue near Cairo who saved this particular letter centuries ago appeared to feel that its potential reference to God made it worthy of reverential treatment, or perhaps we would now say, made it "religious."[62])

Some of the most difficult questions to grapple with are these: What was religion and how did it matter – or not matter – in everyday lives? When did religious identity (based on adherence to a creed or identification with an associated group or sect) matter more than other forms of identity in motivating individuals or propelling events? How ethical is it for historians to assume (and thereby in some sense impose) identities, of a religious nature or otherwise, in describing individuals and groups? To what extent can the historian speak of common "Christian," "Jewish," and "Muslim" experiences, given that communities – and individuals – were so complicated? What about subsidiary or divergent communities and identities, for example, among Greek Orthodox, Shi'i, Sephardi, Yezidi, and other people? And how is it possible to pin down a narrative of Muslim, Christian, and Jewish relations considering that circumstances varied by time and place, and that evidence for day-to-day interactions is often scattered and anecdotal? This book grapples with these questions by emphasizing, rather than eliding, the complexities within the history, and by emphasizing the remarkable and ever-evolving variety of Muslim, Christian, and Jewish cultures that persisted side by side.

Many theologians and scholars of comparative religion now use the term "Abrahamic religions" to suggest historical genealogies connecting Islam, Christianity, and Judaism. The term signals the common recognition, among adherents of these three faiths, of the patriarch Abraham and his legacies, especially regarding belief in a single god (monotheism). Some scholars have used the term to suggest the potential for Muslim, Christian, and Jewish solidarity, or interfaith cordiality through scriptural and theological affinities.[63] Others, by contrast, have pointed to the importance of "Abrahamic kinship" for asserting Muslim, Christian, or Jewish singularity with reference to the other two in the triad, that is, by *sharpening* family rivalries in ways that have translated during the past century into scripturally based land claims in Israel and Palestine.[64] Since this book is not a study of comparative theology, it does not use "Abrahamic religions" as an analytical device. Instead, the book focuses on what men, women, and children have done – on social lives rather than religious dogmas. It explores the warts-and-all history of real people who lived in challenging times, as opposed to what scriptures, theologians, and other religious authorities have told them to do, while questioning the invocation or imagination of religious identity in policies and behaviors.

Five chapters and an epilogue follow. Chapter 2 traces the formation of early Islamic society and the elaboration of policies toward Christians and Jews. These policies went on to shape the policies and ideologies of many Islamic states as they emerged in different places and periods. Chapter 3 examines the Ottoman Empire, its modes of managing religious diversity (including its so-called *millet* system), and the accelerating social changes of the eighteenth century. Chapter 4 studies the nineteenth-century period of Ottoman reform, the efforts of Ottoman sultans and statesmen to promote a new understanding of what it meant to be an Ottoman subject, and the reception of their attempts. Chapters 5 and 6 focus on the decisive reign of Sultan Abdulhamid II, who emphasized the Islamic credentials of the Ottoman state while suppressing political participation and dissent. These chapters also trace the mounting social tensions and resentments that beset diverse peoples of the Ottoman Empire during an era of territorial losses and incipient nationalisms. The Epilogue concludes by considering methods of approaching this history and by mulling over the relevance of this history for how we will make sense of things that have happened – in other words, for the future of the past.

Conclusion

In 1876, the Ottoman Empire had a population that was estimated to be 25 percent Christian, 1 percent Jewish, and 74 percent Muslim.[65] Today, outside Israel, Jewish populations in Middle Eastern countries are minute to nonexistent, while Christian communities have greatly diminished, largely as a result of migration for economic and political reasons, and as an outgrowth of wars.

In 2008, according to the Institute of Muslim Minority Affairs in London, one-third of the world's 1.5 billion Muslims were living as minorities in predominantly non-Muslim countries.[66] Hindu-majority India claimed the largest Muslim minority,[67] although by 2015, Muslim populations in Europe and North America were growing quickly, as a result of economically and politically motivated migrations and higher birthrates relative to non-Muslims. In places like Amsterdam and New York, Muslims were striving to affirm their religious identities and to find their social footing while sharing spaces and cultures with non-Muslims, crossing paths in places like grocery stores, and building friendships in schools. Muslims in diasporic communities were also welcoming new members into their communities through conversion, or were themselves exiting Islam for other religions.[68] In short, people of Muslim origins were contributing to the cultural richness and sophistication of the countries that had received them – much as Christians, Jews, and others once enhanced the cosmopolitanism of the societies where Islamic states prevailed.[69]

Amidst these changing currents, does the history of intercommunal relations in the Middle East have lessons to impart? Certainly this history can tell us something about where "we" (meaning denizens of the world, and inheritors of the past) have been, and how we have arrived where we are now. As this book will show, the history, in a nutshell, went something like this: Beginning in the seventh century, when the religion of Islam and the Muslim empire were born, Muslim-ruled states developed a system for integrating Christians and Jews. That is, they made a pact called the *dhimma*, so that in return for accepting Muslim rule and respecting Islam's cultural supremacy, Christians and Jews could continue to worship as they had done and pursue livelihoods without interference from Muslim authorities. This system worked reasonably well as a model of Islamic imperial rule for many centuries. Yet this system proved untenable in the modern period, as ideas about nationalism and national participation, new cultures of mass consumption, and changing distributions of education and wealth led some Christians, Jews, and Muslims to question old forms of imperial rule as well as traditional social hierarchies. Indeed, the *dhimma* system in the Middle East may have once worked well as a means of managing religious diversity, but it cannot suffice today when ideals of nationalism, citizenship, and national belonging are globally pervasive, and when nation-states, not empires, are normative units of political culture. People, worldwide, want to be told they are equal. In today's world, any state that upholds one religion, sect, or ethnic group in the presence of others, and assumes hierarchies of citizenship accordingly, is bound to chafe the subordinated.

"Redescribing a world," Salman Rushdie suggested, "is the necessary first step towards changing it." Does this mean that history gives room for maneuver? If we look back without flinching, then the answer may be yes. Working from this assumption, this book describes the social circumstances that both drew Middle Eastern peoples together and pushed them apart within the fray of everyday life.

NOTES

1 Sami Zubaida and Richard Tapper, eds., *Culinary Cultures of the Middle East* (London: I.B. Tauris, 1994).
2 Two works that creatively explore the apartment building as a shared space are Joelle Bahloul, *The Architecture of Memory: A Jewish-Muslim Household in Colonial Algeria, 1937–1962*, trans. Catherine Du Peloux Ménagé (Cambridge: Cambridge University Press, 1992); and *Camondo Han*, DVD, directed by Peter Clasen (Istanbul, 2005).
3 "Egypt," in US Department of State, *International Religious Freedom Report for 2014*, www.state.gov/j/drl/rls/irf/religiousfreedom/index.htm?year=2014&dlid =238452#wrapper (accessed February 29, 2016).
4 Gudrun Krämer, *The Jews in Modern Egypt, 1914–1952* (London: I.B. Tauris, 1989), p. 9; S. D. Goitein, *A Mediterranean Society: The Jewish Communities of the Arab World as Portrayed in the Documents of the Cairo Geniza*, 6 vols. (Berkeley: University of California Press, 1967–93).
5 US Department of State, *2009 Report on International Religious Freedom*, www .state.gov/g/drl/rls/irf/2009/index.htm (accessed January 21, 2010).
6 "Turkey," in US Department of State, *International Religious Freedom Report for 2014*.
7 "Iran," in US Department of State, *International Religious Freedom Report for 2014*.
8 In 1950, the United Nations Relief and Works Agency for Palestine Refugees in the Near East (UNRWA) catered to about 750,000 "Palestine" refugees. In 2016, UNRWA estimated that five million Palestine refugees were eligible for its services. United Nations Relief and Works Agency for Palestine Refugees in the Near East (UNRWA), "Palestine Refugees," www.unrwa.org/palestine-refugees (accessed February 29, 2016).
9 Andrea Pacini, ed., *Christian Communities in the Arab Middle East: The Challenge of the Future* (Oxford: Clarendon Press, 1998).

10 Charles D. Smith, *Palestine and the Arab-Israeli Conflict*, 3rd edition (New York: St. Martin's Press, 1996), p. 32; "Israel and the Occupied Territories," in US Department of State, *International Religious Freedom Report for 2014*. On broader trends in Christian demographics, see Philippe Farguès, "The Arab Christians of the Middle East: A Demographic Perspective," in *Christian Communities in the Arab Middle East: The Challenge of the Future*, ed. Andrea Pacini (Oxford: Clarendon Press, 1998), pp. 48–66; and Heather J. Sharkey, "Christianity in the Middle East and North Africa," in *Introducing World Christianity*, ed. Charles Farhadian (Oxford: Wiley-Blackwell, 2012), pp. 7–20.

11 Simon Payaslian, *The History of Armenia* (New York: Palgrave Macmillan, 2007), p. 115. Payaslian gives the figure of "about 2 million" for Armenians living in Ottoman territory in 1876.

12 "Turkey," in US Department of State, *International Religious Freedom Report for 2014*.

13 Bernard Heyberger, *Les chrétiens au Proche-Orient: De la compassion à la compréhension* (Paris: Éditions Payot & Rivages, 2013), pp. 39–41.

14 For example, Jack Healy, "Exodus from North Signals Iraqi Christians' Slow Decline," *New York Times*, March 10, 2012; Susanne Güsten, "Christians Squeezed Out by Violent Struggle in North Syria," *New York Times*, February 13, 2013. See also "Syria," in Central Intelligence Agency, *The World Factbook*, www.cia.gov/library/publications/the-world-factbook/geos/sy.html (accessed February 29, 2016); and United Nations High Commissioner for Refugees, *Syria Regional Refugee Response*, http://data.unhcr.org/syrianrefugees/regional.php (accessed February 29, 2016).

15 Human Rights Watch, *World Report 2015*, www.hrw.org/world-report/2015 (accessed April 6, 2016). See the accounts of migrant workers in each country report.

16 Robert Fisk, "The Never-Ending Exodus of Christians from the Middle East," *The Independent* (London), January 23, 2010, p. 46.

17 This is my adaptation of Arendt's notion of the "banality of evil," which emphasized the functioning of evil through thoughtlessness. Hannah Arendt, *Eichmann in Jerusalem: A Report on the Banality of Evil* (New York: Viking Press, 1963).

18 Salman Rushdie, *Imaginary Homelands: Essays and Criticism* (London: Granta, 1991), pp. 13–14. I am indebted to Joel Beinin for drawing attention to Rushdie's essay: see Joel Beinin, *The Dispersion of Egyptian Jewry: Culture, Politics, and the Formation of a Modern Diaspora* (Berkeley: University of California Press, 1998), p. 28.

19 Paul Ricoeur, *Memory, History, Forgetting*, trans. Kathleen Blamey and David Pellauer (Chicago: University of Chicago Press, 2004), pp. 56, 320.

20 Chocolaterie d'Aiguebelle, "Massacres d'Armenie" and "Guerre Gréco-Turque", parts of two series of collecting cards issued by the firm, c. 1896–98, Kislak Center for Special Collections, Rare Books and Manuscripts, University of Pennsylvania Libraries.

21 From the late nineteenth through the mid-twentieth century, the D'Aiguebelle chocolate company (founded 1869) published more than 6,000 different images on its "chromos," covering broad themes of natural

history, geography, human society, history, and "fantaisies" (perhaps best translated here as "pretty scenes"). Bernard Delpal, "Les 'chromos' du choc-olat: Quand le monastère d'Aiguebelle utilisait la 'réclame' pour ses ventes," *Études Drômoises*, 26 (2006), pp. 28–33.

22 Virginia Westbook, "The Role of Trading Cards in Marketing Chocolate dur-ing the Late Nineteenth Century," in *Chocolate: History, Culture, and Heritage*, ed. Louis Evan Grivetti and Howard-Yana Shapiro (Hoboken, NJ: Wiley, 2009); and Peter C. Marzio, *The Democratic Art: Pictures for a 19th-Century America: Chromolithography, 1840–1900* (Boston: D.R. Godine, 1979).

23 Delpal, "Les 'chromos' du chocolat," p. 32.

24 Malek Alloula, *The Colonial Harem*, trans. Myrna Godzich and Wlad Godzich, intro. Barbara Harlow (Minneapolis: University of Minnesota Press, 1986), p. 4.

25 Susan Sontag, *On Photography* (New York: Picador, 2001), p. 3.

26 Samuel P. Huntington, "The Clash of Civilizations?," *Foreign Affairs*, 72:3 (1993), pp. 22–49.

27 An earlier use of this term appears in Bernard Lewis, *The Jews of Islam* (Princeton: Princeton University Press, 1984). Fernand Braudel wrote, in a similar vein, that "the entire Mediterranean was an area of constant con-flict between two adjacent and warring civilizations." Fernand Braudel, *The Mediterranean and the Age of Philip II* (New York: Harper, 1972), Volume 2, p. 866.

28 Gordon N. Bardos, "Jihad in the Balkans," *World Affairs*, 177:3 (2014), pp. 73–79; Jennifer Mustapha, "The Mujahideen in Bosnia: The Foreign Figure as Cosmopolitan Citizen and/or Terrorist," *Citizenship Studies*, 17:6/7 (2013), pp. 742–55.

29 Public Broadcasting Service (PBS), "Osama bin Ladin vs. the U.S.: Edicts and Statements," *Frontline*, www.pbs.org/wgbh/pages/frontline/shows/binladen/who/edicts.html (accessed March 11, 2013).

30 For example, Bernard Lewis, *The Crisis of Islam: Holy War and Unholy Terror* (New York: Modern Library, 2003); John L. Esposito, *Unholy War: Terror in the Name of Islam* (New York: Oxford University Press, 2003); Seyyed Hossein Nasr, *Islam: Religion, History, and Civilization* (San Francisco: HarperSanFrancisco, 2003); Richard W. Bulliet, *The Case for Islamo-Christian Civilization* (New York: Columbia University Press, 2006).

31 Iraq Body Count, "Documented Civilian Deaths from Violence," www.iraqbodycount.org/ (accessed February 4, 2010, and April 7, 2016). On February 4, 2010, this organization estimated a death toll somewhere between 95,309 and 103,982. On April 7, 2016, it estimated 242,000 "total violent deaths, including combatants" or between 156,400 and 174,941 "docu-mented civilian deaths from violence."

32 "Une Marocaine en burqa se voit refuser la nationalité française," *Le Monde* (Paris), July 11, 2008.

33 Just as worrisome to many, in the aftermath of the Danish cartoon con-troversy, was the way some scholars and institutions began to self-censor. Consider Yale University Press, which published an academic study of the Danish cartoons of Muhammad in 2009 but with the cartoons themselves expunged from the book. Jytte Klausen, *The Cartoons That Shook the World*

(New Haven: Yale University Press, 2009); Yale University Press, "Statement by John Donatich (Director of Yale University Press) [about the decision to not print the Danish cartoons of Muhammad], September 9, 2009, http:// yalepress.yale.edu/yupbooks/KlausenStatement.asp (accessed February 5, 2010); Patricia Cohen, "Yale Press Bans Images of Muhammad in New Book," *New York Times*, August 12, 2009; and Thomas Buch-Andersen, "Denmark Row: The Power of Cartoons," *BBC News*, October 3, 2006, http://news.bbc.co.uk/2/hi/europe/5392786.stm (accessed April 7, 2016).

34 Mohamed Zayani, ed., *The Al Jazeera Phenomenon: Critical Perspectives on New Arab Media* (Boulder, CO: Paradigm, 2005); Philip Seib, *The Al-Jazeera Effect: How the New Global Media Are Reshaping World Politics* (Washington, DC: Potomac Books, 2008).

35 Lizzy Davies, "Pope Francis Completes Contentious Canonisation of Otranto Martyrs," *The Guardian*, May 12, 2013.

36 Constance Classen, *Worlds of Sense: Exploring the Senses in History and Across Cultures* (London: Routledge, 1993).

37 Samir [sic] (Director), *Forget Baghdad*, DVD (Seattle: Arab Film Production, 2004); Miriam Meghnagi, *Dialoghi Mediterranei*, Compact Disc (Rome, 2004).

38 Nefissa Naguib, "The Fragile Tale of Egyptian Jewish Cuisine: Food Memoirs of Claudia Roden and Colette Rossant," *Food & Foodways*, 14 (2006), pp. 35–53.

39 See, for example, this discussion of "Thursday Bread" (*Khubz al-Khamis*) and its affinity to *Qurban*, the Holy Communion bread of the Greek Orthodox church, as produced in Tripoli, Lebanon: Anissa Helou, *Mediterranean Street Food* (New York: HarperCollins, 2002), p. 112; see also pp. 114 and 218 for kindred Ramadan delicacies.

40 Ramin Farahani (Director), *Jews of Iran*, DVD (The Netherlands: NIKmedia, 2005).

41 Sontag, *On Photography*, p. 3.

42 University of Pennsylvania Museum of Archaeology and Anthropology, Archives, Bonfils Collection, Image 165914: "Guard turc à la porte de St. Sepulchre," elsewhere listed as "Portiers musulmans du St. Sepulcre [sic]," circa 1885–1901.

43 Brian Stanley, *The World Missionary Conference, Edinburgh 1910* (Grand Rapids: William B. Eerdmans Publishing Company, 2009), p. 258; see also pp. 252–53.

44 Zachary Lockman, *Contending Visions of the Middle East: The History and Politics of Orientalism* (Cambridge: Cambridge University Press, 2004), pp. 96–97.

45 Roby Carroll Barrett, *The Greater Middle East and the Cold War: U.S. Foreign Policy under Eisenhower and Kennedy* (London: I.B. Tauris, 2007), p. 331, endnote 3. Note that Greece and Turkey joined the Council of Europe at the same time, on August 9, 1949. Council of Europe, *Council of Europe in Brief*, www.coe.int/ (accessed January 27, 2010).

46 Anthony Pagden, ed., *The Idea of Europe: From Antiquity to the European Union* (Cambridge: Cambridge University Press, 2002).

47 L. Carl Brown, ed., *Imperial Legacy: The Ottoman Imprint on the Balkans and the Middle East* (New York: Columbia University Press, 1996).

48 On the significance of silent, private reading, and its contrast to earlier forms of reading aloud, see Marshall McLuhan, *The Gutenberg Galaxy: The Making of Typographic Man* (Toronto: University of Toronto Press, 1962), pp. 92–93.

49 Abd al-Rahman al-Jabarti (1754–1822), *Napoleon in Egypt: al-Jabarti's Chronicle of the First Seven Months*, trans. Shmuel Moreh, intro. Robert L. Tignor (Princeton: Markus Wiener, 1993); Ami Ayalon, *The Press in the Arab Middle East* (Oxford: Oxford University Press, 1994); and Donald Malcolm Reid, *Whose Pharaohs? Archaeology, Museums, and Egyptian National Identity from Napoleon to World War I* (Berkeley: University of California Press, 2002).

50 Among social and political historians, the most influential challenger of the 1798, Napoleon-as-modernizer paradigm has been Peter Gran. See Peter Gran, *Islamic Roots of Capitalism: Egypt, 1760–1840*, new edition, intro. Afaf Lutfi al-Sayyid Marsot (Syracuse: Syracuse University Press, 1998), pp. xi, xiv. See also Nelly Hanna, *Making Big Money in 1600: The Life and Times of Ismail Abu Taqiyya, Egyptian Merchant* (Syracuse: Syracuse University Press, 1998).

51 M. M. Badawi, *A Critical Introduction to Modern Arabic Poetry* (Cambridge: Cambridge University Press, 1975); Albert Hourani, *Arabic Thought in the Liberal Age, 1798–1939* (Cambridge: Cambridge University Press, 1983).

52 McLuhan, *The Gutenberg Galaxy*.

53 Bernard Heyberger, "Livres et pratique de la lecture chez les chrétiens (Syrie, Liban), XVIIe – XVIIIe siècles," *Revue des Mondes Musulmans et de la Méditerranée*, 87–88 (1999), pp. 209–23.

54 Roger Allen, "The Post-Classical Period: Parameters and Preliminaries," in *Arabic Literature in the Post-Classical Period* (The Cambridge History of Arabic Literature), ed. Roger Allen and D. S. Richards (Cambridge: Cambridge University Press, 2006), p. 5.

55 Bernard Lewis captured this idea in *The Jews of Islam* (1984) when he described "the Jews of Islam" and the "Judeo-Islamic tradition" that emerged from the cultural symbiosis of Jewish life in predominantly Muslim societies.

56 A clear discussion of Jewish diversity appears with regard to Egypt in Beinin, *The Dispersion of Egyptian Jewry*.

57 Ussama Makdisi, *The Culture of Sectarianism: Community, History, and Violence in Nineteenth-Century Ottoman Lebanon* (Berkeley: University of California Press, 2000).

58 Edward W. Said, *Orientalism* (New York: Pantheon Books, 1978).

59 Ussama Makdisi in Philip Benedict, Nora Berend, Stephen Ellis, Jeffrey Kaplan, Ussama Makdisi, and Jack Miles, "AHR Conversation: Religious Identities and Violence," *American Historical Review*, 112:5 (2007), see pp. 1437–38 within the group article of pp. 1432–81.

60 Brent Nongbri, *Before Religion: A History of a Modern Concept* (New Haven: Yale University Press, 2013), pp. 4, 7.

61 Salamah ben Musa ben Yitshak to Judah ben Moses ben Sujmar of Fustat (near Cairo), dated Mazara (Sicily), 1064 CE, in the Cairo Genizah Collection (University of Pennsylvania, Katz Center for Advanced Judaic

Studies), Halper 389, http://hdl.library.upenn.edu/1017.4/4452-record (accessed April 6, 2016).

62 A fuller discussion of the Geniza records of Fustat (now part of Cairo) appears in Chapter 2.

63 For example, Karen Armstrong, *A History of God: The 4,000-Year Quest of Judaism, Christianity, and Islam* (New York: A.A. Knopf, 1993).

64 Peter Beyer, *Religions in Global Society* (Abingdon, UK: Routledge, 2006), p. 118; David Leeming, "Abraham," in *The Oxford Companion to World Mythology* (Oxford: Oxford University Press, 2005), pp. 1–2.

65 Stanford A. Shaw and Ezel Kural Shaw, *History of the Ottoman Empire and Modern Turkey*, Vol. 2 (Cambridge: Cambridge University Press, 1977), p. 240.

66 Institute of Muslim Minority Affairs, "Muslim Minority Communities," www.imma.org.uk/plannedvolume.htm (accessed November 21, 2008).

67 Syed Z. Abedin and Saleha M. Abedin, "Muslim Minorities in Non-Muslim Societies," in *The Oxford Encyclopedia of the Modern Islamic World*, ed. John L. Esposito, Vol. 3 (New York: Oxford University Press, 1995), pp. 112–17; and Alan Yuhas, "Muslim Population in Europe to Reach 10% by 2050, New Study Shows," *The Guardian*, April 2, 2015.

68 See, for example, Nadia Marzouki and Olivier Roy, eds., *Religious Conversions in the Mediterranean World* (Houndmills, UK: Palgrave Macmillan, 2013).

69 Marshall G. S. Hodgson, *Rethinking World History: Essays on Europe, Islam, and World History*, ed. Edmund Burke, III (Cambridge: Cambridge University Press, 1993), p. 97.

2   The Islamic Foundations of Intercommunal Relations

Introduction: Islamic Societies and the Politics of Inclusion

In what is now the Middle East, early Islamic states and legal systems worked on the assumption that Christians and Jews lived among Muslim believers as integral parts of the social landscape. In fact, Islamic states assigned Jews and Christians a special status, calling them *ahl al-dhimma* or *dhimmi*s, meaning "people of the pact." In this sense, Islamic societies included Jews and Christians from the very beginning of Islam itself. Yet, although Islamic states tolerated Jewish and Christian *dhimmi*s, they prescribed for them a subordinate social status and imposed restrictions in law and policy.[1]

This chapter will explain how the concept of the *dhimmi* arose and what it initially meant on the ground. It will study how and on what terms non-Muslims secured the protection of Islamic states and societies while recognizing their political and cultural hegemony. Over a remarkably long period, from the seventh century to the nineteenth and twentieth centuries and stretching in some respects to the present day, early Islamic mechanisms for managing Muslim-*dhimmi* relations influenced policy, attitudes, and assumptions about how intercommunal relations should work. To be sure, Islamic societies changed significantly across time and place. Nevertheless, as this book will show, Muslim rulers and ordinary people across the centuries invoked Islamic tradition, as they perceived it, to justify policies and behaviors toward non-Muslims. Likewise, many Muslims still invoke this perceived tradition today.

This chapter surveys the historical foundations of intercommunal relations as they developed following the seventh-century debut of Islam. The survey starts by clarifying the terms "Islam," "Muslims," and "Islamic societies," and then provides a thumbnail sketch of early Islamic history with attention to initial Muslim encounters with Jews and Christians. After examining the social pact of the *dhimma* and what it entailed in practice, the chapter continues by reflecting on how Muslims began to assert a distinct identity as the size of their community grew. Ultimately, this account explores the meaning, nature, and bounds of social inclusion for non-Muslims in the early Islamic empire.

Islam, Muslims, and Islamic Societies: Coming to Terms with History

"Recite! In the name of your Lord, who created – created man from a blood-clot!"[2] With these words, Muslims have believed, Muhammad received the first in a series of revelations that God intended for humankind. The year was 610 CE. From then until his death twenty-two years later, Muhammad conveyed the messages that, gathered together as the Qur'an (meaning "Recitations"), became the foundational text of Islam. In the Arabian peninsula, where most people at the time were venerating various astral deities and natural spirits, but where small communities of Jews, scattered Christians, and others were embracing the idea of a single divine figure, these words inspired a new monotheistic religious community – a community of believers who became known as Muslims, literally "those who submit" to God.

In some respects, the date of Muhammad's first revelation in 610 marks the conception of Islam. Yet Muslims have identified another seminal date, in 622, when the first group of these new believers left Mecca for Medina in order to escape from repression. Their emigration or *hijra* came to mark the start of the Islamic calendar, and signaled the date after which the first Muslims were able to organize collectively. From then on, the development of Islamic religious culture occurred in tandem with the growth of an Islamic political life.

The coincident development of religion and polity among Muslims has often prompted observers to use "Islam" to refer to two things at once: on the one hand, a system of belief and devotion, and on the other, a series of historical states endowed with bodies of law. The latter usage is problematic because it ascribes complicated political actions to a religion, thereby obscuring the role of human agency in driving them. Scholars have sometimes gone still farther by using "Islam" to convey a whole civilization – a congeries of states and societies with their associated cultures and peoples. In his now-classic, three-volume study titled *The Venture of Islam* (published posthumously in 1974), the historian Marshall Hodgson grappled with this problem of wording and observed, "Not only what may be called the religion proper, then, but the whole social and cultural complex associated with it – indeed, at the most extreme extension, the totality of all the lifeways accepted among any Muslims anywhere – may be looked on as Islam and seen as a self-contained whole, a total context within which daily life has proceeded in all its ramifications."[3] In an effort to achieve greater clarity, Hodgson experimented with words. He used the clunky "Islamdom" to refer to domains under Islamic rule, and "Islamicate" (a term, as he acknowledged, that had a "double adjectival ending, setting the reference at two removes from the point referred to") to cover cultures that may have emerged in an Islamic milieu but that did not necessarily follow standard, orthodox, or explicitly Muslim practices. For example, whereas the phrase "Islamic law" tended to imply Shari'a law (which in turn implied an ideal, divinely sanctioned law), Hodgson suggested that the phrase "Islamicate law" could more flexibly describe law that evinced both conventionally Islamic *and* distinctively local or customary values.[4]

These pages will use the term "Islam" in a particular, restricted, and abstract sense, to refer to a religion that gained expression, historically and in practice, by diverse people who understood or implemented it in different ways. This religion, of course, provided important cultural underpinnings for societies that developed under its influence. Used as a noun or adjective, the term "Muslim" will refer specifically to people, that is, adherents of Islam (e.g., "Muslim merchants") and their customs or deeds (e.g., "Muslim holidays," "Muslim prayers"). Finally, the adjective "Islamic" will have a broader usage, since it is capable of covering Muslims and non-Muslims alike (e.g., Islamic art, Islamic civilization, and above all Islamic history) in cultural spaces where Muslim peoples and their associated cultures were influential. Thus employed, these terms make it possible to distinguish religion (as an ideal and abstraction) from people (as historical actors in flesh and blood) and from cultures (as the intellectual and material expressions of human societies). This usage also makes it possible to articulate two important premises: first, the formation of Islam as a religion was related, but not identical, to the formation of Islamic societies and Muslim communities; and second, with regard to intercommunal relations, Islam (the abstract religious entity) neither helped nor harmed Jews or Christians, though individual Muslims could sometimes do both.

The formative period of Islam lasted for the first four to five centuries after the death of Muhammad. The first significant portion of this era stretched from 610 to 632. Short but utterly decisive, this was the period of Muhammad's prophecy, and the period when Islam, as a religion, was born. Muhammad articulated the messages that Muslims later gathered and recorded as the text of the Qur'an. During this period, Muhammad and his followers also organized an incipient Islamic polity around the fledgling Muslim collective or *umma*.

The second portion of this era, stretching from 632 to 661, followed Muhammad's death. In these years, four companions of the Prophet (remembered by many Muslims as *Rashidun* or "rightly-guided" ones) sought to preserve both the Muslim message and Muslim community while expanding the territories and populations under their rule. By authorizing conquests that extended the Islamic state beyond Arabia, into Egypt and greater Syria (Byzantine or Late Roman imperial territory), and into Iraq and Iran (Sassanian Persian imperial territory), these four *Rashidun* helped to make the Islamic state into an Islamic empire. This period also witnessed the outbreak of disputes that roiled the Muslim community, as Muslims disagreed about who exactly Muhammad's successors (*khalifas*, or caliphs) should be and how they should lead. These disputes escalated into civil wars that produced, over time, sectarian distinctions among Muslims – above all, among those who became known as "Sunnis" and "Shi'is" respectively. The term "Sunni" came from the Arabic word *sunna*, meaning custom or practice, with the implication being that Sunnis tried to emulate the exemplary behavior of the Prophet Muhammad. The term "Shi'i," meanwhile, came from the Arabic word referring to a cause or party. It originally referred to a person who supported the cause of 'Ali, Muhammad's cousin and son-in-law, when 'Ali made what was initially an unsuccessful bid for leadership over the Muslim community, before finally winning recognition as the *khalifa* in 656 CE.

A shift in leadership in 661 CE – caused by the slaying of the caliph Ali by members of a third, much smaller Muslim sect known as the Kharijites[5] – gave rise to the third major portion of this formative era. This was the Umayyad period, which lasted from 661 to 750. Muslim rule became dynastic under members of one family, who belonged to the Umayya clan (hence the dynasty's name) of the Arab Quraysh tribe (the same tribe whose elites in Mecca had originally rejected the message of Muhammad). The Umayyads moved the center of the Islamic empire out of Arabia and into Damascus, Syria (which had formerly been part of the Byzantine Empire). This dynastic turn marked a dramatic change from Arab tribal and early Islamic political practice, which had depended to a large degree on consultative or consensus-based decision making. Meanwhile, following the shift to Syria, the Muslim community that formed there "inherit[ed] the mores ... of the dominant, Christian population," ensuring cultural continuity but also – and arguably to the detriment of women – reinforcing restrictive patriarchal values and customs.[6]

The Umayyad rulers presided over further conquests, so that by 711, the Islamic empire stretched from the southern tip of Iberia (Spain) to the edges of Sind, roughly along what is now the India-Pakistan frontier.

Under the Umayyads, Arabic gained ground as the language of Islamic imperial statecraft, even among the Christian, Jewish, and (in the former Persian imperial territories) Zoroastrian bureaucrats whom Muslim rulers employed, while the construction of mosques gave tangible expression to the religious movement of Islam. After a deputy of the Umayyad state killed Husayn (who was the son of 'Ali and the grandson of the Prophet Muhammad) in a battle at Karbala (in what is now southern Iraq) in 680 CE, incipient Shi'i movements sharpened further. In subsequent centuries, Shi'ism appealed strongly to members of various rural protest movements (suggesting its potential as a vehicle for popular resistance), even as it splintered into a variety of branches or sects among followers who recognized different descendants of 'Ali as their leaders. Over time, these various Shi'i sects developed distinct doctrinal positions, while confirming the oppositional coalescence of Sunnism.

In 750, a revolution overthrew the Umayyad dynasty, enabling the rise of the Abbasid dynasty, which shifted the center of the Islamic state eastward, into Iraq, and to a purpose-built capital in Baghdad. The Abbasid revolution sprang from grievances that had been swelling for some time among peasants, soldiers, non-Arab Muslims, and others, and in this way reflected the growing size, diversity, and significantly, too, *unwieldiness* of the Islamic empire. During the Abbasid period, Islamic legal practice began to cohere among jurists who formed *madhhabs*, meaning legal communities or schools of law, and who "articulated and recorded the distinctive legal doctrines that ... regulated their adherents' lives down to the most minute details" while founding mosques, centers of learning, and law courts.[7] This process, too, contributed to the consolidation of Sunni Islam – at least among jurists and other scholars – which by the eleventh century was posed strongly and self-consciously in counterpoint to Shi'ism.[8] The Abbasids enshrined what was becoming Sunni Islam as a kind of default Islam.

Conventionally, the Abbasid period is said to have lasted from 750 until 1258, when the Mongols conquered Baghdad, but in fact, the Abbasid rulers exerted a diminishing degree of control over what remained a unitary Islamic empire only in theory. In the corners of the empire that fell beyond the reach of Baghdad, powerful military men seized control and established Abbasid satellite states. Consider, for example, the Samanids of Iran (c. 819–899 CE), patrons of the arts whose distinctive ceramic bowls survive to grace many of the world's finest art museums today. Even more dramatically, in early tenth-century North Africa, and more precisely in what is now Tunisia, a Shi'i separatist-cum-missionary movement emerged. In 969 CE, supporters of this Shi'i movement conquered Egypt from Abbasid control and founded a new city, *al-Qahira* (literally "the victorious"), or Cairo, which they made into the capital of a dynasty and rival caliphate under the Fatimids (969–1171). The Fatimid dynasty took its name from Fatima, the Prophet Muhammad's daughter, the wife of 'Ali, and the mother of the Prophet's grandsons, Hasan and Husayn.

Political vicissitudes aside, the first few centuries of the Abbasid period witnessed steady growth of the Muslim population through conversion in Muslim-controlled territories. Intellectual and cultural life flourished, as Muslim rulers sponsored great thinkers who composed treatises on subjects as varied as mathematics, grammar, and philosophy. The Abbasid caliphs also established a massive translation institute, called *Dar al-Hikma* ("The House of Wisdom") that brought works from Greek, Persian, and Sanskrit into Arabic. Many of the leading scholars in this enterprise were Christians, such as Hunayn ibn Ishaq (809–873), who translated works by Galen, Aristotle, and Plato for his Abbasid patrons. Arabic literature blossomed, not only in Islamic scholarly circles but also among courtly pleasure seekers. Indeed, Abbasid-era *bons vivants* wrote so many treatises on cuisine alone that one historian has recently claimed, "Islam [*sic*] has the richest medieval food literature in the world – there are more cookbooks in Arabic from before 1400 than in the rest of the world's languages put together."[9]

In retrospect, the first half of the Abbasid era was a vibrant era of Islamic arts, letters, and sciences. By the year 1000, the major urban centers of the Islamic world were so full of life, diversity, and intellectual ferment that they were propelling not just an Islamic state or empire, but a full-blown Islamic civilization. At the same time, the very fragmentation of the Islamic empire resulted in regional dynasties that patronized the arts and sciences beyond Baghdad.

Starting Off: Comity and Violence in Initial Relations

The historical record for the early Islamic period is sketchy, in two senses of the term: it is both fragmentary and of uncertain reliability. Most available textual sources derive from chroniclers and commentators who lived long after – in some cases several generations after – the events that they narrated. This sketchiness has prompted one historian, in a recent work on the early Muslim conquests, to conclude that scholars can best approach many of the surviving written sources as simply "an expression of social memory, of how the early Muslims reconstructed their past" and in the process articulated their own "foundation myths."[10] Merely to ask the question, then, "What was the quality of Muslim relations with Christians and Jews, once Muslims embarked upon state-formation and conquest?" immediately presents choices that hinge upon the politics and predilections of remembering, particularly if the historian tries to write from the perspective of both conquered and conquering people.

From the viewpoint of the vanquished, what can we say? Simply that in the earliest years of the Islamic era, members of the fledgling Muslim community behaved variably toward Christians and Jews on different occasions. Two oft-repeated episodes from Islamic history stand in stark contrast to each other, and support the best- and worst-case scenarios of Islamic history as it involved Jewish and Christian people. These are scenarios that sustain, on the bright side, a vision of "interfaith utopia" and, on the bleak side, a "countermyth of Islamic persecution."[11] Commentators have frequently invoked these two episodes to support much bigger claims about Muslim attitudes toward, and relations with, Christians and Jews, or to sustain opposing tropes of Muslim tolerance and aggression.

On the side of the bleak stands the story of the Banu Qurayza, a tribe of Arab Jews who lived in the oasis of Medina where Muhammad and his followers settled following their *hijra* from Mecca. The Banu Qurayza remained in Medina even after the Muslims' relations with two other Jewish tribes had ruptured, leading to the latters' expulsion. In 627 CE, at a time when the early Muslims were at war with the Banu Quraysh (who had made the lives of Muhammad's followers difficult in Mecca some years before), the Banu Qurayza Jews established contacts with the Meccan enemies of the Prophet.[12] Seeing these Meccan contacts as a betrayal, the Muslims placed the Banu Qurayza Jews under a siege which lasted for twenty-five days until the latter agreed to submit to arbitration. The arbitrator, who was appointed by Muhammad and who may have been "dying of wounds received during the siege against the Qurayza,"[13] was brutal: he ordered the Jewish men killed and the women and children sold as slaves or given as booty – in other words, he ordered the annihilation of the tribe. According to the accounts of several Muslim commentators who wrote during the first centuries of the Islamic era, Muslims chopped off the heads of some 400–900 Jewish adult men, and then distributed a thousand or so women and children. The Prophet Muhammad himself is said to have claimed one of these Jewish women as a wife on the night of her husband's execution.[14] Only three Jewish men and a woman avoided these fates by embracing Islam.[15] Meanwhile, two years later, in 629 CE, Muhammad and his supporters led a largely bloodless conquest of Mecca, whereupon their former enemies, the Quraysh Arabs (whose contact with the Banu Qurayza had served as grounds for the annihilation of this Jewish tribe) embraced Islam and swiftly entered the ranks of the Arab Muslim elites.

What does the story of the Banu Qurayza mean? In a study of the legal status of non-Muslims in the Islamic world, the late scholar Antoine Fattal (1918–87) (who went on to become Lebanese ambassador to the Vatican) suggested that the episode – along with the Qur'anic verses which Muhammad incrementally revealed about Jews – signaled that the space for persuasion was narrowing as the Muslim community expanded, and that "Islam would be spread by force of arms."[16] Early Muslim scholars, more simply, described the executions and enslavements as a decisive and legitimate response to the treachery that this Jewish tribe had demonstrated, and accepted that punishment of the whole tribe, rather than of specific perpetrators, was warranted. In modern times, however, some Muslims have expressed discomfort with, or doubt about, such a total response, on the grounds that "killing such a large number of people is diametrically opposed to the Islamic sense of justice and to basic principles laid down in the Qur'an." In other words, reflecting a modern sensibility that emphasizes individualism rather than tribalism, some Muslims have expressed discomfort with the idea of collective punishment. Pursuing the point, some have attempted to question the accuracy of the story as conveyed by early Muslim writers, in spite of the abundance of sources that agree on the basic points of the episode.[17] In modern times, too, both Muslims and Jews have sometimes cited this episode polemically as evidence of something more sweeping: either to support the idea of the timeless treachery of Jews toward Muslims (e.g., in speeches by President Anwar Sadat of Egypt in 1972, and President Pervez Musharraf of Pakistan in 2001) or of the timeless cruelty of Muslims toward Jews in particular and of the intrinsic, intractable violence of Muslims in general.[18] Since the 1990s, with the growth of the World Wide Web and the proliferation of blogs and other Internet-based media, polemical debates over this episode have only intensified.

Many historians agree that Muhammad expected or assumed that Jews and others would embrace the new message of Islam, finding its merits self-evident. The refusal of Jewish Arabs like the Banu Qurayza to reject their old ways and embrace the new ones may have appeared at the time as an affront to a man (Muhammad) or to a group of people (Muslims) who had a universal message to deliver.[19] Yet, in a recent analysis of this episode, the historian Fred Donner suggested that viewers of the past may be mistaken in projecting a distinctly "Muslim" dimension onto this episode. Muslims were not thinking of themselves as Muslims (*muslimun*) when this incident occurred, he argued, but were calling themselves simply "Believers" (*mu'minun*). Thus, when this episode in Medina occurred, these "Believers" were simply projecting a new kind of monotheistic belief that had not yet crystallized as something distinctive and separate vis-à-vis other forms of monotheism. Ascribing "Muslim" and "Jewish" motives to the actors in this episode may therefore be a mistake.[20]

The execution and seizure of the Banu Qurayza Jews – shocking in its scope and totality – underlines a problem that Muslims, in their presentation of Islam to non-Muslims, have sometimes found hard to shake off. This is the idea that Islam (the religion), Muslims (the people), and Islamic states (the political structures) historically developed in a crucible of violence, with warfare having been essential for the territorial and demographic expansion that enabled Muslim communities to grow and thrive. The episode is complicated by the participation of Muhammad, who emerges in the firsthand stories about him that his companions later recounted and preserved for posterity – stories collectively known as the *hadith* – as a vivid, real-life figure. The episode raises further questions about when violence is legitimate, and when it goes too far.

The problem of war and violence, Marshall Hodgson wrote, edging toward this issue, meaning "the readiness on the part of reformers to use physical compulsion to meet and overcome the compulsion used by those already in power," has featured prominently in many if not most successful reform movements across history. In the reform movement of Islam, Muslims were no exception in facing the "temptation to a spirit of exclusivity that went with any vision of a total community and that received appropriate expression in warfare. The resulting problems," Hodgson concluded, "came to form a persistent theme in Islamic history."[21] To be sure, Christian history has continued to grapple with its own records and legacies of violence,[22] though a striking difference in the early history of Christianity is that its followers were weak and thus tended to receive rather than mete out violence, feeding into a culture of martyrdom that had parallels in Islamic history with the experience of Shi'is in the aftermath of the killing of Husayn at Karbala in 680 CE. For the historian, the result of this problem of war and violence is, in any case, twofold: again, it compounds the difficulty of separating a religion from the practices of the people who claim it, while also highlighting the significance of militarism, including justifications or condemnations of violence, for communities as they negotiate borders.

The case of the Jews of Banu Qurayza represents the dark side of early Islamic history. For examples of the bright side – of the conciliatory and magnanimous in Islamic history – historians have often pointed to the Islamic conquests of Egypt and Syria, which brought these two core territories of the Late Roman or Byzantine Empire into Islamic domains. Textbooks have often repeated a standard story: they note that the early Islamic conquests were easy, quick, and relatively painless, and ascribe this to the way that Egyptian or Syrian Christians "welcomed" the Arab invaders.[23] At that time, disputes over the nature of Christ had driven Christian communities apart, while Syrian "Miaphysites" and Egyptian Coptic "Monophysites" (both of whom had ideas about the fusion of the humanity and divinity in Jesus) loathed the Byzantine authorities, who had been persecuting them for their views on this issue. Consider the example of Benjamin (590–661), a patriarch of the indigenous Coptic church (with the word Copt, referring to an Egyptian Christian, having come from the Greek word for Egypt, *Aigyptos*). The patriarch Benjamin had risen to power during an interlude of Persian rule in Egypt (619–29), lost his place when the Byzantine powers returned, and regained it under the Muslims. During the years immediately preceding the Muslim conquest, Byzantine authorities had tortured and killed Benjamin's own brother, Menas: to be precise, they had roasted him, wrenched his teeth out, and then drowned him. Against the climate of fear and hostility that such Byzantine actions elicited, one scholar speculated that, "Many Copts must have thought that anything would be better than this."[24] Indeed, historians have often recounted that when the Muslim Arab invaders arrived in 639, Christians greeted their rule as an improvement that brought freedom from persecution.

The problem is, however, that scholars now express serious doubt about whether the Christian historiographical record can sustain this idea of the "welcome." In a study of Eastern, and specifically Syriac, Christian writing in the early Islamic era, the historian Jan J. van Ginkel noted along these lines, "This image of the Arabs as rescuing the anti-Chalcedonians [including Syriac, Coptic, and other dissident Christians] from the oppression of the Byzantines has been repeated by many, both by Syrian Orthodox authors and by modern scholars writing on the seventh century. It presents the Byzantine empire as an empire at odds with itself, and more particularly with large parts of its population. This in turn is seen as the reason why the Byzantine empire collapsed under the onslaught of the Arabs in the seventh century." However, extant seventh- and eighth-century Syriac sources fail to sustain the idea that Christians greeted the Muslim invaders as liberators. On the contrary, these sources have little positive to say about either the Romans (Byzantine authorities) *or* the Arabs, and suggest that, during the conquest, the Arab invaders made (or were able to make) no distinction between Christian communities that adhered to the official Byzantine interpretation of Christ's nature and those that did not. In other words, it is unclear whether the Arab Muslims on the battlefield were able to appreciate the theological differences among Christians – differences that historians have long hailed as so important in shaping these formative Muslim-Christian relations in the territories of conquest. By this account, Syriac Christians may have been mere bystanders who suffered in a war that led to the replacement of one imperial government (Byzantine) by another (Islamic).[25]

As late as the 1980s, historians accepted a similar welcome narrative with regard to the Copts of Egypt. But then other scholars began to raise similar doubts about the historical record based on Coptic sources, notably by drawing on a text called *The History of the Patriarchs*, a compilation that chronicles church leaders. These scholars reached a more humdrum conclusion: that the initial relationship between the patriarchs and the Islamic authorities was simply lukewarm. One of these scholars observed that by the Umayyad period (661–750) relations between Muslims and Christians in Egypt had deteriorated and Copts had begun to revolt, leading to a "relationship full of suspense."[26] Within a generation of the conquests, too, the Coptic record suggests that Muslims were engaging in polemics with, and applying restrictions on, Christians. During the tenure of the Coptic patriarch Isaac (686–689), for example, the Muslim governor of Egypt ordered the destruction of crosses and placed words on church doors, declaring, "Muhammad is the great Apostle of God and Jesus is also an Apostle of God. Truly God has not been begotten nor does He beget." This challenge to Christian notions of Jesus' divinity and the trinity appears most striking as evidence of a Muslim community that was trying to clarify its own collective identity through the articulation of a distinct Islamic creed. It may have also anticipated the lively atmosphere for enquiry that became a feature of the Abbasid era a century or two later, when "Theological speculation became a pursuit of men in all walks of life."[27]

Where do these two episodes leave us – the Banu Qurayza massacre in Arabia on the one hand, and the Christian reception of Muslim invaders in the eastern lands of the Byzantine Empire, on the other?

In the case of the Banu Qurayza massacre, if we accept that Muslims were thinking as Muslims (*muslimin*) and not as generic monotheistic "Believers" (*mu'minin*) when the incident occurred in Medina in 627, then the destruction of this tribe can stand as a historical benchmark for Muslim-Jewish relations at their worst. But the episode did not presage how Muslim-Jewish relations would generally go on to be. As the historian Mark R. Cohen pointed out, any effort to portray Islam as "an inherently antisemitic religion ignores, one might say suppresses, the substantial security – at times verging on social (though not legal) parity – that Jews enjoyed through centuries of existence under Muslim rule."[28] Such an account would also ignore the fact that the Islamic empire went on to provide fertile terrain for Jewish cultural life, leading to "a time of extraordinary Jewish mobility" and intellectual vitality.[29] Indeed, Islamic rule provided the conditions that enabled "the veritable crystallization and formulation of Judaism as we know it today," with the spread of the Babylonian Talmud (rabbinical commentary on Jewish laws and traditions), the standardization of prayer books for the synagogue service, and the systemization of Halakha (Jewish law).[30]

As far as the Christians of the former Byzantine territories were concerned, the Muslim leaders who conquered and held Egypt and Syria set what would become a pattern: neither then nor later did Muslim leaders persecute Christians for their styles of Christian belief, including their views on the nature of Jesus. However, from early on, Muslims did argue with Christians in an effort to assert their claim to Islam's theological and philosophical superiority (particularly, again, by rejecting the idea of the trinity and a triune God). Muslim leaders thus combined tolerance on the one hand, with a scorn for and persistent mild denigration of Christian beliefs on the other. This treatment, combined subsequently with various inducements (such as tax breaks and professional opportunities), made conversion to Islam quite attractive for the Christian people placed under Muslim rule.

Was it the case, then, that Muslim leaders did not persecute Christians *enough*, to make them either rebel or resist through persistence in their faith? In his historical study of the Jews of the Islamic world, Bernard Lewis argued as much, writing that, "Christianity was defeated, not destroyed, by the rise of Islam and the establishment of the Islamic state." Elaborating, Lewis suggested that by the time of the Muslim conquests, Jews in the region were "more accustomed to adversity" than Christians were. By contrast, for many Christians, "the transition from a dominant to a subject status, with all the disadvantages involved, was too much to endure, and large numbers of them sought refuge from subjection by adopting Islam and joining the dominant faith and community."[31] Jews were fortunate in having a strong collective consciousness that was independent of place and polity.[32] It helped Jews, too, that their conditions improved relative to the Byzantine era, so that the Muslim conquests and Islamic state-building were not as traumatic as they were for Christians.[33]

Taken together, these circumstances may help to explain why, within five centuries of the Muslim conquests of North Africa, Christianity went extinct in Tunisia, even as small Jewish communities continued to prosper in the same place.[34] The disappearance of Christianity in Tunisia was especially striking given that the region had once been home to major Christian theologians like Tertullian (c. 160–220), who had first used the Latin term *trinitas* to explain a god that had "three persons, [but] one substance."[35]

The Deal of the Dhimma

From the beginning, Muslim leaders made a deal, or set of deals, with Christians and Jews, that established terms for coexistence. First, drawing upon the Qur'an, Muslim rulers recognized Christians and Jews as *ahl al-kitab*, that is, as "people of the book" who possessed scriptures and had a kindred belief in God. In former territories of the Byzantine and Persian Empires, this affinity prompted the early Muslim state-builders to reach agreements with the Christians and Jews who submitted to their conquests. They called these Christians and Jews *ahl al-dhimma*, or *dhimmi*s, meaning "people of the pact," and promised them the right to worship and pursue livelihoods without interference, provided that they recognized Muslim hegemony and acceded to various conditions. Muslim rulers also extended many of these privileges to the followers of Zoroastrianism, which had enjoyed favor as the religion of the ruling elites in pre-Islamic Iran, and which claimed a scriptural tradition as well as the notion of a strong and good creator.[36]

The Qur'an contained various clauses that pertained to the appropriate position and treatment by Muslims of Christians and Jews, and these clauses informed Muslim policies toward non-Muslims. For example, the Qur'an advised (5:5) that Muslim men could marry women from the people of the book (i.e., Jewish or Christian women), with it understood (though not explicitly stated) that their children would be Muslim, and that Jewish and Christian men could not marry Muslim females in return.

The Qur'an (9:29) also stipulated that Christians and Jews should pay a special tax called the *jizya*. For *dhimmi*s, this tax (which was eventually applied in practice to Zoroastrians in the former Persian Empire, too) functioned as "material proof of their subjection" and was a "concrete continuation of the taxes paid to earlier [Byzantine and Persian] regimes."[37] In practice, the tax also contributed to the Islamic state that defended them and provided security. Note, however, that the *jizya* neither functioned as, nor was understood by Christians and Jews to be, a substitution for the *zakat*, or alms-tax, which Muslims were expected to pay as one of the religious duties of Islam for the sake of sustaining Muslim public charity (especially by helping the Muslim poor). That is, the *jizya* that Christians and Jews paid went into Islamic state treasuries for state, not charitable, purposes. Any contributions that Christians and Jews made to support charities, or to sustain institutions, within their respective communities occurred in addition to the *jizya* that they owed the Islamic state.

Meanwhile, other policies toward non-Muslims soon became associated with the *dhimma* and with Islamic state policy, even if they did
not derive from specific Qur'anic injunctions. *Dhimmi*s could not insult Islam, nor could they try to convert a Muslim. Jews and Christians
could not inherit from Muslims – not even from a blood relative,
such as a brother, who had converted to Islam. Jews and Christians
could convert to Islam but could not convert between Judaism and
Christianity. Once born or converted into Islam, a person could not
leave it without facing a penalty of death if that person refused opportunities to recant.[38]

Before the conquests, the term *dhimma* had meant something different, and more abstract. As used in the Qur'an and in *hadith* (which
were, again, firsthand accounts of what the Prophet Muhammad and
his companions had said and done), *dhimma* had suggested God's covenant to protect humankind as well as humankind's responsibility to God
to behave honorably toward others. Yet, during the Umayyad period,
dhimma assumed its much narrower meaning and "became reified into
a technical legal concept" that had a bearing specifically on Christians
and Jews.[39] Moreover, in their provisions and format, the practical deals
that Muslim leaders appear to have initially struck with Christians and
Jews followed the pattern of pre-Islamic surrender agreements in the
eastern Mediterranean region, with one significant difference. Whereas
earlier postconquest pacts had been provisional, ad hoc, and inclined to
lapse as political turbulence settled after invasions, the agreements that
Muslim conquerors made with Christians and Jews assumed some fixity.
That is, the Muslims' *dhimma* arrangement endured and became institutionalized. Later generations of Muslims, in various places and periods,
pointed to the existence of a firm pact (in the singular) to claim precedents for their own modes of maintaining control over Christians and
Jews.[40]

The firm, idealized pact to which later generations of Muslims referred
became known as the Pact of Umar. It was ostensibly an agreement that
Muslim authorities had made with the surrendered Christians of Syria at
the time of the Muslim conquest of this region (634–638). Three features
of the pact have led modern scholars to question its historicity, that is, to
suspect that elements may have been "altered ... and sometimes fabricated from the whole cloth."[41] First, there was a long lag time in its documentation: the oldest recorded, integral text emerged only at the end of
the eleventh century, some three and a half centuries after the conquest
of Syria, when an Andalusian philosopher and jurist named Abu Bakr
Muhammad al-Turtushi (1059–1126) recorded it.[42] Second, as it was
eventually passed down, the text appears to have conflated two different

'Umars: 'Umar ibn al-Khattab, who was the Prophet Muhammad's companion and who led the fledgling Muslim state from 634 to 644 during the period of the Syrian conquest; and 'Umar ibn 'Abd al-'Aziz, who served as Umayyad caliph from 717 to 720, and who systematized the privileges to which the growing number of non-Arab converts to Islam were entitled while confirming the disadvantages of *dhimmi*s.[43] And third, variant versions of the text appeared, containing some different provisions.[44]

In the Pact of Umar, the Christians of Syria purportedly agreed not to build or repair churches among Muslims; not to display crosses in roads or markets where Muslims circulated, or to ring church bells loudly; not to ride mounted animals (such as horses); and not to bear arms. The Pact included laws about dress and appearance: "We shall not seem to resemble the Muslims by imitating any of their garments," and, "We shall always dress in the same way wherever we may be, and we shall bind the *zunnar* [a kind of belt] round our waists." Another clause appeared to commit Christian men to a hairstyle: "We shall clip the fronts of our heads." In the Pact, Christians also promised to show respect for Muslims, declaring, "we shall rise from our seats when they wish to sit."[45]

As a roadmap for Muslim-Christian relations, the Pact of Umar, as Muslims later remembered and invoked it, applied with some adaptation to Jews as well (e.g., with reference to synagogues, as opposed to churches).[46] In fact, argued the historian Norman Stillman, many of the restrictions of the Pact "were probably inspired by the discriminatory legislation against Jews that was already in force in the Byzantine lands conquered by the Arabs."[47] Yet while the early Islamic state may have absorbed some of the discriminatory practices of its Christian predecessor state and applied these practices to both Christians and Jews, it also drew inspiration from pre-Islamic Persian, that is, Sassanian, ideology. As the historian Milka Levy-Rubin pointed out, the pact's clauses that asserted visual and spatial differentiation through clothing, hairstyles, and even seating arrangements evoked Persian, more than Byzantine, modes of maintaining social hierarchies.[48]

Again, the Pact of Umar was not full-formed during the conquests, nor was it an ironclad, everlasting agreement. Over the centuries of the Islamic era, for example, churches and synagogues did get built or repaired in various places, when *dhimmi*s secured permission from Muslim rulers.[49] In fact, in the Jazira region (corresponding to what is now northern Iraq and northern Syria), restrictions on church-building began to appear only in the mid-eighth century, that is, after the assertion of Abbasid control from Baghdad. The historian Chase Robinson concluded that, "As far as the Christians were concerned," and judging

from Syriac sources, "controversy lay not in the legality of church building under Islam, but rather in who had the authority over the churches
once built," as leaders of different Christian churches vied against each
other to secure the favor of Muslim authorities.[50] For a few centuries,
he added, the relative aloofness of the Islamic state (in comparison to
its Byzantine predecessor in the region) enabled the Christians of this
region to enjoy local autonomy in a way that helped to sustain "a hardy
and durable Christian identity."[51]

Likewise, notwithstanding the line in the Pact that proclaimed, "We
shall not sell fermented drinks"[52] (reflecting the Qur'an's disapproval of
alcohol) some Christians along with Jews and Muslims did go on to engage in a brisk trade in selling or buying wine or other fermented drinks
such as *buza* in Egypt.[53] Under the Umayyads and the Abbasids, some of
the caliphs were enthusiastic wine-drinkers, while Arabic literature developed a celebrated tradition of wine poetry, associated with men like the
flamboyant Muslim poet, Abu Nuwas (756–814).[54] The tenth-century
Muslim cookbook writer of the caliphs, Ibn Sayyar al-Warraq, even interspersed several recipes for making mead and wine from raisins and
sugar within his section on drinks, while offering tips on the health ben-
efits of wine-drinking as well as some remedies for hangovers.[55] Alcoholic
beverages, in Ibn Sayyar's account, seem as mundane as juice and other
botanically based liquid concoctions. Meanwhile, centuries later, Turkic
cavalrymen who entered the Islamic empire introduced some of their
own alcoholic favorites. Thus the Muslim "Turkish mamluks" or elite
slave soldiers of Mamluk Egypt (1250–1517) brewed and drank "kou-
miss," fermented mare's milk that had an alcohol content of 4–5 percent,
which placed it in the same range as beer.[56]

The Pact of Umar's implicit restriction on using Arabic (contained in
the provision by which the conquered allegedly promised not to "speak
as they [the Muslims] do"[57]) became moot, as more Christians began
to speak Arabic as a mother tongue. In Lower Egypt, Coptic lapsed as a
spoken language as early as the tenth century, though it persisted in some
Upper Egyptian villages as late as the fourteenth or even sixteenth centuries. In Syria, Christians widely spoke Syriac until the eighth century
although use of this language dramatically contracted thereafter, persisting in centuries that followed only as a literary or liturgical language
among church-educated intellectuals.[58]

One point seems clear in the history of intercommunal relations.
Certain Muslims were more eager than others to create or maintain the
distinctions and social hierarchies that kept Christians and Jews separate and subordinate. One twentieth-century historian called these
eager ones the "doctrinaires," including many *qadis* (judges) and *fuqaha'*

Image 4 The Palmer Cup, wine goblet with Arabic inscription, Islamic, c. 1200–1250. Museum Number WB.53. ©The Trustees of the British Museum.

(jurists or law experts), who interpreted the restrictions on *dhimmi*s in ways that fell short of persecution while nevertheless being "vexacious and repressive."[59] Jurists grounded their restrictions in diverse fields of law. In criminal affairs, for example, jurists drew distinctions in the case of *diya*. Often translated into English as the archaic-sounding "blood-wit," *diya* was the compensation paid, by the family of a perpetrator, in cases of wrongful death. Depending on the school of Islamic law (*madh-hab*), to which they adhered, many Muslim jurists assessed the compensatory price for a killed Christian or Jew at two-thirds or half the price of a Muslim.[60] Other policies affected merchants. For example, Islamic law as refined by the jurists set higher customs duties for *dhimmi*s (5 percent) than for Muslims (2.5 percent), leading an eminent Jewish historian to conclude that "the ruling class intended to keep its ascendancy over the

vast subject population not only by taxing it heavily, but also by fur-
thering Muslim trade to the detriment of non-Muslim business."[61] (The
same historian elsewhere noted, however, that the higher tax on Jewish
merchants imitated Byzantine law and lapsed in certain periods and
places in Islamic history, e.g., in Fatimid Egypt.[62]) Approaching the tax
difference from the Muslim perspective, another interpretation is possible: the higher tax on *dhimmi* merchants aimed to provide an incentive
for them to embrace Islam and join the Muslim community.

One point that is *not* clear is whether the provisions of the *dhimma*
sought to humiliate or merely ended up doing so. Consider the *jizya*
again. Some Muslim religious scholars, citing the Qur'an, argued that
payment should entail some ritual to remind *dhimmi*s of their inferior
status, for example, by having the tax collector grab a *dhimmi* by the neck
and slap him during the payment.[63] Occasionally, some rulers insisted
that *dhimmi*s had to hand over annual *jizya* payments in person, rather
than channeling payment through a community leader, perhaps to reinforce the personal immediacy of their subordination, or perhaps simply to provide the ruler with a head-count of his *dhimmi* subjects.[64] Still
other rulers required *dhimmi*s to carry their proof of *jizya* payment while
traveling (with no comparable requirement on Muslims vis-à-vis their
respective tax payments), and subjected *dhimmi*s who failed to produce
a receipt to "severe punishment." Such policies may have made the *jizya*
into a psychological burden, and one that stung more than many other
provisions of the *dhimma*.[65]

As for the financial burden of the *jizya*, it could vary considerably from
one place and time to another (as indeed could the taxes pressed out of
Muslims). In theory, according to the jurists who set out guidelines for
ideal behavior, Islamic states were supposed to charge a reasonable rate
for the *jizya* and to require payment only from adult, able-bodied men.
But practice diverged from theory, as shown by an unusually rich body of
evidence relating to the Jewish community of Cairo. This evidence comes
from a *geniza*, a repository or stash of assorted writings that, according
to Jewish beliefs, had to be set aside for future burial in case they contained the name of God and therefore commanded respect. While there
were many *geniza*s in Jewish lands, the documents in the Cairo Geniza
were exceptional for their mere survival in "a lumber room attached to a
synagogue";[66] for insights they provide into the everyday life of Jews and
into the societies and global trading networks in which they moved;[67]
and for their long range (with documents dating from eleventh century
through the nineteenth). The unrivaled expert on these papers was the
historian S. D. Goitein (1900–85), who drew upon the Cairo Geniza to
write many articles and books, including a six-volume opus magnum

Image 5 *Marriage Contract of Zein, Daughter of R. Aaron Ha-Mumheh (The Expert)*, Fustat, Egypt, c. 1080–1114. Judeo-Arabic manuscript on parchment. Courtesy of the Library at the Herbert D. Katz Center for Advanced Judaic Studies, University of Pennsylvania. Cairo Genizah Collection, Halper 333.

titled *A Mediterranean Society*. Before he had immersed himself in the Geniza papers, Goitein explained, he had assumed that Jews paid the *jizya* on a sliding scale according to their ability. "This impression proved to be entirely fallacious," he later stated, "for it did not take into consideration the immense extent of poverty and privation experienced by the masses, and in particular their way of living from hand to mouth, their persistent lack of cash, which turned the 'season of the tax' into one of horror, dread, and misery." To make matters worse, by the thirteenth century (when the Sunni Muslim Ayyubid dynasty was ruling Egypt), Muslim rulers, backed up by jurists of the Shafi'i school of law, were no longer exempting "the indigent, the invalids, and the old" from the *jizya*.[68] The tax was, or had become, a great strain.

As the generations wore on, too, and the distance from the conquest period lengthened, Muslim rulers periodically invoked the Pact of Umar, as they understood or imagined it, to call for or justify further restrictions on *dhimmi*s. The case of clothing is illustrative. At the time of the conquest of Syria, observed Yedida Kalfon Stillman in a history of Arab dress, differences between the Hellenistic fashions of the conquered people and of the Arab Muslims were obvious. Merely by looking at a person's dress, one would have been able to identify a conqueror from one of the conquered. But as growing numbers of non-Arabs converted to Islam, and as a "new, cosmopolitan, Islamic fashion" emerged, blending "the Arab, the Irano-Turkic, and the Hellenistic Mediterranean," it became harder to use dress as a means of distinguishing people by their religion, particularly since Muslim, Christians, and Jews were tending to converge toward common fashions.[69] Sometime in the late eighth or early ninth century, Abu Yusuf (d. 807), a chief *qadi* for the Abbasids, wrote a treatise on taxation in which he lamented this convergence. In a chapter on "The Dress and Attire of *Ahl al-Dhimma*," Abu Yusuf cited the Pact of Umar to assert that no *dhimmi*s should be permitted to resemble Muslims in dress. In particular, he excoriated Christian men who had abandoned turbans and distinguishing belts and who were wearing their hair long like Muslims.

Texts like Abu Yusuf's may have either fostered or confirmed the climate of opinion in which the Abbasid caliph, al-Mutawakkil (r. 847–861), invoked *ghiyar*, meaning the laws of differentiation by clothing. In 850, Mutawakkil issued a decree stating that Christians, Jews, and Zoroastrians had to wear certain "honey-colored" garments to mark themselves out in public, notably the *zunnar* belt that the Pact of Umar had mentioned, along with two patches, four fingers wide, to be attached to their fronts and backs. Four years later Mutawakkil issued another edict, ordering Christians in particular to wear yellow on outer garments. This policy of color-coding clothes as a means of asserting social status had Persian (Sassanian) roots.[70] Since the Abbasid caliph Muqtadir issued similar decrees less than sixty years later, in 907–8, it appears that the caliphs' injunctions on clothing were neither followed nor enforced so that Muslims, Christians, and Jews continued to dress much alike. Nevertheless, honey, saffron, and other yellow colors became more frequently associated with Jews and Christians in the rules of *ghiyar*. They resurfaced later and elsewhere (such as in required yellow garments or patches for Jews in fourteenth-century Egypt and fifteenth-century Tunis) because of the *hadith* claiming that the Prophet Muhammad had identified yellow as a distasteful color for Muslims.[71]

The fact remained nonetheless: provided that *dhimmi*s paid their *jizya*, treated Muslims with respect, and caused no trouble, Islamic states generally left Christians and Jews unbothered. In an age when Islamic states were not social-service-oriented welfare states and (unlike modern states) lacked the technology and bureaucracy to intrude into the lives of all their subjects, their minimal functions were defending territories on the one hand, and promoting stability and the rule of law on the other. Muslim rulers, moreover, had neither the ability nor the desire to meddle in the daily lives of their subjects – whether Christian, Jewish, or Muslim. As S. D. Goitein concluded, "The far-reaching and well-attested autonomy of the Christian and Jewish communities within the Muslim state had as its main reason the simple fact that the Muslim subjects, too, were mainly left to their own devices."[72]

Ultimately, the very system that subordinated *dhimmi*s may have helped to fortify communal and sectarian solidarity among them, by prompting Christians and Jews to look inward for social support, into their respective religious communities. This tendency toward communalism certainly bound together Jews, who otherwise exhibited a startling degree of socioeconomic diversity. For while some Jews held distinguished positions in Islamic society, for example, as medical doctors, astronomers, and political advisers to the caliphs, most Jews were quite poor, while many held professions that were considered to be at the very bottom of the combined Muslim, Christian, and Jewish social order, working, for example, as tanners, pigeon racers, and executioners. In some cases, Jews did jobs – such as burying excrement – that had been their lot in Roman times as well. The last point suggests, again, the continuities in Islamic historical practice vis-à-vis the Byzantine era, which showed just how much Muslim rulers inherited from their Christian predecessors. Nevertheless, in spite of this broad spectrum of wealth and prestige in employment, Jewish communities in the Umayyad and early Abbasid periods pooled resources, as one scholar argued, so that the rich helped to provide for the poor.[73]

Demographic Shifts, Lines of Distinction, and Points of Convergence

For the two centuries or so after the early Muslim conquests, Muslims comprised a fraction of the population in the lands that they ruled. But one would not know it from the Arabic sources, which "are almost exclusively interested in the doings of Muslims." As the historian Hugh Kennedy pointed out, "The only infidels who get speaking parts in the [Arabic] chronicles are the Byzantine emperors and Persian generals whose deliberations form a prelude to their inevitable defeats." Reading the works of the great Muslim historian, Muhammad ibn Jarir al-Tabari (838–923), one "would have very little idea that the vast majority of the population ruled by the caliphs in the eighth and ninth centuries were not Muslim, still less any understanding of their concerns."[74] Early Islamic policies toward containing non-Muslims may have thereby reflected the anxiety of a small ruling elite that, of necessity, had to make a deal or set of deals with the subordinated non-Muslim majority. By the tenth century, however, the demographic balance had shifted; in core regions of the Middle East and North Africa that had once belonged to the Byzantine and Sassanian Persian Empires, most people had become Muslims.

The process by which mass conversion to Islam occurred is a matter of some debate. Nevertheless, it appears that, in the central lands of the Islamic empire, conversions spiked during the ninth century, when the Abbasid state was at its most powerful.[75] As more people came into contact with Muslims, rates of conversion increased through intermarriage, assimilation, and acculturation.[76] A kind of bandwagon effect may have occurred through peaceful and popular acclaim, producing a strong Muslim majority that only then sustained, in one scholar's view, a truly Islamic society.[77] Reflecting on the conversion of Copts to Islam in Egypt, other historians offered a much less sanguine interpretation, arguing that negative social pressures leveled upon *dhimmi*s were decisive in prompting conversions. In this view, the accumulation of "social restrictions, legal inferiority, Muslim hostility, excessive taxation, and physical insecurity" ultimately compelled Christians to become Muslims, with the ninth century, again, as "the great watershed" for conversions.[78] Such conversions in Egypt gained particular momentum among Christian farmers, who faced a land tax as well the *jizya*, and who found themselves compelled to pay a higher amount of tax, per capita, as the number of *dhimmi*s declined.[79]

In some ways, and in spite of differences of timing and impetus, this scholarship on conversion to Islam in the Abbasid period resembles the scholarship on conversion to Christianity in nineteenth- and early twentieth-century Africa. Both historical processes of conversion occurred in imperial settings where ruling powers used elements of coercion to effect social policies, and where professional and economic opportunities – and not only perceptions of spiritual or devotional merit – appear to have made conversion to the religion of the ruling powers seem attractive to individuals or families.[80] Of course, in colonial Africa – in contrast to the early Islamic Middle East – there was no official, tiered system of taxes or social rights that hinged upon conversion.

Nevertheless, twentieth-century converts to Christianity often did expect to enjoy a higher degree of social mobility relative to those who continued to adhere to the faiths of their ancestors. Conversion led to a kind of membership that carried social privileges.

Even if the "Age of Conversions"[81] in the Islamic Middle East peaked in the ninth century, a critical juncture for converts and *dhimmi*s had occurred a century earlier, during the brief reign of the Umayyad caliph 'Umar ibn 'Abd al-'Aziz (r. 717–20). In the years following the conquests, non-Arabs had begun to embrace Islam, and yet many Arab Muslims (i.e., immediate descendants of the conquerors) appeared to feel that the advantages of Islam were theirs alone, and that, in effect, all non-Arabs (converts to Islam or not) should be treated as *dhimmi*s. 'Umar ibn 'Abd al-'Aziz changed this situation by exempting non-Arab converts to Islam from the *jizya* and recognizing them as *bona fide* Muslims. Thus, if Islam had begun as an Arab religion, 'Umar ibn 'Abd al-'Aziz helped to fulfill its universal potential by extending the perquisites of membership in the Muslim community to newcomers. At the same time, this caliph also sharpened the lines of distinction that separated Muslims from other believers in God, by expelling some non-Muslims from government office, and by forbidding, perhaps for the first time, the construction of new churches and synagogues.[82] He also reportedly forbade Christians employed by the state from wearing a specific style of robe, turban, and silk cloth that Muslims were wont to wear.[83] Again, with the steady increase in the number of conversions to Islam, it had become harder by the early eighth century to tell Muslims and non-Muslims apart in markets and on streets. In this sense, 'Umar ibn 'Abd al-'Aziz's policies helped to reassert the kind of tangible or visual differences that had once enabled people to recognize Muslims and non-Muslims at a glance.[84] Thus when the scholar Abu 'Abd Allah Muhammad ibn Idris al-Shafi'i (767–820) later wrote a treatise elaborating the Pact of Umar and its restrictions for *dhimmi*s, he was building on the legacy of 'Umar ibn 'Abd al-'Aziz.[85] Note that al-Shafi'i went on to achieve renown as a path-breaking scholar of *fiqh*, or Islamic jurisprudence, and as the eponymous founder of one *madhhab*, or school of Islamic law.

Indeed, in the Umayyad and Abbasid periods, "Shari'a-minded pietists" tried to bring Muslims into line, enjoining them to follow the example of the Prophet Muhammad and his companions (the *sunna*) and promoting or inventing rituals and customs that would enable Muslims to behave in distinctly Muslim ways.[86] In Egypt, for example, at a time when many Coptic Christians were converting to Islam, jurists discouraged Muslims from preserving certain Christian customs, such as carrying candles in funerary processions. Jurists also disagreed with each other over whether *dhimmi*s could wash the corpses of Muslims, or even attend Muslim funerals as mourners. Many said no – *dhimmi*s could not or should not prepare Muslims for burial or participate in their funerals – suggesting the very physicality of the limits that jurists and pietists were trying to impose between Muslims and others.[87] The consequences of these limits may have been especially troubling and traumatic for divided families, in which partial conversions to Islam occurred.

Of course, what ordinary Muslims said and did was often not what the jurists wanted or expected. Regarding the middle centuries of the Islamic era, the historian Jonathan Berkey observed that, "Reports of Muslims participating in the religious festivals of their Jewish and Christian neighbors ... remained common ... and provided the foundation for a sustained polemic on the part of Muslim scholars."[88] Sometimes, Muslims too followed Christian customs simply because they liked them or found them useful. "So, for example, according to the tenth-century geographer al-Muqaddasi, the Muslims of Syria participated in the celebration of Easter, Christmas, and other Christian feast-days, in part because their more-or-less regular appearance according to the solar calendar helped to mark the agricultural seasons more accurately than the Muslim holidays, which ... moved forward each year according to the lunar Muslim calendar."[89]

Likewise, many Muslim, Christian, and Jewish intellectuals sought out or welcomed contact across religious lines. Leading Jewish philosophers, who were interested in "what it is rational to believe – about God, the world, and human beings – and ... what is right to do and good to pursue in our lives"[90] – refined their ideas amidst exchanges with Muslims. Sa'adiya ben Gaon (882–942) and later Moses Maimonides (1135–1204) were prime examples in this regard.[91] Among Christians, meanwhile, intellectual exchanges with Muslim thinkers inspired a new Christian Arabic literary tradition, which often addressed philosophical and theological issues.[92] The Christian and Jewish adoption of Arabic offers powerful linguistic evidence for cultural rapport as well. Note, for example, that the papers of the Cairo Geniza were written in Arabic, Hebrew, and also Judeo-Arabic, that is, Arabic rendered in Hebrew characters and possessing some Hebrew and Aramaic grammatical and lexical elements.[93] As a vehicle for expression, Judeo-Arabic had spoken forms as well, and came to flourish among Jews as far west as Morocco.

One can find further evidence of rapport in books by Muslim lovers of the culinary arts, who regarded the traditions of the Christians and Jews around them with a keen interest and familiarity. Thus, an entire chapter in the tenth-century *Kitab al-Tabikh* (Book of Cookery), which is the oldest surviving (though not the first-ever-written) Arabic cookbook, attributed to Ibn Sayyar al-Warraq, concerns the vegetarian dishes that the Christians of Syria and Iraq cooked during Lent, in lieu of meat. These were the same vegetarian dishes that Christian doctors, employed by the Abbasid caliphs, were known to recommend as foods for the sick.[94] While most cookbook authors of the Abbasid era were high-ranking Muslims, who had some connection to Abbasid court life, Jewish and Christian writers produced many scholarly treatises during this period on issues of diet and hygiene, which Muslim gastronomes read. For example, there was the tenth-century Jewish doctor, Abu Ya'qub Ishaq ibn Sulayman al-Isra'ili (also known as Yitzhak ben Shlomo ha-Yisraeli; d. 932), who wrote an influential book about dietetics in the city of Qayrawan, which is now part of Tunisia.[95]

Humble people were sharing food customs as well. As archaeologists and art historians have shown, for example, the style of popular ceramics – such as the fired-clay bowls people used for their food – stayed much the same in Syria as the Byzantine imperial era transitioned into the Islamic imperial era. While new ceramic styles emerged among elites in the first few generations that followed the Islamic conquests, the "pottery of everyday life" remained similar.[96]

Among Muslim literati, music lovers were among the most cosmopolitan and inclusive in their attitudes toward non-Muslim traditions. Consider a remarkable epistle on music, written in tenth-century Baghdad as part of an encyclopedic survey of "all the fields of knowledge and research of its time." Apparently the work of several authors or "brothers" (ikhwan), this epistle emphasized the universalism of music ("all the peoples of the world have recourse to music and even many animals find pleasure in it"), its value as a window into "the wonders of creation," and its magnificent variety. "Know, my brother – may God assist you and assist us through the spirit [emanating] from Himself – that each people of the earth possesses melodies, songs, and rhythms different from each other, and so great in number, that only the great God who created, formed and fashioned men different in character, language and colour, is able to count them." The authors acknowledged the devotional power of Muslim, Christian, and Jewish music alike, by writing about the "art of music in the sanctuaries and the sacred places at the moment of the solemn reading of the prayers, the sacrifices, invocations, supplications and lamentations" as done by "the prophet David – may he be blessed – during the reading of the Psalms and as the Christians do in their churches, [and] the Muslims in their mosques."[97] In commenting further on the "great musical tradition" that emerged under the Umayyads and blossomed under the Abbasids, the musicologist

Amnon Shiloah noted that Muslim commentators on music lavished special attention on David, king of ancient Israel recognized as a prophet in the Qur'an, observing that his beautiful psalm-singing was said to have attracted birds, humans, and other animals.[98] Recurrent high praise for David may help to explain why the books of Abbasid-era Muslim musicologists had such an influence on Jewish scholars who were writing musical treatises in the same period.[99]

To summarize, widescale conversions to Islam had occurred by the tenth century, placing Muslims in positions of greater power vis-à-vis Christians and Jews. Muslims thus came to enjoy what one sociologist, writing a work of comparative world history, described as two types of power. The first type of power, which had been manifesting itself since the Muslim conquests, was authoritative power, "willed by groups and institutions," in this case by Islamic states backed up by law courts and weapon-bearing forces, which could issue "definite commands and [demand] conscious obedience." What the demographic shift to Islam enabled was the second kind of power – "diffused power," or popular power – of the kind that "spreads in a more spontaneous, unconscious, decentered way throughout a population, resulting in similar social practices that embody power relations but are not explicitly commanded."[100] By the tenth century, too, popular devotional practices, bodies of legal interpretation, and other cultural forms had cohered, fostering Muslim identities that were increasingly distinct from those of Christians and Jews. These trends confirmed social hierarchies and cleavages.

Nevertheless, people, communities, and cultures still intersected – in conversations among scholars, or in the circulation of books; in the celebration of popular holidays; and through trading networks and common patterns of cultural consumption. The many points of cultural convergence that tied Jews into Islamic society prompted S. D. Goitein, in his study of the Cairo Geniza, to conclude that Muslims, Christian, and Jews lived together in a kind of "cultural symbiosis" that was often mutually beneficial and enriching. Islamic law consistently tried to enforce the "segregation and subservience" of *dhimmi*s to Muslims, but in practice, Muslims, Christians, and Jews lived in close proximity, often renting houses or apartments from each other in the same city streets or buildings. In the eleventh, twelfth, and early thirteenth centuries, too, a "flourishing middle class and a brisk international trade made for free intercourse between various segments of the population."[101] In this social environment, Christians, Jews, and Muslims lived their lives in Islamic societies, albeit while belonging on different terms of inclusion.

Conclusion: Societies in Formation

In a book titled *The Formation of Islamic Art*, the art historian Oleg Grabar posed an intriguing question: When does it make sense to speak of an Islamic art in *formation*, as opposed to an Islamic art that has *formed*?[102] At what point, in other words, can we say that the changes of history had created something distinctly "Islamic" in art? Scholars may agree on certain key features that eventually emerged to typify Islamic art – the ornamental use of Arabic calligraphy, for example, or the application of arabesque or geometric motifs in lieu of figurative representation. But searching for clean breaks in the record may be futile when so many artworks (including buildings) suggest continuity vis-à-vis earlier traditions. The Dome of the Rock, in Jerusalem, is an obvious example: sponsored by the Umayyad caliph, 'Abd al-Malik, and completed in 691, this mosque sports a dome in the style of a Byzantine *martyrium* (i.e., a church built to honor Christ or another martyr).[103] It is a cultural hybrid, a somewhat church-like mosque, illustrating the blending of new and old cultures. Focusing on the former lands of the Byzantine and Sassanian Empires, and thinking about examples like the Dome of the Rock, Grabar described a history of Islamic artistic formation that went something like this: The early Muslim conquerors swept through quickly but without engaging in massive destruction; a considerable amount of infrastructure, both physical (such as churches) and cultural (such as "collective memories, legends, and myths") remained intact; Islamic states and societies inherited this infrastructure; Muslims and other members of Islamic societies then went on to use, adapt, and reconfigure much of this "material, aesthetic, and emotional order," endowing it with new qualities along the way.

This lesson about the formation of Islamic art applies to the formation of Islamic societies more broadly. Islamic societies emerged out of and evolved from existing social contexts; they absorbed the influences and ideas of Christians, Jews, and others, and then moved in new directions. Likewise, embracing Islam through conversion, many Christians and Jews joined and helped shape Muslim communities that were in flux. Some converts from Judaism to Islam proved to be "spectacularly influential" in the Muslim communities that they joined, by assimilating Jewish legal scholarship – including "reams of Halakha [meaning laws and traditions] and Aggada [meaning exigetical texts and rabbinic homilies]" – into Muslim scholarly traditions. A key example of such a Jewish convert to Islam was the Yemeni, Wahb ibn Munabbih, who died around 720 and who became an important transmitter of stories (*hadith*) about the Prophet Muhammad's companions.[104] Jewish converts to

Islam exerted influence in other social spheres, too. Consider Ya'qub ibn Killis (930–991), at one time leader of merchants in Syria, who helped to mastermind the Fatimid conquest of Egypt in 969 and then "brilliantly revamped the financial structure of the country."[105]

This rumination on the meaning and nature of cultural "formation" raises deeper epistemological questions. What are the decisive markers in the past, when do we begin stories and end them, and when do we declare something complete or full-formed? The same questions that we may address to the study of Islamic art are critical for the study of Muslim relations with Christians and Jews, because the way history looks – grim or cheerful, calm or chaotic, and so on – depends on the event, place, or era that we choose as the end of our story. In this respect, the cinematographer's dilemma, where to cut and splice a film, closely resembles the challenge facing the history-writer.

If we were to examine documents from the Cairo Geniza that mention clothing, for example, what would we see? If we cut to the eleventh century, we could find trousseau lists indicating the garments that Jewish brides were taking into marriage. When compared with Arabic literary sources from the period, these trousseau lists confirm that moderately prosperous urban Jewish and Muslim women were dressing alike in Fatimid Egypt, notwithstanding the Pact of Umar's ostensible injunction against *dhimmis* resembling Muslims in dress.[106] Jump two centuries ahead, however, and the Geniza records show something different: under the successor dynasties of the Ayyubids (1169–1250) and Mamluks (1250–1517) in Egypt and Syria, differentiation by clothing was quite pronounced, since Muslim rulers were now enforcing the laws of *ghiyar*. For example, beginning in 1301, the Mamluks required Christians men to wear blue turbans, and Jews to wear yellow; later they required Christian and Jewish women to wear wraps in these same identifying colors.[107] The increasingly tight enforcement of clothing rules appeared to reflect a calcification of Muslim attitudes toward non-Muslims which the Crusades, the Spanish Reconquista, and economic strains reinforced and which Muslim clerics supported.[108] Indeed, from then until the nineteenth century, most Jewish and Muslim women in Egypt, and arguably throughout the Arab world, dressed sufficiently *unlike* each other that one look at their garments would have been enough to tell them apart by religion.[109] Once again, merely choosing where we stop or start telling a narrative makes a major difference to how hopeful or bleak, harmonious or conflict-ridden, a history looks from our vantage point.

Analyzing population data and rates of conversion from Christianity to Islam in Egypt, two historical demographers have also identified the twelfth and thirteenth centuries as a period of strain. They, too, have connected this strain to the Crusades. The Roman pope, Urban II, launched the Crusades in 1096, ostensibly for the sake of recovering Christian property and defending Christianity or Christian people.[110] He was responding, in particular, to a plea for help from the Christian rulers of the much-truncated Byzantine Empire, which was then occupying parts of Asia Minor and southeastern Europe from its capital at Constantinople, but which was facing pressure from Turkic nomads who were relatively recent converts to Islam. These Turks had begun to migrate from Inner Asia into the Anatolian plateau, in search of new lands for pasture and new opportunities for looting from settled agricultural peoples in the region. They were the precursors to, or perhaps even the forebears of, a certain family of Turks – the Ottomans – who began their rise to power in the region some two centuries later, and went on to establish what became known as the Ottoman Empire.

The European Crusaders – who in various phases of their warfare struck Asia Minor, the Levant, and North Africa (notably, Egypt and, abortively, Tunisia), leaving aside their deeds in Europe – slaughtered local Muslims, Christians, and Jews with little distinction, and undermined the already fragile Byzantine Empire by laying waste to its territories.[111] They struck at a time of political fragmentation in the Islamic world: Muslim control over Spain and Sicily was diminishing, while the Fatimids in Egypt were weakening, too.[112] During the Crusades, local Christians became vulnerable to attack by Muslims, who suspected them of aiding or sympathizing with their ostensible co-religionists. For this reason, indeed, some Christians in Mamluk Egypt tried to pose as Jews when they walked down the street, believing that this impersonation would make them safer.[113] As a series of holy wars initiated by Christians of western Europe, the Crusades raise a question that resurfaces time and again, with regard to the modern period of Middle Eastern history: namely, did European agents of intervention help Middle Eastern Christians in any way, or rather weaken them, by stirring up mistrust and resentment among Muslims who came to question the loyalty of the Christians around them? Certainly, the Crusaders of the twelfth and thirteenth centuries, like Western interventionists in the modern period, posed challenges to the Islamic order as it regulated relations between Muslims and others.

The Crusaders appear to have increased the vulnerability of Christians in Egypt and Syria, particularly following the rise of the Mamluk dynasty, which established a base in both regions and quickly uprooted the last Crusader kingdom from Jerusalem. Coptic chroniclers described the Mamluk period (1250–1517) as an age of persecution and martyrs, when Muslim authorities fired Christians from government jobs and when Muslim mobs destroyed churches, killed Copts, and created an atmosphere of fear in which many Christians converted to Islam. On one occasion, authorities destroyed a church claiming that the sound of the wooden clappers (*naqus*), which Christians used in lieu of bells to summon worshippers, interfered with the ability of Muslims to hear sermons in a nearby mosque.[114] This was also a period when many *muhtasib*s (Muslim inspectors of public places) regularly invoked the Pact of Umar to justify measures that included requiring Christians and Jews to travel around Cairo only on foot, and only on donkeys, side saddle, beyond the city perimeter.[115] By the time the Mamluk era ended in 1517, Christians had shrunk to perhaps 7 percent of Egypt's population – about the same proportion as in late twentieth-century Egypt.[116]

Of course, many measures that left Christians feeling beleaguered also affected Jews. Decrees issued against *dhimmi*s were many and varied in Mamluk Egypt, which was beset by strains arising not only from the Crusades, but also from the mid-fourteenth-century pandemic outbreak of the bubonic plague known as the Black Death that struck the country – and the wider region. In 1354, for example, less than a decade after the Black Death had struck Egypt, one Mamluk ruler became concerned about the inability of Muslims and *dhimmi*s to distinguish one another when naked. Thus, he ordered *dhimmi* men (Jews and Coptic Christians who practiced, like Muslims, male circumcision[117]) to wear a metal ring around their necks in the public bathhouse, and forbade *dhimmi* women from bathing with Muslim women at all. In 1419, other rules stipulated that Christian and Jewish men and women should wear distinguishing colored buttons (blue for Christians, yellow for Jews) and a bell around their necks in the bathhouse or at market. On one occasion, Muslim female bathhouse attendants beat up Christian and Jewish women who had avoided these orders.[118] Meanwhile, another fifteenth-century rule barred Jewish and Christian doctors from treating Muslim patients. In the face of these humiliations, and "within an atmosphere of progressively heightening religious consciousness and cultivated contempt," many Jews, like many Christians, converted to Islam.[119]

In spite of the variations and vicissitudes like the ones highlighted here, relations between Muslims, on the one hand, and Christians and Jews, on the other, continued to follow certain patterns that went back to the early Islamic era, when rulers of the fledgling Islamic empire devised ways of including Jews and Christians as fellow "people of the book." Recall that Muslim rulers of this empire had made a deal of protection, establishing terms for coexistence. For the beneficiaries of this deal, the *dhimmi*s, they devised institutions and practices that confirmed an order and hierarchy of social relations. In this way, to use a present-day turn of phrase, Islamic states "managed diversity." And the diversity they managed looked, in broad strokes, like this: Christians and Jews pursued lives and livelihoods within Islamic societies, which had pronounced social hierarchies. These hierarchies placed Muslims at the top while providing a variety of social and economic incentives to encourage non-Muslims to convert to Islam. In the Middle East and North Africa, these conditions, in the long run, enabled Muslim communities to grow at the expense of Christian and Jewish communities, which remained (in the case of Jews) and became (in the case of Christians) minorities, in the sense of being both socially subordinate and numerically small. The boundaries of religion, maintained through law and practice, encouraged communities to remain distinct, as did laws and policies that sought to reinforce the social subordination of Christians and Jews in relation to Muslims. And yet, neighbors found opportunities for social contact across religious lines, and merchants engaged in trade. Intellectuals shared ideas, and the evidence survives in musical, culinary, philosophical, architectural, and other works that bear the mark of production through interplay. The result may indeed have been cultural symbiosis, a kind of living together that entailed mutual benefit and interdependence for communities of Muslims, Christians, and Jews.

During the early fourteenth century, around the very time that the Mamluks in Egypt were trying to reassert clothing distinctions for *dhimmi*s in bathhouses, the family of Turks known as the Ottomans was rising to power in western Anatolia. In 1453, an Ottoman sultan conquered Constantinople, extinguishing the Byzantine Empire. Yet, it was only in the years from 1517 to 1520 that another Ottoman sultan wrested greater Syria and Egypt from the Mamluks and thereby extended Ottoman control into the historic heartlands of the early Islamic world. We can say in retrospect that this conquest, of what were by now largely Arabic-speaking territories, marked the debut of the Ottoman Empire as a "Middle Eastern" power.

NOTES

1 Lewis, *The Jews of Islam*, p. 8.
2 Qur'an 96:1–2.
3 Marshall G. S. Hodgson, *The Venture of Islam: Conscience and History in a World Civilization, Volume 1: The Classical Age of Islam* (Chicago: University of Chicago Press, 1974), p. 75.
4 Hodgson, *The Venture of Islam*, Vol. 1, pp. 3, 57–59.
5 The noun Kharijite derives from the Arabic verb *kharaja*, meaning to exit. As their name suggests, the Kharijites opted out of the emerging Muslim order – although critics who regarded them as extremists said that they went beyond the pale.

6 Leila Ahmed, *Women and Gender in Islam: Historical Roots of a Modern Debate* (New Haven: Yale University Press, 1992), p. 33.
7 Nimrod Hurvitz, "From Scholarly Circles to Mass Movements: The Formation of Legal Communities in Islamic Societies," *American Historical Review*, 108:4 (2003), pp. 985–1008, see especially pp. 986–87.
8 George Makdisi, *History and Politics in Eleventh-Century Baghdad* (Aldershot, UK: Variorum, 1990), see the chapter titled, "The Sunni Revival," pp. 155–68.
9 Lilia Zaouali, *Medieval Cuisine of the Islamic World: A Concise History with 174 Recipes*, trans. M. B. DeBevoise, foreword by Charles Perry (Berkeley: University of California Press, 2007), p. ix.
10 Hugh Kennedy, *The Great Arab Conquests: How the Spread of Islam Changed the World We Live In* (Philadelphia: Da Capo Press, 2007), p. 2.
11 Mark R. Cohen, *Under Crescent and Cross: The Jews in the Middle Ages* (Princeton: Princeton University Press, 2008), pp. ix–xi.
12 Norman A. Stillman, *The Jews of Arab Lands: A History and Sourcebook* (Philadelphia: Jewish Publication Society of America, 1979), pp. 14–15.
13 Stillman, *The Jews of Arab Lands*, p. 15.
14 M. J. Kister, "The Massacre of the Banu Qurayza: A Re-Examination of a Tradition," *Jerusalem Studies in Arabic and Islam*, 8 (1986), pp. 61–96.
15 Antoine Fattal, *Le statut légal des non-musulmans en pays d'Islam*, second edition (Beirut: Dar El-Machreq Sarl Éditeurs, 1995), p. 5.
16 Fattal, *Le statut légal des non-musulmans en pays d'Islam*, p. 3.
17 Kister, "The Massacre of the Banu Qurayza," p. 66. Kister is summarizing and critiquing the account of W. N. Arafat, "New Light on the Story of Banu Qurayza and the Jews of Medina," *Journal of the Royal Asiatic Society of Great Britain and Ireland*, 2 (1976), pp. 100–107.
18 Regarding accounts stressing Jewish duplicity, see Cohen, *Under Crescent and Cross*, p. 11; and "Partial transcript of Pakistan President Musharraf's televised speech asking the people of Pakistan to support his course of action," *The Washington Post*, September 19, 2001, www.washingtonpost.com/wp-srv/nation/specials/attacked/transcripts/pakistantext_091901.html (accessed June 1, 2011). Regarding accounts stressing Muslim persecution and violence, see, for example, Andrew G. Bostom, MD [*sic*], *The Legacy of Jihad: Islamic Holy War and the Fate of Non-Muslims*, foreword by Ibn Warraq (Amherst, NY: Prometheus Books, 2005), and the works of Bat Ye'or, such as *The Dhimmi: Jews and Christians under Islam* (Rutherford, NJ: Fairleigh Dickinson University Press, 1985).
19 See, for example, Stillman, *The Jews of Arab Lands*, pp. 10–13.
20 Fred M. Donner, *Muhammad and the Believers: At the Origins of Islam* (Cambridge, MA: Harvard University Press, 2010), pp. 68–74.
21 Hodgson, *The Venture of Islam*, Vol. 1, p. 186.
22 For a candid look at the violence in Christian history, see Stephen Tomkins, *A Short History of Christianity* (Grand Rapids, MI: William B. Eerdmans, 2006).
23 See, for example, Barbara H. Rosenwein, *A Short History of the Middle Ages*, third edition (Toronto: University of Toronto Press, 2009), p. 74.
24 Kennedy, *The Great Arab Conquests*, pp. 145–46.

25 Jan J. van Ginkel, "The Perception and Presentation of the Arab Conquest in Syriac Historiography: How Did the Changing Social Position of the Syrian Orthodox Community Influence the Account of their Historiographers?," in *The Encounter of Eastern Christianity with Early Islam*, ed. Emmanouela Grypeou, Mark Swanson, and David Thomas (Leiden: E.J. Brill, 2006), pp. 171–84.

26 Harald Suermann, "Copts and the Islam of the Seventh Century," in Grypeou, Swanson, and Thomas, *The Encounter of Eastern Christianity with Early Islam*, pp. 95–109.

27 David Thomas, ed. and trans., *Anti-Christian Polemic in Early Islam: Abu 'Isa al-Warraq's 'Against the Trinity'* (Cambridge: Cambridge University Press, 1992), p. 4.

28 Cohen, *Under Crescent and Cross*, p. x.

29 Steven M. Wasserstrom, *Between Muslim and Jew: The Problem of Symbiosis under Early Islam* (Princeton: Princeton University Press, 1995), p. 11.

30 Stillman, *The Jews of Arab Lands*, pp. xv, 31–34, 40–41.

31 Lewis, *The Jews of Islam*, pp. 17–18.

32 Stillman, *The Jews of Arab Lands*, p. 27.

33 Jonathan P. Berkey, *The Formation of Islam: Religion and Society in the Near East, 600–1800* (Cambridge: Cambridge University Press, 2003), p. 96.

34 Youssef Courbage and Philippe Fargues, *Christians and Jews under Islam*, trans. Judy Mabro (London: I.B. Tauris, 1998), pp. 29–43.

35 François Decret, *Early Christianity in North Africa*, trans. Edward Smither (Eugene, OR: Cascade Books, 2009); Geoffrey D. Dunn, *Tertullian* (London: Routledge, 2004).

36 Jamsheed K. Choksy, "Zoroastrians in Muslim Iran: Selected Problems of Coexistence and Interaction during the Early Medieval Period," *Iranian Studies*, 20:1 (1987), pp. 17–30 (see p. 17); and Jamsheed K. Choksy, *Conflict and Cooperation: Zoroastrian Subalterns and Muslim Elites in Medieval Iranian Society* (New York: Columbia University Press, 1997).

37 Cl. Cahen, "Djizya," in *The Encyclopaedia of Islam*, ed. B. Lewis, Ch. Pellat, and J. Schacht, new edition, Vol. 2 (Leiden: E.J. Brill, 1983), pp. 559–62.

38 Cl. Cahen, "Dhimma," in *The Encyclopaedia of Islam*, ed. B. Lewis, Ch. Pellat, and J. Schacht, new edition, Vol. 2 (C–G) (Leiden: E.J. Brill, 1983), pp. 227–31; Yohanan Friedmann, *Tolerance and Coercion in Islam: Interfaith Relations in the Muslim Tradition* (Cambridge: Cambridge University Press, 2003).

39 Mahmoud Ayoub, "Dhimmah in Qur'an and Hadith," in *Muslims and Others in Early Islamic Society*, ed. Robert Hoyland (Aldershot, UK: Ashgate, 2004), pp. 25–35.

40 Milka Levy-Rubin, *Non-Muslims in the Early Islamic Empire: from Surrender to Coexistence* (Cambridge: Cambridge University Press, 2011), Chapter 1, "The Roots and Authenticity of the Early Conquest Agreements," pp. 8–57.

41 Cahen, "Dhimma," p. 227.

42 Cahen, "Dhimma," p. 228; Fattal, *Le statut légal des non-musulmans en pays d'Islam*, p. 60.

43 The classic modern study of the Pact of Umar, first published in 1930, is A. S. Tritton, *The Caliphs and Their Non-Muslim Subjects: A Critical Study*

of the Covenant of 'Umar (London: Frank Cass, 1970). See also Cahen, "Dhimma," p. 227.

44 Fattal, *Le statut légal des non-musulmans en pays d'Islam*, pp. 60–69.

45 "The Pact of Umar," in Bernard Lewis, ed. and trans., *Islam from the Prophet Muhammad to the Capture of Constantinople*, Vol. 2 (New York: Oxford University Press, 1987), pp. 217–19.

46 Lewis, *The Jews of Islam*.

47 Stillman, *The Jews in Arab Lands*, p. 26.

48 Levy-Rubin, *Non-Muslims in the Early Islamic Empire*, see Chapter 5, pp. 113–63 and especially pp. 146–49, 154–57.

49 Berkey, *The Formation of Islam*, p. 161.

50 Chase Robinson, *Empire and Elites after the Muslim Conquest: The Transformation of Northern Mesopotamia* (Cambridge: Cambridge University Press, 2000), 13–15, 19.

51 Robinson, *Empire and Elites after the Muslim Conquest*, pp. 168–69.

52 "The Pact of Umar," in Lewis, *Islam from the Prophet Muhammad to the Capture of Constantinople*, Vol. 2, p. 218.

53 Omar D. Foda, "Grand Plans in Glass Bottles: A Social, Economic, and Technical History of Beer in Egypt, 1880–1970," PhD diss., University of Pennsylvania, 2015 (see Chapter 2, "The Pharaoh's Homebrew and Muslim Moonshine: The History of Buza in Egypt").

54 Robert Hamilton, *Walid and His Friends: An Umayyad Tragedy* (New York: Oxford University Press, 1988); Abu'l-Faraj al-Isfahani, *The Book of Strangers: Medieval Arabic Graffiti on the Theme of Nostalgia*, trans. Patricia Crone and Shmuel Moreh (Princeton: Markus Wiener, 2000); Philip F. Kennedy, *Abu Nuwas: A Genius of Poetry* (Oxford: Oneworld, 2005).

55 Nawal Nasrallah, ed. and trans., *Annals of the Caliph's Kitchens: Ibn Sayyar al-Warraq's Tenth-Century Baghdadi Cookbook* (Leiden: E.J. Brill, 2007), pp. 450–80, see especially pp. 460–64, 468–72, and on hangover cures, pp. 458–59. The glossary in Nasrallah's volume suggests that Abbasid-era Baghdad had a rich Arabic vocabulary for the types of wines and other alcoholic drinks! See, for example, pp. 554–55.

56 Paulina B. Lewicka, *Food and Foodways of the Medieval Cairenes: Aspects of Life in an Islamic Metropolis of the Eastern Mediterranean* (Leiden: E.J. Brill, 2011), pp. 484–85; and on the alcoholic drink scene of medieval Cairo in general, pp. 483–550.

57 Lewis, "The Pact of Umar," p. 218.

58 Kees Versteegh, *The Arabic Language* (New York: Columbia University Press, 1997), pp. 94–95. On nineteenth-century, missionary-led efforts to revive "Classical Syriac" as a modern literary language, see H. K. Murre-van den Berg, *From a Spoken to a Written Language: The Introduction and Development of Literary Urmia Aramaic in the Nineteenth Century* (Leiden: Nederlands Instituut voor het Nabije Oosten, 1999).

59 Cahen, "Dhimma," p. 227.

60 Cahen, "Dhimma," p. 228.

61 S. D. Goitein, "The Rise of the Near Eastern Bourgeoisie in Early Islamic Times," *Cahiers d'Histoire Mondiale*, 3:3 (1957), pp. 583–603, see p. 594.

62 S. D. Goitein, *A Mediterranean Society: The Jewish Communities of the Arab World as Portrayed in the Documents of the Cairo Geniza*, Volume 2: *The Community* (Berkeley: University of California Press, 1971), p. 289.

63 Lewis, *The Jews of Islam*, p. 9. See also Cohen, *Under Crescent and Cross*, p. 69.

64 Cahen, "Djizya," p. 561.

65 Berkey, *The Formation of Islam*, pp. 161–62.

66 S. D. Goitein, *A Mediterranean Society: The Jewish Communities of the Arab World as Portrayed in the Documents of the Cairo Geniza*, Volume 1 (Berkeley: University of California Press, 1967), pp. 1–3.

67 The Geniza documents tell stories that stretch as far as the Malabar coast of India. See Amitav Ghosh, *In an Antique Land* (New York: A.A. Knopf, 1993).

68 S. D. Goitein, "Evidence on the Muslim Poll-Tax from Non-Muslim Sources: A Geniza Study," *Journal of the Economic and Social History of the Orient*, 6:3 (1963), pp. 278–95, especially p. 279.

69 Yedida Kalfon Stillman, *Arab Dress: A Short History*, ed. Norman A. Stillman (Leiden: E.J. Brill, 2000), pp. 39, 41.

70 Levy-Rubin, *Non-Muslims in the Early Islamic Empire*, pp. 148–49.

71 Stillman, *Arab Dress*, pp. 52–53, 102–4, 109, 111.

72 S. D. Goitein, "Minority Self-rule and Government Control in Islam," in Hoyland, *Muslims and Others in Early Islamic Society* (Aldershot, UK: Ashgate, 2004), pp. 159–74.

73 Wasserstrom, *Between Muslim and Jew*, pp. 19–24.

74 Kennedy, *The Great Arab Conquests*, p. 30.

75 Michael G. Morony, "The Age of Conversions: A Reassessment," in *Conversion and Continuity: Indigenous Christian Communities in Islamic Lands, Eighth to Eighteenth Centuries*, ed. Michael Gervers and Ramzi Jibran Bikhazi (Toronto: University of Toronto Press, 1990), pp. 135–50.

76 Richard W. Bulliet, *Conversion to Islam in the Medieval Period: An Essay in Quantitative History* (Cambridge, MA: Harvard University Press, 1979).

77 Bulliet, *Conversion to Islam*, pp. 1–2.

78 Ira M. Lapidus, "The Conversion of Egypt to Islam," *Israel Oriental Studies*, Vol. 2 (1972), pp. 248–62 – see p. 260.

79 Courbage and Fargues, *Christians and Jews under Islam*, p. 23. See, too, Stillman, *The Jews of Arab Lands*, pp. 28–29.

80 A classic study of African conversion to Christianity in the modern period, emphasizing the role of economic and professional advantage in eliciting conversions, is T. O. Beidelman, *Colonial Evangelism: A Socio-Historical Study of an East African Mission at the Grassroots* (Bloomington: Indiana University Press, 1982). Even accounts that are more sympathetic to Christianization acknowledge that conversion was often a "strategic response" to new conditions. See Dana L. Robert, *Christian Mission: How Christianity Became a World Religion* (Chichester, UK: Wiley-Blackwell, 2009), p. 49.

81 Morony, "The Age of Conversions."

82 Cohen, *Under Crescent and Cross*, pp. 5, 66.

83 Stillman, *Arab Dress*, p. 103.

84 Stillman, *Arab Dress*, pp. 104–5.

85 Cohen, *Under Crescent and Cross*, p. 69.

86 Leor Halevi, *Muhammad's Grave: Death Rites and the Making of Islamic Society* (New York: Columbia University Press, 2007), pp. 3–4.
87 Halevi, *Muhammad's Grave*, pp. 69, 149–51, 156–57.
88 Jonathan P. Berkey, *The Formation of Islam: Religion and Society in the Near East, 600–1800* (Cambridge: Cambridge University Press, 2003), p. 251.
89 Berkey, *The Formation of Islam*, pp. 160–61.
90 Steven Nadler and T.M. Rudavsky, "Introduction," in *The Cambridge History of Jewish Philosophy*, Volume 1: *From Antiquity through the Seventeenth Century* (Cambridge: Cambridge University Press, 2008), p. 2.
91 Sarah Stroumsa, *Maimonides in His World: Portrait of a Mediterranean Thinker* (Princeton: Princeton University Press, 2009); Sarah Stroumsa, "The Muslim Context," in *The Cambridge History of Jewish Philosophy*, ed. Steven Nadler and T.M. Rudavsky, Volume 1: *From Antiquity through the Seventh Century* (Cambridge: Cambridge University Press, 2008), pp. 39–59.
92 Sidney H. Griffith, *The Church in the Shadow of the Mosque: Christians and Muslims in the World of Islam* (Princeton: Princeton University Press, 2007), p. 4.
93 Benjamin H. Hary, *Multiglossia in Judeo-Arabic* (Leiden: E.J. Brill, 1992).
94 Zaouali, *Medieval Cuisine of the Islamic World*, pp. x–xi, xxiii. By some accounts, the first Arabic cookbook, which no longer survives, was written by Ibrahim ibn al-Mahdi (779–839), "poet, professional singer and gourmet" who was also "half-brother of [the Abbasid caliph] Harun al-Rashid"! Ibn Sayyar al-Warraq, *Kitab al-tabikh*, ed. Kaj Öhrnberg and Sahban Mroueh, Studia Orientalia 60 (Helsinki: The Finnish Oriental Society, 1987), p. v.
95 Zaouali, *Medieval Cuisine of the Islamic World*, pp. xxiii–xxiv.
96 Kennedy, *The Great Arab Conquests*, p. 33.
97 Amnon Shiloah, *The Epistle on Music of the Ikhwan al-Safa (Baghdad, 10th century)* (Tel Aviv: Tel Aviv University, Faculty of Fine Arts, School of Jewish Studies, 1978), pp. 6, 15–16.
98 Amnon Shiloah, *Music in the World of Islam: A Socio-Cultural Study* (Detroit: Wayne State University Press, 1995), p. 33.
99 Shiloah, *The Epistle on Music of the Ikhwan al-Safa*, p. 11.
100 Michael Mann, *The Sources of Social Power, Volume 1: A History of Power from the Beginning to A.D. 1760* (Cambridge: Cambridge University Press, 1986), p. 8.
101 Goitein, *A Mediterranean Society*, Vol. 2, pp. 289–91.
102 Oleg Grabar, *The Formation of Islamic Art*, revised and enlarged edition (New Haven: Yale University Press, 1987), p. 9.
103 Grabar, *The Formation of Islamic Art*, p. 49.
104 Wasserstrom, *Between Muslim and Jew*, p. 26.
105 Stillman, *The Jews in Arab Lands*, p. 43.
106 Stillman, *Arab Dress*, p. 56. On the relative liberalism of the Fatimids vis-à-vis *dhimmi*s, see Stillman, *The Jews in Arab Lands*, pp. 43–44.
107 Stillman, *The Jews in Arab Lands*, pp. 69–70.
108 Stillman, *Arab Dress*, pp. 108–9.
109 Stillman, *Arab Dress*, pp. 161–74.
110 For a definition of the Crusades, see Jonathan Riley-Smith, *The Crusades: A Short History* (London: The Athlone Press, 1987), pp. xviii–xix.

111 A vivid work of historical fiction, purporting to tell this story, is Amin Maalouf, *The Crusades through Arab Eyes*, trans. Jon Rothschild (New York: Schocken Books, 1984). See also Carole Hillenbrand, *The Crusades: Islamic Perspectives* (London: Routledge, 2000).

112 Paul M. Cobb, *The Race for Paradise: An Islamic History of the Crusades* (New York: Oxford University Press, 2014).

113 Kristen Stilt, *Islamic Law in Action: Authority, Discretion, and Everyday Experiences in Mamluk Egypt* (Oxford: Oxford University Press, 2011), p. 110.

114 Stilt, *Islamic Law in Action*, p. 111.

115 Stilt, *Islamic Law in Action*, p. 119.

116 David Thomas, "Arab Christianity," in *The Blackwell Companion to Eastern Christianity*, ed. Ken Parry (Oxford: Blackwell Publishing, 2007), pp. 1–22, see especially p. 19; and M. Martin, "Statistiques chrétiennes d'Égypte," *Travaux et jours* (Beirut), 24 (1967): 65–75.

117 On the Coptic Christian practice of male circumcision in Egypt, and on its practice by some other Christians in western Asia, see Sami al-Dhib, *Khitan al-dhukur wa al-inath, 'inda al-yahud wa al-masihiyyin wa al-muslimin: al-jadal al-dini*, preface by Nawal al-Sa'dawi (Beirut: Riad El-Rayyes Books, Ltd., 2000), pp. 217–52.

118 Stilt, *Islamic Law in Action*, p. 119.

119 Stillman, *The Jews in Arab Lands*, pp. 70–75.

3   The Ottoman Experience

Introducing the Ottoman Empire

The Ottoman Empire was vast. At its peak in the sixteenth century, it stretched from what is now Algeria in the west to Iraq in the east, and from Hungary in the north to Yemen in the south. It possessed a richness and diversity of culture that came from the dizzying array of people it ruled: Muslims, Christians, and Jews; speakers of Turkish, Greek, Arabic, Armenian, and more. "Cosmopolitan, sophisticated, and multilingual":[1] the words that one scholar used to describe Sultan Suleyman the Magnificent (r. 1520–66) can apply to the empire at large.

The grandeur of the Ottoman Empire also arose from its remarkable perseverance and continuity in the midst of strains and changes. Founded around the year 1300 in the western marches of Anatolia (today's Turkey), the empire made the transition into the modern period and persisted into the second decade of the twentieth century. Two centuries ago, the Ottoman Empire claimed authority over most of the settled regions of the Middle East and North Africa. (Recall that the only exceptions were Morocco and Iran, which remained independent under Islamic dynasties of their own.) The Ottoman experience, here meaning the shared networks of administration, trade, and learning as well as the common policies and institutions that bound the empire together, helped to set the stage for much of Middle Eastern and North African history as it played out in the nineteenth and twentieth centuries.

How did Muslims, Christians, and Jews live together in this Ottoman Empire? And how successful was the empire in managing diversity over time, particularly as the forces of foreign intervention grew stronger in the eighteenth century? This chapter addresses both questions in the period before 1800. It sketches features that made the empire distinctive: its administrative policies toward religious communities, or *millet*s; its absorption of converts to Islam within the ruling class; and its continued engagement with Europe and with the people, goods, and ideas emanating from it. After looking more closely at how *dhimmi* society functioned, it examines the eighteenth century as a pivotal period of cultural ferment and heightened interaction with western Europe to see how daily lives changed among both the ruling elites and the tax-paying commoners – or *reaya* (flock), as the Ottoman state called its subjects. As the sense of continuity associated with "tradition" began to erode, the social landscape stood poised to shift between and within communities of Muslims, Christians, and Jews.

An Empire of Distinction

Writing in 2004, more than a decade after the acrimonious breakup of Yugoslavia, one Turkish scholar and diplomat maintained that Ottoman rule in the Balkans had been exceptional in promoting harmony in the midst of diversity. Inspired by books that praised tolerant Islamic rule over Muslims, Christians, and Jews in what is now Spain during the centuries after 711 (when the first Muslim army reached Gibraltar) and before the culmination of the Reconquista in 1492 (when the armies of Aragon and Castile defeated the last Muslim stronghold in Granada), this writer argued that the Ottoman Empire was similar in its openness. In his view, the "peaceful coexistence and mutual influence" that Ottoman rule promoted among "Muslims, Christians, Jews and various ethnic communities," amounted to a "Pax Ottomanica."[2] However, by recalling other periods of ostensible imperial peace – such as the Pax Romana of the first- and second-century Roman Empire, the Pax Mongolica of the late thirteenth- and fourteenth-century Mongol Empire, and the Pax Britannica of the nineteenth- and twentieth-century British Empire – his very phrasing betrayed an awkward truth. Namely, empires are not voluntary formations. They expand through conquest, and persist through coercion. In this regard, the Ottoman state was *un*exceptional in its use of violence for asserting and preserving the empire.

In many ways, too, the Ottoman Empire was unexceptional as an Islamic empire. It was a successor to other great Islamic empires, rivaling in its sheer scale the Abbasid domains (750–c. 1258). It also eventually followed some of the practices and precedents of earlier Islamic states, especially in policies toward Muslims and non-Muslims. With few exceptions across the six-century span of the empire's existence (c. 1300–1920), Ottoman rulers were tolerant in the classic Islamic sense of the term: once they conquered a territory and its people acquiesced, the state left them largely alone, in large part (as with earlier Islamic states) because its technological capacity to intrude was so limited. In time, the Ottomans recognized Jews and Christians as *dhimmi*s and collected special taxes from them, including the *jizya*.

In its treatment of *dhimmi*s, the Ottoman rulers followed historical precedents in quirkier ways as well. Like the Abbasids of tenth-century Baghdad and the Mamluks of fourteenth-century Cairo, the Ottomans occasionally invoked, but irregularly enforced, rules about dress, that is, about the color and cut of robes, headwear, and shoes, which could mark Christians and Jews apart from Muslims and from each other. Of course, rulers sometimes invoked restrictions on women's clothing, too, or on the clothes that rich men and poor men could wear. For example, in the late eighteenth century, Ottoman authorities ordered humble Muslim men to stop wearing robes embellished with the fur of ermine, sable, otter, and fox (which were supposed to be the preserve of high officials) and to restrict themselves to pelts from more common animals, like rabbits and squirrels.[3] As this example shows, religion was neither the only important marker of identity nor the only determinant of social hierarchy.

The Ottoman state nevertheless devised distinctive means of administering its Christian, Jewish, and Muslim subjects on the basis of their religious communities, or *millet*s. Historians call this the Ottoman "*millet* system," and regard it as a defining feature of the Ottoman Empire. The term "system" can be somewhat misleading, though, since Ottoman practice entailed arrangements that were of a somewhat flexible, *ad hoc* nature. For example, Ottoman authorities were ready to acknowledge changing sectarian allegiances among Christians, whom the Ottoman state never treated as members of a single community or *millet*. Although the Ottoman Empire began to form as a frontier state in western Anatolia as early as 1300, Ottoman policy toward non-Muslims gained coherence only after 1453, when the Ottoman sultan Mehmet II conquered and occupied Constantinople (Istanbul), and made it into his capital. At this juncture, facing a diverse urban population that was largely Greek and Christian, Mehmet II devolved authority to leaders of religious communities, who then liaised with the state in the collection of taxes. Applied beyond the imperial capital, this Ottoman mode of devolving authority persisted with modifications over the centuries.

The Ottoman Empire was also distinctive because it became a *European* empire, and retained control over massive Christian populations, large segments of which had not converted to Islam by the time Ottoman dominion lapsed. Indeed, for two centuries, until it absorbed the Mamluk Empire by conquering Syria and Egypt in 1517, the Ottoman Empire had a larger Christian population than a Muslim one. The Ottoman Empire's positions in southeastern Europe meant that the empire was constantly rubbing against competing Christian-ruled states. The result of this friction was not only conflict, but also intimacy. The Ottoman ruling classes and its subject population became "familiar" with Europe, not only in the sense of knowing it, but of being related to it in the family way – a situation that was enhanced by the frequency of individual conversions to Islam through choice or force. Of course, occasionally people resisted conversion to Islam. The case of more than 800 Christians of Otranto (now in southern Italy), stands out as an example. When Ottoman forces conquered this town in 1480 and demanded that survivors convert to Islam, they reportedly executed the refusers en masse. Or maybe not. One historian questioned the veracity of the account of the Ottoman slaughter of the "Otranto martyrs" and concluded that, instead of killing the locals, Ottoman troops probably took them hostage and then sold them into slavery abroad.[4] Either way, retrospective accounts of this episode went on in centuries that followed to rally Christians around historical perceptions of religiously motivated bloodshed that Ottoman imperial expansion entailed.

In its method of forced conversion, the Ottomans devised another striking system, and one that was both unique in Islamic history and an aberration from Islamic law. For more than three centuries in its Balkan territories, beginning in the reign of Murat I (r. 1361–89), Ottoman authorities applied a system known as the devşirme, by which they extracted a periodic tax of young Christian men. Upon reaching villages, they marched out village priests with their baptismal rolls, demanded to examine all the males between the approximate ages of 10–20, and chose those who seemed like the best and the brightest – leaving the others to tend farms and pay taxes.[5] Ottoman authorities enslaved these youths, converted them to Islam, and trained them for the elite artillery corps known as the Janissaries. In practice, many of these new Janissary converts gravitated to Sufism, an approach to Muslim worship that emphasizes the role of prayer in humankind's relation to God. In particular, they leaned toward the Bektashi order of Sufism, which, with its emphasis on a loving and beloved God who was unitary but yet had three parts in Allah, Muhammad, and Ali, may have "served to draw in Christians and to make them feel at home within the order."[6]

Another significant source of involuntary, *de facto* conversion occurred through slave concubinage, as Ottoman Muslim male elites took into their households non-Muslim women whom they had captured in raids. With these women they fathered children whom Islamic law deemed to be Muslim. Slave concubinage was not unique to the Ottomans – countless rulers of Islamic states had engaged in this practice before. What *was* remarkable in the Ottoman case, however, was the sheer extent of it among the most powerful, as sultans came to prefer these exogamous liaisons as a way of producing their heirs. Ottoman chroniclers later rewrote history to suggest that these concubine mothers had been

Chorbadgi en cérémonie.

Image 6 "Chorbadgi en cérémonie" (Janissary colonel in ceremonial dress), watercolor painting on paper, 1790. Museum Number
1974,0617,0.12.1.85. ©The Trustees of the British Museum.

free Muslims from the start. A historian of the Ottoman imperial harem
concluded, instead, that aside from six or so marriages contracted during the early Ottoman period with the daughters of Anatolian Muslim
potentates, all of these women – with one exception – were non-Muslims
by birth.[7] These concubine consorts were almost always of Christian origin, like the mother of sultan Selim II (r. 1566–74), "Roxelana," who was
born Alexandra Lisowska in what is now Ukraine and was later known in
the palace as Hürrem Sultan. An exception to this pattern of Christian
mothers was the mother of sultan Murad III (r. 1574–95), who appears
to have been Jewish.[8] The prevalence of concubinage among the sultans
and among the Ottoman ruling classes as a whole helps to explain how it
could be that, by the mid-seventeenth century, so many Muslim political
office holders were the sons or grandsons of Christian females.[9]

Of course, the Ottoman Empire was an Asiatic empire, too, having been founded around 1300 by Turks whose forebears had migrated from Inner Asia into western Asia sometime around the eleventh century. After Ottoman forces conquered Egypt in 1517, the empire also became African, a claim it soon strengthened by recognizing military delegates who installed themselves along the North African coast. One of the most successful of these delegates was a Mediterranean privateer named Hizir Reis (c. 1478–1546), who was the son of a Greek Christian woman whom his father, an Ottoman Muslim cavalryman, had seized from the island of Lesbos (now in Greece) following the Ottoman conquest of Mytilene in 1462.[10] Later known as the naval commander Khayr al-Din ("goodness of the faith") to his Ottoman supporters, but as the pirate Barbarossa ("redbeard") to his European foes, Khayr al-Din Barbarossa used his base in Algiers to raid the shore of what is now Italy, seizing objects and people as booty in the name of the Ottoman state.[11] His life and career illustrate how the Asiatic, European, and African elements of the empire converged.

Finally, the Ottoman Empire was also modern, which, to historians, means more than merely that it came up close to present-day times. With reference to European history, many historians point to watersheds that marked the start of a "modern" period around 1500. They cite the printing of the Gutenberg Bible, the first moveable-type book, in 1454, and the voyages of Christopher Columbus to the Americas, in 1492, with the one signaling the rise of a new age of mass communication and literacy, and the other a new age of global exploration and long-distance trade. The Ottomans did not discover new territories, nor did they widely embrace the new printing technology. In the view of some influential historians who wrote in the mid-to-late twentieth century, Ottoman inaction in these spheres delayed the empire's "modern" experience, and pushed it into a long stretch of decline that began once the reign of Suleyman the Magnificent ended in 1566. Perhaps the most forceful proponent of this view in the past half century was Bernard Lewis (b. 1916), who argued that New World explorations, together with the opening of western European maritime trade with Africa and Asia, made the Ottoman Empire into a backwater. Lewis argued further that the influx of New World silver, which had a devastating impact on Ottoman currency, confirmed the empire's weakness and pushed it farther into decline.[12]

To be sure, after Suleyman, the empire did not expand its territories and faced a series of military defeats. The Ottoman state periodically raised taxes to levels that caused great distress among peasants and urban workers, especially in Anatolia. Distress erupted in rural and urban revolts that punctuated the history of Istanbul, Anatolia, and its environs in the sixteenth, seventeenth, and eighteenth centuries. Nevertheless, even amidst these strains, the empire remained culturally vibrant and productive, as a wealth of new studies – on Ottoman art, poetry, cuisine, and more – has shown in the past twenty years.[13] These studies make it hard to sustain the earlier view of chronic Ottoman decline, when Ottoman history from 1500 to 1800, studied up close, looks so stunning, eventful, and creative. For this reason, historians today are more likely to emphasize the empire's adaptation in the face of crisis over the older model of decline, while noting the empire's transition from externally driven militarism toward a more internally focused bureaucratization.[14]

Developments that occurred in the "modern world system"[15] in the realms of travel, trade, technology, and learning certainly reverberated into the Ottoman Empire. For example, the empire received New World agricultural commodities, such as tobacco and corn (maize), through contacts with the new western European imperial powers of Britain, Spain, Portugal, the Netherlands, and France. Records from Topkapı Palace, residence of the sultans in Istanbul, show that in 1694 the imperial kitchens even received a ton of tomatoes, in a green variety called *kavata*.[16] The Ottoman Empire gave things back in return. In the sixteenth and seventeenth centuries, for instance, the empire transmitted a new bean that grew in Yemen – a bean that once roasted, ground, and made into a drink, had energizing properties.[17] This was coffee, which spawned a new institution – the coffeehouse – that soon became popular not only in Istanbul but also in cities like London and Paris (where it eventually helped to brew a revolution).[18] And then, too, there were Ottoman carpets, items holding such high prestige that sixteenth-century western European artists painted them into their portraits in order to dignify kings (as Hans Holbein did when painting Henry VIII of England, arms akimbo and legs planted on a rug), to exalt the Virgin Mary and baby Jesus (as Lorenzo Lotto did, following a convention set already in the Renaissance art of the previous century by artists like Gentile Bellini), or to complement the beauty of subjects captured in scenes from everyday life (as Nicolaes Maes and Johannes Vermeer did, in the paintings of young women peeling apples or dozing at a table after work).[19] All of these exchanges occurred even as the Ottoman Empire continued to engage in trade with other, more established trading partners to its east, receiving silk textiles from Safavid Iran (its imperial arch-rival, but a trading partner nonetheless) and cottons from Mughal India.[20]

Modernity was not just a matter of new technologies and global economies; it was also a state of mind and a set of ideas. Central to these ideas, and to the European Enlightenment with which the modern period became closely tied, was a belief in the importance of the individual

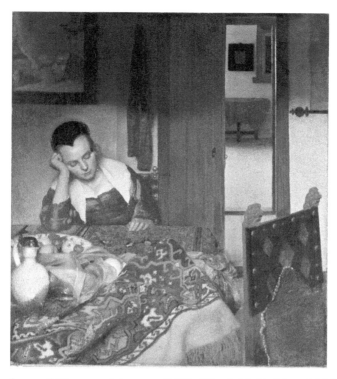

Image 7 Vermeer, Johannes (1632–75). *A Maid Asleep.* 1656–57. Oil on canvas, 34 1/2 × 30 1/8 in. (87.6 × 76.5 cm). Bequest of Benjamin Altman, 1913 (14.40.611). The Metropolitan Museum of Art. Image copyright ©The Metropolitan Museum of Art. Image source: Art Resource, NY.

person, who possessed a capacity for reasoned thinking and constructive reform. This aspect of modernity – its elevation of the individual, openness to the new, and critical inquiry – had a subversive potential because it carried a readiness to question established orthodoxies. In the eighteenth century, the Ottoman Empire, which had its own partial and ambiguous place within Europe, became more caught up in this kind of modernity.

Turkish, Muslim, and Anatolian: The Heart of the Ottoman State

To appreciate the cultural contours of the Ottoman Empire – its Turkishness, its Muslimness, and its ambiguous Europeanness, one can look first to Istanbul before widening the gaze. Istanbul today claims the distinction of being the only city in the world to straddle two continents: Europe and Asia. Its historic center sits across from the westernmost edge of Anatolia, or Asia Minor, where the Ottomans traced their beginnings as a dynasty. As the crucible of the Ottoman state, Istanbul and Anatolia more broadly were places where the empire absorbed diverse peoples and cultures, and in the process, helped to forge new identities.

The family of Osman (1258–1326), whose military successes in western Anatolia initiated the empire and gave it the "Ottoman" name, claimed descent from Turkic nomadic peoples who shared close linguistic and cultural affinities, and who relied on the horse for their livelihoods. (Note that the term "Turkic" refers to a cluster of peoples, originally from Central or Inner Asia, who spoke or who speak a set of related Altaic languages. "Turkic" is a broader term than "Turkish," since scholars nowadays use the latter to refer to the language spoken in the Republic of Turkey and to the people and culture associated with this state, and not to speakers of Turkic languages in countries like Uzbekistan and Azerbaijan.) The historic homelands of these nomads were the steppes of Inner Asia, a region centered in present-day Tibet and Mongolia, where people spoke languages belonging to the Uralic and Altaic language families. This was a region which, "at any given time, lay beyond the borders of the sedentary world," and which Chinese, Greek, and other chroniclers over the centuries had portrayed as the "antithesis" to their civilizations.[21]

The precursors to the Ottoman Turks migrated from Inner Asia westward into Central Asia (the region to the northeast of what is now Iran), probably in the first three centuries of the Islamic era. Originally shamanists, they converted to Islam under the influence of itinerant preachers. It was then, in Transoxania (the region across the Oxus River, now the Amu Darya, which roughly marks the southern border of Uzbekistan), that the newly converted Turks began to call themselves *ghazi*s, or warriors for the faith, as they raided settled communities. As one historian observed, "Early Turkic Muslims ... probably understood the *ghaza* [a religious war akin to jihad] not in Islamic legal scholars' terms," but rather as a more dignified name for an old practice that they associated with the horsemen's heroic ideal.[22] It sounded better to call oneself a *ghazi* – a man with a noble cause – than a mere marauder in search of loot and lucre. The Ottomans, whose immediate forebears probably moved beyond the Caspian Sea to reach Anatolia in the eleventh century, embraced the *ghazi* ideal as well, as they attacked settled populations of Greeks, Armenians, and others who inhabited domains over which the Byzantine Empire was losing control. These raids made the early Ottoman Empire what it was, even if the true extent of the *ghazis*' conviction as Muslims is impossible to gauge.

The Byzantine defeat at the hands of the family of Turks known as the Seljuks – a defeat marked in 1071 at the Battle of Manzikert – allowed Turkic horsemen to migrate into the Anatolian plains unhindered. By the twelfth century, so prolific were the Turks in Anatolia that Latin sources began to use the term "Turchia" – suggesting a place of the Turks – to refer to the areas that they had overtaken.[23] This usage spread, and entered English as early as 1369, when Geoffrey Chaucer (1343–1400) dropped a reference to "Turkye" [*sic*] into his poem called *The Book of the Duchess*.[24] The important point here is that "Turchia" or "Turkey" was a term that foreigners devised, not one that the Ottomans coined. Turkey existed in the European imagination until the twentieth century – and arguably until the end of World War I – when locals embraced this place name themselves.[25] The name gained formal status in 1923, when the post-Ottoman republic that emerged in Anatolia and eastern Thrace proclaimed itself "Türkiye" on the international stage.

Ideas of "Turkey" aside, how "Turkish" were the Ottoman state and the Turkish-speaking population of Anatolia, in the sense of retaining connections to the ancestral Turks of Inner Asia? While some scholars maintain that a distinctively Turkish patrimony persisted, the answer is elusive.[26] The Ottoman state adopted and adapted so much from the Byzantine Empire that it supplanted in Anatolia (even appointing some court personnel), that the Ottoman hybrid incorporated much of Byzantine and pre-Ottoman Anatolian culture.[27] There also occurred considerable intermingling – to use a delicate term for an often crude process – as conquered, captured, or converted non-Turkish people entered the Ottoman Muslim ruling class or became assimilated into Muslim, Turkish-speaking families among the commoners. Along the way the very nature of Turkishness changed.

The question of numbers and assimilation – "how many Turks came to Asia Minor, how many Anatolians converted [to Islam], what is the ratio of 'real' Turks to converts in the composition of the later 'Turkish' society under the Ottomans?"[28] – carries such a heavy political charge that many historians mention the issue and quickly move on. Certainly in the post-Ottoman world today, people who do not identify themselves as "Turks" may perceive their forebears as having been on the receiving end of unwanted Ottoman advances, and such a perception can carry a sense of resentment and shame. The historian Cemal Kafadar likened these feelings about Ottoman cultural influence to those that may emerge from an "unequal sexual relationship" in which "[t]he influencer is like the one who penetrates and is proud, and the influenced is like the one who is penetrated and thus put to shame."[29]

Evidence from genetic anthropology, which entails the study of molecular change among populations through the analysis of DNA and blood groups, suggests that the biological connection of Anatolian Turks (now the Turks of Turkey) to the Turks of Inner Asia became very tenuous, occurring through historically sporadic and limited migrations that left few traces through "gene flow." One study from 1998 even concluded "that Anatolian populations … were less genetically distant from British than from Central Asian populations" and that they had more in common genetically with Basques and Sardinians, too.[30] Self-identified Turks in present-day Anatolia appear to share the closest genetic relationship to Jordanians, Assyrians, and Armenians.[31] The last two of these groups were Christian peoples who faced massacres during the 1890s and again during World War I – massacres that many Armenians and Assyrians have described as Ottoman Turkish (and Kurdish) efforts to eliminate them. In short, the historical shifts that constituted a large "Turkish" population in Anatolia resulted from what two biological anthropologists have called a "conversion": a conversion that occurred less through immigration and interbreeding (as one can trace it genetically, through the decoding of blood), and more through intangible processes of cultural and linguistic absorption.[32]

Cultural assimilation, in the case of Turks, included change of religion, for although there were non-Muslim Turkic peoples (Buddhists, Orthodox Christians, shamanists, and even some Jews) in parts of Eurasia, Turks identified closely with Islam in the Ottoman territories.[33] A Christian or Jew could "become" a Turk, if one was not born identifying as a Turk, by converting to Islam. In various European languages, the association of conversion to Islam with the Ottomans became so strong that "Turk … even became a synonym for Muslim, and a convert to Islam was said to have 'turned Turk' wherever the conversion took place."[34] Thus, for example, a Greek verb for converting to Islam was *tourkevo*, meaning literally "to become a Turk." To signal conversion, converts changed their clothes to brighter Muslim clothes – in the sixteenth century, for example, by abandoning the gray outer coats and black, flat-topped shoes that an edict prescribed for Christian and Jewish men.[35] They also changed their names to Muslim names. In 1669, for example, a Jewish physician known as Moses, son of Raphael Abravanel, converted to Islam and became Hayatizade Mustafa Fevzi Effendi; in a similar manner, around 1700, the French military advisor to the Ottoman state named Claude Alexandre Comte de Bonneval (1675–1747) converted to Islam and became "Ahmet."[36] Those who "turned Turk" could even build their homes differently, since color rules pertained to buildings and not only to clothes. That is, they could incorporate into their edifices "the vivid colouring (reserved for Muslims, throughout the Empire) ... as opposed to the grey of 'minorities' (Greeks and, here, especially Jews)."[37] Presumably, however, for most converts, the shift of language to Turkish fluency – an important step in Turkification – was not, and could not be, as sudden.

So heterogeneous did the "Turkish" population of the Ottoman Empire become in its first centuries that Turkish solidarity eroded. Of course, this assumes – as Ottoman intellectuals themselves assumed – that a degree of Turkish solidarity had existed in the first place, in the form that the fourteenth-century historian, Ibn Khaldun (1332–1406) of Tunis, called 'asabiyya and identified as a critical ingredient in state-building.[38] Class distinctions soon divided Turks, with rulers and the rich controlling the means of production (above all land) and wealth (much of it from taxes) as poor subjects strove to eke out an existence through their labor. There were also geographic differences distinguishing city- and town-dwellers from those in the countryside. These distinctions grew clearer as early Ottoman state-builders settled down, devised an administration, assumed the pomp of an imperial court, and came to enjoy urban luxuries.[39] Finally, Turks were heterogeneous in the nature of the Islam they practiced. In particular, they belonged to a variety of Sufi orders – Bektashi, Naqshbandi, Helveti, Mevlevi, and more. Among rural-dwellers in eastern Anatolia, many identified with what became known as Alevism – a form of Islam that reflected the strong influence of both Sufi and Shi'i ideas.[40]

By the sixteenth century, the social distinctions within the Turkish-speaking population were manifesting themselves in different forms of Turkish language. Elites came to employ a Turkish variant called Osmanli, or Ottoman, which drew upon many Persian and Arabic loan-words and used Arabic script for its writing. For example, a linguist who analyzed one text by a respected Ottoman "prose stylist" of the early seventeenth century found that 5 percent of its vocabulary was of Turkish origin; 20 percent was of Persian origin; and 75 percent was of Arabic origin.[41] This Ottoman language arguably achieved its most elevated or obfuscatory form in poetry. So rarified was Ottoman court poetry by the sixteenth century that another literary scholar has specu-lated that Ottoman elites may have been more interested in the "music" of the verse – meaning its assonance, alliteration, and rhythm – than in the meaning of its words, which they may have struggled to grasp.[42] Meanwhile, Ottoman elites came to look down upon Turkish Muslim commoners as bumpkins – albeit as bumpkins who had their own thriving oral cultures of troubadour poetry. For the sixteenth or seventeenth century, then, it may make sense to reserve the term "Ottoman," when describing people, for the ruling classes, who were associated with the Ottoman state. Thus, one could speak about an Ottoman sultan, an Ottoman scribe (producing calligraphic documents for the administration), an Ottoman court poet, or the Ottoman 'ulama (Muslim religious scholars)[43] – but not about an Ottoman peasant or fishmonger. Once again, social hierarchies distinguished Turks – and Muslims – from each other, and not only Muslims from Christians and Jews.

In theory, even more than Turkishness, Islam provided a source of solidarity to Muslims of the empire. And indeed, in the fifteenth century, Ottoman authorities insisted on speaking about and treating Muslims as one religious community or *millet*, which, in some sense, recalled the early Islamic ideal of the *umma* as a community of believers. This insistence in official discourse on Muslim singularity – despite variations in Muslim practice – contrasted with policy toward Christians, among whom the Ottoman state always recognized sectarian differences. The Ottoman state's recognition of diversity may have had a self-serving and ideological purpose. The historian Tijana Krstic argued that "religious diversity among Ottoman non-Muslim subjects remained the cornerstone of Ottoman imperial identity" and offered "testimony to Ottoman prestige and ability to bring about the unity of religious groups under the umbrella of Islam." Krstic suggested that the Ottomans drew their inspiration for governing diverse peoples from "a pre-Christian ideal of Roman imperial rule," although one can also point to the Islamic historical legacy of the Umayyads and Abbasids.[44]

Meanwhile, in its official refusal to recognize Muslim differences, the Ottoman state revealed its own sectarian biases. That is, the Ottoman Empire defined itself as a Sunni Muslim empire, as had most of the major Islamic empires in history, even though sympathy for, or adherence to, Shi'ism or to Shi'i ideals (reflecting special esteem for 'Ali, the prophet Muhammad's cousin and son-in-law, and his heirs) was widespread throughout Anatolia.

The Ottoman Empire did not begin as an adamantly Sunni empire, though circumstances pushed it to identify more strongly with Sunnism following the rise on its eastern flank of the Safavid Empire (1501–1722) of Iran. The Safavids embraced Shi'i Islam of the Imami or "Twelver" variety, thus called because of the twelve spiritual leaders, or *imam*s, whom its adherents revered, beginning with the prophet Muhammad's cousin and son-in-law 'Ali and ending with a twelfth imam who vanished in 874. Shah Isma'il (r. 1501–24), the Safavid Empire's founder, was a

Muslim whose mother came from one of the Turkoman tribes of eastern Anatolia, who himself spoke a Turkic tongue, and who regarded himself and his followers as *ghazi*s (attacking Georgian Christians and other non-Muslims). The fact that Shah Isma'il and his heirs spoke the same cultural "language" as the evocatively named and independently minded "Black Sheep Turks" and "White Sheep Turks" of eastern Anatolia made them dangerous rivals to the Ottoman state. Consider, for example, that Shah Ismail was able to communicate with his illiterate Turkish tribal followers through poetry that used simple language to convey complex ideas[45] – something that the Ottoman sultans would have been unable to do at that stage with the esoteric poetry of the Ottoman court. Safavid and Ottoman armies fought war after war against each other, in the sixteenth and seventeenth centuries, most heatedly over the region between the Tigris and Euphrates rivers (present-day Iraq), which the Ottomans eventually won. The two enemy empires managed nonetheless to continue exchanging Safavid silks for Ottoman silver. However, fearing that Shi'i traders might try to proselytize among and stir up rural Muslim tribesmen in their domains, Ottoman authorities insisted that only non-Shi'i merchants conduct their mutual trade. Armenian Christians benefitted and assumed a privileged position within Safavid-Ottoman commerce.[46]

In his insistence on Shi'ism, Shah Ismail became more committed to doctrinal rigor than either the Ottomans to his west or the Mughals in India to his east. He forced Sunni Muslims to "convert" to Shi'ism, as did his son, Shah Tahmasp (r. 1524–76), who also ordered mosques to lead a ritual cursing of the first three Sunni caliphs – that is, the prophet Muhammad's successors Abu Bakr, Umar, and Uthman. (Note that the fourth caliph recognized by Sunnis, namely, 'Ali, had been the favorite of the Shi'is in the first place.) Later, in the seventeenth century, the Safavids forced the conversion of many Armenian Christians and Jews, some of whom remained loyal to their old faiths by faking religious conformity in a way that resembled the Shi'i practice of *taqiyya*, or dissimulation (a self-preservation measure for Shi'is who found themselves among Sunnis).[47] Despite the original idiosyncracies of Safavid religion, which drew on a mix of Islamic and pre-Islamic ideas, Safavid state-sponsored religious scholars accentuated differences between Shi'i and Sunni Muslims, and between Muslims and non-Muslims. Non-Muslims in the Safavid context included not only Christians and Jews, but also Zoroastrians (who were indigenous to Iran) as well as a small number of traders, mediating trade with India, whom we would now call Hindus and Jains.[48] In time, and perhaps under the influence of Zoroastrianism, some of Iran's Shi'i scholars theorized differences between Shi'is and non-Muslims in terms of ritual purity. Thus, they emphasized the defiling nature of physical contact with non-Muslims and with their sweat, saliva, and other bodily fluids.[49] These ideas translated into stricter dietary practices for Shi'is vis-à-vis non-Muslims, which theoretically made commensality, or meal-sharing, less conceivable between a Christian or a Jew and a Shi'i cleric than between a Christian or a Jew and a Sunni.[50]

The Safavids made the Ottomans look easy-going in their attitudes toward Muslim conformity and interaction with non-Muslims. The Ottomans, for example, tolerated Shi'ism in practice. Along these lines, the historian Stefan Winter concluded that, "the Ottoman state, contrary to conventional assumptions, was ideologically too heterogeneous and politically too pragmatic to follow an actual policy against Shiism [*sic*]," with the result that it devised working relationships with the leaders of Shi'i communities in specific places like Mount Lebanon.[51]

Among the Ottoman sultans, however, there was one exception: Mehmet IV (r. 1648–87), who relished converting Christians and Jews to make them "honored by the glory of Islam," in Ottoman parlance of the day. Mehmet IV took pleasure in promoting a kind of Muslim public piety, by banning the use of coffee, wine, and tobacco, and executing transgressors. In this regard, he broke from Ottoman state practice, which had conventionally allowed a wide berth to Christians, Jews, and Muslims in their devotions.[52] Mehmet IV's mother, herself a convert to Islam who had entered the Ottoman court as a Christian slave concubine of Ukrainian origin, was even more enthusiastic about demonstrating public piety. Following the great fire that devastated Istanbul in 1660, she prevented Jews from rebuilding their burnt synagogues in the city's Eminönü district and forced them to sell or abandon their properties. She went on to "convert ... a Jewish landscape into a Muslim landscape" by building an enormous mosque complex on the site where Jews had lived and worshipped.[53]

More representative of the Ottoman way was Mehmet II (r. 1451–81), the conqueror of Constantinople, who effected conversions that looked more like incremental absorption. His approach was manifest in his conversion of buildings. Unlike his contemporary Babur (1483–1530), the founder of the Mughal Empire, whose memoirs suggest that he did not really like India but just needed a kingdom and wanted its wealth, Mehmet the Conqueror was delighted with his conquest of, and subsequent residence in, Constantinople.[54] He did not destroy the city; he simply adopted it and made it his own. Upon entering Constantinople, the first thing he did was visit Hagia Sophia, the church that symbolized the power of the Eastern Roman Empire, and convert it into a mosque. Yet while he removed many icons and Christian liturgical objects, and installed a prayer niche and pulpit for Muslim worship, he kept most of the mosaics in place, including those depicting the Virgin Mary and Christ over the apse and Christ Pantokrator (an adult, almighty Christ) in the dome. In this way, noted the art historian Çiğdem Kafescioğlu, the building "preserved to a remarkable degree its Byzantine Christian identity."[55]

The Ottoman conquerors converted other churches in the city: for example, the Dominican church of Genoese merchants became the Friday mosque of Galata district.[56] But not all churches became mosques. By the late sixteenth century, the Ottomans had converted at least one Byzantine church in Istanbul into a zoo for the sultans, whose menagerie, housing hyenas, lions, elephants, and other exotic creatures, became a "must see" for elite European visitors.[57]

As with Ottoman society more generally, the work of absorbing, internalizing, and "converting" so many people and institutions changed Turkish Muslims as well. Indeed, the Islamic devotional practices of the Ottoman ruling classes showed signs of Christian influences that converts to Islam may have carried into Muslim practice. Above all, there was a tendency to focus on Muhammad and his corporeal personhood in a way that recalled the Christian preoccupation with Jesus. In a study of Ottoman illustrated prayer manuals, one scholar concluded that Ottoman Islamic piety in the sixteenth century revolved around stories about the Prophet Muhammad and textual portraits, so to speak, that conveyed him. Written texts presented Muhammad as the "embodiment of the vessel of God's divine logos" in his capacity as transmitter of the Qur'an, and treated his sayings as conveyed in the stories of his companions (the *hadith*) as if they were oral relics. The same period saw the flourishing of a kind of visual poem, called the *hilye*, which entailed physical description of the Prophet based on accounts of those who had known him. Many appeared to believe that poems recalling the Prophet, sometimes written with the lines arranged like the outline of a human body, had a protective power akin to an amulet.[58] Against the context of an Islamic visual tradition that often shunned the figurative representation of beings, such word poems functioned as a kind of textual iconography and, again, recalled Christian devotions.

Central to official Ottoman-Islamic piety, and another reflection of Christian influence, was the veneration of relics that had Christian, Judaic, and Muslim associations. The sultans took an active role in collecting these. For a start, Mehmet II reportedly "showed deep respect" toward what he believed to be "Christ's stone of nativity and an arm bone and part of the skull of St. John the Baptist," which he secured during the capture of Constantinople.[59] Eventually the Ottomans also secured what they identified as the staff that Moses had used to part the Red Sea, and a marble cooking vessel that had belonged to the Prophet Abraham. Many of the later acquisitions bore a special significance to Muslims, possibly suggesting the consolidation of a distinctly Muslim (and less convert-influenced) piety in ruling circles. Sultan Selim I (r. 1512–20) secured the most prestigious relics of all when he conquered Cairo in 1517, and took items that the Mamluks had taken from the Abbasids, who had taken them from the Umayyads before them. These were relics of the Prophet Muhammad – his mantle, sandals, standard (war flag), prayer beads, and more. As late as 1783 the Ottomans secured what they identified as a footprint of the Prophet, etched into rock, which they found in Syria and transferred to Istanbul. They also acquired a rock impression of the Prophet's elbow.[60]

In the Ottoman royal palace, the sultans built a special room to hold these relics. They added to the collection, until it included more than 600 items. They also hired craftsmen to make beautiful reliquaries to hold them; they nestled a tooth fragment from the Prophet, for example, in a jewel-encrusted gold box.[61] The sultans and their advisors visited the relics ceremoniously, "on Fridays, holidays, before embarking on military campaigns, during state ceremonies (such as accessions to the throne), and at the annual cleaning of the relics' room."[62] These relics played an important role in Ottoman state religion. At the start of military campaigns, for example, Ottoman authorities paraded the Prophet's standard in Istanbul (along with miniature Qur'ans that they attached to poles, to symbolize the major districts of the empire[63]). People pushed to see the Prophet's standard; some appeared to believe that the mere sight of it conferred blessings.[64] Of course, only the people of Istanbul saw this spectacle. Even a city like Aleppo (which is today less than thirty miles from the Turkish border, in Syria), was more than a month's journey away from the imperial capital during the eighteenth century.[65] Nevertheless, what happened in Istanbul was important for the rest of the empire. The capital was "a bottomless pit of consumption" that drew goods from the empire at large, "displayed the pomp of an imperial nerve center … , set trends in fashion and refinement[,] and made the momentous decisions of peace and war."[66] Its actions, and its circumstances, influenced the rest of the empire.

Istanbul was also an excellent laboratory for experimenting in how to manage religious and cultural diversity. The population of Byzantine Constantinople had dwindled to some 70,000 when the Ottoman conquest began. In 1453, Mehmet II entered the city to find that all but 10,000 had fled. To repopulate his new capital, he forcibly settled some Anatolian and Balkan peoples and attracted others – Muslims,

Christians, and Jews – by offering land or opportunities. Conditions for Jews, in particular, were so congenial that many came from as far as western Europe.[67] Mehmet II's repopulation policies were so successful that within a generation, the population had risen to some 100,000.[68] By 1477, the inhabitants of Istanbul were 60 percent Muslim, 21.5 percent Greek Orthodox, and 11 percent Jewish, along with smaller populations of Armenians, Gypsies (Roma), and others. Meanwhile, the neighboring district of Galata (a trading hub that became a *de facto* part of the city) had a population that was 35 percent Muslim, 39 percent Greek Orthodox, 22 percent foreign European (consisting of merchants from cities like Genoa), and 4 percent Armenian, with many Jews living just outside the district's walls, in the village of Hasköy.[69] The district of Galata retained its diversity, and by the seventeenth century, claimed 200,000 non-Muslim and 64,000 Muslim residents, spread across "eighteen Muslim, seventy Greek, two Armenian, one Jewish, and three Frankish quarters."[70] It was here, at the heart of the empire, that Mehmet II devised an Ottoman mode for administering religious communities or *millet*s.

The *"Millet* System," or the Ottoman Mode of Dealing with Groups by Religion

History books used to aver – and some still aver – that the Ottoman state had a *"millet* system": a way of dealing with non-Muslims as religious communities or *millet*s that granted them considerable autonomy. However, for many years now, scholars who study Ottoman history closely have acknowledged that this version of the story is not quite right for the period before 1800.

For a start, there is a problem of semantics: the word *millet* is slippery, because official Ottoman sources used it in variable ways.[71] Ottoman sources applied the term *millet* to Muslims, and not only to Christians and Jews, for indeed, the Ottoman state regarded Muslims as a community, too. In general, they left Muslim groups to themselves, though they expected Shi'is, in particular, to remain discreet about their religious practices, and regarded Shi'i expression in eastern Anatolia as a worrisome possible sign of pro-Safavid political sentiment.[72] In other contexts, the word *millet* bore connotations of sovereignty, which the empire's subjects lacked. Thus, for example, after a treaty with France in 1536, which granted extraterritorial rights to foreign Christian merchants, Ottoman authorities referred to the "Franks" of Istanbul as a *millet*.[73] In this context, *millet* served as a polite term within diplomatic correspondence, but did not mean (as European diplomats assumed) that Ottoman authorities were using it as a blanket term for the empire's own Christian subjects. In fact, Ottoman authorities often used two different words to refer collectively to people in their empire: they called them *taife*s or *cemaat*s, both simply meaning "groups."[74] Official documents sometimes used one of these words for a religious group, as when they referred to a *taife* of Jews. But sometimes documents applied *taife* to a professional group, for example, by referring to a *taife* of butchers.[75] The latter usage is not so surprising when one considers that, in cases of petitions or disputes, Ottoman Islamic courts typically described men not only by religion, but also by profession and place of residence, suggesting how multiple elements combined to produce a person's public, social identity.[76]

The projection of the *millet* system onto the Ottoman past may be a distortion caused by viewing earlier periods through the lens of the nineteenth century.[77] Yet, even if nineteenth- and twentieth-century observers of the past were more inclined to detect a "*millet* system" than Mehmet II or his successors would have been, the term still has utility. The Ottoman authorities consistently, across the generations, had modes of interacting with communities or groups through religious leaders, who exercised considerable autonomy over social affairs, for example, in regulating marriages. And while the policies of authorities toward Muslims and non-Muslims evoked Islamic historical precedents, their practices were often so distinctive that they set the Ottoman experience apart. By using the term "*millet* system," we can acknowledge more effectively both the Ottoman mode of categorizing people by religion and the quirks of the Ottoman experience, as long as we recognize, first, that practice changed over time and varied somewhat from place to place; and second, that the *millet* was an administrative interface of a religious community and not the community itself.[78]

For the Ottoman state, the *millet* system functioned as a "strategy of empire."[79] The state tolerated diverse religious communities but the religious communities had to tolerate each other, too: they all had a stake in keeping the peace and maintaining public order.[80] Christian and Jewish leaders tried to resolve intracommunal conflicts or handle their own misbehavers within individual congregations or in larger rabbinical and ecclesiastical courts, and declared penalties for transgressors that could include jail, excommunication, or refusal of religious burial.[81] At the same time, the *millet*s provided social services to their constituents. Many of these services depended on *waqf*s, or religious endowments, which pious individuals bequeathed to fund schools, places of worship, soup kitchens, public water fountains, and more. *Waqf*s began in the early Islamic era as Muslim institutions, although Jews and Christians embraced the term and the practice as well.[82]

Non-Muslim religious leaders benefitted from the Ottoman system in important ways. Greek-speaking Orthodox Christians, for example, secured a deal with the Ottoman state that gave them a privileged position vis-à-vis Catholics. This privilege was manifest in Istanbul, where Mehmet II granted the Patriarch of the Orthodox Church a position of leadership over all Orthodox Christians. Successive patriarchs, who were always Greek speakers, asserted their claims over many Orthodox Christian Slavs in the Balkans and later (after the conquest of Egypt and Syria in 1517) over many Orthodox Christian Arabs in the Levant. The Orthodox advantage was also clear in places like Crete, an island that Venice had ruled from 1204 until an Ottoman conquest that culminated in 1669. Under Ottoman rule, Islam spread on Crete, as many local Christian men converted to secure posts in the Ottoman military. But Orthodox Christianity spread under Ottoman rule, too, taking back ground that it had lost to Catholicism during the four centuries of rule under Venice.[83]

The steady support that the Ottoman sultans lent to Orthodox Christian churches, and their commitment to "suppressing, in principle, the Catholic Church throughout their realms" proved so popular among the ordinary people that it helped the Ottoman Empire to expand rapidly in the Balkans during the fifteenth and sixteenth centuries. So argued the Turkish historian Halil İnalcık, who described the Ottoman state as the "protector of the Orthodox Church and millions of Orthodox Christians" – and not only as a state of and for Muslims.[84] Certainly the Orthodox-Ottoman alliance made sense in another respect: the Greeks were locals, the Ottoman Turks were becoming locals, and the sultans were making Istanbul home. Perhaps the Ottoman rulers of Istanbul shared with Greek Orthodox Christians a sense of sympathy – in the literal, Greek-root sense of "fellow feeling" – based on territory and an attachment to place.

The Ottoman policy of investing the Greek Patriarch of Istanbul with an aura of power was tactically wise. It helped to win the cooperation of a hefty local Christian population in a context where foreign Catholic or "Latin" powers – notably, Venetians and Habsburgs in the sixteenth century – were posing a constant threat both to the empire and to Eastern churches. In 1529, Mehmet II's great-grandson, Sultan Suleyman the Magnificent, set siege to Vienna. So imminent, and so frightening, was his near-capture of the city, that Charles V felt compelled "to make concessions to the Protestants in Germany to gain their support, a major factor in the subsequent survival and expansion of the Lutheran movement in western Europe."[85] In this way, Ottoman tensions with Catholic powers had far-reaching consequences for other Christians, both within and outside Ottoman domains – showing once again how the Ottoman Empire was a participant and an agent in European history.

Ecclesiastical silverware, which Orthodox Christian artisans made in Ottoman lands, offers material evidence to support claims for the vitality of Christian Istanbul. This silverware included intricately decorated items used in churches, such as chalices (for communion wine), dishes (for communion bread), and bowls (for the water that priests used in baptisms). Patterns of production and circulation for this silver indicate that, until the end of the empire in the early twentieth century, Ottoman Istanbul remained a critical node and vibrant center for Orthodox Christians across Europe.[86]

Mehmet II extended the bargain he made with the Greeks in Istanbul to Jews. Jews found their situation under Ottoman rule so tolerable that many Jews from farther afield gravitated to Istanbul and other major cities of the realm to seek livelihoods. They tended to settle in large urban areas, and even grew to become the majority in Salonika (now Thessaloniki, Greece). Some of those who came were Ashkenazi Jews, escaping persecution in central Europe (notably, in Poland, Austria, and Bohemia [now the Czech Republic]). Many others were Sephardic Jews, who sought refuge upon their mass expulsion from Spain during the Reconquista of 1492.[87] In Ottoman Jerusalem alone, the influx of Sephardic immigrants more than quadrupled the local Jewish population by 1550, and transformed Jewish life in the city.[88]

Two points stand out here regarding the Jews of the Ottoman Empire. First, Jews were communities in the plural, not one community as the singular term *millet* implied. Nevertheless, Jews appear to have been amenable to this single-*millet* status, for although their practices were diverse, they "preferred to present a united front when dealing with the authorities."[89] Together, their numbers were tiny, and this made cooperation with the state seem worthwhile. In addition to Ashkenazi and Sephardic Jews in the empire, for example, there were indigenous Jews, whom today one would call "Mizrahi" Jews but who were known in Arabic-speaking territories as *Musta'rab* (Arabized) Jews. There were also Kara'ites, who rejected the Talmud as a source of legal authority. More ambiguously still, there was a small community of Samaritans living north of Jerusalem, who practiced a religion that was close to, but not firmly part of, Judaism. Eventually, too, there were "Francos": Jewish immigrants from parts of western Europe, who began to arrive in the late eighteenth century and who enjoyed the protected status of non-Ottoman European merchants. (As non-Ottoman subjects, these Francos were not *dhimmis*, and so did not have to pay the *jizya*, much to the annoyance of local Jews.[90])

The second point is that the very conditions that made Ottoman cities so congenial to Jews stoked resentment toward them among diverse Christians, who perceived Jews as Ottoman lackeys. As seventeenth- and eighteenth-century folksongs attest, Christians harassed and vilified Jews in ways that they could never have done to Muslims, while Orthodox ecclesiastical authorities arguably abetted these actions.[91] In the sixteenth century, meanwhile, foreign Catholic visitors to the Ottoman Empire – such as a Portuguese Franciscan priest living in Jerusalem in 1546 – sometimes approached Ottoman Muslim authorities in cases where a Christian person went missing, to accuse Jews of murdering the missing person in order to extract his or her blood for ritual purposes.[92] This was "blood libel," a stock feature of European anti-Semitism, which Christians tried to pass on to Muslims.

Besides Greek Orthodox Christians and Jews, there were Christian Armenians, with whom Mehmet II dealt separately. He understood (as the early Arab Muslim conquerors of seventh-century Syria and Egypt had apparently not) that there were multiple Christian sects that called themselves "Orthodox," and that cooperation among Christians was difficult, even unlikely, amid their competing truth claims. In particular, the Armenian Apostolic Church adhered to a creed called Miaphysitism, or more broadly, Monophysitism (postulating a fusion of the human and divine natures of Christ in one body), which was a doctrine that Greek Orthodoxy dismissed as heretical. Thus, in 1461, Mehmet II appointed the Armenian archbishop of Bursa as the patriarch of Armenians and gave him powers equivalent to those of the Greek Patriarch of Istanbul.

The historian Stanford Shaw suggested that the Armenian *millet* was an umbrella covering every other non-Muslim group that did not fit into the Greek Orthodox or Jewish *millets*. Among these others were "Gypsies (called *Kibti*, or Copts, by the Arabs and Ottomans, apparently because of a mistaken identification with the original inhabitants of Egypt), the Assyrians, the Monophysites of Syria and Egypt, and the Bogomils of Bosnia, who were in fact doctrinally related to the Manicheans." Before the nineteenth century, Shaw wrote, there were also some Christian Catholic groups that recognized Vatican authority while preserving their own eastern rites, such as the Maronites of Mount Lebanon (a region incorporated into the Ottoman Empire after the Syrian conquest of 1517), and the Latin Catholics of Croatia, Hungary, and Albania.[93] However, there is scant evidence for a coherent "Armenian *millet*" possessed with real authority over these enormously diverse, non-Armenian groups. Over Armenians in Istanbul alone, the Armenian patriarch's influence may have been "purely symbolic," in part because historic centers of the church were elsewhere, deep in Anatolia. Likewise, until the mid-nineteenth century, the influence of an Ottoman-state-recognized chief rabbi (appointed from 1835 onward, in a formalization of the Jewish *millet*) also extended little beyond Istanbul.[94]

From the perspective of the Ottoman state, Christian and Jewish leaders who really mattered included laymen who helped the state to generate revenue. These lay leaders included merchants, financial advisors, tax collectors, and moneylenders. Two people who fit this profile were the aunt-and-nephew banking duo, Doña Gracia Nasi (c. 1510–69) and Don Joseph Nasi (c. 1520–79), both Sephardic Jews who found refuge in the Ottoman Empire upon their expulsion from Spain and whose family owed much of its fortune to the international spice trade.[95] In fact, the family had been *conversos*, converts to Christianity, who reclaimed their Judaism upon finding haven in Ottoman lands.[96] The two Nasis lent a lot of money to the Ottoman palace and arguably attained "more influence with the sultan and his family than any other Jewish or Christian subject in Ottoman history."[97] Indeed, they won so much appreciation from Sultan Suleyman the Magnificent that he agreed to lease them the ancient city of Tiberias, on the coast of what is now Israel, so that they could restore it and start a *yeshiva*, or Jewish seminary. Don Joseph also had a dream for Cyprus, as the Ottomans stood poised to wrest it from Venice: he hoped to start a sanctuary on the island for Jews, who were fleeing from persecution in Europe.[98] His idea for starting a Jewish homeland in Ottoman Cyprus arguably anticipated an idea that European Jewish Zionists later propounded, vis-à-vis Ottoman Palestine, nearly four centuries later.

From the non-Muslim communities, the Ottoman authorities also wanted men who could lead in collecting the *jizya* tax from *dhimmi*s. The Ottoman state badly needed this income because the *jizya* went directly to the imperial treasury, unlike many other sources of revenue – such as *waqf* funds, which supported religious endowments, and proceeds from *timar*s, or land grants, which sustained Ottoman military men in lieu of a salary. Indeed, during the sixteenth century, the *jizya* constituted the most important source of revenue for the Ottoman state.[99] During the first half of the eighteenth century, at a time when the Ottoman central state was ever more desperate for funds to support its military, the *jizya* amounted to 40 percent of its income.[100]

This reliance on the *jizya*, argued the historian Jane Hathaway, explains why the Ottoman central state cultivated ties to leading Jewish and Christian merchants or bankers, even more than rabbis, bishops, and the like: simply, the former were better at mustering taxes from the community. Thus in Cairo during the seventeenth century, for instance, the Ottoman governor's banker functioned as the head of the Jewish

community.[101] But Islamic court judges, or *qadi*s, played an important role in this process, too. Ottoman tax records show that in some
rural, agricultural areas, where non-Muslim populations were generally Christian, *qadi*s compiled registers every few years in which they
recorded the names of able-bodied non-Muslim adult men who were
liable to pay the *jizya*. Their registers accounted for changes through
death, maturity (of boys to adulthood), relocation, and conversion to
Islam (in which case responsibility for payment ceased). In some places,
households paid according to the number of adult males within them;
elsewhere communities collected payments based on a lump sum that
authorities demanded. Either way, and in theory, tax collectors were supposed to consider the ability of men to pay on a scale of low, medium, or
high according to their means.[102] However, evidence from one particular
Anatolian town, Kayseri, in the early seventeenth century, shows that the
jizya there took no account of poverty: everyone paid the same.[103]

Islamic law and historical precedent was not the only source of
Ottoman fiscal policy. In the Balkans especially, taxes reflected arrangements that the early Ottoman state had made with local Christians
in light of pre-Ottoman customs. Thus, in Hungary, for example, the
Ottomans charged Christians a special tax on foraging pigs, while along
the Danube, they charged Christians a tax on pigs that were slaughtered
during Christmas. (Before the Ottomans, Christians had paid this tax in
meat, but since Muslims were not supposed to eat pork, Ottoman collectors assessed it in cash.) In Bulgaria, they expected Christian farmers to supplement their annual agricultural taxes with "a gift to the fief
holder of a hen and a pastry." Sunni Muslim scholars, learned in Islamic
jurisprudence, might have found some of these tax customs odd or even
amusing, though they might have winced to hear of others that impinged
on the privilege of Muslims. For example, in the Balkans, Ottoman collectors forced "Muslim gypsies" to pay the *jizya*, suggesting the ambiguous social position of the Roma in general. In Macedonia, they assessed
the *jizya* on Muslim cavalrymen who claimed fiefs on lands that Christian
peasants inhabited, making the status of the land, and not of the person,
the determining factor for tax liability.[104]

Another point worth making about the *jizya*, and about other taxes
which Muslims paid, is that the Ottoman treasury appears to have aimed
for fairness in collection – although what actually happened in the provinces was another story. During the sixteenth and seventeenth centuries, the Ottoman treasury recorded thousands of petitions "from all
over the empire ... year after year," in which Ottoman subjects objected
to their tax assessments. The steady recurrence of such petitions suggests
that Ottoman subjects found the government reasonably responsive and

accountable.[105] In the seventeenth century, however, subjects were pro-
testing not just the *jizya*, but even more importantly, the "extraordinary
levies and dues" (*avariz*) that the Ottoman state began to apply – in
cash, kind, and labor – at a time when military campaigns were emptying
the imperial coffers. These new taxes could include "providing chickens
or onions for the imperial kitchens; supporting post horses; maintaining roads, bridges, and watercourses; guarding mountain passes; providing grain for the horses of the army on the march; sending oarsmen to
the naval galleys; or giving cash for paying soldiers or purchasing provisions in time of war."[106] Such "extraordinary" taxes became ordinary,
that is, distressingly regular, as the Ottoman state demanded more and
more. Unpaid, demobilized, and armed soldiers were distressed, too,
and vented their frustrations on villagers and townspeople throughout
Anatolia, making "banditry, brigandage, and depradations" a hallmark
of the early seventeenth century.[107] These circumstances propelled many
peasants (Muslim and Christian) to flee for Istanbul, although Ottoman
authorities tried to push them back to their villages. Meanwhile, "The
considerable internal migration made it virtually impossible to keep
track of people" for tax-collecting purposes. It has also made it virtually
impossible for historians today to deduce the size of Christian populations on the basis of *jizya* assessments.[108]

Significantly, Ottoman authorities did not extract the *jizya* from foreign Christians and Jews who were not their subjects. Above all, they
exempted foreign European merchants and consular officials who
enjoyed privileges that Ottoman sultans awarded in treaties, called *ahd-
name*s in Ottoman Turkish (deriving from an Arabic root meaning "covenant") and Capitulations in English, referring to the chapters or clauses
(*capitula*s in Latin) of their texts. The Ottomans had extended comparable privileges informally to Genoese merchants in the fifteenth century,
and soon extended them to Venetians. France secured a formal treaty in
1535 and extended its privileges in subsequent treaties. England secured
a treaty in the late sixteenth century, the Netherlands got one in the
early seventeenth century, and in the eighteenth century, so did a host of
other entities – the Habsburg Empire, Sweden, the Kingdom of the Two
Sicilies, Tuscany, Denmark, Russia, and Spain.[109] Until the eighteenth
century, the Ottoman Empire did not demand reciprocal privileges
abroad because it did not formally manage trade within Europe and
assumed that few of its Muslim merchants would venture into Christian
lands.[110] That situation appeared to be changing in the seventeenth century, however, as some Ottoman subjects – and especially Armenian and
Greek Christian merchants – ventured to cities like Amsterdam, where
they founded trading colonies in the far corners of the Ottoman world.[111]

Dhimmi **Life in Practice**

In the big cities, *dhimmi* life and the *millet* system often assumed a spatial dimension. In some areas, Muslim, Christian, and Jewish families inhabited the same city streets. In others, *dhimmi*s clustered together in districts that became known for the religion of their people. The legacy of this kind of communal geography remains visible today in the historic center ("Old City") of Jerusalem, which claims a "Muslim Quarter," "Jewish Quarter," "Christian Quarter," and "Armenian Quarter" (with the distinctiveness of the last of these relative to the other Christian district expressing the spatial, social, and not only doctrinal differences that could keep members of Christian sects apart). In many cities, the non-Muslims gathered in districts that were close to the seat of Muslim rulers, for example, in Baghdad, Aleppo, Cairo, Tunis, and Algiers.[112] Proximity to Muslim rulers may have conferred a greater sense of protection.

Clustering together by religion had its advantages. It made communal worship, the observation of major holidays, and the finding of marriage partners easier. It also ensured some safety in numbers and less fear of facing harassment as *dhimmi*s, particularly during times of social distress. The seventeenth century witnessed one such period, when Muslim supporters of the Kadizadeli movement, in Istanbul, tried to impose their puritanical and populist code and to extirpate what they deemed un-Islamic customs. Tellingly, Kadizadelis called non-Muslims *kefere* (infidels) rather than *dhimmi*s (protected people) and engaged in behavior that compromised "the famous religious tolerance of the Ottomans," in the tactful words of one scholar.[113] In the wake of the great Istanbul fire of 1660, in particular, when many Jews experienced displacement, Islamic courts registered cases where Muslims and Christians objected to Jews moving into their neighborhoods. In another case, an unhappy Muslim neighbor went so far as to secure a *fatwa* from the *shaykh al-Islam* (the chief of the *'ulama*) affirming that Muslims could force a Christian to sell his home to a Muslim if the Christian performed Christian rituals in a home located in a "Muslim" neighborhood.[114]

As in earlier periods of Islamic history, Muslims, Christians, and Jews were able to distinguish each other by appearance, and not merely by custom. Beginning in the latter part of the reign of Suleyman the Magnificent (r. 1520–66), Ottoman authorities more rigidly enforced dress codes that sought to separate Muslims and non-Muslims while emphasizing the inferiority of the latter.[115] In the early sixteenth century, a French diplomat reported, Jewish men wore yellow turbans; Armenians, Greeks, Copts, and other Christians wore bluish turbans; and "Turks" wore white turbans.[116] The robes of Jewish and Christian

Image 8 Opaque watercolor and ink on paper showing a Bekci, or Ottoman night watchman, carrying a club and a lantern, including pink and yellow tulip cut-outs on either side. Folio from an album titled, "A briefe relation of the Turckes, their kings, Emperors, or Grandsigneurs, their conquests, religion, customes, habbits, etc," Istanbul, 1618. Museum Number 1974,0617,0.13.32. ©The Trustees of the British Museum.

men and women were generally dark, in the blue to black range, because Ottoman Muslims deemed these colors to be of "ill omen." Wealthy Muslims opted for bright colors such as "carmine red," "lilac" and "violet," and "cinnamon," while humble Muslims went for more subdued colors but still not black or dark blue.[117] In footwear, however, Ottoman Muslim elites came to "prize yellow, particularly for their slippers," while non-Muslims had to wear black.[118] That Ottoman custom was the opposite of conventions in the Abbasid era, when Muslim ruling classes and jurists had deemed yellow an inauspicious color that was suitable only for *dhimmi*s.[119]

In a context where public baths drew together people of all religions and walks of life, there remained the problem – with which the fourteenth-century Mamluk rulers of Egypt and Syria had also grappled[120] – of how to distinguish between Muslims and *dhimmi*s when they were naked. In sixteenth-century Jerusalem, public bathhouses required a Jewish man to wear a bell around his neck "to announce his arrival and warn the Muslims to hide their nakedness"; in seventeenth-century Egypt, a Jewish man had to wear a red or black necklace instead. Significantly, too, bath-houses issued different towels for Muslims and *dhimmi*s – reflecting an order that the Ottoman sultan Selim I (r. 1512–20) had issued.[121] Islamic court records detail cases like the one that arose in Jerusalem in 1547, when prosperous Muslim clients pressed charges against a bathhouse operator, who allegedly gave everybody the same shabby towels, thereby failing to distinguish between clients on the basis not only of religion (Muslim vs. *dhimmi*) but of rank (so as to distinguish rich Muslims from poor ones).[122] In 1640, in Istanbul, regulations stipulated that *dhimmi* men and women alike had to distinguish themselves from Muslims in the bathhouse by wearing a ring on their towels. "They were [also] to change in a different place, were not to be given clogs [for their feet], and had to wash at separate spots." In 1761, in Aleppo, Syria, Muslim authorities solved the problem of visual differentiation by specifying different days on which Muslims, Christians, and Jews could go to the bath house at all.[123] The frequent restatement of dress codes in Istanbul, over the course of many generations, suggests that regulations about dress often lapsed or went unheeded, especially in the "noisy commotion" of the public bath. Nevertheless, even as late as the early twentieth century – the eve of the collapse of the Ottoman Empire – prevailing custom in Istanbul baths still dictated that Muslims and non-Muslims should change their clothes in separate areas.[124]

Sultans sometimes responded to the pressures of Muslim hardliners, who were keen to enforce social hierarchies, by attending more seriously to dress codes. An edict of 1577, for example, declared that *dhimmi*s who violated dress codes would face execution. In the 1650s, another French traveler observed that the "Christians do not dare to wear an all-white turban, because if one caught a Christian with it on, subject of the Sultan or not, he would have to turn Turk [convert to Islam] or die" – a phenomenon confirmed by Islamic court records.[125] Occasionally, while traveling through dangerous areas, *dhimmi*s – who, by the terms of Islamic law, could not bear arms to defend themselves – were able to secure documents from Muslim authorities permitting them to wear Muslim clothes temporarily, as a way of avoiding extra harassment from bandits.[126] Meanwhile, in the Ottoman provinces, local Muslim officials sometimes announced new clothing rules as a way of squeezing money out of non-Muslims who then paid to have the rules cancelled. On one occasion, in Aleppo, Syria, in 1775, Christian negotiators haggled with Muslim officials for eleven days to get new clothing restrictions repealed, and succeeded in bargaining them down to one-third of the amount originally

Image 9 Nineteenth-century bath clogs, wood with leather strap covered in metallic thread, Ottoman Empire. Museum Number 2013,6008.1.a-b. ©The Trustees of the British Museum.

demanded. Most of the city's Christians stayed indoors throughout their negotiations as a sign of protest.[127]

Despite the physical and cultural barriers to interaction, Muslims, Christians, and Jews did mix in various settings. They mixed, for a start, in bars and brothels, like the ones that flourished so dramatically in the Galata district of Istanbul, which was located along the inlet of the Bosphorus known as the Golden Horn. The well-known Ottoman traveler, Evliya Çelebi (1611–89), estimated that along the coast at Galata during the mid-seventeenth century, there were 200 brothels and taverns, mostly run by Greeks and Jews, and each catering to several hundred Muslim and non-Muslim customers.[128] The assumption in Istanbul was that non-Muslims ran the "vice trade" – a trade that Ottoman authorities both tolerated and taxed – and that Muslims could partake of, but not offer, its services. Yet, in the eighteenth century, there were Muslim female sex workers, too, while former Janissaries ran "bachelor houses" that were used for smuggling and prostitution. The result, observed the historian Fariba Zarinebaf, in a social history of the Ottoman underworld, was that "Istanbul was the scene of many kinds of sexual encounters between members of various nations and communities," as the literature of the period describes.[129]

Evidence from the Syrian city of Aleppo, during the same period, suggests that sex workers – Muslims and non-Muslims alike – were not necessarily family renegades or outcasts. Indeed, a study of 300 years' worth of Ottoman court records for Aleppo concluded that 42 percent of cases of alleged *zina* (fornication) involved family businesses, in which husbands, wives, and other relatives engaged in sex work as procurers, managers, or prostitutes. One case, for example, involved a Muslim man named Mustafa ibn Fathi and his wife Fatima bint Musa whom angry neighbors charged with running a brothel from their home. Legal records from Ottoman Aleppo support two claims: first, that the standard judgment against those whom judges found guilty of *zina* was eviction, in this case, banishment to another district of the city; and second, that neighbors – not judicial or religious authorities – initiated cases against those believed to be disturbing public order by behaving inappropriately.[130] The result was what another scholar, in a study of court cases from eighteenth-century Damascus, characterized as "quarter solidarity": a form of collective identity, based on residence in a common neighborhood, that often transcended religion. Quarter solidarity was on show in Damascus, for example, when a delegation of Jewish and Muslim neighbors persuaded their local court to evict five Jews whom they felt were discrediting the district by selling wine within it.[131]

Muslims, Christians, and Jews mixed, too, in some professional guilds that were important to life in the cities, such as the guild of the "round cake-makers." One study, based on a sampling of Islamic court records from Istanbul, concluded on the basis of the cited names of guild members that perhaps a third of Istanbul's guilds were religiously mixed in the seventeenth century; the remaining two-thirds were Muslim-, Christian-, or Jewish-only, perhaps because it was easier to work with people who had the same holidays.[132] Guilds that were made up of non-Muslims – such as a guild of Greek candlestick makers in the 1660s – sometimes appointed Muslims as their spokesmen, perhaps because they felt that Muslims could advocate for them more effectively in an Islamic court. In other cases, single-religion guilds cooperated with each other: in one instance, a wholly Muslim guild came to court to advocate for its equivalent Jewish guild of "smallware-dealers" (specializing in cups, plates, and the like) over the latter's right, vis-à-vis other guilds, to sell European-made glass. Guilds functioned in some ways like *millet*s supposedly did. Guild leaders, for example, collected certain taxes, notably the "extraordinary" taxes that Ottoman authorities added in the seventeenth century.[133] They also engaged in acts of collective piety and social service, with Christian-only guilds, for example, pooling funds to buy the elaborate silver items for churches, as well as their icons, liturgical vestments, lamps, and furnishings. In this way, Christian guilds invigorated church life in the city.[134]

This history of guilds points to another place where non-Muslims interacted: the Islamic (Shari'a) law courts. Following a long precedent in Islamic law, Ottoman Islamic courts worked on the premise that Christians and Jews could seek justice, on their own initiative, within them. And indeed, much to the chagrin of religious leaders, Christians and Jews availed themselves of the opportunity, with Jewish and Christian women, in particular, often seeking out the more liberal Muslim laws on marriage, divorce, and inheritance. For example, in the central Anatolian town of Kayseri, during the period from 1600 to 1625, 27 percent of female litigants were *dhimmi*s.[135] Records from Ottoman Damascus show, likewise, that many other *dhimmi*s came to register property titles and commercial transactions, with the Islamic courts functioning as *de facto* public record offices.[136] In another case from the seventeenth century involving a guild dispute, a non-Muslim "shoe-tip maker" even brandished in court a *fatwa* that he had secured from a Muslim *shaykh*, challenging the Muslim leaders of the relevant guild who had previously denied his application to join.[137]

Not only were the Islamic courts often more generous to Jewish and Christian women than their own communal courts could be (particularly vis-à-vis inheritance), but they also had a reputation for fairness in claims between Muslims and non-Muslims and between humble and powerful people.[138] Sometimes, even Jewish and Christian religious leaders sought help from the Islamic courts after failing in their own efforts to handle a problem. In one case from eighteenth-century Istanbul, five district rabbis, joined by more than twenty Greek, Armenian, and Muslim residents of a mixed neighborhood, begged an Islamic court to sentence a Jewish woman named Rifke (Rivka), claiming that she had "intermingle[d] with Muslim, Armenian, and Greek men against the shari'a." The police register noted that Jewish community leaders had tried to punish her, and to expel her from the neighborhood, but she "continue[d] her prostitution day and night and refuse[d] to improve her conduct." The court complied and sentenced her to banishment, which was, in Istanbul as in Ottoman cities like Aleppo, the common Islamic court punishment in this period for "moral misconduct."[139] It is hard to decide what was most remarkable about Rifke's case: that she had sex with so many different kinds of men, and lived to tell the tale; that so many different kinds of neighbors joined to protest against her;

or that everyone, rabbis and residents together, sought and found help from the Islamic court judges.

Of course, the case of the promiscuous Rifke may seem remarkable now, but it was probably not unusual, as court records from other cities, such as Damascus and Jerusalem attest. *Dhimmi*s sought out the Muslim courts time and time again: the courts functioned as what one would call today a "civic space." Thus while religion kept Muslims, Christians, and Jews apart in some ways, common cultural assumptions and practices brought them together in others. Writing about Ottoman Aleppo, the historian Abraham Marcus may not have been too romantic when he mused that, while people showed differences in class, sex, and religion, "common collective heritage and experience of the townspeople far outweighed these differences; a concord on essentials united all groups."[140]

The Eighteenth Century and the Acceleration of Social Change

The eighteenth century was a pivotal period in Ottoman social and political affairs; it was also an era of cultural ferment. Long an imperial aggressor, the Ottoman Empire became subject to an imperialism that scholars vaguely call "Western." In the process, the Ottoman Empire experienced military defeats and signed treaties that gave other European powers claims over some of its lands, and some of its peoples. Representatives of other European countries cited long-standing trade agreements with the Ottoman Empire – the Capitulations – to push their privileges farther by officially recognizing a select number of the empire's Jews and Christians as protégés. Foreign European customs, ideas, and people, coming from well beyond the Balkan territories that belonged to "Ottoman Europe," began to impinge upon everyday life, leading to changes in realms ranging from the economic (as manifest in Egypt, for example, in the consolidation of private land-ownership) to the literary (where new subjects and prose styles drew attention to the mundane or quirky experiences of individuals)[141]. The culture of scholarly writing expanded beyond the ranks of religious experts, enabling historians to engage in more than just "ulamalogy" (the study of *'ulama*), as the historian Dana Sajdi called it, after she discovered an eighteenth-century Arabic chronicle of Damascus written by a barber – a newcomer to the world of literary authority.[142] At the same time, Roman Catholic missionaries appeared in numbers from countries like France and what is now Italy, persuading many Christians of the Islamic world to change their churches and arguably, too, their political allegiances. To the historian, these cultural changes make the eighteenth-century Ottoman Empire look very "modern," in the sense of reflecting assertions of personal (as opposed to collective or corporate) interest amidst the global circulation of goods and practices.

Militarily and diplomatically, there were three watershed events that bore upon the Ottoman Empire broadly and upon the political status of *dhimmi*s more narrowly. The first was the Treaty of Karlowitz of 1699, which followed an Ottoman defeat by the Habsburg Empire (Austria) and the loss of territories in parts of what are now Serbia, Bosnia, Croatia, Romania, and Hungary. Karlowitz put the Ottomans on the defensive in Europe. In the treaty, the sultan also confirmed the rights of Catholics in Ottoman domains, thus giving the Habsburg emperor, Leopold I (c. 1658–1705), who also held the title of Holy Roman Emperor (r. 1658–1705), a pretext to intervene on behalf of Catholics.[143] In the long run, however, as the number of Catholics grew among Ottoman Christian communities, France became the major beneficiary of this provision.

The second watershed was the Treaty of Kujuk Kaynarca of 1774. This treaty acknowledged the Ottoman Empire's defeat by Russia and its loss of Crimea, whose Muslim rulers – the Crimean Tatar khans – had recognized Ottoman suzerainty since the sixteenth century. The treaty's terms gave Russia the right to build an Orthodox church in Istanbul, which Russia then interpreted to mean a Russian right to protect all Orthodox Christians in the Ottoman Empire – a pretext, in this case, for Russian meddling in Ottoman affairs.[144]

The third watershed was Napoleon's invasion of Egypt in 1798, which inaugurated a French occupation of the country that lasted for three years. The French regime introduced an Arabic printing press – looted from the Vatican – and started an Arabic government gazette, which endured long after an Anglo-Ottoman expedition forced France to withdraw in 1801. Napoleon's forces briefly overturned centuries-old Islamic conventions regarding *dhimmi* behavior by appointing Coptic Christians to high ranks and equipping others with horses and weapons.[145] As short as it was, the French occupation set the stage for major changes in Egypt during the nineteenth century.

In the eighteenth century, too, European foreigners began to exploit one of the privileges granted to them in the Capitulations: namely, the right to appoint Ottoman Christian or Jewish subjects as translators (known as dragomans), and in so doing to grant each a certificate, called a *berat*, which gave foreign protection as well as a degree of legal and fiscal autonomy. In practice, this arrangement brought a *de facto* end to the *dhimmi* status of *berat*-holders and thus their obligation to pay the *jizya* and other taxes. This process was especially marked in the Syrian city of Aleppo, as "consuls, especially the French and English, dispensed them with abandon to the employees and relatives of their dragomans, to the host of clerks, agents, and salesmen employed by their merchants, and to numerous wealthy non-Muslims."[146] Indeed, rather than bestowing these privileges on genuine employees, as the Capitulations had intended, European ambassadors, and sometimes their consuls or even their dragomans, began to sell them to the highest bidder as a way of padding their incomes. In one case from 1783, for example, a Catholic dragoman named Nasrallah A'idah, who worked for the Dutch consulate in Aleppo, sold a *berat* to a rabbi named Ifraim son of Salomon Lagniado, making him an "hononary dragoman" or what the Ottoman authorities called a *berath*.[147]

Many historians have identified the practice of *berat*-selling as a symptom of the mounting weakness of the Ottoman state, which began to lose not only tax revenues but also, and more abstractly, power and influence over some of its wealthiest Christians and Jews.[148] In fact, most Jews in the empire, during the eighteenth century, were traders, artisans, and laborers, while most Christians, similarly, were humble urbanites or peasants, so that the vast majority were unable to buy a *berat*.[149] But for the rich who *could* afford it, the *berat* may have seemed like a back door out of *dhimmi* status, a way of escaping the "principle of inequality that the non-Muslims disliked but were in no position to undo" by acquiring a kind of diplomatic immunity.[150]

It is perhaps no surprise that eighteenth-century Aleppo was such a lively center for the buying and selling of *berat*s: taxes there were exorbitant. The city's ruling classes were rapacious in demanding taxes from Muslims, Christians, and Jews alike, and their policies exacerbated the widespread food shortages of the period. Public outrage reached such a pitch in 1751, a year of famine, that Muslim women occupied the minaret of the city's Great Mosque where they shouted insults at the governor for doing nothing while people starved. But extortion appears to have struck non-Muslims particularly hard, argued Abraham Marcus, since Christians and Jews were easy targets who, as *dhimmi*s, had no arms for self-defense. During the late eighteenth century, Christians and Jews of this city were reduced to selling off silver from their churches and synagogues in order to cover their taxes, while in the 1790s, authorities even forced Jews to pay for the privilege of burying their dead.[151]

Aleppo was the scene for another major development of the Ottoman eighteenth century. It witnessed the rise of sustained activity on the part of Catholic missionaries, who had been working in the city from the 1630s with support from France, appealing to Orthodox Christians. Catholic missionaries in this same period were becoming active elsewhere in the Ottoman Empire, such as in Anatolia, among Armenians, and in Egypt, among Copts. Still, their impact was particularly strong in

Aleppo and other parts of Syria, where, by the eighteenth century, most local Christians became Catholic adherents. Local Christians may have found Catholic doctrines or modes of worship attractive, but Catholic missionaries also offered this-worldly advantages, including schools for children, diplomatic protection, and even, for merchants, insurance on Mediterranean shipping.[152] By the mid-eighteenth century, Catholics had been so successful that all the major Eastern churches had manifested new breakaway churches that recognized Rome (such as the Melkite church, which broke off from Greek Orthodoxy in Syria, or the new Coptic Catholic church in Egypt).[153]

French Catholic missions were also starting to change behaviors and expectations among women, with broader implications for families and gender relations. As the historian Bernard Heyberger observed in his study of these missions in seventeenth- and eighteenth-century Aleppo, "The missionaries tended to valorize the place of women in society, and to make certain taboos fall away regarding their impurity and ignorance."[154] Under missionary influence, and much to the dismay of local families, some young women began to avoid marriage by choosing lives of celibacy – that is, by choosing careers in the church. At a time when Catholic missions were emphasizing an individual culture of Christian devotion, many of these female devotees learned not only to read, but also to write – whereupon some began recording their innermost thoughts in personal diaries. Catholic missionaries reported to their superiors in Rome that some of these same women were staying too long in the confessional, taking advantage of a Catholic system that gave them the chance to talk about themselves and to pour out worries, misdeeds, and desires.[155] We can see in these developments, too, the emergence of a very modern culture of individualism, as well as the beginnings of a new kind of activism and professional life among women.

Again, Catholic missions were expanding in the eighteenth-century Middle East, and new churches were forming. The Ottoman state probably underestimated the importance of these developments, although their consequences proved momentous. The Greek and Armenian patriarchs in Istanbul took action in the face of the Catholic whittling of their communities by demanding and pursuing the centralization of authority in a process that led by the mid-eighteenth century to what the historian Bruce Masters called the "definitive establishment of the Armenian and Greek Orthodox *millet*s, backed by the sultan's writ." The Greek Orthodox patriarch, in particular, began to pursue a process of Hellenization that entailed sending out Greek-speaking ecclesiastical authorities from Istanbul to run churches in Slavic lands and in islands like Crete and Cyprus. In 1776 and 1777, the Greek Orthodox patriarch also managed to have the Ottoman authorities announce the abolition of the independent Orthodox patriarchates in Peć (now in Kosovo) and Ohrid (now in the Republic of Macedonia). The Serbian patriarch simply responded by withdrawing into Habsburg territory, beyond Ottoman control. A similar backlash occurred among Orthodox Bulgarians, who reacted to Greek centralization by evincing a new interest in Bulgarian history and language. "The struggle over the centralisation of church authority in both the Orthodox and the Armenian *millets*," Masters concluded, "inadvertently sparked the growth of ethnic consciousness that would emerge as the Romantic nationalisms of the nineteenth century."[156] To wit, nationalism among Christians sprang from tensions among Christians themselves. Meanwhile, in Egypt, Catholic missionary activity inspired the assertion of Coptic Orthodox ecclesiastic authority, setting the stage for a Coptic revival that would stretch into the nineteenth and twentieth centuries.[157]

Protestant Christians began to trickle into the Ottoman Empire in this century, too. In 1752, for example, the first Protestant missionaries reached Egypt: these were a small group of Moravian Pietists.[158] The Moravians' lack of connection to a European power, and their small-scale, non-polemical efforts to promote an ethic of manual labor and piety among Copts without converting them, occasioned no apparent resistance – which is probably why historians know so little about them.

One of the most interesting Protestant Christians to enter the Ottoman Empire in this period eventually converted to Islam and became known as Ibrahim Müteferrika (c. 1674–1745). Born in Kolozsvár, Transylvania (now part of Romania) when the region was under Hungarian control, this man was in training for church ministry when an Ottoman patrol seized and enslaved him along the Habsburg frontier in 1692. Judging from a treatise that he later wrote, which was a "polemic against Papism [Catholicism] and the doctrine of the Trinity," Ibrahim Müteferrika's own prior Protestant inclinations may have leaned toward Unitarianism (a Christian theology emphasizing the oneness of God) – a tendency that may have eased his transition into the Sunni Islam of learned Muslims, with its unequivocal emphasis on monotheism.[159] Evincing what was arguably a Protestant enthusiasm for print culture, Ibrahim Müteferrika went on to make his mark on Ottoman history by leading the first Islamic-state-approved press in the world, dedicated to publishing works for a Muslim audience in Ottoman Turkish.[160]

That said, Ibrahim Müteferrika did not start the first printing press in the Ottoman Empire. This distinction goes instead to two Jewish

brothers, David and Samuel ibn Nahmias, who started a Hebrew printing press in Istanbul in 1493 – just one year after their expulsion from
Spain – and who published the Torah along with other major works of
Jewish law and tradition.[161] Christians started presses well before the
venture of Ibrahim Müteferrika, too. In 1627, for example, the Greek
Orthodox patriarch in Istanbul made what Bruce Masters called an
"opening salvo in the defence of Orthodoxy" against Catholic missionary overtures by approving the establishment of a Greek-language press
in the Ottoman capital. French authorities, offended by the anti-Catholic
polemical works that it produced, persuaded the Ottoman authorities to
shut down this press one year later.[162] Note that this Greek Orthodox
press was responding to publications emanating from Roman Catholic
sources in Rome – for by the early seventeenth century, the missionary
wing of the Roman Catholic church, the Propaganda Fide, was printing
works in Greek and Arabic, Syriac, and Armenian, too.[163]

Notwithstanding these precedents, Ibrahim Müteferrika's launch-
ing of his press in 1727 – one year before Benjamin Franklin's press in
Philadelphia, noted the Turkish Cypriot historian Niyazi Berkes – was a
real watershed for Ottoman print culture.[164] His printed volumes resembled manuscripts but contained features common to the modern book,
such as page numbers, titles, and tables of contents.[165] In a work that he
wrote himself in Ottoman Turkish and printed in 1731, entitled *Rational
Bases for the Polities of Nations*, Ibrahim Müteferrika urged Ottomans to
borrow worthwhile ideas and practices from Christian Europe.[166] He also
published a book about the Americas called, *A History of Western India,
Known as the New World*. Likewise, he published scientific books that conveyed the ideas of Galileo, Descartes, and others, prompting one scholar
to credit him for helping to spark an "Ottoman Enlightenment."[167]
However, Ibrahim Müteferrika did not have an easy time with his venture – in part because his books were expensive, reflecting the high
cost of paper – and his press languished after his death. Content posed
another barrier, for while he had managed to secure both a firman from
the sultan and a fatwa from the head of the 'ulama, allowing his press to
move forward, these permissions barred him from publishing works of
an Islamic nature. Thus his press yielded no Müteferrika Qur'an to rival
the Gutenberg Bible.[168]

Still, the fact that Ibrahim Müteferrika was able to print books at all
attests to the openness that prevailed during the tenure of Ibrahim Pasha,
who from 1718 to 1730 served as grand vizier (meaning chief minister)
to Sultan Ahmet III (r. 1703–30). Ibrahim Pasha may have been the
first Ottoman official to think that Ottoman foreign policymakers should

have a firm knowledge of Europe. He was also the first grand vizier to send Ottoman ambassadors to Paris and Moscow; before then, Ottoman sultans had expected emissaries to come to them. Those Ottomans who went to Paris, in particular, returned inspired by French art, architecture, fashion, and culture, and introduced new practices within the ruling classes.[169]

Historians call the years of Ibrahim Pasha's vizierate the "Tulip Period," referring to both the lush array of tulips that the sultan and Ottoman elites planted in their gardens as well as to the mood of vivid flamboyance that these flowers evoked. During these years from 1718 to 1730, tulips became a status symbol and "helped elaborate a diplomatic language for [Ottoman] political elites who transferred part of their ideological competition from the battlefield to the palace, garden, and parade ground."[170] The grandest tulip garden of them all was at Sa'adabad, the pleasure palace that Sultan Ahmet III built to resemble the palace of France's kings at Versailles. French culture manifested its influences in other ways as well – for example, in the Baroque or Rococo design of public fountains, and in the adornment of palace walls with murals, which western European artists came to paint.[171] Two art historians speculated that the Ottomans may have embraced Rococo so readily because the "scrolling leafs and flowers of the rococo [already had] a close affinity with the traditional, stylized, vegetal vocabulary" of the Ottoman tradition. In any case, Rococo motifs trickled down to Orthodox Christian artists too – suggesting that the cultural influences of the Tulip Period extended beyond the range of Ottoman Muslim elites – by leaving a discernible mark on the design of the precious silver objects produced for churches in the century that followed.[172]

The Tulip Period was an age when the Ottoman ruling classes attended lavish garden parties wearing clothes to match the tulips, and when turtles carried candles on their backs to light these gardens at night.[173] But in this era, beyond the walls of Istanbul's palaces, the urban poor were growing poorer, more desperate, and more crowded together as taxes spiked, food grew scarce, and the population burgeoned. Against this context, in 1730, an urban revolt erupted under the leadership of a man known as Patrona Halil, a one-time Janissary of Albanian origin, who ran a coffeehouse in Istanbul. The revolt nipped the Tulip Period in the bud. Rioters stormed Topkapı Palace in Istanbul and seized and executed the sultan; they burned down Sa'adabad palace. Some Jews and Christians saw their shops looted, or received threats reminding them to dress only in the dark clothes and shoes of *dhimmi*s, but other Jews and Christians joined the rioters. In short, the rioters were diverse, like Ottoman urban society at large; they were responding to the acute cleavages of wealth and privilege that marked this era; and some were evoking discourses of public order and propriety that harkened back to earlier Islamic tradition.[174] The fact that so many of the rioters were former Janissaries also shows how the Ottoman state and its military were changing. Once part of an elite military cadre, Janissary veterans had come to swell the ranks of Istanbul's "poor working class and criminal underworld" while providing leadership for the revolt.[175]

One historian has called the Tulip Period "an engaging label for an era of self-indulgence that symbolized the loss of imperial dynamism."[176] This assessment goes too far. The developments that Ibrahim Müteferrika made with his press, and the openness that Ottoman ruling elites evinced toward western European high culture, suggest that the Ottoman Empire in the Tulip Period was entering a more energetic era of exchange with parts of Europe. This exchange, which was largely cultural – for example, in the borrowing of building and landscape architecture[177] – provided models for a kind of give-and-take that later assumed other guises. In 1797, for example, sixty-eight years after the end of the Tulip Period, Ottoman authorities intervened diplomatically for the first time on behalf of some of its merchants, who were Greek Orthodox Christians trading in Amsterdam, by demanding tax advantages comparable to those that European merchants had long been claiming in Ottoman domains.[178] Such developments suggest that the Ottoman Empire was becoming cosmopolitan in new ways, and as this last detail about Amsterdam suggests, that some of its non-Muslim subjects were becoming "Ottoman merchants" on the international stage. Or maybe merchants like these were becoming part of a new social species, which some have called "Homo Ottomanicus." Members of the species included Muslims, Christians, and Jews, as well as Ottoman subjects and permanent foreign residents who were moving around in the world but who were anchored in Ottoman society.[179]

The Tulip Period, as well as the Patrona Halil Revolt that ended it, arguably marked, too, the debut of a modern culture of popular mass consumption centered on global trade. This culture of consumption was not only a preserve of the early eighteenth-century Ottoman elites, who coveted tulips much as the Amsterdam rich had done a century before. Rather, by the early eighteenth century, this culture of consumption was reaching even into the lives of humble people, many of whom were able to afford cups of the roasted bean beverage that Patrona Halil and other men of his ilk were selling in their coffeehouses.[180] The consumption of these goods was helping to form the common cultural landscape in which the diverse peoples of the Ottoman Empire mixed.

Conclusion: The Case of the Green Tomato

"Tradition limits change, but does not exclude it," observed the textile historian Charlotte Jirousek in a study of Ottoman clothing. "In fact," she continued, "the only thing about traditional culture that is static might be the *perception* that tradition is static."[181]

It was precisely this problem about the perception of tradition that bothered the historian Tülay Artan when she surveyed the kitchen registers of Topkapı Palace in Istanbul for clues about what Ottoman sultans and their households were eating and drinking; how their patterns of consumption were changing, especially in the eighteenth century; and more broadly, how the empire fit into global networks of exchange.[182] Thinking like a food detective – tracing the arrival of a new comestible and then following it to see where it went – Artan found one character particularly elusive. This was the American tomato.[183]

This much seems clear: In 1694, for the first time, the kitchens of Topkapı Palace received a ton of tomatoes, called *kavata*, in a variety that dictionaries from the period described as having "green and slightly bitter" fruits and as being good for pickling with its leaves.[184] But from there the trail faded. Nearly two centuries passed, and the tomato began to resurface in cookbooks – although in recipes assuming its ripened red fruit form, minus the leaf. Artan gleaned a sliver of anecdotal evidence from a woman – an oral informant – who remarked that in her great-grandmother's generation, in late nineteenth-century Edirne (now northwestern Turkey, near the border with Greece and Bulgaria), people still used to prepare and eat tomato fruits only when green, tossing out those that had reddened. This led Artan to wonder: if Turks for a century or more have been expecting to eat the ripe red fruits of the tomato plant, and if no recipes survive for the old green kind, then "When and how did the double change come – that is, replacing *kavata* by other, reddening varieties, and then accepting the habit of picking and eating them after they had ripened?" Her puzzlement led to a much deeper question: "How much else of what we take for granted is actually of very recent origin?"[185]

To rephrase the question that the tomato elicited, how much of what people assume as traditional now is the product of accumulated (or still accumulating) change from the past? When do little changes, piled up, lead to much bigger ones? These musings are pertinent to many of the big questions of Ottoman social history. Who was a Turk, and when? What did it mean to be Ottoman? How did Muslims understand and "live" their Islam in an empire of constant conversion? What were the boundaries of religious communities – *millet*s – and to what extent did they mediate corporate authority and forge internal feelings of solidarity? What was it like, in this place or that, to live as a Christian or Jew; as a peasant, soldier, concubine, guild member, or poet; as a woman or man; as a young person or old one? And to return to the perennial question of this study, how did people get along, in the scrimmage of daily existence?

Certainly, there is material evidence to suggest a degree of broad continuity – that is, tradition – in some aspects of Ottoman material culture. Consider clothing again. "The cut of Ottoman official garments changed very little between 1550 and 1800," noted Charlotte Jirousek. "The consistency is great enough ... that an observer from the court of Mehmed II (1451–1481) would have been able to identify the status of many citizens should he have been transported to the Istanbul of Murad III (1574–1595), Ahmed II (1691–1695), or even of Selim III (1789–1807)." The basic shape of garments persisted, while differences in color, material, and the style of shoes and headgear were coded to mark out social ranks and religious differences. These consistencies in clothing remained even while new materials appeared on the scene – such as French silks, first imported after 1700.[186]

One of the great accomplishments of the Ottoman Empire, and the key to its longevity across six centuries, may have been that its sultans managed to retain the allegiance of its "multifarious inhabitants ... even [if] this consisted usually of no more than [their] not rebelling and paying taxes."[187] The sultans created, in other words, a sense that the empire was there, solid, and that it was meant to be there, holding up traditions rooted in the heritage of Islamic religion and statecraft. Policies toward Jews and Christians as *dhimmi*s were central to this Islamic tradition, which bolstered the empire from within, and ascribed an implicit historical stability to intercommunal relations. And yet, amidst it all, changes were constant. People converted, as from Christianity and Judaism to Islam, or from Orthodox Christianity to Catholicism (in Syria) or the opposite (in Crete); imperial boundaries swelled and contracted in the aftermath of battles; taxes rose (more than they seemed to fall); and things moved – including goods, ideas, and people. All of these changes occurred within established frameworks that gave a semblance of continuity, while offering opportunities not just for exchange, but more intimately, for sharing, across the social spectrum.

The historian Carter Vaughn Findley has argued that the "Turkish carpet" exemplifies the interwoven quality of Ottoman society. Sephardic Jews who fled from Spain to Ottoman domains at the end of the fifteenth century brought rugs, from their synagogues, which were woven with a typically Iberian architectural design: a "triple-arch motif often with a hanging lamp in the center." By the sixteenth century, this motif was appearing in Ottoman court carpets; soon it was appearing in village carpets, too, and in carpets made for Muslim and Christian worshippers. It became a beloved design among Turkish-speaking peoples. Findley has concluded that, "The reworking of this design in the Ottoman world and its widespread appropriation in synagogues, churches, and mosques speaks of a Mediterranean cultural synthesis," and typifies the empire's inclusiveness and adaptive character.[188]

Historians used to say that the Ottoman Empire settled into torpor once the age of major conquests closed at the end of Sultan Suleyman's reign in 1566. Foreign powers began to chip away at the empire's territories in the late seventeenth and eighteenth centuries, and Ottoman armies racked up defeats. And yet, the panorama of this Ottoman era remains so dazzling that the image of decline is hard to sustain. Cultures seethed on the ground in the empire, and history galloped along. In the eighteenth century, Ottoman history seemed to be galloping faster than ever before. And what about the broader landscape against which this history was running? Many fine-grained social changes were adding up, poised to produce major shifts in the groundwork of Ottoman societies.

NOTES

1 Donald Quataert, *The Ottoman Empire, 1700–1922* (Cambridge: Cambridge University Press, 2000), p. 5.
2 Ekmeleddin İhsanoğlu, *A Culture of Peaceful Coexistence: Early Islamic and Ottoman Turkish Examples* (Istanbul: Research Centre for Islamic History, Art, and Culture [IRCICA], 2004), p. 7. İhsanoğlu may have been thinking of the widely acclaimed book by María Rosa Menocal, titled, *The Ornament of the World: How Muslims, Jews, and Christians Created a Culture of Tolerance in Medieval Spain* (Boston: Little, Brown, 2002), which appeared shortly after (and which responded to) the events of September 11, 2001, in the United States.
3 Madeline C. Zilfi, "Whose Laws? Gendering the Ottoman Sumptuary Regime," in *Ottoman Costumes: From Textile to Identity*, ed. Suraiya Faroqhi and Christoph K. Neumann (Istanbul: Eren, 2004), p. 132.
4 Nancy Bisaha, *Creating East and West: Renaissance Humanists and the Ottoman Turks* (Philadelphia: University of Pennsylvania Press, 2004), p. 158.
5 Godfrey Goodwin, *The Janissaries* (London: Saqi Books, 2006), pp. 34, 36.
6 John Kingsley Birge, *The Bektashi Order of Dervishes* (London: Luzac & Co., 1937), p. 215.
7 Leslie P. Peirce, *The Imperial Harem: Women and Sovereignty in the Ottoman Empire* (New York: Oxford University Press, 1993), p. 37. The preference for concubines (who as slaves lacked an extended family to defend them) may have had a practical motive insofar as it ensured that, during the fratricidal bloodbath following the death of a sultan, candidate brothers for the throne (each of whom was generally, as a matter of policy, from a different mother) could kill each other without fearing retaliation from avenging relatives.

 8 Stanford J. Shaw, *History of the Ottoman Empire and Modern Turkey*, Volume
    1: *Empire of the Gazis: The Rise and Decline of the Ottoman Empire, 1280–1808*
    (Cambridge: Cambridge University Press, 1976), p. 178.
 9 Colin Imber, *The Ottoman Empire, 1300–1650: The Structure of Power*, second
    edition (Houndmills, UK: Palgrave Macmillan, 2009), p. 2.
10 Tijana Krstic, *Contested Conversions to Islam: Narratives of Religious Change
    in the Early Modern Ottoman Empire* (Stanford: Stanford University Press,
    2011), pp. 64–65.
11 See Mustafa ibn Abd Allah Haji Khalifa, aka Katib Çelebi, *The History of the
    Maritime Wars of the Turks*, trans. James Mitchell, Chapters I–IV (London:
    Oriental Translation Fund, 1831).
12 Bernard Lewis, *The Muslim Discovery of Europe* (New York: W.W. Norton
    1982), p. 48.
13 Consider, for example, Christiane Gruber, ed., *The Islamic Manuscript
    Tradition: Ten Centuries of Book Arts in Indiana University Collections*
    (Bloomington: Indiana University Press, 2010), which focuses largely on
    Ottoman book arts; Walter G. Andrews and Mehmet Kalpakli, *The Age of
    Beloveds: Love and the Beloved in Early-Modern Ottoman and European Culture
    and Society* (Durham: Duke University Press, 2005), which focuses largely on
    poetry; Suraiya Faroqhi and Christoph K. Neumann, eds., *The Illuminated
    Table, the Prosperous House: Food and Shelter in Ottoman Material Culture*
    (Würzurg: Ergon Verlag Würzburg, 2003); and Amy Singer, ed., *Starting with
    Food: Culinary Approaches to Ottoman History* (Princeton: Markus Wiener,
    2011).
14 Jane Hathaway, *The Arab Lands under Ottoman Rule, 1516–1800* (Harlow,
    UK: Pearson Education Limited, 2008), p. 8.
15 Immanuel Wallerstein, *The Modern World-System* (New York: Academic
    Press, 1974).
16 Tülay Artan, "Aspects of the Ottoman Elite's Food Consumption: Looking
    for 'Staples,' 'Luxuries,' and 'Delicacies' in a Changing Century," in
    Consumption Studies and the History of the Ottoman Empire: An Introduction,
    ed. Donald Quataert (Albany: State University of New York Press, 2000),
    p. 112.
17 Ralph S. Hattox, *Coffee and Coffeehouses: The Origins of a Social Beverage in the
    Medieval Near East* (Seattle: University of Washington Press, 1985).
18 Brian Cowan, *The Social Life of Coffee: The Emergence of the British Coffeehouse*
    (New Haven: Yale University Press, 2005).
19 John Mills, "The Coming of the Carpet to the West," in *The Eastern Carpet
    in the Western World: From the 15th to the 17th Century*, ed. Donald King and
    David Sylvester (London: Arts Council of Great Britain, 1983), pp. 11–
    23; Rosamond E. Mack, *Bazaar to Piazza: Islamic Trade and Italian Art,
    1300–1600* (Berkeley: University of California Press, 2002), p. 5; see also
    p. 83, plate 76; and Marika Sardar, "Carpets from the Islamic World," The
    Metropolitan Museum of Art, www.metmuseum.org/toah/hd/crpt/hd_crpt
    .htm (accessed March 6, 2016). This convention proved so influential that
    art historians came to describe some Ottoman rug patterns after the names
    of artists who rendered them in paintings. The Philadelphia Museum of Art,
    for example, holds specimens of what it calls "Lotto" and "Holbein" rugs.

20 Rudolph P. Matthee, *The Politics of Trade in Safavid Iran: Silk for Silver,*
    1600–1730 (Cambridge: Cambridge University Press, 1999), p. 22; Stephen
    Frederic Dale, *The Muslim Empires of the Ottomans, Safavids, and Mughals*
    (Cambridge: Cambridge University Press, 2010), p. 128.
21 Denis Sinor, *The Cambridge History of Early Inner Asia,* Vol. 1 (Cambridge:
    Cambridge University Press, 1990), pp. 16, 18.
22 Carter Vaughn Findley, *The Turks in World History* (Oxford: Oxford University
    Press, 2005), p. 65.
23 Cemal Kafadar, *Between Two Worlds: The Construction of the Ottoman State*
    (Berkeley: University of California Press, 1995), p. 4.
24 "Turkey," *Oxford English Dictionary Online,* December 2011.
25 Kafadar, *Between Two Worlds,* p. 4.
26 For example, Findley argues for persisting Turkishness in his book, *The Turks*
    in World History.
27 Findley tackles this debate broadly in *The Turks in World History* (and insists,
    by way of conclusion, that the distinctively Turkish dimension of Ottoman
    culture persisted) while Shaw refers to "Byzantinization" as a bureaucratic
    process without assessing its larger significance. See Shaw, *History of the*
    Ottoman Empire and Modern Turkey, Vol. 1, p. 29, on the policies of Sultan
    Bayezit (r. 1389–1402).
28 Kafadar, *Between Two Worlds,* p. 23.
29 Kafadar, *Between Two Worlds,* p. 25.
30 See Aram Yardumian and Theodore G. Schurr, "Who Are the Anatolian
    Turks? A Reappraisal of the Anthropological Genetic Evidence,"
    Anthropology & Archeology of Eurasia, 50:1 (2011), pp. 6–42, especially p. 22.
31 Yardumian and Schurr, "Who Are the Anatolian Turks?," p. 7.
32 The term "conversion" is one that Yardumian and Schurr use themselves: see
    "Who Are the Anatolian Turks?," p. 19.
33 Findley, *The Turks in World History,* p. 18.
34 Bernard Lewis, "Europe and Islam," The Tanner Lectures on Human Values,
    Delivered at Brasenose College, Oxford University, February 26, March 5,
    and March 12, 1990, p. 85.
35 Charlotte Jirousek, "The Transition to Mass Fashion System Dress in the
    Later Ottoman Empire," in Quataert, *Consumption Studies and the History of*
    the Ottoman Empire, p. 225.
36 On Moses, later known as Hayatizade, see Marc David Baer, *Honored by the*
    Glory of Islam: Conversion and Conquest in Ottoman Europe (Oxford: Oxford
    University Press, 2008), p. 134. On the French count who became Ahmet,
    see Shaw, *History of the Ottoman Empire and Modern Turkey,* pp. 241–42.
    Historians know this detail about Bonneval only because he was an aristocrat
    who had an earlier career as a courtier to Louis XIV of France; most converts
    to Islam in the Ottoman Empire, like most people in general, remain name-
    less in the historical record.
37 Pierre Pinon, "The Ottoman Cities of the Balkans," in *The City in the Islamic*
    World, ed. Salma K. Jayyusi, Renata Holod, Attilio Petruccioli, and André
    Raymond, Vol. 1 (Leiden: E.J. Brill, 2008), pp. 147–48.
38 Ibn Khaldun, *The Muqaddimah: An Introduction to History,* trans. Franz
    Rosenthal, abridged by and ed. N. J. Dawood (Princeton: Princeton

University Press, 1969); Virginia H. Aksan, "Ottoman Political Writing, 1768–1808," *International Journal of Middle East Studies*, 25 (1993), pp. 53–69, see p. 54. Aksan notes that, beginning in the sixteenth century, Ottoman intellectuals invoked Ibn Khaldun's theory of dynastic deterioration when writing advice manuals for sultans in the face of Ottoman military defeats.

39 Cafadar, *Between Two Worlds*, pp. 16–17.

40 Hamit Bozarslan, "Alevism and the Myths of Research: The Need for a New Research Agenda," in *Turkey's Alevi Enigma: A Comprehensive Overview*, ed. Paul J. White and Joost Jongerden (Leiden: E.J. Brill, 2003), pp. 3–16.

41 Christine Woodhead, "Ottoman Languages," in *The Ottoman World*, ed. Christine Woodhead (London: Routledge, 2012), pp. 143–58 (see p. 152).

42 Kemal Silay, *Nedim and the Poetics of the Ottoman Court: Medieval Inheritance and the Need for Change* (Bloomington: Indiana University Turkish Studies, 1994), p. 18.

43 Madeline C. Zilfi, "The Ottoman *Ulema*," in Faroqhi, *The Cambridge History of Turkey*, Vol. 3, pp. 209–25.

44 Krstic, *Contested Conversions to Islam*, p. 96.

45 Dale, *The Muslim Empires of the Ottomans, Safavids, and Mughals*, p. 69.

46 Matthee, *The Politics of Trade in Safavid Iran*, p. 22.

47 Vera B. Moreen, "The Problems of Conversion among Iranian Jews in the Seventeenth and Eighteenth Centuries," *Iranian Studies*, 19:3/4 (1986), pp. 215–28.

48 Dale, *The Muslim Empires of the Ottomans, Safavids, and Mughals*, pp. 120, 124–25. On the construction of Hinduism, see Peter van der Veer, *Religious Nationalism: Hindus and Muslims in India* (Berkeley: University of California Press, 1994).

49 Lewis, *The Jews of Islam*, pp. 33–34.

50 David M. Freidenreich, *Foreigners and Their Food: Constructing Otherness in Jewish, Christian, and Islamic Law* (Berkeley: University of California Press, 2011); see chapter 11 on Shi'is.

51 Stefan Winter, *The Shiites of Lebanon under Ottoman Rule, 1516–1788* (Cambridge: Cambridge University Press, 2010), p. 5.

52 Marc Baer, Ussama Makdisi, and Andrew Shryock, "Tolerance and Conversion in the Ottoman Empire: A Discussion," *Comparative Studies in Society & History*, 51:4 (2009), pp. 927–40, see especially pp. 930–31; and Marc David Baer, *Honored by the Glory of Islam: Conversion and Conquest in Ottoman Europe* (New York: Oxford University Press, 2008).

53 Baer, *Honored by the Glory of Islam*, pp. 81–89.

54 Dale, *The Muslim Empires of the Ottomans, Safavids, and Mughals*, p. 73.

55 Çiğdem Kafescioğlu, *Constantinopolis/Istanbul: Cultural Encounter, Imperial Vision, and the Construction of the Ottoman Capital* (University Park: Pennsylvania State University Press, 2009), pp. 18–20.

56 Kafescioğlu, *Constantinopolis/Istanbul*, pp. 21–22.

57 Suraiya Faroqhi, "Introduction," in *Animals and People in the Ottoman Empire*, ed. Suraiya Faroqhi (Istanbul: Eren, 2010), pp. 11–54, see p. 23 for this detail.

58 Christiane Gruber, "A Pious Cure-All: The Ottoman Illustrated Prayer Manual in the Lilly Library," in Gruber, *The Islamic Manuscript Tradition*, pp. 130–32.

59 Gruber, "A Pious Cure-All," p. 133. The skull fragment of St. John the Baptist had many adventures, wandering from Istanbul to Serbia (in the hands of Mehmet II's Serbian stepmother) and then to a Greek monastery, where an Ottoman force from Algiers finally claimed it. The commander of this force, one Hasan Pasha, "kept it in his home, with a candle in a silver candlestick always burning nearby," until he died and the skull returned to Istanbul. Hilmi Aydın, *The Sacred Trusts: Pavilion of the Sacred Relics, Topkapı Palace Museum, Istanbul* (Somerset, NJ: Light, 2004), pp. 150–51.

60 For another example of Muslim popular attitudes toward a sacred rock, see Ibn Battuta's description of "Adam's Peak" in what is now Sri Lanka: Ross E. Dunn, *The Adventures of Ibn Battuta, a Muslim Traveler of the Fourteenth Century* (Berkeley: University of California Press, 1986), p. 241.

61 Aydın, *The Sacred Trusts*, pp. 61, 79–81, 115, 138–39, 144–47.

62 Gruber, "A Pious Cure-All," pp. 133–34.

63 Heather Coffey, "Between Amulet and Devotion: Islamic Miniature Books in the Lilly Library," in Gruber, *The Islamic Manuscript Tradition*, pp. 79–115.

64 Aydın, *The Sacred Trusts*, pp. 79–80.

65 Abraham Marcus, *The Middle East on the Eve of Modernity: Aleppo in the Eighteenth Century* (New York: Columbia University Press, 1989), p. 27. Marcus notes that the trip from Aleppo to Izmir took one month; Istanbul was further north still.

66 Marcus, *The Middle East on the Eve of Modernity*, p. 16.

67 Halil İnalcık, "Foundations of Ottoman-Jewish Cooperation," in *Jews, Turks, Ottomans: A Shared History, Fifteenth through the Twentieth Century*, ed. Avigdor Levy (Syracuse: Syracuse University Press, 2002), pp. 3–14.

68 Shaw, *History of the Ottoman Empire and Modern Turkey*, Vol. 1, pp. 59–60.

69 Kafescioğlu, *Constantinopolis/Istanbul*, p. 178; Fariba Zarinebaf, *Crime and Punishment in Istanbul, 1700–1800* (Berkeley: University of California Press, 2010), p. 25.

70 Zarinebaf, *Crime and Punishment in Istanbul*, p. 25.

71 Benjamin Braude, "Foundation Myths of the *Millet* System," in *Christians and Jews in the Ottoman Empire*, ed. Benjamin Braude and Bernard Lewis, Vol. 1 (New York: Holmes and Meier, 1982), pp. 69–88.

72 Shaw, *History of the Ottoman Empire and Modern Turkey*, Vol. 1, p. 86.

73 Shaw, *History of the Ottoman Empire and Modern Turkey*, Vol. 1, p. 97.

74 Braude, "Foundation Myths of the *Millet* System," p. 72.

75 Molly Greene, "Beyond the Community: Writing the History of the Greeks under Ottoman Rule," paper presented at the Annenberg Seminar in History, University of Pennsylvania, November 16, 2010.

76 Eunjeong Yi, *Guild Dynamics in Seventeenth-Century Istanbul: Fluidity and Leverage* (Leiden: E.J. Brill, 2004), p. 241.

77 Braude, "Foundation Myths of the *Millet* System," p. 72.

78 Daniel J. Schroeter, "The Changing Relationship between the Jews of the Arab Middle East and the Ottoman State in the Nineteenth Century," in

Jews, Turks, Ottomans: A Shared History, Fifteenth through the Twentieth Century, ed. Avigdor Levy (Syracuse: Syracuse University Press, 2002), p. 92.

79 Baer, Makdisi, and Shryock, "Tolerance and Conversion in the Ottoman Empire," pp. 928–29.

80 Karen Barkey, "Islam and Toleration: Studying the Ottoman Imperial Model," *International Journal of Politics, Culture, and Society*, 19:1/2 (2005), pp. 5–19, see especially p. 17.

81 Zarinebaf, *Crime and Punishment in Istanbul*, p. 147. In Istanbul, each Jewish congregation managed its legal affairs until the late seventeenth century, when three major rabbinical courts coalesced. Minna Rozen, "The Ottoman Jews," in *The Cambridge History of Turkey, Volume 3: The Later Ottoman Empire, 1603–1839*, ed. Suraiya N. Faroqhi (Cambridge: Cambridge University Press, 2006), p. 266.

82 André Raymond, "The Management of the City," in *The City in the Islamic World*, ed. Renata Holod, Attilio Petruccioli, and André Raymond, Vol. 2 (Leiden: E.J. Brill, 2008), pp. 775–93; and Randi Deguilhelm, "The Waqf in the City," in Holod, Petruccioli, and Raymond, *The City in the Islamic World*, Vol. 2, pp. 923–50.

83 Molly Greene, *A Shared World: Christians and Muslims in the Early Modern Mediterranean* (Princeton: Princeton University Press, 2000), pp. 5, 41.

84 Halil İnalcık, *The Ottoman Empire: The Classical Age, 1300–1600* (London: Phoenix, 2000), pp. 7, 13.

85 Shaw, *History of the Ottoman Empire and Modern Turkey*, Vol. 1, p. 94.

86 Brigitte Pitarakis and Christos Merantzas, *A Treasured Memory: Ecclesiastical Silver from Late Ottoman Istanbul in the Sevgi Gönül Collection* (Istanbul: Sadberk Hanım Museum, 2006), p. 14.

87 Shaw, *History of the Ottoman Empire and Modern Turkey*, Vol. 1, p. 152.

88 Ruth Lamdan, *A Separate People: Jewish Women in Palestine, Syria and Egypt in the Sixteenth Century* (Leiden: E.J. Brill, 2000), pp. 6–7. Lamdan noted that Jews in Palestine numbered some 2,000–2,500 by about 1500, and 10,000–12,000 by 1550.

89 Amnon Cohen, *Jewish Life under Islam: Jerusalem in the Sixteenth Century* (Cambridge, MA: Harvard University Press, 1984), p. 7.

90 Rozen, "The Ottoman Jews," pp. 256–57, 268.

91 Rozen, "The Ottoman Jews," pp. 262–63.

92 Cohen, *Jewish Life under Islam*, p. 125.

93 Shaw, *History of the Ottoman Empire and Modern Turkey*, Vol. 1, pp. 152–53.

94 Hathaway, *The Arab Lands under Ottoman Rule*, p. 191; and Jacob M. Landau, "Changing Patterns of Community Structures, with Special Reference to Ottoman Egypt," in Levy, *Jews, Turks, Ottomans*, pp. 77–87, see especially pp. 81–82.

95 İnalcık, "Foundations of Ottoman-Jewish Cooperation," in Levy, *Jews, Turks, Ottomans*, p. 10.

96 Yaron Ben Naeh, "The Nasi Family, or the Dream of Tiberias," in *A History of Jewish-Muslim Relations from the Origins to the Present Day*, ed. Abdelwahab Meddeb and Benjamin Stora, trans. Jane Marie Todd and Michael B. Smith (Princeton: Princeton University Press, 2013), pp. 220–21.

97 Hathaway, *The Arab Lands under Ottoman Rule*, p. 193–94.
98 Shaw, *History of the Ottoman Empire and Modern Turkey*, Vol. 1, p. 177.
99 Linda T. Darling, *Revenue-Raising and Legitimacy: Tax Collection and Finance Administration in the Ottoman Empire, 1560–1660* (Leiden: E.J. Brill, 1996), pp. 26–27.
100 Linda T. Darling, "Public Finances: The Role of the Ottoman Centre," in *The Cambridge History of Turkey*, ed. Suraiya Faroqhi, Vol. 3 (Cambridge: Cambridge University Press, 2006), pp. 118–31, see p. 125.
101 Hathaway, *The Arab Lands under Ottoman Rule*, p. 192.
102 Darling, *Revenue-Raising and Legitimacy*, pp. 82–83, 104.
103 Ronald C. Jennings, "Zimmis (Non-Muslims) in Early 17th Century Ottoman Judicial Records: The Sharia Court of Anatolian Kayseri," *Journal of the Economic and Social History of the Orient*, 21:3 (1978), p. 233.
104 Imber, *The Ottoman Empire*, pp. 241–42, 245.
105 Darling, *Revenue-Raising and Legitimacy*, p. 281.
106 Darling, *Revenue-Raising and Legitimacy*, p. 27.
107 Jennings, "Zimmis (Non-Muslims) in Early 17th Century Ottoman Judicial Records," p. 227. See also Shaw, *History of the Ottoman Empire and Modern Turkey*, Vol. 1, p. 196.
108 Jennings, "Zimmis (Non-Muslims) in Early 17th Century Ottoman Judicial Records," p. 238; Suraiya Faroqhi, "Rural Life," in Faroqhi, *The Cambridge History of Turkey*, Vol. 3, pp. 376–90, see p. 377.
109 Maurits H. van den Boogert, *The Capitulations and the Ottoman Legal System: Qadis, Consuls, and Beratlis in the 18th Century* (Leiden: E.J. Brill, 2005), p. 7.
110 J. C. Hurewitz, *Diplomacy in the Near and Middle East: A Documentary Record, 1535–1914*, Vol. 1 (Princeton: D. van Nostrand, 1956), p. 1 (in the preface to the text for the "Treaty of Amity and Commerce: the Ottoman Empire and France, February 1535"), pp. 1–5.
111 Ismail Hakkı Kadı, "On the Edges of an Ottoman World: Non-Muslim Ottoman Merchants in Amsterdam," in *The Ottoman World*, ed. Christine Woodhead (London: Routledge, 2012), pp. 276–88.
112 Raymond, "The Management of the City," pp. 782–83.
113 Yi, *Guild Dynamics in Seventeenth-Century Istanbul*, pp. 37–39.
114 Baer, *Honored by the Glory of Islam*, pp. 102–3.
115 Suraiya Faroqhi, "Introduction, or Why and How One Might Want to Study Ottoman Clothes," in Faroqhi and Neumann, *Ottoman Costumes: From Textile to Identity*, pp. 15–48, see especially p. 22.
116 Matthew Elliot, "Dress Codes in the Ottoman Empire: The Case of the Franks," in Faroqhi and Neumann, *Ottoman Costumes: From Textile to Identity*, pp. 103–23, see especially pp. 105–7.
117 Faroqhi, "Introduction, or Why and How One Might Want to Study Ottoman Clothes," pp. 25–26.
118 Elliot, "Dress Codes in the Ottoman Empire," p. 105; Faroqhi, "Introduction, or Why and How One Might Want to Study Ottoman Clothes," p. 25.
119 Stillman, *Arab Dress*, pp. 52–53, 102–4, 109, 111.
120 Stillman, *The Jews of Arab Lands*, pp. 70–75.

121 Ebru Boyar and Kate Fleet, *A Social History of Ottoman Istanbul* (Cambridge: Cambridge University Press, 2010), p. 258.

122 Cohen, *Jewish Life under Islam*, pp. 73, 138, 239 (footnote 2).

123 Bernard Heyberger, *Les Chrétiens du Proche-Orient au temps de la Réforme Catholique (Syrie, Liban, Palestine, XVIIe–XVIIIe siècles)* (Rome: École Française de Rome, 1994), pp. 51–52.

124 Boyar and Fleet, *A Social History of Ottoman Istanbul*, p. 259.

125 Quoted in Elliot, "Dress Codes in the Ottoman Empire," p. 106.

126 Elliot, "Dress Codes in the Ottoman Empire," pp. 106–7.

127 Marcus, *The Middle East on the Eve of Modernity*, p. 99.

128 Zarinebaf, *Crime and Punishment in Istanbul*, p. 26.

129 Zarinebaf, *Crime and Punishment in Istanbul*, pp. 41, 87–88.

130 Elyse Semerdjian, *"Off the Straight Path": Illicit Sex, Law, and Community in Ottoman Aleppo* (Syracuse: Syracuse University Press, 2008), pp. xvii, 94, 119, 159.

131 Abdel-Karim Rafeq, "Public Morality in 18th Century Ottoman Damascus," *Revue du monde musulman et de la Méditerranée*, 55:1 (1990), pp. 180–96, see p. 182.

132 Yi, *Guild Dynamics in Seventeenth-Century Istanbul*, p. 68.

133 Yi, *Guild Dynamics in Seventeenth-Century Istanbul*, pp. 69, 83.

134 Pitarakis and Merantzas, *A Treasured Memory*, pp. 16, 86–88, 92.

135 Ronald C. Jennings, "Women in Early 17th Century Ottoman Judicial Records: The Sharia Court of Anatolian Kayseri," *Journal of the Economic and Social History of the Orient*, 18:1 (1975), pp. 53–114, see p. 59.

136 Najwa Al-Qattan, "Dhimmis in the Muslim Court: Legal Autonomy and Religious Discrimination," *International Journal of Middle East Studies*, 31:3 (1999), pp. 429–44.

137 Yi, *Guild Dynamics in Seventeenth-Century Istanbul*, p. 208.

138 Lamdan, *A Separate People*, p. 137; Al-Qattan, "Dhimmis in the Muslim Court," p. 430; Cohen, *Jewish Life under Islam*, pp. 113, 127–37.

139 Zarinebaf, *Crime and Punishment in Istanbul*, p. 92, 168.

140 Marcus, *The Middle East on the Eve of Modernity*, p. 220.

141 Nelly Hanna, *In Praise of Books: A Cultural History of Cairo's Middle Class, Sixteenth to Eighteenth Century* (Syracuse: Syracuse University Press, 2003), p. 1; Gran, *Islamic Roots of* Capitalism, p. xiii.

142 Dana Sajdi, *The Barber of Damascus: Nouveau Literacy in the Eighteenth-Century Ottoman Levant* (Stanford: Stanford University Press, 2013), pp. 1–9.

143 Shaw, *History of the Ottoman Empire and Modern Turkey*, Vol. 1, p. 224.

144 Shaw, *History of the Ottoman Empire and Modern Turkey*, Vol. 1, p. 250.

145 Aziz S. Atiya, *A History of Eastern Christianity* (London: Methuen, 1968), pp. 101–3.

146 Marcus, *The Middle East on the Eve of Modernity*, p. 46.

147 Van den Boogert, *The Capitulations and the Ottoman Legal System*, pp. 69, 76–78.

148 For a discussion of these debates, see van den Boogert, *The Capitulations and the Ottoman Legal System*, pp. 8–9; he casts doubt on whether the *berats* really "nullified the sultan's authority."

149 Rozen, "The Ottoman Jews," p. 269; Bruce Masters, "Christians in a Changing World," in *The Cambridge History of Turkey*, Volume 3: *The Later Ottoman Empire, 1603–1839*, ed. Suraiya N. Faroqhi (Cambridge: Cambridge University Press, 2006), pp. 272–79, see p. 272.
150 Marcus, *The Middle East on the Eve of Modernity*, p. 41.
151 Marcus, *The Middle East on the Eve of Modernity*, pp. 90, 99–100.
152 Marcus, *The Middle East on the Eve of Modernity*, p. 47.
153 Masters, "Christians in a Changing World," p. 277.
154 Heyberger, *Les Chrétiens du Proche-Orient au temps de la Réforme Catholique*, pp. 559–60.
155 Bernard Heyberger, "Individualism and Political Modernity: Devout Catholic Women in Aleppo and Lebanon between the Seventeenth and Nineteenth Centuries," in *Beyond the Exotic: Women's Histories in Islamic Societies*, ed. Amira El-Azhary Sonbol (New York: Syracuse University Press, 2005), pp. 71–85, see p. 79.
156 Masters, "Christians in a Changing World," pp. 276–78.
157 Alastair Hamilton, *The Copts and the West, 1439–1822: The European Discovery of an Egyptian Church* (Oxford: Oxford University Press, 2006); Febe Armanios, *Coptic Christianity in Ottoman Egypt* (Oxford: Oxford University Press, 2011); Paul Sedra, *From Mission to Modernity: Evangelicals, Reformers, and Education in Nineteenth-Century Egypt* (London: I.B. Tauris, 2011); and S.S. Hasan, *Christians versus Muslims in Modern Egypt: The Century-Long Struggle for Coptic Equality* (Oxford: Oxford University Press, 2003).
158 David D. Grafton, *Piety, Politics, and Power: Lutherans Encountering Islam in the Middle East* (Eugene, OR: Wipf and Stock, 2009), pp. 17–18, 81–82.
159 Niyazi Berkes, *The Development of Secularism in Turkey* (Montreal: McGill University Press, 1964), pp. 36–47.
160 Yasemin Gencer, "Ibrahim Müteferrika and the Age of the Printed Manuscript," in Gruber, *The Islamic Manuscript Tradition*, pp. 155–93, see p. 155.
161 Yaron Ben Na'eh, "Hebrew Printing Houses in the Ottoman Empire," in *Jewish Journalism and Printing Houses in the Ottoman Empire*, ed. Gad Nassi (Istanbul: Isis Press, 2001), pp. 73–96, see especially p. 79.
162 Masters, "Christians in a Changing World," pp. 276–77.
163 Heyberger, "Livres et pratique de la lecture chez les chrétiens (Syrie, Liban), XVIIe – XVIIIe siècles."
164 Berkes, *The Development of Secularism in Turkey*, p. 41.
165 Gencer, "Ibrahim Müteferrika and the Age of the Printed Manuscript," p. 180.
166 Berkes, *The Development of Secularism in Turkey*, p. 42.
167 Shaw, *History of the Ottoman Empire and Modern Turkey*, Vol. 1, pp. 237–38.
168 Indeed, Ottoman scribes managed to keep the Qur'an out of printers' hands in Istanbul until 1871. Gencer, "Ibrahim Müteferrika and the Age of the Printed Manuscript," pp. 183, 199, footnote 99.
169 Shaw, *History of the Ottoman Empire and Modern Turkey*, Vol. 1, p. 233.
170 Ariel Salzmann, "The Age of Tulips: Confluence and Conflict in Early Modern Consumer Culture (1550–1730)," in *Consumption Studies and*

the History of the Ottoman Empire: An Introduction, ed. Donald Quataert (Albany: State University of New York Press, 2000). pp. 83–106, see p. 84.

171 Shaw, *History of the Ottoman Empire and Modern Turkey*, Vol. 1, p. 237.

172 Pitarakis and Merantzas, *A Treasured Memory*, pp. 101–3.

173 Zarinebaf, *Crime and Punishment in Istanbul*, p. 17; Shaw, *History of the Ottoman Empire and Modern Turkey*, Vol. 1, p. 234.

174 Zarinebaf, *Crime and Punishment in Istanbul*, p. 58.

175 Zarinebaf, *Crime and Punishment in Istanbul*, p. 68.

176 Dale, *The Muslim Empires of the Ottomans, Safavids, and Mughals*, p. 247.

177 Suraiya Faroqhi, *Subjects of the Sultan: Culture and Daily Life in the Ottoman Empire*, trans. Martin Bott (London: I.B. Tauris, 2007), p. 19.

178 Kadı, "Non-Muslim Ottoman Merchants in Amsterdam," pp. 284–85.

179 Meropi Anastassiadou and Bernard Heyberger, ed., *Figures anonymes, figures d'élite: pour une anatomie de l'homo ottomanicus* (Istanbul: Isis Press, 1999); and Maurits H. van den Boogert, "Defining Homo Ottomanicus: How the Ottomans Might Have Done It Themselves," www.academia.edu/1009873/Defining_Homo_Ottomanicu_How_the_Ottomans_might_have_done_it (accessed April 18, 2013).

180 Dana Sajdi, "Decline, Its Discontents and Ottoman Cultural History: By Way of Introduction," in *Ottoman Tulips, Ottoman Coffee: Leisure and Lifestyle in the Eighteenth Century*, ed. Dana Sajdi (London: I.B. Tauris Academic Studies, 2007), pp. 1–40.

181 Jirousek, "The Transition to Mass Fashion System Dress," p. 204.

182 Artan, "Aspects of the Ottoman Elite's Food Consumption," pp. 112–13. Another historian describes kitchen registers as the "deliveryman's entrance" into Ottoman court history and mines them for information about not only food and drink, but also health and medicine. Christoph K. Neumann, "Spices in the Ottoman Palace: Courtly Cookery in the Eighteenth Century," in Faroqhi and Neumann, *The Illuminated Table*, pp. 127–60.

183 The wild tomato originated in South America (the Peruvian highlands) but became a domesticated, edible fruit in North America (Mexico). Alan Davidson, *The Oxford Companion to Food*, ed. Tom Jaine, second edition (Oxford: Oxford University Press, 2006), pp. 802–3.

184 Arif Bilgin, "Refined Tastes in a Refined Palace: Eating Habits of the Ottoman Palace from the 15th–17th Centuries," *Turkish Cultural Foundation: Turkish Cuisine*, www.turkish-cuisine.org/english/article_details.php?p_id=20&Pages=Articles&PagingIndex=6 (accessed June 1, 2012).

185 Artan, "Aspects of the Ottoman Elite's Food Consumption," pp. 112–13.

186 Jirousek, "The Transition to Mass Fashion System Dress," pp. 209–10, 217.

187 Imber, *The Ottoman Empire*, p. 3.

188 Findley, *The Turks in World History*, pp. 97–99.

The Ottoman Empire in an Age of Reform:
From Sultan Mahmud II to the End
of the Tanzimat Era, 1808–1876

Introduction: The Empire's Showcase Reforms

On November 3, 1839, European diplomats gathered with Ottoman officials, provincial notables, and Muslim religious scholars (*'ulama*) in an
inner chamber of Topkapı Palace in Istanbul. There they listened to the
reading of an imperial edict – the first ever proclaimed in a public ceremony.[1] Known to historians as the Hatt-ı Şerif of Gülhane – or in English
as the "Noble Rescript of the Rose Chamber," the "Rose Chamber
Edict," or simply, the reform of 1839 – its content was unprecedented
in Ottoman history.[2] Later, the sultan, Abdulmajid I (r. 1839–61), confirmed the edict in a private ceremony in the room of the sacred relics –
that is, the room containing the mantle of the Prophet Muhammad,
which Sultan Selim I (r. 1512–20) had secured during his conquest
of Egypt three centuries earlier.[3] This edict initiated the Tanzimat, or
"Reorganization" era, during which the Ottoman state changed its philosophy and practice of government and enacted many reforms. The goal
of these measures was to make the empire more "modern," as that term
was variously interpreted, and to gird it against interference from other
European powers.

The 1839 edict was remarkable in more ways than one. It couched
its commitment to good government in lofty language that drew inspiration from both the French *Déclaration des droits de l'homme et du
citoyen* (Declaration of the Rights of Man and of the Citizen, 1789),
and the Virginia Bill of Rights of 1776 (which influenced the American
Declaration of Independence, drafted shortly thereafter).[4] "[A]re not
life and honor the most precious gifts to mankind?," its text enquired,
with a flourish.[5] The edict's language reflected the Western cultural fluency of the sultan's advisers who drafted the text, and by extension, the
changes that had brought a distinct western European and especially
French influence to bear on elite Ottoman education during the previous generation. The edict promised the regularization of taxation and
military service, and the honoring of "life, liberty, and property," but did

so without either privileging Muslims or specifying conditions for *dhim-mi*s. On the contrary, the edict proclaimed that, "These imperial concessions are extended to all our subjects, of whatever religion or sect they may be."[6] In this regard, as the historian M. Şükrü Hanioğlu argued, the edict's universalism represented "a change in the official ideology of the [Ottoman] state" and "a significant first step toward the transformation of hitherto Muslim, Christian, and Jewish subjects into *Ottomans*."[7]

In 1856, one month before the Treaty of Paris concluded the Crimean War (in which Britain and France fought with the Ottoman Empire against Russia), Sultan Abdulmajid I issued another proclamation. This reform edict of 1856, known as the Hatt-ı Hümayun, confirmed all the traditional privileges of the empire's non-Muslim communities while guaranteeing them equal opportunities in education, government service, and the military, as well as continued freedom in religious practice. It, too, used lofty language: "I desire to increase well-being and prosperity," the sultan averred, "to obtain the happiness of all my subjects who, in my eyes, are all equal and equally dear to me."[8] At the same time, the 1856 edict raised the prospect of legal action against anyone who used "any injurious or offensive term" toward an Ottoman subject of another religion, language, or race. This clause was understood to mean, for example, that Muslims should no longer call Christians or Jews *kafir*s (infidels) if they had tended to do so before.[9] It may have also signaled a broader, goodwill effort on the part of the Ottoman state to discourage the common tendency among some Muslims of using mildly derogatory language to distinguish themselves from Christians and Jews. The historian Selim Deringil has referred along these lines to the "little barbs" and "small insults of everyday life" that non-Muslims faced in this period, reflected in the discursive tendency of official documents to list a dead Christian or Jew as *mürd* (a term akin to "croaked" or "kicked the bucket" in English, and also used to describe the death of animals) but a dead Muslim as *merhum* (more politely suggesting something like "deceased" or "passed away").[10]

Against this context, the reform edicts of 1839 and 1856 raise a host of questions. Were the edicts merely attempts at window-dressing, to make the empire look modern on the world stage and to curry favor with the powers of Europe, while actually sticking to old ways beneath the surface?[11] Did they represent a sincere belief on the part of Sultan Abdulmajid and his statesmen in egalitarian ideals, or simply a pragmatic effort to make inclusion in the empire more appealing at a time when ethnic nationalist movements were gaining momentum among some of the empire's Christians? Did Ottoman Muslim bureaucrats and humble Muslim people throughout the empire welcome, oppose, or even pay much heed to the edicts, which theoretically rendered obsolete the sub-ordination of non-Muslims as *dhimmi*s? And did Christians and Jews appreciate the concessions that the edicts were trying to make? Further questions relate to the edicts' implementation and consequences. Did the edicts improve conditions for Christians and Jews in the long run, or merely aggravate existing tensions between Muslims and (former) *dhimmi*s?

In debates that stretch over decades like long-running conversations, historians have hazarded answers to these questions about the reality, practice, and long-term impact of the nineteenth-century Ottoman reforms. One historian argued that despite reform efforts that included the drafting in 1876 of an Ottoman constitution, which declared all subjects "*Osmanli* ['Ottoman'], whatever religion or creed they hold," equality between Muslims, Christians, and Jews failed to materialize.[12] (It was a bad sign, he concluded elsewhere, that the Muslim preacher appointed to give the closing prayer after the reading of the 1856 edict called upon God to "have mercy on the people of Muhammad" and to preserve them – referring to Muslims alone.[13]) This "failure" of equality to materialize, cautioned another scholar, was not only the product of Ottoman government or Muslim popular unwillingness to extend privi-leges to non-Muslims. Non-Muslims played a role in its shortcomings, too, by proving reluctant to yield whatever autonomy they could eke out through their *millet*s or, for some individuals, through status holdings as *berath*s (protégés and affiliates of foreign European consular pow-ers).[14] In a related vein, a third scholar offered an observation about nineteenth-century Middle Eastern and North African Jews that argu-ably applied to Christians as well. Jews "wanted two incompatible things at the same time," he wrote. These were "equality within their Islamic states and … special privileges through their connection to the outside forces that were penetrating their world."[15] These outside forces came above all from western Europe, and gave non-Muslims "a way out of, or at least an improvement of, their own traditional and subordinate status as *ahl adh-dhimma*."[16]

Between some Muslims and Christians in particular, intercommunal relations in the Balkans, Anatolia, and greater Syria worsened in the nine-teenth century, and hampered Ottoman reforms of the period.[17] Egypt was an exception, as Muslim-Christian relations entered an era of cor-diality, a period that one chronicler hailed as one of "striving, of notable achievements and of progress in all fields of life," and that another cited as a period of increased opportunities for Copts under the rule of Muhammad Ali and his heirs.[18] By contrast, Muslim-Jewish relations proceeded in this period with relative calm, while Jews evolved into what the historian Julia Phillips Cohen called a "model minority" and "model *millet*." As a sign of their keen support of the Ottoman state, Jews in this period even began to incorporate Ottoman Islamic symbols, such as crescent and star, and the sultan's insignia, into their ritual objects. It probably helped that Jews throughout this period continued to keep a low profile.[19] For example, Jews continued to worship in discreet synagogues even as Christians inclined toward a more "triumphalist architecture," by building larger and more ostentatious churches, inspired by western European Gothic and Baroque styles.[20] The construction of monumental synagogues occurred much more rarely – examples being the Baron Jacob Menashe Temple in Alexandria, built in 1863, and the synagogue in Oran (in French-controlled Algeria), which began in 1880.[21] Jews kept quiet in a more literal sense as well: they did not disturb the traditional Islamic soundscape as Christians in greater Syria were starting to do when they rang metal church bells instead of merely striking a semantron (an instrument, known in Arabic as *naqus*, which was made of wood and struck with a mallet).[22] Small changes in such things as church bell ringing signaled much larger developments at play.

The pages that follow examine the trajectory of Ottoman reforms while focusing mainly on the period from the ascension of Sultan Mahmud II in 1808 to the end of the Tanzimat era in 1876. They consider the blend of high idealism and hard-core political pragmatism that led Ottoman statesmen to promote reforms; the complex factors that inhibited the reforms from living up to their promises; and the brew of ingredients, some local, others originating from far away, that swirled new tensions into relations between Muslims and those who were once, but who by mid-century were technically no longer, their *dhimmi*s.

"Modern" Times: Culture and Politics across the Sweep of the Nineteenth Century

The conventional approach to the history of the nineteenth-century Middle East starts with major late eighteenth-century treaties and wars that set the stage for regional politics in this period. The Treaty of Kujuk Kaynarca (1774), by which Russia claimed the Crimea from the Ottoman Empire, as well as the right to act as "protector" of the empire's Orthodox Christians, stands out. So does the Napoleonic conquest of Egypt (1798), which France staged without notice or provocation to secure this strategic territory on the eastern Mediterranean, thereby challenging Britain's access to the Red Sea and Indian Ocean. A less conventional entry into the nineteenth century focuses on changes in everyday life and behavior that signaled larger cultural developments at play, and attested to the remarkable, if bewildering, changes that Muslim, Christian, and Jewish people were together experiencing.

To take this less conventional, cultural route, consider the behavior of Mahmud II, who ascended the Ottoman throne as sultan in 1808 and ruled until 1839: Unlike his predecessors, who had eaten their meals in the traditional way, seated on cushions around a low tray or *sofra*, Mahmud II preferred to eat at a table with a chair. He ate *alla franca* as the Ottomans called it, meaning in the style of Europeans.[23] Mahmud II also liked to wear tailored trousers and jackets, to shave his beard, and to drink champagne.[24] Sultan Mahmud's dining, furniture, and personal tastes suggest how western European practices and paraphernalia were beginning to pervade the daily life of the Ottoman sultan and, increasingly, too – as travel accounts, paintings, material objects, and other sources from the period show – of humbler men and women in his realm.[25]

Over the course of the nineteenth century, the Ottoman state became "modern" by embracing new technologies, centralizing its government, and again, enacting myriad reforms. For example, following the lead of many European contemporaries, Ottoman authorities began to stake out claims to both modernity and antiquity by endorsing the new science of archaeology, and by invoking historical and territorial claims to the physical remnants of the Islamic, Byzantine, Hellenistic, and earlier civilizations that had existed on Ottoman lands.[26] A law issued in 1869 signaled this change by regulating the excavation and collection of antiquities, which British, French, and other foreign collectors had been taking – or as it increasingly now seemed to Ottoman officials, looting – for years, since the establishment of the British Museum in London in 1753.[27] In other words, during the century that saw the rise of romantic nationalism in Europe (based on conceptions of people, or "nations," within fixed territories, sharing cultural patrimonies rooted in history, language, and folklore), the Ottoman Empire tried to join the club by emphasizing its own newness in light of its oldness.

The nineteenth century was certainly replete with new contrivances, many of which seemed to speed up the pace of life. Thanks to railways, tramways, and the extension of paved roads, people traveled faster, farther, and more often. By mid-century, steamships were bringing hordes of European and American travelers into the Middle East, thereby fostering the growth of the modern tourist industry, which fed on a popular fascination for archaeology and the lands of the Bible, and which emerged from the traditions of pilgrimage. First as a trickle in the 1860s, and then in a growing stream during the three decades that followed, the same steamships began carrying economic migrants *out* of the

The Excavations at the Temple Court in Nippur

Image 10 Excavations of the Nippur Temple Court, photograph by John Henry Haynes, 1893. Image Number 185157. Courtesy of the Penn Museum.

region, and particularly from what is now Lebanon. These migrants, who included moderately skilled or educated Christians, and to a lesser extent Muslims and Jews, sailed for the United States, Mexico, Argentina, and elsewhere in the Americas in search of opportunity.[28] Another important technological breakthrough was the telegraph, which made its debut in Istanbul in 1855. The telegraph's very rapidity increased the workload of Ottoman state employees, who found themselves racing to process and respond to the flurry of messages that now dashed between Istanbul, the empire's major cities, and new embassies in places like London.[29]

In the nineteenth century, global networks of trade accelerated the popular consumption of goods that came from all over the world. For example, while chairs were rare in early nineteenth-century Istanbul, estate inventories (used to determine inheritance) show that by the end of the century, Muslim and non-Muslim members of the middle classes frequently owned chairs, as well as sofas, china sets, French-style consoles (mirror-topped wooden cabinets), and other bulky items of decor.[30] European manufactured goods flooded into the Middle East, displacing locally made items and hurting artisans. Thus imported metal spoons from Europe supplanted spoons made locally from horn, wood, or shell; while after 1860, "[f]ingers fell from fashion and were replaced by the fork," a utensil that had hitherto been little known in the Ottoman lands.[31] Even more dramatic were changes in the cut, color, and style of clothing, which erased many of the differences that had marked Muslims, Christians, and Jews, as well as high-status and low-status people, apart from each other. Obvious changes appeared first in men's apparel, although women's dress was changing in the nineteenth century, too, most conspicuously among elites. Beginning in the 1830s (when regular steamship traffic began between Istanbul and western Europe) wealthy Greek and Armenian Christian women in the Ottoman capital abandoned the traditional loose-robed styles of Ottoman clothing, substituting French designs instead. They adopted tailored dresses, which were constructed from pieces of fabric that had been cut and sewn to fit the contours of the individual women who wore them. In the 1860s, affluent Muslim women began to wear such dresses as well, copying designs from Paris and London. By 1896, as the century ended, fashion trends among elite women had changed so much that the Muslim wife of a high-ranking Ottoman military officer wore to her daughter's betrothal ceremony "a white dress of finest Brussels lace called Point d'Angleterre over cream satin ... [with] white roses [that] edged the low-necked bodice."[32]

Again, Mahmud II offers a useful point of departure for making sense of these changes, because he did so much to set the mood, and the stage, for the Ottoman nineteenth century. Mahmud II appreciated the many challenges that his empire was facing. To start, the Janissaries, who formed the core of the empire's military, were corrupt and inept. By 1800, only 10 percent of the Janissaries who were collecting government salaries and rations were alive and ready to serve.[33] Many members of the Janissary corps were at this stage full-time shop-owners or artisans, while in cities like Istanbul and Aleppo, some were even mafia-style thugs who claimed money in return for "protecting" other shop-owners and guildsmen.[34] At the same time, Western powers were chipping away at Ottoman territories and meddling in its affairs, while claiming a new language of "humanitarianism," especially where the empire's Christian subjects were concerned.[35] In the process, the Ottoman Empire was losing its hold over the Balkans, and also over North Africa, as signaled by France's invasion and seizure of the empire's westernmost territory,

Algeria, in 1830, near the end of Mahmud II's reign. Adding to the strain of the period was that large Christian populations, such as Greeks and Serbs, were becoming restless under Ottoman rule, and were drawing inspiration from nationalist ideas that made them yearn for independence. The empire ran the risk of falling to pieces.

As the nineteenth century opened, the Ottoman Empire also faced a challenge from a formidable Muslim adversary. This was Muhammad Ali (1769–1849), as his name is known in Arabic, or Mehmet Ali, in Ottoman Turkish. He was an Ottoman officer variously described as having been of Albanian or Macedonian extraction, who went to Egypt in 1801 to restore order following the joint Ottoman-British campaign that evicted France's army of occupation. Muhammad Ali proved to be so talented – and ruthless – in administering Egypt that within a few years of his appointment he was asserting *de facto* autonomy from the Ottoman Empire while also expanding his own domains. In 1820, he launched an invasion into the interior of the Sudan, which the Ottoman Empire had never previously claimed. Muhammad Ali used his military to collect Egyptian peasants and to coerce them into working on a variety of massive labor schemes, whether growing cash crops like cotton, digging irrigation canals, manning new textile factories, or serving as conscripts in his armies.[36] Thinking of Egypt relative to the larger continent of which it is part, one can legitimately identify Muhammad Ali as the first modern empire-builder in Africa to perfect the use of forced labor as a tool of domination and exploitation within the modern global economy. In this regard, his efforts anticipated by several decades what the French, British, Belgian, and other European imperial powers later did with so-called corvée schemes in their African colonies.[37]

Three other aspects of Muhammad Ali's enterprising behavior warrant attention. First, Muhammad Ali offered a role model for the Ottoman state that technically employed him. From the imperial center in Istanbul, Sultan Mahmud II and his successors copied many of the military, economic, and educational reforms that Muhammad Ali first implemented in Egypt – for example, by sending delegations of students to France for advanced training in fields such as engineering and translation, and then hiring them to staff new government initiatives upon their return. Second, Muhammad Ali actively strove to be modern, as the Ottoman state from Istanbul was striving as well. Aware, for example, that an outbreak of the plague had hampered Napoleon's troops in their effort to control Egypt after 1798, Muhammad Ali in Egypt ordered the adoption of the western European tactic of quarantine, which had first been developed in Venice, and applied it to outbreaks of diseases like cholera. Muhammad Ali did so even though the French doctor, Antoine Barthélémy Clot (1793–1868), who was the chief medical officer in charge of his new medical school, did not believe in the efficacy of quarantine. In this case, the differences of opinion between Muhammad Ali and Clot Bey (as the doctor was known) on public health policy show that what it meant to be modern, even in the realm of science, was up for grabs.[38] Third, the very success of Muhammad Ali's military campaigns prompted the European powers – and especially Russia, France, and Britain – to intervene. Worried by Muhammad Ali's expansion into Syria in 1831, and by the threat that this foray posed to the Ottoman core and the political *status quo*, the European powers coaxed him to withdraw in 1840, promising him in return the right to pass his Egyptian governorship dynastically to his sons.

This effort to persuade Muhammad Ali to leave Syria represented the so-called Eastern Question in action. Implicit in the Eastern Question, as the phenomenon of foreign European diplomacy vis-à-vis the Ottoman Empire was known, was the issue of how to keep the Ottoman Empire – also in this period dubbed "the Sick Man of Europe" – alive and afloat, thereby avoiding wars between the various parties of Europe. For while France and Britain had their own ongoing history of mutual enmity and competition, they both worried about Russia, whose expanding empire directly abutted the Ottoman territories as well as Iran. France and Britain feared that if the Ottoman Empire collapsed, then Russia would be well placed to snatch up the pieces. Russian expansion was a source of particular worry to Britain, which depended on, and obsessed over, accessing all sea and land routes to India. The fact that the Eastern Question "produced a Russo-Turkish [*sic*] war every 20 or 25 years in the period between Peter the Great [r. 1682–1725] and the Eastern crisis of 1875–78" only added to Franco-British concerns about Russian expansion.[39]

Against this context of war, the threat of territorial erosion, and European interference, Mahmud II stood ready to make reforms. However, he proceeded with caution in view of the fate of his predecessor, Sultan Selim III (r. 1789–1807), whose experiences were instructive. Before his accession in 1789, "[e]ven while he was a prince incarcerated in the palace [which was the common lot of potential contenders to the Ottoman throne], Selim corresponded with Louis XVI, the model of the enlightened monarch he hoped to be, asking for French help in rebuilding the Ottoman army and regaining the territories previously lost to Russia."[40] Rather inauspiciously, in other words, the French role model of the future Sultan Selim III was the same reformist monarch who later lost his head to the guillotine in the wake of France's revolution.

Nevertheless, in 1792 (just months before Louis XVI's demise), Selim III formed a new military corps with French assistance. Called the Nizam-ı Jedid or "New Order," it drew on Anatolian Muslim peasant boys as conscripts. It soon grew to become a disciplined corps of nearly 23,000 men and more than 1,500 officers.[41] Of course, the Janissaries saw this force as a threat to their position. They denounced it as a foreign innovation and violation of tradition, and attracted the support of leading *'ulama*, who condemned it in a fatwa.

Under the pressure of condemnation, Selim III stepped down from the throne in 1807, and was murdered one year later. But what exactly had offended and roused the *'ulama* against Selim III? It may have been that Christians, that is, unconverted foreigners, were assuming positions of influence in the military of an Islamic state, an institution that had been reserved for Muslims since the age of the Prophet Muhammad and his earliest successors. The Ottoman military had always welcomed men of non-Muslim origin into its ranks, but in the past such men had converted to Islam first. Recall, for example, that when the French officer, Claude-Alexandre Comte de Bonneval (1675–1747), had assumed his position as military advisor to Sultan Mahmud I (r. 1730–54) (see Chapter 3), Bonneval had "turned Turk," that is, embraced Islam, as a prerequisite for Ottoman service. He also adopted the name Ahmet and assumed the appropriate dress for a Muslim man of his station. A well-known pastel portrait by the French-Swiss painter Jean-Étienne Liotard (1702–89) shows the converted Bonneval *qua* Ahmet clad in a convincingly Ottoman-style turban, robe, and beard. In Bonneval's day, as one historian put it simply, "The Ottomans still were not ready to accept the services of an unconverted Christian."[42]

But that was no longer true by the time Selim III recruited French officers, less than a century later, to aid him in forming his army – for Selim III's Frenchmen stayed French, that is, Christian, in the Ottoman understanding of the term. As technical advisors, Shaw added, these Frenchmen "comprised the first Western social group ever thrust into Ottoman society without special arrangements to limit their contact with Ottomans.... They roamed openly in the streets. They gave parties to which some Ottomans were invited, thus enabling the latter to observe their homes and ways of life."[43] In other words, the unconverted French officers appointed by Selim III began to fraternize with Muslims. Their social contacts may have made it conceivable, a half century later, for Sultan Abdulmajid (who issued the 1839 and 1856 reform edicts) to break from custom among sultans by attending non-Muslims' festivities, including in 1851 or 1852 a Greek Orthodox wedding (involving the daughter of an influential Greek diplomat in Ottoman service), and in

1856, a ball, which various local non-Muslims, European diplomats, and the British ambassador Stratford Canning also attended.[44]

The Ottoman sultans and their advisers in the nineteenth century felt an urgent need for reform, for change toward something new and different. But many humbler Muslims did not see things the same way. By mid-century, the urban Muslim rich were flourishing – enjoying with affluent non-Muslims a new western-European-inspired culture of shopping for entertainment, which enabled them to buy everything from parasols and bow-ties to watches, "sock suspenders," and lavender water[45]. By contrast, in this same period, when Tanzimat reforms were at their peak, many Muslim workers in the empire were facing rising taxes, meager meals, and shrinking prospects in their trades – and all this at a time when local Christians appeared to be growing wealthier than Muslims, and when European goods and businesses were edging out local manufactures.[46] For Muslims who were feeling economic distress of this kind, the idea of adhering or returning to tradition – perceived as an older and better way – may have offered comfort and a sense of stability. Their search for comfort in some ideal of tradition may have contributed to the feelings, ranging from ambivalence to antipathy, with which many of the empire's Muslims regarded the efforts of the Ottoman government as it sought to innovate and to open itself to more exchange with the rest of Europe.

Mahmud II, the Greek Revolt (1821–1832), and Precursors to Reform

For Mahmud II, reform probably seemed critical at a time when the empire was facing grave challenges from Christian nationalist groups whose members aimed for secession. Serbs had revolted in 1804, prompting Russian intervention on their behalf. By the Treaty of Bucharest of 1812, Serbia won concessions that led to its virtual autonomy. More dramatic still was the "Greek Revolt," or the Greek War of Independence, which began in 1821, and attracted British, French, and Russian support. A popular element propelled France's and Britain's support, namely, Philhellenism, a romantic fascination with ancient Greece that inspired intellectuals like the English poet Lord Byron and that grew out of eighteenth-century Enlightenment thinking.[47] This foreign support boosted the Greek rebels diplomatically and eventually helped them to achieve independence in 1832 from the Ottoman Empire and from what some Greeks later decried as "Turkocracy."

In fact, Greeks had conflicting attitudes toward secession. For example, Greek merchants involved in trade with Russia and western Europe were particularly enthusiastic about secession, whereas church leaders connected with the Greek Orthodox Patriarchate in Istanbul (which had long enjoyed the Ottoman state's recognition as a supreme ecclesiastical authority) opposed it.[48] Indeed, as the revolt began, the Greek Orthodox patriarch in Istanbul, Gregory V, threatened to excommunicate anyone who agitated against Ottoman rule. But the patriarch's protestations of allegiance to the empire were not enough. Sultan Mahmud II and his advisers were so enraged by reports of Greek attacks on Ottoman officials and on Muslim communities in Thrace and the Morea that "the Ottoman authorities hanged the patriarch at the gate of his own palace at the end of April 1821 and let his body and those of a number of bishops be dragged through the city and thrown into the Bosphorus."[49]

Mahmud II went even further: he ordered Ottoman authorities throughout his realm to publicly humiliate Greek Orthodox Christians and possibly to execute church leaders as well. In what is now Lebanon, authorities in Beirut responded to this directive by jailing Orthodox clergymen and those who knew Greek, while in Sidon, the governor ordered Christians to pay extra taxes in a humiliating ceremony that entailed slapping their necks (suggesting a practice that some early Islamic jurists had advised as part of the proper mode of *jizya*-paying by *dhimmi*s[50]). But Muslim leaders in Damascus sent a message to the sultan explaining their unwillingness to implement these orders; they "asserted that the Christians of the city were loyal; they had paid their taxes; [and] the Qur'an forbade that their lives be forfeit without cause."[51] Instead, authorities in Damascus simply ordered the Christians of the city to wear the dark clothes that tradition assigned to *dhimmi*s. They even dropped this recourse to an old "sumptuary regime" when Christians paid a large sum of money instead.[52] This much is clear: Ottoman policies implemented in response to the Greek Revolt show just how much events in the Balkans affected life in the Arab provinces.

Today, few people would see the Arabic-speaking people who belonged to the Greek Orthodox Church as having been "Greek" at all, even if almost all high-level clergymen in their church were products of a Greek-speaking, and Greek-literate, ecclesiastical culture. Ottoman reactions to the Greek Revolt in the 1820s certainly prompted some Arabic-speaking Christians to question the "Greekness" of Greek Orthodoxy and to assert claims for church autonomy. Consider the case of the "*Rum*" Catholics (with "*Rum*" here literally meaning "Rome" but referring to the territory of what had been the eastern Roman Empire, that is, the former Byzantine Empire in the Levant). In the 1820s, *Rum* Catholics began increasingly to call themselves Melkites, using a word that derived from the Syriac *malka*, meaning king, suggesting their distant historic association with the Byzantine Empire. These *Rum* Catholics came from Arabic-speaking families that had historically adhered to Greek Orthodoxy but that embraced Catholicism under the sponsorship of Roman Catholic missionaries while nevertheless retaining Orthodox liturgies and practices. Prominent members of the *Rum* Catholic community, including wealthy Syrian merchants, responded to the Greek Revolt by stressing their loyalty to the Ottoman state, and by lobbying for recognition as a separate community (in part, and again, by making large gifts of money). Ottoman authorities rewarded these *Rum* Catholics or Melkites by announcing their autonomy from Greek Orthodoxy in 1841 and by recognizing a separate *millet* for them in 1848. Significantly, Syrians, not Greeks, were in charge of this *millet*, while members of the associated Melkite church embraced Arabic, not Greek, for their liturgy.[53] Ultimately, this struggle over church authority amounted to what the historian Bruce Masters called a series of "*millet* wars" that stimulated ethnic awareness and nationalist consciousness among certain Christian groups in Ottoman domains (see also Chapter 3). This consciousness included, in the case of the Melkites, an Arabic cultural affinity that ultimately transcended the confines of their church to fuse with the Arab nationalism that some Muslim, Christian, and Jewish literati began to espouse later in the nineteenth century.[54]

The Greek Revolt prompted the Ottoman state to make administrative changes as well. Historically, Ottoman authorities had relied heavily on Greek Christians as dragomans or translators. However, in 1821, when the revolt began, authorities decided to form a new translation corps and to staff it with Muslims instead. "The first translator, who was appointed in 1821, was Yahya, a Turkish Greek [*sic*] convert to Islam," who taught at the government's new engineering school and who apparently translated works into Ottoman from French and Italian. The second official appointed, in 1823, was an even more remarkable translator and scholar named Ishaq (d. 1834), who was variously described as the son of a convert from Judaism to Islam, or as a convert from Judaism himself. Ishaq reportedly knew "Arabic, Persian, Greek, Latin, French, and Italian, in addition to Turkish … [while h]is work entitled *Mecuma-ı Ulum-u Riyaziye* (Book of Mathematical Sciences) was published in 1831 in four volumes."[55] Men like Yahya and Ishaq helped to teach French, Italian, and other European languages to a new generation of Muslim intellectuals, and seeded a culture of literary translation that changed the books that educated Ottomans read for edification and pleasure.[56] In decades that followed, many of the leading thinkers, policy-setters, and reformers in Istanbul were graduates of the translation bureau.[57] Merely by translating European works into Ottoman Turkish, these translators encountered, spread, and perhaps absorbed the Enlightenment ideas regarding liberty, egalitarianism, and individual rights, which made their way into Tanzimat edicts.

The Greek Revolt also impressed upon Sultan Mahmud II the need for military reform. In 1826, therefore, he formed a modern European-trained army akin to the thwarted Nizam-ı Jedid of Selim III. This time, members of the *'ulama* were more supportive of the sultan – and more cognizant of the need for a stronger military – so that when the Janissaries reacted by revolting, the *'ulama* issued a fatwa permitting the Ottoman authorities to slaughter and suppress them.

Once upon a time, the mere sound of approaching Janissaries, who played a distinctive percussive music to accompany their military marches, had struck fear into enemies' hearts. But by the time of their demise in 1826, the Janissaries, or rather their musical forms, were already echoing in less threatening ways beyond Ottoman borders. Notably, their influence was resounding through the adoption of percussion instruments, march-like beats, and "Turkish" styles that were adding verve to the orchestral and chamber music of Western Europe. Works like Mozart's jolly "Rondo alla Turca" in his Sonata no. 11 in *A Major* (1783), and like Beethoven's Ninth Symphony (1824), replete with clashing cymbals, testified to the diffuse cultural impact of the Janissaries.[58]

Back on the ground in Ottoman domains, however, the abolition of the Janissaries had consequences of a more serious economic and political nature, which showed how the different groups within Ottoman society fit together and shared common destinies. For example, in the city of Salonika (now Thessaloniki, in Greece), Jews had formed deep economic connections to the Janissaries, even if Jews also suffered from their depredations.[59] From the early sixteenth century, for example, Salonika Jews, who came to constitute the largest religious group in this city, had held the rights to produce the woolen textiles from which Janissary uniforms were made. The abolition of the Janissaries had grave consequences for the Jewish artisans who made this cloth, not to mention the merchants who sold it.[60] Moreover, in Salonika in 1826, one of the wealthiest and most influential leaders of the Jewish community was Behor Isaac Carmona, banker to the Janissaries. So closely allied was he with these troops that when the sultan abolished the Janissaries, he ordered Carmona's execution, too, as another measure in the curtailment of Janissary influence.[61]

Meanwhile, the abolition of the Janissaries benefited Armenian Christians. Armenian bankers and moneylenders stepped in to replace Jewish bankers in service to the Ottoman state.[62] Armenian workers benefitted, too. Consider that when Mahmud II crushed the Janissaries in

1826, he struck more broadly at the Muslim artisans and guild members with whom they had close links, and went so far as to expel thousands of ethnic Turkish and Kurdish day laborers from Istanbul to eastern Anatolia. The sultan then had Armenians brought in to replace them, engaging in a population swap that bred resentments between working-class eastern Anatolian Turks and Kurds, on the one hand, and Armenians, on the other. These resentments simmered, the historian Donald Quataert suggested, until seventy years later, when eastern Anatolian Kurds replaced Armenian laborers who were attacked by lower-class Muslim mobs in Istanbul during the massacres of the mid-1890s.[63] By fanning ethnoreligious and class-based hostility, Ottoman authorities used a classic tactic of imperialism – divide and rule among subjects.

Finally, the abolition of the Janissaries weakened the position of the 'ulama and shifted power in the Ottoman state. For generations, the 'ulama had been able to ally with the Janissaries to "make or break" a sultan, but with the Janissaries gone, they lost leverage. From then until 1908, the sultan and his palace staff, on the one hand, and civil bureaucrats, on the other, were the chief players in Ottoman politics.[64] Indeed, the Sublime Porte – as the grand vizier's council was called from the mid-seventeenth century, in a metonymical reference to the elegantly constructed gate that opened onto Topkapı Palace in Istanbul – gained increasing influence during the nineteenth century, as the Ottoman bureaucracy swelled into a vast complex of buildings and functions.[65] Scholars debate the question of who was really leading the Ottoman state during the Tanzimat era of reforms: the sultans or their ministers? Many lean toward the latter view and present the period from 1839 to 1876 as one of "bureaucratic ascendancy," when the ministers of revamped government departments were gaining power while the number of petty and middle-rank civil officials multiplied many times over.[66] This growth in the bureaucracy reflected a broader trend of the nineteenth century. Namely, the Ottoman state, meaning the collective apparatus of the central government, was growing bigger and more complicated, and was trying to insert itself into the lives of the people whom it claimed to administer. The state was intruding even into matters as intimate as what people put on their heads.

Turbans Make the Man? Headgear Reform (1829) and the Politics of Dress

"Clothes make the man. Naked people have little or no influence in society."[67] So remarked Mark Twain, the American novelist, essayist, and wit, who was coincidentally one of the new breed of tourists to go on a

"Great Pleasure Excursion" to the Ottoman world via steamboat in the late 1860s.[68]

Ottoman gentlemen would have agreed with Twain's assessment of dress, though some might have argued that turbans, more than any other item of apparel, were what really made a man. For centuries in the Ottoman Empire, turbans had marked men apart from each other in terms of religion, profession, and rank. The turban was so powerful a symbol of social position that Ottoman Muslim men literally had their headgear carved into the top of their tombstones, so that visitors to a cemetery could "read" the turbans to identify the status of men in their graves.[69]

Mahmud II tried to change all that in 1829 when he "sought to eliminate the visual differences among males by requiring the adoption of identical headgear."[70] This move, which was arguably as important and radical a maneuver as the 1839 and 1856 Tanzimat reform decrees, attempted to enforce a visual uniformity and equality of all male subjects of the empire – Muslim, Christian, and Jew – in the eyes of the sultan, and perhaps too, in the eyes of each other. The sultan accomplished this move by banning the turban for most men (specifically exempting only the *'ulama*) and ordered them to adopt instead the fez. This was a brimless, conical, flat-topped hat associated with the city of Fez in Morocco, and introduced to the heart of the Ottoman Empire by members of the Ottoman navy, some of whom had returned from the western Mediterranean wearing it on their heads.

The 1829 headgear reform casts light on everyday social relations, as Donald Quataert argued in a significant article on the subject. Christian and Jewish men, he contended, accepted the fez gladly, welcoming the opportunity to look like Muslim men and thereby to escape from discrimination, which the traditional clothing markers of *dhimmi* status had facilitated. Thus, he reasoned, headgear reform "worked" in the upper echelons of society, in the sense that it erased visible distinctions of religion. However, nonelite, working-class, urban Muslim men, that is, tradesmen and artisans, resisted the headgear reform, or rather, undermined the state's efforts to foster a new culture of parity through dress. They did so by twisting fabric in different colors or styles around their fezzes to mark working groups (such as glass sellers and weavers) apart from each other, in a manner that may have sought to substitute for the crumbling structures of guilds.[71]

Two factors, Quataert argued, propelled the resistance of these working-class Muslim men. The first was their resentment over the leveling changes of the headgear reform, which undermined the traditional system that had made their Muslim-ness, and therefore their superiority over non-Muslims, visibly manifest regardless of their own relative wealth or poverty. (Along these lines, the British physician Alexander Russell, who left an account of his life in Aleppo during the eighteenth century, noted that poor Muslim women and children were the most likely to harass *dhimmi*s and foreigners, on the basis of their clothing, and to try to enforce distinctions of dress among non-Muslims.[72]) The second factor propelling their resistance was the negative association that the fez of Mahmud II bore in relation to this sultan's *laissez-faire* economic policies, which were leaving them more vulnerable to competition from cheap European manufactured imports. The British-Ottoman trade agreement of 1838, known as the Anglo-Turkish Convention or as the Treaty of Balta Liman, later confirmed these policies. Mahmud II's fez may have become the symbol of a new economic order in Ottoman lands, which appeared by the early nineteenth century to be benefitting Christian merchants far more than their Muslim counterparts.[73]

Indeed, Mahmud II's 1829 headgear reform may not have been as much of a leveling device in practice as it seemed to be on paper. During the years immediately after the reform, men continued to mark their fezzes with colored ribbons that signaled religion and rank. Jews, for example, marked theirs with blue and Christians with black.[74] Whether they did so as a result of personal choice, social pressure, or explicit orders from authorities is difficult to determine in retrospect. It appears, in any case, that the ribbons, color-coded by religion, disappeared from men's fezzes only after the issuing of the Hatt-ı Hümayun decree in 1856.

The 1829 reform of headgear was erratic in other respects. In 1842, the grand vizier (who was also known at this time as the prime minister) apparently felt uneasy about the way the fez was minimizing visible religious differences, and thus ordered non-Muslim men to wear the kalpak instead of the fez. Originally a cone-shaped sheepskin hat that had once been popular among Central Asian Turks, the kalpak by about 1800 had become distinctive to Armenian men, including Armenian translators, moneylenders, and doctors who were in service to the Ottoman state. By this time, too, the kalpak had changed form, becoming "swollen almost like a melon," in the opinion of one historian, and made out of a black felt that was "too hot and uncomfortable for indoor wear."[75] The kalpak certainly made its wearers stand out. Perhaps it was against the context of the grand vizier's call for the kalpak's return that Charles White, a British colonel living in Istanbul in the 1840s, recorded his exchange with an Armenian Christian man. Why don such an ugly and inconvenient hat like the kalpak, White asked this Armenian; why not wear something nicer (like the fez)? "Are we not Rayas?," the Armenian was said to reply. "Do not the Turks desire to blacken our heads as well as our faces?"[76]

The Armenian's response alluded to an important change that had occurred in the usage of the term "Raya" or "*reaya*." For centuries, the Ottoman ruling classes had addressed all Muslim and non-Muslim tax-paying commoners as part of the "flock," as the term *reaya* suggests, and treated them much the same, with the exception that non-Muslims, as *dhimmi*s, paid the *jizya* tax. In this regard, the Ottoman Empire's Muslims, Christians, and Jews had shared a "common subjecthood." However, beginning in the eighteenth century, popular and official usage changed as the term *reaya* began to pertain primarily to Christian tax-paying subjects only. Muslims continued to pay taxes but as "Muslims," not as part of the *reaya*, and in this regard Muslims identified more closely with the ruling classes and, in the words of one scholar, "moved up to become citizens of sorts" even as Christians (and Jews) remained subjects.[77] In other words, even as some Christians – and notably members of the urban Christian merchant classes – were becoming discernibly wealthier than Muslims, their political status was arguably deteriorating vis-à-vis Muslims on the ground. This situation may explain the growing alienation that some Christians felt from the Ottoman polity as well as the element of urgency, and the protestations of equality, which pervaded mid-nineteenth-century Ottoman reforms. Circumstances arguably remained different for Jews throughout the nineteenth century because Jews in places like Syria appeared to Muslims to be apolitical and more accepting of their subordinate status.[78]

The checkered application of the 1829 reform raises another perennial question in late Ottoman history: how much power did the central Ottoman state really have in changing society? Certainly historians of consumption, who study how people ingested, wore, read, bought, sold, swapped, or otherwise used material things, question the influence of the Ottoman state.[79] It is not simply that people resisted the state's dictates, as the case of clothing shows – although some resistance was always at play. It is rather that people had their own ideas, likes, and dislikes, and exercised choice accordingly – particularly as imported foreign textile and other fashion goods made choice in clothing more abundant and individual. For example, the way women arranged their hair, trimmed their dresses (e.g., with lace or macramé beading), or dressed for a wedding (perhaps endeavoring to look like Britain's Queen Victoria, who was a global trendsetter for brides in this century), all reflected small but cumulative choices that Muslim, Christian, and Jewish women were increasingly making, often in the privacy of their own homes.[80]

Image 11 "Femmes juives en costume de sortie" (Jewish women in out-door clothes), c. 1876–85, Bonfils Collection, Image Number 165856. Courtesy of the Penn Museum.

Then, too, not all Christians and Jews *wanted* to look like either Muslims or universal Ottoman subjects. Still others faced pressures to conform to the expectations of dress that arose from *within* Jewish and Christian communities. For example, in the nineteenth century, one prominent rabbi from Izmir, Hayyim Palaggi (1788–1868), claimed that "changing one's mode of dress was an act of apostasy" and that any Jew who tried to dress like a non-Jew "would bring down the wrath of God." Palaggi's colleague and fellow rabbi, Raphael Asher Sovo of Salonika, felt much the same and "declared his [own] efforts to restore [Jewish] women's modesty in dress, to stop [their] Europeanizing and exposure of hair."[81]

Of course, Jewish opinions varied, and other rabbis tried to encourage their followers to adhere to Ottoman reforms. Reportedly, for example,

Reşid Paşa (1800–1858), one of the chief architects of the Tanzimat reforms and at various times grand vizier, asked the Chief Rabbi of Istanbul to advise Jewish women to stop wearing the *hotoz*, a large, balloon- or melon-shaped, and shawl-wrapped headdress that marked its wearers apart as Jews. (Reşid Paşa was apparently aiming for a kind of greater uniformity among women that would suggest, perhaps, a common female "Ottoman" dress.) The Chief Rabbi complied, and many Jewish women heeded his call to stop wearing the *hotoz*. But an ominous development then followed, as stories spread about a mysterious woman who appeared in a boat outside Istanbul, presented herself to Jews, and called herself cholera, a scourge who had come to punish the Jewish people for abandoning their old ways. The legend of the cholera lady hints at the social anxieties that were besetting Jews and others in this era of sartorial change. Meanwhile, as for the *hotoz*, it disappeared slowly from Istanbul and its environs as a head covering for Jewish women, although photographs of women wearing it suggest that it was persisting in Istanbul and Bursa as late as 1873.[82]

It is telling that the Ottoman state tried to reform men's clothing but never applied drastic reforms to women (the detail of Reşid Paşa and the Jewish *hotoz* notwithstanding). Women's clothing was a touchy subject. In the early to-mid-nineteenth-century, Ottoman authorities repeatedly criticized Muslim women for making European-style changes to their clothing even as they were intervening to change men's dress, beginning with their military uniforms, which became styled in the French manner. This situation led one historian of Ottoman society to conclude that Muslim women increasingly shouldered the burden of maintaining communal distinction, and that ostensible continuities in their modest apparel helped to deflect attention from the social changes that the state had a hand in producing.[83] Amid dizzying social changes, in other words, Muslim women assumed greater responsibility for embodying tradition through dress.

To repeat: in the late 1820s, Mahmud II presented himself as a modern ruler and man. Clean-shaven and betrousered, he made public speeches and cut ribbons at opening ceremonies, much like the politicians and rulers who were his contemporaries in Europe and North America.[84] Mahmud II knew that his reform of men's headgear, far from being trivial, drove at matters of substance. He belonged to a long series of rulers in the Ottoman Empire (as well as in the earlier Byzantine and Abbasid Empires) who had recognized clothes – or more specifically, rights to wearing certain clothes – as political weapons.[85] Like his distant successor, Mustafa Kemal Ataturk (1881–1938), who led the infant republic of Turkey more than a century later and who banned the fez while ordering men, this time in 1925, to adopt instead a hat with a brim, Mahmud II knew that clothing was a critical means of social control and an emotive force among the people.[86] Through his own clothing choices and through the headgear reform that he promoted, Mahmud II tried to use dress as a tool for social engineering.

Religious Equality and Liberty; Idealism and Realpolitik

The Ambiguities of the Ottoman Reform Edicts (1839 and 1859)

There were myriad Ottoman reforms besides the ones that reorganized the military and the translation corps, and that refashioned headgear for men. In the second quarter of the nineteenth century, the Ottoman state also reorganized the empire's postal system, began issuing passports to subjects traveling abroad, devised a system of government ministries (apportioning the bureaucracy in new ways), and initiated the custom of hanging the sultan's portrait in government offices (the last in a clear attempt to assert the ubiquity of state power).[87] At the same time, the government founded schools that promoted new forms of inquiry within them. For example, in 1847, an imperial decree approved the use of human corpses in medical schools for the purposes of performing autopsies and dissections, disregarding long-standing objections of the *'ulama*. This measure obviated the need for wax models, of the kind that emerged in what is now Italy in the eighteenth century and that one can still see on display at La Specola, the natural history museum founded by the Medici family in Florence.[88] Considering the fraught history of human dissection throughout Europe –including, for example, in Britain, where the only corpses that surgeons could legally dissect until 1832 were those of executed murderers – the timing of this Ottoman decree was in step with changes proceeding elsewhere in Europe vis-à-vis medical studies.[89]

These changes notwithstanding, the real centerpieces of the Ottoman Empire's nineteenth-century reforms were, again, the 1839 reform (the Hatt-ı Şerif of Gülhane or "The Rose Chamber Edict") and the 1856 reform, or the Hatt-ı Hümayun, which Sultan Abdulmajid I issued. Both extolled the idea of equality among the empire's Muslim, Christian, and Jewish subjects, but had murky motives and consequences. Studying them more closely reveals the underlying political tensions of the Ottoman nineteenth century.

Recall that in the 1839 Rose Chamber Edict, the Ottoman state promised better systems of government vis-à-vis the judicial system, tax collection, and military service, and declared these applicable to all. The 1839 edict seemed to address a new kind of Ottoman: someone who would belong to the empire not through coercion or religious allegiance, but through membership, choice, and participation. This new Ottoman sounded less like a subject, and more like a citizen. The Ottoman state followed through on its commitment to religious equality when, in 1847, it created a system of mixed courts that were ordered to value testimony from Christians, Jews, and Muslims equally. This last measure represented a break from the Ottoman Islamic legal tradition, which had barred *dhimmi* witnesses from testifying against Muslims in court (but which had allowed Muslims to witness against Christians or Jews even in disputes among fellow *dhimmi*s).[90]

Again, the 1856 Hümayun decree elaborated on these promises while confirming the extant rights of non-Muslim subjects. In so doing, the edict implicitly abandoned the practice of classifying non-Muslims as *dhimmi* subordinates – suggesting instead social parity among all Ottoman subjects. It is worth emphasizing, nevertheless, that the Ottoman state after 1856 continued to recognize non-Muslims as members of *millet*s, that is, religious communities endowed with corporate identities resting on the cultural life of their places of worship and associated institutions (such as church-run schools).

The 1856 edict stressed universal religious liberty, but in retrospect, its vision of what religious liberty meant, and the change it intended relative to historical precedent, remain uncertain. One can see this uncertainty in its statements on building and repairing places of worship. Like the great Islamic empires that had preceded it, the Ottoman Empire had long adhered to an Islamic state tradition, ascribed to the Pact of Umar, which barred Christians and Jews from building or repairing churches or synagogues. In practice, Muslim rulers in various times and places had occasionally offered exceptions, so that new churches and synagogues were sometimes built and old ones renovated. Exceptions aside, deep-rooted assumptions about the Islamic topography of religious construction generally curtailed the building of churches and synagogues, with restrictions emanating not only from Muslim authorities but also, on the ground, from Muslim villagers and townspeople. An American missionary who visited Upper Egypt in 1860 noted this phenomenon after meeting one group of Coptic Christians, living near Abu Tig, who reported that their village had 4,000 Christians "but they had no church: the Moslems would not allow them to build."[91]

By specifically confirming that subjects were free to build or repair places of worship, the 1856 Ottoman edict seemed, at first glance, to be lifting one of the centuries-old restrictions on *dhimmi*s. The edict declared that, in villages, towns, cities, and urban quarters, "where the whole population is of the same religion, no obstacle shall be offered to the repair, according to their original plan, of buildings set apart for religious worship, for schools, for hospitals, and for cemeteries." But the edict contained a critical caveat: in mixed communities, it declared, where both non-Muslims and Muslims lived, residents would need to appeal to the Sublime Porte for permission to build and repair any churches. This provision was important, for in the Ottoman territories of the Middle East and North Africa, Christians did not live cordoned off from Muslims. Rather, they shared villages in rural areas, and shared neighborhoods and even apartment buildings in urban areas, as they had been doing for centuries. This Ottoman "mixity," as one might call it, stood in marked contrast to urban Morocco (which was never an Ottoman territory, and which lacked an indigenous Christian population) in the same period. That is, in many cities of Morocco, first Fez, from as early as 1437, and later others, such as Marrakesh and Meknes, successive Muslim rulers had required local Jews and foreign Christian visitors to live in enclosed neighborhoods, called *mellah*s, apart from Muslims.[92] This policy of enclosure in Moroccan *mellah*s continued through the nineteenth century and persisted, under the rulers of the Alawite dynasty, until France and Spain imposed protectorates on Morocco in 1912.

The Ottoman context was different: both Christians and Jews in Ottoman domains lived jumbled with Muslims. For this very reason, the 1856 decree's stipulation, requiring non-Muslims in mixed neighborhoods to appeal to the Sublime Porte for permission in building or repairing their places of worship, meant that the *status quo* was actually continuing. So what, if anything, was changing here? Perhaps, on this point, the innovation rested merely in the sultan's open articulation of goodwill toward non-Muslims, as well as in his solicitous recognition of their concerns. For the edict vowed to take "energetic measures to insure to each sect, whatever be the number of its adherents, entire freedom in the exercise of its religion."[93]

Of course, the Ottoman decree of 1856 was more than a spontaneous outpouring of the sultan's goodwill. It was also the product of the political moment, an expression of *realpolitik*. The Crimean War (1853–56) was winding down; peace negotiations were proceeding. The Ottoman sultan and his statesmen were eager to maintain support from allies, especially Britain. The empire was also anxious to counteract Russian claims both to its territory and to the allegiance of its Orthodox Christians, whose ostensible protection had figured in Russian policy as well as in the outbreak of the Crimean War.[94] Indeed, the *casus belli* for the Crimean War had been an episode known as the "monk's dispute," which centered on arguments over which Christians (local Catholics, backed by France, or local Orthodox Christians, backed by Russia) should control the keys to the church and grotto of the Nativity in Bethlehem, and which should maintain the Church of the Holy Sepulchre in Jerusalem. (Technically, two Muslim families – the Nuseibehs and the Joudehs – had for centuries held the keys to the Church of the Holy Sepulchre, and they still do so today, in an arrangement that gives access to the diverse Christians who wish to enter the church.[95]) With this "monk's dispute," the Ottoman sultan and his advisors had found themselves stuck with an explosive combination of Christian sectarianism and Great Power politics – and had tried and failed to placate France and Russia, Orthodox Christians and Catholic Christians, at the same time.[96]

France and Russia were always major political players in nineteenth-century Ottoman affairs. But in the drafting of the 1856 edict, Britain was the biggest foreign player. Its ambassador and intermediary in Istanbul was Stratford Canning (1786–1880), who became known officially as Viscount de Radcliffe following his elevation to the peerage and to membership in Britain's House of Lords in 1852. So influential and aggressive was Canning during this period that some historians have argued that the 1856 decree was the direct product of Canning's diplomatic "prodding" and "blackmail" of the sultan, which assumed a distinctly "Protestant colouring."[97] Indeed, Canning prioritized the concerns of Protestant missionaries, who, backed by strong financial and moral support from their home constituencies, were expanding across the world in this period. Constituted as "voluntary societies" that often represented multiple churches, Protestant missions accelerated their work in the Ottoman Empire during the nineteenth century. The pioneer in this regard was an organization known as the American Board of Commissioners for Foreign Missions (ABCFM), which blazed trails following the arrival of its first two missionaries in Izmir and then Jerusalem in 1820.[98]

The changing contours of Christian missionary activity during the nineteenth century help to explain Canning's maneuvers. Protestant missionaries who arrived in Ottoman lands during the nineteenth century shared some important things with their Catholic counterparts. Above all, Protestant missionaries, like Catholics, were drawing converts from local Christian communities, for example, among Armenians. But Catholic missions were tending to focus almost completely on people who were Christian already. This effort formed part of a larger Catholic policy of connecting "Eastern" Christians to the Holy See in Rome, or strengthening the allegiance of Eastern Rite or "Uniate" Christians, such as Maronites and Melkites, as well as Catholic Copts and Catholic Armenians, who recognized papal authority in Rome.[99] By contrast, Protestant missionaries adhered to universal aspirations that were an outgrowth of their evangelicalism. In the Ottoman lands, Protestants hoped to convert not only local Christians (Orthodox and Catholic included), whom they believed had fallen into a state of spiritual and intellectual torpor under centuries of Islamic rule, but also Muslims, Jews, and others.[100] For Protestants, herein was a problem: the universalism of Protestant missions collided with traditional Islamic state policies, which regarded Christian attempts to convert Muslims, and indeed, according to many Muslim jurists, any other non-Christians in Islamic domains, as taboo.[101]

This was the broader context for Stratford Canning's "Protestant diplomacy" vis-à-vis the Ottoman sultan. At a time when Protestants were increasingly forging connections to each other across national and sectarian lines, and conferring over issues of common concern, many missionaries had begun to question Ottoman Islamic policy, which was inhibiting their efforts to convert people, and were pressing their consular representatives into their struggles. Protestant missionaries' questioning led, in turn, to debates over religious liberty and its relationship to what was becoming known as "humanitarianism" or "human rights."

To missionaries looking at the Ottoman Empire the question of religious liberty was more than an abstraction: the lives of real people were at stake. Canning and his superior, Lord Clarendon (Britain's Secretary of State for Foreign Affairs), were aware of four occasions, in the years leading up to the issue of the Hatt-ı Hümayun reform of 1856, when Muslim authorities in Ottoman lands had executed men on the grounds of apostasy. Two cases had occurred in 1843, when an Armenian and Greek duo had converted to Islam but then recanted, only to face death by beheading. (A British mission executive later cited consular reports to claim that at least one of these men had uttered the oath of conversion to Islam under the influence of alcohol, suggesting that he saw a distinction between the sincerity as opposed to the formality of conversion and assumed that religious profession was or should be voluntary.[102]) Two other executions had occurred in 1852 and 1853, when Muslim men, in Aleppo and Adrianople (now Edirne) respectively, had embraced Christianity and faced death as their punishment. In a letter to Canning written in 1855, and later cited approvingly by British and American mission executives, Lord Clarendon noted these incidents in relation to Britain's defense of "Turkey" against Russia in the Crimean War. Why should Britain bother to "save Turkey" if its laws entailed what he called the insult and persecution of Christians? "The Christian Powers," Clarendon concluded, "are entitled to demand, and Her Majesty's Government to distinctly demand, that no punishment whatever shall attach to the Mohammedan who becomes a Christian, whether originally a Mohammedan or originally a Christian, any more than any punishment attaches to a Christian who embraces Mohammedanism."[103]

Writing in 1899, Eugene Stock, secretary and chronicler of the largest Anglican mission of Britain, namely, the Church Missionary Society (CMS), looked back on Stratford Canning's overtures to the Ottoman sultan with approval, by observing that "the time and opportunity had come for a direct missionary attack upon Mohammedan Turkey."[104] His use of militant language was common among nineteenth-century Protestant missionaries, who were becoming more interested in the history of the Crusades as it related to their own work.[105] After "long negotiations," this chronicler added, "in which the skill and firmness of Lord Stratford de Redcliffe were tested to the utmost," the Ottoman sultan inserted new wording into his draft of the 1856 edict, so as to include an affirmation of religious liberty. "As all forms of religion are and shall be freely professed in my dominions," declared the sultan's text, "no subject of my empire shall be hindered in the exercise of the religion that he professes, nor shall he be in any way annoyed on this account. No one shall be compelled to change their religion."[106]

Protestant missionaries celebrated this text and cited the 1856 Hatt-ı Hümayun as a statement in support of the kind of religious liberty that would enable individuals of whatever religion, sex, age, or social status to change and proclaim their creeds. Indeed, missionaries were still hopefully referring to this text in the opening decades of the twentieth century.[107] But even at the time of the edict's issue, its meaning and impact were ambiguous. Consider, again, the words of the British mission chronicler Eugene Stock who, in 1899, observed that missionaries in the Levant "knew well that the Hatti-humayûn [sic] proclaimed in state at Constantinople under the eye of the British Ambassador was one thing, and that the same decree as interpreted by pashas and cadis [Islamic court judges] in a distant part of the Empire was quite another thing."[108] More than a century later, another writer agreed that the 1856 decree was part of a bid for Ottoman imperial self-preservation that ostensibly "dismantled the legal hierarchy governing the relations between Muslims and non-Muslims established by the Pact of 'Umar" but that "sounded better on paper than was the reality of its implementation in the provinces."[109] Certainly, British government records show that two years after its issue, Stratford Canning conveyed to a colleague the "widespread feeling of disappointment, and almost of despair" that was spreading in Europe given that so "little had been done in execution of the [decree] since its promulgation."[110]

Missionaries, in the long run, were disappointed, too, because the edict did not open the floodgates for conversion as they had hoped or anticipated, even though Ottoman authorities stopped executing apostates after 1856, and adopted a policy that amounted to looking the other way in cases of conversion out of Islam.[111] Ultimately, Muslim popular antipathy proved to be just as potent – if not *more* potent – than state-directed sanctions in deterring acts of apostasy from Islam. Muslim families, neighbors, and local policemen took matters into their hands to stop aspiring converts from leaving Islam, using physical assault, house arrest, unilateral marriage (in the case of females), and, in extreme cases, death (e.g., by poisoning) to prevent the perpetuation of apostasy.[112] This power of deterrence attests to the critical role of the general Muslim populace (the *'amma* in Arabic), as opposed to the ruling elites, in making Islamic societies.[113] It suggests the importance of neighborhoods as political communities, capable of marshaling district or "quarter solidarity" to coerce perceived transgressors.[114] It also helps to explain how or why debates over the practical and theoretical exercise of religious liberty continued unabated throughout the nineteenth and twentieth centuries (long after the Ottoman Empire's demise). Even in the early twenty-first century, many political and religious figures in the post-Ottoman Islamic world continued to insist that people were born into the religions of their fathers, that they were required to stay Muslim if they were born Muslim, and that the exercise of personal religious choice could or should occur only within limits – notably, being acceptable if it entailed the choice among non-Muslims to convert *to* Islam.[115]

Close examination of the 1856 edict reveals another striking feature. When the text promised continuity of privileges, "*ab antiquo* ... to all Christian communities or other non-Mussulman persuasions established in my empire," it did not mention Jews directly. Jews featured, if anything, as an afterthought in the edict, much to the concern of some European Jewish observers.[116] That is because Christians (and arguably European Christians) were the driving forces behind the movement to extract official declarations of religious equality – and Muslims knew it to be so. Tellingly, when sectarian violence broke out in the Syrian city of Aleppo in 1850, and in Damascus in 1860, Muslim mobs vented their frustrations over Ottoman reforms by attacking local Christians, but not local Jews.[117]

Finally, Christian missionaries and Britons like Stratford Canning were not the only ones to harbor disappointment about the outcomes of the 1856 edict. The sultan and his ministers had grounds for disappointment as well. For there were clauses in the 1856 edict that reflected the

Ottoman leadership's own hopes for reform, and these, too, yielded little. Notable, in this regard, were lines pertaining to the expansion of military recruitment, which suggested the possibility that Christian and Jewish men could bear arms in defense of the empire.

Bearing Arms: Muslims, Non-Muslims, and Citizenship

In a tradition stretching back centuries and attributed, again, to the Pact of Umar, Islamic states had barred Christians and Jews from the military – and also, in a related vein, from riding horses. Convention held that *dhimmi*s could, however, ride donkeys, which were slow but suitable for transport.[118] "We shall not mount on saddles, nor shall we gird swords nor bear any kinds of arms nor carry them on our persons," a version of the pact had declared.[119]

Exceptions to this rule were historically rare in the Ottoman Middle East and North Africa. The following three examples are illustrative.

First, in extremely remote, tribally organized parts of northern Yemen, Jewish men were known to ride horses and carry rifles along with Muslim companions. But elsewhere in Yemen, the subordination of Jews as *dhimmi*s was much harsher than in core areas of the Ottoman Empire. For instance, in the same period in central Yemen, Jews had to dismount from their donkeys when they passed Muslims along the way.[120]

Another exception to the rule involved Napoleon. During his conquest of Egypt in 1798, Napoleon recruited a Coptic Christian named Mu'allim Ya'qub Hanna for the French army of occupation, and, radically within the context of Islamic Egypt, authorized this man to form a "Coptic Legion" out of some 2,000 Upper Egyptian Christian men.[121] When a joint Ottoman-British expedition evicted France's army from Egypt, however, the experiment in recruiting Coptic Christians for military service in Egypt ended, and the collaborators were left exposed. Consequently, General Ya'qub (as he was by then known) fled with other leading Arabic- and Ottoman Turkish-speaking supporters of the French military (including Christians and some Muslims) on a ship bound for France. The survivors, henceforth known to the French government as the "Egyptian refugees," disembarked at Marseilles and settled there permanently in 1801.[122]

But Napoleon planted an idea, as a third example suggests. Thirty years after the joint Ottoman-British force had expelled the French army from Egypt, Muhammad Ali sent his son, Ibrahim, to invade Syria on his behalf. During this "Egyptian" occupation of Syria, which lasted from 1831 to 1839, Ibrahim Pasha tried the same tactic that his father had become notorious for using among Egyptian peasants: expanding the army by engaging in large-scale conscription, in this case, among Druze men of Mount Lebanon. The Druze (who belonged to a religious group that had historically branched off from Isma'ili Shi'i Islam during the eleventh century, and who tended not to identify with Islam) rebelled against this conscription policy in 1837. With Muhammad Ali's approval, Ibrahim Pasha decided to crush their insurgency by enlisting support from Maronites, and distributed 16,000 rifles among them. In other words, Christians got arms and used them to help a regime that was trying to impose a much-hated draft on Druze men. Within a year, Muhammad Ali's regime had crushed the Druze rebels, and Ibrahim Pasha ordered the Maronites to relinquish their weapons. But the damage was done to relations between Maronite and Druze communities, precipitating communal conflicts that began in the region in 1841 and reached a crescendo in 1860.[123]

Against the context of the traditional ban on arming non-Muslims, it was certainly a bold move for the 1856 Ottoman edict to break from historical precedent by calling for the recruitment of Christians and Jews into the military of an avowedly Islamic state. The edict reasoned that, "The equality of taxes entailing equality of burdens, as equality of duties entails that of rights, Christian subjects, as those of other non-Mussulman sects ... shall, as well as Mussulmans, be subject to the obligations of the law of recruitment."[124] The Ottoman state was arguably presenting here a notion of citizenship for Muslims and non-Muslims alike, based on the premise that they should all share rights and responsibilities alike.[125] But this plan for universal male recruitment – and by extension, its conception of citizenship – did not materialize in the nineteenth century. Instead, the military remained a Muslim preserve, with partial exceptions for a small number of Christian Greeks and Armenians who served the Ottoman military as non-combatant doctors.[126]

This much is clear: the 1856 edict's call for universal male recruitment was, once more, the product of *realpolitik*. The Ottoman Empire needed soldiers; it was waging many wars. These wars were of a defensive nature, against threats from other European powers. Internal cohesion – that is, strong support for the empire *within* the empire – seemed critical for survival. The Ottoman Empire also needed more soldiers because the nature of its military was shifting.[127] By the late 1830s it was moving away from a model that treated military service as a prestigious and potentially lucrative profession, and toward one that emphasized the mass recruitment of low-paid, thinly trained soldiers. Having 24,000 personnel in 1837, the Ottoman military multiplied almost fivefold to include approximately 120,000 soldiers by the 1880s.[128] The military was also shifting toward the recruitment of free Muslim *locals*, from core areas of the empire, such as Anatolia and greater Syria. This policy contrasted with the practice of earlier centuries, when the Ottoman Empire (like many other Islamic empires in history) had favored the recruitment of men from imperial peripheries and frontier zones. Recall here the Janissaries, whose members had originally hailed from Christian communities in the Balkans, before Ottoman authorities enslaved, converted, educated, and mobilized them within this elite infantry corps.[129]

In its turn toward the massive recruitment of locals during the middle decades of the nineteenth century, Ottoman authorities were to some degree following the example of their governor in Egypt, Muhammad Ali. But the example of France was also critical. French military experts had been advising the Ottoman state since the days of Bonneval Pasha in the early eighteenth century. By the early nineteenth century, French military advisors arrived in Istanbul familiar with the massive draft that France's revolutionary government had instituted in 1793 for men whom it deemed citizens and called "volunteers."[130]

For most Muslim men, a career in this modern conscription army was neither lucrative nor glamorous. Military conditions were often so brutal (entailing chronic hunger, disease, and discomfort, not to mention the risk of injury or death in battle) that many men regarded recruitment as a death sentence. In Muhammad Ali's Egypt, recruits were so desperate to avoid military duty that many maimed their own limbs or had relatives gouge out or pour poison into their eyes in an effort to render themselves unfit for service.[131]

Military recruitment – in the Ottoman core as well as in Egypt – was also *longer* in practice than it was supposed to be in theory.[132] It was standard in the nineteenth century for Ottoman recruits to serve for twenty years in active service and the reserves. Considering that life expectancy for Anatolian Muslims in the late nineteenth century averaged from twenty-seven to thirty-two years, it was no wonder that songs of the period lamented the military draft as a death sentence.[133] (Note, however, that substantial infant mortality rates sharply reduced the average lifespan.) As a result of all these changes – and against the context of persistent foreign wars – the burden of military service in the nineteenth-century Ottoman Empire was falling heavily on Muslim men (not to mention their families) – and there were few if any compensations or perquisites to make it seem worthwhile. Meanwhile, the Ottoman Empire's limited industrial base continued to impede the state's ability to provide for recruits throughout the nineteenth century and even into the early twentieth, so that, "in the 1877–8 Russian war, in the Balkan war of 1912–13 and in World War I, large parts of the [Ottoman] army were starving and many more soldiers died of cholera, typhus and dysentery than of wounds."[134]

Faced with such bleak realities, Ottoman authorities in the mid-nineteenth century may have seen Christian men, in particular, as an untapped source of military labor, whose recruitment could assuage the chronic shortage of military manpower while lifting some of the burden on Muslims. Recall here that while Jews accounted for a tiny fraction of the Ottoman Empire's population in the late nineteenth century – perhaps 1 percent overall – the Christian population was hefty, ranging, according to various estimates, from a quarter to nearly a third of the total population.[135] In this regard, drafting non-Muslims, as the 1856 edict proposed to do, would have been not only fair (signaling the equal rights, and responsibilities, of Ottoman subjects) but practical, too.

But again, a universal draft did not go into effect. This disjuncture between the theory and practice of Ottoman conscription was the result of several interrelated factors. First, it appears that many Muslims did not feel comfortable with the idea of allowing non-Muslims to bear arms and serve in the military. It violated tradition and the social order; the idea seemed as outlandish as drafting women. Moreover, many Muslims feared that conscripting Christians and Jews would damage or destroy the morale of Muslim troops. "This was a serious point," averred the military historian Erik Jan Zürcher, "because, as all observers of the Ottoman army between 1850 and 1918 agree, the fighting spirit of the Ottoman troops was to a very high degree religious" and based on Islam.[136] Also, Muslims may have doubted how loyal Christians would be after living as *dhimmi* subordinates for so many centuries. The record of Greek and Serbian separatism, and the close ties that "Ottoman" Christians had to foreign European Christians, added to these doubts.

But if Muslims were unenthusiastic about non-Muslim conscription, then Christians and Jews were equally or more so. Their lack of enthusiasm for joining may have reflected the known brutality of military service. But it may have also signaled that Christians and Jews felt more like social subordinates than like Ottoman equals – and more like subjects than citizens.[137] Some non-Muslims doubted the welcome they were likely to receive from Muslims within the army or the pressures to convert to Islam that they might face; others preferred to stay with their families and to focus on their farms, businesses, or trades. Whatever their motives, few clamored to enlist.

There was a final reason for the non-recruitment of Christians and Jews: the Ottoman state wanted or needed their taxes.[138] Consider that the *jizya*, which was historically a tax paid by defended, not defending, people, constituted the second largest source of tax revenue for the

Ottoman treasury during the early nineteenth century. But by proclaiming the equality of non-Muslims, including their equal responsibility to serve in the military and thereby fight to defend the empire, the 1856 edict ended *dhimmi* status for non-Muslims and, with it, the obligation to pay the *jizya*. Eager to retain this revenue, Ottoman authorities decided that the taxes that non-Muslims were willing to pay to avoid military service were worth more than the value of their soldiering. And so, from 1856, the Ottoman state began to accept an "exemption tax" (*bedel-i askeri*), which enabled Christians and Jews to pay for the right of *not* serving in the military. An expert on the history of taxes in the Ottoman Empire has pointed out that, "The fact that the *jizya* was no longer levied [after 1856], may well have been perceived as an important symbolic step towards full legal equality, but financially one tax had merely been replaced with another."[139] The exemption tax was the *jizya* in a new guise.[140]

Christians preferred to pay an exemption tax rather than serve in the military. Muslims preferred Christians to share the burdens of military service but did not want to give equal access to the officer corps or to see Muslims ranked below Christians.[141] The bottom line was that Muslims and Christians were refusing to come together in a military that forced soldiers to serve under abysmal conditions in an era of recurring warfare, at a time when those who did serve were growing ever more resentful. By being able to avoid military service Christians may have been able to flourish more in agricultural pursuits than they would otherwise have done, and this may have helped them to rebound in numbers after centuries of demographic contraction.[142] The ability of Jews to avoid military service may have helped their relative numbers to grow in this period, too.[143] By contrast, Muslim communities were hard hit by military service. An English traveler who toured central and eastern Anatolia in 1879, just after the end of the Russo-Turkish War of 1877–78, noted that many places seemed empty of Muslim men, while in other places, fewer than 10 percent of the males who were drafted ever returned from the front. For Muslim men, the result of this particular war was a "demographic hemorrhaging."[144]

Lines Sharpen: The Rise of a New Sectarianism

On the second night of the Muslim holiday of 'Id al-Adha, in the Islamic calendar year of 1266 (October 17, 1850), a Muslim mob attacked a Christian neighborhood in the Syrian city of Aleppo. According to Butrus Aratin, a Melkite Catholic bishop of the city who chronicled the events, seven Christians died during the two days of rioting; 300 were injured;

and of the latter, 70 eventually died of their wounds.[145] Never before had Ottoman Aleppo witnessed Muslim-Christian violence of this kind.[146] The Muslim rioters hailed only from the poor, eastern quarters of the city, while the subjects of their rage were Christians who lived in a new, wealthy, and mostly Christian suburb outside the city limits. Christians from poor neighborhoods were left untouched, as were the city's Jews.

The spark that set off the Aleppo riot of 1850 was a report that spread among Muslims of the eastern quarters, to the effect that Ottoman authorities were about to impose a new military draft.[147] Making matters worse was the new Ottoman policy of taxing Muslims directly. Whereas in the past the state had relied on intermediaries to collect taxes from aggregate Muslim communities, leaving some degree of wiggle room for people to pay according to means, the revamped Ottoman system worked on a per capita basis and was both absolute and unforgiving. Indeed, the new taxes resembled the *jizya* that Christians and Jews had traditionally paid, and may have seemed for this reason more humiliating. In a context where traditionally "anonymity had shrouded the sultan's subjects," these new demands from the state may have also seemed unbearable to the Muslims who rioted.[148]

Among the poorer Muslims of Aleppo, the sense of deteriorating privileges appears to have sharpened, too, because many Christians in the city were becoming visibly wealthier as a result of alliances with foreign firms. These wealthy Christians were mostly Melkites who had accepted Catholicism under the earlier influence of French and other missionaries. By 1850, members of this entrepreneurial Christian community of Aleppo looked to Europeans for their business partners – and no longer to local Muslim merchants. Their lack of connections to Muslims in Aleppo left them more isolated and more vulnerable to this attack.[149]

In the mid-nineteenth century, similar political tensions were bearing down upon Mount Lebanon, a region whose residents had historically been able to retain a degree of aloofness from central state control, thanks to the protection that its mountains provided. These nineteenth-century tensions, which gained expression in a series of local conflicts and then, in 1860, in a conflagration that observers later described as civil war, reflected three major developments of the preceding decades.

The first development entailed the assertion of external state power. Historically, Mount Lebanon had been a backwater. In fact, during the Islamic era, its very remoteness vis-à-vis imperial state power had been the source of its appeal for the Druze, who, again, belonged to a sect that developed during the tenth and eleventh centuries as an offshoot of Isma'ili Shi'ism. Druze religion developed such distinctive features that scholars have variously described it as a distinct religion or as a heterodox form of Islam, while Druze people themselves have tended to keep their beliefs and practices secret while practicing *taqiyya*, or dissimulation.[150]

Mount Lebanon became part of the Ottoman Empire after the conquest of greater Syria in 1517. Nevertheless, Ottoman authorities, in practice, had been content to rule it loosely by liaising with an emir from the local population.[151] The Ottoman state only attempted to assert stronger control – and to collect, more energetically, the taxes that it claimed as its due – starting in the early nineteenth century, amidst larger attempts to consolidate the imperial bureaucracy.[152] Outside intervention into Mount Lebanon intensified during the decade after 1830, when Muhammad Ali of Egypt sent his son Ibrahim Pasha to seize the region, claiming it as compensation for having helped Ottoman authorities in their (unsuccessful) efforts to suppress the Greek Revolt of the 1820s. Recall that in Mount Lebanon, Ibrahim Pasha intensified efforts to draft Druze men for the army, thereby adding to popular discontentment that gained expression in revolts. The Ottoman Empire reasserted its control in 1841, but peasants were restless as they struggled to pay onerous taxes.

A second development affecting Mount Lebanon was the demise of its feudal order and the rise of a new rich. From the 1690s and until the early nineteenth century, this feudal order had revolved around an emir of the predominantly Sunni Muslim Shihab family, who liaised with Ottoman authorities.[153] The emir worked in concert with the leaders or *shaykh*s of several prominent Druze, Maronite Christian, Sunni, and Shi'i Muslim families, who in turn collected taxes from peasants. This feudal society was intensely status-conscious. For example, Shihab emirs had recognized social rank in terms of whether the emirs greeted visitors by standing or staying seated, and whether the emirs allowed visitors either to kiss them on their shoulders or hands, or not to kiss them at all. Even the way a letter was written or folded conveyed information about the social positions of the writer and the recipient.[154] Traditionally, family lineage determined social status, and money could not buy rank. The situation began to change, however, in the middle decades of the nineteenth century, as a new class of entrepreneurs began to purchase titles as *shaykh*s or to marry their children into high-status families.[155]

This *nouveau riche* consisted of Maronite Christians, who had benefitted from silk production and the silk trade with France. This trade dramatically expanded following the advent of steamship travel between the French Mediterranean coast and the Levant during the 1830s. Culturally speaking, Maronites, as Eastern Rite Catholics, were well positioned socially to engage in trade with French businessmen (many of whom were Catholic by background, too). At the same time, through their contacts with Catholic missionaries who operated schools, and who were disproportionately of French origin, Maronites gained an exposure to the French language, which proved valuable in business dealings.[156] Even Maronite peasants benefitted from the silk industry, insofar as they proved willing to work – and soon, to send their unmarried daughters to work – in French-owned silk factories. While this factory work did not make Maronite textile workers rich, it did make them more prosperous.[157] By contrast, the Maronites' immediate neighbors in Mount Lebanon, the Druze, were not engaging in these new economic enterprises even though Maronites produced some of their silk on land that they leased or bought from Druze people.[158] At the same time, a population increase was prompting Maronites to migrate into predominantly Druze areas during the eighteenth and early nineteenth-centuries.[159] Their needs or demands for space placed pressure on land as a resource.

The third major development to affect Mount Lebanon during the nineteenth century was sectarianism. Sectarianism meant more than mere sect-membership – more, in other words, than adherence to one variant of a religion (such as, in the case of Mount Lebanon, Sunni as opposed to Shi'i Islam, or Maronite Christianity as opposed to Greek Orthodoxy). As its suffix "-ism" hints, this sectarianism carried an ideological charge and reflected the politicization of communal identity. It was similar, in this regard, to "confessionalism," another term often applied to Mount Lebanon, which suggests adherence to bodies of religious doctrine. Of course, the phenomenon of sectarianism was not unknown in Islamic history. The reign of Shah Isma'il (r. 1501–24), founder of the Safavid dynasty in Iran, stands out as a vivid example: Shah Isma'il had forced Sunni Muslims to embrace Imami (Twelver) Shi'ism while reportedly taking an "obscene delight in torturing Sunni dissenters, [and] burning some alive, as part of his effort to establish Shi'i religious uniformity."[160] Nevertheless, what was new about the sectarianism that emerged in nineteenth-century Mount Lebanon was, first, that it reflected a calcification of religious, communal borders in places that had previously tolerated some movement across them, and, second, that it developed at the grass roots. That is, in contrast to the sectarianism of sixteenth-century Safavid Iran, the sectarianism of mid-nineteenth-century Mount Lebanon was not the result of top-down policies issued by the Ottoman sultans in their imperial center, but rather emerged from diffuse local conditions. And some of the locals had a stake in it – embracing a language and logic of sectarianism to lobby external powers, as many Christians of the region arguably did when they appealed to France for support.[161]

To illustrate the kind of fluidity that was possible before communal borders hardened, consider the Shihab emir, Bashir II (1788–1841), who had both a mosque and a church built at his palace.[162] Indeed, by some accounts, Bashir II was a Sunni Muslim convert to Maronite Christianity, in a Mount Lebanon context where his conversion from Islam to Christianity had elicited little in the way of social sanction from Muslim communities.[163] This emir's behavior and religious ambiguity prompted a French observer to remark that Bashir II "appeared to be a Druze to the Druzes, a Christian to the Christians, and a Muslim to the Muslims." Some of Bashir II's contemporaries evinced a similar catholicity in piety, outlook, and practice. For example, Christian and Druze notables often swore oaths at the same shrine to the Virgin Mary, "one loyal Shi'a emir was buried in the Sunni Shihab family cemetery," and "a Christian merchant funded the construction of a mosque."[164] Of course, the sharing of shrines and other holy places in this manner, among Muslims, Christians, and Jews, was common throughout the Middle East, while in some places, such as Cairo and Istanbul, the popular practice of sharing persisted into the twenty-first century.[165] Nevertheless, in Mount Lebanon, the options for or likelihood of sharing appeared to narrow considerably as the nineteenth century proceeded.

What caused communal borders to harden in this way? Foreign missionaries, and especially French Catholics and British and American Protestants, certainly played a part in this process. They competed for converts, looked askance at any expressions of religious hybridity, and saw, or insisted on seeing, "the pure communal actor," such as the hermetically sealed Maronite or the absolute Druze. Illustrating this tendency were two Jesuit priests, Riccadonna and Louis Abougit, who were appalled by the practice of some Christians in Mount Lebanon of giving their children "Muslim" names, singing "Muslim" songs, and joining Muslim neighbors in religious festivities. Both missionaries were among those who tried to halt such crossovers.[166]

The 1860 Maronite-Druze skirmishes escalated into massacres, including one that killed 5,000 people on a single day in July. They sprang, again, from the collapse of the feudal order, changes in Ottoman policies, shifts in the local economy, and the rising tide of sectarianism as factors that mixed together and exploded. The result was a civil war.[167] This new form of nineteenth-century sectarianism emerged not only in the rural areas but also in Beirut, a burgeoning city on the coast, where growing economic disparities between diverse Muslim and Christian communities increased social tensions. By some accounts, this sectarianism was at its sharpest *among* Christians (especially of the Greek Orthodox, Maronite, and Greek Catholic or Melkite variety), even if most accounts, then as today, concentrated primarily on tensions *between* Druze, Muslim, and Christian people. There was also a strong element of class conflict, with sectarianism arguably stronger among the poor for whom the slightest shift in status could make their vulnerability feel more acute.[168]

The sectarian bloodletting of 1860 did not stop in Mount Lebanon, but spread later in the same year to Damascus. Notably, when a group of some 6,000 Maronite refugees arrived in Damascus after Druze forces had crushed them in a place called Zahle, they received a chilly reception. Reports had reached the Muslims of Damascus to the effect that the Christians in Mount Lebanon had been attacking mosques and massacring Muslims. It made matters worse that the Muslims of Damascus harbored resentments toward their own local Christian populace as well – notably, again, regarding the wealth they had accrued from their intimate involvement in the French silk trade that had crushed textile manufacturing in Damascus. But in Damascus, unlike in Mount Lebanon, the focus of Muslim resentment was not on the Maronite community, but on the Melkites or Greek Catholics.[169]

Violence exploded in Damascus after an incident in July 1860, involving a group of Muslim boys, who began to bother local Christians by using chalk or coal to mark out their doors and by drawing crosses on the pavement – and then taunting Christians when they stepped over them. When the local Ottoman governor attempted a clumsy crackdown on the perpetrators, the situation exploded. Over the course of eight days, Muslim and Druze mobs consisting of perhaps 20,000–50,000 men – mostly artisans, tradesmen, and soldiers – poured into neighborhoods inhabited by affluent Melkite Christians, and killed, maimed, plundered, and raped with abandon, while also carrying off women and children. At the same time the mobs torched houses, churches, foreign consulates, and even a leper hospital with the lepers still in it. They left behind smoldering ruins. Recall that, as one of the terms of *dhimmi* status, Christians had traditionally lacked the right to bear arms. At this moment in 1860, they still had few weapons to defend themselves.[170] Note, too, that the mobs attacked neither Jews nor Christians of poor neighborhoods, but only affluent Christians, suggesting that factors of wealth (and poverty) were intersecting with religion.[171]

Ottoman authorities in Istanbul were reportedly shocked and appalled by the carnage. Under threat of heavy reprisals, they ordered Muslims who had abducted women and children to give them up, regardless of whether the abductees had converted (or been declared converted) to Islam or whether Muslim men had sexually assaulted them and claimed them as wives. The authorities arrested hundreds of Muslim men, and publicly executed scores of them. Records identified the executed by their professions, thereby offering some insight into class origins: they included lemonade sellers, barbers, bead traders, carpenters, and other assorted shopkeepers and artisans. On one day in August 1860 alone, Ottoman authorities executed 167 men as their families and other members of the public looked on; they then suspended the corpses of 57 of them in bazaars and streets, and on gate-posts, as grisly memorials of the punishment. During ensuing weeks, the authorities executed many more, and sentenced hundreds of others to exile or hard labor. Meanwhile, "half-starved and half-naked," Christian survivors left homeless "survived on coarse bread and cucumbers," while many Muslims who had played no part in the violence looked with "shame and amazement ... at what had happened" on their home turf. Soon the Ottoman authorities also set about rebuilding the shattered economy. They attempted to dissuade members of the Christian entrepreneurial class from abandoning the city for good, but some of these measures caused anguish for others. In some cases, for example, the authorities seized the houses of Muslims and turned them over to homeless Christians. More broadly, the authorities demanded indemnity payments from all the non-Christians of Damascus, that is, from all Muslims and Jews.

Historically, Muslim thinkers had identified the prevention of *fitna*, or public disorder, as one of the main responsibilities of an Islamic state. One could certainly read the harsh measures of the Ottoman authorities in the wake of the 1860 Damascus massacres, and their efforts to restore balance for Christian residents, as part of measures to restore order in the wake of a terrible outbreak of *fitna*. But there was more to it than that – it was more complicated and more was at stake. The massacres called the policies of idealistic reformers into question. They ruptured relations along religious sectarian lines in a way that had never been seen before in the Islamic history of Damascus. And to make it more difficult, European and American observers, linked to powerful countries behind them, were watching. Indeed, more than watching: the Russian, French, Dutch, Austrian, Belgian, and American consulate buildings were all plundered and burnt to the ground.[172] The massacres were a colossal source of humiliation for the Ottoman state that aimed to preserve order within its domains. The massacres, or rather their aftermath, also caused deep anguish for residents of Damascus and their successors. Even coping with the indemnity payments was difficult. "To put up with the practical burdens of the fine was bad enough, but to live with its implications was still more painful. Were all the non-Christian Damascenes liable to a fine because, in effect, they were all guilty? Even today," mused a historian in 1994, "it is a sensitive subject."[173]

"Emancipation," Anti-Semitism, and the New Jewish Activism

With rare exceptions, relations between Jews and Muslims in the late eighteenth- and nineteenth-century Ottoman Empire were calm and steady. But political and intellectual changes in Europe were transforming Jewish communities in ways that would have far-reaching consequences for the Islamic world. Developments in France proved to be especially important. Through a train of circumstances connected to French engagement abroad, changes inside France eventually reverberated outward to affect Jews living in the Ottoman domains of western Asia, southeastern Europe, and North Africa. They even reached Iran, where shahs of the Qajar dynasty (c. 1796–1925) were ruling, and Morocco, which remained independent under the Alawite dynasty (1631–present). Most significantly, these changes affected the Jews of Algeria, which France wrested from the Ottoman Empire in 1830 and transformed into a colony for settlers from France as well as from places like Malta and Sicily.[174]

The life and career of Adolphe Crémieux (1796–1880) illustrates this story of Jewish engagement in broad and vivid strokes. A French Jewish patriot and lawyer who was a firm republican and lifelong admirer of Napoleon, Crémieux came from a family that derived its livelihood from the silk trade – the western end of the same Mediterranean silk trade that was doing so much to transform greater Syria during the nineteenth century.[175] Crémieux embodied a new form of Jewish activism that sought to promote modern French values, both in France and the Islamic world, while advocating for Jewish people. Yet, unlike the leaders of the Zionist movement, which emerged during the generation after his death, Crémieux was an optimist, or at least the product of an optimistic age. He believed that Jews could and should flourish *in situ*, by staying put and improving their political and social circumstances, wherever they might be.[176] To understand Crémieux as well as the spirit of his age as it related to Jews in Ottoman lands, one must start by considering the French Revolution, and how it did and did not improve the situation for Jews in France and the region.

Issued in 1789, the *Déclaration des droits de l'homme et du citoyen* (Declaration of the Rights of Man and of the Citizen) represented the high ideals of the French Revolution. With its emphasis on "natural, inalienable, and sacred rights," it later inspired the Ottoman reform edicts of 1839 and 1856. However, like these two Ottoman edicts, with their affirmations of religious equality, the French *Déclaration des droits de l'homme et du citoyen* promised more than some of its supporters had originally intended. Certainly its authors seemed surprised by the "onslaught of unanticipated petitions [they received] from groups across the [French] empire – from peasants and Jews to people of color and actors – using the [National] Assembly's new language to declare that they too were 'men' and deserved the same rights as 'all other Frenchmen'."[177]

At the time of the French Revolution, some 40,000 Jews were living in France, out of a total population of about 28 million, and they were eager to secure their position. Their mere presence in France was still technically illegal; King Charles VI's edict of 1394, which had expelled all the Jews from the realm, had never been annulled.[178] Conditions were somewhat better by this time in Britain, where a positive sentiment toward Jews, or "philo-Semitism," had taken hold among some sectors of the Protestant population. This climate of philo-Semitism had enabled Jews, during the Protectorate era of Oliver Cromwell (1653–58), to secure tacit permission to live in England, in spite of King Edward I's expulsion decree of 1290.[179] Meanwhile, in contrast to the situation in France and Britain, Jews in the Ottoman domains and in Alawite Morocco enjoyed recognized positions as well as the freedom to live and practice their trades.[180]

In retrospect, most observers recall 1791 as the year when a decree from the French National Assembly granted the Jews of France their "emancipation" along with the privileges and responsibilities of citizenship. (Note that this was less than two years after French Protestant Christians had won their own "emancipation" in France after centuries of persecution, thereby giving Protestants a major stake in the French Revolution, too.[181]) For Jews, circumstances after 1791 improved dramatically. Consider that, in Paris before the revolution, some 500 Jews had been living in a semi-clandestine condition under the surveillance of the same bureau of police that was charged with responsibility for prostitutes.[182] After the revolution, Paris became a congenial center of Jewish life, attracting diverse Jews from elsewhere in France and abroad, and allowing a cadre of professionals and entrepreneurs to emerge.[183]

The French Revolution occurred at a time when many Jewish intellectuals were eager for change. In the last quarter of the eighteenth century, a new philosophical movement, known as the Haskalah or Enlightenment, was energizing Ashkenazi Jewish thinkers in Europe – including those of eastern French cities like Metz. Haskalah intellectuals were trying to take Jewish debate out of the synagogues and away from the rabbis, and into newspapers, clubs, cafés, homes, and other venues where they swapped ideas. Calling for the modernization and uplift of Jewish society, Haskalah thinkers embraced values such as free, rational thought and liberal inquiry that resonated with those of the French philosophers who inspired the Revolution.[184] By the mid-nineteenth century, the legacies of both the Haskalah and the French Revolution were together producing a new Jewish leadership of men who were enthusiastically and idealistically French. Adolphe Crémieux was born into this exciting world of postrevolutionary France, where, at least in republican circles, his Jewishness posed few barriers to advancement.

Historically, Islamic states had offered Jews a kind of security and official acceptance that was lacking in France before the 1790s, but postrevolutionary France now seemed to offer something much better: citizenship and opportunity, based on the idea of equal membership. To many Jews, this new deal looked better than either traditional *dhimmi* subjecthood or the revamped *millet* arrangement of the 1839 and 1856 Ottoman decrees.

And yet, with its capacity for inserting a note of doubt, the verb "seemed" – as in "postrevolutionary France *seemed* to offer Jews something much better" – is important, for two reasons. First, even those French revolutionary leaders who issued statements calling for Jewish "regeneration" or Jewish rights, such as the universalist thinker Abbé Henri Grégoire (1750–1831) and Napoleon Bonaparte himself – acknowledged ambivalence about making a place for Jews within the French "family."[185] Indeed, such leaders expressed the hope or expectation that Jews would "abandon their particularities," and "dissolve ... into the national mass" – that is, become more French, and less Jewish.[186] Second, anti-Jewish sentiment – or anti-Semitism, as it was becoming known in the mid-to-late nineteenth century – persisted, despite the leveling rhetoric of the revolutionary credo, while discrimination disappeared from laws, but not minds.[187] Church leaders, who were heirs to a long history of Christian vilification of Jews, continued to play critical roles in maligning Jews and stirring up public sentiment against them. Meanwhile, new anticlerical, secular, and racial (i.e., nontheological) expressions of anti-Semitism were also gaining a voice.[188]

There were two anti-Semitic incidents of the mid-nineteenth century – both abetted by Christians closely linked to the Roman Catholic Church – that pushed Adolphe Crémieux and some of his colleagues into action. The first incident occurred in Syria in 1840 and became known as the Damascus Affair. The second occurred in Bologna in 1858, and became known as the Mortara Affair. Neither occurred on French soil, showing how, in this age of quickening communication, more history was "transnational" – that is, spanning and jumping borders.

The Damascus Affair began in 1840, when a group of European Catholic missionaries and doctors approached the French consul of the city to report the absence of a Capuchin priest named Père Thomas. They averred that people had last seen Père Thomas – as well as his servant, Ibrahim Amara, who was also missing – in a Jewish quarter of the city. The French consul, the Comte de Ratti-Menton, took action. For although Père Thomas was Sardinian and not French in origin, he qualified for French protection according to the terms of the Franco-Ottoman Treaty of 1740, which recognized France's right to protect all Catholic clergy in the Ottoman Empire.[189] Presuming from the start that Jews had murdered the priest and his servant, Ratti-Menton began by apprehending suspects from the Jewish quarter and turning them over to the Muslim governor of the city for interrogation. This Muslim governor was Sherif Pasha, and he was a high-ranking appointee (and son-in-law) of Muhammad Ali of Egypt, whose regime at this moment still held the Syrian territory that its armies had wrested from Ottoman control in 1831.[190]

Like the French consul, Sherif Pasha presumed foul play. He ordered his subordinates to round up dozens more Jews – including, for example, all Jewish butchers and gravediggers (who might have had something to do with the presumed dismemberment and disposal of the priest and his servant), and had them flogged with a whip, called the kurbash, which was made from hippopotamus leather. These floggings elicited confessions: certain Jews had first killed Père Thomas and his servant, then collected their blood in a copper basin, and finally used it to make matzoh bread for their Passover ritual. This macabre account may have seemed novel to many Muslims in Damascus. But it was a familiar story in Europe, where "blood libel" narratives had been circulating since the twelfth century. While a variety of Catholic popes over the centuries (such as Innocent IV, Gregory X, and Nicholas IV) had dismissed these stories as unfounded, the basic narrative persisted and gained support, high and low, in church circles, to the extent that the church ultimately recognized some of the alleged child victims as saints.[191] For example, there was Little Saint Hugh, who had died in Lincoln, England, in 1255, and whose alleged Jewish killer was said to admit, according to the 1910 edition of the *Catholic Encyclopedia*, that "it was a Jewish custom to crucify a boy once a year."[192]

The Damascus Affair added one more to the list of 150 or so documented cases of Christian blood libel cases that had resulted in Jewish deaths. In this case, the Jewish dead included "two witnesses whose stories did not accord with the story of ritual murder and two of the accused."[193] In addition, Sherif Pasha and his underlings subjected dozens of Jews to sustained violence – making the proceedings of the Damascus Affair, from today's perspective, a case study in the psychopathology of forced confessions. For example, a 22-year-old man, who claimed to see Père Thomas leaving the city, "died after 5,000 lashes [that were] administered under orders of Sharif Pasha," prompting a contemporary source to record that afterward, "the Jews had great difficulty in conducting the customary purification of the corpse … since the flesh fell entirely off from the bones."[194] At the same time, local Christians joined in on the violence, sacking synagogues, desecrating Jewish cemeteries, and in one case, "snatch[ing] Jews] off the streets, [… and then] subject[ing them] to forced labor in building a church."[195]

What really happened to the priest and his companion? Authorities eventually turned up some scraps of cloth and some bones, which they claimed to be human, as proof of their death and dismemberment, but no convincing answer was ever found. So much time has elapsed that no one is likely to solve the case. But scholars can analyze the behavior of the actors involved in the investigation.[196] For example, the French consul, Ratti-Menton, arguably seized upon the case of Père Thomas as a way of rallying Arab Christians, and especially Maronite Catholics, to France, and reciprocally, of rallying sympathy from Christian audiences in France to the cause of Arab Christians.[197] Sherif Pasha, whose zeal in pursuing the case against the city's Jews might otherwise seem inexplicable, may have thought that his energetic pursuit of the Damascus case would curry favor with the French consul, at a time when France seemed to be Muhammad Ali's only hope of keeping Syria as an adjunct to Egypt, apart from Ottoman control. Indeed, in this period, Muhammad Ali was supporting a policy of cultivating the goodwill of local Syrian Christians, whom he recognized as a useful conduit to France. The Jews of Damascus, by contrast, had a reputation for loyalty to the Ottoman authorities and were politically of no use to Sherif Pasha and the Muhammad Ali regime.[198]

For Adolphe Crémieux, and indeed for all educated Jews who followed these events from some distance, the Damascus Affair elicited "shock," "extreme shock," and more shock again.[199] It was difficult to fathom how, in an age of reason, a representative of the French government in Syria could take a story so preposterous, so rooted in medieval traditions of diabolizing Jews, and use it to round up and torture random assortments of schoolboys, rabbis, butchers, and others, in a case in which even the fact of a crime was uncertain. It came as even more of a shock when both the French foreign minister and the French king, Louis Philippe, ignored appeals to condemn the French consul in Damascus. For Jews like Crémieux, the Damascus Affair therefore planted doubt about the durability of their own newly won rights within France.[200]

Rather than succumb to this worry, Crémieux and some of his colleagues from France and Britain took action. They wrote to newspapers, appealed to other governments (notably Britain), staged public protests, and more. By coordinating efforts to rally public opinion, both within and beyond Jewish circles, Crémieux and his colleagues initiated a new culture of Jewish activism and lobbying.[201]

The story of the Mortara Affair, which took its name from a Jewish boy named Edgardo Mortara, was just as bizarre and as sad. It started in Bologna in 1858 at a moment of political flux. Conquered by Napoleon in 1796 and turned into a short-lived republic, Bologna reverted after 1815 to the Papal States, a theocratic entity ruled by the Roman Catholic papacy. When the Mortara Affair began, Bologna was still technically under the rule of Pope Pius IX (1792–1878), and not yet part of the Kingdom of Sardinia (the precursor to unified Italy) as it would be one year later.

The Mortara Affair began when Edgardo was six years old. A Christian servant, employed by the family, retroactively claimed that she had secretly baptized the boy on an earlier occasion when he was grievously ill. Accepting both the claim to, and the legitimacy of, this woman's "emergency conversion," papal authorities seized the boy, took him to Rome, and installed him in a hospice for instructing new converts. Papal authorities rebuffed the family's efforts to reclaim Edgardo on the grounds that, as Jews, the Mortaras were merely guests of a Christian polity and had in any case broken the law by engaging a Christian as a servant. While newspapers across western Europe expressed dismay or outrage over the seizure of Edgardo Mortara, most Catholic authorities either supported his Christian conversion, or, being too afraid to gainsay the pope, kept quiet.[202]

The Mortaras never got their child back, despite years of entreaties. Edgardo Mortara eventually became a Catholic priest, adopting the name of his patron, Pope Pius IX, to become "Pio Maria." He spent a long career in the church, working in part as a missionary to Jews. In March, 1940, Edgardo, or Pio Maria, died at age eighty-eight in an abbey in Liège, just two months before Nazi forces occupied Belgium and began to round up all people whom they deemed Jews by profession or birth.[203]

Again, the Mortara Affair in 1858 elicited shock from Jews across Europe, who regarded the case as one of kidnapping and forced conversion. The incident galvanized Adolphe Crémieux, who established with colleagues in 1860 a new organization called the Alliance Israélite Universelle (AIU). The AIU dedicated itself to the education of Jews and to the amelioration of their conditions, while focusing efforts on the southern and eastern Mediterranean rim. It did so by developing a network of French-medium schools for girls and boys, beginning with a school in Tetuan, Morocco, which opened in 1862. The AIU also ventured into French-controlled Algeria and eastward, into Ottoman domains. It opened its first schools in Istanbul in 1864. In 1873, the AIU reached Iran. By 1914, the AIU was running 183 schools with a total enrollment of 43,700 students.[204]

The AIU was a Jewish missionary movement. Its delegates spoke often about their own "civilizing" or "regenerating" mission among fellow Jews whom they hoped to convert from "tradition" into what they regarded as modernity and progress.[205] At the same time, AIU delegates were "missionaries of France," who promoted French language and French culture in their schools and who often presented the Jewish traditions of Islamic lands as primitive, uncultured, and ignorant.[206] The AIU's culture of French-style *laïcité* or secularism, as well as its discourse of cultural conversion, prompted some local Jewish critics in North Africa and western Asia to dismiss AIU schools as centers of "irreligion."[207] And perhaps this charge was not wholly unfounded: in Turkey, argued one scholar, AIU educations "weakened the chain of transmission of the past and contributed to the secularization of large sections of the community."[208]

The AIU certainly left Jewish communities "Frenchified" (*francisés*): speaking French, dressing like people in metropolitan France, and giving their children French names – such as Caroline, Eugénie, and Jacqueline for girls.[209] The evidence of their Frenchness was literally carved into rock. For just as one can scan the Ottoman-era tombstones of Muslims in Istanbul for information about changing indices of social status, so one can read Jewish tombstones from the same city, where French displaced Hebrew and Ladino as the language for epitaphs during the nineteenth century.[210] Linguists have noted, too, that throughout North Africa, French spread so fast and so far among Jews that it displaced the language of their daily discourse. For many Jews, this language had been some form of Judeo-Arabic, again, an Arabic used by Jews, containing Hebrew and Aramaic lexical influences, and written in Hebrew script.[211] Looking, in particular, at the case of Tunis, one linguist has argued that the gender parity of AIU schools – their enrollment of girls who were as likely as boys to become literate and fluent in French – enabled French not only to become a lingua franca among Jews but also to become, by the interwar era of the twentieth century, the native tongue of the city's Jewish community.[212]

If the Mortara Affair, which occurred in Bologna under papal rule, was the spark that lit the AIU, then why did the AIU focus on Jews in Islamic countries, and not on Jews in western Europe? Men like Crémieux, who served as the AIU's first president, would have probably used a French Orientalist discourse (emphasizing France's modernizing and liberalizing role in addressing the imputed tyranny inherent in Islamic societies[213]) to suggest that the Jews of the Islamic world faced persistent disabilities as *dhimmi*s, and therefore needed the benign intervention of the AIU and France more acutely than the Jews of "civilized" Europe. In Morocco, for example, where the first AIU school opened, they might have pointed out that Jews in many cities were still required to live in the walled-off districts called *mellah*s and to mark their Jewishness by removing their shoes and walking barefoot when they ventured into Muslim neighborhoods.[214]

But, of course, another equally important reason for the AIU's projection into the Islamic world was that it reflected positively on Jews in France and neighboring countries. In the post-Damascus Affair, post-Mortara Affair period, European Jews were desperate to keep, earn, and prove their rights of national belonging. The AIU's service in projecting French culture overseas earned its representatives in France considerable goodwill. Nevertheless, the complete non-involvement of Muslims in the Mortara Affair in Bologna – the affair that set the AIU into motion – shows how the Islamic world was becoming drawn, inextricably, unwittingly, and unavoidably, into deep currents of European history that involved relations between Christians and Jews.

In 1870, as the Franco-Prussian War raged, Adolphe Crémieux became the minister of justice in France, and in this capacity promoted what he saw as another boon to Jewish peoples. This was the Crémieux Decree, by which the French government unilaterally declared the Jews of Algeria – a total of some 35,000 people – to be French citizens. Writing in 2004, an Algeria-born French historian described this decree in glowing terms, mentioning that it transformed Algerian Jews from "a humiliated and inferiorized people," stuck with *dhimmi* status, into "free and liberated" French people. "For the Jews of Algeria," she concluded, "France, an abstract and idealized entity, had liberated them and they loved her."[215] But writing in 2010, another scholar took a much dimmer view of the Crémieux Decree and its implications: "In their effort to secure full citizenship for Algerian Jews, [French] colonial officials helped develop a mythology holding Algerian Jews to be more intelligent, faithful, and redeemable than Muslims, their supposedly less-gifted former oppressors." In this way, the French government's unilateral imposition of citizenship on Algerian Jews "obscured their ancestors' deep connections to North African society."[216] France drove a wedge between Algerian Jews and Muslims, who respectively became, by virtue of Crémieux's decree, the "haves" and the "have-nots" of French citizenship.

In a similar vein, a second Algeria-born French historian, Benjamin Stora, concluded that the 1870 Crémieux Decree ruptured Jews from Algerian Islamic society so sharply that their shift of status amounted to an internal exile. Stora called this exile the first of three for Algeria's Jews. The second exile, he argued, occurred in 1940, when France's Vichy regime (working in collaboration with the Nazis) revoked the Crémieux Decree of 1870 and thereby cancelled the citizenship of Algerian Jews; the third occurred in 1962, when Algerian Jews, once again "French," left en masse for France in the wake of the Algerian War for Independence.[217]

For Muslims, French policy in Algeria was harsh. After invading and occupying the country in 1830, France constructed a regime based on a form of settler colonialism that subjected the Muslim majority population to land seizures, forced resettlements, the closure of Islamic schools, and stiff penalties for a host of infractions ranging from failure to serve on forced-labor schemes to failure to stand when a French officer went by. This scheme of punishments, which was originally devised for the Muslims of Algeria, became a model for all of French colonial Africa.[218] On top of this "legal caste system," Muslims experienced "humiliating social hierarchies, impoverishment, wide-scale sexual abuse, and massacres" perpetrated by colonial military authorities and settlers.[219] For all these reasons, Algeria became a huge blind spot – and source of hypocrisy – in incipient French and British debates about human rights. The result was that men like the Briton, Stratford Canning, were able to make claims about Muslim tyranny and to press the Ottoman sultan to issue his edict of equality in 1856 even while, at the same time, French rule in Algeria was more oppressive than anything that the Ottomans had concocted.[220]

Did Adolphe Crémieux and his colleagues in the AIU not see the injustices of French rule in Algeria – or did they just *choose* not to see them? It is hard to say. Certainly in this period when the Ottoman Empire, as well as Alawite Morocco and Qajar Iran, were growing weaker on the international stage, it was more convenient to lambast Muslims in the Islamic world for injustices meted out to Jews, than to address the anti-Semitism that continued to pervade the now powerful, historically Christian states of western Europe. In fact, this same anti-Semitism pervaded Algeria, too, among the French-speaking settler population and especially among French military officers.[221] The anti-Semitism of these constituencies in Algeria left authorities from metropolitan France later unwilling to extend French citizenship to Jews in Morocco when the issue arose, out of a fear of offending French (Christian) sensibilities.[222]

French Algeria went on to play a striking cameo role in the history of French anti-Semitism. For in the small grape-growing town of Miliana, southwest of Algiers, the Crémieux Decree of 1870 prompted settlers in 1871 to form an anti-Jewish league that aimed to discourage Jews from voting during parliamentary elections. This anti-Jewish league anticipated the first anti-Semitic league founded in France in 1889, and arguably marked the debut of "institutionalized French anti-Semitism."[223] Later, in 1897, in the Algerian town of Oran, settlers rioted against Jews as "capitalists" (notwithstanding the fact that some 44,000 out of 53,000 Jews in Algeria at the time counted among the poor) and demanded the cancellation of the Crémieux Decree. "Behind the declared anti-Semitism of the Europeans in Algeria," argued Benjamin Stora again, "the fear of the 'Arab peril' was lurking." His comment suggests that the phenomena of French Christian anti-Jewish sentiment, and French Christian anti-Arab or anti-Muslim sentiment, may have been twins joined at the hip.[224]

Conclusion: How Was Religion Important?

The violence that ravaged Mount Lebanon and Damascus in 1860 occurred against the backdrop of massive social changes that included the collapse of the feudal order; the growing assertion of the central Ottoman state and of France, Britain, and their emissaries in local affairs; and widening disparities in wealth between the mostly Christian beneficiaries of foreign trade on the one hand, and humble Muslim members of the agricultural and artisanal sectors, on the other. But what about religion? How important was religion as a force behind these events?[225]

Perhaps it is more useful to ask, "How was religion important?" as opposed to "How important was religion?." That is, how had religion mattered in the past, and how was it mattering in new or old ways in 1860, when violence rocked Mount Lebanon and Damascus and when Jewish activists in France established the AIU, with its new, pan-Jewish ideals? In response to this inquiry, some general trends stand out.

First, there were some areas in which religion was, and remained, unimportant. Continuing a pattern set by other Islamic states in history, the Ottoman state did not use religion as grounds for restricting non-Muslims in commerce. As long as Christians and Jews paid their taxes, their merchants were able to engage in business and flourish – although the tacit assumption was that they would use their wealth with discretion. This policy remained the same in the nineteenth century, as far as Ottoman authorities were concerned. However, some Christians (even more so than Jews) began to demonstrate their wealth publicly, for example, by building more flamboyant houses and churches. Instead of stepping aside when a Muslim passed by, one scholar suggested, some of these non-Muslims now stayed put on the pavement.[226]

Second, there were some areas of partial change in the sphere of religion, as the case of law suggests. For example, during the mid-nineteenth century, Ottoman authorities created mixed courts, where Jews and Christians could give testimony on the same footing as Muslims. At the same time, however, nineteenth-century Ottoman reforms left Islamic laws about marriage, divorce, child custody, inheritance, and family matters largely unchanged. These family laws continued to distinguish different rights for Muslims, Christians and Jews as well as for men and for women. For example, according to Islamic law as practiced, Muslim men in Ottoman domains could still legally marry Jewish and Christian women, while Jewish and Christian men could not marry Muslim women. Ottoman reforms also continued to recognize Christian and Jewish *millets* as communities in which religious authorities exercised some power, for instance, while regulating marriages among adherents.

In one important respect, however, the Ottoman state *did* begin to intervene in marriage. Namely, in 1869 the state passed an Ottoman Law of Nationality, the ulterior motive of which, in the view of the historian Karen Kern, was to thwart marriages between Sunni and Shi'i Muslims. This change occurred at a time when many ostensibly Sunni Muslims, in what is now southern Iraq, were beginning to embrace or convert to the Imami or Twelver form of Shi'ism that Iranian rulers had been promoting since the time of the Safavids. In 1874, Ottoman authorities went one step further by passing another law that banned marriages outright between Ottoman women and Iranian men whether they were Muslim, Christian, or Jewish.[227] Ottoman-Iranian rivalry was not new: it went back centuries. What *was* new at this juncture, however, was the growing intervention of modern states across the world – the Ottoman state, like the United States of America, and others – in issuing passports, determining residency rights, and controlling borders in a mid- to late nineteenth-century era of massive migration.[228]

In other ways, nineteenth-century reforms meant that religion stopped mattering as much as it had done. This process arguably began in 1829, in a way that was at once dramatic and mundane, with Mahmud II's headgear reform, a leveling measure that put the same type of hat on the heads of most Muslim, Christian, and Jewish men. The subsequent 1839 and 1856 edicts indirectly set the stage for other changes in clothing, by stressing a culture of parity among Ottoman subjects. To be sure, there was a period of mismatch, when some markers of religion (such as color-coded ribbons on fezzes[229]) persisted, and when, as the historian

Niyazi Berkes put it wryly, "People appeared incognito in apparel of their own invention."[230] Nevertheless, the trend toward convergence persisted, especially among the more prosperous classes of Muslim, Christian, and Jewish men and women, all of whom dressed increasingly like western Europeans.[231] As the nineteenth century proceeded, it became harder to judge the religious identity of a man or woman by taking a swift look at his or her clothing while, as portrait photographs show, changes began to distinguish family members (grandparents, parents, and children) from one generation to another.[232]

There were other spheres of social life in which religion had been important, supposedly stopped being important in the nineteenth century, but remained important nonetheless. The most obvious case in the Ottoman Empire involved military service. Historically, Islamic states had allowed only Muslims to bear arms; indeed, arms-bearing (like horse-riding) was an assumed feature of Muslim control over non-Muslim *dhimmi*s. This part of the social contract "worked" as long as military service was reasonably advantageous for Muslims. But with the rise of its modern conscription army in the early nineteenth century, the Ottoman military became a machine that chewed up and spit out Muslim men. It left Muslim conscripts weakened, maimed, or dead (more often from diseases than from battle wounds), and left families bereft of their labor and income-generating capacity, with little compensation in either wealth or honor to make up for their losses.[233] Military service became so loathed that the mere rumor of a new draft of Muslim men was enough to precipitate the Aleppo riots of 1850.[234] The 1856 Ottoman reform edict addressed this issue, by declaring, again, that "equality of taxes entail[ed] equality of burdens" so that "Christian subjects, as those of other ... sects ... [should, like Muslims] be subject to the obligations of the law of recruitment."[235] But the recruitment of Christians and Jews did not occur: for just as Muslims could not imagine having Christians and Jews in the army, Christians and Jews could not imagine it, either, preferring to pay taxes rather than serve.

As the Tanzimat era drew to a close in the third quarter of the nineteenth century, the Ottoman Empire was changing, but changing to what? The vagueness of this question hints at the depth of the identity crisis that was besetting the empire. During the Tanzimat era, the empire abandoned the emphasis on Islamic tradition and statehood that had long endowed its state with legitimacy through its perceived connection to a tried-and-true past. But what new ideology could sustain a polity that had been forged through coercion and conquest, like all other empires in history? The Ottoman reformers never answered this question convincingly. Nor did the Ottoman state decide how to treat or regard its Muslim and non-Muslim people in practice: were they subjects (whom they could order around) or citizens (who could talk back)? Throughout the Tanzimat period, the Ottoman state also wavered over whether to treat people as individuals, with personal rights (in accordance with Enlightenment ideals), or as members of larger religious collectives (in keeping with established tradition). The elimination of clothing distinctions according to religion may have made it easier to see a man as an individual rather than to read (or to be able to read) him as a "Jew," "Christian," or "Muslim." But in other ways, Ottoman authorities persisted in treating people as parts of collectives, such as when they forced *all* Jews and *all* Muslims to pay indemnities to the Christians of Damascus after the 1860 massacres. Meanwhile, to some degree, reforms may have remained unrealized because Christians and Jews mistrusted the Ottoman state's sudden calls for equality after centuries of official subordination as *dhimmi*s.[236]

Amidst the reforms, Christians and Jews retained their *millet*s as intermediate and collective sources of religious structure and authority. By contrast, Muslims, who had always been much more heterogeneous in practice than the empire's Islamic ideology had acknowledged, did not even have that. By some accounts, this lack of guidance from a no-longer-very-Islamic state left many Muslims feeling unmoored.[237] Meanwhile, with the 1839 and 1856 edicts, Muslims lost even the credential of religious superiority that had traditionally placed them – regardless of their relative wealth – on a rung above all *dhimmi*s. It made matters worse that Christians and Jews were becoming visibly wealthier. Confusion, rootlessness, discontentment, and psychological shock: historians use these words and others to describe the feelings that beset Muslims as the nineteenth century neared its last quarter.[238]

In 1876, against the context of myriad changes, a new sultan named Abdulhamid II ascended to the Ottoman throne. Foreign European observers, and even Ottoman statesmen, knew remarkably little about this man who had grown up in the imperial palace in a state of near-seclusion.[239] Would he stick with the Tanzimat program, observers wondered at the time; would he continue to promote modernizing reforms? Events would soon show that, no, Abdulhamid II would not stick with the Tanzimat program, but yes, he would continue to support modernizing reforms, and especially those that enabled him to tighten his grip over the government, the people, and the lands within his domains. He would do all these things while trying to reaffirm and reassert the Islamic identity of the Ottoman state.

NOTES

1 J.C. Hurewitz, ed., *Diplomacy in the Near and Middle East: A Documentary Record, 1535–1914,* Vol. 1 (Princeton: D. Van Nostrand, 1956), p. 113.

2 M. Şükrü Hanioğlu, *A Brief History of the Late Ottoman Empire* (Princeton: Princeton University Press, 2008), p. 72.

3 Roderic H. Davison, "Turkish Attitudes Concerning Christian-Muslim Equality in the Nineteenth Century," *The American Historical Review,* 59:4 (1954), p. 847. On the larger collection of sacred relics in the palace, see Aydın, *The Sacred Trusts.*

4 Hanioğlu, *A Brief History of the Late Ottoman Empire,* p. 73.

5 Hurewitz, *Diplomacy in the Near and Middle East,* p. 114.

6 Davison, "Turkish Attitudes," p. 847.

7 Hanioğlu, *A Brief History of the Late Ottoman Empire,* pp. 73–74.

8 Roderic H. Davison, *Reform in the Ottoman Empire, 1856–1878* (Princeton: Princeton University Press, 1963), p. 3.

9 Davison, "Turkish Attitudes," pp. 847, 859.

10 Selim Deringil, "'There Is No Compulsion in Religion': On Conversion and Apostasy in the Late Ottoman Empire, 1839–1856," in Selim Deringil, *The Ottomans, the Turks, and World Power Politics: Collected Studies* (Istanbul: Isis Press, 2000), p. 102.

11 Bernard Lewis, *The Emergence of Modern Turkey,* third edition (New York: Oxford University Press, 2002), pp. 165, 170, and 211.

12 Davison, "Turkish Attitudes," p. 848.

13 Davison, *Reform in the Ottoman Empire,* p. 3.

14 Bruce Masters, *Christians and Jews in the Ottoman Arab World: The Roots of Sectarianism* (Cambridge: Cambridge University Press, 2001), p. 139.

15 Norman A. Stillman, "Middle Eastern and North African Jewries Confront Modernity: Orientation, Disorientation, Reorientation," in *Sephardi and Middle Eastern Jewries: History & Culture in the Modern Era,* ed. Harvey E. Goldberg (Bloomington: Indiana University Press, 1996), p. 62.

16 Stillman, "Middle Eastern and North African Jewries," p. 60.

17 Quataert, *The Ottoman Empire,* p. 173.

18 Iris Habib el Masri, *The Story of the Copts* (n.p. [Beirut]: The Middle East Council of Churches, 1978), p. 507; Hasan, *Christians versus Muslims in Modern Egypt,* pp. 33–34.

19 Julia Phillips Cohen, *Becoming Ottomans: Sephardi Jews and Imperial Citizenship in the Modern Era* (Oxford: Oxford University Press, 2014), p. xii–xiii, 1, 4. See also Moshe Ma'oz, "Changing Relations between Jews, Muslims, and Christians during the Nineteenth Century, with Special Reference to Ottoman Syria and Palestine," in *Jews, Turks, Ottomans: A Shared History, Fifteenth through the Twentieth Century,* ed. Avigdor Levy (Syracuse: Syracuse University Press, 2002), pp. 108–18; and Gudrun Krämer, "Moving out of Place: Minorities in Middle Eastern Urban Societies, 1800–1914," in *The Urban Social History of the Middle East, 1750–1950,* ed. Peter Sluglett (Syracuse: Syracuse University Press, 2008), p. 221.

20 Compare, for example, Joshua Schreier, *Arabs of the Jewish Faith: The Civilizing Mission in Colonial Algeria* (New Brunswick: Rutgers University

Press, 2010), p. 11, with Masters, *Christians and Jews in the Ottoman Arab World*, p. 158. The term "triumphalist architecture" comes from Bernard Heyberger, who contrasted nineteenth-century Levantine churches with the much more modest churches of earlier centuries. Heyberger, *Les Chrétiens du Proche-Orient au temps de la Réforme Catholique*, p. 57.

21 Dominique Jarrassé, "Synagogues in the Islamic World," in *A History of Jewish-Muslim Relations from the Origins to the Present Day*, ed. Abdelwahab Meddeb and Benjamin Stora, trans. Jane Marie Todd and Michael B. Smith (Princeton: Princeton University Press, 2013), pp. 911–921, see especially pp. 912–13, 920.

22 Heyberger, *Les Chrétiens du Proche-Orient au temps de la Réforme Catholique*, pp. 58–59; Masters, *Christians and Jews in the Ottoman Arab World*, pp. 159, 162.

23 Suraiya Faroqhi, "Introduction," in *The Illuminated Table, the Prosperous House*, ed. Suraiya Faroqhi and Chrisoph K. Neumann (Würzburg: Ergon Verlag Würzburg, 2003), p. 22. On the evolving concept of "alla franca," see Hanioğlu, *A Brief History of the Late Ottoman Empire*, p. 100.

24 Berkes, *The Development of Secularism in Modern Turkey*, p. 122; François Georgeon, "Ottomans and Drinkers: The Consumption of Alcohol in Istanbul in the Nineteenth Century," in *Outside In: On the Margins of the Modern Middle East*, ed. Eugene Rogan (London: I.B. Tauris, 2002), p. 15.

25 Jennifer Scarce, *Women's Costume of the Near and Middle East* (London: Unwin Hyman, 1987), pp. 66–67.

26 Wendy M. K. Shaw, "From Mausoleum to Museum: Resurrecting Antiquity for Ottoman Modernity," in *Scramble for the Past: A Story of Archaeology in the Ottoman Empire, 1753–1914*, ed. Zainab Bahrani, Zeynep Çelik, and Edhem Eldem (Istanbul: SALT, 2011), pp. 423–31.

27 Zainab Bahrani, Zeynep Çelik, and Edhem Eldem, "Introduction: Archaeology and Empire," in Bahrani et al., *Scramble for the Past*, pp. 15–16, 32–33, 35.

28 Extant scholarship on "Syrian" migration to the Americas has emphasized the importance of Arabic-speaking Christians in this process. In fact, many Jews and Muslims migrated, too, although it appears that some tried to pass as Christians or later assimilated into Christian communities. See Kemal H. Karpat, "The Ottoman Emigration to America, 1860–1914," *International Journal of Middle East Studies*, 17:2 (1985), p. 182; and Theresa Alfaro-Velcamp, *So Far from Allah, So Close to Mexico: Middle Eastern Immigrants in Modern Mexico* (Austin: University of Texas Press, 2007), passim. Although the first "pioneers" of Lebanese emigration left in 1871, emigration to the Americas only accelerated in the late 1880s. Akram Fouad Khater, *Inventing Home: Emigration, Gender, and the Middle Class in Lebanon, 1870–1920* (Berkeley: University of California Press, 2001), p. 48.

29 Roderic H. Davison, "The Effect of the Electric Telegraph on the Conduct of Ottoman Foreign Relations," in *Nineteenth-Century Ottoman Diplomacy and Reforms* (Istanbul: Isis Press, 1999), pp. 371–83.

30 Hanioğlu, *A Brief History of the Late Ottoman Empire*, pp. 28, 105–6.

31 Boyar and Fleet, *A Social History of Ottoman Istanbul*, p. 293. On the fork, which was known by eighteenth-century Polish aristocratic visitors to

Istanbul, but not by their Ottoman hosts, see Darius Kolodziejczyk, "Polish Embassies in Istanbul, or How to Sponge on Your Host without Losing Your Self-Esteem," in *The Illuminated Table, the Prosperous House*, ed. Faroqhi and Neumann, pp. 51–58.

32 Nancy Micklewright, "Women's Dress in Nineteenth-Century Istanbul: Mirror of a Changing Society," PhD diss., University of Pennsylvania, 1986, pp. 146–47, 156–57, 192, 206, 208.

33 Virginia H. Aksan, "Ottoman Military Recruitment Strategies in the Late Eighteenth Century," in *Arming the State: Military Conscription in the Middle East and Central Asia, 1775–1925*, ed. Erik J. Zürcher (London: I.B. Tauris, 1999), pp. 24–25.

34 Quataert, *The Ottoman Empire, 1700–1922*, p. 135.

35 Davide Rodogno, *Against Massacre: Humanitarian Interventions in the Ottoman Empire, 1815–1914: The Emergence of a European Concept and International Practice* (Princeton: Princeton University Press, 2012). The *Oxford English Dictionary* cites an example from 1850 for the earliest use in English of the word "humanitarianism," meaning "concern for human welfare as a primary or pre-eminent moral good." "Humanitarianism," *Oxford English Dictionary Online*, July 2012.

36 Khaled Fahmy, *All the Pasha's Men: Mehmed Ali, His Army, and the Making of Modern Egypt* (Cambridge: Cambridge University Press, 1997).

37 Heather J. Sharkey, "African Colonial States," *The Oxford Handbook of Modern African History*, ed. John Parker and Richard Reid (Oxford: Oxford University Press, 2013), pp. 151–70.

38 Anne Marie Moulin, "The Construction of Disease Transmission in Nineteenth-Century Egypt and the Dialectics of Modernity," in *The Development of Modern Medicine in Non-Western Countries: Historical Perspectives*, ed. Hormoz Ebrahimnejad (London: Routledge, 2009), pp. 42–58, see p. 56.

39 Winfried Baumgart, *The Crimean War, 1853–1856* (London: Arnold, 1999), p. 3.

40 Shaw, *History of the Ottoman Empire and Modern Turkey*, Vol. 1, p. 260.

41 Erik Jan Zürcher, "The Ottoman Conscription System in Theory and Practice, 1844–1918," in *Arming the State: Military Conscription in the Middle East and Central Asia, 1775–1925*, ed. Erik J. Zürcher (London: I.B. Tauris, 1999), p. 79.

42 Shaw, *History of the Ottoman Empire and Modern Turkey*, Vol. 1, p. 241.

43 Shaw, *History of the Ottoman Empire and Modern Turkey*, Vol. 1, p. 265. See also Hanioğlu, *A Brief History of the Late Ottoman Empire*, p. 44.

44 Roderic Davison, "The *Millets* as Agents of Change in the Nineteenth-Century Ottoman Empire," in Davison, *Nineteenth-Century Ottoman Diplomacy and Reforms*, pp. 413–14. The father of the bride was Istefanaki Vogorides, who features prominently in Christine M. Philliou, *Biography of an Empire: Governing Ottomans in an Age of Revolution* (Berkeley: University of California Press, 2011).

45 Boyar and Fleet, *A Social History of Ottoman Istanbul*, p. 286.

46 Reşat Kasaba, *The Ottoman Empire in the World Economy: The Nineteenth Century* (Albany: State University of New York Press, 1988), pp. 102–3;

Donald Quataert, "Clothing Laws, State, and Society in the Ottoman Empire, 1720–1829," *International Journal of Middle East Studies*, 29 (1997), pp. 414–16; Abdul-Karim Rafeq, "Craft Organization, Work Ethics, and the Strain of Change in Ottoman Syria," *Journal of the American Oriental Society*, 111:3 (1991), p. 509; and Bruce Masters, "The 1850 Events in Aleppo: An Aftershock of Syria's Incorporation into the Capitalist World System," *International Journal of Middle East Studies*, 22 (1990), pp. 4, 13, 16. One can identify a similar pattern in this period among the Druze of Mount Lebanon as well: Leila Tarazi Fawaz, *An Occasion for War: Civil Conflict in Lebanon and Damascus in 1860* (London: I.B. Tauris, 1994), pp. 24–25.

47 David Roessel, *In Byron's Shadow: Modern Greece in the English and American Imagination* (New York: Oxford University Press, 2001); Henry Laurens, "La projection chrétienne de l'Europe industrielle sur les provinces arabes de l'Empire ottoman," in *Le choc colonial et l'islam: les politiques religieuses des puissances coloniales en terres d'islam*, ed. Pierre-Jean Luizard (Paris: La Découverte, 2006), p. 44.

48 Kasaba, *The Ottoman Empire in the World Economy*, pp. 29–31.

49 Rodogno, *Against Massacre*, p. 65–67.

50 See, for example, Lewis, *The Jews of Islam*, p. 9.

51 Masters, *Christians and Jews in the Ottoman Arab World*, pp. 106–7.

52 The phrase "sumptuary regime" comes from Zilfi, "Whose Laws?," pp. 125–41; Masters, *Christians and Jews in the Ottoman Arab World*, p. 107.

53 Masters, *Christians and Jews in the Ottoman Arab World*, pp. 107–12.

54 Masters, "Christians in a Changing World," p. 278. On the emergence of this shared Arab nationalism, see Albert Hourani's now-classic work, *Arabic Thought in the Liberal Age*.

55 Berkes, *The Development of Secularism in Turkey*, pp. 118, 128.

56 On the shift toward reading European-language books and translations, see Hanioğlu, *A Brief History of the Late Ottoman Empire*, pp. 63–64.

57 Berkes, *The Development of Secularism in Turkey*, p. 128.

58 Arynne Wexler, "Clash between Europe and the Ottoman Empire: How Percussive Instruments Set the Beat for Ottoman Influence in the 18th and 19th Centuries," *Journal of International Relations*, 17 (2015), pp. 182–93.

59 Aron Rodrigue, *French Jews, Turkish Jews: The Alliance Israélite Universelle and the Politics of Jewish Schooling in Turkey, 1860–1925* (Bloomington: Indiana University Press, 1990), p. 26.

60 Mark Mazower, *Salonica, City of Ghosts: Christians, Muslims, and Jews, 1430–1950* (New York: Alfred A. Knopf, 2005), p. 54.

61 Rodrigue, *French Jews, Turkish Jews*, p. 27.

62 Rodrigue, *French Jews, Turkish Jews*, p. 27.

63 Quataert, "Clothing Laws, State, and Society in the Ottoman Empire," pp. 404, 420.

64 Hanioğlu, *A Brief History of the Late Ottoman Empire*, p. 59.

65 Gábor Ágoston, "Grand Vizier," in *Encyclopedia of the Ottoman Empire*, ed. Gábor Ágoston and Bruce Masters (New York: Facts on File, 2009), pp. 235–36; Carter V. Findley, *Bureaucratic Reform in the Ottoman Empire: The Sublime Porte, 1789–1922* (Princeton: Princeton University Press, 1980), pp. 5–6.

66 Quataert, *The Ottoman Empire*, p. 64. He added, "The number of civil officials that totaled perhaps 2,000 persons at the end of the eighteenth century, reached 35,000 in 1908, virtually all of them males (p. 63)."
67 John Bartlett, *Bartlett's Familiar Quotations*, gen. ed. Justin Kaplan, seventeenth edition (Boston: Little, Brown, 2002), p. 563.
68 Mark Twain, *Innocents Abroad, or the New Pilgrim's Progress* (Hartford, CT: American Publishing Company, 1869).
69 Edhem Eldem, *Death in Istanbul: Death and Its Rituals in Ottoman-Islamic Culture* (Istanbul: Ottoman Bank Archives and Research Centre, 2005), p. 52.
70 Quataert, *The Ottoman Empire*, p. 65.
71 Quataert, "Clothing Laws," pp. 417–18.
72 Elliot, "Dress Codes in the Ottoman Empire," p. 117.
73 See, for example, Charles Issawi, *An Economic History of the Middle East and North Africa* (New York: Columbia University Press, 1982), p. 89; and Kasaba, *The Ottoman Empire in the World Economy*, pp. 28, 102.
74 Esther Juhasz, *Sephardi Jews in the Ottoman Empire: Aspects of Material Culture* (Jerusalem: Israel Museum, 1990), pp. 130–31.
75 Fr. Babinger, "Kalpak," in *E.J. Brill's First Encyclopaedia of Islam, 1913–1936*, ed. M. Th. Houtsma, Vol. 4 (Leiden: E.J. Brill, 1993), p. 701.
76 Elliot, "Dress Codes in the Ottoman Empire," pp. 105–6.
77 Baki Tezcan, "Ethnicity, Race, Religion and Social Class: Ottoman Markers of Difference," in *The Ottoman World*, ed. Christine Woodhead (London: Routledge, 2012), pp. 166–68.
78 Ma'oz, "Changing Relations between Jews, Muslims, and Christians during the Nineteenth Century," p. 114.
79 Donald Quataert, "Introduction," in *Consumption Studies and the History of the Ottoman Empire: An Introduction*, ed. Donald Quataert (Albany: State University of New York Press, 2000), p. 10.
80 Zilfi, "Whose Laws?," p. 129; Micklewright, "Women's Dress."
81 Juhasz, *Sephardi Jews in the Ottoman Empire*, p. 127.
82 Osman Hamdy [sic] Bey and Marie de Launay, *Les costumes populaires de la Turquie en 1873: Ouvrage publié sous le patronage de la Commission impériale ottomane pour l'Exposition universelle de Vienne* (Constantinople: Levant Times & Shipping Gazette, 1873), Plate 36 and pp. 285–485; Juhasz, *Sephardi Jews in the Ottoman Empire*, p. 141.
83 Zilfi, "Whose Laws?," p. 136.
84 Berkes, *The Development of Secularism in Turkey*, p. 122.
85 Philip Mansel, *Dressed to Rule: Royal and Court Costume from Louis XIV to Elizabeth II* (New Haven: Yale University Press, 2005), p. 39.
86 Jirousek, "The Transition to Mass Fashion System Dress in the Later Ottoman Empire," in Quataert, *Consumption Studies*, p. 237.
87 Hanioğlu, *A Brief History of the Late Ottoman Empire*, p. 62.
88 Berkes, *The Development of Secularism in Turkey*, pp. 115–16; and R. Ballestriero, "Anatomical Models and Wax Venuses: Art Masterpieces or Scientific Art Works?," *Journal of Anatomy*, 216:2 (2010), pp. 223–34; and J. C. Chen, A. P. Amar, M. L. Levy, and M. L. Apuzzo, "The Development of Anatomic Art and Sciences: The Ceroplastica Anatomical Models of La Specola," *Neurosurgery*, 45:4 (1999), pp. 883–91.

89 Helen Macdonald, *Human Remains: Dissection and Its Histories* (New Haven: Yale University Press, 2005), p. 2.
90 Rudolph Peters, *Crime and Punishment in Islamic Law: Theory and Practice from the Sixteenth to the Twenty-First Century* (Cambridge: Cambridge University Press, 2006), p. 178; Timur Kuran and Scott Lustig, "Judicial Biases in Ottoman Istanbul: Islamic Justice and Its Compatibility with Modern Economic Life," *Journal of Law and Economics*, 55:3 (2012), pp. 631–66; see especially 647–48.
91 Gulian Lansing, *Egypt's Princes: A Narrative of Missionary Labor in the Valley of the Nile*, second edition (Philadelphia: William S. Rentoul, 1864), p. 36.
92 Jane S. Gerber, *Jewish Society in Fez, 1450–1700: Studies in Communal and Economic Life* (Leiden: E.J. Brill, 1980); Emily Gottreich, *The Mellah of Marrakesh: Jewish and Muslim Space in Morocco's Red City* (Bloomington: Indiana University Press, 2007).
93 Hurewitz, *Diplomacy in the Near and Middle East*, p. 151.
94 Hurewitz, *Diplomacy in the Near and Middle East*, p. 149.
95 Custodia Terrae Sanctae (Franciscan Missionaries Serving the Holy Land), "'Opening' of Church of the Holy Sepulchre," www.sepulchre.custodia.org/default.asp?id=4127 (accessed April 27, 2016).
96 Baumgart, *The Crimean War*, pp. 10, 12.
97 The term "prodding" comes from Hurewitz, *Diplomacy in the Near and Middle East*, p. 149. The other terms come from Berkes, *The Development of Secularism in Modern Turkey*, p. 152.
98 Mehmet Ali Doğan, "From New England into New Lands: The Beginning of a Long Story," in *American Missionaries and the Middle East: Foundational Encounters*, ed. Mehmet Ali Doğan and Heather J. Sharkey (Salt Lake City: University of Utah Press, 2011), pp. 3–32.
99 Chantal Verdeil, "Introduction: La mission en terre de l'Islam dans le renouveau de l'histoire missionaire," in *Missions chrétiennes en terre d'islam, Moyen-Orient, Afrique du Nord (XVIIe-XXe siècles): Anthologie de textes missionnaires*, ed. Chantal Verdeil (Turnhout, Belgium: Brepols, 2013), pp. 5–59. There were occasional exceptions of Catholic missionaries who did aspire to the conversion of Muslims, such as French Lazarists who were active in Damascus in the 1870s. See Jérôme Bocquet, "Le rôle des missions catholiques dans la fondation d'un nouveau réseau d'institutions éducatives au Moyen-Orient arabe," in Luizard, *Le choc colonial et l'Islam*, p. 334.
100 For an articulation of such ideas about Eastern Christianity, see, for example, this work by a German missionary: Julius Richter, *A History of Protestant Missions in the Near East* (New York: Fleming H. Revell, 1910), pp. 36, 62.
101 Friedmann, *Tolerance and Coercion in Islam*.
102 Eugene Stock, *The History of the Church Missionary Society: Its Environment, Its Men, and Its Work*, Vol. 2 (London: Church Missionary Society, 1899), p. 149.
103 For citations of this correspondence, see Robert E. Speer, *Christianity and the Nations* (New York: Fleming H. Revell, 1910), pp. 228–29; and Stock, *The History of the Church Missionary Society*, Vol. 2, pp. 149–50.

104 Stock, *The History of the Church Missionary Society*, Vol. 2, p. 148.

105 Bernard Lewis, *The Crisis of Islam: Holy War and Unholy Terror* (New York: Modern Library, 2003), pp. 50–51; Heather J. Sharkey, "A New Crusade or an Old One?," *ISIM Newsletter* (Leiden: International Institute for the Study of Islam in the Modern World), 12 (June 2003), pp. 48–49.

106 Hurewitz, *Diplomacy in the Near and Middle East*, Vol. 1, p. 151.

107 Heather J. Sharkey, *American Evangelicals in Egypt: Missionary Encounters in an Age of Empire* (Princeton: Princeton University Press, 2008), pp. 55–58.

108 Stock, *The History of the Church Missionary Society*, Vol. 2, p. 151.

109 Masters, *Christians and Jews in the Ottoman Arab World*, pp. 137–39.

110 Viscount Stratford de Redcliffe to the Earl of Malmesbury, Constantinople, October 6, 1858, Document #10 in Kenneth Bourne and D. Cameron Watt, eds., *British Documents on Foreign Affairs: Reports and Papers from the Foreign Office Confidential Print*, Part 1: *From the Mid-Nineteenth Century to the First World War*, in David Gillard, ed., Series B: The Near and Middle East, 1856–1914, Vol. 1: *The Ottoman Empire in the Balkans, 1856–1875* (Lanham, MD: University Publications of America, 1984), pp. 18–19.

111 Selim Deringil, *The Well-Protected Domains: Ideology and the Legitimation of Power in the Ottoman Empire, 1876–1909* (London: I.B. Tauris, 1999), p. 91.

112 Sharkey discusses this phenomenon in her book, *American Evangelicals in Egypt*.

113 For a discussion of this point in another context, see Amira El-Azhary Sonbol, *The New Mamluks: Egyptian Society and Modern Feudalism*, foreword by Robert A. Fernea (Syracuse: Syracuse University Press, 2000), p. xxxix.

114 Semerdjian, *"Off the Straight Path,"* p. xix, building on Rafeq, "Public Morality in 18th Century Ottoman Damascus."

115 Ann Elizabeth Mayer, *Islam and Human Rights*, fifth edition (Boulder: Westview Press, 2013).

116 Rodrigue, *French Jews, Turkish Jews*, p. 14.

117 Anh Nga Longva, "From the *Dhimma* to the Capitulations: Memory and Experience of Protection in Lebanon," in *Religious Minorities in the Middle East: Domination, Self-Empowerment, Accommodation*, ed. Anh Nga Longva and Anne Sofie Roald (Leiden: E.J. Brill 2012), p. 51.

118 Lewis, *The Jews of Islam*, p. 36; Masters, *Jews and Christians in the Ottoman Arab World*, p. 22.

119 "The Pact of Umar," in Lewis, ed. and trans., *Islam from the Prophet Muhammad to the Capture of Constantinople*, Vol. 2, p. 218.

120 Bat-Zion Eraqi-Klorman, "Yemen," in *The Jews of the Middle East and North Africa in Modern Times*, ed. Reeva Spector Simon, Michael Menachem Laskier, and Sara Reguer (New York: Columbia University Press, 2003), p. 391.

121 el Masri, *The Story of the Copts*, pp. 501–2.

122 Ian Coller, *Arab France: Islam and the Making of Modern Europe, 1798–1831* (Berkeley: University of California Press, 2011).

123 Makdisi, *The Culture of Sectarianism*, pp. 53–57.

124 Hurewitz, *Diplomacy in the Near and Middle East*, Vol. 1, p. 152.

125 Richard Bellamy, *Citizenship: A Very Short Introduction* (Oxford: Oxford University Press, 2008), pp. 114–15.
126 Zürcher, "The Ottoman Conscription System in Theory and Practice," p. 89.
127 Jan Lucassen and Erik Jan Zürcher, "Introduction: Conscription and Resistance: The Historical Context," in *Arming the State: Military Conscription in the Middle East and Central Asia, 1775–1925*, ed. Erik J. Zürcher (London: I.B. Tauris, 1999), pp. 1–20.
128 Quataert, *The Ottoman Empire*, p. 63.
129 Even Muhammad Ali of Egypt, in the 1820s and 1830s, had raided non-Muslim areas of what is now Sudan and South Sudan, in order to seize men as slaves for his military.
130 Lucassen and Zürcher, "Introduction: Conscription and Resistance," in Zürcher, *Arming the State*, pp. 8–9.
131 Khalid Fahmy, "The Nation and Its Deserters: Conscription in Mehmed Ali's Egypt," in Zürcher, *Arming the State*, pp. 59–77.
132 Fahmy, "The Nation and Its Deserters," p. 72, and Lucasson and Zürcher, "Introduction: Conscription and Resistance," p. 12, both from Zürcher, *Arming the State*.
133 Quataert, *The Ottoman Empire*, pp. 63, 111–12.
134 Zürcher, "The Ottoman Conscription System in Theory and Practice," in Zürcher, *Arming the State*, p. 85.
135 Twenty-four percent (c. 1876) is the figure for Christians cited in Shaw and Shaw, *History of the Ottoman Empire and Modern Turkey*, Vol. 2, p. 240. Zürcher suggests "nearly 30 percent" during the era of Abdulhamid II (r. 1876–1909). Zürcher, "The Ottoman Conscription System in Theory and Practice," p. 88.
136 Zürcher, "The Ottoman Conscription System in Theory and Practice," p. 88.
137 Zürcher, "The Ottoman Conscription System in Theory and Practice," p. 88.
138 Zürcher, "The Ottoman Conscription System in Theory and Practice," pp. 88–89.
139 Maurits H. van den Boogert, "Millets: Past and Present," in Longva and Roald, *Religious Minorities in the Middle East*, p. 38.
140 The same point is made in Hanioğlu, *A Brief History of the Late Ottoman Empire*, p. 90.
141 Davison, "Turkish Attitudes," p. 859.
142 Davison, "The *Millet*s as Agents of Change," pp. 416–17 on agriculture. On this idea of Christian demographic growth, see Thomas, "Arab Christianity," pp. 19–20.
143 Yaron Ben-Naeh [*sic*], "Jews on the Move during the Late Ottoman Period: Trends and Some Problems," in *A Global Middle East: Mobility, Materiality, and Culture in the Modern Age, 1880–1940*, ed. Liat Kozma, Cyrus Schayegh, and Avner Wishnitzer (London: I.B. Tauris, 2015), 134–62, see pp. 136–37.
144 François Georgeon, *Abdülhamid II: Le sultan calife (1876–1909)* (Paris: Libraire Arthème Fayard, 2003), p. 106.
145 This analysis of the Aleppo riot draws upon Masters, "The 1850 Events in Aleppo"; see p. 17, footnote 2 on the casualties.

146 Masters, "The 1850 Events in Aleppo," p. 4.
147 Masters, "The 1850 Events in Aleppo," p. 12.
148 Masters, "The 1850 Events in Aleppo," pp. 13–14.
149 Masters, "The 1850 Events in Aleppo," pp. 16–17.
150 Kais M. Firro, *A History of the Druzes* (Leiden: E.J. Brill, 1992), pp. 20–23.
151 Fawaz, *An Occasion for War*, p. 15.
152 Fawaz, *An Occasion for War*, p. 15.
153 Khater, *Inventing Home*, p. 23.
154 Makdisi, *The Culture of Sectarianism*, p. 34.
155 Khater, *Inventing Home*, pp. 20, 41; Makdisi, *The Culture of Sectarianism*, p. 34.
156 Laurens, "La projection chrétienne," p. 51. On the growth of French mission school network in greater Syria and Egypt during the nineteenth century, see Bocquet, "Le rôle des missions catholiques dans la fondation d'un nouveau réseau d'institutions éducatives au Moyen-Orient arabe," in Luizard, *Le choc colonial et l'islam*, pp. 327–42.
157 Khater, *Inventing Home*, p. 27.
158 Ahmad Beydoun, "Movements of the Past and Deadlocks of the Present: Did the Violence of the Nineteenth Century Generate a Society Prone to Civil War?," in *Breaking the Cycle: Civil Wars in Lebanon*, ed. Youssef M. Choueri (London: Stacey International, 2007), p. 4; Fawaz, *An Occasion for War*, p. 24.
159 Meir Zamir, *The Formation of Modern Lebanon* (London: Croom Helm, 1985), pp. 5, 8.
160 Dale, *The Muslim Empires of the Ottomans, Safavids, and Mughals*, p. 56.
161 Eugene L. Rogan, "Sectarianism and Social Conflict in Damascus: The 1860 Events Reconsidered," *Arabica*, 51:4 (2004), p. 498.
162 Makdisi, *The Culture of Sectarianism*, p. 35.
163 Leila Tarazi Fawaz, *Merchants and Migrants in Nineteenth-Century Beirut* (Cambridge, MA: Harvard University Press, 1983), p. 108; Fawaz, *An Occasion for War*, pp. 15–16.
164 Makdisi, *The Culture of Sectarianism*, p. 35.
165 Dionigi Albera and Maria Couroucli, eds., *Sharing Sacred Spaces in the Mediterranean: Christians, Muslims, and Jews at Shrines and Sanctuaries* (Bloomington: Indiana University Press, 2012).
166 Makdisi, *The Culture of Sectarianism*, pp. 69, 88, 91. See also Ussama Makdisi, *Artillery of Heaven: American Missionaries and the Failed Conversion of the Middle East* (Ithaca: Cornell University Press, 2009).
167 Beydoun, "Movements of the Past and Deadlocks of the Present," especially pp. 10–11.
168 Fawaz, *Merchants and Migrants*, pp. 112, 114.
169 Fawaz, *An Occasion for War*, pp. 25, 78–79; Beydoun, "Movements of the Past and Deadlocks of the Present," p. 10.
170 Fawaz, *An Occasion for War*, p. 87.
171 This summary relies on Fawaz, *An Occasion for War*, pp. 84–100. The quotation comes from p. 100.
172 Fawaz, *An Occasion for War*, pp. 89–90.
173 Fawaz, *An Occasion for War*, pp. 139–41, 160.

174 Julia C. Clancy-Smith, *Mediterraneans: North Africa and Europe in an Age of Migration, c. 1800–1900* (Berkeley: University of California Press, 2010).

175 Georges Renauld, *Adolphe Crémieux, Homme d'État Français, Juif, et Franc-maçon: Le combat pour le République* (Paris: Detrad, 2002), p. 14; and Daniel Amson, *Adolphe Crémieux: L'Oublié de la Gloire* (Paris: Éditions du Seuil, 1988), pp. 13–18.

176 These optimistic ideas were reflected in the Alliance Israélite Universelle, which Crémieux helped to establish. Rodrigue, *French Jews, Turkish Jews*, p. 138; and on the tensions with Zionism, Michael M. Laskier, *The Alliance Israélite Universelle and the Jewish Communities of Morocco, 1862–1962* (Albany: State University of New York Press, 1983), pp. 194–95.

177 Alyssa Goldstein Sepinwall, *The Abbé Grégoire and the French Revolution: The Making of Modern Universalism* (Berkeley: University of California Press, 2005), pp. 90–91.

178 Michel Winock, *La France et les juifs de 1789 à nos jours* (Paris: Éditions du Seuil, 2004), p. 11.

179 David S. Katz, *Philo-Semitism and the Readmission of the Jews to England, 1603–1655* (Oxford: Clarendon Press, 1982).

180 See, for example, Daniel J. Schroeter, *The Sultan's Jew: Morocco and the Sephardi World* (Stanford: Stanford University Press, 2002), pp. 55–56.

181 Arno J. Mayer, "The Perils of Emancipation: Protestants and Jews," *Archives des sciences sociales des religions*, 90 (1995), pp. 5–37, see p. 9.

182 Jean-Marc Chouraqui, "Les communautés juives face au processus de l'Émancipation: des stratégies centrifuges (1789) au modèle centralisé (1808)," *Rives Nord-méditerranéennes*, 14 (2003), http://rives.revues.org/407 (accessed November 29, 2012), see paragraph 6 for the source of the quotation. This article discusses the various arrangements of the revolutionary French state with Jews who were living in France.

183 Michael Graetz, *Les Juifs en France au XIXe Siécle: de la Révolution française à l'Alliance Israélite Universelle*, trans. Salomon Malka (Paris: Éditions Seuil, 1989), pp. 63–65.

184 Shmuel Feiner, *The Jewish Enlightenment*, trans. Chaya Naor (Philadelphia: University of Pennsylvania Press, 2004), pp. xii, 1–2.

185 Winock, *Le France et les juifs de 1789 à nos jours*, p. 24.

186 The first quotation comes from Chouraqui, "Les communautés juives face au processus de l'Émancipation," paragraph 53; the second from Sepinwall, *The Abbé Grégoire and the French Revolution*, p. 95.

187 Winock, *Le France et les juifs de 1789 à nos jours*, p. 27.

188 Walter Laqueur, *The Changing Face of Antisemitism: From Ancient Times to the Present Day* (Oxford: Oxford University Press, 2006), pp. 4, 21, 55–57.

189 Jonathan Frankel, *The Damascus Affair: "Ritual Murder," Politics, and the Jews in 1840* (Cambridge: Cambridge University Press, 1997), p. 20.

190 Frankel, *The Damascus Affair*, p. 60.

191 Laqueur, *The Changing Face of Antisemitism*, pp. 56–57.

192 Richard Urban Butler, "St. Hugh," *The Catholic Encyclopedia*, Vol. 7 (New York: Robert Appleton, 1910), www.newadvent.org/cathen/07515b.htm (accessed December 4, 2012).

193 Mary C. Wilson, "The Damascus Affair and the Beginnings of France's Empire in the Middle East," in *Histories of the Modern Middle East: New Directions*, ed. Israel Gershoni, Hakan Erdem, and Ursula Wocöck (Boulder: Lynne Rienner, 2002), pp. 63–74, see p. 65.

194 Frankel, *The Damascus Affair*, pp. 37–40.

195 Frankel, *The Damascus Affair*, p. 151.

196 Wilson, "The Damascus Affair and the Beginnings of France's Empire in the Middle East," p. 64.

197 Wilson, "The Damascus Affair and the Beginnings of France's Empire in the Middle East," pp. 69–70.

198 Frankel, *The Damascus Affair*, pp. 60–62; see also Moshe Ma'oz, "Changing Relations between Jews, Muslims, and Christians during the Nineteenth Century, with Special Reference to Ottoman Syria and Palestine," in *Jews, Turks, Ottomans: A Shared History, Fifteenth through the Twentieth Century*, ed. Avigdor Levy (Syracuse: Syracuse University Press, 2002), pp. 108–18.

199 Frankel, *The Damascus Affair*, p. 5.

200 Rodrigue, *French Jews, Turkish Jews*, pp. 1–3.

201 Rodrigue, *French Jews, Turkish Jews*, p. 3.

202 Winock, *La France et les juifs de 1789 à nos jours*, pp. 53–55.

203 David I. Kertzer, *The Kidnapping of Edgardo Mortara* (New York: Alfred Knopf, 1997).

204 Rodgrigue, *French Jews, Turkish Jews*, p. xii.

205 Élizabeth Antébi, *Les Missionaires Juifs de la France, 1860–1939* (Paris: Calmann-Lévy, 1999), pp. 11–12.

206 Laskier, *The Alliance Israélite Universelle*, p. 3.

207 Gottreich, *The Mellah of Marrakesh*, p. 89.

208 Rodrigue, *French Jews, Turkish Jews*, p. 119.

209 Rodrigue, *French Jews, Turkish Jews*, p. 119; Laskier, *The Alliance Israélite Universelle*, p. 271.

210 Eldem, *Death in Istanbul*, on Muslims; Juhasz, *Sephardi Jews in the Ottoman Empire*, p. 61.

211 Hary, *Multiglossia in Judeo-Arabic*; Moshe Bar-Asher, *La composante hebraïque du judeo-arabe algerien (communautés de Tlemcen et Aïn-Témouchent)* (Jerusalem: Hebrew University, 1992).

212 Keith Walters, "Education for Jewish Girls in Late Nineteenth- and Early Twentieth-Century Tunis and the Spread of French in Tunisia," in *Jewish Culture and Society in North Africa*, ed. Emily Benichou Gottreich and Daniel J. Schroeter (Bloomington: Indiana University Press, 2011), pp. 257–81.

213 Said, *Orientalism*.

214 As Emily Gottreich noted along these lines in a study of Marrakesh, it was "what Jews wore on their feet (more generally, who could wear shoes of what kind where) ... that serve[d] as an uncanny indicator of the state of Jewish-Muslim relations at any given moment." Gottreich, *The Mellah of Marrakesh*, p. 94.

215 Joëlle Allouche-Benayoun, "Les enjeux de la naturalisation des Juifs d'Algérie: du dhimmi au citoyen," in Luizard, *Le choc colonial et l'islam*, pp. 179, 188.

216 Schreier, *Arabs of the Jewish Faith*, pp. 2, 11.

217 Benjamin Stora, *Les Trois Exils: Juifs d'Algérie* (Paris: Stock, 2006).

218 Gregory Mann, "What Was the *Indigénat*? The 'Empire of Law' in French West Africa," *Journal of African History*, 50 (2009), pp. 331–53, see p. 333.

219 Schreier, *Arabs of the Jewish Faith*, p. 7.

220 Berkes, *The Development of Secularism in Turkey*, pp. 149–50, on Canning; Rodogno, *Against Massacre*, p. 11.

221 Allouche-Benayoun, "Les enjeux de la naturalisation des Juifs d'Algérie," p. 184.

222 Laskier, *The Alliance Israélite Universelle and the Jewish Communities of Morocco*, pp. 168–71.

223 David Cohen, "Algeria," in Simon, Laskier, and Reguer, *The Jews of the Middle East and North Africa in Modern Times* (New York: Columbia University Press, 2003), p. 463.

224 Benjamin Stora, "The Crémieux Decree," in Meddeb and Stora, *A History of Jewish-Muslim Relations from the Origins to the Present Day*, pp. 286–91, see especially p. 291.

225 Rogan, "Sectarianism and Social Conflict in Damascus," pp. 493–94, 507–8.

226 Krämer, "Moving out of Place," p. 218. On churches, see Heyberger, *Les Chrétiens du Proche-Orient au temps de la Réforme Catholique*, p. 57.

227 Karen M. Kern, "Rethinking Ottoman Frontier Policies: Marriage and Citizenship in the Province of Iraq," *Arab Studies Journal*, 25:1 (2007), pp. 8–29; and Karen Kern, *Imperial Citizenship: Marriage and Citizenship in the Ottoman Frontier Provinces of Iraq* (Syracuse: Syracuse University Press, 2011).

228 See Ian Goldin, Geoffrey Cameron, and Meera Balarajan, *Exceptional People: How Migration Shaped Our World and Will Define Our Future* (Princeton: Princeton University Press, 2011). They describe the period from 1840 to 1914 as the "age of mass migration" (p. 58) that prompted states to seek regulation. They do not explicitly mention the Ottoman Empire, but its regulatory behavior fits this pattern perfectly. On the rise of documentation and rights for traveling across borders or staying put within them, see Will Hanley, "Papers for Going, Papers for Staying: Identification and Subject Formation in the Eastern Mediterranean," in Kozma, Schayegh, and Wishnitzer, *A Global Middle East*, pp. 177–200.

229 Juhasz, *Sephardi Jews in the Ottoman Empire*, pp. 130–31.

230 Berkes, *The Development of Secularism in Turkey*, p. 124.

231 Stillman, *Arab Dress*, pp. 161–63.

232 See, for example, the family photographs in Musée d'Histoire d'Art et d'Histoire du Judaisme, *Juifs d'Algérie* (Paris: Skira Flammarion, 2012); and Léone Jaffin, *Algérie Aimée: Mes souvenirs et 222 recettes de là-bas!* (Paris: Le Courrier du Livre, 2012).

233 Zürcher, "The Ottoman Conscription System in Theory and Practice."

234 Masters, "The 1850 Events in Aleppo," p. 5.

235 Hurewitz, *Diplomacy in the Near and Middle East*, Vol. 1, p. 152.

236 See also Davison, "Turkish Attitudes," p. 853; Quataert, "Clothing Laws, State, and Society in the Ottoman Empire," p. 420; Berkes, *The Development of Secularism in Turkey*, pp. 158–59, 202, 204–5.

237 Berkes, *The Development of Secularism in Turkey*, pp. 158–59.

238 Davison, "Turkish Attitudes," p. 856.

239 Georgeon, *Abdülhamid II*, pp. 24, 54–55.

5 The Pivotal Era of Abdulhamid II, 1876–1909

Introduction: Setting the Tone

In 1880, the archaeologist Henry Layard (1817–94), who three decades earlier had excavated the ancient Assyrian city at Nimrud (now in Iraq), was serving as Britain's ambassador to the Ottoman Empire. One day, Layard recalled, he entered the Ottoman palace of Yildiz for an audience with Sultan Abdulhamid II (r. 1876–1909), to find the latter scrutinizing rules for the cabarets of Istanbul's Pera district. When Layard expressed astonishment that the sultan should bother with such a triviality, rather than leave the task to a secretary, Abdulhamid II replied that there was no one whom he could trust with such a matter.[1]

Layard's anecdote captured an important aspect of Abdulhamid II's personality, which set the tone for his reign. Namely, the sultan was a micro-manager and workaholic who sifted through mounds of paperwork, reportedly up to 1,200 papers a day, attending to the minutest details of his empire.[2] Abdulhamid II was also mistrustful – the word that now hovers around him is "paranoid" – and used the powers of his modernizing state to construct an elaborate spy network and surveillance system in order to monitor and control what was happening in his realm.[3] His paranoia extended even to the coffee that he drank in profusion: he insisted on watching his servants prepare each cup, to make sure that no one could poison him.[4]

Abdulhamid II struggled during his reign with a fear of untimely death. It was not just that both of Abdulhamid II's parents had died of tuberculosis, or that sixteen of his twenty-two sisters and six of his own thirteen daughters died young, mostly from endemic childhood diseases like diphtheria. It was also that the two sultans who preceded him had met such bad ends. His uncle, Sultan Abdulaziz (r. 1861–76), either slashed his own wrists with scissors (as the official autopsy report claimed),[5] or was the victim of a murder staged to look like a suicide, as many observers believed at the time. The Paris correspondent of the *New York Times*, for example, reported Abdulaziz's death in 1876 as an "assassination" that "caused no surprise ... since everyone [had] expected it" as part of a *coup d'état* to unseat this sultan, who had persisted in financial recklessness even as a budgetary crisis loomed.[6] After Abdulaziz's death, Abdulhamid II's older brother ruled as Murad IV for a few months before a nervous breakdown prompted advisors (possibly egged on by Abdulhamid II himself) to dethrone him on grounds of insanity. Abdulhamid II had still other reasons for worry. Looking beyond Ottoman borders, to the north, east, and west, he followed with dread the assassinations that successively felled Alexander II (1881) of Russia, Nasir al-Din Shah (1896) of Iran, James A. Garfield (1881) and William McKinley (1901) of the United States, Empress Elizabeth ("Sisi") (1898) of Austria, King Umberto of Italy (1900), and other leaders of this era.[7] Seeking protection from personal attack, Abdulhamid II hunkered down on the outskirts of Istanbul, in his palace at Yildiz. He rarely ventured beyond its walls without taking elaborate security precautions that included sweeping roads for bombs and sending male and female informants into buildings that abutted the scheduled routes of his excursions, which included a weekly Friday trip to the mosque.[8]

Abdulhamid II came to the throne just as the Ottoman state was defaulting on foreign loans that his immediate predecessors had accumulated. These loans had funded such things as Dolmabahçe Palace in Istanbul, which boasted the largest and heaviest crystal chandelier in the world, weighing over four tons.[9] And yet Abdulhamid II himself was thrifty. He insisted, for example, on marketing the wool from sheep that grazed on his fields at Yildiz, as well as white lead (a paint ingredient) mined from his soil. With the help of his Greek agent, and using his own funds, he amassed a tidy fortune through speculation in Istanbul markets.[10] For relaxation in odd hours, he dabbled in gardening and watercolor painting, or did carpentry in his workshop, where he enjoyed constructing exotic wood desks and tables inlaid with mother of pearl. With his do-it-yourself ethos, relentless work schedule, and enthusiasm for personal money making, Abdulhamid II would have excelled as a Wall Street tycoon if he had lived under different circumstances in New York City half a century later.

Who was this man – this Ottoman sultan, spymaster, woodworker, wool-seller, and private investor? British and French politicians of the period described him as an advocate of "pan-Islam" – an ideology promoting political unity among all Muslims everywhere – who was ready to take any means, including war in the guise of jihad, to rally Muslims worldwide against Christian peoples and powers. The critics who hated him most eventually dubbed him the "Monster of Yildiz" and the "Red Sultan," suggesting that he was bloodthirsty, or had blood on his hands, particularly in relation to attacks on Armenian Christians that accelerated during his reign in the 1890s. Either way, pan-Islamic jihadist or red-monster sultan, such portrayals have made Sultan Abdulhamid II seem like a puppet master who pulled the strings of major events of his reign.

But how much did Abdulhamid II actually control? For example, to what extent did he support or abet in the violence of the 1890s that struck small contingents of Armenian nationalist militants, along with much larger populations of unarmed Armenian men, women, and children, who were simply trying to get on with their lives? The French historian François Georgeon, who set his magisterial and meticulously researched biography of Abdulhamid II (published in 2003) against the panorama of the times, concluded that the man was a puzzle: too private, and too secretive, to fathom.[11] One of Abdulhamid II's contemporaries, the Egyptian intellectual Ibrahim al-Muwaylihi (1844–1906) who spent time in Istanbul during the early 1890s, explained his mindset more simply. "It is almost as if he thinks some trap has been set for him with every single step he takes," so that "all the energy he does devote to state matters is actually intended to protect himself" and not his people or the empire at large. But the sultan's paranoia backfired, Muwaylihi suggested, because his spies fabricated stories with abandon in order to justify their jobs and win promotions.[12] The barrage of their bogus intelligence reports left the sultan numb and blind to what was really going on.

What is certainly clear is that during his reign, which lasted from 1876 to 1909, Abdulhamid II assumed close direction over the Ottoman state, and promoted a Sunni Muslim official culture. He did so by emphasizing the empire's affinity to the Arabic-speaking territories where Islam had historically emerged; by sponsoring the construction of a railway for transporting Muslim pilgrims from Damascus, through the western Arabian desert, to Mecca and Medina; and by promoting the inculcation of Sunni Muslim doctrines and practices among some of the empire's non-Christian, non-Jewish, and therefore ostensibly Muslim populations whose various religious practices were distinctive enough to call their Islam into question. He consolidated control where he could, even as the empire lost its hold over some lands inhabited primarily by Muslims. Notable in this regard were Tunisia and Egypt, which France and Britain quasi-officially grabbed or, to use the colonial lingo of the time, "occupied," in 1881 and 1882, respectively.

Observers of the Ottoman past often cite Mehmet II (1432–81), the conqueror of Constantinople, and Suleyman the Magnificent (1494–1566), the besieger of Vienna, as contenders for the title of most powerful Ottoman sultan in history. Abdulhamid II belongs in this lineup, too – even if he reigned over an empire that was losing territories around its edges. In contrast to the sultans of the mid-nineteenth-century Tanzimat period, who had followed the cues of their reform-minded bureaucrats, Abdulhamid II called the shots. He set policy. He shuffled his ministers, so that no bureaucrat could challenge his power. Though his empire lost some territories, he strengthened its hold over lands that remained. He authorized his underlings to intrude into the daily lives of ordinary people, Ottoman subjects, to a degree unprecedented in history, and the result was that paperwork stacked up on desks all over the empire, including his own. He followed world news closely and attempted to groom the empire's image – for example, by sending a gift of 1,819 photographs of the empire and its modernization projects (schools and military academies, naval frigates, bridges, and whatnot) to the US government, which preserves them as the "Abdul Hamid II Collection" in the Library of Congress.[13] And again, he set the tone for an Ottoman state that was, if not pan-Islamic in the way that some western European governments feared, then decidedly Muslim nonetheless. Critics attested to the grip of his one-man show by devising an adjective from his name, "Hamidian," which they used to describe his reign, as in phrases like "Hamidian despotism" and "Hamidian persecution."[14]

The pages that follow examine the Abdulhamid II period more closely. They consider how the distinctly Muslim tone that Abdulhamid II tried to set was a defensive calculation, designed to bolster Muslim popular support against the context of growing foreign cultural, political, and economic intervention and a string of military defeats. Near zones of conflict along the empire's northern and northwestern perimeters, Muslim-Christian relations grew more tense and fraught during his reign, even as the empire's Muslim population grew proportionally bigger relative to the total Christian population as a result of territorial losses and migrations. By contrast, Muslim-Jewish relations remained steady in the major urban centers of the empire, and Jews persisted as loyal, and increasingly patriotic, Ottoman subjects.[15] This was true even as a new Jewish nationalist movement, the Zionist movement, gained ground abroad in parts of eastern and western Europe where some Jews were beginning to imagine escapes from anti-Semitism.

During the reign of Abdulhamid II, did religious identities matter more or less than before? The answers tug in both directions. In places where empires were colliding, where ethnic nationalist ideologies were finding adherents, and where discrepancies in wealth were widening along religious lines – in other words, places like eastern Anatolia – religious identities mattered *more*. And yet, in urban areas like Cairo and Istanbul, and especially among highly educated and affluent people, religion in the Abdulhamid II era mattered *less* than ever in Ottoman history. Prosperous, city-dwelling Muslims, Christians, and Jews were mingling in a growing array of social spaces, including social clubs, restaurants, schools, and department stores, and as result of their contacts new forms of solidarity were able to take shape.[16] Conflict *and* conviviality: inter-communal relations in the Abdulhamid II era covered the spectrum from one end to the other.

The Shifting Terrain: Debt, War, and Migration

Abdulhamid II came to the throne at a difficult moment in 1876. He faced financial problems, a refugee crisis, and, almost immediately, too, a new war with Russia. The fallout from these events jolted the Ottoman Empire out of the Tanzimat era, and had lasting repercussions for Ottoman politics, international affairs, and social relations between Muslims and Christians especially.

The first problem that faced Abdulhamid II reared up three years before his accession: it was a financial crisis, soon to be known as the "Great Depression" of its time, that broke out in Europe and North America just as famine afflicted eastern Anatolia.[17] Unable to make payments on the high-interest loans that it had drawn after the Crimean War (1854–56), the Ottoman state defaulted in 1876. This financial trauma precipitated the overthrow and demise of Sultan Abdulaziz, but its repercussions went farther than that: arguably, it left the empire unable to strengthen its military sufficiently in the remaining forty-odd years of its existence.[18] Meanwhile, within five years of bankruptcy, the European powers imposed a Public Debt Administration (PDA), made of representatives of the debt's bond-holders, 80–90 percent of whom were British, French, and German.[19] In 1881, as one historian observed, no one would have foreseen that the PDA would "become what it would be twenty years later: a masterpiece of western imperialism in the Empire, a sort of financier state within the state controlling nearly a quarter to a third of the empire's revenues and employing nearly 7,000 people."[20] Its presence poked a hole into Ottoman sovereignty, and tethered the empire more tightly to the foreign powers that Abdulhamid II wished to elude.

The second problem was that, during the fifteen years before Abdulhamid II's accession, the Ottoman Empire had begun to receive huge waves of Muslim refugees from areas to the north where the Russian Empire was expanding. During the early 1860s, Muslim Tatars had fled into the Ottoman heartlands, accounting for perhaps 200,000 out of a total Tatar population of 300,000 that had been living in Crimea beforehand. These Tatars had faced accusations of treasonous behavior on the part of Russian authorities with regard to the Crimean War, even though most of them appear to have been unarmed peasant bystanders during this conflict.[21] (In this regard, their situation resembled that of Armenians, who in eastern Anatolia fifty years later, faced accusations of disloyalty toward the Ottoman Empire in the context of World War I, in this case by ostensibly siding with Russia. As with the Armenians, accusations of treason provided pretexts for Tatar displacement.) During the 1860s, too, tens of thousands more Muslims – this time Circassians living on the northeast shore of the Black Sea, in the Caucasus Mountains – fled into Ottoman domains in the wake of pogroms and massacres.[22] Ottoman authorities struggled to accommodate these traumatized people, whom an Armenian activist, writing from New York in 1908, called "bands of paupers, half-clad, penniless and wild with hunger," amounting to "an immense army of destructive robbers."[23] Historians have since agreed that some of these refugees were dangerous, violent, and inclined to push residents off the land that they wanted.[24] Others posed risks to public health, because in their weakened states they contracted and spread diseases like typhus.[25]

The third problem arose one year into Abdulhamid's reign. This was the Russo-Turkish War of 1877–78, which Slavic Christian nationalists in the Balkans launched at what seemed like an opportune moment of Ottoman weakness. Russia lent immediate and active support. Although the Ottoman state looked to Britain for assistance, Britain waited until Russian armies reached within seven miles of Istanbul before calling on Russia to halt. In fact, rather than just showing the extent to which the Ottoman state had become "a hostage to British whims,"[26] Britain's tardy response also showed how its foreign policy was paralyzed by domestic sparring that bore some relation to Britain's own history of intercommunal, and in this case, Christian-Jewish, relations. For when the Russo-Turkish War started, Britain's Conservative prime minister, Benjamin Disraeli (1809–98), saw the conflict in terms of the territorial standoff known as the Eastern Question and was anxious to support "the Turks" against Russian expansion.[27] And yet, Disraeli, who had converted from Judaism to Anglican Christianity at age twelve, was struggling at home in the United Kingdom with a pervasive anti-Semitism that his critics used to ridicule and discredit him. One writer, for example, dubbed Disraeli "Ben Ju-Ju." Another, a church minister, published a letter in a Sheffield newspaper in 1876 dismissing Disraeli as a "Jew Earl, philo-Turkish Jew and Jew Premier" (with the first epithet referring to his status as the first Earl of Beaconfield).[28] In this context, the treatise that Disraeli's old rival, the evangelical Christian and Liberal politician William Gladstone (1809–98) published on the "Bulgarian horrors" – by which Gladstone meant Muslim atrocities against Christians in this war, and not also Christian atrocities against Muslims – is striking on three grounds. First, the treatise tapped into anti-Semitic and anti-Muslim discourses; second, it questioned Britain's alliance with the Ottoman Empire; and third, it suggested the influence of a popular pan-Christian ideology in Britain that mirrored the pan-Islam which observers later attributed to Abdulhamid II and his circle.

When the war ended, Russia pushed through a quick treaty – the Treaty of San Stefano of March 1878 – though Britain immediately demanded its revision at the Congress of Berlin (June–July 1878) in order to curtail Russian influence. The subsequent Treaty of Berlin confirmed how much the Ottoman Empire lost in this war – namely, control over two-fifths of its territory and one-fifth of its population.[29] Romania, Serbia, and Montenegro became independent, while Montenegro, in particular, tripled its territory and gained access to the Adriatic Sea. Bulgaria emerged autonomous, paying only a tribute to the Ottoman state, and with access to the Aegean. Austria-Hungary occupied Bosnia-Herzegovina. And even Britain, which claimed to be negotiating on behalf of the Ottoman Empire, extracted Cyprus as a Mediterranean naval base.

The Ottoman territory that emerged from this Russo-Turkish War was less European and more Asiatic and North African: we would now call it more "Middle Eastern." At the same time, its population was more Muslim and less Christian. In religious terms, for example, Muslims had accounted for perhaps 60 percent of the empire's population in the 1850s, but represented some 72 percent after this war.[30] Contributing to this development was the fact that some 2 million Muslim refugees from the Balkans and Russia staggered into what was left of the Ottoman Empire in the wake of this conflict.[31] The 515,000 or so Muslims who left Bulgaria alone were fleeing from massacres perpetrated by local Bulgarian Christians as well as by Russian and Bulgarian soldiers.[32] All told, these Russo-Turkish War refugees appeared to have been part of a larger population of five million or so Muslims, who, during the 1854 to 1908 period, entered the Ottoman heartlands from the Balkans, Crimean peninsula, and Caucasus region combined. In some places (including certain villages in eastern Anatolia) where 90 percent of the Muslim men who had left for the front in 1877 or 1878 had died from war wounds and from diseases like cholera and plague, these refugees helped to offset the drop in Muslim numbers.[33] Considering that the Ottoman population consisted of approximately 17.4 million people in 1893, the Muslim refugees from the Balkans and Caucasus regions came to represent a hefty part of the total.[34] Their descendants accounted for an estimated 30 percent of the population in the Republic of Turkey nearly a century later in 1970.[35]

Judging from nationalist, postimperial histories, which recalled the Ottoman period as a capital-D "Dark Age" full of forced conversions, many Serbian, Montenegrin, and other Balkan Christian peoples were happy to see the Ottomans go in 1878.[36] Many Armenians came out of the Russo-Turkish War heartened as well. For although the San Stefano Treaty, which Russia had tried to push through, never technically went into effect, many Armenians drew hope from its Article 16, which called upon the Ottoman state to undertake "ameliorations" among Armenians in its domains. The best amelioration of all would have been a government crackdown on the Kurds and Circassians who preyed on Armenians in the Ottoman domains of eastern Anatolia, attacking Armenians' villages, burning their farms, and raping and abducting their women in acts that had become part of an everyday culture of violence.[37]

If we look back, we can see that the Russo-Turkish War and its ensuing treaties ravaged the late Ottoman state so badly that it ended the Ottoman Empire's status as a serious European power.[38] It had significant long-term implications for intercommunal relations, too. Whereas in the mid-nineteenth century, Ottoman authorities had described Armenian Christians as "the loyal millet"[39] – notably in relation to the Greeks who had revolted in the 1820s – after this war the Ottoman authorities and many Muslims in Anatolia more broadly began to look upon Armenians as a problem. Many Muslims took particular offense at actions of the Armenian Orthodox patriarch, Nerses Varjabedian (1837–84), who promoted Armenian interests at the Congress of Berlin by courting Russian support, and who hoped to secure a degree of Armenian autonomy in eastern Anatolia under Russian protection.[40] For Armenians, Varjabedian catalyzed a new culture of Armenian international lobbying.[41] His efforts came to an abrupt end, however, in 1884, when he died, according to one Armenian writer, after being poisoned on orders from the sultan.[42]

The Russo-Turkish War and its settlements had weighty implications for British and French imperialism as well. Writing in Cairo in 1895, the Egyptian journalist Ibrahim al-Muwaylihi suggested that when France had signaled at the Congress of Berlin that Egypt (as well as Syria and Jerusalem) should remain outside the scope of negotiations, British strategists got the message that they should claim Egypt before France could do so.[43] Thus Britain invaded and occupied Egypt in 1882, an event that historians of the British Empire have long identified as a trigger for the European colonial partition or "Scramble" for Africa.[44]

Leaving aside Great Power politics, treaties, and statesmen, what did the Russo-Turkish War of 1877–78 mean to ordinary Muslims in the Ottoman heartlands? Recalling the violence that devastated Balkan Muslim communities, many Muslims (and especially those who had witnessed the violence or its aftermath firsthand) emerged from this conflict with a growing sense that, to powerful countries like Britain and France, suffering and death did not count for the same among Muslims as they did among Christians.[45] In the long run, these feelings of beleaguerment produced a siege mentality vis-à-vis the "Christian world," from the proverbial men and women on the street up to the sultan, and did more than any demographic shift to harden Muslim attitudes toward Christians where refugees were arriving.

Abdulhamid II and the End of the Tanzimat Era

Historians have tended to see the year 1876 as such a sharp break from what came before it that they have end-dated the Tanzimat period there. The following section explains why and in what sense this era of reform ended, and what Abdulhamid II, who became sultan that year, had to do with it.

When Abdulhamid II came to the throne in 1876, Ottoman reformers were busy drafting a constitution that they modeled on the Belgian constitution of 1831.[46] This Ottoman constitution advanced lofty ideals. While confirming that Islam was the religion of the state, the constitution of 1876 declared that "All Ottomans" – here meaning all the empire's people – "are equal in the eyes of the law," endowed with "the same rights and duties without prejudice regarding religion."[47] The Ottoman constitution represented a high-water mark of Ottomanism, a budding ideal of Ottoman belonging. This ideal placed less stress on the empire – given that empires, by definition, depend on coerced inclusion – and more on the nation, insofar as it implied voluntary incorporation among people who shared, or with some effort *could* share, common social and political aims.

Ahmed Şefik Midhat Pasha (1822–83), a leading Tanzimat-era statesman who also served briefly as one of Abdulhamid II's grand viziers, expressed hope that this constitution could stave off foreign European intrusion into Ottoman internal affairs by making the empire look progressive, strong, and kindly toward its Christians. Conveying this impression of kindliness was crucial at a time when Russia stood poised to claim Ottoman abuse of Christians as an excuse to jump into the Balkans and into Armenian zones of Anatolia. In 1876, Midhat Pasha hoped to cultivate a more durable Ottoman sentiment in another way, too. Namely, in keeping with the constitution's emphasis on equal rights and responsibilities, he supported "mixed" education in places where Muslims and Christians lived side-by-side. Thus, he urged the government to open its military academies, in particular, to Ottoman Christian men.[48]

Midhat Pasha was working from a pragmatic assumption that some earlier Tanzimat reformers had shared – the idea that the Ottoman Empire could best defend itself from external imperial aggression and internal separatist nationalism by bolstering goodwill from within.[49]

Two points are worth noting here. First, while the empire's Christian populations caused some concern for Ottoman authorities like Midhat Pasha in the context of Great Power diplomacy, Jews did not. Accounting for just 1 percent of the total Ottoman population in 1876, Ottoman Jews were quiet and concentrated in cities – not spread out like Christians.[50] Second, recall that Ottoman reformers had toyed with the idea of extending military opportunities and military service to Christians (and Jews) before, at the time of the 1856 reform decree. Such a measure would have broken from Islamic traditions of statecraft and from popular attitudes among Muslims and non-Muslims alike, which had kept military service a Muslim preserve. It would have also eased the burden of military service on Muslims in an age of mass conscription and debilitating defensive wars, while giving Christians and Jews a sense of opportunity, equity, and stakeholding within the empire.[51] But just as the 1856 proposal came to naught, this one led nowhere, too. A major force against change this time was Abdulhamid II himself, who went on to maintain – and more than that, to emphasize – principles of Muslim exclusivity in certain social arenas.

The constitution of 1876 provided for a parliament of elected provincial delegates, consisting of a mixture of Muslim, Christian, and Jewish men in proportion to the size of these religious communities. In fact, the parliament that met in 1877 claimed to give Christians an edge beyond their officially estimated numbers so as to convince foreign European powers of the Ottoman state's generosity. The result was that there were seventy-one Muslims, forty-four Christians, and four Jews among the delegates.[52] The parliament kept busy during its first session in 1877. Its members debated taxes and budgets, called for cuts in the civil service, and tried to show prudence in light of the financial crisis that had arisen from the state's defaulting on earlier loans.[53]

In debating taxes and payrolls, the parliament may have started as little more than a "chamber of 'yes-men'" who were ready to pass along "pleasant advice to the sovereign."[54] But its tone changed with the onset of the Russo-Turkish War when some deputies questioned Ottoman military strategy. One delegate, a Muslim baker who was the head of the baker's guild, went so far as to chide the sultan as Russia advanced. "You have asked for our opinions too late"; this baker-parliamentarian said, "you should have consulted us when it was still possible to avert disaster."[55] Irked by the criticism and unwilling to receive more,

Abdulhamid II decided to cut off the flow.[56] "I now understand," the sultan declared, "that it is not possible to move the peoples whom God has placed under my protection by any means other than force."[57] Using the power that the constitution granted him, Abdulhamid II terminated the parliament during its second session in 1878. The sultan did not call parliament back in session, at least not until a military coup d'état in 1908 forced him to do so at the end of his reign.

The dissolution of the parliament was one sign that the Tanzimat period was over, although scholars have argued that economics played a role in ending it, too. In the aftermath of both the 1876 bankruptcy and the Russo-Turkish War of 1877–78, the Ottoman state lacked funds to make all the infrastructural additions and refurbishments that it would have liked to do, or perhaps needed to do.[58] It did not help that the first twenty years of Abdulhamid II's reign coincided with the "Great Depression" or "Long Depression" of 1873–96, a downturn which began at the Vienna Stock Exchange in 1873 and which caused crises and downturns around the world.[59] The tight financial circumstances of these years curbed reforms, forced the state to set priorities, and signaled the end of the Tanzimat era in which opportunities had seemed more abundant and accessible.

More than money and projects, however, the real ending of the Tanzimat reflected a change in political mood. And here, Abdulhamid II – the man, the quirky person – set the tone in two ways. First, he confirmed Muslim privilege in state institutions and projects, thereby upholding something like the *status quo ante* of the pre-Tanzimat period. Second, he curtailed political expression for Muslims and non-Muslims alike. Abdulhamid II not only scotched the parliament, but also muzzled intellectuals who spoke, wrote, and, above all, published in Ottoman Turkish, Arabic, Armenian, and other languages. In a period when rates of printing, literacy, and reading were soaring, and when novels and detective stories were the rage (with Abdulhamid II himself a fan of Sherlock Holmes stories in translation), intellectuals had to deal with Ottoman government censors who forced them to expunge basic words from their dictionaries, lest readers get dangerous ideas.[60] Thus the words for "revolution," "democracy," and "republic," which made it into the 1882 edition of a Turkish-French dictionary, disappeared from the 1898 version, while the 1901 edition lost entries for words like "parliament," "despot," and "liberty."[61] Fear of words and their power prompted the sultan to ban the use of the word "Macedonia" in official correspondence, because he feared that using it would boost separatist nationalism in the Ottoman territory where an ancient kingdom of that name had once existed.[62]

Abdulhamid II's Egyptian critic, Ibrahim al-Muwaylihi, recounted in 1895 a similar story about the Ottoman government censors who ordered the authors of a Turkish-Armenian dictionary to expunge the word for "sword," since no Armenian should have one. Muwaylihi demanded of his readers, "What can be the effect of such a ridiculous decision, on a people who are well aware of the way things are in the world and have excelled in American schools?" He was referring to the fact that so many Armenians in this period attended Christian mission schools in Anatolia.[63]

In addition to scrapping the parliament and imposing surveillance, Abdulhamid II dramatically shrank the influence of grand viziers and high-level bureaucrats. During the first five years of his reign (1876–81) he flipped through twelve different grand viziers, each lasting an average of four months – too short a time for anyone to get a grip on the job.[64] Only a tiny inner circle retained the sultan's trust over the years. This circle included a British advisor, a French advisor, a Greek doctor, and a Sufi Muslim sheikh who served as his astrologer.[65]

Meanwhile, Abdulhamid II exiled potential challengers to the far corners of the empire. He used Tripolitania, corresponding to what is now the western coastal region of Libya, as a common site of exile. In this way, Libya functioned like a "Siberian Sahara" for disfavored intellectuals, military officers, and functionaries whom he ejected from Istanbul.[66] Similarly, he disposed of one of his former grand viziers, the urbane and progressive Midhat Pasha, by first convicting him of assassinating the late Sultan, Abdulaziz, and then exiling him to Taif, in what is now Saudi Arabia. There, while languishing from an untreated case of what was apparently cutaneous anthrax, Midhat Pasha thwarted attempts by his Ottoman military keepers to poison him, before one of these keepers eventually strangled him with a cord.[67] Years later, at the time of Abdulhamid II's final ouster in 1909, a *New York Times* article added a sordid detail to this last story. Abdulhamid II not only had Midhat Pasha killed, its author claimed, but also had his head "cut off, pickled, and sent [back] to the Sultan in a box labeled, 'Old Japanese ivory. With Care.'"[68]

The Ottoman State and the "Imperial Revival"

Of course, by the late 1870s, when Midhat Pasha was stuck in his Arabian exile, places like Taif were no longer as remote as they had been. For even as the Ottoman Empire was losing land along its edges, it was also strengthening its hold over Libya and Arabia, regions which it had loosely claimed in the sixteenth century. By making its position firmer and clearer in what lands it had left, the Ottoman Empire effected what some have called an imperial revival.[69]

Just as the Ottoman state under Abdulhamid II expanded its influence over residual territories and subjects, it also implemented new scientific, educational, and organizational practices to keep the empire *au courant* in the world. In many respects, Abdulhamid II neither worked from scratch nor broke from precedent. Rather, he built upon measures that dated from the eras of his grandfather, father, and uncle – the sultans Mahmud II, Abdulmajid, and Abdulaziz – thereby suggesting continuities that threaded Abdulhamid II's reign to the Tanzimat period and to the era that had directly preceded it.

Consider Libya more closely. The hereditary Karamanli dynasty had ruled the coast around Tripoli (though not much of the Saharan interior) after 1711 while giving nominal allegiance to Ottoman authorities. But in 1835, the Ottoman state of Sultan Mahmud II took direct control of this territory and in 1841, amidst a larger reorganization of the imperial military, installed a new army unit in Tripoli.[70] Arabia was similar. Before the mid-nineteenth century, the only part of Arabia that the Ottomans had consistently controlled over the generations was the Hijaz in the west, which contained the holy cities of Mecca and Medina and therefore conferred great prestige. After the 1517 conquest of Syria, Ottoman authorities had secured a pilgrimage route from Mecca to Damascus by building a string of fortresses that doubled as travelers' rest stops. Yet their claims to al-Hasa (the eastern region of Arabia) and Yemen, in southern Arabia, had all but lapsed in the late sixteenth and early seventeenth centuries.[71] This situation began to change in 1869, during Abdulaziz's sultanate, when the redoubtable Midhat Pasha became the Ottoman *vali* or governor of Baghdad and closed in on what is now Iraq while advancing or renewing Ottoman claims in Kuwait, Bahrain, al-Hasa, and Yemen.

Driving these changes was the fact that foreign empire builders were encroaching onto Ottoman turf. The Ottoman retrieval of Libya in 1835 occurred shortly after France invaded Algeria in 1830. Likewise, Midhat Pasha's efforts in Arabia and Iraq responded to a British threat that became more urgent in 1869, when the Suez Canal opened to traffic and dramatically shortened the sailing time between Britain and India. By 1869, in any case, Britain was already installed at the southern tip of Arabia, having annexed Aden, now in Yemen, in 1839. Britain had also been busy making truces with Arab potentates on the Arabian coast, eventually giving rise to the "Trucial States" that were precursors to the United Arab Emirates. Meanwhile, in 1862, a British mail service linked Ottoman Baghdad to the British Empire in India, while a British telegraph network connected Baghdad not only to India and Istanbul but also to Tehran in Iran, which was ruled by the Qajar dynasty (c. 1796–1925).[72]

Enforcing claims to territory required a bigger military. In 1837, when Mahmud II was on the throne, the army had numbered 24,000 men. By the 1880s, that number had quintupled to 120,000.[73] The number of bureaucrats expanded, too, because the Ottoman imperial state needed many more highly literate office workers. That is, it needed men who could receive and process instructions from the center, and send reports back in return; keep track of income and revenues; and through it all, handle the paperwork – now emerging in handwritten, printed, typed, and telegraphed forms – that the system was churning out. The Ottoman state had employed some 2,000 civil administrators in 1789, but was employing many, many more by 1900. Estimates vary a lot: perhaps 35,000–50,000 employees; perhaps 50,000–100,000; maybe half a million.[74] Whatever it was, by 1900, the cumulative, century-long increase in the number of state employees had been substantial.

The Ottoman state was also doing more things. Its regulatory functions had increased steadily from the 1830s onward, as a result of policies that Abdulhamid II's predecessors initiated and upon which he built. In the 1830s, for example, the state initiated more regular census-keeping, to help assessing taxes and military drafts.[75] Starting with Black Sea ports, authorities imposed quarantine measures to guard against diseases like cholera.[76] In 1857, it devised a Refugee Code to coordinate the entry and resettlement of displaced people; this code later structured policies toward refugees of the Russo-Turkish War.[77] In 1858 it passed a Land Law that provided for privatizing and registering property in ways that transformed land tenure. This law outlasted the empire: its impact was evident, for example, in post–World War I Palestine under British rule, when arguments over land sales and settlement arose against the context of Jewish Zionist immigration.[78]

To appreciate how the Ottoman state expanded its functions and staked claims on the ground, consider an example from what is now Jordan. Two centuries earlier, Ottoman authorities had assessed the predominantly Sunni Muslim settled population of this region for taxation and military conscription in *collective* terms by liaising with leaders of villages and town quarters. But in the late nineteenth century, the Ottoman state increasingly treated the people as solo actors. In Jordan, this process of individual counting and treatment or "individuation" began in the towns of Irbid and Salt during the reign of Abdulaziz, when Ottoman administrative posts opened in these places, making it possible to keep direct tabs on the locals (as opposed to farming out administration or tax collecting to others). The process continued under Abdulhamid II, during whose reign Ottoman authorities settled some Circassian and later Chechen refugees in Jordan.[79] Ottoman authorities in Jordan, as in Iraq, also began to press in on the nomadic tribes: to count them, conscript them, and take as taxes the revenues that tribesmen had traditionally extracted for their own use from settled peoples around them.[80]

All of this bureaucratic growth depended on an expanding school system that was capable of producing employees for the state. Here the government of Abdulhamid II turned "the largely paper plans of his [Tanzimat-era] predecessors into bricks and mortar." The Ottoman state built some 10,000 new government schools of varying levels during the Abdulhamid II era alone. These schools taught academic subjects and skills, but also modes of learning and living, such as how to use wall maps, blackboards, and European-style desks and beds, and how to eat from single plates with knives and forks, rather than using hands from common trays.[81]

New nineteenth-century technologies boosted Abdulhamid II's government in other ways as well. Photography, for example, was critical. Continuing the precedent set by his uncle Abdulaziz, Abdulhamid II retained official photographers at court, including men like the Armenian brothers known as Abdullah Frères, who had counted many distinguished people among their subjects. (Even the American novelist, Mark Twain, had sat for an Abdullah Frères portrait in 1867, when he sailed into Istanbul on *The Quaker Queen* during his tour of the Holy Land.[82]) Like his contemporary, Queen Victoria (r. 1837–1901) of the United Kingdom, Abdulhamid II appreciated photography as a technology that had both artistic and political potential. Although he did not handle the camera himself, this "sultan of photography" spent spare moments surveying everything from the portraits of his children to the mug shots of convicts – even studying the latter, in the twenty-fifth year of his reign, to award amnesties after "examining the convicts' faces in the light of physiognomy."[83] Unlike Queen Victoria, however, who used photographs to project her evolving image as "loving mother, devoted wife, grieving widow, and powerful sovereign,"[84] Abdulhamid II was not interested in staging pictures of himself for public consumption, apparently because he feared the publicity. Unlike his predecessors, beginning with Mahmud II, he refused to have his portrait (either painted or photographed) hung in public places, but instead endorsed the hanging of banners with a slogan that read, "Long live the sultan!"[85] Along these lines, Ibrahim al-Muwaylihi observed in 1895 that none of the Istanbul residents he asked could tell him what the sultan looked like.[86] And while some observers may have interpreted his renunciation of public portraits as a sign of respect for the traditional Muslim ban on portraiture, others ultimately attributed his behavior to a combination of paranoia (the fewer people who could recognize him, the better) and to the public performance of ostensible piety.

Abdulhamid II preferred, above all, to use photographs for intelligence purposes. He encouraged photography as a mode of imperial record-keeping[87]. From the early 1880s, he hired landscape photographers and sent them into the corners of his empire.[88] In this way he amassed a collection of more than 30,000 negatives, and from the privacy of Yildiz palace, pored over prints to go on vicarious "tours of inspection." Through photographs, he saw how things looked, who was doing what, and how they were doing it.[89] "He had a reputation for bringing together seemingly unimportant events and small details in photographs," observed a historian of his photographic collection, "like a detective working to solve mysteries"[90] – perhaps like a Sultan Sherlock Holmes.

In addition to documenting roads, bridges, schools, hospitals, and other evidence of infrastructural development,[91] Abdulhamid II's photographers took pictures of "representative trophies" from the empire's pre-Islamic civilizations.[92] These trophies consisted, for example, of statues, urns, and other relics from Greco-Roman, Trojan, Babylonian, and Phoenician sites – that is, the kinds of objects that European and American archaeologists were beginning to excavate, and where possible, to export, to museums, universities, and private collections abroad.[93] In fact, the Ottoman state was becoming interested in archaeology, too. In 1869, during the reign of Abdulaziz, the state implemented the first antiquities law, to regulate exports from excavation sites, and to make sure that the Ottoman state got a share of the spoils. Under Abdulhamid II, these antiquities laws grew stricter in iterations of 1874, 1884, and 1906.[94] During an age when museum-building was a means of asserting national or imperial claims, the Ottoman Empire organized its own imperial museums, which enabled it to stake out ownership of its territory and of the "multiple pasts" stored within it.[95] Representing the Ottoman state in many of these efforts was Osman Hamdi Bey (1842–1910), an archaeologist in his own right and discoverer at Sidon (now in Lebanon) of the *Alexander Sarcophagus*, which dates from the fourth century BC and which depicts Alexander the Great battling the Persians.

In fact, Osman Hamdi Bey was also a fine artist. Trained in Paris, he is celebrated in Turkey today for his magnificent oil paintings of idealized Ottoman scenes.[96] His paintings captured something of the spirit of the Ottoman Empire in its age of imperial revival. Lush in detail and deeply romantic, works like *At the Mosque Door* (painted for the Ottoman

Image 12 *At the Mosque Door*, oil painting by Osman Hamdi Bey, 1891, Image Number 184892. Courtesy of the Penn Museum.

government's display at the World Columbian Exposition in Chicago in 1893) and his 1906 painting *The Tortoise Trainer* (which fetched a record-breaking sum for a "Turkish" painting at auction in 2004),[97] recall the art of his contemporary, the French painter Jean-Léon Gérôme (1824–1904), and the similarity is no accident. Gérôme was one of Osman Hamdi Bey's teachers in Paris, and both men approached the subjects of their paintings with an Orientalist gaze. That is, they painted from the view of the rational observer surveying native people and places that were at once beautiful and exotic but yet stuck in some other time – and needing outsiders, armed with the genius of modern civilization, to push them ahead.

Strikingly, the paperback cover of Edward Said's book *Orientalism* used one of Gérôme's paintings – *The Snake Charmer* (c. 1879), featuring a naked boy performing before men in a tiled, mosque-like interior – to illustrate its point about the nature and expression of imperial hauteur in this period.[98] Edward Said focused in his book on French, British, and to some extent, too, American expressions of Orientalism. And yet, as the historian Ussama Makdisi argued, Ottoman imperialists in this period had their own brand of "Ottoman Orientalism," and with it a belief in the need for the modernization or nudging forward of subject peoples. While Britain and France had colonies in Asia and Africa as testing grounds for their "civilizing missions," the Ottoman Empire had its Arab provinces to uplift – and began to write about them during this period in patronizing and culturally imperious tones that recall British and French texts from this period. Osman Hamdi Bey exemplified this phenomenon of Ottoman Orientalism. For even as he was protecting excavation sites from unlimited European and American takeaways by applying Ottoman antiquities laws, he was hauling off treasures from places like Sidon to the imperial museum in Istanbul, where he felt that they could be more appropriately tended and appreciated. And so today, even as a place like postimperial London has trophies like the Elgin Marbles (sculptures from the Parthenon which once-Ottoman Greece has been trying to claim as its birthright), postimperial Istanbul, and not Beirut, now has the *Alexander Sarcophagus*.[99] As the historian Selim Deringil observed, returning to the sultan who set the tone of this age, "Abdülhamid would almost certainly have agreed with Edward Said 'that struggle [for empire] is … not only about soldiers and cannons but also about ideas, about forms, about images and imaginings'."[100]

Ottomans Abroad

The same imperial revival that occurred within the empire led to more active engagement in the world beyond it. Under Abdulhamid II, the Ottoman state opened new consulates. In Asia, consulates opened in places like Singapore, Karachi, Madras, and Calcutta, where there were Muslim trading diasporas. In the Americas, they opened in places like Havana and Buenos Aires.[101] Diplomacy expanded in other ways, too, as Abdulhamid II cultivated relations beyond the old cast of characters, with emerging powers like Germany and the United States. In 1894, for example, Abdulhamid II gave aid to victims of US forest fires as a gesture of Ottoman goodwill, while reciprocally, the US government called on the sultan during the Spanish-American War of 1898, by asking him to discourage Muslims in the Philippines from fighting American soldiers who were waging war against Spain.[102]

Of course, the Ottoman Empire's connections to the United States as well as to countries like Mexico, Cuba, Brazil, and Argentina were becoming more significant in this period because so many Ottoman subjects were migrating to the Americas during this age of mass migration, when people around the world faced few barriers to immigration and limited demands for documentation.[103] About one-third of Mount Lebanon's population migrated to the Americas between 1880 and 1914; others left Anatolia and what is now Syria; occasional migrants set out, too, from British-occupied Egypt and from Libya.[104] Consider the example of Rose Cohen Misrie. Born to Syrian Jewish parents in Tripoli, Libya and having a surname that meant "Egyptian" (*misri*) in Arabic, she moved with her family to New York in 1906 and opened "The Egyptian Rose," a kosher and self-styled "Syrian" restaurant, where she served canonical Levantine dishes like *mujaddara* (rice and lentils with caramelized onions) and *sambusak* (savory cheese-filled turnovers) to a mostly male clientele of "Syrian, Turkish, and Greek Jews."[105] The case of Rose Cohen Misrie, who was in some sense simultaneously Libyan, Egyptian, and Syrian in origin, suggests the multiplicity of regional affinities that were possible for people who came from families that lived within an Ottoman orbit.

About 1.2 million Ottoman subjects migrated to the Americas in the half century after 1860, equivalent to about 5 percent of the total Ottoman population in 1914. Some three-quarters of emigrants were men. Most were Christians, although Jews and Muslims (both Sunnis and Shi'is) left, too. In all, perhaps 15–20 percent of the Ottoman migrants to the United States were Muslims.[106] For example, consider the Muslim migrant to the United States who became known as "Hi Jolly" – an Anglicized form of "Hajj Ali." A specialist in training camels, Hi Jolly formed an experimental camel corps in the American Southwest on behalf of the US War Department. When he died in 1902, he was buried in Quartzsite, Arizona, in a tomb shaped like a pyramid and topped with a camel. Today, the town of Quartzsite maintains the "Hi Jolly Monument" within the "Hi Jolly Cemetery," which is the resting place for the town's pioneer settlers, Hi Jolly included.[107]

The religious demographics of Ottoman émigrés to the Americas are hard to know with precision for a few reasons. First, on the American end, documentation was uneven. Many North and South American locals did not see or care about the religious differences among Ottoman immigrants, and often lumped Muslim, Christian, and Jewish immigrants together as "Semites," "Arabs," or "Turks." Second, on the sending Ottoman side, authorities may have undercounted or not realized the extent of Muslim emigration from Mount Lebanon especially. Certainly Ottoman authorities were unhappy to see Muslims go, because it reduced the number of men whom they could draft for the army. And third, judging from the case of Mexico, many migrants in the Americas settled down and married across religious and sectarian lines, so that with time, many descendants of Ottoman migrants blended into local Christian communities regardless of the religious affiliations they had before their arrival.[108] In short, religious life, and often, too, religious identity, worked differently in the American diaspora, as individuals refashioned their lives in foreign places. In fact, the camel corps leader and pioneer settler of Quartzsite, Arizona, illustrates the religious ambiguity of the Ottoman immigrant perfectly, for Hi Jolly sometimes went by a Muslim name, "Hajj Ali" (suggesting that he had performed the pilgrimage to Mecca), and sometimes by a Christian one, "Philip Tedro." But who was Philip Tedro, and when in his life did Hi Jolly go by that name? Was Philip Tedro "a Greek born in Syria" who later converted to Islam, as the town of Quartzsite suggested on its website?[109] Or was Philip Tedro merely an alias – a name of convenience – that Hi Jolly sometimes used to ease his movement through, and integration into, a largely Christian social terrain? A third possibility is that this man was born Muslim and became a Christian abroad. It may be impossible now to know.

From the perspective of the Ottoman state, migrants to the Americas caused worry for two reasons. First, some Christians who emigrated to the United States spread stories there about Ottoman and Muslim tyranny against them. This was especially true after 1900, when certain Maronite and Armenian activists (from Mount Lebanon and Anatolia respectively) began to publish books and articles that had nationalist overtones.[110] Second, not all émigrés stayed where they went. Perhaps as many as one-third returned from the Americas,[111] and brought new ideas and habits back with them. Concerned by these migrants but at the same time eager to deter Ottoman subjects from securing European passports on their way out (perhaps working on the assumption, again, that many would come back), Ottoman authorities during the Abdulhamid II era tightened procedures for travel documents – that is, for passports – to monitor entries and exits of subjects and aliens. This concern with documenting migration helps to explain why the Ottoman state in this period opened new consulates in Barcelona, Spain, and in various American cities.[112] Such consulates helped the Ottoman state to keep tabs on its subjects as they traveled hither, yon, and sometimes back again.

Railways, schools, and quarantine stations; museums and photographs; consulates and passports; with all this and more, Abdulhamid II confirmed the Ottoman Empire's status as a "modern" state enmeshed in the web of the world. But just as circumstances – including foreign debts – tethered the Ottoman Empire to other countries in this period, so were circumstances tethering other countries to the Ottoman Empire. To rule India, for example, Britain depended on 1,800 miles of telegraph lines that stretched across the Ottoman Empire, even as the Ottoman Empire, in turn, depended on Italy for the telegraph lines that maintained its contact with Libya.[113] Railway and shipping lines, likewise, connected some Ottoman towns to western European commercial hubs like Manchester, Hamburg, and Marseille more quickly than to their own hinterlands.[114] Meanwhile, as news spread (whether sent along steamship postal routes or conveyed with the lightning speed of the telegraph), the Ottoman sultan perched in his palace at Yildiz was as likely to receive an intelligence report from, say, his emissaries in Washington, DC, regarding the affairs of Mormons in distant Utah, as he was to get news from the Yemeni interior.[115]

The Enemy Example: Christian Missionaries in Ottoman Lands

In fact, Ottoman diplomats in Washington, DC, had been dispatching news about Mormons to Istanbul since 1871, five years *before* Abdulhamid II reached the throne. At a time when an estimated 2 percent of Muslim households in Istanbul, and 16 percent of those in Nablus (now in the West Bank of Palestine) were polygamous, Ottoman diplomats were fascinated by news of the Mormons' battles with the US government as Mormon men flouted laws by marrying multiple women.[116] In fact, the diplomats' reporting had a practical basis: Ottoman authorities were concerned by the presence of American missionaries in the Ottoman Empire, and were following news about all mission-minded groups.[117] In this case, the reports proved useful to Abdulhamid II in 1884, when Mormons sent their first missionary, a man born in Switzerland, to Istanbul following an "invitation" from an Armenian. (This was sixty-four years after the first American Protestant missionaries of the ABCFM, a joint Congregationalist and Presbyterian enterprise, had arrived in the Ottoman lands.) Later Mormons made Antep (now Gaziantep, in southeastern Turkey) into an Ottoman base for activities while venturing into a few other Anatolian and Syrian towns where Armenians were living.[118] Following the pattern common to both Catholic and Protestant missionaries in this period, Mormons justified starting their work on the basis of a Christian presence in the region and then appealed mainly to people who were Christians already, even while remaining theoretically open to the conversion of Muslims and others.[119]

Compared to other Catholic and Protestant missions, the Mormon presence was miniscule. But for a man like Abdulhamid II, who wanted to monitor everything and who worried about foreign meddling in his empire, even a small clutch of evangelists was part of the big bundle – the colossal headache – that Christian missionaries were creating. As Abdulhamid II knew, Christian missionaries across the Catholic and Protestant spectrum were difficult to follow and to control. They represented a polyglot assortment of churches, orders, and societies; they came from many countries; they spread out in cities, towns, and villages all over the empire; and they were engaged in providing a huge range of educational and social services, for men and women, boys and girls, of all social classes and backgrounds. They had a frustrating tendency to do what they wanted, with scant attention to conventions or regulations. It made matters worse that so many missionaries presented models of excellence in their schools, hospitals, and other institutions. They were "the enemy who was also the example,"[120] inspiring and vexing at the same time.

Consider, for example, the field of medicine. At institutions like the Syrian Protestant College (founded by American Presbyterians in 1866, and renamed the American University of Beirut [AUB] in 1920), and at the Université de Saint-Joseph in the same city (founded by French Jesuits in 1875), missionaries taught medicine and trained men as future doctors beginning in 1873 and 1883 respectively. But missionaries exerted their greatest medical influence in public health, via outreach to people in villages, towns, and urban quarters, where they introduced measures to prevent disease and promote good health. In a period when women were beginning to exceed men on mission rosters, and when Catholic and Protestant missions alike were devoting over half of their funds to work among women and girls, much of this public health work benefitted women and their children.[121] Particularly significant were missionaries' prenatal and postnatal care programs that included vaccination and training in domestic hygiene. Such programs appear to have had a discernible impact on Christians, who were becoming visibly healthier – not to mention wealthier, better educated, and more prolific – than some of the Muslim populations around them.[122]

With regard to public health among Christians, Anatolia was striking. According to a Russian consul in the region who wrote before World War I, about half of Kurdish Muslim babies in eastern Anatolian villages died at birth because of the lack of medical assistance to their mothers, while another 30 percent of Kurdish infants died before age three, often from endemic diseases like smallpox, scarlet fever, and typhoid, or from the bites of snakes and insects.[123] During a period when Anatolian Muslims lived for an average of twenty-seven to thirty-two years (or, if they survived to age five, for an average of forty-nine years),[124] Armenians, by contrast, were apparently avoiding or surviving many of the childhood illnesses that were lowering life expectancies in the region. An awareness of these discrepancies in well-being may have contributed in this period to anti-Armenian sentiment among Muslims.

Missionaries were also known for their schools, many of which taught skills – everything from knowledge of foreign languages, to facility with telescopes or printing presses – that boosted their graduates' social ambitions and career prospects. Catholic mission institutions were so numerous that they reportedly accounted for more than half of all enrolled schoolchildren in what is now Syria, Lebanon, and Israel/Palestine together by the eve of World War I, at all levels of instruction.[125] Catholic schools represented a large array of religious orders: between 1870 and 1910, twenty-five different orders installed themselves in the Holy Land alone.[126] Protestant missions were prolific, too. By 1905, British Anglican missionaries of the Church Missionary Society (CMS) were operating 120 schools and enrolling nearly 10,000 students in the Ottoman Empire. By 1914 (five years after Abdulhamid II's reign had ended), American missionaries of the ABCFM and the Presbyterian Board of Foreign Missions were operating 473 elementary and 54 secondary schools, along with 4 theological schools and 11 colleges in Ottoman lands, while enrolling a total of 32,252 students.[127] These figures did not include American Presbyterian institutions in Egypt, which contributed to a high rate of literacy among Egyptians who belonged to the Evangelical (Presbyterian) church. A Presbyterian source claimed that while some 12.5 percent of Egyptian men and 1 percent of Egyptian women were literate in the overall population by 1900, the rates were 52 percent for men and 20 percent for women among Evangelicals.[128]

In important respects, the experiences of Jews vis-à-vis missions ran parallel to the experiences of Christians during this period. Among Jews, standards of health were improving, infant mortality rates were dropping, and the result was a demographic boost that paralleled the Christian experience.[129] At the same time, the schools of the Alliance Israélite Universelle (AIU), which had as their mission the modernization of Jews by Jews (see Chapter 4) and the inculcation of French culture, were raising educational levels and social prospects.[130] This was the case even among children who came from the poorest working classes and who attended vocational programs. In Istanbul and Edirne, for example, AIU schools after 1873 were taking the sons of Jewish cigarette-makers, boat-rowers, and others who "eked out a miserable livelihood" and training them via apprenticeships to become typesetters, watchmakers, mechanical metal forgers, and more.[131] To be sure, the AIU also educated elites. The point here is simply that Christian and Jewish missionaries effected mobility even through programs that involved manual training (as one can also see from the example of the Italian Salesian Catholic missionaries who taught manual trades like woodworking, shoe-repairing, and book-binding at their schools in Egypt[132]). Whether literary or artisanal, the education offered in mission schools gave Jewish and Christian students a marked degree of social mobility relative to the Muslim population.[133] Yet while AIU schools tended to educate only Jewish children, Christian mission schools enrolled Jewish and increasingly Muslim pupils as well – making their impact on Ottoman society broader.

Christian missionary education had a particularly strong impact on social aspirations and expectations for girls. For a start, missionaries planted the idea that girls *belonged* outside of their homes, in schools but also with adult women in churches – and this, in social contexts where public collective worship for indigenous Christians (as for Muslims) had traditionally been a men's affair.[134] Among wealthy urban Muslim families, as among Christian and Jewish families, fluency in French (more so than in English, Italian, or German) became a social credential that parents wanted for their daughters.[135] Meanwhile, with so many mission-ary women working as teachers (not to mention as translators, nurses, and sometimes, too, as certified doctors) missionaries presented models of professionalism to the girls who passed through their schools, thereby suggesting to Ottoman females that matrimony was not the only route to achievement.[136] Among the formidable women that missions presented as role models was the American Mary Eddy, who was born in Beirut in 1864 to missionary parents and who later earned a medical degree in New York. Eddy had her credentials confirmed by the Ottoman state after passing a six-hour examination before a committee of twenty-four "Turkish" physicians at the imperial medical college in Istanbul. She went on to found eye clinics, hospitals, and a tuberculosis sanatorium, and often traveled on horseback around villages in Syria providing med-ical care and performing surgery on those in need.[137]

Protestant women missionaries (unlike Catholic nuns in their habits) were fashion models, too: literally, they modeled everyday "Western" clothing to students in their schools. Like other western European and North American women in this period, they wore dresses with highly shaped and fitted bodices that accentuated the curves of breasts and buttocks. Of course, relative to their home societies, missionaries wore clothes that were quite staid and unlikely to match up to the Parisian styles that some members of the Ottoman elite were avidly following. Perhaps because of this perception of their dowdiness, historians have paid little attention to missionaries as fashion-setters. Nevertheless, judging from photographs, missionaries set *de facto* dress codes, including tailored dresses in girls' schools. Even certain hairstyles caught on. Meanwhile, missionaries taught girls literacy and arithmetic while devoting hours of instruction to embroidery, lacemaking, and other "needle arts" which parents appeared to value as skills that enhanced marriageability. Girls learned to make such things as decorative doilies for end tables (with a kind of Victorian home decor in mind), finely crocheted collars for their own dresses, and monogrammed handkerchiefs for their fathers (perhaps to sport in the front pockets of tailored jackets).[138] These details suggest how Christian missionaries were projecting aspects of western European and American *material* culture into the most intimate domestic scenes.

Abdulhamid II worried about the impact that Christian missionaries had on the behavior and dress of Muslim girls. He also worried about the impact of Christian governesses, whom rich Muslims in Istanbul were importing from France, Germany, and other western European countries, to teach their daughters languages, piano, needlework, and manners. Continuing in a long line of Ottoman sultans who had attempted to preserve social and gender hierarchies via clothing,[139] Abdulhamid II eventually spoke up. He did so by publishing an order in the newspaper that women should stop wearing tailored, tight-waisted jackets and thin veils, and by warning Muslim parents against hiring Christian governesses and sending daughters to Christian mission schools.[140] But continuing in an even longer line of Muslim rulers going back to the early Islamic era (see Chapter 2), Abdulhamid II may have issued his warnings about dress more as a public performance of piety than with the expectation that people would listen.

Finally, many mission schools also modeled a kind of confidence along with a readiness to question, and if necessary to revise or discard established traditions. American missionaries seemed especially adept or at ease in refusing "to defer to learned theologians and traditional orthodoxies," perhaps as an outgrowth of the populist and pluralistic impulses motivating their brands of Protestant religion.[141] This lack of deference went on spectacular display at the Syrian Protestant College in Beirut (the future AUB), in 1882, when the American faculty and their Arab students (the latter already armed with experience from leading college-sponsored debate clubs and journals) clashed with members of the institution's Board of Trustees, who were based in New York.[142] This conflict arose when trustees forced the resignation of an American professor after learning that he had favorably, and very publicly, discussed theories of evolution as presented in Charles Darwin's book, *On the Origin of Species* (1859) – first in an Arabic commencement speech, and later, in print, in a college-sponsored Arabic journal. When the trustees continued by ordering faculty and students to sign a pledge affirming God's role as the "Creator and Supreme Ruler" of the universe and rejecting the idea that "man descended from lower animals," many refused, prompting suspensions of several students and resignations of a few professors.[143]

The Darwin controversy largely occurred within the Arab-American circles of the Syrian Protestant College. But in fact, arguments over science had stretched beyond this American college to include the French Jesuit institution, Saint Joseph's, across town in Beirut. Indeed, members of the two schools had waged long-running arguments on the pages of their respective journals, with associates of the Jesuit college having accused the Arab students, graduates, and tutors at the Syrian Protestant College of heresy for ridiculing the notion that there could be supernatural spirits at work in the world. (Clearly, some French Catholics were caught up in their own struggles to reconcile science and religion in this period.) Strikingly, the Ottoman government censor who watched these debates, as they occurred on the pages of journals, appeared to be more concerned by their acrimony than by their content. Meanwhile, on the pages of the Syrian Protestant College–sponsored journals, Muslim students and scholars were joining actively in debates about science and religion, with many arguing for the compatibility between the two.[144] In short, and with regard to these scientific debates as they occurred within learned societies, Catholic-Protestant rancor was sharp even while Muslim-Christian relations were amicable.

Christian Missionaries, Muslim Audiences, and Nationalism

A professor of medicine and author of Arabic scientific textbooks on subjects ranging from chemistry and astronomy to internal medicine, the missionary Cornelius Van Dyck (1818–95) resigned his position at the Syrian Protestant College in light of the Darwin affair. Yet while Van Dyck was a scientific polymath open to ideas about evolution, he was no liberal firebrand. In addition to having a medical degree, this native New Yorker was an ordained minister of the Dutch Reformed Church, and a missionary originally sent by the ABCFM, who two decades earlier had led a team in Beirut to translate the Bible into modern Arabic. Published in 1865, during the reign of Sultan Abdulaziz, this text became known as the "Van Dyck" Arabic Bible or as the "Van Dyck-Smith" Arabic Bible, the latter in a reference to the missionary Eli Smith (1801–57) who had started the translation project in 1848 and who had led it for nine years until his death.[145] Today, for many Arabic-speaking Christians, including Coptic Orthodox Christians in Egypt, this 1865 Bible translation and an updated version remain influential.[146]

Two trends in Protestant missions of the period informed the political tone of the Abdulhamid II era. The first trend was Bible translation and mass publishing, which helped to seed different forms of nationalism by making books cheaper and literacy more accessible, thus stimulating the formation of "imagined communities" among readers of the languages rendered in print.[147] The second trend was a growing resolve to appeal to Muslims and to try to convert them to Christianity, in spite of Islamic traditions that had historically forbidden such action.

In their translation work, Protestant missionaries were acting from a premise – even more, an evangelical principle – that people deserved Bibles in languages that they could understand for themselves. They usually focused on the "vernacular" or everyday spoken languages of the kind that people used, say, to negotiate the price of wheat and apricots at market, or to speak with family at home. They worked from the assumption that reading and understanding a text was much easier, and literacy was much more accessible, if a written text followed ordinary speech.

The Van Dyck Bible was a partial exception to this vernacular policy, insofar as its translators tried to strike a balance between accessibility and loftiness. The issue of this balance was particularly acute for Arabic, which evinced a multitude of registers along the spectrum from colloquial language or dialects to the high literary language (*al-fusha*). There was a reason for this Arabic Bible's elevated tone: namely, its American translators saw the Qur'an as a rival text – just as they saw Islam as a rival religion – and wanted their Bible to convey a spirit that was more august than homey.[148] In fact, Van Dyck relied heavily on insights from a Muslim scholar named Yusuf al-Asir (1815–90), who became a member of the translation team. A graduate of al-Azhar in Cairo who authored works on Arabic grammar and other subjects,[149] Yusuf al-Asir brought his knowledge of the Qur'an to bear on this Bible's literary style.

Two other important members of this Arabic Bible translation team were Nasif al-Yaziji (1800–71), a Melkite (Greek Catholic) Christian, and Butrus al-Bustani (1819–83), a Maronite Catholic convert to Protestantism. The energies that these men dedicated to the Bible translation project later extended into other works of publishing, authorship, and translation. Indeed, both Bustani and Yaziji became leading figures in the late nineteenth-century *Nahda*, or Arabic literary revival, which the intellectual historians George Antonius (1891–1942) and Albert Hourani (1915–93) both hailed in now-classic works as the spark that lit up the late nineteenth- and early to mid-twentieth-century Arab nationalist movement.[150] Bustani, in particular, was to the Arabs what Denis Diderot (1713–84) had been to the French: he attempted to grapple with the expanse of knowledge by producing the first Arabic encyclopedia for what he believed was a modern, enlightened age. On the basis of a close study of the early Van Dyck Bible manuscripts, some scholars now believe that Butrus al-Bustani played a bigger role than anyone else on the translation team – Smith and Van Dyck included – with the result that some have begun to refer to the "Bustani-Van Dyck Bible."[151]

In the 1860s (around the same time that the Van Dyck Bible debuted), the Bulgarian scholar Petko Slaveykov (1827–95) worked closely with American and British missionaries on a modern Bulgarian Bible. These efforts influenced Slaveykov as he helped to shape an incipient Bulgarian nationalist movement that had its foundations in Bulgarian Orthodox Christianity (and not, ironically, in missionary-style Protestantism) and in the educational mobilization of women and men. By emphasizing the Bulgarian vernacular as a language worthy for the Bible and for books and newspapers, the Bulgarian nationalist movement of the period also distanced itself from Greek-dominated ecclesiastical culture and from the Greek language, which had previously been the lingua franca of Bulgarian intellectuals. Significantly, Slaveykov worked on this translation not in Sofia, but in Istanbul, which in the 1860s had the biggest concentration of ethnic Bulgarians in any Ottoman city.[152] The locus of his translation work also serves as a reminder that late nineteenth-century Istanbul remained a cultural and intellectual hub within the world of Orthodox Christianity as it extended into the Balkans and beyond throughout Europe.[153]

English may have been the lingua franca of Protestant missions, equivalent to French and sometimes Italian for Catholics, and yet Protestant missions often used the mother tongues of their students (and especially Arabic and Armenian) as media of instruction in schools. Like Catholic and Jewish AIU schools in this period, they did not use Ottoman Turkish, attesting to the still quite limited currency of this language of state among non-Muslims and beyond the high social circles of Muslims who had ties to the government. Missionaries' use of local vernaculars in academic contexts appeared to encourage nationalism in practice.[154] And yet, in a period when nationalist identities were up for grabs, and when lingering Tanzimat-era ideals held out hopes for some kind of Ottoman identity and citizenship that could stretch across Muslim, Christian, and Jewish lines, the process of nation-building through vernacular print culture was not always clear-cut. Consider in this regard the Bible versions that Protestant missionaries (at different times and representing different missions) prepared just for Armenians – with each translation suggesting a potential nation or "imagined community" of readers that existed at the time. During the last years of the nineteenth century and opening years of the twentieth, Protestant missionaries produced and circulated Bible texts in "Ancient Church" Armenian, modern "Eastern" Armenian, modern "Western" Armenian, and both Kurdish and Turkish in Armenian characters (for Armenian Christians who spoke forms of Kurdish and Turkish in everyday parlance but who were literate in the Armenian script). Similarly, missionaries published a Turkish-language version written in the Greek alphabet, for Greeks who came from the central Anatolian region of Cappodocia.[155]

These particular Turkish-language Bible versions for Greeks and Armenians were not as obscure as they may now seem; they represented significant vernacular communities. As the historian M. Şükrü Hanioğlu observed, "The first novels published in the Ottoman Empire in the mid-nineteenth century were by Armenians and Cappodocian Greeks [who] wrote them in Turkish, using the Armenian and Greek alphabets."[156] The subject of the first Armenian-Turkish novel was telling. "It was an Armenian Romeo and Juliet," Hanioğlu explained, "depicting a love affair between two Armenians of different denominations – Armenian Apostolic and Catholic – and touching upon the sensitive question of sectarianism" – and one could add, missionary intervention, among Armenians. (Strikingly, the first novel written by a Muslim in Ottoman Turkish, dating from 1875, dealt with gender relations, too, suggesting how opportunities for girls and women in this period were testing social assumptions throughout Ottoman society.)[157] Once upon a time, the Armenian- and Greek-scripted Turkish Bibles suggest, Armenians and Greeks could have been Turks – after all, they read, wrote, and spoke in Turkish, and they thought about God in Turkish, too. These translations suggest possible histories of a multiethnic Anatolia that could have been or might have been, if the paths that history later took (during and just after World War I) had not obliterated their possibilities.

Returning again to the Van Dyck Bible, one can see how this published text of 1865 anticipated by nearly two decades a *second* trend among Protestant missions: the tendency to focus on Muslims. For when Eli Smith began the Arabic translation that Van Dyck later completed, Smith wrote to sponsors in New York, explaining that the Maronite and Melkite Catholics living in and near Beirut "actually form but a very small portion of the people for whom we labor," insofar as "the mass of the great Arab family are Muhammadans, whose sacred book [the Qur'an] is the standard of grammar & taste for the language." In short, Smith nodded to the ideal of universal evangelization (spreading the Christian message to everybody), which was inspiring Protestant missionaries in this period, and admitted that he was aiming for an Arabic Bible that would appeal both in the clarity of its message and in the eloquence of its language to Muslims.[158]

Smith wrote this letter in 1848, when the Tanzimat reforms were gaining momentum. Eight years later, the Ottoman sultan Abdulmajid issued the reform decree of 1856, which included language that affirmed freedom of religion. Then and for years to follow, Protestant missionaries took heart from this decree and interpreted it as a move toward complete freedom in religious choice.[159] However, the edict sustained another reading, one that suggested an affirmation of the *status quo ante* of Islamic tradition (see Chapter 4). This tradition, again, had historically upheld the freedom of Muslims, Christians, and Jews to practice the religions into which they were born, or alternately, the freedom of Christians and Jews to join the Muslim community via conversion. In any case, regardless of what the sultan had intended in his edict or of the mixed messages that the edict sent, Christian missionaries in the post-1856 period seemed to feel freer and bolder in evangelizing.

As the nineteenth century advanced, Protestant missionaries also grew bolder because they had foreign advocates to stand up for them: consuls on the ground, and political leaders from afar, who were ready to entreat, persuade, protest, or threaten on their behalf. This had not been the case even in 1830, when American missionaries had lacked the diplomatic power and gumption to intercede on behalf of As'ad al-Shidyaq (1798–1830), their first convert from Maronite Catholicism, who died alone in jail, tortured by Maronite ecclesiastical authorities who had interpreted his turn to Protestantism as a crime of apostasy.[160]

In the years after the 1856 Ottoman reform edict, however, matters were obviously changing. An illustrative case involved another former Maronite – a "Syrian" priest-turned-Protestant named Faris al-Hakim – who lived in Upper Egypt, where he worked closely with American Presbyterian missionaries. In 1861, this former priest appeared at court in Assiut. He aimed to defend a Coptic woman who had converted to Islam upon marrying a Muslim man but who wanted to leave her husband and return to the Christian community. According to a missionary source, "a crowd of [Muslim] men at the court tied up, assaulted, and bastinadoed Faris al-Hakim with the judge goading this on, and threw him in jail." American missionaries immediately contacted the American consul-general in Egypt, who paid a visit to the Ottoman viceroy, Said Pasha (1822–63), as he was about to leave for Istanbul. Not only did

Said Pasha order Faris al-Hakim's release, but he also commanded the Muslim ringleaders of the attack to pay a massive fine and serve a year in jail. Shortly afterward, US president Abraham Lincoln (1809–65) wrote a follow-up letter to Sa'id Pasha about the matter.[161] In short, this case from Egypt showed not only that missionary (and American) influence was growing by 1861, but also that a Christian could publicly aid a Muslim apostate, live to tell the tale, and go on to prosper.

Another event emboldened missionaries as the nineteenth century ended: this was the British invasion and "Occupation" of Egypt in 1882. The event reverberated into Syria, where in the words of the Palestinian historian Abdul Latif Tibawi (1910–81) "Anglo-Saxon missions" – meaning the members of British and American missions alike – "were jubilant." In a period when Protestant missionaries were beginning to use increasingly militant, neocrusader language to describe their relations with Muslims, one American missionary in Beirut hailed the British invasion of Egypt as "another phase of the great, inevitable conflict between Christianity and Mohammedanism."[162] British and American missionaries had reason to be happy, since British imperialism offered them protective cover in this period, and the British Occupation made the armor stronger. Meanwhile, by the early 1880s, the British CMS mission was beginning to pursue an official policy in Egypt and the Levant aiming exclusively for the conversion of Muslims. Some smaller British missions followed a similar policy of focusing on Muslims, even as certain other English and Scottish societies specialized in missions to convert Jews.[163] Catholic missions, once again, did not prioritize work among non-Christians, although in practice they welcomed converts from Judaism and Islam as did all Protestant missions.[164]

As the nineteenth century ended, some missionaries began to take their support for religious choice to its logical conclusion by admitting that belief in *anything* was optional. In Egypt in 1862, for example, Andrew Watson (1834–1916), who was a leading figure in the American Presbyterian mission to Egypt, intervened with European and American consuls to defend an Egyptian man of Muslim origin who had declared himself an atheist after studying abroad in France. In a context where many Muslims deemed rejection of God as the worst form of apostasy, theoretically punishable by death,[165] Egyptian authorities were going to punish this man by sending him southward up the Nile into what is now South Sudan, for exile and (Watson believed) probable drowning. Thanks to the missionaries' intercession, the man escaped that fate and by 1897 was still living in Cairo. "I am sorry to add, however," Watson wrote in his chronicle of the mission, published in 1904, "that the man [still] does not seem to have any religion, though he is a man of good moral character, and occasionally pays a visit to our Cairo bookshop."[166] Could a person be good and moral without believing in God whatsoever? This missionary concluded yes.

To be sure, Catholics and Protestants had not always held such liberal views about religious choice. Yet following civil wars and revolutions, countries like Great Britain and France had come far since their own days of burning accused heretics and witches at the stake, so that the eras of Mary Tudor or "Bloody Mary" (1516–58) and Elizabeth I (1533–1603) of England seemed long over. By the closing years of the late nineteenth century, it was hard to imagine how representatives of Henry VIII (1491–1547) could have executed a man for producing an English translation of the Bible. (This was William Tyndale [1494–1536], whom English authorities strangled and then immolated.) By the late nineteenth century even a new Joan of Arc (1412–31) would have been able to survive announcing visions of angels – not to mention dressing like a man – in France! Likewise, by the last quarter of the nineteenth century, Ottoman Muslim supporters of the mid-nineteenth-century Tanzimat reforms were thinking differently from their forebears who had lived in the times of Mehmet the Conqueror (1432–81). Yet while Ottoman Muslim intellectuals of the Abdulhamid II era were likely to agree that the state should not be in the business of judging and punishing apostates, the idea of a free-for-all in religious choice appeared to leave even the most liberal Ottoman Muslims uneasy. Among Muslims of all social ranks, traditional assumptions about conversion, apostasy, and the inescapability of Islam persisted.

How many full-fledged, baptism-and-all conversions from Islam to Christianity actually occurred in the Ottoman Empire in this period? Any number is a guess: a few dozen, a few hundred, maybe more, on the part of Protestant and Catholic missions together? Whatever they were, the numbers were minute, as missionaries readily admitted. Missionaries concluded that conversion from Islam remained so taboo, and so likely to provoke intense opposition and physical violence from families and neighbors, that few Muslims were ready to chance it. Their critics, on the other hand, concluded that missionary Christianity was so unappealing and such a big social step down from Islam that no sane person was likely to bother. Either way, these assumptions help to explain why conversions from Islam to Christianity were so exceedingly rare during the last quarter of the nineteenth century, despite the attention that they received from both missionaries and their critics. Of course, even conversions from one form of Christianity to another – say, from Orthodox or Eastern-Rite Catholic Christianity to Roman Catholicism and to Protestantism – were small in number relative to the total population. According to one estimate, for example, there were only 65,000 Protestants in the entirety of the Ottoman Empire by 1914, out of 18 million people total – and most of these were Armenians who had left the Armenian Apostolic Church.[167] Ottoman Protestants accounted, in other words, for just one-third of 1 percent of the Ottoman population. Yet, while Protestants had a minute presence in the Ottoman Empire, Protestant missionaries cast a long shadow with their new ideas, foreign diplomatic and imperial contacts, readiness to dismantle or break from traditions, opportunities for females, promotion of printing and reading, and ability to equip students and protégés with skills in a world that was tipping in favor of western Europe and North America.[168]

In 1883, a British CMS school in Salt, in what is now Jordan, reported the conversion of two Muslim boys in their school. News of this case appeared to confirm widespread fears among some Muslims about the subversive agendas of Christian missionaries, and provoked a government crackdown. For a start, in 1884, Ottoman authorities issued orders forbidding Muslims in the region from attending Christian schools, and rushed to fund construction instead of many more government schools, in which Islam, as the state religion, prevailed. At the same time, the government initiated efforts to distribute Qur'ans as a way of countering missionaries' distribution of Bibles.[169]

In 1886, the Ottoman government took measures further by requiring mission schools – both Christian and Jewish (AIU) institutions – to submit to regular inspections, thereby enabling the government to monitor not only the quality but also, and perhaps more importantly, the potentially political content of schools.[170] At the same time, Ottoman authorities investigated whether missionary teachers had teaching qualifications (as opposed to a general college or university education), and reportedly found that only 1 out of 345 teachers in Protestant schools in Syria, Lebanon, and Palestine had any kind of teaching diploma.[171] Authorities also found that out of some 400 American mission schools operating on Ottoman terrain, 341 lacked official licenses to operate, leading them to examine American institutions with particular scrutiny.[172] In fact, the Ottoman state had been trying to exert greater control over foreign schools from the days of Sultan Abdulaziz: a rule requiring foreign schools to be licensed dated from 1869. Yet even by 1894 (eight years after the inspection rule went into effect, and eighteen years into the reign of Abdulhamid II), only 37 percent of foreign schools had licenses to operate.[173] These figures testify to how evasive foreign missionaries could be in their dealings with the Ottoman state.

In the first year after the new inspection rule went into effect, some inspectors were Christians or Jews. But from then on, the Ottoman authorities appointed only Muslims, as if to suggest that only Muslims could reliably look out for the state by inspecting foreign Christian and Jewish institutions. This small detail about the Muslim-only status of school inspectors was an important sign of the times. Suspicious and on the defensive, Abdulhamid II was making efforts to strengthen the Sunni Muslim, as opposed to broadly Ottoman or generally Islamic, foundations of his state in facing threats that he now deemed to be both foreign and internal at once.[174]

Abdulhamid II and the Politics of Pan-Islam

In tracing the development of twentieth and early twenty-first-century Islamist movements among Sunni Muslims (with the Muslim Brotherhood, founded in Egypt in 1928, offering the most influential and obvious example), historians have often pointed to Abdulhamid II. Abdulhamid II, they say, introduced "pan-Islam," an ideology that stressed unity among Muslims from the Middle East and India to Southeast Asia and beyond, in the face of foreign imperialist threats and modern social conditions.[175] (In fact, the word "pan-Islam" first came into circulation in 1877, one year after his ascension.[176]) Certainly Abdulhamid II blended two qualities that came to distinguish Islamist movements during the century after his death in 1918. The first quality was an official respect for Islamic traditions of statehood, including traditions that privileged Muslims and Islamic legal conventions and that regarded non-Muslims as social subordinates.[177] In Abdulhamid II's case, this privileging of Muslims was implicit, for he did not abrogate the 1839 and 1856 Ottoman reform decrees which had stressed religious equality, nor did he explicitly revive earlier discourses about *dhimmi*s and the *jizya* tax. The second quality was a readiness to embrace cutting-edge technologies, particularly when these served either to maintain the force of the state or to project its image abroad.

A key example of Abdulhamid II's embrace of technology was the Hijaz Railway (constructed after 1900), which he ostentatiously presented as a Muslim-financed, Muslim-engineered, and Muslim-built effort in an age when foreign European concerns otherwise dominated the construction and management of Ottoman railways. Ottoman authorities did not even allow non-Muslims to own or buy land abutting the rail lines.[178] But in fact, and despite official rhetoric about its Muslim-only support base, Ottoman Christians and Jews contributed to this railway, too, because for many years authorities required all civil employees to give up one month of their salaries as a "donation" to the project.[179] At once an act of piety and a technological feat, this line cut across the arid expanses between Damascus and Mecca in a way that made pilgrimage easier, quicker, and cheaper for many Muslims.[180]

The Hijaz Railway also helped to consolidate Abdulhamid II's fan base among Muslims outside the empire, especially in British-controlled India (now independent Pakistan, India, and Bangladesh), where many admired him for leading the most powerful Islamic state that was still standing in the world. This degree of goodwill enabled him to make rhetorical claims to the caliphate, that is, to being the leader of all Muslims everywhere. Note that Ottoman rulers had historically used the title "sultan," which suggested the temporal nature of their rule. By contrast, the term "caliph" (from the Arabic word *khalifa*, meaning simply "successor") had originally signaled religious and political leadership over the unitary Muslim state and community, in the era that followed the Prophet Muhammad's death in 632 (See Chapter 2). In other words, as a title that the Prophet's companions Abu Bakr, 'Umar, 'Uthman, and 'Ali had first held in the mid-seventh century, and that successive rulers of the Umayyad and Abbasid dynasties had gone on to claim in centuries that followed, "caliph" suggested a level of Muslim probity that gave its bearer enormous prestige. Ottoman sultans had occasionally invoked the discourse of the caliphate before – in the text of the 1774 Treaty of Kujuk Kaynarca, for example, and occasionally during the 1860s and 1870s, relative to the sultan Abdulaziz. But Abdulhamid II expanded its use. Aspiring to a kind of figurehead-style eminence among Muslims not only within the Ottoman Empire, but also beyond its borders, Abdulhamid II welcomed the title of caliph, even though its practical function by the late nineteenth century was purely symbolic.

Claiming to be caliph had an ideological and psychological purpose, too. It gave Abdulhamid II a way to claim a residual moral, if not political, authority over Muslims living in Balkan and North African territories that the Ottoman Empire had lost. This justified, in turn, the maps produced for Ottoman government schools – maps that "clung to the fig-leaf of the empire's de jure borders" by including Algeria (conquered by France in 1830) and Tunisia (a French protectorate since 1881).[181]

British, French, Dutch, and Russian authorities were anxious about Abdulhamid II precisely because he attracted so much respect from Muslims in their own imperial domains. They worried that this sultan-caliph would rouse Muslims to a state of anticolonial jihad.[182] But in fact, Abdulhamid II never called for jihad, and there was no sign that he ever considered plotting one, either. Nevertheless, the fear among foreign European authorities that "when two Muslims meet in a café, they make pan-Islamism"[183] was not wholly unfounded in this period. Many Muslim thinkers were entering into a state of intellectual ferment;

Image 13 "Cawas et employé du consulate de France" (Guard and employee at the French consulate), c. 1885–1901, Bonfils Collection, Image Number 165926. Courtesy of the Penn Museum.

they were beginning to think more carefully about how to act and react politically and socially during an age when Muslim-inhabited lands from Algeria and Zanzibar to Bengal, the Deccan plateau, and Malaya had fallen, or were falling, under Western imperial control. The feeling of being on the defensive, of being subordinates – in this case colonial sub-jects – under the control of ostensibly "Christian" powers, was difficult for these activists to swallow. Against this political context, Abdulhamid II served as a face for the movement of Muslim political solidarity or pan-Islam that was building momentum.

One of the leading pan-Islamic activists of this era – and certainly the most flamboyant – was Jamal al-Din al-Afghani (1839–97). Accounts

of Afghani's career read like a "Who's Who" and a "What's What" of
intellectuals, venues, and events from the last quarter of the nineteenth
century. Although his name appeared to suggest an Afghan and perhaps therefore Sunni Muslim origin, Afghani came from a Shi'i Muslim
family in Asadabad, Iran – a fact that he concealed during a career that
he spent moving in mostly Sunni circles, as he hopped from India and
Afghanistan to Istanbul, Egypt, beyond and back again, urging Muslims
to mobilize against European (and for Afghani, especially British) imperialism.[184] Would his Sunni Muslim peers have taken him less seriously
or embraced him less warmly if they had known of his Shi'i origins?
Probably, yes, and this answer suggests the practical limits of the pan-
Islamic movement in bridging historical Sunni-Shi'i sectarian divisions.

The time that Afghani spent in Egypt in the 1870s proved to be
especially significant for his career. In Cairo, Afghani forged a close
relationship with a younger Egyptian intellectual named Muhammad
Abduh (1849–1905), who went on to become a distinguished scholar
and reformer of modern Islamic law. After British authorities in Egypt
decided that Afghani's speeches and writings had become too strident,
Afghani went into exile in France, and 'Abduh joined him there. Together
in Paris they produced an Arabic journal called al-'Urwa al-Wuthqa –
the "strongest bond" – with essays that called not only for unity among
Muslims, but also for a return to the foundational principles of early
Islamic society amidst life in the modern age. This notion of selectively
emulating the ways of early Muslims while living in modern conditions
(and in some cases, while emigrating to "Western" and predominantly
non-Muslim countries) became known as "salafism" (from the Arabic
word salaf, meaning ancestors) and went on to inspire Sunni Islamists in
the generations that followed.[185] During his time in France, too, Afghani
staged what became a famous debate with the French philosopher Ernest
Renan (1823–92), in which Afghani insisted on the compatibility of Islam
and modern science. In this speech (later published) and in other writings, he evinced another characteristic of the budding pan-Islamic movement, namely, a readiness to engage in the intellectual defense of Islam
against European claims to its backwardness, while using the Arabic
periodical press as a forum for political expression.[186] Afghani paved the
way for future Islamists like the Syrian Rashid Rida (1865–1935) and the
Egyptian Hasan al-Banna (1906–49), who also proved deft at conveying
their arguments in print.[187]

During his lifetime and after his death, observers reached mixed ver-
dicts on Afghani's character. His admirers cast him as a genuine, committed Muslim who was dedicated to defending and rallying Muslims
against the excesses of Western imperialism.[188] His critics dismissed him

as a rabblerouser and charlatan who was more enthusiastic about political agitation and the *idea* of Muslim unity than about Islam as a devotional system.[189] In 1877, a young American missionary named Anna Young Thompson (1851–1932) overheard a private discussion that Afghani had in Cairo with her colleague and fellow missionary, Andrew Watson (the same man who had helped the Egyptian Muslim-turned-atheist some years before). That night, Thompson captured Afghani's slippery character in her diary, when she wrote about the visit to the mission building of this "learned Moslim [*sic*] man known as 'The Philosopher' for his much & overwhelming talk & arguments, from Persia or Afghanistan ... who can argue that there is a God or that there is none."[190] She concluded that Afghani did not believe in much of anything at all.

Why was it that some people who met Afghani believed him to be a truly devout Muslim, whereas others concluded that he was apathetic or even hostile to religion? Writing a century later, a biographer tried to explain: Grounded in a certain tradition of Islamic philosophy and Iranian Shi'i disputation, Afghani adhered to the idea that only learned elites could understand ultimate truth, and that ordinary people needed and wanted literalist religion.[191] In other words, he tailored his commentaries according to whether he was addressing the cognoscenti or the hoi polloi, perhaps leaving the latter more convinced than the former of his adherence to Muslim principles. Another possible reason for the uncertainty that Afghani elicited may have derived from his use of *taqiyya*: the practice of dissimulation, of not speaking and acting openly but instead of pretending to think or to be something else, to which Shi'i Muslims had historically resorted for the sake of surviving in hostile Sunni milieus. In other words, when Afghani told different audiences different things – shaping his comments to suit his hearers, and leaving those who compared notes afterward confused about his sincere beliefs – he may have been performing his Shi'i-style *taqiyya*.[192] Certainly some critics have argued that Afghani bequeathed his own brand of *taqiyya* to some of the leaders of twentieth-century Sunni Islamist movements, who sometimes hid, minimized, or publicly misrepresented their actual views and intentions for the sake of political survival.[193]

And what about Abdulhamid II? How did he regard Afghani, this other exemplar of pan-Islam? It appears that Abdulhamid II appreciated Afghani's talents as an activist, but mistrusted him to the core. In 1892, the sultan invited Afghani to come to Istanbul, and Afghani, honored, accepted. In return for a house and a salary, Afghani helped the sultan by writing letters to various Shi'i *'ulama*, entreating them to recognize the Sunni sultan as the caliph of all Muslims. But Afghani found that once installed in Istanbul as the sultan's guest, he was stuck there; his days of hopping countries were over. With his keen attention to surveillance, Abdulhamid II was surely aware of reports suggesting that Afghani was or had variously been a spy for Russia or Britain, or both. The sultan would have been aware, too, that Afghani abetted in the long-distance plan that led to the assassination of Nasir al-Din Shah of Iran in 1896. As a man who prized stability – and especially the stability of his own regime – Abdulhamid II appeared to conclude that Afghani could be dangerous. Thus, the sultan kept Afghani in a state of *de facto* house arrest in Istanbul until the activist's death from cancer in 1897.

Of course, pan-Islam was more than Afghani, just as it was more than Abdulhamid II. Pan-Islam, again, was a mood that extended throughout Ottoman domains and beyond while drawing upon broad Muslim support. Writing in 1964, the historian Niyazi Berkes did not hide his scorn when mentioning that overblown, even hypocritical, religiosity was a hallmark of the Abdulhamid II period. And yet, Berkes continued, the ordinary Muslim people of the Ottoman Empire genuinely appreciated and admired Abdulhamid II, who projected himself as a capable, confident, and self-sufficient Muslim ruler.[194] Many Arabic-speaking Muslims appeared to appreciate, too, the way that Abdulhamid II reversed earlier policies by stressing the centrality of the Arab provinces (and not the empire's European districts) to the empire, by listing Arab provinces first among Ottoman provinces in the sultan's imperial yearbooks, and by assigning higher salaries for Arab regions, so that, say, an official posted to Baghdad received more than an official of commensurate rank and position in Albania.[195] Under Abdulhamid II, the Arabic-speaking regions of the empire were no longer imperial backwaters; they represented the heart of the empire.

Did ordinary Muslims in the empire know that the sultan appreciated an occasional glass of cognac or champagne "to settle his nerves," despite the Qur'an's discouragement of drinking intoxicants (5:90, 2:219)? Did they know that he looked the other way when Muslim employees in his palace broke or ignored the daytime fast of Ramadan, so that they could keep up with their paperwork?[196] It is unlikely that they knew, though whether they would have cared if they *had* known is another question. Certainly people knew that Abdulhamid II regularly left the palace to attend Friday prayers; that during Ramadan he visited the sacred relics (including the Prophet Muhammad's mantle) and hosted fast-breaking meals for Ottoman and foreign dignitaries; that he refrained from posting his image around the empire, opting for a sober calligraphic insignia instead; that he declared bans on the public consumption of alcohol in Muslim urban districts (even if enforcement was uneven); and that he worked harder and lived more simply than his predecessors.[197] In short, many Muslims appreciated his emphasis on the Islamic foundations of the Ottoman state and his personal habits of quiet and regular Muslim piety.[198] Niyazi Berkes – again, no admirer of Abdulhamid II and his regime – concluded that, "The foundation of Hamidian rule was the great mass of the [Muslim] people – with all their beliefs and superstitions, and also their sense of honour and decency."[199]

Becoming (More) Muslim

Deference to tradition in the thick of modern life was a hallmark of Abdulhamid II's reign and a feature of the pan-Islamic movement and all Islamist movements that followed. And yet, focusing on the activities of super-literati like Afghani and Abduh can obscure an equally important aspect of pan-Islamic politics in the Abdulhamid II era, namely, the Ottoman state's policies toward members of certain offbeat Muslim or quasi-Muslim communities that were living inside the empire. These policies, which reflected the changing attitudes on the part of the sultan and his supporters toward who and what was Muslim, entailed sending out preachers and teachers to draw certain communities toward state-sanctioned Sunni Islam while buffering them from the appeals of Christian missionaries.

Abdulhamid II's approach to the Muslim practices of his subjects marked a shift from the laissez-faire policies of his predecessors. During its period of territorial expansion, the Ottoman Empire had been an "empire of conversions"[200]: large numbers of people entered Islam, the religion of state, by some combination of choice and force, and through intermarriage, professional opportunity seeking, and different forms of slavery. Amidst so much conversion, Ottoman Islam – to use a singular noun for a polymorphous entity – had been a religion in flux. Consider, for example, that in 1555, when a group of disgruntled Janissaries wrote to the Ottoman grand vizier to complain about unfair treatment from their superior officer (who, like them, was Christian-turned-Muslim), they lambasted this officer as a "Hungarian infidel who converted to Islam only yesterday and whose breath still reeks of pork."[201] It would have been hard to imagine such a cavalier remark appearing in a letter to a high state official in the 1880s and 1890s, if only because the Ottoman Empire under Abdulhamid II was losing its tolerance for religious ambiguity while conversion was becoming more serious.

In fact, Ottoman Islam accommodated a lot of diversity in practice during the 1880s and 1890s. It encompassed robust traditions of Sufism, as represented by Bektashi, Mevlevi, and other orders. In what is now southern Iraq and Lebanon, there were populations that adhered to Shi'ism of the Twelver variety, which Shah Isma'il had promoted in Iran after 1501. Especially in Istanbul and its environs, and among the ruling classes and military elites, Muslims included many people whose forebears had converted from Christianity and to a lesser extent Judaism in the not-too-distant past and who sometimes preserved vestiges of Christian or Jewish practices.[202] The Dönme exemplified this last trend: they were descendants of a small community (originally numbering 200–300 families or perhaps 1,000–1,500 people) who had converted from Judaism to Islam in 1666, after the Ottoman sultan of the time gave their leader, Rabbi Sabbatai Sevi (1626–76), an ultimatum to convert to Islam or face death. The rabbi, who had offended many Jews and who had worried Muslim authorities by claiming to be a messiah, chose conversion, prompting his most loyal supporters to follow him into Islam.[203] Memories of this rabbi-messiah-turned-Muslim enabled the Dönme to keep a sense of communal cohesion across the three centuries that followed even as they remained firmly apart from the Jewish community to which their families had once belonged. As the nineteenth century ended, the Dönme gave their sons Muslim names like Muhammad and Ahmad, scrupulously observed the Muslim fast of Ramadan, and visited mosques to pray, even while among themselves they recited additional liturgies in Hebrew and Ladino (also known as Judeo-Spanish), that is, the language of Sephardic Jews.[204] In public, the Dönme did what faithful Muslims were supposed to do; in private, they did things of their own.

Descendants of Greek Orthodox Christians who had converted to Islam in the seventeenth century, the Stavriotae or Istavri were another case of religious hybrids. In the nineteenth century, Stavriotae men bore Muslim names and served as Muslims in the Ottoman military. Yet unlike the Dönme, who kept apart from Jews, the Stavriotae maintained close contact with Greek Orthodox Christian people and appear to have practiced Christianity at home.[205] For this reason, the term "crypto-Christians," meaning secret Christians, suited the Stavriotae in a way that the term "crypto-Jews" did not apply to the Dönme, who did not consider themselves Jewish.[206] And while the Dönme never renounced their public identities as Muslims, many Stavriotae tried to do just that during the half century after the 1856 reform decree, which they interpreted as signaling openness to a new kind of religious choice.[207]

The Ottoman Empire included some other groups whose religious beliefs were hard to classify. In Albania, for example, there were people who had Muslim public names and Christian domestic ones; went to village churches and city mosques; had sons confirmed, christened, but also circumcised; married according to both Muslim and Christian rituals; observed Christian fasts but went to mosque during Ramadan;

and asked for Christian last rites but were buried in Muslim grave-yards. Sometimes strategic reasons affected which religion they publicly expressed: in some Albanian villages, for example, people professed to be Muslims when Ottoman tax collectors arrived (so that they could pay less tax) but Christians when military recruiters came (so that they could avoid being drafted).[208]

In rural parts of Anatolia and greater Syria, where access to literacy had been historically minimal, some people followed religious practices that blended special respect for Ali (the prophet Muhammad's son-in-law and cousin whose cause, again, had inspired the *shi'a* or cadre of early Islamic partisans who gave Shi'ism its name), along with many other religious elements. These elements included aspects of Sufism; local or "folk" customs; and influences from Christianity, Judaism, Zoroastrianism, and pre-Islamic, nature-centered religion. The Alevis (natives of what became Turkey after World War I), the Druze (natives of what became Lebanon, Syria, and Israel), the Yezidis (natives of what became Iraq, Syria, and Armenia), and the Nusayris or Alawites (natives of what became Syria) fell into this ambiguous category.

In the late nineteenth century, were the Dönme, Stavriotae, Alevis, Druze, Yezidis, and Alawites Muslim? The answer to this question is some combination of technically yes, maybe, maybe not, not really, and "sort of." Outside observers differed in their assessments, while even members of these groups appeared to vary in the extent of their identification with Islam and Muslims. These groups were endogamous – they married among themselves – and that preserved their cohesion. With the exception of the Dönme, who lived mostly in Salonika and Istanbul, and the Stavriotae, who lived in the Black Sea region around Trebizond (now Trabzon, Turkey) and by the nineteenth century, too, in the central Anatolian town of Yozgat, these groups tended to live far from state control. They were adept at obscuring or keeping secret their true religious practices or beliefs. Indeed, their inclination toward a kind of *taqiyya* or dissimulation, which functioned as a kind of "everyday political opportunism" and tactic of survival "in an environment which expelled them as heretics,"[209] helps to explain why observers often placed the Alevis, Druze, Yezidis, and Alawites along the Shi'i spectrum. (The Dönme certainly dissimulated, but in their lack of special deference for Ali, they fell into the Sunni camp. The same applied to the Stavriotae.)

What did it mean for a group to be maybe Muslim, maybe not? Writing in 1709, a Carmelite priest named Elia Giacinto di Santa Maria wrote to Rome about a journey he had made to an Alawite village in Syria, in which he grappled with this question. This priest reported that the Alawites whom he had met were "Muslim" insofar as they studiously abstained from pork, practiced male circumcision, and dressed like Muslims. If "Turks" were around, they observed the fast of Ramadan. Like mainstream Muslims, they denied notions of the Trinity while professing respect for Jesus as a prophet. But otherwise, Father Giacinto reported, his Alawite contacts regarded Sunni Muslims with contempt and mistrust, and in a departure from normative Islam, believed in "metempsychosis," or human reincarnation after death into animals like lions and gazelles. They engaged in certain Christian-like practices, which Father Giacinto attributed to the influence of Crusaders of yore. They seemed to love Palm Sunday, for example, and happily marched into church, palm fronds aloft, with Christians neighbors on that day; they also engaged in a secret, nighttime communion ritual involving drinking wine and eating bread.[210] Jump forward to 1855, and one can find a remarkably similar account – this time about the Kurdish-speaking Alevis – coming from American Protestant missionaries of the ABCFM in Arabkir (now Arapgir, in eastern Turkey). Alevis were Muslim, American missionaries reported, and yet Alevis did not fast during Ramadan, nor did they perform the five daily prayers common to Muslims. Rather, they devised extemporaneous prayers of their own. And instead of avoiding pork in their diets, Alevis avoided fish. At the same time, Alevis seemed to believe in Christ and to invoke him in an annual bread-making ritual.[211] Like Father Giacinto who wrote about the Alawites, American missionaries concluded that the not-wholly-Muslim religious practices of the Alevis made them promising targets for Christian missionary appeals.

An Alawite fondness for palm rituals? An Alevi aversion to fish? One wonders whether Father Giacinto in 1709 and the American ABCFM missionaries in 1855 conveyed accurate information, or if they merely mistook the quirks of individuals for those of an entire community. Anyone who has worked closely with Christian missionary reports or with travel accounts more broadly knows that such sources can be hit-or-miss in their details. And yet, with regard to these groups, the intelligence that Ottoman Muslim authorities had at their disposal was not necessarily much better than what Christian missionaries were able to gather. The Turkish historian Ilber Ortaylı, who formerly directed the Topkapı Palace museum complex in Istanbul (home of generations of Ottoman sultans), acknowledged as much. Ottoman authorities, he wrote, had long known what the religion of the *dhimmi*s – the empire's Christians and Jews – was about. But even by the Abdulhamid II era, authorities did *not* know much about the beliefs of the Alawites, Yezidis, Alevis, and Dönme, who were secretive and kept to themselves.[212]

For most of Ottoman history, the beliefs of groups like these had not mattered. Ottoman authorities assessed religious identity in terms of what people said and professed, and how they acted in public. Authorities did not barge into back rooms and cellars to check up on how people were praying. Nor did they function like the "Thought Police" whom George Orwell (1903–50) conjured in his novel *1984*; they did not stand ready to pounce upon people for "thoughtcrimes."[213] Moreover, Ottoman authorities had worked on the straightforward assumption that the empire's subjects included three basic types of religious characters: Christians; Jews; and everyone else, meaning Muslims. To be Muslim was the default. In this rough scheme, the Ottoman state refused to recognize sectarian distinctions among Muslims, and accepted that groups like the Alawites and Alevis were Muslims, or at least Muslim enough, even if some of their ideas and practices may have seemed weird from the outside.[214]

"Weird" is a word that scholars tend not to use to describe religious groups; as a comment on strangeness, it sounds disrespectful and almost slangy in its candor. In academic parlance, the fancier word "heterodox" is more common.[215] But in implying deviation from some kind of "orthodox" norm, the "heterodox" label has discursively shackled groups like the Yezidis, Alawites, and Dönme to Islam, making it difficult for scholars to imagine accounting for, or speaking about, the beliefs and practices of these groups as anything other than deviant versions of Islam. The word heterodox also squashes the possibility of considering Alawism, Alevism, Yezidism, and Dönmism as autonomous religions that possessed internal coherence for their followers. In short, "heterodox" may sound more rarified than "weird," but "weird" is more open in practice.

Terminology aside, the fact is that Ottoman authorities found it hard to account for the Yezidis as Muslims. Perhaps it was the Yezidi belief in the figure known as Malak Tawus, or the "Peacock Angel," that flummoxed them most and made them think that Yezidis might be something other than Muslims entirely. (Yezidis looked to the Peacock Angel as God's primary intermediary with humankind on Earth, and sometimes represented him in bronze icons.[216]) Indeed, while some Sunni Muslim religious authorities characterized the Yezidis as heretics at best, and devil worshippers at worst, Ottoman authorities remained more ambivalent.[217]

As the nineteenth century wore on, this ambivalence gained expression in a set of policies that zigzagged. For example, after 1839, during the early years of the Tanzimat era, as the tax-collecting prowess of the central Ottoman state advanced, authorities decided to make Yezidis pay the *jizya* along with Christians and Jews as though they were not Muslims but belonged to a religious category of their own. (Note that they did not extract *jizya* from either the Druze or the Alawites.)[218] And yet, as the state became more desperate for Muslim men to serve in the army, authorities reconsidered. And so, starting in the mid-1850s – around the time that

Sultan Abdulmajid issued his reform decree affirming the equal rights and responsibilities of Muslim and non-Muslim subjects – the Ottoman state began to demand regular conscripts from Yezidi communities, which proved to be highly unpopular (as all Ottoman military drafting was in this period). Concluding that Yezidi money may have been more valuable than Yezidi service, Ottoman authorities wavered again. For at least one decade, from 1875 to 1885, the state allowed Yezidis to pay the military exemption tax, that is, the *jizya* substitute that Christians and Jews were now making.[219] Muslims or not Muslims? Ottoman authorities could not make up their minds but were determined to squeeze out of the Yezidis the best deal that they could get in money or manpower.

Abdulhamid II came to the throne, and the wavering stopped. Under his leadership, the Ottoman state refused to accept the exemption tax from Yezidis and forced Yezidi men to serve in the military.[220] Under Abdulhamid II, too, authorities decided that if the Yezidis were not really Muslims, then it was about time that they *became* Muslims. Beginning in the early 1890s the sultan sent Sunni clerics as Muslim missionaries to Yezidi areas and entrusted them with the "rectification" (*ihtida'*) of Yezidi beliefs through a process that aimed for *de facto* conversion to Sunni Islam[221]. Authorities wooed some Yezidi leaders to Istanbul by offering them honors, gifts, and financial incentives, and then placed them under house arrest (using much the same tactic that the sultan had tried on Jamal al-Din al-Afghani several years before). At the same time, Abdulhamid II sent the Ottoman military to crush Yezidi resistance and to force compliance with state demands. Heads fell. After one raid in 1892, Ottoman forces literally carried into Mosul the remnants of Yezidi men from the neck up. Ottoman-state-sanctioned Sunni clerics also organized a public ceremony that called on Yezidi chiefs to embrace Islam, while authorities beat up those who refused to participate. Finally, the Ottoman state built mosques and madrasas to inscribe Sunni Islam into the landscape of Yezidi communities.[222]

The historian Selim Deringil has called these measures part of the sultan's policy of the "new orthodoxy," which entailed using the powers of the Ottoman state to promote and enforce Sunni Islam of the Hanafi *madhab* (referring to the particular tradition of Sunni Islamic jurisprudence that the Ottoman Empire followed). Against this political climate, one set of Stavriotae who petitioned the state to revert formally to Christianity – and thereby to become exempt (as Christians effectively were) from the military draft – came up against stiff resistance. Authorities threatened to draft Stavriotae and send them to Libya, Yemen, and the Hijaz, and warned Stavriotae parents to send their sons to government schools where they could gain exposure to the Islam to which, in the state's view, they were forever bound.[223] During the Abdulhamid II era, when the empire was so desperate for money, manpower, and a sense of political and cultural coherence, shrugging off Islam was not an option.

As part of the program to promote a new Sunni orthodoxy, Abdulhamid II also sent teacher-preachers, who constituted a *de facto* "religious secret police-cum-missionary organization," to a variety of other "heretics" during the 1890s. These included Arabic-speaking bedouin in the Ma'an Valley (an area that now overlaps Jordan, the West Bank of Palestine, and Israel), whose lack of literacy and nomadic lifestyles may have contributed to what Ottoman authorities regarded as their lax performance and understanding of Islam. These Muslim missionary campaigns also extended to Zaydis, members of a small and distinct branch of Shi'ism who lived in Yemen, where the Ottoman state was busy asserting its territorial claims. Ottoman missions in this decade included Alawites in Syria, too.[224] In fact, some Alawites in Antioch who formally embraced Sunni Islam under Ottoman pressure complained afterward that other Sunnis ("real" Sunnis?) rejected their conversions and treated them as badly as ever. An Ottoman investigation substantiated these claims, observing that Muslim notables in the area had traditionally used Alawites like a slave-labor force.[225] This case suggests the limits of state power in this context. For while the sultan's delegates could try to "rectify" Alawite beliefs in the direction of Sunni Islam, they could not as easily overcome the skepticism and mistrust of Sunni Muslims who were expected to receive Alawites into their fold.[226]

Converting people like the Alawites, who were experts at dissimulation, posed problems for gauging sincerity. If an Alawite man claimed to embrace Sunni Islam, how could one be sure that he would not revert to old ways? How could one know that he really meant it, and *believed*?

Belief: to quote Hamlet, "Aye, there's the rub!" The attitudes of Abdulhamid II and his supporters were changing with regard to religious belief, and in this sphere, Christian missionaries once again exerted an influence. Religion, Christian missionaries of the nineteenth century maintained, was neither an unshakeable inheritance nor a public veneer; it was instead a matter of private belief and inner conviction, subject to change, and involving some combination of the thoughts inside one's head plus the feeling in one's heart.[227] Under the influence of evangelical and pietistic strands of Christian thought, Protestants were more vocal than Catholics during this period in expounding ideas about individual choice, change, and heartfelt religion vis-à-vis Islamic societies, although Catholic missionaries were arguably converging with Protestants in their underlying assumptions.[228] As the nineteenth century ended and the twentieth began, some Protestant missionaries were beginning to reason, too, that religion, as a fundamentally interior experience, could be secret, so that a person could theoretically act Muslim on the outside but yet "think" and "feel" Christian on the inside, by believing in Christ and perhaps, too, in a notion of fellowship with other Christians.[229] Some missionaries were recognizing, in short, a possible Christian variety of dissimulation that would enable Muslims-turned-Christians to avoid the stigma of public apostasy and the harassment that it would entail.

Ultimately, Ottoman officials came to see Muslim religion in a similar manner as Christian missionaries – as something mutable, subject to change or abandonment, and operating inside – and this realization frightened them. It deepened their fears to see foreign Christian missionaries in this same period spread out across Ottoman domains to set up schools, hospitals, and other institutions while elaborating on their hopes for mass conversions in material that they wrote for home audiences.[230] The attempted public shift of the Stavriotae from Islam to Christianity may have compounded officials' concerns. Abdulhamid II and his supporters also worried about the Alevis, some of whom had in the 1850s and 1860s expressed a desire to develop a closer connection or alliance to the Protestants, or at least to the Protestant *millet* that seemed to afford its members more autonomy from the Ottoman state.[231] Against this context, Abdulhamid II's policies of building many more schools and mosques, and sending Muslim missionaries to groups deemed deviant in their Islam, represented an act of "aggressive counterpunching" to Christian missionary threats.[232]

The Ottoman government began to envision its new schools not as sites for a broadly *Islamic* culture (in the umbrella sense of including Muslims and non-Muslims; see Chapter 1), but rather as sites dedicated to promoting *Muslim* culture for Muslim students. In this way, government schools partly supplanted mosques as centers of religious education, where Muslim teachers on state salaries could teach, review, and test Islam as a modern academic subject on a par with history and geography.[233] Meanwhile, non-Muslims in government schools could find that they were rare creatures. For example, one Greek Orthodox Christian noted that in 1895, he and his brother were the only non-Muslims in a government school of 250 students in Latakia, Syria, while a Jewish memoirist named Sam Lévy recalled of his youth in the 1880s that he was the only non-Muslim at a government boarding school in Salonika (a city that otherwise had a large Jewish population) and so the Muslim students "baptized" him Kemal![234]

Again, Abdulhamid II tried to make groups like the Yezidis and Alawites either Muslim or more Muslim, depending on one's perspective. He did so for three reasons. First, Ottoman armies desperately needed more

Image 14 *Students, imperial military middle school* Halep [Aleppo],
c. 1890–93. Albumen photographic print by Abdullah Frères. Library
of Congress, Washington, DC. Abdul Hamid II Collection.

manpower at a time when many Muslim families regarded the draft as
a virtual death sentence (thereby making all recruitment into an act of
coercion). Second, the sultan disapproved of the continuing idiosyn-
crasies of hybrid religious communities in an empire where a mood of
Muslim reform and rigor was on the upswing. And third, he feared that
Christian missionaries would get to the idiosyncratic groups first – and
perhaps succeed in attracting them. In fact, Christian missionaries were
not terribly successful at wooing converts from groups like the Yezidis
and Druze. (Another way of saying this is that the bread-and-butter work
of Christian missions continued to be among local Christians – and this
point applied to Protestants and Catholics alike, in spite of the loud talk

among Protestants about their missions to Muslims, Jews, and others.) These points suggest that fears more than realities shaped Ottoman policy, and that communities of Alevis, Alawites, and others remained robust in the face of both Muslim and Christian missionary appeals.

In fact, the Yezidi experience suggests how Ottoman policies to convert or rectify religious groups had the potential to backfire. For when some Yezidis who survived the Ottoman military attacks of the early 1890s arrived as refugees among fellow Yezidis in the Jabal Sinjar region of what is now northern Iraq, they spread news of what the government's forces had done to them. Their reports contributed to the spread of millenarian ideas and anti-Ottoman and anti-Muslim propaganda, and this fired, in turn, a Yezidi religious revival.[235] Far from weakening Yezidi identity, Abdulhamid II's attempts at "Sunnification" made Yezidism stronger.

Conclusion: Continuity, Rupture, and Islamic Reform

In 1862, five years before Sultan Abdulaziz took his nephew Abdulhamid to witness the Exposition Universelle in Paris, and fourteen years before this nephew claimed the throne,[236] Ottoman police stumbled into a Dönme community center in Salonika (now Thessaloniki). Searching for a missing person, they found something else instead: implements of torture, covered in blood. Upon investigating, police ascertained that this group of Dönme (who represented one of three Dönme sects) had been using this space as a secret court, where they beat transgressors from their community and killed those who leaned too far toward non-Dönme Islam, for example, by trying to marry a Muslim outsider. Protestant missionaries had been calling the Dönme "Jewish Turks" since the 1820s, perhaps to elide their Muslim-ness and to justify proselytization among them. According to the historian Marc David Baer, this incident from 1862 may have marked the moment when Ottoman officials began to see the Dönme differently, too. For indeed, the report identified the Dönme as those "who appear in public as Muslims yet actually follow a Jewish sect."[237]

The tendency on the part of government officials to recognize religion as a matter of inner belief and not merely of public profession, which became clear during the Abdulhamid II era, had been gaining ground for some time. One can say the same about many other developments of the Abdulhamid II era: they built on what came before. As the nineteenth century advanced, the administrative reach of the Ottoman Empire grew, the bureaucracy expanded, Ottoman subjects traveled farther (and sometimes settled permanently on the other side of the world), and more elements originating in western Europe and North America exerted charm and issued threats. France, for example, fielded both Sarah Bernhardt (1844–1923), the stage actress, as well as many of the bankers who hammered on the empire's portals once bankruptcy struck in 1876. Abdulhamid II himself was a great fan of the actress, whom he invited to Istanbul for a private performance, but not of the bankers, who set up the Public Debt Administration on Ottoman turf to wring out the money that they considered their due.[238]

And yet, despite these continuities in trends, policies, and connections, two converging factors made the post-1876 period qualitatively different from what came before. These were the darker mood of the times, occasioned by territorial and financial losses, and the personality of the sultan, who worked hard but lived as if he were huddled under permanent siege. The empire that started Abdulhamid II's reign in 1876 had been still substantially European and North African, though within the space of six years, it became more narrowly "Middle Eastern" in a way that one would recognize today. At the same time, the Ottoman Empire was more *Muslim* in its demographic profile than it had ever been in its history. These circumstances influenced Abdulhamid II's turn toward pan-Islam or the "new [Sunni] orthodoxy," which included, among other things, efforts to make people he deemed "bad" Muslims into "good" Muslims while keeping Christian missionaries in check. The fact that Muslim intellectuals like Muhammad Abduh and Jamal al-Din al-Aghani had begun to call for Islamic reform and for an Islamic modernity built on tradition – all while agitating against foreign (non-Muslim) imperialism on the part of powers like Britain and France – sharpened pan-Islamic activity in this period.

During the late nineteenth century, there were two other features of the cultural landscape that set the stage for the Muslim and pan-Islamic politics of the era. The first feature was nationalism, which threatened to break the empire into big pieces or "nations" made of people who shared some combination of language, religion, and historical memory of togetherness in a particular place. For much of the nineteenth century, nationalism in the Ottoman Empire had been a Christian phenomenon. Think of the Greeks, some of whom in the 1820s imagined and realized a new Greece built on the ideal of the ancient one. Serbs, Armenians, and other Christians later caught the "bug" of nationalism, too. By the late nineteenth century, however, nationalism was no longer just a Christian problem for the Ottoman state. Some highly literate Muslims were beginning to express nationalist ideas, based not on religion per se but on language communities of writers and speakers.

The other feature of the political landscape that set the stage for Sunni pan-Islamic politics in this period was Wahhabism, an ideology and religious culture that arose in the central Arabian region of Najd (now in Saudi Arabia), which had always remained beyond effective Ottoman control. The influence of Wahhabism showed that Abdulhamid II's pan-Islam was not a hermetic development – that is, it did not arise within the sealed borders of the Ottoman Empire – but rather took shape amidst reformist currents that were swirling in the larger Muslim world, and within Asia and Africa especially.[239]

Wahhabism took its name from an eighteenth-century Muslim thinker named Muhammad ibn 'Abd al-Wahhab (1703–92) who had forged an alliance with a tribal chief named Muhammad ibn Sa'ud (d. 1765). Ibn 'Abd al-Wahhab called for a return to the fundamentals of Islamic religion by means of strict adherence to Qur'anic teachings and to the personal example of the Prophet Muhammad's behavior (his *sunna*). He criticized popular Muslim practices such as shrine worship and saint worship (i.e. the informal acclamation of holy men and women who demonstrated religious charisma), and saw these as infringements on the monotheistic principle, enshrined in Islam's credo, that "there is no god but God." In short, he advocated an austere Sunni practice that led him to denounce Sufis, Shi'is, and all other Muslims who diverged from his model Islam, to the extent that he readily called such Muslims infidels and hence legitimate targets for war. Ibn 'Abd al-Wahhab's supporters and allies, including the family of Ibn Sa'ud, had briefly threatened Ottoman territory during the opening years of the nineteenth century, when they tried to conquer western Arabia. Unwilling to brook the loss of Mecca and Medina, the holy cities of Islam, whose control gave the Ottoman Empire enormous prestige, Ottoman authorities had sent the governor of Egypt, Muhammad Ali, to crush the Wahhabis in the Hijaz. This war, which lasted from 1811 to 1818, would have amounted to little more than a footnote in the history books except that the Sa'udis rebounded, and after World War I won international recognition for a kingdom in Arabia under their leadership.

These details are worth mentioning here because the Wahabbis stimulated two significant developments among adversarial Muslim groups during the late nineteenth century. First, and despite their anti-Sufi sentiments, the Wahhabis inspired reforms within Sufi movements, including some that were active in Ottoman territories and others that were not.[240] Beyond the coast of what is now Libya, for example, one of these reformed Sufi organizations, led by the Sanusi family, was winning adherents and developing an economic and social network that extended deep into the Sahara desert to parts of what are now Chad and Niger.[241] Years later, after Italy invaded Libya in 1911 and forced Ottoman forces to withdraw after a short war, members of the Sanusiya brotherhood led the anti-Italian resistance. And, second, the Wahhabis' intermittent attacks on areas corresponding to southern Iraq, including the shrine centers of Najaf and Karbala, where the caliph Ali (d. 656) and his son, the Prophet Muhammad's grandson, Husayn (d. 680), were buried, set in motion a mass shift toward Shi'ism. This shift occurred among Arabic-speaking Muslims. It involved especially Arab Muslims who were turning from pastoral nomadism to settled agriculture and who were cultivating protective alliances with Persian-speaking *ulama* (from what is now Iran) whose presence in Najaf and Karbala had been growing since the eighteenth century.[242]

Thus, in the very period when Abdulhamid was sending out Muslim teachers and preachers to bring groups into greater conformity with Hanafi-style Sunni Islam, Shi'ism was spreading at breakneck speed among Arabic-speaking Muslims in the Ottoman territory that now corresponds to southern Iraq. In this case, the spread of Shi'ism had more to do with Wahhabi-Saudi attacks coming out of Arabia than with the tactics of the Ottoman state emanating from Istanbul. Whether one employs the word "conversion" to describe this shift toward Shi'ism depends on how substantial one considers the change. This much is clear: in this corner of the Ottoman Empire during the nineteenth century, sectarian borders among Muslims were proving to be relatively porous, while "Sunni" as a sect identity was not rock-solid. Some 2,500 years before, Persian Empire builders had conquered Mesopotamia, forging links between what we now call "Iraq" and "Iran." In the late nineteenth century, political circumstances associated with the militant Sunni ideology of the Sa'udi family were confirming the cultural ties that linked Iraq and Iran while guaranteeing that Shi'ism as a way of understanding Islamic history on the one hand, and Muslim life and devotion on the other, would not just persist but expand.

Abdulhamid II was still going strong twenty years into his reign. In some ways, the social circumstances of his era were enabling Muslims, Christians, and Jews to fraternize – literally, to act like brothers – more than ever before. Females were also involved, so that circumstances were increasingly allowing Muslims, Christians, and Jews to "sororize," or act sisterly, too. Yet, tensions were building. During the 1890s circumstances in Anatolia were becoming more precarious for Armenian Christians, in spite of – or precisely because of – their greater prosperity. Meanwhile, in western Europe, some Jewish thinkers were beginning to question whether the popular anti-Jewish sentiment pervasive among Christian people – a sentiment increasingly known as anti-Semitism – would ever stop shadowing Jews. Their pessimism gave rise to the Zionist movement, which stood poised to reconfigure the Middle East as the Ottoman Empire neared its end.

NOTES

1 Georgeon, *Abdülhamid II*, p. 149.
2 Georgeon, *Abdülhamid II*, p. 149.
3 Erik J. Zürcher, *Turkey: A Modern History*, second edition (London: I.B. Tauris, 1998), p. 84.
4 Findley, *Bureaucratic Reform in the Ottoman Empire*, pp. 228–29; Georgeon, *Abdülhamid II*, p. 140.
5 Ali Haydar Midhat Bey, *The Life of Midhat Pasha: A Record of His Services, Political Reforms, Banishment, and Judicial Murder, Derived from Private Documents and Reminiscences by His Son Ali Haydar Midhat Bey* (London: John Murray, 1903), pp. 89–91. A multinational panel of doctors, including those of the British and Austro-Hungarian embassies, signed this autopsy report.
6 "The Turkish Revolution: The Death of Abdel Aziz," *New York Times*, June 19, 1876; Christopher Clay, *Gold for the Sultan: Western Bankers and Ottoman Finance, 1856–1881* (London: I.B. Tauris, 2000), pp. 334–35. On the suicide-versus-murder debate, see also Eliakim Littell, ed., *Littell's Living Age*, Fifth Series, Vol. 23, July, August, September 1878 (Boston: Littell and Gay, 1878), pp. 678–79.
7 Georgeon, *Abdülhamid II*, pp. 25, 48–50, 389.
8 Ibrahim al-Muwaylihi, *Spies, Scandals, and Sultans: Istanbul in the Twilight of the Ottoman Empire*, trans. Roger Allen (London: Rowman & Littlefield, 2008), pp. 108–9. On his Friday processions to the mosque, which European tourists would line up to see, Deringil, *The Well-Protected Domains*, pp. 22–23.
9 Ihsan Yücel, *Dolmabahçe Palace*, second edition (Istanbul: TBMM Department of National Palaces, 1995).
10 Georgeon, *Abdülhamid II*, pp. 30–31.
11 Georgeon, *Abdülhamid II*, p. 55.
12 Muwaylihi, *Spies, Scandals and Sultans*, pp. 164–65. Carter Findley offered a similar assessment in *Bureaucratic Reform in the Ottoman Empire*, pp. 228–33.
13 Carney E. S. Gavin and the Harvard Semitic Museum, *Imperial Self-Portrait: The Ottoman Empire as Revealed in the Sultan Abdul Hamid II's Photographic Albums* (Cambridge, MA: Harvard University Press, 1988).
14 For example, consider how these phrases appear in this classic exposition on late nineteenth- and early twentieth-century Arab nationalism: George Antonius, *The Arab Awakening: The Story of the Arab National Movement* (Philadelphia: J.B. Lippincott, 1939), pp. 61, 79.
15 Cohen, *Becoming Ottomans*.
16 François Georgeon and Paul Dumont, eds., "Introduction," in *Vivre dans l'Empire Ottoman: Sociabilités et relations intercommunautaires (XVIIIe–XXe siècles)* (Paris: Editions L'Harmattan, 1997), pp. 9–11.
17 Şevket Pamuk, *The Ottoman Empire and European Capitalism, 1820–1913* (Cambridge: Cambridge University Press, 1987), p. 13.
18 Clay, *Gold for the Sultan*, pp. 1–2.

19 Donald Quataert, "The Age of Reforms, 1812–1914," in *An Economic and Social History of the Ottoman Empire, Vol. 2 1600–1914*, ed. Suraiya Faroqhi, Bruce McGowan, Donald Quataert, and Şevket Pamuk (Cambridge: Cambridge University Press, 1994), pp. 773–74.

20 Georgeon, *Abdülhamid II*, p. 122.

21 Brian Glyn Williams, "Hijra and Forced Migration from Nineteenth-Century Russia to the Ottoman Empire: A Critical Analysis of the Great Crimean Tatar Migration of 1860–1861," *Cahiers du Monde russe*, 41:1 (2000), pp. 79–108; see especially pp. 79, 90.

22 Stephen D. Shenfield, "The Circassians: A Forgotten Genocide?," in *The Massacre in History*, ed. Mark Levene and Penny Roberts (New York: Berghahn Books, 1999), pp. 149–83.

23 Vahan Cardashian, *The Ottoman Empire of the Twentieth Century* (New York: J.B. Lyon Company, 1908), pp. 183–84.

24 Dawn Chatty, *Displacement and Dispossession in the Modern Middle East* (Cambridge: Cambridge University Press, 2010), pp. 99, 108–9.

25 Kemal H. Karpat, *Ottoman Population, 1830–1914: Demographic and Social Characteristics* (Madison: University of Wisconsin Press, 1985), p. 27; Georgeon, *Abdülhamid II*, p. 92.

26 M. Hakan Yavuz, "The Transformation of 'Empire' through Wars and Reforms: Integration vs. Oppression," in *War and Diplomacy: The Russo-Turkish War of 1877–87 and the Treaty of Berlin*, ed. M. Hakan Yavuz with Peter Sluglett (Salt Lake City: University of Utah Press, 2011), pp. 23–24.

27 Justin McCarthy, *The Ottoman Peoples and the End of Empire* (New York: Oxford University Press, 2001), p. 46.

28 Anthony S. Wohl, "'Dizzi-ben-Dizzi': Disraeli as an Alien," *Journal of British Studies*, 34:3 (1995), p. 378. With reference to his career and to the Russo-Turkish War, see also Anthony S. Wohl, "'Ben Ju-Ju': Representations of Disraeli's Jewishness in the Victorian Political Cartoon," *Jewish History*, 10:2 (1996), pp. 89–134.

29 Shaw and Shaw, *History of the Ottoman Empire and Modern Turkey*, Vol. 2, p. 191.

30 Quataert, "The Age of Reforms," p. 782.

31 Quoted in Reşat Kasaba, *A Moveable Empire: Ottoman Nomads, Migrants, and Refugees* (Seattle: University of Washington Press, 2009), p. 117.

32 McCarthy, *The Ottoman Peoples and the End of Empire*, p. 48.

33 Georgeon, *Abdülhamid II*, pp. 106–8; Quataert, "The Age of Reforms," p. 789; Karpat, *Ottoman Population*, p. 55.

34 Quataert, "The Age of Reforms," p. 792.

35 Cited in Pamuk, *The Ottoman Empire and European Capitalism*, p. 205.

36 Sylvie Gangloff, ed., *La perception de l'héritage ottoman dans les Balkans* (Paris: L'Harmattan, 2005), p. 19.

37 Georgeon, *Abdülhamid II*, pp. 91, 109, 257.

38 Yavuz, "The Transformation of 'Empire' through Wars and Reforms," p. 18; Shaw and Shaw, *History of the Ottoman Empire and Modern Turkey*, Vol. 2, p. 195.

39 Ronald Grigor Suny, "Religion, Ethnicity, and Nationalism: Armenians, Turks, and the End of the Ottoman Empire," in *In God's Name: Genocide*

and Religion in the Twentieth Century, ed. Omer Bartov and Phyllis Mack (New York: Berghahn Books, 2001), p. 35.

40 Yavuz, "The Transformation of 'Empire' through Wars and Reforms," pp. 41–43.

41 Armenian National Education Committee (United States), "The Congress of Berlin," *Milwaukee Armenian Community*, http://milwaukeearmenians .com/tag/nersess-varjabedian/ (accessed May 20, 2014).

42 Cardashian, *The Ottoman Empire of the Twentieth Century*, p. 184.

43 Muwaylihi, *Spies, Scandals, and Sultans*, p. 88.

44 Ronald Robinson and John Gallagher, *Africa and the Victorians: The Climax of Imperialism* (New York: Anchor Books, 1968).

45 See Rodogno, *Against Massacre*.

46 Hanioğlu, *A Brief History of the Late Ottoman Empire*, p. 117.

47 Shaw and Shaw, *History of the Ottoman Empire and Modern Turkey*, Vol. 2, p. 177.

48 Midhat Bey, *The Life of Midhat Pasha*, pp. 141–43.

49 Davison, "Turkish Attitudes concerning Christian-Muslim Equality in the Nineteenth Century," pp. 850–53.

50 Shaw and Shaw, *History of the Ottoman Empire and Modern Turkey*, Vol. 2, p. 240; Cohen, *Ottoman Citizens*.

51 Zürcher, "The Ottoman Conscription System in Theory and Practice."

52 "The Jews were given one [delegate] for every 18,750 males (4 deputies in all); the Christians, one for every 107,557 males (44 deputies in all), and the Muslims, one for every 133,367 males (71 deputies in all)." Shaw and Shaw, *History of the Ottoman Empire and Modern Turkey*, Vol. 2, pp. 181, 200. As this source noted, Ottoman authorities calculated the Armenian population at less than half of what European travelers and Christian missionaries estimated, so that the numbers are open to debate.

53 Shaw and Shaw, *History of the Ottoman Empire and Modern Turkey*, Vol. 2, p. 185; Clay, *Gold for the Sultan*, p. 335.

54 M. Şükrü Hanioğlu, "The Second Constitutional Period, 1908–1918," in *The Cambridge History of Turkey*, ed. Reşat Kasaba, Vol. 4 (Cambridge: Cambridge University Press, 2008), p. 63.

55 Shaw and Shaw, *History of the Ottoman Empire and Modern Turkey*, Vol. 2, p. 187.

56 Hanioğlu, "The Second Constitutional Period," p. 63.

57 Quoted in Findley, *Bureaucratic Reform in the Ottoman Empire*, p. 221.

58 Clay, *Gold for the Sultan*, p. 1.

59 Hanioğlu, *A Brief History of the Late Ottoman Empire*, p. 135.

60 On changing cultures of reading, see Ami Ayalon, *Reading Palestine: Printing and Literacy, 1900–1948* (Austin: University of Texas Press, 2004), p. 1; on novels, see Hanioğlu, *A Brief History of the Late Ottoman Empire*, pp. 98–99; on Sherlock Holmes, see Georgeon, *Abdülhamid II*, p. 141.

61 Georgeon, *Abdülhamid II*, p. 388.

62 İpek Yosmaoğlu, *Blood Ties: Religion, Violence, and the Politics of Nationhood in Ottoman Macedonia, 1878–1908* (Ithaca: Cornell University Press, 2014), pp. 9–11.

63 Muwaylihi, *Spies, Scandals, and Sultans*, p. 26.

64 Georgeon, *Abdülhamid II*, p. 116.
65 Georgeon, *Abdülhamid II*, pp. 116–19, 151–52.
66 Georgeon, *Abdülhamid II*, p. 157.
67 Midhat Bey, *The Life of Midhat Pasha*, pp. 242–56.
68 Francis McCullagh, "What Was Found in the Lair of Abdul Hamid: Amazing Discoveries in the Yildiz Kiosk Following the Fall of Turkey's Sultan Reveal a Condition Surpassing Fiction," *New York Times*, June 6, 1909, Magazine Section p. SM3.
69 A.C.S. Peacock, "Introduction: The Ottoman Empire and Its Frontiers," in *The Frontiers of the Ottoman World*, ed. A. C. S. Peacock (Oxford: Oxford University Press, 2009), pp. 10–11.
70 Shaw and Shaw, *History of the Ottoman Empire and Modern Turkey*, Vol. 2, p. 85.
71 Andrew Petersen, "The Ottoman Conquest of Arabia and the Syrian Hajj Route," in Peacock, *The Frontiers of the Ottoman World*, pp. 86–87, see map on p. 91.
72 Gökhan Çetinsaya, "Challenges of a Frontier Region: The Case of Ottoman Iraq in the Nineteenth Century," in Peacock, *The Frontiers of the Ottoman World*, pp. 283–85.
73 Quataert, *The Ottoman Empire*, p. 63.
74 Frederick Anscombe, "Continuities in Ottoman Centre-Periphery Relations, 1878–1915," in Peacock, *The Frontiers of the Ottoman World*; p. 235; Quataert, *The Ottoman Empire*, p. 62; Georgeon, *Abdülhamid II*, p. 153; Quataert, "The Age of Reforms," p. 765.
75 Karpat, *Ottoman Population*, pp. 20–21.
76 Aysegül Demirhan and Oztan Oncel, "Development of the Foundations of Quarantine in Turkey in the Nineteenth Century and Its Place in the Public Health [*sic*]," *Journal of the International Society for the History of Islamic Medicine*, 2:4 (2003), pp. 42–44.
77 Chatty, *Displacement and Dispossession in the Modern Middle East*, p. 97 and passim; and Martin Bunton, "Inventing the Status Quo: Ottoman Land-Law during the Palestine Mandate, 1917–1936," *International History Review*, 21:1 (1999), pp. 28–56.
78 The 1858 Land Law, its purpose in ensuring the Ottoman tax base and rural stability, and its implications for landowners and sharecroppers remain subjects of debate. Quataert, "The Age of Reforms," pp. 856–61.
79 Eugene L. Rogan, *Frontiers of the State in the Late Ottoman Empire* (Cambridge: Cambridge University Press, 1999), pp. 51, 72–74.
80 Rogan, *Frontiers of the State in the Late Ottoman Empire*, p. 13; Çetinsaya, "Challenges of a Frontier Region," p. 276.
81 Benjamin C. Fortna, *Imperial Classroom: Islam, the State, and Education in the Late Ottoman Empire* (Oxford: Oxford University Press, 2002), pp. 4, 10, 99, 145–47.
82 "Mark Twain Signed Photo by Abdullah Frères in Constantinople," Shapell Manuscript Foundation, www.shapell.org/manuscript.aspx?mark-twain-signed-photo-from-constantinople (accessed June 2, 2014).
83 Gültekin Çizgen, "Abdülhamid and Photography," in *The Family Album of Abdülhamid II*, ed. Nevzat Bayhan (Istanbul: İstanbul Büyükşehir Belediyesi, 2009), pp. 13, 15; and Georgeon, *Abdülhamid II*, p. 162.

84 The J. Paul Getty Museum, "A Royal Passion: Queen Victoria and Photography," www.getty.edu/art/exhibitions/victoria/ (accessed June 1, 2014). See also John Plunkett, *Queen Victoria: First Media Monarch* (New York: Oxford University Press, 2003).
85 Deringil, *The Well-Protected Domains*, pp. 18, 22.
86 Muwaylihi, *Spies, Scandals and Sultans*, p. 110.
87 Wendy M.K. Shaw, *Possessors and Possessed: Museums, Archaeology, and the Visualization of the Ottoman Empire* (Berkeley: University of California Press, 2003), p. 142.
88 Shaw, *Possessors and Possessed*, p. 142.
89 Georgeon, *Abdülhamid II*, pp. 161–62.
90 Çizgen, "Abdülhamid and Photography," p. 14.
91 See Gavin and the Harvard Semitic Museum, *Imperial Self-portrait*, for a selection of such photographs.
92 Shaw, *Possessors and Possessed*, p. 149.
93 See, for example, Bruce Kuklick, *Puritans in Babylon: The Ancient Near East and American Intellectual Life, 1880–1930* (Princeton: Princeton University Press, 1996).
94 Zeynep Çelik, "Defining Empire's Patrimony: Late Ottoman Perceptions of Antiquities," in *Scramble for the Past: A Story of Archaeology in the Ottoman Empire, 1753–1914*, ed. Zainab Bahrani, Zeynep Çelik, and Edhem Eldem (Istanbul: SALT, 2011), pp. 446–47.
95 Renata Holod and Robert Ousterhout, "Osman Hamdi Bey and the Americans," in *Osman Hamdi Bey and the Americans*, ed. Renata Holod and Robert Ousterhout (Istanbul: Pera Museum, 2011), pp. 16–35; see especially p. 21.
96 Emine Fetvaci, "The Art of Osman Hamdi Bey," in Holod and Ousterhout, *Osman Hamdi Bey and the Americans*, pp. 118–36; and Heather Hughes and Emily Neumeier, "From Istanbul to Philadelphia: The Journey of 'At the Mosque Door'," in Holod and Ousterhout, *Osman Hamdi Bey and the Americans*, pp. 102–17.
97 Ihsan Yılmaz, "Osman Hamdi's 'Lost' Masterpiece in Action," *Hürriyet Daily News*, April 28, 2014.
98 Said, *Orientalism*; and Jonathan Jones, "Jean-Léon Gérôme: Orientalist Fantasy among the Impressionists," *The Guardian*, July 3, 2012.
99 Ussama Makdisi, "Ottoman Orientalism," *The American Historical Review*, 107:3 (2002), pp. 769–70, 783–84.
100 Deringil, *The Well-Protected Domains*, p. 15.
101 Georgeon, *Abdülhamid II*, p. 210; Karpat, "Ottoman Emigration to America."
102 Deringil, *The Well-Protected Domains*, p. 143; Georgeon, *Abdülhamid II*, p. 211.
103 Golden, Cameron, and Balarajan, *Exceptional People*, p. 58.
104 Khater, *Inventing Home*, p. 48; Karpat "Ottoman Emigration to America." On Egypt, for example, see Sharkey, *American Evangelicals in Egypt*, p. 3.
105 Joan Nathan, "The Legacy of Egyptian Rose, in Time for Passover," *New York Times*, March 20, 2002.
106 Quataert, "The Age of Reforms," p. 792.

107 Quataert, "The Age of Reforms," p. 791; Quartzsite, Arizona, "Hi Jolly Cemetery," http://ci.quartzsite.az.us/index.php/2013-01-08-06-33-10/hi-jolly-cemetary-2 (accessed July 13, 2014).

108 Alfaro-Velcamp, *So Far from Allah, So Close to Mexico*, especially pp. 50–51, 56, 123, 149.

109 Quartzsite, Arizona, "Hi Jolly Cemetery."

110 Khater, *Inventing Home*, p. 49; and Karpat, "Ottoman Emigration to America," p. 179. An example of such writing by an Armenian would be Cardashian, *The Ottoman Empire of the Twentieth Century*.

111 Karpat, "Ottoman Emigration to America," p. 179.

112 Karpat, "Ottoman Emigration to America," p. 184.

113 Zeynep Çelik, *Empire, Architecture, and the City: French-Ottoman Encounters, 1830–1914* (Seattle: University of Washington Press, 2008), p. 7.

114 Pamuk, *The Ottoman Empire and European Capitalism*, p. 3.

115 Karen M. Kern, "'They Are Not Known to Us': The Ottomans, the Mormons, and the Protestants in the Late Ottoman Empire," in *American Missionaries and the Middle East: Foundational Encounters*, ed. Mehmet Ali Doğan and Heather J. Sharkey (Salt Lake City: University of Utah Press, 2011), pp. 122–63.

116 Kern, "They Are Not Known to Us," pp. 127–29; and Quataert, *The Ottoman Empire*, p. 112.

117 Kern, "They Are Not Known to Us," p. 127.

118 Brigham Young University, *Global Mormonism Project: Turkey*, http://globalmormonism.byu.edu/?page_id=169 (accessed July 14, 2014).

119 On these common tendencies across Christian missions, see Chantal Verdeil, "Introduction," in *Missions chrétiennes en terre d'islam (XVIIe–XXe siècles)*, ed. Chantal Verdeil (Turnhout, Belgium: Brepols, 2013), pp. 5–59, see especially pp. 6–7, 30.

120 Deringil, *The Well-Protected Domains*, p. 14.

121 Heleen Murre-van den Berg, "Nineteenth-Century Protestant Missions and Middle Eastern Women: An Overview," in *Gender, Religion and Change in the Middle East: Two Hundred Years of History*, ed. Inger Marie Okkenhaug and Ingvild Flaskerud (Oxford: Berg, 2005), pp. 103–22.

122 Verdeil, "Introduction," pp. 41–42.

123 Michael A. Reynolds, *Shattering Empires: The Clash and Collapse of the Ottoman and Russian Empires, 1908–1918* (Cambridge: Cambridge University Press, 2011), p. 25.

124 Quataert, *The Ottoman Empire*, p. 111.

125 Mehmet Ali Doğan, "Missionary Schools," in *Encyclopedia of the Ottoman Empire*, ed. Gábor Ágoston and Bruce Masters (New York: Facts on File, 2009), pp. 385–89.

126 Verdeil, "Introduction," p. 20.

127 Doğan, "Missionary Schools."

128 Wallace N. Jamison, *The United Presbyterian Story: A Centennial Study, 1858–1958* (Pittsburgh: Geneva Press, 1958), p. 86.

129 Ben-Naeh, "Jews on the Move during the Late Ottoman Period: Trends and Some Problems," pp. 136–37.

130 Jérôme Bocquet, ed., *L'enseignement français en Méditerranée: les mission-aires et l'Alliance Israélite Universelle* (Rennes: Presses universitaires de Rennes, 2010).

131 Rodrigue, *French Jews, Turkish Jews*, pp. 101–3.

132 Annalaura Turiano, "De la pastorale migratoire à la coopération tech-nique: Missionnaires italiens en Égypte; Les salésiens et l'enseignement professionel (1890–1970)," PhD diss. (History), Aix-Marseille Université, 2015.

133 Stillman, "Middle Eastern and North African Jewries Confront Modernity," p. 64.

134 Verdeil, "Introduction," pp. 13, 44; Sharkey, *American Evangelicals in Egypt*, p. 219.

135 Bocquet, "Le rôle des missions catholiques dans la fondation d'un nou-veau réseau d'institutions éducatives au Moyen-Orient arabe," in Luizard, *Le choc colonial et l'islam*, p. 338.

136 Ellen L. Fleischmann, "Our Moslem Sisters: Women of Greater Syria in the Eyes of American Protestant Missionary Women," *Islam and Christian-Muslim Relations*, 9:3 (1998) pp. 307–23.

137 Ellen Fleischmann, "I Only Wish I Had a Home on This Globe: Transnational Biography and Dr. Mary Eddy," *Journal of Women's History*, 21:3 (2009), pp. 108–30.

138 Historians have rarely discussed the social import of needlework for girls' education. See, however, Heather J. Sharkey, "Christians among Muslims: The Church Missionary Society in the Northern Sudan," *Journal of African History*, 43 (2002), pp. 51–75, and especially pp. 60–61 including foot-note 47. Photographs in the CMS archives in Birmingham, UK, and at the Presbyterian Historical Society in Philadelphia confirm this impression of mission schools as propagators of Anglo-American-style dress.

139 Zilfi, "Whose Laws?," pp. 125–41.

140 Boyar and Fleet, *A Social History of Ottoman Istanbul*, pp. 297–302.

141 Nathan O. Hatch, *The Democratization of American Christianity* (New Haven: Yale University Press, 1989), pp. 9–10.

142 Marwa Elshakry, "The Gospel of Science and American Evangelism in Late Ottoman Beirut," in Doğan and Sharkey, *American Missionaries and the Middle East*, pp. 167–210; and Betty S. Anderson, *The American University of Beirut: Arab Nationalism and Liberal Education* (Austin: University of Texas Press, 2011), pp. 40–46.

143 Elshakry, "The Gospel of Science," pp. 191–93.

144 Elshakry, "The Gospel of Science," pp. 188–90.

145 Isaac H. Hall, "The Arabic Bible of Drs. Eli Smith and Cornelius V. A. Van Dyck," *Journal of the American Oriental Society*, 11 (1882–85), pp. 276–86.

146 David D. Grafton, "A Critical Investigation into the Manuscripts of the 'So-Called' Van Dyck Bible," *Cairo Journal of Theology*, 2 (2015), pp. 56–64.

147 On this idea of "print languages" and "imagined communities" as the basis of nationalist movements, there are two seminal works: Marshall McLuhan, *The Gutenberg Galaxy: The Making of Typographic Man* (Toronto: University of Toronto Press, 1962), see especially p. 199; and Benedict Anderson,

Imagined Communities: Reflections on the Origin and Spread of Nationalism, revised edition (London: Verso, 1999).

148 Heather J. Sharkey, "The Gospel in Arabic Tongues: British Bible Distribution, Evangelical Mission, and Language Politics in North Africa," in *Cultural Conversions: Unexpected Consequences of Christian Missionary Encounters in the Middle East, Africa, and South Asia* (Syracuse: Syracuse University Press, 2013), pp. 203–21.

149 Clément Huart, *A History of Arabic Literature* (New York: D. Appleton and Company, 1915), pp. 419–20.

150 Antonius, *The Arab Awakening*; Hourani, *Arabic Thought in the Liberal Age*.

151 Grafton, "A Critical Introduction to the Manuscripts of the 'So-Called' Van Dyck Bible"; and Leirvik Oddbjørn, *Human Conscience and Muslim-Christian Relations: Modern Egyptian Thinkers on Al-Damir* (London: Routledge, 2007), p. 75.

152 Barbara Reeves-Ellington, "Petko Slaveykov, the Protestant Press, and the Gendered Language of Moral Reform in Bulgarian Nationalism," in Doğan and Sharkey, *American Missionaries and the Middle East*, pp. 211–36, see especially p. 216.

153 Pitarakis and Merantzas, *A Treasured Memory*, p. 14.

154 Bruce Masters, "Missionaries," in Ágoston and Masters, eds., *Encyclopedia of the Ottoman Empire*, pp. 384–85.

155 British and Foreign Bible Society, *The Gospel in Many Tongues: Specimens of 872 Languages in Which the BFBS Has Published or Circulated Some Portion of the Bible* (London: British and Foreign Bible Society, 1965), pp. 12, 84, 161.

156 Hanioğlu, *A Brief History of the Late Ottoman Empire*, p. 36.

157 Hanioğlu, *A Brief History of the Late Ottoman Empire*, pp. 98–99.

158 American Bible Society Library, New York, RG#17.01, Correspondence Files, Levant/Near East Versions: Letter from Eli Smith to Rev. Dr. Brigham, Bhamdun, Mount Lebanon, 26 October 1848.

159 A. L. Tibawi, *American Interests in Syria 1800–1901: A Study of Educational, Literary and Religious Work* (Oxford: Clarendon Press, 1966), p. 171.

160 Makdisi, *Artillery of Heaven*.

161 Earl E. Elder, *Vindicating a Vision: The Story of the American Mission in Egypt, 1854–1954* (Philadelphia: United Presbyterian Board of Foreign Missions, 1958), pp. 31–34.

162 Tibawi, *American Interests in Syria*, p. 255.

163 On missions to Jews, see Michael Marten, *Attempting to Bring the Gospel Home: Scottish Missions to Palestine, 1839–1917* (London: Tauris Academic Studies, 2006); and W. T. Gidney, *The History of the London Society for Promoting Christianity amongst the Jews, from 1809 to 1908* (London: London Society for Promoting Christianity amongst the Jews, 1908).

164 See, for example, H. E. Philips, *Blessed Be Egypt My People: Life Studies from the Land of the Nile* (Philadelphia: Judson Press, 1953), pp. 17–43, on the case of Muhammad Mansur, who became Mikha'il Mansur after converting from Islam in the 1890s. This man first converted to Catholicism but then turned to Protestantism.

165 See the chapter on apostasy in Friedmann, *Tolerance and Coercion in Islam*, pp. 121–59.

166 Andrew Watson, *The American Mission in Egypt, 1854 to 1896*, second edition (Pittsburgh: United Presbyterian Board, 1904), pp. 151–52; and Heather J. Sharkey, "Muslim Apostasy, Christian Conversion, and Religious Freedom in Egypt: A Study of American Missionaries, Western Imperialism, and Human Rights Agendas," in *Proselytization Revisited: Rights, Free Markets, and Culture Wars*, ed. Rosalind I. J. Hackett (London: Equinox, 2008), p. 158.

167 Masters, "Missionaries," p. 385.

168 On their impact on cultures of reading, see Ami Ayalon, "New Practices: Arab Printing, Publishing, and Mass Reading," in Kozma, Schayegh, and Wishnitzer, *A Global Middle East*, pp. 321–44, see especially pp. 325 and 338.

169 Rogan, *Frontiers of the State in the Late Ottoman Empire*, pp. 137–38, 143.

170 Rodrigue, *French Jews, Turkish Jews*, p. 157.

171 Tibawi, *American Interests in Syria*, p. 267.

172 Fortna, *Imperial Classroom*, pp. 77–79.

173 Georgeon, *Abdülhamid II*, pp. 238–39.

174 Fortna, *Imperial Classroom*, pp. 47, 77–79, 96–98.

175 John Obert Voll, *Islam: Continuity and Change in the Modern World* (Syracuse: Syracuse University Press, 1982), p. 90.

176 Georgeon, *Abdülhamid II*, p. 208.

177 Georgeon, *Abdülhamid II*, p. 323.

178 Çelik, *Empire, Architecture, and the City*, p. 35.

179 Quataert, "The Age of Reforms," pp. 808–9.

180 Quataert, "The Age of Reforms," p. 814. Note, however, that the railway was never completed to the extent originally planned, in part because local Arab Muslim tribes sabotaged some of the lines out of a not-unfounded fear that the railway would enable the Ottoman state to intrude more deeply into their lives. See Çelik, *Empire, Architecture, and the City*, p. 39.

181 Georgeon, *Abdülhamid II*, pp. 193, 198, 444; and Fortna, *Imperial Classroom*, p. 190.

182 Georgeon, *Abdülhamid II*, p. 209.

183 Georgeon, *Abdülhamid II*, pp. 208–9.

184 Nikki R. Keddie, *Sayyid Jamal al-Din al-Afghani: A Political Biography* (Berkeley: University of California Press, 1972); and Nikki R. Keddie, *An Islamic Response to Imperialism: Political and Religious Writings of Sayyid Jamal al-Din al-Afghani* (Berkeley: University of California Press, 1983).

185 Gilles Kepel, *Jihad: The Trail of Political Islam* (London: I.B. Tauris, 2002), pp. 219–20; and Henri Lauzière, *The Making of Salafism: Islamic Reform in the Twentieth Century* (New York: Columbia University Press, 2016).

186 Voll, *Islam*, p. 91.

187 Umar Ryad, *Islamic Reformism and Christianity: A Critical Reading of the Works of Muhammad Rashid Rida and His Associates (1898–1935)* (Leiden: E.J. Brill, 2009); and Brynjar Lia, *The Society of the Muslim Brothers in Egypt: The Rise of an Islamic Mass Movement, 1928–1942*, foreword by Jamal al-Banna (Reading, UK: Ithaca Press, 1998).

188 For an account by a contemporary admirer, see Tariq Ramadan, *Western Muslims and the Future of Islam* (New York: Oxford University Press, 2004).

189 Elie Kedourie, *Afghani and 'Abduh: An Essay on Religious Unbelief and Political Activism in Modern Islam* (New York: Humanities Press, 1966).
190 Heather J. Sharkey, "An Egyptian in China: Ahmed Fahmy and the Making of World Christianities," *Church History*, 78:2 (2009), p. 316.
191 N. R. Keddie, "Afgani, Jamal-al-din," *Encyclopædia Iranica*, Vol. 1, Fascicle 5, (1983), pp. 481–486.
192 Keddie, *Sayyid Jamal al-Din al-Afghani*.
193 Paul Landau, "Islamic 'Reformism' and Jihad: On the Discourse of Tariq Ramadan," *Transatlantic Intelligencer* (2005), www.trans-int.com/wordpress/index.php/islamic-"reformism"-and-jihad-on-the-discourse-of-tariq-ramadan/ (accessed August 12, 2014). The clandestine militant wing of the mid-twentieth-century Muslim Brotherhood in Egypt – of whose existence, in fact, many members of the movement appear to have been wholly unaware – exemplified this use of hiding and misrepresentation. See Richard P. Mitchell, *The Society of the Muslim Brothers* (New York: Oxford University Press, 1993).
194 Berkes, *The Development of Secularism in Turkey*, pp. 255, 259.
195 Hanioğlu, *A Brief History of the Late Ottoman Empire*, pp. 129–30; Georgeon, *Abdülhamid II*, p. 184.
196 Georgeon, *Abdülhamid II*, pp. 140, 332; Benjamin C. Fortna, "The Reign of Abdülhamid II," in *The Cambridge History of Turkey*, Vol. 4: *Turkey in the Modern World*, ed. Reşat Kasaba (Cambridge: Cambridge University Press, 2008), p. 41; Quataert, *The Ottoman Empire*, p. 166.
197 Berkes, *The Development of Secularism in Turkey*, p. 255; Georgeon, *Abdülhamid II*, pp. 199, 332.
198 Masters, *Christians and Jews in the Ottoman Arab World*, p. 170.
199 Berkes, *The Development of Secularism in Turkey*, p. 258.
200 Marc David Baer used this phrase at the workshop on "The Politics of Conversion: Historical Perspectives, Sociological and Anthropological Insights," Middle East and Middle Eastern American Center (MEMEAC), the City University of New York (CUNY) Graduate Center, October 14, 2011.
201 Krstic, *Contested Conversions*, p. 1.
202 Krstic, *Contested Conversions*, p. 2 and elsewhere.
203 Marc David Baer, *The Dönme: Jewish Converts, Muslim Revolutionaries, and Secular Turks* (Stanford: Stanford University Press, 2010), p. 4.
204 Baer, *The Dönme*, p. 17.
205 Deringil, *The Well-Protected Domains*, p. 78; and Selim Deringil, "Redefining Identities in the Late Ottoman Empire: Policies of Conversion and Apostasy," in *Imperial Rule*, ed. Alexei Miller and Alfred J. Rieber (New York: Central European University Press, 2004), pp. 107–30, see especially pp. 119–21.
206 Baer, *The Dönme*, p. 15.
207 Deringil, *The Well-Protected Domains*, p. 78.
208 Maurus Reinkowski, "Hidden Believers, Hidden Apostates: The Phenomenon of Crypto-Jews and Crypto-Christians in the Middle East," in *Converting Cultures: Religion, Ideology and Transformations of Modernity*, ed. Dennis Washburn and A. Kevin Reinhart (Leiden: E.J. Brill, 2007), pp. 409–33, see p. 420.

209 The quotations are respectively from Kais M. Firro, "The Attitude of the Druzes and 'Alawis vis-à-vis Islam and Nationalism in Syria and Lebanon," in *Syncretistic Religious Communities in the Near East*, ed. Krisztina Kehl-Bodrogi, Barbara Kellner-Heinkele, and Anke Otter-Beaujean (Leiden: E.J. Brill, 1997), pp. 87–99; and from the opening essay in this same volume, Krisztina Kehl-Bodrogi, "Introduction," pp. xi–xvii.

210 Bernard Heyberger, "Missions catholiques en Syrie à l'époque moderne," in Verdeil, *Missions chrétiennes en terre d'islam*, pp. 61–94, see especially pp. 80–86.

211 Hans-Lukas Kieser, "Missionaires américaines en terre ottomane (Anatolie)," in Verdeil, *Missions chrétiennes en terre d'islam*, pp. 94–126, see especially pp. 108–13.

212 Ilber Ortaylı, "Les groupes hétérodoxes et l'administration ottomane," in *Syncretistic Religious Communities in the Near East*, ed. Krisztina Kehl-Bodrogi, Barbara Kellner-Heinkele, and Anke Otter-Beaujean (Leiden: E.J. Brill, 1997), p. 205.

213 George Orwell, *Nineteen Eighty-Four* (London: Secker & Warburg, 1949).

214 In the Turkish republic that emerged after World War I, the state essentially continued this policy of overlooking sectarian distinctions among Muslims and attributed religious distinctions among the Alevis to their "folklore." Kabir Tambar, *The Reckoning of Pluralism: Political Belonging and the Demands of History in Turkey* (Stanford: Stanford University Press, 2014), pp. 2–3.

215 Scholars who come from a western European Christian tradition sometimes resort to other terms – notably, "nonconformist," in the mode of a British Protestant, or "dissident," in the mode of a French Catholic – to refer to the Alawites, Yezidis, and others.

216 Nelida Fuccaro, *The Other Kurds: Yazidis in Colonial Iraq* (London: I.B. Tauris, 1999), pp. 15–17.

217 Georgeon, *Abdülhamid II*, p. 273.

218 Ortaylı, "Les groupes hétérodoxes et l'administration ottomane," pp. 207–9.

219 Fuccaro, *The Other Kurds*, pp. 31–33, 40.

220 Fuccaro, *The Other Kurds*, p. 40.

221 Ortaylı, "Les groupes hétérodoxes et l'administration ottomane," pp. 206–7.

222 Deringil, *The Well-Protected Domains*, pp. 69–74.

223 Deringil, *The Well-Protected Domains*, p. 78.

224 Deringil, *The Well-Protected Domains*, pp. 75–77.

225 Deringil, *The Well-Protected Domains*, p. 83.

226 American missionaries reported a similar problem during this period and later, when trying to persuade indigenous Middle Eastern Christians to overcome mistrust by accepting the rare Muslim converts to Christianity.

227 On missionaries' attitudes in this period towards belief see, for example, Carolyn Goffman, "From Religious to American Proselytism: Mary Mills Patrick and the 'Sanctification of the Intellect'," in Doğan and Sharkey, *American Missionaries and the Middle East*, pp. 84–121, especially pp. 85, 91.

228 The essays in Verdeil, *Missions chrétiennes en terre d'islam*, suggest the convergences in Catholic and Protestant missionary thought vis-à-vis the Islamic societies of the Middle East and North Africa. On evangelicalism, see

Sharkey, *American Evangelicals in Egypt*. Pietistic strands of thought influenced Lutherans especially: see Grafton, *Piety, Politics, and Power*.

229 This idea of secret believers or "secret disciples" gained expression in the works of the American missionary Samuel M. Zwemer (1867–1952), such as in his book *Islam: A Challenge to Faith* (New York: Student Volunteer Movement for Foreign Missions, 1907), p. 218.

230 Tibawi, *American Interests in Syria*, pp. 256–57; Deringil, *The Well-Protected Domains*, pp. 91–92.

231 Hans-Lukas Kieser, *Nearest East: American Millennialism and Mission to the Middle East* (Philadelphia: Temple University Press, 2010), pp. 51–55.

232 Fortna, *Imperial Classroom*, p. 4.

233 Fortna, *Imperial Classroom*, p. 176.

234 Selçuk Akşin Somel, *The Modernization of Public Education in the Ottoman Empire, 1839–1908: Islamization, Autocracy, and Discipline* (Leiden: E.J. Brill, 2001), p. 241; Julia Phillips Cohen and Sarah Abreyava Stein, *Sephardi Lives: A Documentary History, 1700–1950* (Stanford: Stanford University Press, 2014), p. 72–75.

235 Fuccaro, *The Other Kurds*, pp. 34–35.

236 Georgeon, *Abdülhamid II*, pp. 31–32.

237 Baer, *The Dönme*, pp. 11–12.

238 Hanioğlu, *A Brief History of the Late Ottoman Empire*, p. 141; Clay, *Gold for the Sultan*.

239 Voll, *Islam: Continuity and Change in the Modern World*.

240 Voll, *Islam: Continuity and Change in the Modern World*.

241 E. E. Evans-Pritchard, *The Sanusi of Cyrenaica* (Oxford: Clarendon Press, 1954); Knut S. Vikør, *Sufi and Scholar on the Desert Edge: Muhammad B. 'Ali al-Sanusi and His Brotherhood* (Evanston: Northwestern University Press, 1995).

242 Yitzhak Nakash, *The Shi'is of Iraq* (Princeton: Princeton University Press, 1994), pp. 3, 15–16, 28–29.

6 Coming Together, Moving Apart: Ottoman Muslims, Christians, and Jews at the Turn of the Century

Introduction: Changes Afoot

During the sixteenth century, when a kind of yellow leather shoe became popular in the Ottoman Empire, Ottoman authorities enforced a rule that restricted this footwear to Muslims. The same authorities required Christians and Jews to wear black on their feet instead.[1] Jump forward to the late nineteenth century, and the "footscape" was different. In an Ottoman government bureau – say, a foreign ministry office in Istanbul circa 1890 – educated Muslim male employees were wearing the same kind of dark-hued shoes as their Christian and Jewish counterparts – and the same kind of trousers and jackets, too.[2] Once a sign of *dhimmi* drabness, a dark suit had become *de rigueur* for the successful office-going man of the late nineteenth century, making religious identity harder to discriminate at a quick glance. Changes were afoot among women, too, as fashionable Muslim, Christian, and Jewish females abandoned flatsoled slippers for Parisian-style heeled shoes and ankle-boots.[3] In some of the small details of everyday life, things were looking more equal.

Dress had once sent sharp signals about who people were in the Ottoman Empire – potentially conveying information not only about such things as religion, but also about town or village of origin, profession, and even age or marital status[4] – but distinctions had eroded over the nineteenth century. Sultan Mahmud II's ban on the turban (1829), the egalitarian rhetoric of the major Tanzimat reforms (1839 and 1856), the influence of European and American people and culture in mission schools and other venues, and the industrial manufacture of clothing combined to have this effect. A photograph that Sultan Abdulhamid II gave to the US government, preserved at the Library of Congress, illustrates mass production.[5] Dating from the early 1890s, it shows the high-ceilinged, big-windowed interior of "the Ottoman Fez Factory" with rows of heavy machinery capable of turning out the brimless fez hat (also known as the *tarbush*) in quick, identical succession. But how much did these changes in clothing mean? This simple question leads to a much

Image 15 *Interior of the Imperial Fez Factory*, c. 1890–1983. Albumen photographic print by Abdullah Frères. Library of Congress, Washington, DC. Abdul Hamid II Collection.

larger debate about whether changes on the surface accompanied deeper equality underneath – that is, about what was superficial, and what was substantial.

This chapter examines the question of social parity and disparity on the one hand and social contact and distance on the other during the latter years of Abdulhamid II's reign. It goes just beyond 1908, when a group of military officers called the Young Turks staged a coup d'état ostensibly to restore the Ottoman constitution and parliament, which the sultan had suspended in 1878. Two opposing trends – one that favored more mingling among Muslims and non-Muslims, and another that stressed distinctions among them – occurred at the same time but unevenly, with differences according to place and time. I call these two opposing trends "convergence" and "divergence," and advance several arguments about them.

First, religion in certain respects was becoming harder to see in public, suggesting the existence of or potential for greater social parity among people of different religions. The example of dress, again, is telling: among prosperous urbanites especially, clothing was doing little, in theory, to mark people out as ambulatory exemplars of Muslim, Christian, and Jewish collectives.[6] "Western" clothing, argued one scholar, freed Christians and Jews from humiliations historically associated with *dhimmi* status; signaled their "civil emancipation," which had begun during the Tanzimat period; and gave Christians and Jews a better chance of walking down a street unmolested.[7] Such clothing certainly signaled their sophistication – or perhaps even their embodiment of "the idea of modernity and Europe."[8] Another historian suggested that, dressed in "modern" clothes that did not blare out the religion of their wearers, Christians and Jews in cities like Cairo and Damascus felt more confident. The result? They "no longer stepped down from the pavement when a Muslim came along."[9]

The power of clothes to blur religious status allowed some Muslims to act differently, too. In *fin-de-siècle* Istanbul, for example, Muslim men in "Western" dress sometimes slipped into neighborhoods where Christians and Jews lived in order to drink alcohol in taverns or eat undetected during the Islamic month of Ramadan, when observant Muslims fasted in daytime.[10] Besides dress, other restrictions were falling away, affecting how things looked from the outside – for example, rules that limited the color of a non-Muslim's house and the number of oars on a non-Muslim's Bosphorus fishing vessel.[11]

This first point leads to the second: secular spaces emerged where religion intruded less often. People within "secular" spaces did not necessarily believe less strongly in God or identify less firmly with a religious group or sect. And anyway, who could know what was inside people's heads if one reckoned religion in terms of belief? "Secular" meant only theoretical neutrality in matters of religion, with religious identities and practices becoming less overt, ostentatious, or restrictive. Secular spaces existed outside institutional venues of mosque, church, synagogue, and prayer hall, and were open to different people. To paraphrase a historian writing about the Arab middle classes, secular spaces were also those where modes of behavior, and not religious allegiances, were "the price of admission."[12]

The third argument of the chapter runs against the first two. Despite convergence in how things looked, religion as a mode of social classification was *not* fading as the nineteenth century closed. Mutual prejudices and old grudges persisted. Assumptions swirled below the surface about social hierarchies and the roles Muslims and non-Muslims should play relative to each other. In an everyday context, these assumptions restricted people's options. Most obviously, the Islamic legal tradition continued to enshrine inequality between Muslims and non-Muslims on the one hand, and men and women on the other, so that courts allowed Muslim men to marry Christian or Jewish women while forbidding the reverse within a social order so ingrained and authoritative that few people thought to question it. In this milieu, it was possible, for example, for a Kurdish Muslim militia man in rural eastern Anatolia to take – and in practice during the 1890s, to grab – an Armenian Christian woman as a wife, though the reverse for an Armenian man relative to a Muslim woman remained out of the question. Old attitudes continued to shape Ottoman military culture, too (see Chapter 5), with military service remaining almost completely a Muslim preserve. Until the end of Abdulhamid II's reign, Christians and Jews paid a tax, akin to the *jizya* of old, for the military exemptions that they wanted and that Muslims expected them to take.[13]

The fourth point is that religion was in some respects calcifying, growing less flexible and more clearly bounded. The result, in Ottoman lands as in places as far afield as Britain and British-ruled India, was what some anthropologists and historians have called "a conversion to modernities," which entailed a growing public consciousness of large-scale corporate religion – "modern" Islam, Christianity, Hinduism, and so forth.[14] While one would go too far to suggest, as one scholar did, that speaking of Jews, Christians, and Muslims before the twentieth century is anachronistic, on the grounds that most people "lived far away from any institutional religion" and practiced "largely a syncretic amalgamation of local traditions and superstitions,"[15] policy setters were certainly promoting standardization through a steadily growing network of schools. Consider, for example, what the Egyptian Muslim reformist, Muhammad Abduh, began to do at al-Azhar (the venerable university for Islamic studies in Cairo, founded around the year 970 by the Fatimid rulers of Egypt). During the 1890s, Abduh endeavored to standardize al-Azhar's curriculum, a measure of "modernization" that reified, or perhaps even invented, Islamic tradition as a self-consciously modern academic subject.[16] He also set regular class times, organized a central library, and hired a school doctor to monitor students' health and hygiene.[17] Likewise, Abduh endeavored to reform the Shari'a court system in Egypt to project greater uniformity in Islamic law – a measure that he implemented, in part, by requiring the inclusion of indices in compendia of new legal rulings,[18] so that tradition, as it formed, would become searchable. Taken together, and thinking more generally, the following occurred: as school systems expanded and as literacy became a popular (as opposed to elite) skill, many bureaucrats, teachers, journalists, and others promoted what some call a communalistic sense of religion, which potentially privileged the identity of the religious group over the identity of the empire or nation.[19]

Finally, this chapter argues that the Abdulhamid II era was a period of high anxiety among segments of the empire's Muslim populace who felt socially and economically beleaguered. These anxieties limited the scope of a secular public culture that could transcend religious and sectarian distinctions. As Chapter 5 showed, the Russo-Turkish War of 1878 had led to severe territorial and financial losses for the Ottoman Empire and had prompted the influx from the Caucasus and Balkan regions of hundreds of thousands of Muslim refugees, who struggled to build new lives. Far from bringing closure, the Russo-Turkish War left the future looking shaky, with the "Great Powers" of Europe – and even some of the not-so-great powers of Europe – perching over the Ottoman Empire like hawks ready to pounce for land, wealth, and power. Abdulhamid II was anxious himself. Concerned for his own security and for the empire's territorial integrity, he relied on reports from spies, officers, and bureaucrats who stoked his fears.

Complicating social relations, Christians and Jews were beginning to expect more within Ottoman society. Through the efforts of diplomats, merchants, and missionaries, European and American influences were mounting, buoying Christians and Jews in their education, prosperity, and hopes. Non-Muslims thus became less willing to play the subordinate roles which Islamic states had assigned them for centuries, and more willing to embrace reforms that worked to their advantage. They increasingly refused to accept the principle of Muslim supremacy. These developments grated on many Muslims and compounded their sense of unease.

Meanwhile, the sultan stressed the Sunni Muslim dimensions of the Ottoman state in ways that diminished the egalitarian impulses of the Tanzimat era, although without explicitly reverting to the pre-Tanzimat-era language of *dhimmi*-ness to describe his Christian and Jewish subjects. His privileging of Islam and Muslims had direct consequences for policy. For example, in 1890, partly as a cheap way of shoring up the empire's military strength, Abdulhamid II sponsored a militia filled with Kurdish Muslim pastoralists and deployed them in eastern Anatolia, a region where Kurds had traditionally demanded protection money – an informal tax – from historically unarmed Armenian Christians. The sultan named this militia after himself: they were the "Hamidiye" cavalry. Poorly paid and just as poorly supervised, men in this militia stepped up raids on Armenian communities, taking food, goods, and women in what a British consul, writing in 1891, called "a system of military robbery."[20] Of course, raiding had occurred in the past: what was new was that the Hamidiye enjoyed state sponsorship – even if the central state barely controlled them. Amid thwarted hopes and rising aspirations, Armenian nationalism began to simmer, even as Kurdish Muslims, who were mostly poor, grappled with resentments and fears of their own. This mix of circumstances exploded in the mid-1890s, when Armenians fell to a series of massacres in which the official religious and therefore legal status of Armenians as Christians played a role, for example, in making it possible for Muslim attackers to haul off Armenian females as wives.

In the increasingly urban places where Jews lived, Muslim-Jewish relations remained generally calm, as they had been in earlier periods of Ottoman history. And yet, important events were occurring off-stage, meaning that they happened beyond Ottoman borders but had direct repercussions for the empire. In 1894, for example, a military officer of Jewish origin, Albert Dreyfus (1859–1935), faced an accusation of treason in France. Disgusted by the anti-Semitic dimensions of the "Dreyfus Affair," a Viennese Jewish journalist named Theodor Herzl (1860–1904) wrote a treatise called *The Jewish State* urging fellow Jews to form a polity of their own somewhere else. Like the Mortara Affair (see Chapter 4), the Dreyfus Affair and reactions to it stimulated a new form of Jewish activism. In this case the activism centered on a Jewish nationalist ideology, Zionism, which came to focus its energies on a corner of Ottoman territory around Jerusalem where formative events for Jews had transpired millennia before. The Zionist movement had little impact on Muslim-Jewish relations within the Ottoman Empire during the years when Abdulhamid II was ruling. Nevertheless, because Zionism went on to have a momentous impact on the post–Ottoman Middle East, and ultimately inspired the formation of Israel in 1948, its inception in this era is worth signaling.

For historians wanting to understand how individuals and groups related to each other as Muslims, Christians, and Jews, the Abdulhamid II era is confusing. Religion seemed to matter more and less at the same time. Another way of explaining this situation, again, is in terms of convergence and divergence: Muslims, Christians, and Jews were coming together in some ways and places, and moving apart in others.

Camaraderie: More than Commerce and Natural Disasters?

Go back 250 years from the 1890s, and consider an episode that occurred in 1641, when locusts struck the Syrian city of Aleppo. According to contemporary reports of Christian travelers and ecclesiastics, local Muslim leaders responded to this calamity in two steps. First, they secured from Persia a water renowned for special powers that included attracting birds to devour these insects. Next, they arranged a parade, during which Muslim, Christian, and Jewish religious dignitaries – in that order – marched for hours around the city, with the Christian clergy wearing liturgical robes, carrying crosses and icons, and chanting in Greek, Syriac, and Armenian according to their churches. The parade ended when dignitaries hung a receptacle of the Persian water on the minaret of a mosque.[21]

In the seventeenth- and eighteenth-century Levant, Christians and Muslims rarely marched together in processions as they did on this occasion in Aleppo, remarked the historian Bernard Heyberger. Only exceptional circumstances and a need for affirming collective security joined them in "shared public sacralities" like this one.[22] Throughout most of the Ottoman era, members of the different religious groups lived in the same urban communities, and yet in the words of historian Bruce Masters, found "little to draw them[selves] together, beyond commerce or natural disasters."[23]

In the 1890s, by contrast, and in spite of Sultan Abdulhamid II's renewed public emphasis on Sunni Islam, educated urban and urbane Muslims, Christians, and Jews appeared to be drawing together over much more than trade and catastrophe. For non-Muslims, new spaces for sociability opened and forced old boundaries to give way.[24] These new spaces included public venues like French-style cafés and parks, and private clubs like masonic lodges, which fostered togetherness while allowing people to spend leisure hours on a flatter social terrain.

Many Ottoman musicians, in particular, seemed to confound the "commerce and natural disasters" model of Muslim, Christian, and Jewish social relations by seeing and hearing across religious lines – especially starting in the eighteenth century when Ottoman music entered a robust period under court patronage. Recall that in the early Islamic era, musicians of different religions had merrily consorted, perhaps because, as the authors of a tenth-century, Abbasid-era treatise on music maintained (see Chapter 2), they considered music a wonder of God's creation, shared by humans, birds, and other animals.[25] Many Ottoman-era musicians evinced a collaborative, universalist ethos as well.

Consider, for example, the Jewish poet-composer Isaac Najara (c. 1555–c. 1625), who drew inspiration from what Janissary soldiers sang in Damascus coffeehouses to compose songs in Turkish, Arabic, and Greek. Najara's students devised a choral tradition in Jewish devotional music that adapted Turkish melodies to Hebrew prayers and spread to Istanbul, Salonika, and Izmir. Over a century later, another Jewish musician named Tanburo Isak (c. 1745–1814) taught the *tanbur* (a long-necked, stringed lute) to Sultan Selim III, and "apparently developed a distinctive school of playing which was transmitted through the Armenian [Christian] jeweler Oskiyam to the Nakshibandi [Muslim] Sheikh Abdulhalim," starting a chain of discipleship that continues among (Muslim) musicians in Turkey today. During the eighteenth century in Istanbul, meanwhile, a Greek Orthodox Christian man named Petros the Pelopponesian studied music in Istanbul with Mevlevi Sufi Muslims (sometimes known in English as the "Whirling Dervishes," and reputed for the music and dance that accompanied their *dhikr*s or prayer sessions). This Greek musician, in turn, brought Mevlevi styles and melodies into Orthodox Church music, enabling a kind of Neo-Byzantine church music to flourish. In Istanbul, Muslim, Christian, and Jewish composers sometimes attended each other's worship services just to hear the music. Some Mevlevi Muslims even went to synagogues to hear and later hang out with their friends, who were Jewish cantors.[26] Not all religious leaders were happy about this kind of social and musical mixing – judging, at least, from the reactions of one rabbi in late nineteenth-century Salonika – but musicians generally went ahead and did it anyway.[27]

The musicologist Walter Zev Feldman suggested that, during the eighteenth century, this practice of listening to the music of other religious communities had the effect of secularizing church and synagogue music as leading cantors became "stars" among Muslim audiences.[28] During the last third of the nineteenth century, something else changed, too. Ottoman sultans stopped patronizing composers, prompting Christian and Jewish musicians to seek careers in "*gazinos*," meaning casinos or nightclubs that had large musical ensembles. Perhaps because Muslim composers continued to have Mevlevi Sufis as patrons, Muslim composers did not move to *gazinos* as readily during this period. As a new social space, which replaced "older Greek taverns and Turkish coffee-houses," *gazinos* "offered a venue for a new middle-brow form of the older court music, suited to the taste of the middle classes."[29]

This last point about "middle-brow" culture is critical. The nineteenth century saw the debut of an Ottoman middle class which flourished in secular spaces where religion mattered less. To be sure, middle class groups in their various global manifestations have been notoriously hard to identify, perhaps because their constituents have kept changing. Explaining them has been as tricky in, say, France, the United States, Peru, and India, as in the late Ottoman Empire and the post–World War I Middle East.[30] What was the middle class exactly? When was it born; how did it grow? Is it better or more accurate to speak of a single "middle class" in a certain place, or of plural "middle classes"? For convenience more than conviction, I use the singular "middle class" here.

The Ottoman middle class of the 1890s had several recognizable features. Its members lived in cities and towns. Distinct from old, aristocratic elites, most men in its ranks earned incomes in commerce, professional service (i.e., in law, medicine, or government administration), or the military officer corps. Well off, if not downright rich, its members had money to spend on "extras," like nice socks, and not only on urgent necessities, like wheat and barley as food staples.[31] They also had money for leisure, some of it in the guise of domestic or personal improvement, such as interior decorating or piano and dance lessons.[32] Educated and literate, middle-class people read a lot, especially in "vernacular print languages" – literary forms of the languages that they studied, which were probably related or close to what they spoke at home – Turkish, Arabic, Armenian, or otherwise. Unlike Ottoman literati of the eighteenth century, they were unlikely to read hand-penned and costly manuscripts. Rather, they read cheap texts from printing presses – magazines, newspapers, and books – including romance, adventure, and detective stories that entertained more than they edified. Helping all of these developments was the increasing accessibility in this period of eyeglasses, a small-scale technology and increasingly mass-produced and affordable item, which enabled people with poor vision to read.[33]

Applying theories about how print culture seeds nationalism, one could say that the reading habits of "typographic man," or more accurately, typographic person, primed these middle-class readers to accept the premises of incipient linguistically based nationalisms, as Turks, Arabs, and so on.[34] Consider that from 1830 to 1870, about a hundred Armenian newspapers appeared in Istanbul (many for fleeting print runs) stimulating what Armenian nationalists later called the *zartonk* or renaissance.[35] This Armenian *zartonk* had its parallel among what Arabic literati, precursors to Arab nationalism, came to call their *nahda*. This Arabic *nahda* also depended on access to printing presses, which flourished in Beirut and later, after 1882, in Egypt (where British authorities of the Occupation allowed a freer press than Abdulhamid II was willing to tolerate).[36]

The emergent Ottoman middle class included women, who were increasingly literate and in some cases literati in their own right. Having attended schools, they could read with ease; some among them began to write and publish, too. In retrospect, the growth of female authorship has made women's lives and thoughts more accessible, making historians less likely in the long run to narrate the past as a purely men-made affair.[37]

These developments have also made it easier to track how masculine and feminine roles evolved in society. It appears, for example, that during this *fin-de-siècle* Ottoman period, educated women increasingly expected to have a say in choosing husbands, while as a memoirist recalled, "love and love marriages blossomed in Istanbul."[38] Missionaries helped to speed up these changes among Christian women in particular, by sponsoring church journals that welcomed female contributors and by encouraging women to read devotional texts on their own and to think more critically about their place at home, at church, and beyond.[39]

Finally, the members of this middle class had knowledge of the world beyond Ottoman borders, and especially western Europe and North America – both sources of styles and behaviors that became subjects of emulation. Many also claimed fluency in foreign European languages like French and German (as opposed to Ottoman European languages like Greek or Bulgarian) because of their access to foreign schools or tutors. The middle class made its strongest showing in coastal towns like Beirut and Istanbul that opened onto the Mediterranean. This sea was the source of a western-leaning form of "port-city cosmopolitanism" that depended both on Europeans and Americans (merchants, missionaries, diplomats, and others) coming eastward, and on "Ottomans" migrating westward, notably to seek futures in the Americas.[40]

Well-off, literate, and open to the world, the late Ottoman middle class was disproportionately Christian and Jewish. The nineteenth-century proliferation of Christian and (in the case of the Alliance Israélite Universelle) Jewish mission schools had endowed Christians and Jews with the *savoir-faire* and *savoir-vivre* that were prerequisites for middle-class membership. The mission schools' provision of literacy – which in Jewish and Catholic schools occurred largely in French – benefitted females substantially, helping to explain the importance of Christian and Jewish *women*, again, to the reading middle class.[41] Christian and Jewish men, meanwhile, gained skills that boosted them in the new middle-class "liberal professions" of the nineteenth century, as photographers, printers, engineers, and more. Arabic-speaking Christians especially were prolific writers and prolific readers alike.[42]

Some Muslims in this period joined the middle class, too. But Muslims had less to gain from middle-class membership where religious distinctions were muted. The historian Keith David Watenpaugh advanced an explanation. "[An] insistence on equality and cooperation bereft of religious distinction," he wrote, "held little appeal for members of the Muslim elite or even portions of the Muslim middle class, as for them equality represented the surrender of privileges and customary patriarchy." Pointing to the close connection between middle class and secular culture, he added, "Secularism held out the promise of empowerment only for non-Muslims."[43] Bernard Lewis made a similar, though broader, claim about social dynamics in the post–Tanzimat Ottoman Empire. "The equalization of the non-Muslims," Lewis wrote, "meant [for Muslims] the loss of the supremacy which they had long regarded as their right."[44] For many Muslims, in other words, shifts in the social pile were likely to cause a slide down.

Coming Together: Sites of Convergence

Consider again the *gazinos* that emerged as "middle brow" or "middle class" venues in Istanbul. Like the composers who sought careers there, many *gazinos'* owners were Greeks, Armenians, and Jews. So were many customers, though Muslims frequented them, too. In contrast to taverns and coffeehouses, where performances of local music occurred, *gazinos* blended the foreign and local. They combined what another musicologist called a "Turkish-style (*alaturka*) music program and [a] European-style (*alafranga*) space," whose well-to-do customers were able to order alcoholic drinks for refreshment. *Gazinos* were still mostly-male social spaces, though with their *alafranga* ambience, they began to draw females. To be sure, many religiously observant Muslim, Christian, and Jewish families regarded the mixed-sex, alcohol-purveying milieu of *gazinos* with suspicion and disapproval.[45] And yet, during this period when "drinking came out of hiding," with consumption of alcoholic beverages such as raki (a locally produced aniseed liqueur) becoming a sign of "modern" behavior, *gazinos* were sites of shared conviviality among Muslims, Christians, and Jews. A ladies' etiquette manual, published in the Ottoman language during this period, suggested how routine drinking had become in affluent circles: its advice on dinner parties included a matter-of-fact suggestion not to seat drinkers beside pious abstainers.[46]

More mundanely, leisured shopping – browsing or buying for pleasure – brought people together in ways that confirmed the notion that people are what they eat, wear, and use.[47] Picture postcards, which enjoyed their heyday in the 1890s, were an archetypal consumer product from this period. Bought to send or collect, postcards reflected the interplay of printing advances and quickening global travel, often across empires.[48] Whether they depicted, say, dancing girls or ships in a harbor, postcard images and their captions had the power to conjure the world as it was or, in fantasies, could be.[49] A recent study of Egyptian cosmopolitanism suggested as much by starting with a discussion of cards that depicted Cairo streets in the 1890s and of the two Jewish entrepreneurs who produced them.[50] Within post-1869 (post–Suez-Canal-opening)

Egyptian society, postcards of Cairo and of other cities presented very different views of what it meant to be "modern" versus "traditional." Consider, for example, photographs of the Suez Canal city of Port Said from the 1880s or 1890s, which a company called Photochromie Zürich produced in beautiful colorized prints. Images of "modern" Port Said feature a glistening harbor lined with majestic, multi-storied buildings like the Grand Continental Hotel. By contrast, images of the "Arab quarters," or the "traditional" city – which was in fact built at the same time as the harbor district – show muddy streets and squat clay buildings filled with boys clad in ankle-length gowns, or *jallabiyya*s.[51]

Postcard shops, like the one that flourished in the Beyoğlu district of Istanbul at the turn of the century,[52] brought well-off men, women, and children together in amicable proximity. And yet, since postcard shoppers could mingle without much interaction, how significant was their activity to forging a common culture based on consumption? If one accepts Bruce Masters's premise that the "routinization of inter-personal relations across religious lines" made it less likely for people to withdraw at night "behind their locked quarter gates, with the confidence borne of deep conviction that theirs alone was the true faith," then even a trivial endeavor like postcard shopping may have helped to develop a sense of community.[53] That said, without chatting among fellow browsers, shopping was unlikely to forge what the philosopher Jürgen Habermas (b. 1929) called a "public sphere," where diverse people considered common interests apart from the state and helped to create "civil society." To be effective as a public sphere, the philosopher Nancy Fraser elaborated, a space needed to function as "a theater ... in which political participation [was] enacted through the medium of talk." Just as important as talking was the possibility – in theory, if not always in practice – that "inequalities of status were to be bracketed, and discussants were to deliberate as peers."[54]

Freemasons' lodges, which reached the Ottoman Empire as European imports, fit the bill in fostering togetherness within a theater of vigorous talk. As a secret society for men, Freemasonry promoted "truth-seeking," "interreligious sociability," religious tolerance, and personal responsibility.[55] Aware that Freemasons swore oaths of loyalty with each other regardless of religious identities, and that some scorned established religion, many clerics disapproved of them, even though a handful of Muslim *'ulama* and Christian ecclesiastics became Freemasons. The first lodges founded in Cairo (1845) and Istanbul (1855) drew French, British, Italian, and other expatriates; before long they attracted middle-class Christians, Jews, and Muslims and occasional aristocrats, too. For example, 'Abd al-Halim Pasha, youngest son of Muhammad Ali of Egypt, joined the Freemasons in Egypt after attending Saint-Cyr military academy in France. So did Murat IV, who reigned as sultan for three months in 1876 until a nervous breakdown enabled his brother to step up to the throne or to seize it (with the correct verb for what Abdulhamid II did – step up or seize – remaining in doubt).[56] Freemasons attracted "radicals" and "leftists," too, including those who espoused anticlerical ideas, considered anarchism and socialism, and advocated international reform. Among the latter were Arabic writers from Beirut, Cairo, and Alexandria who contributed to the literary flowering or *nahda* of the period.[57]

Jamal al-Din al-Afghani, the peripatetic ideologue who touted Muslim solidarity in the face of Western imperialism (see Chapter 4), joined the Freemasons. In fact, he was so enthusiastic that he became chairman of the major Cairo lodge in 1878, whereupon he shifted its patronage from the United Grand Lodge of England to the Grand Orient de France, considering the latter more open to political debate.[58] Afghani's role in a society marked by its mixed membership and Franco-British allegiances seems at odds with the reputation he later earned as the forerunner to twentieth- and early twenty-first-century Islamism, with its built-in anti-"Western" credentials. How could a society famed for skepticism about religious dogmas and identities draw the late nineteenth century's most flamboyant Muslim activist? It helped that Freemasons' lodges were a crucible for making elites: in this way they offered something that Afghani wanted, even craved. That Afghani could be both a pan-Islamic ideologue and a Freemason also suggests the capacity of secular spaces to foster religious agendas. This tendency was as true of the Ottoman Empire as it was of, say, early twentieth-century India, where secular middle-class spaces provided a culture – here meaning a biological growth medium – for a Hindu nationalism that drew partly on anti-Muslim sentiment.[59] In short, religious neutrality and chauvinism could persist together as if on a palimpsest, scraped and reused many times and preserving traces of earlier texts.[60] In this case, new ideas about social parity and camaraderie did not fully efface old ideas about religious hierarchies, but rather faded in and out on the same plane.

With its mixture of secrecy, debate, and Enlightenment thought, Freemasonry helped to shape another group of Muslim thinkers who regarded Islam as a touchstone.[61] These were the Young Ottomans, members of a clandestine society that emerged in Istanbul in 1865 among employees of the state Translation Bureau – men whose jobs immersed them in Ottoman-language print culture. The Young Ottomans advocated constitutional government while extolling patriotism and the idea of *vatan*, or homeland. No fans of rule by monarchs (including sultans), they were frustrated by the intrusion of foreign European powers in

Ottoman affairs, by the empire's territorial losses, and by the breakaway threats of Balkan nationalisms. At the same time, while they claimed to support Ottoman identity for all subjects of the realm as well as rule by consent, they privileged Islam and therefore Muslims in the government that they imagined. Seeing inconsistency, the historian Niyazi Berkes described their ideas with wry bluntness as an "amalgam of constitutionalism and [Muslim] religious nationalism" that amounted to "ideological confusion."[62] Strikingly, the Young Ottomans expressed deep dissatisfaction with the Tanzimat reforms. They appeared to feel, first, that the reforms had only emboldened the Great Powers to meddle more on the Christians' behalf, and, second, that Christians had gained new rights while keeping old privileges as members of non-Muslim *millet*s. Among the new rights Christians gained was the freedom to have *millet*-based constitutions and assemblies, with the latter functioning like churchy parliaments.[63] Referring to these frustrations, one Turkish scholar recently described the Young Ottomans as forerunners to Turkish Muslim nationalism of the post–World War I variety whose Islamization of the concept of *vatan* (meaning homeland or nation) grew sharper in the late 1860s partly in reaction to "the privileged status of Christian *millet*s and Balkan nationalism."[64] The Young Ottomans movement contained strains of anti-Christian sentiment and Muslim self-affirmation, which it passed on to political successors.

Ironically, some of the most deeply sectarian institutions of the late nineteenth-century Ottoman Empire – foreign Christian mission schools – offered prime opportunities for religious mixing. Most mission schools had first catered to local Christians but increasingly admitted Muslims, too. Vivid examples include two American institutions, the Syrian Protestant College (opened to male students in 1866, and renamed the American University of Beirut in 1920), and Robert College in Istanbul (opened, also for males, in 1878 as an outgrowth of Bebek Seminary, founded in 1866). Eager to keep and attract more Muslims, both schools toned down the explicit Christian elements of their programs over time and became more secular. In return, many middle-class and elite Muslims favored these Christian schools because their programs were strong in subjects and pedagogies; because they had a reputation for treating students with respect regardless of their religious affinities; and because, by cultivating knowledge and know-how, they enabled students to connect to the big world beyond. Mission schools also appealed to Muslim parents because many – the two examples above notwithstanding – catered to females in a period when girls' schools were still few. Notions held by Protestant and Catholic missionaries in this period – notably, that religion could change through conviction, and that belief was personal and potentially private – helps to explain why so many mission schools were able and willing to accommodate non-Christians.[65] For indeed, judging from their own writings, missionaries hoped that the subtlety of their teachings or personal examples could sway students toward their brand of Christianity, whether they officially converted or not. Sultan Abdulhamid II feared exactly this possibility of partial or unwitting transformation. For this reason, he forbade Muslims from attending Christian mission schools, although the persistence of Muslim enrollments suggests that some parents paid him no heed.[66]

In general, Abdulhamid II appeared uneasy about how religious distinctions were blurring. He was also unhappy that urbane Muslims, Christians, and Jews were increasingly dressing alike in explicitly European fashions, making their bodies into sites of convergence. It bothered him, for example, that some Ottoman Muslim officials in consulates abroad, along with some Christian and Jewish men living in Ottoman cities, had begun to wear European brimmed hats. Hence, like Sultan Mahmud II before him (1839) and Mustafa Kemal Ataturk (1881–1938) of the Republic of Turkey after him (1925), he issued an edict on men's headgear near the start of his reign. In this case, Abdulhamid II banned the brimmed hat and upheld the fez as the official headgear of Ottoman men, "in the name," as one scholar recently put it, "of national [sic] and Islamic tradition."[67] (This Islamic "tradition" stretched only to the early nineteenth century, when the fez supplanted the turban!) Given how Abdulhamid II ascribed symbolic power to the fez, it is no wonder that he included a picture of the "Imperial Fez Factory" within the hefty fifty-one photograph albums sent in the 1890s as a gift to the US government.[68] It is no wonder, too, that the few available photographs of Abdulhamid II – a man who loved photography but hated having his picture taken[69] – show him fez-topped as well.

Without a doubt, the higher level of social convergence during the Abdulhamid II era owed something to western European and American cultural norms, drawn from the mix of schools, shops, clothing, Freemasons' lodges, and the like, that loosened old hierarchies while enabling people to consort in neutral spaces. And yet "Western" culture and secular socializing did not lead ineluctably to universal fellowship, the *fraternité*, of French revolutionary ideals. Men could, say, join a Freemasons lodge, talk blithely, and still walk out the door as religious chauvinists. Immersion in Western culture did not guarantee that people would or could flow freely across lines of religion.

Likewise, immersion in local Ottoman culture did not trap people inside the walls of religion, either. Consider the late Ottoman musical scene. Abdulhamid II is said to have had some knowledge of playing the *bağlama* or *saz*, a long-necked lute, but generally found Ottoman music a bore. His real love was for Italian operas by Rossini, Bellini, Donizetti, and Verdi. He even invited great foreign singers, like the Belgian soprano Blanche Arral (1864–1945), to perform for him.[70] Once, by contrast, courtiers invited the Ottoman musician Tanburi Cemil Bey (1873–1916) to the palace but ended his performance when the sultan dozed off. Indignant nearly a century later at this affront to one of the greatest Ottoman composers and *tanbur* players of all time, the musicologist Walter Feldman dismissed Abdulhamid II as "the sleeping sultan" and argued that his behavior during Tanburi Cemil's performance amounted to an "abdication of responsibility" over the patronage of Ottoman music, which entered a long period of "somnolence" under his watch. What became known as "Turkish art music" withered and almost died in the twentieth century, Feldman added, but gained a boost in the 1980s, when Greek musicians from Greece ventured to Istanbul, imperial capital of yore, to study it as part of "their own pre-modern secular art music tradition."[71]

What can one conclude from these details? For all his commitment to a Sunni Muslim ideal of Ottoman Islamic statehood, Abdulhamid II himself was a firm fan of what Ottomans called culture "allafranca," that is, "Western" culture, in his home life.[72] He loved Italian operas, as well as gripping yarns by Arthur Conan Doyle and Gaston Leroux; he admired pop culture icons like the French actress Sarah Bernhardt (see Chapter 5). Given his predilections, Ottoman musical culture persisted in spite of, and not because of, "this bourgeois king ... this bourgeois sultan,"[73] while owing some of its vigor to the non-Muslim artists who appreciated and practiced it with their Muslim colleagues. To put it another way: Abdulhamid II may have tried to ban hats, discourage Muslim parents from sending their children to Christian schools, and conjure an image of Islamic tradition, but he was as attracted to aspects of western European and American culture as many other affluent Ottoman urbanites of his time. Perhaps two lessons to draw are these: first, just as the Ottoman Empire was a European empire, not to mention an Asian and African empire, too, so Ottoman culture was integrally both "Western" and "Eastern"; and second, culture was much more than religion.

Thinking about chances for Muslims, Christians, and Jews to mix on cordial terms, the historian François Georgeon looked back on the Abdulhamid II era and claimed to see a *brassage* or new brew that was breaking down clumps of religious communities. Georgeon called the result *convivance*, meaning not just living together (as the Latin roots, *con* and *vivere*, suggest) or putting up with each other out of need or by happenstance, but rather living together in good cheer.[74] To be sure, the imperial capital of Istanbul showed many signs of conviviality. There, Christian professionals and businessmen socialized in masonic lodges with Muslim and Jewish colleagues. There, Muslim and Christian school friends sometimes fasted in solidarity during Ramadan and shared sweets during Easter.[75] Those Muslims, Christians, and Jews who had money to spare converged in the same shops to buy their suspenders, parasols, and *eaux de cologne*.[76] Historians have had another way to describe this array of *bonhomie*: they have called it "Ottomanism," suggesting that it held promise for a kind of transreligious, supra-ethnic identity based on common residence and fellow feeling within the Ottoman Empire.

Of course, these ideals were by and large city values that flourished in cosmopolitan, middle-class circles where Muslims, Christians, and Jews converged. A place like Yemen, where congeniality had much more trouble crossing religious lines, was a different story and is worth examining as a contrast to Istanbul. Indeed, observers reported that social boundaries in Yemen between Muslims and Jews remained so sharp during the late nineteenth century that if a Jew brushed against a Muslim by mistake, the Muslim could demand that he pay for soap to have the Muslim's clothing washed and decontaminated. And while sharing sweets from a common tray may have been commonplace for Muslim, Christian, and also Jewish friends or colleagues in convivial Istanbul, Muslims in the Yemeni city of Sana'a not only refused to eat or drink with Jews, but stood ready to smash utensils that Jews defiled by touching.[77] Inside one Ottoman Empire, different worlds were spinning.

Dung and Dead Bodies: Jews and the Limits of Ottoman Reform

Even in its truncated shape after the Russo-Turkish War, the late nineteenth-century Ottoman Empire can seem too big to fit on the stage of one history. In terms of state-society relations, Istanbul obviously differed from Nablus, just as Mecca differed from Mosul and Benghazi, any city differed from any village or tribal encampment, and so on. Egypt had its own complexities: it managed to be Ottoman, quasi-autonomous, and, after 1882, British-occupied at the same time, leaving students of history to scratch their heads over the timing and nature of its colonial past. Appreciating these distinctions, and yet seeking to tidy history as a way to contain it, the historian Cem Emrence suggested that late nineteenth-century Ottoman history happened along three "imperial paths" (leaving Egypt aside). There was a coastal path, he claimed, in places like Beirut, where middle-class Christians and Jews were increasingly prominent; an interior path in places like Damascus, where a locally rooted Sunni Muslim bloc ran affairs in collaboration with Ottoman bureaucrats; and a frontier path. The frontier included restive places like Yemen, Libya, and parts of what are now Iraq, eastern Turkey, and Syria, where Ottoman authorities hammered on Muslim solidarity and struck bargains with local Muslims in an effort to avoid losing control.[78] This scheme for thinking about Ottoman history has advantages. It can help to explain, for example, why as the century ended, circumstances for non-Muslims seemed rosy in Beirut, where Arabic-speaking Christian intellectuals were enjoying prominence as cultural luminaries and activists, but bleak in places where Ottoman rule was thin on the ground.[79]

Consider Yemen, a frontier that the Ottoman state never fully controlled. Much of the population in northwest Yemen, which included Sana'a and its hinterlands, followed Zaydi Islam and recognized an *imam*, meaning a holder of political and religious authority in the Shi'i sense of the term. (To Sunnis, by contrast, *imam* meant simply a prayer leader in a mosque.) Forebears of the Zaydis had split from what became the two major branches of Shi'ism (Ismaili Shi'ism and Imami or Twelver Shi'ism, the latter dominant in Iran) during the eighth century. As a result of their sectarian specificity and geographical isolation, Zaydi Muslims followed certain customs that diverged from those of Sunni and other Shi'i Muslims. Some of their quirkiest customs involved Jews, who were the only non-Muslims in a place that lacked indigenous Christians. During the late nineteenth century, Jews numbered about 60,000–80,000 people in Yemen, with some 85 percent of them living scattered in villages and the remainder inhabiting towns like Sana'a (where Jews accounted for a fifth of the population), Ibb, and Dhamar.[80] Suffice it to say that the Ottoman Tanzimat decrees of 1839 and 1856, with their language of religious inclusion and parity, had not "happened" in regions of Yemen where the Zaydi imam held sway and where Muslims maintained stiff restrictions on Jews as *dhimmi*s that recalled the Pact of Umar (see Chapter 2). For example, Jews could not ride saddled animals (i.e., they could ride donkeys but not horses), build houses higher than those of Muslims, blow loudly their shofars (arguably the closest Jewish equivalent to a church bell), or dress like Muslims. They had to wear distinguishing dark clothing and hairstyles – which for Yemeni Jewish men meant curled side-locks.[81] In areas of Yemen where most Muslims followed Sunni Islam of the Shafi'i *madhhab* or legal variety, policies and attitudes toward Jews as *dhimmi*s were by some accounts less restrictive – although this difference may have been due as much to the more relaxed norms of tribal society and to the distance from Sana'a as it was to sectarian attitudes.[82]

In 1872, during the reign of Sultan Abdulaziz, Ottoman forces conquered – or in their official view, reconquered – Yemen as part of the policy of controlling peripheries more closely (see Chapter 5). Recall that Britain had annexed Aden, on Yemen's southern coast, in 1839; the Suez Canal had opened in 1869 and benefitted British shipping especially. Heavily invested in India, Britain had interests in the Red Sea, Arabia, Persian Gulf, and Indian Ocean – and these interests were likely to grow. Against this context, securing Yemen became a priority for Ottoman authorities who arrived to find Yemeni Jews anxious for change. British rule in Aden had not only removed debilities on Jews in that enclave, but had also opened contact via letter writing between Yemeni Jews in the interior and European activists, especially those from the Alliance Israélite Universelle in Paris and the Anglo-Jewish Association, a kindred organization founded in London in 1871. The Suez Canal also eased and quickened communication between Jews in Yemen and in Ottoman locales like Salonika, Hebron, and Cairo. In this way, Yemeni Jews heard about the Tanzimat reforms and sensed that conditions for Jews elsewhere were good, improving, or at least better than what they were facing. When the Ottoman governor, Ahmad Mukhtar Pasha, arrived with troops in Sana'a, they were desperate to see improvements themselves.[83]

Jewish leaders hoped that reform-minded Ottoman authorities would overturn two Zaydi policies in Yemen. The first was the "Orphans Decree," which dated from the eighteenth century. This ruling empowered Zaydi Muslim authorities to seize Jewish children whose fathers had died, convert them, and raise them as Muslims. In a land where drought, food shortages, and disease ran rampant and left many young children bereft of their fathers, the Orphans Decree instilled dread in Jewish families. The second policy was the Dung-Gatherers Decree, also known as the Latrine or Scrapers Edict. Issued in the seventeenth or eighteenth century, and applied in Sana'a before extending to other towns, the Dung-Gatherers Decree required Jews to clear from sewers and latrines human feces which, when burned, fueled Muslim and Jewish communal baths.[84] The ruling also required them to remove carcasses and non-Muslim corpses (as happened on one occasion, when two Christian travelers wandered into Ibb and expired).[85] Theoretically the obligation to collect waste applied to all Jews, rabbis included, though in practice responsibility fell on the poorest who received payment from fellow Jews but who became like a kind of shunned caste. Other Jews refused to marry or eat with dung-gatherers, to let their men read the Torah in synagogue, and to enroll their children in schools.[86] Jews at large nevertheless admitted feeling the sting of the dung-gatherers' humiliation, which Muslims reinforced by jeering the Jews who did this work.[87]

By some accounts, the Ottoman governor, Ahmad Mukhtar Pasha, genuinely believed in reform and sympathized with Yemeni Jews. Under his leadership Ottoman authorities ended the seizure of orphans. Otherwise, good intentions collided with the Ottoman need to win local Muslim support, or at least not to alienate Muslims too much. For when the pasha tried to end the Dung-Gatherers' Decree, Zaydi Muslims howled: it was tradition, they insisted, and who else could do a job so degrading? In the end, Ahmad Mukhtar bowed to local Muslim pressure and in the words of one historian, "persuaded the Jewish notables that it would be in their own interest to maintain the status quo."[88] "The Turks found themselves confronted with relentless guerrilla attacks by the [Muslim] tribes," a second historian reflected, "and had to expend most of their energy and resources in attempting to suppress the revolt against their rule." At least Ottoman authorities made sure that the Jews got some outside payment for the work, "whereas under the Arab rule [sic] they never saw even a copper coin."[89]

Jews in Sana'a held another, more general grievance, which Ottoman authorities did not address. More than the Dung-Gatherers Decree, some Jews reported in the 1870s that the worst of their daily tribulations was that Muslim children pelted them with stones, yanked men's sidelocks, and insulted them as they passed in the streets, but convention barred them from striking back. "The Turkish [sic] Governor attempted to bring an end to it," another reported, "but was told by a Zaydi jurist that the practice was 'an age old custom' (in Arabic *Ada*) and that therefore it was unlawful to forbid it."[90]

Keeping the status quo was one thing; making things worse was another. Ottoman authorities proved so ruthless in extracting taxes and labor that they saddled Yemeni Jews with new burdens. Never mind that the *jizya* had supposedly lapsed in the heart of the empire: in Yemen, Ottoman authorities demanded *jizya* from Jews and more than doubled the sum. On one occasion in 1890 they arrested and tortured ten Jewish men – community leaders – for failing to pay enough *jizya*.[91] And whereas Zaydi authorities had scrupulously respected Jewish observation of holidays and Sabbath days, Ottoman authorities proved simultaneously lax and draconian. They forced Jews to grind grain for Ottoman troops during Passover, when Jews otherwise cleaned and stopped using their millstones.[92] On one Sabbath during the Sukkot holiday, they forced dozens of Jewish men to carry injured Ottoman soldiers on stretchers over a route so rugged and strenuous that several bearers died.[93] Jewish chroniclers later remembered this episode of the "Stretcher-Bearers' Decree" as a low point of their history in Yemen.[94] Of course, Yemen was a tough place for the Ottoman forces, too. They were constantly sparring with

local Muslims including those who supported their chief rival, Yahya
Muhammad Hamid al-Din (1869–1948), who wanted to rule as Zaydi
imam. When their soldiers suffered injuries, it was a struggle to keep
them alive.

Finally, while Yemeni society observed sharp religious distinctions, the
droughts and famines that hit the region in the 1890s failed to discriminate. A Jewish source reported that "thin, cadaverous, virtual skeletons,
wander[ed] like ghosts through the town [of Sana'a] in search of something to eat" while some adults, starving and desperate, ate their own
children.[95] As far-fetched and horrific as this last claim may sound, it was
conceivable: "Famine cannibalism has [had] a long history" in societies
around the world, one scholar recently argued, and occurred during the
past two centuries in diverse places like Ireland, China, and Nigeria.[96]
Some twenty years after these events in Yemen, during the chaos of World
War I, isolated cases of famine cannibalism occurred in Ottoman Syria,
too.[97] Returning to Yemen, the point is that living conditions were bad
during the late nineteenth century for Muslims and Jews alike. People
suffered amidst political instability caused by constant, low-grade warring; food shortages; high, even harsh taxes; and impoverishment, the last
aggravated by imports of cheap manufactured goods from Europe and
India which gutted Yemen's artisanal economy.[98] If Jews had it worse than
other Yemenis, it was because they were *dhimmi*s, regarded by Muslims
as lowly, dirty creatures whose lot in life should be shoveling shit.

Yemeni Jews began to see an exit from these hardships during the
last two decades of the nineteenth century. Some moved to British-
controlled Aden; others literally jumped ship. A new era in Yemeni
Jewish migration began in 1881, when a couple of families left Sana'a
for the shoreline and sailed on dhows for Jerusalem. In time, some
ventured east to Bombay on India's Arabian Sea coast, while many
others headed northwest through the Suez Canal and onward to Egypt
and to Jaffa and Jerusalem. Jews remaining in Yemen faced hefty communal *jizya* bills that did not shrink to account for the émigrés, and
this prompted more to leave. By 1884, about 400 Yemeni Jews had
reached Jerusalem; by 1888, the number had grown to 650; by 1908,
there were 2,500.[99] By 1914, the Yemeni Jewish population had doubled again around Jerusalem.[100] These figures did not include Yemenis
who settled elsewhere, for example, Egypt, which was drawing immigrants (including many southern Europeans) to the Suez Canal Zone,
Alexandria, and Cairo.[101] These early trickles gave way to a steady flow
decades later.

In hailing modern Jewish migration to Jerusalem and its environs as
a "return" to ancient Israel after two millennia – a return that enabled

the emergence of the State of Israel in 1948 – many twentieth- and early twenty-first century Jewish thinkers have celebrated the arrival in 1881 of a group called Bilu, which took its name from letters in the biblical verse Isaiah 2:5 ("O, house of Jacob, come, let us walk in the light of the Lord!"[102]). Fourteen students belonging to this Bilu group reached Ottoman Palestine from the Russian Empire, where anti-Semitic laws and pogroms were targeting Jews. Indeed, in 1881, sixteen years before the Dreyfus Affair in France prompted the Viennese journalist Theodor Herzl to write *The Jewish State* (1896), a Russian Jewish thinker named Leo Pinsker published a pamphlet called *Auto-Emancipation* even as another set of Russian-speaking Jews formed a group called Hibbat Zion, meaning "Lovers of Zion." In short, members of the Bilu group came out of a milieu where early Zionist thought was taking shape as a proactive yet pessimistic response to anti-Jewish sentiment, which was starting to go by the pithier name of "anti-Semitism."[103] Zionist thought started from a number of premises, including these: that anti-Semitism would not go away; that Jews should take charge to improve their conditions, and not wait passively for improvement to happen; that leaving and going to some place new was preferable to sticking things out where they were; and that ancient Jewish political history offered lessons on how to be strong. Zionism entailed a search for self-respect.[104]

In fact, Yemeni Jews who set out from Sana'a reached Jerusalem several months *before* the Bilu group. And yet these Yemenis were not Zionists, nor have Jewish writers tended to hail them as initiators of the "First Aliyah" (literally, the first ascent, with the Hebrew term *aliyah* used by Zionists to suggest a migration representing a lofty achievement or higher calling). Even if some literate leaders in the Yemeni Jewish community were aware of intellectual currents swirling among Jews in Europe, a more important and recurrent intellectual input for rank-and-file Yemeni Jews had been messianism, that is, ideas about the end of time and Judgment Day. Such ideas had been circulating among Yemeni Jews since the days of Sabbatai Sevi (1626–76)[105] in the seventeenth century, giving hope amidst dire conditions.[106] Nevertheless, by getting jobs in the new agricultural projects or *moshavot* that European Jewish settlers were starting in Palestine, Yemeni Jewish farmworkers bolstered Zionism's back-to-the-land ideal of "Hebrew labor."[107] Yemeni Jews in Palestine thus became actors in the Zionist movement, even if they did not arrive that way.

Back in Yemen, Ottoman rule began to fizzle after 1908. In 1910, a year that one historian associated with a "Turkish capitulation," the Zaydi claimant to the imamate, Yahya Muhammad Hamid al-Din, issued an edict reinstating old policies toward Jews as *dhimmi*s.[108] Imam Yahya consolidated his rule after the Ottoman Empire's collapse amidst World War I, so that his rulings applied in Sana'a and outlying regions until his death by assassination in 1948. Imam Yahya restored the Orphans Decree, which Ottoman authorities had suspended. In addition to clarifying payment of *jizya*, he decreed, inter alia, that Jews must not "raise their voice against a Muslim," "construct houses higher than those of Muslims," and "brush against Muslims in the street." He also ordered that "Jews must always get to their feet before Muslims." Stipulations like these made it easier for Jews, who claimed an ancient heritage in Yemen, to pick up and leave. A major opportunity to vacate Yemen arose in 1949 – one year after both Imam Yahya's death and the emergence of Israel. This was when Israeli authorities sent airplanes to fetch Yemeni Jews in a two-year staged migration, which they called "Operation Magic Carpet." The Orientalist name of this enterprise, which recalled fanciful tales of the Arabian Nights, reflected the attitudes of Israel's mostly European (Ashkenazi) Jewish founders toward "Eastern" Jewish others.[109]

While surveying Jewish societies in the modern Middle East and North Africa during the nineteenth century, the historian Reeva Spector Simon contended that life for Jews "remained stagnant or worsened" in three places that witnessed forced conversions to Islam and the reassertion of *dhimmi* rules. (Her remark implied that elsewhere in this large region, situations for Jews generally improved.) Yemen was one of the places on her three-worst list; so were Morocco and Iran – neither of them Ottoman territories.[110] Strikingly, Libya did *not* make the list even though it was an Ottoman edge-zone where local Muslims held deep-rooted attitudes toward Jews as *dhimmi*s. The experiences of Jews in Libya are worth considering briefly for the sake of comparison and contrast with Yemen, and for showing that not all frontiers were alike, even in places where the Ottoman presence was slim.

After having ceded Libya to the Karamanli dynasty through a kind of subcontracting agreement after 1711, the Ottoman state asserted direct control in 1835. Ottoman officials sent from Istanbul thereafter brought the reformist spirit of the Tanzimat era to bear on the coastal region where the Ottoman presence was strong. A Jewish chronicler and rabbinic court clerk named Mordechai Ha-Cohen (1856–1929) observed that in nineteenth-century Tripoli, many "Muslim Turks" defended the Jews from local Muslims, prompting Jews to see themselves as partners in Ottoman reform.[111] "From the time that Tripoli came under the protection of Turkey [sic]," Ha-Cohen wrote, "the Jews began to shake off the dust of their lowliness, for the ruling Turks did not have strong hatred of the Jews as did the [local] Arabs."[112] Before the Ottomans came, he explained, local Muslims sometimes tried to trap Jews into converting to

Islam "like a bird in a snare." They also insisted that Jews, as *dhimmis*, honor Muslims, refrain from riding horses or bearing arms, and more, even as the Ottoman Empire showed signs of relaxing some traditional restrictions.[113] And yet, Libyan Muslims sometimes mixed with Jews in a congenial way. For example, Libyan Muslims appeared to have none of the Shi'i-style purity taboos that informed Zaydi attitudes in Yemen – nothing to prevent them from eating with Jews and sharing utensils.[114] Ha-Cohen certainly praised the generosity of Libyan Muslim hosts toward travelers, especially in villages. "[I]f a mounted [Muslim] warrior comes to their house, or even an ordinary Jew," he observed, "they earn a good name by greatly honoring him" with a fine meal.[115] His account suggests that while Ottoman rule may have offered new opportunities for Jews (prompting migration from the interior to coastal towns and villages), Libyan Muslim society already had standards of hospitality that crossed religious lines.[116]

If there was one long-term problem for Libyan Jews associated with Ottoman rule, it may have been simply the following: that the Ottoman authorities' more equitable attitudes toward Jews stoked resentment among many local Muslims who sensed the relative erosion of their own higher status. This resentment persisted beyond 1911, when Italy invaded Tripolitania and put a *de facto* end to Ottoman rule in the territory.[117]

However far it lurks below the surface, resentment has the power to drive history. Resentment certainly drove the massacres that struck Armenians in the 1890s. Whether one ascribes these massacres to a toxic brew of "jealousies, frustrations of all sorts, social, cultural, even sexual," or simply to a broad social and economic envy that left sectors of the Muslim population deeply disgruntled, the underlying point is the same. Massacres happened, and were able to happen because of the predilections of a government whose delegates looked away when violence broke loose.[118]

Resentment: The Story of the 1890s Armenian Massacres

Recall a bleak moment in Syrian history: the week in July 1860 when a mob of some 20,000–50,000 men plundered, killed, and raped their way through a neighborhood of Damascus, leaving thousands dead. The attackers were Muslim men from the laboring and artisanal classes who lived elsewhere in the city. The victims were well-to-do Christians, mostly Melkites, whose Catholicism arose from missionary encounters. Compared to the massacres that struck Armenian Christians in Anatolia during the 1890s, this Damascus massacre was remarkable, in part, because Ottoman authorities took such rapid measures to stop them by punishing marauders and by forcing them to return abducted females. Meanwhile, Damascus Christians hailed many Muslims who had helped them in their dark hours. Heroes included humble people, like a grocer, and distinguished figures, like 'Abd al-Qadir al-Jaza'iri (1808–83), exiled leader of the resistance to France's conquest of Algeria. (For organizing the rescue of thousands in Damascus, 'Abd al-Qadir received accolades from a host of foreign leaders, including Pius IX of the Vatican and Abraham Lincoln of the United States. The fact that he later joined the Freemasons suggests that he was open to mixing with Christians.)[119]

Move northeast into Anatolia, jump ahead thirty-five years, and behold what a difference place, time, and sultan could make. Between 1894 and 1897, large-scale plunder, rape, assault, and abduction occurred in towns and villages throughout eastern Anatolia. The attackers were mostly Kurdish Muslims, including members of Abdulhamid II's eponymous Hamidiye regiments, although Muslim Turkish speakers and *muhajirs* (refugees from the Balkans and Caucasus) counted among them as well. The victims were Armenian Christians engaged in farming, trade, and other pursuits, along with a much smaller number of Kurds who died in reprisals. Lacking heartwarming tales of rescue, historical accounts more often mention that Armenians lived in fear of Kurdish neighbors. Ottoman authorities did not suppress the violence and made no moves to punish marauders. Nor did they dismiss officials on whose watch atrocities occurred. By allowing attacks to drag on for years, authorities broke from three ideals of Ottoman statecraft. Two had deep roots in Islamic history: first, the notion of protecting non-Muslim subjects and, second, the idea of maintaining public order whenever possible to avoid strife, or *fitna*. The third was the newer Tanzimat notion of treating non-Muslims and Muslims equitably in relation to the state.

Estimates for death tolls vary widely, but whatever they were, they make the 1860 Damascus massacre look trifling. American missionary sources suggested in 1896 that 37,000 Armenians had died along with 1,800 Kurds, and that 300,000 were "reduced to misery" from injury and destroyed property. Other sources have cited much higher figures for Armenian dead – 100,000–300,000.[120] Figures for the total number of Kurds killed and injured are lacking, although one source claimed, "In the vast majority of massacres, Armenian victims exceeded Muslims in the range of hundreds to one."[121] One of the most notorious events of this period happened in Urfa in which 3,000 Armenians died, incinerated in the cathedral where they sought refuge.[122] The *New York Times* in 1896 reported that the aggregate attacks had turned 50,000 Armenian children into orphans.[123]

Rape and abduction featured strongly in the violence. Kurdish tribesmen seized many Armenian females making them *de facto* wives and
Muslim converts. "Females" is a more accurate word here than "women"
because some of the abducted were girls as young as nine.[124]

Many thousands of Armenians, meanwhile, converted to Islam amidst
the strife – entire villages of men, women, and children totaling some
25,000 across Diyarbekir province alone. Ottoman officials insisted that
such conversions were voluntary and, sometimes, so did Armenians
when pressed. The historian Selim Deringil, however, scrutinized mass
conversions during this conflict and demurred: he called these conversions forced, and attributed them to the terror that prevailed among
Armenians even after raiding had ended. For Deringil, the fact that so
many Armenian adult men arranged for hasty circumcisions to prove
their shift to Islam, and that some changed their churches into mosques
overnight and began to engage in ostentatious, five-times-a-day praying within them, betrays desperation – a hope that Kurdish Muslims
would stop attacking them if they were Muslim, too. Strikingly, Ottoman
authorities "rejected" some of these mass conversions, fearing that they
would draw bad publicity or unwanted diplomatic pressure from foreign observers. This rejection left Armenian quasi-converts in dangerous
limbo: vulnerable to Muslim attacks as apostates if they went back to
Christianity, yet lacking official Muslim status. Deringil also questioned
the individual conversions of Armenian females whom marauders had
seized. When located afterward, a few of these insisted that they preferred to remain with their abductors, married and Muslim. The shame
of their rape was likely so intense, he argued, and their prospects for
future marriage within the Armenian community so dim, that submitting
to the situation foisted upon them may have seemed better than returning home sullied.[125]

Precisely because officials did not quell the violence that beset eastern
Anatolia during the mid-1890s, historians have continued to debate the
role of the sultan behind it. Pause to consider the sources, which do not
easily settle the matter: they have gaps and are prone to charges of bias
whether they are Armenian memoirs, Christian missionary accounts,
European consular reports, or Ottoman state correspondence. The fact
that Abdulhamid II was so secretive, covering his tracks while trying to
spy on everyone else, dooms historians to speculate even more.

Against this context, three questions about the sultan recur. Did
Abdulhamid II order these attacks on Armenians? Given his lack of
effort to suppress the raiding, did he *want* these attacks to happen? Did
he even control the frontier where they transpired – an area containing
Kurds and Armenians who lived in tense and awkward proximity? Likely

answers, in order, are these: No, the sultan did not appear to order the attacks. To judge from past behavior, he was too cautious to do something so rash. He did, however, give support throughout his reign to the idea of Muslim preeminence, and this seemed to make it easier for some Muslims on the ground – including urban notables, Kurdish chiefs, members of Sufi brotherhoods, and *'ulama* – to justify actions against Armenians in terms of bringing out-of-control people back into line. (Indeed, raids on Armenians often began on Fridays after Muslim men gathered in mosques for congregational worship, when preachers delivered inflammatory sermons.[126]) The answer to the second question – did the sultan want these attacks to occur? – seems to have been yes. For reasons considered below, he seemed to think that Armenians deserved what they got. And third, to the question of whether he had a tight grip on eastern Anatolia, the answer is not fully. Although the region was much closer to Istanbul than, say, Yemen, the Ottoman central state found the Kurdish tribes of the region perennially hard to control, which is partly why Abdulhamid II had devised the scheme of roping Kurds into the Hamidiye in the first place.[127] By and large, the Hamidiye fighters did what they wanted and stayed "almost completely impervious to the discipline of a modern army."[128] Ottoman authorities nevertheless shortened their tether, and made their collaboration worthwhile, by giving them weapons and a *carte blanche* to despoil Armenians.[129]

Many who blamed Abdulhamid II for what befell the Armenians portrayed him as a bloodmonger and dubbed him "the red sultan." Such claims can mislead by assigning too much credit to the sultan, who did not operate solo. Abdulhamid II had delegates on the ground – not only Kurds running amok but also educated, Ottoman Turkish-speaking, imperial men on the spot who made decisions and who conveyed reports that he seemed ready to believe. There were men like Eniş Pasha, governor of Diyarbekir, who appeared to incite attacks on Armenians while insisting to Istanbul that all criticism was "the slander of enemies."[130] The same Eniş Pasha made the hundreds of abducted Armenian females sound like stolen chickens, by referring in official correspondence only to "Armenian women who were dispersed here and there during the troubles"[131] – suggesting that what happened to them was no big deal. Still other functionaries may have crafted exaggerated reports of Armenian perfidy for the banal reason that they wanted promotions and therefore needed to seem busy and important to authorities in Istanbul.[132]

Abdulhamid II's attitudes toward Armenians appeared to move in step with those of many Anatolian Muslims in this period, and these attitudes were built on resentment. As one scholar argued, this resentment extended even to "liberal and Westernizing Ottoman Turks," who had ostensibly been the strongest supporters of the Tanzimat-era reforms.[133] Parsing the sultan's intentions is therefore an exercise in cultural metonymy: his thoughts were of a piece with a popular mood. Together he and many Anatolian Muslims seem to have shared *Schadenfreude* toward Armenians. This satisfaction at seeing them suffer helps to explain, again, why the government allowed the violence to occur and stretch on as it did.[134]

At century's end, Anatolian Muslims resented or even feared Armenians on many counts. To repeat, as Christians, Armenians did not perform military combat in a period when mass conscription hit Muslims hard. Armenians' exposure to mission schools placed them ahead of Muslims in male and female literacy, while their knowledge of hygiene and access to medical care enabled their children to evade illness at much higher rates than Kurds, who lost as many as half of their babies in childbirth.[135] Armenian adults, too, were on average healthier than Kurds, many of whom suffered from blindness-inducing trachoma.[136] When cholera struck Diyarbekir, more Muslims than Armenians died.[137] Thanks to the 1858 Land Reform Law and émigré remittances, more Armenians in eastern Anatolia were buying land, often from Turkish- and Kurdish-speaking Muslims who had fallen into debt.[138] In this economy, many Armenians became debt-holders, or as some sources describe them, moneylenders or "usurers," with the last term especially suggesting the unethical charging of interest.[139] Exclusive claims of Armenians to land challenged what had historically been "many overlapping rights such as rights to passage, poaching, [and] grazing ... on a single plot," to the disadvantage of pastoralist Kurds and newer refugees from the Caucasus and Balkans.[140] Some Muslims even seemed to think that Armenians were becoming savvier in agriculture so that their farmers got more from the land.[141] In the last quarter of the century, Armenians were becoming more visible in certain places, too. In Diyarbekir, again, "whole quarters of the city ... changed from Turkish to Christian" as Armenians bought "Turkish" houses.[142]

While some scholars have suggested that Armenians – like Greek and Arab Christians – were enjoying a population "renaissance"[143] in this period, another trend may have driven Armenian house purchases in Diyarbekir. This was the migration of eastern Anatolian Armenians from rural areas into towns and cities, as Kurds and Caucasus refugees pushed them off their lands.[144]

The vague perception that Armenians were teeming while Muslims were dwindling led some Anatolian Muslims to hold a grudge.[145] Certainly in Istanbul, Muslim "middle strata" couples were having fewer children, continuing a trend in family planning that had begun in the

1860s. Small nuclear families were becoming normal. Beyond Istanbul, too, Muslim women were limiting offspring. As early as 1878, a British consul claimed that Muslims were having so many abortions that their population was shrinking. Whether this was true or not is irrelevant (and in any case, it seems that abortions were common before then, too).[146] The point is that the sultan became concerned about abortion and population trends, and hired a German doctor to do an assessment. The doctor, in turn, issued a verdict: Anatolian Muslims, he declared, were approaching extinction because of disease, birth control, and military fatalities. Panicked by this report, Ottoman authorities declared abortions illegal. They also approved publications like the one in 1889, which called abortion a crime while stating that, "A child is a creature of God from the very moment it is conceived." This position on conception and terminating pregnancy departed from what Muslim jurists had historically concluded about fetal viability, and suggested an incipient pronatalist policy. It also suggested that a kind of demographic anxiety was taking hold in some Muslim circles – and this, even though Muslims in Istanbul – if not in Diyarbekir – appeared to be growing relative to Christians and Jews in both number and as a proportion of the population,[147] partly, perhaps, because of migration into the capital.

Anatolian Muslims' anxieties about Armenians and their ostensible expansion extended to other Christians, such as Greek inhabitants of the Ottoman Empire. Indeed, one Turkish historian described Ottoman Greeks in this period as having been "free of military obligations and paying insignificant taxes in proportion to their incomes, [so that they] could afford to raise large families."[148] Yet, not all historians have agreed that Christian numbers were growing. One argued, on the contrary, that such claims were based on shaky "retro-projections,"[149] while two others suggested that urban Christians (like Jews) were likely planning their families, too.[150] Still, perceptions of rampant breeding by non-Muslims stoked resentments and led to a kind of divergence in mentalities, while confirming the Ottoman state's open door policies toward Muslim refugees who could offset declining Muslim numbers.[151]

Another fear gripped many Muslims in eastern Anatolia: that Britain, France, and Russia would help Armenians to seize power and land at Muslims' expense. Rumors spread that Armenians would make Anatolian Muslims refugees – *muhajirs* – like the Chechens and Circassians. These fears intensified in 1895 when the sultan seemed ready to yield to Russian, French, and British diplomats who called for pro-Armenian reforms. Changes would have given Armenians access to police jobs in proportion to their numbers, suppressed Kurdish raids, regularized taxes, allowed Armenians greater autonomy in six eastern provinces, and formed a commission in Istanbul with Muslim and non-Muslim members to guarantee compliance. Many Ottoman Muslims found these proposed reforms offensive: they threatened to hack away at Ottoman sovereignty while giving a lot to Armenians. Their news set off "riots that spread like a shockwave across the totality of eastern Anatolia," with violence in each area often starting with the pillage of Armenian shops.[152] Attacks on commercial sites underscored the economic underpinnings of social divergence, especially for impoverished Kurds. Attacks were par-lays by the "have-nots" against people who seemed to have more.[153]

Just as one can point to recurring patterns in European anti-Semitic portrayals of Jews, so one can point to recurring discourses in emerg-ing late Ottoman Armenophobia. (In fact, to the north in the Russian Caucasus, tropes took hybrid form: Russians sometimes called Armenians "Caucasian Jews" and portrayed them as "wily commer-cial types."[154]) Some Ottoman Muslims and European foreigners alike claimed that Armenians flaunted their wealth.[155] Others claimed that they were arrogant and considered themselves superior to, and more civilized than, Muslims.[156] "To religious Muslims," one scholar argued, "the visibility of better-off Armenians in the capital and towns appeared as an intolerable reversal of the traditional Muslim-*dhimmi* hierarchy."[157] Sentiments like these fueled a movement, expressed in advertisements within Ottoman Turkish periodicals, to avoid Armenian (and Greek) products and shops and to patronize Muslims instead.[158] Still others suggested that Armenians were impatient in demanding equality, and expected too much, too fast.[159] Some suggested that they had forgotten their rightful, that is, subordinate place in society.[160] Taken together, these attitudes enabled Ottoman authorities to devise a "blame-the-victim" narrative[161] or perhaps a "they-brought-it-on-themselves" narrative, in relation to the violence of the 1890s. Both terms capture the tendency of Ottoman authorities (and sometimes twentieth- and early twenty-first century historians) to imply that Armenians invited attacks through their own imprudent behavior. Pervasive assumptions of Armenian excess – they had too much, they did not know their station, they were haughty and demanding – informed a popular Muslim Armenophobia. This Armenophobia, in turn, helps to explain the behavior of Ottoman authorities who stood aside as Armenians fell. In short, the inaction of Ottoman authorities was an action, a choice, a government policy, which reflected a tacit cow-and-cull strategy that the sultan supported: a strat-egy to intimidate Armenians, and thin down their numbers.[162]

Armenians, for their part, harbored deep resentments of their own. Many felt that Islamic courts discriminated against them as Christians in land disputes. Using government-issued guns, Kurdish militiamen seized

Armenian properties, and Ottoman authorities did nothing. Even when a court decided in a landowner's favor, thugs with guns were likely to show up and make the verdict moot.[163] Pastoralist Kurds imposed a much-hated custom on Armenian farmers called *kişlak*, which forced them to provide winter shelter and fodder.[164] Kurds ran a long-standing protection racket, too: they made Armenians pay a "tax" in return for either defending them or not attacking them. The Ottoman state demanded taxes, too. After 1890, when Abdulhamid II created the Hamidiye regiments, the situation worsened: more armed Kurds wrested more "tax" from Armenians with impunity.

This protection racket stalled in 1894 when some Armenians in Sasun refused to pay the two taxes – one for the Kurds, the other for the Ottoman state – when representatives of both fiscal constituencies showed up to collect. On this occasion, instead of resisting with hammers, cutting knives, iron bars, and other weapons of the weak, some Armenians brandished rifles, which a clandestine band of revolutionaries had somehow procured.[165] Perceiving a grievous threat to public order and state authority in the form of gun-toting Armenians, the Ottoman regional governor, with support from the sultan in Istanbul, sent forces to suppress the tax rebels, who agreed to put down their weapons for amnesty. Savagery ensued – soldiers and militiamen let loose a riot of plunder, rape, and murder. By the time the hemorrhage ended, an estimated 3,000 Armenians, or a quarter of the town's residents, were dead. British, French, and Russian diplomats demanded to participate in an inquiry, but the sultan refused to include them. Instead, Ottoman authorities issued their own report, which concluded that Armenians had engaged in sedition on a scale that required this crackdown.[166] Sasun was a turning point: the anti-Armenian violence that exploded there – on that occasion with the government's authorization – spiraled to outlying regions.[167]

In eastern Anatolia, among poor Armenian farmers and humble artisans, grievances over low-grade Kurdish raids and land grabs had begun by the 1890s to push a small number toward anticlerical, revolutionary socialism inspired by the writings of Karl Marx (1818–83), Friedrich Engels (1820–95), and others. Some of these revolutionaries joined a group known as the Hunchaks (also known as the Social Democrat Hunchakian Party, originally founded by Russian Armenians studying abroad in Geneva, Switzerland, in 1887) who reversed the centuries-old tradition of *dhimmi* disarmament while resorting to occasional terrorism in the form of attacks on Muslims. The Hunchaks, indeed, were the revolutionaries who featured in the resistance at Sasun in 1894. Hunchaks were also behind a momentous attack on the Ottoman Bank in Istanbul.

This assault occurred in 1896, when 26 revolutionaries descended on this bank with guns and bombs, killed a few guards and bystanders, took 150 hostages among employees and customers, and threatened to blow up the building. They demanded, among other things, the appointment of a European high commissioner to oversee Armenian affairs in the east. In the end, the revolutionaries "accomplished" three things with their assault on the Ottoman bank. First, they enraged the Muslim populace in Istanbul and set off a bloodbath in the city. Mobs killed about 8,000 random Armenians, mostly humble laborers, whom they "chased like rabbits" in the streets, according to an eyewitness.[168] Second, they triggered the spread of further violence out of eastern Anatolia and into Istanbul, the beating heart of the empire. And third, they deepened the ill will and mistrust toward Armenians that had begun to sink roots in parts of the Muslim population.

"I have dined out with them at the palace," an American diplomat in Istanbul reflected on Armenian elites in the 1890s, "where they sat wearing decorations conferred by the sultan and mingling on terms of equality with the Mahommedan pashas."[169] While it would be a stretch to say that the sultan's best friends were Armenians (if he had any best friends to speak of), his chief architect at Yildiz was certainly Armenian – and responsible for elements of the palace that may have reminded the sultan of what he had seen during his trip to Paris with his uncle, Sultan Abdulaziz, in 1867.[170] But Istanbul was not Diyarbekir, illustrious urbanites were not struggling peasants, and wealthy and well-connected Armenians in the capital were not vulnerable Armenians scraping by and striving to build better lives in the hinterlands.

Most scholars have described the violent events of the mid-1890s as "massacres"; some have called them "pogroms" as well.[171] The term "massacres" suggests that perpetrators did not necessarily have the sanction of higher powers. "Massacres" also implies disproportionate strength in number or weaponry among one group that repeatedly attacked another, more vulnerable group, inflicting great bloodshed and harm. "Pogroms," by contrast, suggests that state agents abetted in or incited the violence. "Pogroms" also recalls contemporary attacks on Jews in the Russian Empire, like those that prompted the Bilu group (see above) to migrate to Jerusalem in 1881. By associating Armenian history with Jewish history, the term "pogroms" may also imply that sporadic, state-abetted attacks – against Jews in the Russian Empire and Armenians in the Ottoman Empire – were precursors to larger genocidal assaults in subsequent history. Whether or not the word "pogroms" suits what happened in the 1890s depends, again, on how we see Abdulhamid II and his delegates in relation to these attacks. Even

Image 16 "Jeune arménienne" (Young Armenian woman), c. 1876–85, Zangaki Brothers Collection, Image Number 291176. Courtesy of the Penn Museum.

if we conclude that he did not explicitly orchestrate the attacks, can we call them pogroms if we believe that he set the tone that made them possible both by "inculcating the atmosphere of anti-Christian, Islamic chauvinism in which the massacres took place" and by turning a blind eye to marauding?[172] Word choice, finally, may depend on the size of one's window for viewing Armenian history. If our vision encompasses the annihilating violence of 1915, also known as the Armenian Genocide, and if we see the violence of the 1890s as a precursor to the later event, then "pogroms" as a descriptor makes sense.

Regardless of what one calls them, the events of the 1890s seem so egregious that even after running through the grudges that had mounted on multiple sides, the same question returns: why did something so awful happen? Eastern Anatolia was not Kent or Sussex, the historian Jeremy Salt tried to answer, in a reference to two British counties known for being bucolic and calm to the point of boring.[173] The state's power was limited on this frontier, he implied, summoning the argument that apologists have used to exonerate the state. And yet, infrastructural developments in roads, telegraph lines, and railways were beginning to draw the region more closely to Istanbul while enabling the Ottoman state to tax and keep tabs on the region more closely. So in that sense, eastern Anatolia in its relation to Istanbul *was* becoming more like Kent and Sussex vis-à-vis London. Certainly control over eastern Anatolia had never been stronger in Ottoman history.

Of course, spreading roads gave resentments greater passage for travel. Thus noted the historian Leila Fawaz about the Beirut-Damascus Road, which opened to traffic in 1863, shortening a three-to-four-day journey to a thirteen-hour trip. Paved roads quickened the flow of information in the late Ottoman period, she wrote, and made people – and especially rural "have-nots" – acutely aware of the greater prosperity and "Westernization" on show in urban centers.[174] News from convivial Istanbul may have likewise traveled by road to places like Diyarbekir and its outskirts, adding heat to resentments that were already simmering.

The Ottoman Empire had historically depended on some combination of coercion, collaboration, and acceptance to survive. By the time the violence of the mid-1890s ended, Armenians emerged culled, but not cowed – and less inclined to accept the empire's legitimacy. Turkish-speaking Anatolian Muslims, on the contrary, seemed ready to continue their compact with Ottoman imperial rule. Nationalism was no longer a European import or a Balkan phenomenon, but was coursing through the empire.

Imperial Nation? Young Turks Shaking the Empire

Abdulhamid II was so paranoid – so afraid some person or group would try to kill or, just as bad, overthrow him – that he forbade the Ottoman navy from leaving its docks in Istanbul lest its ships aim guns at his palace. For the same reason, he made his army in the capital practice musketry without real bullets.[175]

The sultan's mistrust was well founded. Discontentment had been stewing in the military for some time among well-educated, well-read Ottoman officers who loved the empire but thought that they could do better than he did at running it. Thirty years into Abdulhamid II's reign, many young officers belonged to a secret organization of dissenters who were tired of the regime and raring for change. Dubbed the "Committee of Union and Progress" – the CUP for short – this organization had been founded in 1889, the centennial year of the French Revolution.[176]

The spark that set the CUP moving in 1908 came from an unlikely place near the western edge of the empire. This was Macedonia, one of the first Ottoman gains in the fourteenth century, and one of its last remaining European holdings in the twentieth. (Note that the Ottoman Empire had controlled Macedonia for about a century and a half *longer* than it had held Arabic-speaking regions like Syria.) When the British king and the Russian czar met in June 1908, in the Baltic port of Reval (now Tallinn, in Estonia) to discuss their "spheres of influence" in Persia (now Iran) – that is, the parts of Persia that each wanted to control without officially controlling them – a clutch of CUP officers jumped into action, fearing that Britain and Russia would next scheme to divide Macedonia – one of the Ottoman borderlands from which some leading CUP officers hailed. The officers executed a military uprising that aimed to take control of the empire in order to keep it intact.[177] As rebellion spread, the sultan yielded to its leaders' chief demand: to restore the parliament that he had put on hold in 1878.

Supporters of this 1908 rebellion called its leaders the Young Turks and their maneuver a "revolution," although the rebels at first kept Abdulhamid II on the throne. Critics, who included Muslim conservative supporters of the sultan, saw it as a mere insurrection. Drawing upon a wide base of popular support, the Young Turks proposed a general election several months later. Many middle-class Muslims, Christians, and Jews were excited, even euphoric, about reviving the Ottoman constitution, holding elections, and sending delegates to represent them.

Consider, for example, the case of a Jewish lawyer named Shlomo Yellin, whom the historian Michele U. Campos discussed in a book about this period, titled *Ottoman Brothers*. Yellin knew many languages. He was fluent in Ottoman Turkish and Arabic, Yiddish and Polish, and comfortable in English, French, Ladino, and Hebrew. Born in Jerusalem and educated at the elite Galatasaray lycée and imperial law college of Istanbul, Yellin lived in Beirut when the Young Turks staged their uprising. Yellin, who had recently applied for membership in the Freemasons, addressed fellow CUP members and middle-class professionals in 1909, using terms that showed his faith in the empire. "In the Ottoman Empire," he declared, "the different peoples are equal to one another and it is not lawful to divide according to race; the Turkish, Arab, Armenian, and Jewish elements have mixed with one another, and all of them are connected together, molded into one shape for the holy *vatan*."[178] This homeland (*vatan*), this nation, was the Ottoman Empire in its entirety.

Yellin was no outlier among Jews in his enthusiasm for the empire and for how the Young Turks seemed poised to revise it. As the historian Aron Rodrigue observed, Jews throughout the empire greeted the Young Turks' entry with "jubilation ... [and] with high expectations about new opportunities for Jews in all areas of public life in Turkey [sic]." There was a sudden demand among them for more Ottoman Turkish instruction in schools: they wanted to be fluent in the language of state.[179] The Jewish sense of Ottoman pride at this moment rested, too, on recollections of 1492 – the year when Spain had expelled all its Jews. The Ottoman Empire had offered the refugees an immediate and lasting haven, and on the basis of this memory, argued the historian Julia Phillips Cohen, Jews felt a gratitude that anchored their Ottoman patriotism.[180]

Another historian, Bedross Der Matossian, studied three "nondominant groups" – Jews, Armenians, and Arabs – who initially celebrated the Young Turks.[181] Juxtaposed to Campos's *Ottoman Brothers*, Der Matossian's book, *Shattered Dreams of Revolution*, describes how and why men went from feeling giddy, fraternal, and, well, Ottoman, to feeling alienated within a few years as the Young Turks became increasingly autocratic. "Men" is the appropriate word here, since this revolution was an androcentric affair: its supporters' essays and speeches were full of talk about "brotherhood."

The initial enthusiasm of Christians and Jews for the Young Turks suggests that Ottomanism, as an ideal of imperial belonging or even nationalism that could span religious, linguistic, and geographical divides, was alive when the twentieth century began. Some spirit of the Tanzimat reforms carried on. And yet, as Yellin's speech hinted, Ottomanism was facing many contenders – other ways for the empire's religious and linguistic groups to imagine themselves as Arabs, Armenians, or Jews; or, for that matter, as Albanians, Kurds, or Macedonians. The epithet of the revolution's leaders pointed to problems ahead. They were Young *Turks*, steeped in Ottoman Turkish-language print culture and in the oral culture of spoken Turkish. They either were, or were becoming, self-aware "Turks" instead of Ottomans, with consequences for how they would run what was left of the empire.

The revolution first lost luster at Adana, near Anatolia's southern Mediterranean coast. In April 1909, local Muslim resentments toward Adana's Armenians (many of whom had supported the Young Turks revolution) escalated as rumors spread, suggesting that Armenians were planning to rise up to advance their own cause. Mobs exploded in pillage, rape, and murder in an "Adana Massacre" that left thousands of Armenians dead.[182] Evoking the "they-brought-it-on-themselves" narrative about the Ottoman Armenian past, the historian Dawn Chatty remarked that "most accounts lay some blame on the Armenian prelate of Adana, Bishop Mushegh" for declaring that "the centuries of Armenian servitude had passed." "For Muslims," she added simply, "this new era of constitutionality appeared threatening to their traditional relationship with Armenians"[183] – a tradition rooted in Muslims' expectations that they would sit atop the social pile while Armenians stood somewhere below. In fact, economic factors featured strongly in the mob violence. Armenian innovations in agriculture – which included the introduction of steam ploughs, steam threshers, and reaping machines – had begun to imperil the livelihoods of Muslim migrant farm workers, some 60,000 of whom had come to depend on seasonal work near Adana. Migrants were indeed among the agitators. A headline in the *New York Times* issue of April 25, 1900, blared, "ARMENIAN WEALTH CAUSED MASSACRES."[184]

Adana was a moment of rupture for Armenians – one of a series of turning or turning-away points that sharpened Armenian nationalism in lieu of an Ottoman alternative.[185] The Young Turks did not prosecute the marauders, and their inaction spoke volumes. It told Armenians once again that in relation to the state and to Muslim society they should not expect much to change; the Young Turks had not staged a revolution to benefit *them*. The historian Erik Jan Zürcher has argued, indeed, that the Young Turks (who were nearly all Muslims, with an occasional Jew who had proven his mettle) harbored many resentments toward Christians. Many came from towns along the Ottoman borderlands, especially in the Balkans, where highly educated and upwardly mobile non-Muslims dominated private sector jobs in railways, department stores, factories, export firms, and more. The Young Turks, by contrast, had found opportunities in the state bureaucracy or military officer corps, but still had to scrape by when the Ottoman state fell behind on salary payments. Their resentment toward Christians may have sprung from the frustration of feeling almost-powerful and almost-poor at the same time.[186]

In October 1909 – six months after events at Adana – the Young Turks declared that the Ottoman state would begin drafting all men into the military regardless of their religion. On the surface their announcement fulfilled the egalitarian aspirations of the 1856 Tanzimat edict, which had edged toward describing Ottoman subjects as rights-and-duties-sharing citizens. The Grand Rabbi in Istanbul declared his support for this draft; so did some Christian leaders. Fearful of how service would work, however, and aware of the historic power of Muslim culture within the military of the Ottoman state, some Greek and Armenian leaders tried to secure guarantees. They wanted ethnically and religiously separate units commanded by Christian officers and staffed by priests, a ban against converting Christians to Islam during military service, and spaces for

Image 17 *Armenian Widows, with Children, Turkey*, near Adana, April or May 1909. Glass negative by Bain News Service. Library of Congress, Washington, DC. George Grantham Bain Collection.

Christian worship in barracks. In 1910, one Jewish recruit named Abram Aruh was enthusiastic about life in the barracks with seven Greeks, two Bulgarians, thirty-seven Muslims, and one other Jew. "We live like brothers," he declared, although mealtimes were hard: the food was not kosher, and so he found it hard to eat.[187]

Judging from how the CUP later treated Christian and Jewish conscripts when World War I broke out – that is, by disarming them and forcing them to work on road-digging crews and in other hard-labor projects within "labor battalions" – Christian skeptics were right to be worried. "Regarding the inclusion of different religious and ethnic elements of the empire into the conscription system and their treatment," the historian Mehmet Beşikçi observed, "the CUP's perspective and practice were discriminatory from the beginning ... never based on equality and always characterized by deep distrust." Pragmatism drove their inclusion – not any sense of "constitutional Ottoman equality" toward non-Muslims. The need for more bodies in a modern army also prompted the CUP to extend the draft to previously exempt Muslim groups, including theology (*medresa*) students (especially those who had failed examinations) and residents of Istanbul.[188] Christians were not the only ones to feel uneasy: news of the draft left many Kurds uneasy, too, even appalled, as they considered the prospect of Christians (especially Armenians) armed by the state. Aware of these sensitivities, the Young Turks in 1910 sent Christians from the Balkans to serve in Van, in order to acclimate Kurds to the change.[189]

In practice, CUP officers remained ready to bargain: the very rich, whether Muslim, Christian, or Jewish, could buy exemptions after 1909.[190] Non-Muslims who were desperate to avoid conscription, but who lacked money to buy their way out, found two other escapes: securing a foreign passport, or emigrating.[191] Indeed, the 1909 conscription law caused a wave of Ottoman Christians – especially Greeks, Armenians, and "Syrians" (including many from what is now Lebanon, Palestine, and Israel) – to sail for the Americas. Between 1910 and 1912, about 45,000 men from Lebanon and Syria left for Argentina alone.[192] Others went to Mexico and the United States.[193] US government census figures showed that from 1909 to 1910 the number of immigrants arriving from "Asian Turkey" doubled.[194] Of those who reached the United States from "Syria," 95 percent claimed to be joining friends and relatives who were already there, suggesting how well-trodden the American path had become.[195] Of course, Muslims emigrated, too, driven by the same mix of opportunity seeking and draft evasion as Christians. In fact, Muslims accounted for 43 percent of the Syro-Lebanese migrants to Argentina in 1909.[196] Some Jews, by contrast, seemed optimistic amidst this transition, which many saw as a final emancipation from *dhimmi*-style disabilities.[197] In Tripoli, Libya, for example, they seemed to welcome the chance to enlist – perhaps, again, because Jews there saw themselves as partners in Ottoman reform, and had faith in the ameliorative motives of the Ottoman state.[198]

That one historian called Armenians "nondominant" in 1908 hardly seems surprising, since attitudes about the subordination of Christians lingered among many Muslims. The same applies to Jews, historically another *dhimmi* group.[199] By contrast, calling Arabs "nondominant," as this scholar did, may seem – indeed, *should* seem – more surprising. Most Arabs, after all, were Sunni Muslims, adherents of the Ottoman religion of state. Arabs were heirs to the language of the Qur'an; Arabic was the vehicle for what Muslims everywhere acknowledged as God's message to humankind.[200] Arabs were also cultural successors of the early Islamic empire (think of the Rashidun caliphs, the Umayyads, and the Abbasids) – and this was a source of prestige for the Ottoman Empire, particularly in an age when its sultan styled himself a latter-day caliph.[201] In more concrete terms within Ottoman history, Arab Muslims had

featured prominently as Ottoman imperial collaborators from the sixteenth century onward.[202] As "notables" (*'ayan*) in places like Damascus,
they had been linchpins of Ottoman rule, mediating between Istanbul
and Arab people on the ground.[203]

And yet, by the time of the Young Turks revolution, some Arab thinkers had begun to *feel* nondominant – or at least, to express a sense of
marginalization and difference relative to "Turks" who were running the
empire.[204] Some alienation may have arisen at the grass roots as a result
of conscription, which Ottoman authorities exacted upon the Arab provinces for the first time with the outbreak of the Russo-Turkish War in
1877.[205] Some alienation may have arisen, too, among Arab notables,
long-standing collaborators of the Ottoman state, who were eager to
retain or expand their influence on the ground.[206] Above all, the sense
of detachment had something to do with Arab nationalism: a feeling of
peoplehood among those who claimed to share an illustrious "Arab" past
and a promising "Arab" future and who hankered (as all nationalists
seem to do) after autonomy. This feeling had grown during the nineteenth century with the growth of Arabic printing and literacy.

Without a doubt, Arabic readers had raw material for nationalism at
hand. They had a rich literary history that stretched back to pre-Islamic
poetry and that had flourished without pause since the dawn of Islam.
As the twentieth century opened, they enjoyed access to a growing array
of printed journals, novels, and academic books (including science textbooks), which confirmed the depth of their heritage and its capacity for
progress in the modern age.[207] Raw materials for their nationalism were
visual, too, and included still images, like book and magazine illustrations, and later moving images, after the "cinématographe" debuted in
Alexandria, Egypt in 1896, within a year of its first showing in France.[208]

If Arab literati felt "nondominant" as the twentieth century opened,
perhaps it was also because so many of them were Christians and
Jews – that is, "Arabs" and "non-Muslims" at the same time. Prominent
Christian thinkers included Butrus al-Bustani (1819–83), author of the
first Arabic encyclopedia, and a man whose various writings helped to
establish a kind of nonsectarian, even "ecumenical" nationalism;[209] and
Jurji Zaydan (1861–1914), whose novels celebrated great characters and
events in Islamic history in ways that appealed to Muslims and non-
Muslims alike.[210] Among Jews, Baghdad sustained a particularly lively
Arabic literary scene, leading many to call themselves "Arab Jews" and
later, during the interwar period of the twentieth century, "Iraqi Jews"
as well.[211] In short, the active and broad-based participation of Christian
and Jewish thinkers in this incipient movement may help to explain why
Arab nationalism managed to transcend religion in ways that Armenian

nationalism, Turkish nationalism, and Zionism (as a form of Jewish nationalism), did not – and this, even though Arab nationalists recognized the centrality of Islamic civilization to Arab history and culture. Yet, even in incipient Arab nationalism the prominence of Christian and Jewish thinkers appeared to elicit pushback from some Muslims. In an influential article first published in 1961 and reissued in 1973, the historian C. Ernest Dawn suggested that the "Syrian Moslem Arabs" were not happy with the "Christian version of Arabism." "In fact," he added, "Moslem Arabs of Syria were outraged at the spectacle of Christians assuming the air of Arab learning," to the extent that "[a]ttacks on the pretensions of [thinkers like Ibrahim al-] Yaziji and other Christian Arab literary men were popular" for a time in the late nineteenth century. "Arabic shall not be Christianized," went a Muslim "battle cry," as he called it, from the late nineteenth century.[212]

In a classic work about the Arab "awakening" published in 1939, the Lebanese Christian writer George Antonius claimed that late nineteenth-century Arab thinkers explored the grandeur of Arabic literature and history even while considering how to "shake off the Turkish yoke," as Ibrahim al-Yaziji (the very same Beiruti poet and Christian thinker that C. Ernest Dawn mentioned) urged in 1857.[213] Antonius's claims about longstanding Arab resistance to "the Turks" sounded heroic, even romantic, in retrospect and worked well in a book that aimed to make Arab nationalism appear triumphant. And yet, Arabic literati were neither staging revolts against the sultan nor plotting for the empire's demise before 1908, even if many intellectuals resented Abdulhamid II and his spy-ridden, tight-fisted rule. Regarding this resentment, think again of the Egyptian Muslim litterateur, Ibrahim al-Muwaylihi (see Chapter 5) whose Arabic account of the sultan's rule was so scathing, so darkly funny in sketching the absurdities of his rule, that Abdulhamid II tried to get the British in Egypt to seize and destroy all its copies. A typically barbed observation from Muwaylihi was one from 1895 describing how the sultan's spies harassed Armenians in Istanbul: "If a spy discovered a drawing on a cigarette carton or box of matches that looked like a sail, oar, rudder, or any other part of a ship, he would immediately take the item away. He would then write a report in which the Armenian would be accused of demanding independence. After all, ... the drawing in question portrayed a ship, which is a symbol of authority in their culture."[214] Appreciating Muwaylihi's satire depends in part on recognizing how land-locked Armenians have historically been.

As a realist who constantly worried, Abdulhamid II appeared to sense the potential for Arab malaise. He strove to keep the Arab provinces lodged firmly within his empire – especially after the losses of the Russo-Turkish

War. He brought Arab Muslim students to study in Istanbul, and showered Muslim Arab notables (as well as Muslim Kurdish and Albanian notables) with honors. In yearbooks published annually from 1846, he reversed the custom of putting the empire's European provinces first and gave top spots to Arab regions. He boosted salaries to make service in, say, Baghdad seem more prestigious than, say, Bitola (in what is now the Republic of Macedonia).[215] He built the famed Hijaz Railway from Damascus toward Mecca to facilitate pilgrimage while binding Arabia to the Levant. Together such measures underlined the centrality of the Arab and mostly Muslim provinces to the empire. At the same time, such measures aimed to halt the spread of nationalism among Ottoman Muslims by prioritizing Islam as a common identity.[216] For similar reasons, Abdulhamid II tried to strengthen ties to Albania, where roughly 70 percent of the population was Sunni Muslim.[217] Albanians had no language as prestigious as Arabic to shield them from cultural makeover. Thus Abdulhamid II's government schools promoted Ottoman Turkish prophylactically against Albanian nationalism, to an extent that they never dared among Arabs.[218]

As the twentieth century began, Arabic-speaking Sunni Muslim literati were increasingly describing the Ottoman Muslim ruling classes as "Turks" (atrak), emphasizing their difference from Arabs in culture, language, and pedigree. This marked a change from the Arab custom, set in the sixteenth century, of identifying the Ottoman ruling classes as rumi or "Roman," in a broader reference to Anatolia as Rum ("Rome"). The names Rum and rumi (which had circulated in the pre-Ottoman Seljuk era as well) nodded to the Byzantine or eastern Roman Empire and the Ottoman succession to it, in a way that privileged history and geography over language and ethnicity. The Arabic shift from "Romans" to "Turks" was another sign that pan-Ottoman identity was fraying among Sunni Muslims in the empire.[219]

It was one thing for Arabs to call the Ottoman ruling classes "Turks"; it was another, bigger development for highly educated Ottoman Muslims (at least, those from Anatolia and the European environs of Istanbul) to call themselves "Turks" as well. To be sure, foreign Europeans had been freely referring to Turks, the Turkish language, and Turkey for centuries – from at least the twelfth century in Latin, for example, and the fourteenth in English.[220] Until this pivotal turn-of-the-century era, however, Ottomans had not used this nomenclature reflexively. For centuries the ruling elites had distinguished themselves from both the rustic Turks of Inner Asia (who had arrived on horseback in the mists of time) and the yokel Turks of Anatolia and other parts of west-central Asia, who spoke a series of related dialects.[221] "Arabs [had] always distinguished themselves from the Turks," claimed the historian Niyazi Berkes in 1964, "whereas the Turks, especially the common people, [had] identified themselves only as Muslims."[222] That began to change in the nineteenth century and the first few years of the twentieth, through the same kind of literary and historical exploration that inspired Greeks, Arabs, and others. In this case, intellectual pioneers included men like Ahmet Cevdet Paşa (1822–95, author of the first Ottoman grammar in 1850), Nemik Kemal (1840–88, author of poems and plays that promoted the idea of *vatan* or fatherland), and Ziya Gökalp (1876–1924, who promoted ideas of modern Turkishness).

Other factors, too, helped a new Turkish consciousness to grow. There was a growing sense of difference among Anatolian Muslims relative to the non-Muslim *millet*s whose members seemed more coherent and confident in the wake of the Tanzimat reforms. There was a search for identity rooted in something more than religion given that Ottoman Islam, in practice, had always been very diverse.[223] Then, too, there was the research of foreign literati who confirmed the coherence of Turkish language and history from the outside while making Turks look cultured and reasonable. According, again, to Niyazi Berkes, three Jewish scholars were among those who offered independent verification of Turkish high culture: these were Arthur Lumley Davids (1811–32, an aspiring lawyer excluded from the bar in his native Britain on the grounds of his Jewishness, who during his short life wrote a Turkish grammar and history);[224] Ármin Vámbéry (1832–1913, who wrote about Turkic languages as they related to his own language, Hungarian); and Léon Cahun (1841–1900, an Alsatian who wrote French historical fiction, including a novel that celebrated Janissaries).[225] The bottom line is that, as the twentieth century opened, "Turk" was becoming a term of pride among urbane Ottoman Muslims, the Young Turks included, who could point to research about their distinction.

The Young Turks had thought they could do better than Abdulhamid II when they forced him to bring back the parliament in 1908. But the challenge of holding the empire together proved bigger and more difficult than they had foreseen. Wars broke out in quick succession after the Young Turks came to power. Italy invaded Libya in 1911 and tried to pad it onto Italian territory while claiming to revive the Roman Empire on the south coast of the Mediterranean. The Ottoman-Italian War lasted for a year until Ottoman authorities, without officially relinquishing their claims, left the Muslims of Libya to carry on fighting alone as events closer to Istanbul seized their attention. For, indeed, a series of Balkan Wars broke out in 1912 and 1913 as four countries – Bulgaria, Greece, Montenegro, and Serbia – used the opportunity of the distractions in

Libya to claim fuller independence or to expand territory. By some accounts the Balkan Wars were the worst defeat in Ottoman history: the empire lost over 60,000 square miles of territory, amounting to 80 percent of its remaining population in Europe.[226] Once again, Muslim refugees flooded in – somewhere between 113,000 and 640,000 of them in total.[227]

The Balkan Wars left the Young Turks embittered, especially since so many members of the CUP came from Balkan lands that the empire had lost. They railed against the atrocities that Christian Balkan peoples inflicted on Muslims, even though, as the historian Michael Reynolds argued, "Balkan Christians inflicted upon each other precisely the same savageries that they exchanged with Muslims."[228] The Balkan Wars also intensified an anti-Christian and generally xenophobic strain within popular Muslim thought and state policy, while increasing the Anatolian Muslim sense of demographic anxiety.[229] These wars, added the historian Mustafa Aksakal, filled the Young Turks with a thirst for revenge. They conveyed these sentiments to the public in works like a geography textbook, printed in 1913, which declared it a "national duty to right this wrong, and to prepare for taking revenge for the pure and innocent blood that has flowed like waterfalls."[230]

Barely had the Balkan Wars subsided when a new war began in 1914. This was the Great War, which was renamed World War I more than two decades later after a second eruption made it look like part of a series. Before the Great War started, approximately a quarter to a third of the eastern Anatolian population had been Armenian.[231] By war's end, the Armenians had almost wholly disappeared from Anatolia. They were dead (with perhaps as many as one million, or half of the pre-1914 population, killed[232]), they had fled, they had been rounded up and sent on a forced march through the desert to Syria, or they were being absorbed via *de facto* marriage, adoption, and conversion into Anatolian Muslim families, many of which claimed to have rescued them.[233] Indeed, in the wake of this violence, Muslim families absorbed perhaps as much as 5–10 percent of the Armenian population, or some 100,000–200,000 women and children.[234] The assimilation of Armenians into Muslim families, argued the historian Taner Akçam, "was as much a structural element of genocide" as killing.[235]

Who was to blame for what happened? During the twentieth and early twenty-first centuries, supporters of successive post–Ottoman Turkish governments often described what had happened as a series of regrettable and unplanned episodes in a brutal war. During this war, the narrative continued, some Armenians had proven disloyalty by favoring Russia over the Ottoman Empire and had incurred popular wrath as a consequence. It was a stock argument of Armenophobia: Armenians had brought the violence on themselves through treasonous sympathies with foreigners. Leaving aside the "veritable industry of Armenian Genocide denial" that followed World War I, the elimination of Armenians, and later of Greeks through a population exchange implemented in 1923, had a practical result for Turcophone leaders.[236] It left the population of Anatolia more wholly and reliably Muslim, in ways that eased the building of the Republic of Turkey after World War I.

From 1910 to 1918, in the midst of the Ottoman-Italian War, the Balkan Wars, and the Great War, representative parliamentary government and the other lofty aims of the 1908 revolution fell by the wayside as the military-led regime turned to dictatorship. More than a century later, observers still muse over a sad, important, but unanswerable question. Did war make the dreams of the revolution impossible, or did the Young Turks turn into hardline, parochial power-mongers as a result of their natural proclivities?[237] (In other words, were impersonal forces of history to blame for what happened, or does the fault fall to the Young Turks themselves?) Romantics may answer one thing and cynics another, although either way the question leads to something bigger. It begs reflection on whether the Ottoman Empire stood a chance in the twentieth century. It forces one to consider whether other circumstances, different leaders, or alternate responses could have enabled Ottoman imperial nationalism to grow and to make people of different languages and religions all feel at home and with hope where they were.

Conclusion: Fuzzy Endings

The Young Turks showed inertia toward Armenians in 1909 when the massacres occurred at Adana. But in other respects, they acted with lightning speed. Seeing that the Muslims who went on the rampage there claimed to support Abdulhamid II, and realizing that the sultan was angling to come back to power, the Young Turks deposed Abdulhamid II and squashed his "counterrevolution" without further ado. They arranged for his brother Reşad to ascend as a figurehead sultan, and guaranteed their own hold on power.

Unlike his uncle, Sultan Abdulaziz, Abdulhamid II did not suffer a probable murder staged to look like a suicide. His dethroning was more like a quiet Shakespearean scene than a high drama: quick exit to the side and off stage. The Young Turks exiled him to Salonika, the provincial city west of Istanbul, where they put him under house arrest with some wives, servants, three daughters, and two sons. "After having governed an immense empire, which extended from the Adriatic to the Persian Gulf and from the Caucasus to the edges of the Sahara," reflected his biographer, "Abdülhamid reigned only over two floors of a villa." Forbidden from reading newspapers or from strolling in his back garden, he kept busy reading novels, watching his daughters play piano, and doing carpentry and building clocks in a workshop that he installed in part of the house.[238] For a sultan whose erection of clock towers in provincial towns throughout the empire had signaled the turn in timekeeping from the traditional *allaturca* style to the modern *allafranca*, this late-life experimentation in *horlogerie* seems quite fitting.[239]

History teachers are notorious for forcing students to memorize dates: clean start- or end-times marking battles, treaties, dynasty changes, and other watershed or waterloo moments. But Ottoman history stymies effort to pin down a moment of closure. A professional historian of the empire could fill a ream with possible imperial end dates. Credible options include 1908, when the Young Turks forced the sultan to restore the Ottoman constitution; 1909, when they booted Abdulhamid II off the throne; the 1912–13 period, when the Balkan Wars arguably ended Ottomanism as a viable, pluralistic, and secular nationalism as the regime veered toward a more Muslim and Turkocentric identity;[240] and 1914, when the Great War broke out, Britain definitively severed Egypt from the empire, and a train of events started that led to the empire's defeat and collapse. The list goes on, with many dates in between for secret treaties and broken promises, land grabs, and partitions. These dates include, for example, the McMahon-Husayn Correspondence of 1915 and 1916 (when Britain promised the family of Sharif Husayn of Mecca an Arab kingdom in return for revolting against Ottoman rule); the Sykes-Picot Agreement of 1916 (when France and Britain discussed Arab territories that each wanted to grab after the war); and the Balfour Declaration of 1917 (when Britain declared support for establishing a Jewish "homeland" in Palestine with apparently little thought for the Muslims and Christians who already called it home).

Possible endings continue into the 1920s, with the declaration of a Turkish republic; the construction of League-of-Nations-approved, French- and British-controlled "mandates" or *de facto* colonies over Arab territories that were (according to the League's covenant) "inhabited by peoples not yet able to stand by themselves under the strenuous conditions of the modern world"[241]); the swapping of "Greeks" and "Turks" between Turkey and Greece; the abolition of the sultanate; and in 1924, the sudden expulsion of the Ottoman family from Turkey. ("The men had one day to leave," a grandson of Abdulhamid II recalled more than eighty years later; "the women had a week."[242]) Perhaps the absolute ending was really in 1926, when it became clear to Muslim delegates at the so-called Caliphate Conference in Cairo that the Ottoman Empire was definitively gone, that the "Ottoman religious [and] political order was dead," and that no single Muslim leader – whether figurehead or autocrat – could practically command the world's Muslims.[243]

The Ottoman Empire had a fuzzy ending, a twenty-year-long unraveling moment. Its end began in 1908 when Abdulhamid II, the last strong sultan in Ottoman history, gave in to the Young Turks' demands. The end stretched on during World War I and afterward, when Britain and France schemed to take the empire apart. In its place emerged many countries, ostensibly nation-states instead of empires, which devised policies toward religious communities that recalled the heritage or betrayed the vestiges of Ottoman rule.[244]

NOTES

1 Faroqhi, "Introduction, or Why and How One Might Want to Study Ottoman Clothes," pp. 18, 22, 25–26.

2 Saleh M. Barakat, "Westernization of Levantine Male Clothing," in *Les Européens vus par les libanais à l'époque ottomane*, ed. Bernard Heyberger and Carsten-Michael Walbiner (Beirut: Orient-Institut, 2002), pp. 203–9.

3 Nora Şeni, "Fashion and Women's Clothing in the Satirical Press of Istanbul at the End of the 19th Century," in *Women in Modern Turkish Society: A Reader*, ed. Sirin Tekeli (London: Zed Books, 1995), pp. 25–45, see p. 30; Stillman, *Arab Dress*, p. 167.

4 Shelagh Weir, *Palestinian Costume* (Austin: University of Texas Press, 1989) (for a discussion of the subtle messages once conveyed by clothing); and Osman Hamdi Bey and Marie de Launay, *Les costumes populaires de Turquie en 1873* (Constantinople [*sic*]: Impr. du Levant Times & Shipping Gazette, 1873) (for a study that claimed to present "traditional" types).

5 Abdullah Frères, "Interior of the Imperial Fez Factory," albumen photographic print, Abdul Hamid II Collection, held by the Library of Congress Prints and Photographs Division, Washington, DC, www.loc.gov/pictures/item/2003675899/ (accessed February 6, 2015).

6 To be sure, clothing was doing less to mark out men by their occupation, too, as it appears to have done in earlier periods when guild-based identities were strong among urban workers and when male members of the Ottoman ruling classes had signaled internal distinctions through the style and folds of their turbans.

7 Stillman, *Arab Dress*, pp. 117–18, 162.

8 Abdelwahab Meddeb, "Introduction: Parallel Memories," in *A History of Jewish-Muslim Relations from the Origins to the Present Day*, ed. Meddeb and Stora, pp. 13–14, reflecting on Tunis.

9 Krämer, "Moving out of Place," p. 218.

10 Georgeon, "Ottomans and Drinkers"; François Georgeon, "Le Ramadan à Istanbul de l'Empire à la Republique," in *Vivre dans l'Empire Ottoman: Sociabilités et relations intercommunautaires (XVIIIe-XXe siècles)*, ed. François

Georgeon and Paul Dumont (Paris: Editions L'Harmattan, 1997), pp. 31–113.

11 Roderic H. Davison, "The Millets as Agents of Change in the Nineteenth-Century Ottoman Empire," in *Christians & Jews in the Ottoman Empire*, abridged edition, ed. Benjamin Braude (Boulder: Lynne Rienner, 2014), p. 190.

12 Keith David Watenpaugh, "Being Middle Class and Being Arab: Sectarian Dilemmas and Middle-Class Modernity in the Arab Middle East, 1908–1936," in *The Making of the Middle Class: Toward a Transnational History*, ed. A. Ricardo López and Barbara Weinstein (Durham: Duke University Press, 2012), p. 277.

13 Zürcher, "The Ottoman Conscription System in Theory and Practice," p. 86.

14 Peter van der Veer, "Introduction," in *Conversion to Modernities: The Globalization of Christianity*, ed. Peter van der Veer (New York: Routledge, 1996), pp. 1–21, especially pp 4–5 and 15; Talal Asad, *Genealogies of Religion* (Baltimore: Johns Hopkins University Press, 1993).

15 These words came from one of the anonymous reviewers of this manuscript.

16 On the reification of religion, see Wilfred Cantwell Smith, *The Meaning and End of Religion: A New Approach to the Religious Traditions of Mankind* (Minneapolis: Fortress, 1991). On the invention of tradition, see Eric Hobsbawm and Terence Ranger, eds., *The Invention of Tradition* (Cambridge: Cambridge University Press, 1983). For a synthetic recent analysis of when religion(s) "happened," see Brent Nongbri, *Before Religion: A History of a Modern Concept* (New Haven: Yale University Press, 2013), and especially the introduction, pp. 1–14.

17 Mark Sedgwick, *Muhammad Abduh* (Oxford: Oneworld, 2010), p. 76.

18 Joachim Langner, "Religion in Motion and the Essence of Islam: Manifestations of the Global in Muhammad 'Abduh's Response to Farah Antun," in Kozma, Schayegh, and Wishnitzer, *A Global Middle East*, pp. 356–64; and Sedgwick, *Muhammad Abduh*, p. 79.

19 Peter van der Veer, "Communalism," in the *International Encyclopedia of the Social and Behavioral Sciences*, ed. James D. Wright, Vol. 4, second edition (Amsterdam: El Sevier, 2015), pp. 263–65.

20 Janet Klein, *The Margins of Empire: Kurdish Militias in the Ottoman Tribal Zone* (Stanford: Stanford University Press, 2011), p. 31; Georgeon, *Abdülhamid II*, p. 257.

21 Heyberger, *Les Chrétiens du Proche-Orient au temps de la Réforme Catholique*, pp. 59–60.

22 Heyberger, *Les Chrétiens du Proche-Orient au temps de la Réforme Catholique*, p. 59.

23 Masters, *Christians and Jews in the Ottoman Arab World*, p. 38.

24 Krämer, "Moving out of Place," p. 218.

25 Shiloah, *The Epistle on Music of the Ikhwan al-Safa*, pp. 15–16, 26.

26 Walter Feldman, Liner notes for Lalezar, *Music of the Sultans, Sufis & Seraglio, Vol. 3: Minority Composers*, Compact Disk (New York: Traditional Crossroads, 2001), pp. 5–6, 8–9.

27 Cohen and Stein, *Sephardi Lives*, pp. 69–72.

28 Feldman, Liner notes for Lalezar, *Music of the Sultans, Sufis & Seraglio*, Vol. 3, p. 9.
29 Feldman, Liner notes for Lalezar, *Music of the Sultans, Sufis & Seraglio*, Vol. 3, pp. 11, 26–27.
30 A. Ricardo López and Barbara Weinstein, eds., *The Making of the Middle Class: Toward a Transnational History* (Durham: Duke University Press, 2012).
31 On socks, see Boyar and Fleet, *A Social History of Ottoman Istanbul*, pp. 286, 299.
32 Haris Exertzoglou, "The Cultural Uses of Consumption: Negotiating Class, Gender, and Nation in the Ottoman Urban Centers during the 19th Century," *International Journal of Middle East Studies*, 35 (2003), pp. 77–101, see p. 81.
33 Uri M. Kupferschmidt, "On the Diffusion of 'Small' Western Technologies and Consumer Goods in the Middle East during the Era of the First Modern Globalization," in Kozma, Schayegh, and Wishnitzer, *A Global Middle East*, pp. 229–60, especially p. 234.
34 McLuhan, *The Gutenberg Galaxy*; Anderson, *Imagined Communities*; and also Ayalon, *Reading Palestine*.
35 Ronald Grigor Suny, *"They Can Live in the Desert but Nowhere Else": A History of the Armenian Genocide* (Princeton: Princeton University Press, 2015), pp. 56–57.
36 Hourani, *Arabic Thought in the Liberal Age*; Ayalon, *The Press in the Arab Middle East*.
37 For example, Beth Baron, *The Women's Awakening in Egypt: Culture, Society, and the Press* (New Haven: Yale University Press, 1994); Marilyn Booth, *May Her Likes Be Multiplied: Biography and Gender Politics in Egypt* (Berkeley: University of California Press, 2001).
38 Alan Duben and Cem Behar, *Istanbul Households: Marriage, Family, and Fertility, 1880–1940* (Cambridge: Cambridge University Press, 1991), p. 99. On changing attitudes toward marriage, see more generally pp. 89–103.
39 Deanna Ferree Womack, "Conversion, Controversy & Cultural Production: Syrian Protestants, American Missionaries, and the Arabic Press, 1870–1915," PhD diss., Princeton Theological Seminary, 2015; Catherine Mayeur-Jaouen, "The Renaissance of Churches at the End of the Ottoman Era (Excluding Egypt) in the 18th and 19th Centuries," in *Christianity: A History in the Middle East*, ed. Habib Badr, Suad Abou el Rouss Slim, and Joseph Abou Nohra (Beirut: Middle East Council of Churches, 2005), p. 767.
40 Cem Emrence, *Remapping the Ottoman Middle East: Modernity, Imperial Bureaucracy, and the Islamic State* (London: I.B. Tauris, 2012), pp. 44–45.
41 Laurens, "La projection chrétienne de l'Europe industrielle sur les provinces arabes de l'Empire ottoman," in Luizard, *Le choc colonial et l'islam*, p. 51.
42 Ayalon, "New Practices," in Kozma, Schayegh, and Wishnitzer, *A Global Middle East*, p. 338.
43 Watenpaugh, "Being Middle Class and Being Arab," pp. 276–77.
44 Bernard Lewis, "The Tanzimat and Social Equality," in *Économie de Sociétés dans l'Empire Ottoman (Fin du XVIIIe – Début du XXe siècle): Actes du colloque de Strasbourg (1er – 5 juillet 1980)*, ed. Jean-Louis Bacqué-Grammont

and Paul Dumont (Paris: Éditions du Centre National de la Recherche Scientifique [CNRS], 1983), pp. 47–54, see p. 53.

45 Maureen Jackson, "The Girl in the Tree: Gender, Istanbul Soundscapes, and Synagogue Song," *Jewish Social Studies*, 17:1 (2010), pp. 31–66, see especially pp. 42–43. Over time, *gazino*s shed their western European dimensions, particularly during the interwar period of the twentieth century, when Turkish Muslim owners took them over. Münir Nurretin Beken, "Musicians, Audience, and Power: The Changing Aesthetics in the Music at the Makzim Gazino in Istanbul," PhD diss. (Ethnomusicology), University of Maryland (Baltimore), 1998.

46 Georgeon, "Ottomans and Drinkers," pp. 16, 18–19; Georgeon, *Abdülhamid II*, p. 332.

47 Quataert, *Consumption Studies and the History of the Ottoman Empire*, p. 1.

48 Christraud M. Geary and Virginia-Lee Webb, *Delivering Views: Distant Cultures in Early Postcards* (Washington, DC: Smithsonian Institution Press, 1998).

49 Alloula, *The Colonial Harem*; Wolf-Dieter Lemke, *Staging the Orient: Fin de Siècle Popular Visions* (Beirut: Éditions Dar An-Nahar, 2004).

50 Deborah A. Starr, *Remembering Cosmopolitan Egypt: Literature, Culture, and Empire* (London: Routledge, 2009).

51 Penn Museum Archives (University of Pennsylvania Museum of Archaeology and Anthropology), Photochrome Collection Box S-28.

52 Boyar and Fleet, *A Social History of Ottoman Istanbul*, p. 318.

53 Masters, *Christians and Jews in the Ottoman Arab World*, p. 38.

54 Nancy Fraser, "Rethinking the Public Sphere: A Contribution to the Critique of Actually Existing Democracy," in *Habermas and the Public Sphere*, ed. Craig Calhoun (Cambridge: MIT Press, 1991), pp. 110, 113, 118–19.

55 Dorothe Sommer, *Freemasonry in the Ottoman Empire: A History of the Fraternity and Its Influence in Syria and the Levant* (London: I.B. Tauris, 2015), p. 5.

56 Karim Wissa, "Freemasonry in Egypt, 1798–1921: A Study in Cultural and Political Encounters," *Bulletin (British Society for Middle Eastern Studies)*, 16:2 (1989), pp. 143–61, see pp. 146–47; Georgeon, *Abdülhamid II*, pp. 38, 55.

57 Ilham Khuri-Makdisi, *The Eastern Mediterranean and the Making of Global Radicalism, 1860–1914* (Berkeley: University of California Press, 2010), pp. 23–24, 44–45.

58 Wissa, "Freemasonry in Egypt," pp. 148–49.

59 Sanjay Joshi, "Thinking about Modernity from the Margins: The Making of a Middle Class in Colonial India," in *The Making of the Middle Class: Toward a Transnational History*, ed. A. Ricardo López and Barbara Weinstein (Durham: Duke University Press, 2012), pp. 29–44, see pp. 39–40.

60 Keith David Watenpaugh, *Being Modern in the Middle East: Revolution, Nationalism, Colonialism, and the Arab Middle Class* (Princeton: Princeton University Press, 2006), p. 23.

61 Thierry Zarcone, "Quand la laïcité des francs-maçons du Grand Orient de France vient aux Jeunes Turcs," in Luizard, *Le choc colonial et l'islam*, pp. 137–58.

62 Berkes, *The Development of Secularism in Turkey*, p. 159.
63 Bedross Der Matossian, *Shattered Dreams of Revolution: From Liberty to Violence in the late Ottoman Empire* (Stanford: Stanford University Press, 2014), pp. 9–11.
64 Behlül Özkan, *From the Abode of Islam to the Turkish Vatan: The Making of a National Homeland in Turkey* (New Haven: Yale University Press, 2012), p. 35.
65 Anderson, *The American University of Beirut*; Doğan and Sharkey, *American Missionaries and the Middle East*. Protestants tended to be more open than Catholics in declaring goals of conversion, and in seeking to enroll non-Christian students, though in practice many Catholics welcomed these possibilities as well. See the essays in Verdeil, *Missions chrétiennes en terre d'islam*.
66 Orlin Sabev, *Spiritus Roberti: Shaping New Minds and Robert College in Late Ottoman Society (1863–1923)* (Istanbul: BÜTEK, 2013), pp. 103–10.
67 Hale Yılmaz, *Becoming Turkish: Nationalist Reforms and Cultural Negotiations in Early Republican Turkey, 1923–1945* (Syracuse: Syracuse University Press, 2013), p. 25.
68 Abdullah Frères, "Interior of the Imperial Fez Factory," albumen photographic print (undated, circa 1880–1893) in the Abdul Hamid II Collection at the Library of Congress, Washington, DC.
69 Çizgen, "Abdülhamid and Photography," pp. 13–20.
70 Georgeon, *Abdülhamid II*, pp. 30, 34.
71 Walter Feldman, *Music of the Ottoman Court: Makam, Composition, and the Early Ottoman Instrumental Repertoire* (Berlin: Verlag für Wissenschaft und Bildung, 1996), pp. 16–17.
72 Hanioğlu, *A Brief History of the Late Ottoman Empire*, p. 141.
73 Georgeon, *Abdülhamid II*, p. 141.
74 Georgeon, *Abdülhamid* II, pp. 223–23. See also the introduction by Georgeon and Dumont in *Vivre dans l'Empire Ottoman*, p. 10.
75 Georgeon, "Le Ramadan à Istanbul de l'Empire à la Republique," pp. 85–86.
76 Boyar and Fleet, *A Social History of Ottoman Istanbul*, p. 286.
77 Tudor Parfitt, *The Road to Redemption: The Jews of the Yemen, 1900–1950* (Leiden: E.J. Brill, 1996), pp. 86, 109; Reuben Ahroni, *Yemenite Jewry: Origins, Culture, and Literature* (Bloomington: Indiana University Press, 1986), p. 102; Yehuda Nini, *The Jews of the Yemen, 1800–1914*, trans. H. Galai (Chur, Switzerland: Harwood Academic Publishers, 1991), p. 102.
78 Emrence, *Remapping the Ottoman Middle East*, p. 2.
79 Emrence, *Remapping the Ottoman Middle East*, pp. 41, 123; Hourani, *Arabic Thought in the Liberal Age*.
80 Eraqi-Klorman, "Yemen," p. 390; and Parfitt, *The Road to Redemption*.
81 Parfitt, *The Road to Redemption*, pp. 94, 97.
82 Laurence D. Loeb, "Gender, Marriage, and Social Conflict in Habban," in *Sephardi and Middle Eastern Jewries: History & Culture in the Modern Era*, ed. Harvey E. Goldberg (Bloomington: Indiana University Press, 1996), p. 260; Eraqi-Klorman, "Yemen," p. 391.
83 Nini, *The Jews of the Yemen*, p. 57.
84 Ahroni, *Yemenite Jewry*, p. 115.

85 The date of 1646 appears in Ahroni, *Yemenite Jewry*, pp. 114–15, 118, 120; the date 1788 appears in Ari Ariel, *Jewish-Muslim Relations and Migration from Yemen to Palestine in the Late Nineteenth and Twentieth Centuries* (Leiden: Brill, 2014), pp. 28–29. On removing non-Muslim corpses, see Parfitt, *The Road to Redemption*, p. 86.

86 Parfitt, *The Road to Redemption*, pp. 87–88.

87 Ahroni, *Yemenite Jewry*, p. 146.

88 Ariel, *Jewish-Muslim Relations and Migration from Yemen*, p. 29.

89 Nini, *The Jews of the Yemen*, p. 67.

90 Parfitt, *The Road to Redemption*, p. 88.

91 Nini, *The Jews of the Yemen*, pp. 62, 64.

92 Nini, *The Jews of Yemen*, p. 71.

93 Ariel, *Jewish-Muslim Relations and Migration from Yemen*, p. 29.

94 Nini, *The Jews of the Yemen*, p. 75.

95 Parfitt, *The Road to Redemption*, p. 37.

96 Cormac Ó. Gráda, *Eating People Is Wrong, and Other Essays on Famine, Its Past, and Its Future* (Princeton: Princeton University Press, 2015), p. 5.

97 Najwa al-Qattan, "When Mothers Ate Their Children: Wartime Memory and the Language of Food in Syria and Lebanon," *International Journal of Middle East Studies*, 46 (2014), pp. 719–36.

98 Ariel, *Jewish-Muslim Relations and Migration from Yemen*, p. 33; Parfitt, *The Road to Redemption*, p. 53.

99 Ariel, *Jewish-Muslim Relations and Migration from Yemen*, pp. 49–52.

100 Ruth Kark and Joseph B. Glass, "Eretz Israel/Palestine, 1800–1948," in Simon, Laskier, and Reguer, *The Jews of the Middle East and North Africa in Modern Times*, p. 338.

101 One memoirist mentioned that her Yemeni Jewish grandfather had moved to British-controlled Aden before settling in the Suez Canal Zone city of Port Said, Egypt, where the family opened a department store. Sylvia Modelski, *Port Said Revisited* (Washington, DC: Faros, 2000), p. 75.

102 *New Revised Standard Version Bible* (New York: The National Council of Churches, 1989).

103 Laqueur, *The Changing Face of Antisemitism*, pp. 21, 26–27.

104 Eyal Chowers, *The Political Philosophy of Zionism: Trading Jewish Words for a Hebraic Land* (Cambridge: Cambridge University Press, 2012), pp. 3–4.

105 Recall that Sabbatai Sevi was the Sephardic mystic whose conversion to Islam, as an alternative to death, prompted some followers in and around Istanbul to peel off from the Jewish community. These became known as the Dönme; see Chapter 5.

106 Ahroni, *Yemenite Jewry*, p. 147. Historians debate the import of messianism for Yemeni Jews. Ari Ariel argues, for example, that scholars have overestimated its role in prompting migration. Ariel, *Jewish-Muslim Relations*.

107 Kark and Glass, "Eretz Israel/Palestine," in Simon, Laskier, and Reguer, *The Jews of the Middle East and North Africa in Modern Times*, p. 338.

108 Parfitt, *The Road to Redemption*, pp. 41–42.

109 Ella Shohat, *Israeli Cinema: East/West and the Politics of Representation*, new edition (London: I.B. Tauris, 2010), p. 134.

110 Reeva Spector Simon, "Europe in the Middle East," in Simon, Laskier, and Reguer, *The Jews of the Middle East and North Africa in Modern Times*, p. 20.

111 Harvey E. Goldberg, *Jewish Life in Muslim Libya: Rivals & Relatives* (Chicago: University of Chicago Press, 1990), pp. 35, 44. See also Harvey E. Goldberg, ed. and trans., *The Book of Mordechai: A Study of the Jews of Libya* (Philadelphia: Institute for the Study of Human Issues, 1980).

112 Quoted in Goldberg, *Jewish Life in Muslim Libya*, p. 38.

113 Goldberg, *Jewish Life in Muslim Libya*, p. 12.

114 On attitudes toward commensality among Sunnis and Shi'is, see Freidenreich, *Foreigners and Their Food*.

115 Goldberg, *Jewish Life in Muslim Libya*, p. 12.

116 During the nineteenth century, the decline of agriculture in the rural interior and the increase of "nomadization" probably contributed to this Jewish migration as well. Goldberg, *The Book of Mordechai*, p. 27.

117 Goldberg, *Jewish Life in Muslim Libya*, pp. 16, 48.

118 Georgeon, *Abdülhamid II*, p. 294; Kieser, *Nearest East*, p. 59.

119 Leila Tarazi Fawaz, *An Occasion for War: Civil Conflict in Lebanon and Damascus in 1860* (London: I.B. Tauris, 1994), pp. 84–160; the quoted phrase is on p. 101.

120 Georgeon, *Abdülhamid II*, p. 292.

121 Donald Bloxham, *The Great Game of Genocide: Imperialism, Nationalism, and the Destruction of the Ottoman Armenians* (Oxford: Oxford University Press, 2005), p. 52.

122 Bloxham, *The Great Game of Genocide*, p. 52.

123 "Fifty Thousand Orphans Made So by the Turkish Massacres of Armenians," *New York Times*, December 18, 1896.

124 Uğur Ümit Üngör, *The Making of Modern Turkey: Nation and State in Eastern Anatolia, 1913–1950* (Oxford: Oxford University Press, 2011), p. 19; Selim Deringil, "'The Armenian Question is Finally Closed': Mass Conversions of Armenians in Anatolia during the Hamidian Massacres of 1895–1897," *Comparative Studies in Society and History*, 51:2 (2009), pp. 360–62.

125 Deringil, "The Armenian Question Is Finally Closed."

126 Georgeon, *Abdülhamid II*, p. 294; see also Deringil, "The Armenian Question Is Finally Closed," p. 367.

127 Klein, *The Margins of Empire*.

128 Fortna, "The Reign of Abdülhamid II," p. 55.

129 Klein, *The Margins of Empire*.

130 Ronald Grigor Suny, *"They Can Live in the Desert but Nowhere Else": A History of the Armenian Genocide* (Princeton: Princeton University Press, 2015), p. 118; Deringil, "The Armenian Question Is Finally Closed," p. 364.

131 Deringil, "The Armenian Question Is Finally Closed," p. 350.

132 Georgeon, *Abdülhamid II*, pp. 283–84.

133 Davison, "The Millets as Agents of Change," pp. 201–2.

134 Deringil, "The Armenian Question Is Finally Closed."

135 Reynolds, *Shattering Empires*, p. 51.

136 Reynolds, *Shattering Empires*, p. 51.
137 Suny, *"They Can Live in the Desert but Nowhere Else,"* p. 116.
138 Suny, *"They Can Live in the Desert but Nowhere Else,"* p. 54; and Davison, "The Millets as Agents of Change," p. 193.
139 Karpat, *Ottoman Population*, p. 24; Özkan, *From the Abode of Islam to the Turkish Vatan*, p. 35.
140 Yücel Terzibaşoğlu, "Struggles over Land and Population Movements in North-Western Anatolia, 1877–1914," *Sociétés rurales ottomanes*, ed. Mohammad Afifi et al. (Cairo: Institut français d'archéologie orientale, 2005), pp. 297–98.
141 Davison, "The Millets as Agents of Change," p. 193.
142 Davison, "The Millets as Agents of Change," p. 193.
143 Mayeur-Jaouen, "The Renaissance of Churches," p. 757.
144 Suny, "Religion, Ethnicity, and Nationalism," p. 39.
145 On the role of demographic anxiety in shaping Anatolian Muslim attitudes towards Armenians before and during World War I, see Taner Akçam, *The Young Turks' Crimes against Humanity: The Armenian Genocide and Ethnic Cleansing in the Ottoman Empire* (Princeton: Princeton University Press, 2012).
146 Quataert, "The Age of Reforms," p. 790.
147 Duben and Behar, *Istanbul Households*, pp. 4–6, 25, 55, 180–82, 242.
148 Karpat, *Ottoman Population*, p. 47.
149 Quataert, "The Age of Reforms," pp. 783–84.
150 Duben and Behar, *Istanbul Households*, p. 7.
151 Georgeon, *Abdülhamid II*, p. 317.
152 Georgeon, *Abdülhamid II*, pp. 292, 294.
153 Edward J. Erickson, "Template for Destruction: The Congress of Berlin and the Evolution of Ottoman Counterinsurgency Practices," in Yavuz and Sluglett, *War and Diplomacy: The Russo-Turkish War of 1877–1878 and the Treaty of Berlin*, p. 369.
154 Nicholas B. Breyfogle, *Heretics and Colonizers: Forging Russia's Empire in the South Caucasus* (Ithaca: Cornell University Press, 2005), p. 189.
155 Jeremy Salt, *Imperialism, Evangelism, and the Ottoman Armenians, 1878–1896* (London: Frank Cass, 1993), pp. 25–27.
156 A discussion of this trope appears in Fatma Müge Göçek, *Denial of Violence: Ottoman Past, Turkish Present, and Collective Violence against the Armenians, 1789–2009* (Oxford: Oxford University Press, 2015).
157 Suny, *"They Can Live in the Desert but Nowhere Else,"* p. 70.
158 Elizabeth B. Frierson, "Cheap and Easy: The Creation of a Consumer Culture in Late Ottoman Society," in *Consumption Studies and the History of the Ottoman Empire: An Introduction*, ed. Donald Quataert (Albany: State University of New York Press, 2000), pp. 243–60.
159 Chatty, *Displacement and Dispossession in the Modern Middle East*, p. 151.
160 For a parallel discussion of Muslim attitudes toward "uppity" Christians in the Ottoman Arab provinces, see Masters, *Christians and Jews in the Ottoman Arab World*, p. 132.
161 Deringil, "The Armenian Question Is Finally Closed," p. 359.

162 The idea of cowing comes from Deringil, "The Armenian Question Is Finally Closed," p. 349. The idea of culling comes from Bloxham, *The Great Game of Genocide*, p. 55.

163 Suny, *"They Can Live in the Desert but Nowhere Else,"* pp. 53–55.

164 Salt, *Imperialism, Evangelism, and the Ottoman Armenians*, p. 24.

165 Georgeon, *Abdülhamid II*, p. 286.

166 Chatty, *Displacement and Dispossession in the Modern Middle East*, pp. 146–47; Erickson, "Template for Destruction," p. 369.

167 Fortna, "The Reign of Abdülhamid II," p. 55.

168 Georgeon, *Abdülhamid II*, p. 300.

169 Salt, *Imperialism, Evangelism, and the Ottoman Armenians*, p. 55.

170 Georgeon, *Abdülhamid II*, p. 131.

171 With regard to the mid-1890s, Suny, for example, used the term "pogroms" broadly in *"They Can Live in the Desert but Nowhere Else."* Georgeon used it, but more sparingly, in *Abdülhamid II*; see, for example, p. 286.

172 Bloxham, *The Great Game of Genocide*, p. 55.

173 Salt, *Imperialism, Evangelism, and the Ottoman Armenians*, p. 156.

174 Leila Fawaz, "The Beirut-Damascus Road: Connecting the Syrian Coast to the Interior in the 19th Century," in *The Syrian Land: Processes of Integration and Fragmentation (Bilad al-Sham from the 18th to the 20th Century)*, ed. Thomas Philipp and Birgit Schaebler (Stuttgart: Franz Steiner Verlag, 1998), pp. 19–27.

175 Zürcher, *Turkey*, p. 84.

176 Erik Jan Zürcher, "The Young Turks: Children of the Borderlands?," *International Journal of Turkish Studies*, 9:1–2 (2003), pp. 275–85.

177 Hanioğlu, *A Brief History of the Late Ottoman Empire*, p. 148; Zürcher, "The Young Turks."

178 Michelle U. Campos, *Ottoman Brothers: Muslims, Christians, and Jews in Twentieth-Century Palestine* (Stanford: Stanford University Press, 2011), pp. 1–2.

179 Rodrigue, *French Jews, Turkish Jews*, p. 125.

180 Cohen, *Becoming Ottomans*, pp. 1, 46–52.

181 Der Matossian, *Shattered Dreams of Revolution*, p. 5.

182 Bedross Der Matossian, "From Bloodless Revolution to Bloody Counterrevolution: The Adana Massacres of 1909," *Genocide Studies and Prevention*, 6:2 (2011), pp. 156–57.

183 Chatty, *Displacement and Dispossession in the Modern Middle East*, p. 151.

184 "Armenian Wealth Caused Massacres," *New York Times*, April 25, 1909.

185 Feroz Ahmad, *The Young Turks and the Ottoman Nationalities: Armenians, Greeks, Albanians, Jews, and Arabs, 1908–1918* (Salt Lake City: University of Utah Press, 2014), p. 14.

186 Zürcher, "The Young Turks."

187 Cohen and Stein, *Sephardi Lives*, pp. 142–43.

188 Mehmet Beşikçi, *The Ottoman Mobilization of Manpower in the First World War: Between Voluntarism and Resistance* (Leiden: E.J. Brill, 2012), pp. 97–100, 126. Beşikçi discusses the labor battalions at some length.

189 Reynolds, *Shattering Empires*, p. 62.

190 Beşikçi, *The Ottoman Mobilization of Manpower*, p. 100.
191 Zürcher, "The Ottoman Conscription System in Theory and Practice," pp. 89–90.
192 Quataert, "The Age of Reforms," p. 792.
193 Işıl Acehan, "Outposts of an Empire: Early Turkish Migration to Peabody, Massachusetts," MA thesis, Bilkent University, 2005, pp. 17–18; Alfaro-Velcamp, *So Far from Allah, So Close to Mexico*, p. 50.
194 Figures cited in Karpat, "The Ottoman Emigration to America," p. 195.
195 Karpat, "The Ottoman Emigration to America," p. 186.
196 Quataert, "The Age of Reforms," p. 792.
197 Rodrigue, *French Jews, Turkish Jews*, p. 125.
198 Goldberg, *Jewish Life in Muslim Libya*, pp. 44, 48–49.
199 Der Matossian, *Shattered Dreams of Revolution*.
200 Niloofar Haeri, *Sacred Language, Ordinary People: Dilemmas of Culture and Politics in Egypt* (New York: Palgrave Macmillan, 2003).
201 Georgeon, *Abdülhamid II*, p. 186.
202 Bruce Masters, *The Arabs of the Ottoman Empire, 1516–1918: A Social and Cultural History* (Cambridge: Cambridge University Press, 2013), p. 7.
203 Albert Hourani, "Ottoman Reform and the Politics of Notables," in *The Modern Middle East*, ed. Albert Hourani, Philip S. Khoury, and Mary C. Wilson (Berkeley: University of California Press, 1993), pp. 83–109.
204 Hasan Kayali, *Arabs and Young Turks: Ottomanism, Arabism, and Islamism in the Ottoman Empire* (Berkeley: University of California Press, 1997).
205 Masters, *The Arabs of the Ottoman Empire*, p. 7.
206 James L. Gelvin, "The 'Politics of Notables' Forty Years After," *Middle East Studies Association Bulletin*, 40:1 (2006), pp. 19–29, especially p. 27.
207 Roger Allen, *The Arabic Literary Heritage: The Development of Its Genres and Criticism* (Cambridge: Cambridge University Press, 1998).
208 Viola Shafik, *Arab Cinema: History and Cultural Identity* (Cairo: American University in Cairo Press, 1998).
209 Makdisi, *Artillery of Heaven*, p. 207.
210 Thomas Philipp, *Ğurği Zaidan, His Life and Thought* (Wiesbaden: Steiner, 1979).
211 Orit Bashkin, *New Babylonians: A History of Jews in Modern Iraq* (Stanford: Stanford University Press, 2012), see Chapter 1, "Brothers and Others: Iraqi Identity and Arab Jewishness," pp. 1–14.
212 C. Ernest Dawn, *From Ottomanism to Arabism: Essays on the Origins of Arab Nationalism* (Urbana: University of Illinois Press, 1973), pp. 122–47, see especially pp. 132–33.
213 Antonius, *The Arab Awakening*, p. 57.
214 al-Muwaylihi, *Spies, Scandals, and Sultans*, p. 80.
215 Georgeon, *Abdulhamid II*, p. 184.
216 Hanioğlu, *A Brief History of the Late Ottoman Empire*, pp. 126, 129–30, 142.
217 Georgeon, *Abdülhamid II*, p. 187.
218 Somel, *The Modernization of Public Education in the Ottoman Empire*, pp. 206–7.

219 Masters, *The Arabs of the Ottoman Empire*, pp. 13–14.
220 "Turkey," *Oxford English Dictionary Online*, December 2011.
221 Lewis, *The Emergence of Modern Turkey*; Findley, *The Turks in World History*.
222 Berkes, *The Development of Secularism in Turkey*, p. 319.
223 On this diversity, and on the historic pragmatism of the Ottoman Empire in accommodating it, see Winter, *The Shi'ites of Lebanon under Ottoman Rule*, pp. 4–8.
224 Joseph Jacobs and Goodman Lipkind, "Arthur Lumley Davids," *JewishEncyclopedia.com*, 1906 edition, www.jewishencyclopedia.com/articles/4987-davids-arthur-lumley (accessed July 30, 2015).
225 Berkes, *The Development of Secularism in Turkey*, pp. 314–15.
226 Akçam, *The Young Turks' Crimes against Humanity*, p. xiv.
227 Zürcher, *Turkey*, p. 114; Akçam, *The Young Turks' Crimes against Humanity*, p. 87.
228 Reynolds, *Shattering Empires*, p. 39.
229 Reynolds, *Shattering Empires*, pp. 38–39; Baer, *The Dönme*, p. 146; and Akçam, *The Young Turks' Crimes against Humanity*, pp. xiv–xv.
230 Mustafa Aksakal, *The Ottoman Road to War in 1914: The Ottoman Empire and the First World War* (Cambridge: Cambridge University Press, 2008), pp. 14–15.
231 Reynolds, *Shattering Empires*, p. 48.
232 Bloxham, *The Great Game of Genocide*, p. 3.
233 Donald E. Miller and Lorna Touryan Miller, *Survivors: An Oral History of the Armenian Genocide* (Berkeley: University of California Press, 1993).
234 Ara Sarafian, "The Absorption of Armenian Women and Children into Muslim Households as a Structural Component of the Armenian Genocide," in *In God's Name: Genocide and Religion in the Twentieth Century*, ed. Omer Bartov and Phyllis Mack (New York: Berghahn Books, 2001), pp. 209–21, see p. 211.
235 Akçam, *The Young Turks' Crimes against Humanity*, p. 314.
236 Akçam, *The Young Turks' Crimes against Humanity*, p. xxvi. See also Renée Hirschon, ed., *Crossing the Aegean: An Appraisal of the 1923 Compulsory Population Exchange between Greece and Turkey* (London: Berghahn Books, 2003).
237 Der Matossian, *Shattered Dreams of Revolution*, p. 2.
238 Georgeon, *Abdülhamid II*, p. 432.
239 Deringil, *The Well-Protected Domains*, p. 29; Avner Wishnitzer, *Reading Clocks, Alla Turca: Time and Society in the Late Ottoman Empire* (Chicago: University of Chicago Press, 2015).
240 Eyal Ginio, "Mobilizing the Ottoman Nation during the Balkan Wars (1912–1913): Awakening from the Ottoman Dream," *War in History*, 12:2 (2005), pp. 156–77; Feroz Ahmad, *The Young Turks: The Committee of Union and Progress in Turkish Politics, 1908–1914* (Oxford: Clarendon Press, 1969).
241 League of Nations, *The Covenant of the League of Nations* (including amendments adopted to December 1924), http://avalon.law.yale.edu/20th_century/leagcov.asp (accessed March 29, 2016).

242 Fred A. Bernstein, "Ertugrul Osman, Link to Ottoman Dynasty, Dies at 97," *New York Times*, September 24, 2009.

243 Israel Gershoni and James P. Jankowski, *Egypt, Islam, and the Arabs: The Search for Egyptian Nationhood, 1900–1930* (New York: Oxford University Press, 1986), p. 73.

244 Samim Akgönül, "Les vestiges du système ottoman dans le traitement des minorités en Grèce et en Turquie," in *La perception de l'héritage ottoman dans les Balkans*, ed. Sylvie Gangloff (Paris: L'Harmattan, 2005), pp. 43–61; see especially p. 43 on the terms "heritage" and "vestiges."

Epilogue

Introduction: The Middle East and "Religious" History

My students over the years have repeatedly said that the Middle East is a very "religious" place – perhaps the most religious in the world. Skeptical about claims to the Middle East's religious exceptionalism (especially given what I know of European, North American, African, and South Asian history), I began investigations that led to this book. I wanted to understand more clearly how and when religion in the Islamic Middle East was important in practice (as opposed to in theory); how it shaped state policies; and, above all, how it affected Muslim, Christian, and Jewish people as they crossed paths in everyday life. My goal was to push aside the sensational history of the Islamic Middle East, to see the mundane and the human more clearly: what people actually did, even if that was not what they were supposed to be doing. Such a study of communal relations in the Middle East could easily fill a multivolume encyclopedia. My aim, however, was to write an accessible distillation, which meant covering some things and leaving out many others.

The book began by surveying early Islamic history from the seventh century onward. It sketched the development of Islam, as a system of belief; of Muslims, as a group of people; and of the early Islamic state, as a polity that included Muslims and non-Muslims alike. In the former lands of the Byzantine and Sassanian Empires, early Muslim rulers drew upon guidance from the Qur'an, insights from the examples of the Prophet Muhammad and his companions, and *ad hoc* policies of the first conquerors toward Christians and Jews within their domains. They called these Christians and Jews *ahl al-dhimma* or *dhimmi*s, meaning people who agreed to a pact, by which they would live protected but subordinate to the Islamic state and to Muslims. These policies proved remarkably durable and offered a rough blueprint that Islamic empires used and adapted in the thousand-plus years that ensued, particularly as more people entered the Muslim fold through marriage (as in the case of Christian and Jewish women, whose children by Muslim fathers were deemed Muslim by law), through free conversions (as when individuals opted to join), and through forced conversions (either from the enslavement of men and women, with many of the latter as concubines, or from other forms of duress).[1]

The bulk of the book focused on the Ottoman Empire, which emerged in the fourteenth century in Asia Minor and southeastern Europe. Beginning with Sultan Mehmet II, who in 1453 overthrew what remained of the Byzantine Empire at Constantinople and made the city into his capital, Ottoman authorities instituted ways of collectively liaising with Christians and Jews. The Ottoman *millet* or community system, as historians retrospectively called it, incorporated many elements of early Islamic state policies (notably, the classification of Christians and Jews as *dhimmi*s who had to pay a special tax called the *jizya*) but tailored them to fit first, the Constantinople milieu, and second and more broadly, the changing social realities of the Ottoman Empire. For example, over time the Ottoman state accommodated new sectarian splits among Christian subjects to recognize multiple Christian *millet*s. It also allowed for the incorporation of Jewish immigrants, especially after 1492 when the empire welcomed Jews whom Spain had expelled. The Ottoman conquests of Syria and Egypt in 1517 signaled a major turning point for the empire in geographic and demographic terms: these conquests made the empire what we would now call "Middle Eastern" while making its population more Muslim. Expansion beyond these areas along the North African coast, toward the Tigris-Euphrates river region (Iraq), and into Arabia, confirmed the empire's transition into being an Islamic Middle Eastern power.

After 1700, the pace of social change quickened in the Ottoman Empire, which arguably entered its "modern" period. The post-1700 period witnessed, for example, the debut of the first Ottoman-government-sponsored printing press (although it proved to be a short-lived venture) as well as the intensification of exchanges with western Europe and the Americas. The Ottoman Empire, in other words, tilted toward a westward form of globalization, marking a change from older eastbound connections of trade and migration that had linked the Islamic empires of western Asia to central, southern, and eastern Asian lands. Thus, in this eighteenth-century age of westward exchanges, "Ottoman" merchants and "Ottoman" coffee beans traveled to places such as Holland, France, and Britain, while French silks, American tomatoes and tobacco, and Dutch tulips increasingly made their way to the Ottoman lands. (For the tulips, at least, the journey was something of a round trip, given that cultivation of this flowering plant had first begun in Persia and then Anatolia several centuries earlier.) In the eighteenth century, too, the Ottoman

Empire began to grapple with military defeats and territorial losses, which persisted until the twentieth-century end of the empire. During this century, the arrival of growing numbers of western European traders, diplomats, and missionaries stood poised to benefit Middle Eastern Christians – and to some extent also Jews – in ways that would shift the balance of intercommunal relations by making non-Muslims more prosperous and more confident.

The nineteenth century was a dramatic and critically important phase of Ottoman history – a period of reforms that reached their peak during the Tanzimat or "Reorganization" era. The bureaucracy grew, paperwork mounted, and the Ottoman state embarked on new ventures that aimed to make the empire more robust on the world stage and more tightly controlled from within. For example, the Ottoman state developed a postal system, began to issue passports and to establish "modern" schools, and confirmed its hold over rural and fringe regions (such as Libya) which the empire had previously controlled very loosely or only in theory. In 1829, Sultan Mahmud II banned the turban for men so that Muslim, Christian, and Jewish employees of the state began to look more alike on the top of their heads. The reform decree of 1856, which many Christian and Jewish observers at the time and later hailed as a move toward social parity, confirmed the influence of egalitarian ideals and ended the practice of officially designating Christians and Jews as *dhimmi*s. However, what some Christians and Jews hailed as their "emancipation" failed to undo social assumptions among many Muslims about the appropriate roles that non-Muslims should play, showing that tangled traditions can prove hard to unknot.[2] Meanwhile, many urban Christians and Jews, and some Muslims, began to flourish economically within a new "middle class" as a result of contacts with European and North American merchants, educators, and missionaries. In the middle class, women began to enter the ranks of the literati and, like men, to change their clothes and their lifestyles in ways that enabled visible and tangible religious distinctions to blur in public arenas.

The long reign of Abdulhamid II, which straddled the period from the end of the nineteenth century into the twentieth, remains as puzzling as the sultan himself. Abdulhamid II dismissed the parliament, devised a vast system of spying and censorship to root out dissent or squash threats to his rule, emphasized anew the Sunni Muslim foundations of the state, and initiated efforts to rein in groups that he considered inadequately or barely Muslim, such as the Alawites and the Yezidis. His Ottoman state proved to be strong, top-heavy, and interventionist, except when it came to the Armenian communities of Anatolia. Indeed, the crowning disaster of his reign occurred in the mid-1890s when many of his Armenian subjects in Anatolia became subject to massacres that he made no efforts to suppress. Viewed dispassionately (which means numbing oneself to the suffering of the Christian and Muslim people involved), these massacres of the 1890s offer a window into the social tensions that were causing late Ottoman society – or perhaps we should say societies, plural – to break down along religious, economic, and ethno-linguistic lines.

The book concludes shortly after the Young Turks Revolution of 1908, which had the immediate goal of restoring parliamentary government. This event proved to be the last hurrah for Ottomanism, a kind of Ottoman imperial nationalism that had the potential to draw the diverse peoples of the empire together. In fact, Ottomanism by this stage was facing many contenders – other incipient nationalisms, among Arabs, Turks, Armenians, and others – who envisioned the empire in terms of smaller pieces or groups. Although Zionism was emerging as a form of Jewish nationalism, it was still at this stage a preponderantly foreign European movement.[3] Indeed, many highly educated Ottoman Jews counted among the most enthusiastic supporters of the Young Turks in 1908.

In universities and colleges throughout the United States, many courses in modern Middle Eastern history now seem to *begin* around the time that this book ends, and then proceed through World War I (1914–18) to decades that followed. Without a doubt, World War I had a cataclysmic impact on the region. It led to the collapse of the Ottoman Empire and the drawing of new borders. Many of the Middle Eastern countries that we see on the map today – Iraq, Syria, and so forth – were concoctions of the post–World War I settlements and of the periodic wars over territory that these unleashed.

However, the eighteenth and nineteenth centuries of the Ottoman Empire were the crucibles for making the modern Middle East. Even after accounting for territorial losses, the Ottoman Empire in this period remained remarkably diverse in its landscapes, peoples, and cultures and had an imperial structure that gave administrative coherence to its domains. This coherence makes the empire meaningful as a unit for historical analysis, and explains why I chose to end this book with the onset of World War I, before the victors chopped the empire into pieces.

The nineteenth-century Ottoman Empire witnessed attempts to revise government and society in ways that could strengthen the empire by giving its residents more of a stake in its well-being. And yet, the Ottoman state struggled to balance two competing needs: respecting tradition and promoting reforms, which was perhaps tantamount to keeping things the same while also changing them. With different degrees of sincerity, commitment, and acceptance among the Muslims, Christians, and Jews of the empire, Ottoman authorities in the early nineteenth century began to reconfigure social hierarchies, including those that privileged Muslims politically and legally over Christians and Jews. However, the state's major reforms – including the landmark Tanzimat decree of 1856, which seemed to promote social parity among Muslim, Christian, and Jewish subjects – revealed a truth that a scholar noted in the context of French history: it was far easier to change rules than mentalities.[4] It was easier to issue edicts with egalitarian language than to undo assumptions about privilege and status. The fact that Christians and Jews in the nineteenth century seemed to be becoming more prosperous relative to Muslims – in other words, that they were amassing economic power – complicated the efforts to promote equity in the political realm.

When the empire came apart, the difficulties of reconciling Islamic tradition with egalitarian values persisted. The Ottoman successor states of the post–World War I and post–World War II Middle East – including Israel, despite its foundation as a Jewish and not Islamic state[5] – inherited many legacies and challenges from the Ottoman Empire, such as the problem of handling religious hierarchies while respecting the rights of nondominant religious communities. With different levels of success and failure, post-Ottoman states have continued to negotiate the place of religion relative to government policy, military service, family law, property rights, school curricula, and more, with implications for how ordinary people are likely to relate as neighbors, as colleagues, and ostensibly, too, as compatriots.

By stopping before World War I this book ends too soon to cover what the British statesman and erstwhile viceroy of India, Lord Curzon (1859–1925), called the "unmixing of peoples" that occurred with the dissolution of the Ottoman Empire in the Balkans.[6] Curzon was referring to the forced migrations that occurred between 1912 and the early 1920s, when perhaps 3.5 million Muslims and Christians fled or were driven from their homes, thereby enabling those who remained to build more ethnically uniform states.[7] Likewise, the book ends too soon to trace the steady attrition that caused Christians and Jews to dwindle or disappear from most Middle Eastern and North African countries between the mid-twentieth century and the early twenty-first. What this book *does* do is to offer a foundation for understanding changing relations among Muslims, Christians, and Jews against a broader sweep of Islamic history.

Historians typically use the word "history" to refer to at least three things at once. First and most obviously, they use "history" to refer to *what happened* – the past as it actually was both in its fine-grained details and in its broad contours. Like the end of a rainbow, however, this kind of history is hard to reach; it requires distance to see, and even then, one is likely to perceive it from only some angles. Scholars also use "history" to refer to the *craft and process* of studying the past. This craft involves methods and, more abstractly, modes of approach. Third, scholars use "history" to mean *the story about the past that one assembles*. This kind of history depends on choice in details, arguments, and narration. The film version of the satirical novel *Lucky Jim*, by the British author Kingsley Amis (1922–95), humorously alluded to a possible fourth meaning for the term, namely, "history" as the egotistical historian. The odious university professor who heads the history department picks up the telephone and answers, "History, Speaking," as if he were capital-H History incarnate, authorized voice of the past.[8] The pages that follow reflect on the second and third kinds of history – that is, history as we approach it and history as we tell it – to conclude this book about the shared past of Muslims, Christians, and Jews. Unlike the department chair in *Lucky Jim*, however, I do not pretend to definitive authority. I expect that different observers of the same past will see other stories in it. Convinced, nevertheless, that the historian's job is to engage in close and rigorous study of previous worlds and to strive for fairness, I advance ideas of a methodological nature, to reflect on what more we can study, how we can study it, and what ambiguities we are likely to face.

The Smell of the Past

Was it possible in the late nineteenth-century Ottoman Empire to tell by a glance if a person was Jewish? The English traveler Edward William Lane (1801–76), who wrote a lively account of the customs of "modern Egyptians" based on his travels in Egypt during the 1820s, thought that he should be able to do so, but confessed that he could not. Women especially baffled him. "[Jewish] women veil themselves," Lane wrote, "and dress in every respect, in public, like the other women of Egypt." Jewish men wore turbans that looked to him like the turbans of Christian men. Perhaps Lane was clumsy at reading the sartorial cues that a local person would have recognized, or perhaps distinctions of dress in the 1820s were already growing more muted among urban Muslims, Christians, and Jews. Whatever the case, Lane insisted that there were other ways to discern. "Oriental Jews," he claimed, showed signs of "sore eyes, and ... bloated complexion[s]; the result, it is supposed, of their making an immoderate use of the oil of sesame in their food."[9]

The sociologist, political scientist, and food historian Sami Zubaida (b. 1937) (who grew up Jewish in Baghdad) picked up Lane's thread about sesame oil and pulled it in another direction. It was true, Zubaida wrote, that Jews throughout Ottoman lands once preferred to cook with sesame oil, which satisfied the kosher dietary prohibition against mixing meat and dairy products while imparting a "distinctive and powerful smell" to their food. Muslims, by contrast, liked to cook their meat with butter; while Christians, who avoided butter (and meat) during Lent and other church fast days, tended toward olive oil. Once upon a time, "Iraqis related that they could smell Jewish houses and streets miles away," because their sesame oil was so pungent.[10] Its scent sometimes seeded a negative stereotype in Iraq as in Egypt: the idea that Jews gave off a whiff of their own. In fact, this stereotype of a Jewish "foul odor" had roots going back to Roman times. Medieval Christian and Muslim writers repeated it, and it went on to surface in many contexts.[11] Assumptions about the smell of Jews prevailed, for example, among Muslims in late nineteenth-century Yemen.[12]

But things changed. "The Jews [in Egypt and Iraq] had apparently internalized their disgrace [… about smell]," Zubaida wrote, "for as soon as factories were established to produce tasteless, odourless vegetable oils [such as corn oil, during the early twentieth century] they switched immediately, thus sacrificing a delicious taste to prejudice." He added that Muslims and Christians soon switched to industrially produced oils, too, mostly because they were cheap and convenient.[13] So it appears that just as Muslims, Christians, and Jews began to converge in their clothing in the nineteenth century, they converged in their vegetable oil in the early twentieth.

These mundane details about cooking fat and food odors have lessons to impart, beyond reminding us of how the Islamic world occasionally inherited anti-Semitic ideas from the Roman Empire and its Christian successors. For a start, these details suggest that residents of an Ottoman city like Baghdad may have been able to *sniff* each other out as Muslims, Christians, and Jews – or perhaps just as importantly, may have believed themselves capable of doing so. They may have detected or claimed to detect each other's membership in one of the three major religious communities by the particular scent of the home cooking – the fried onions and garlic, for example – that clung to their clothes.

"Today's history comes deodorized," the historian Roy Porter (1946–2002) famously observed; we are likely now to forget "the stench of the past."[14] Porter, who was an expert on eighteenth-century England, may have been thinking primarily of the ubiquitous stench of manure in the preautomobile age of horse-drawn carts and wagons, and of human waste tossed out of chamber pots (in the age before flush toilets and extensive plumbing and sewer systems). Regardless, by accentuating the elusive and fleeting nature of smell, Porter's observation can remind us first, of our limits in conjuring the past, and second, of the fact that being Muslim, Christian, or Jewish in an Islamic state may have been more than the sum of praying a certain way, celebrating a given holiday, and having a legal status determined by the religion of one's father. The construction of religious and other identities – such as being Muslim, Christian, or Jewish, or being a man or women from a particular place or with a certain profession – may have depended on the experience of various visual, auditory, haptic (touch-related), and olfactory (smell-related) sensations, too, as well as on cultures of cooking and eating. Along these lines, for example, the male residents of eighteenth-century Aleppo were known to boast about the superiority of the city's females by using a food analogy. "Better Aleppo rye than imported wheat," went a once-common adage, reflecting a shared Muslim, Christian, and Jewish city pride – a sense of masculine territorial identity – that related to home-grown women and grain crops.[15]

Smell, in its capacity as odor or stench, may have pushed people apart, but smell, in its capacity as aroma or fragrance, often drew people together. Judging from what Arabic literati had to say in recipe collections and other food-related manuals produced from the tenth century onward, Muslim writers in places like Baghdad knew a lot about the food of Christians and Jews and wrote about its flavor, scent, healthful qualities, and artistry in highly appreciative tones. For example, Abbasid courtiers recorded recipes for some of the best Sabbath-day dishes of Jews, while Christian doctors treating Muslims at the Abbasid court in Baghdad frequently prescribed the vegan, Lenten-style dishes of observant Christians as a healthy diet for invalids.[16] Muslim gastronomes in Mamluk Egypt, meanwhile, wrote cookery books that included recipes for dishes like "Jewish meatballs," made from pounded meat, pistachios, eggs, and spices and cooked, *bien entendu*, in sesame oil.[17] In short, and at least within the realm of *haute cuisine*, evidence from cookbooks challenges stereotypes about the "foul odor" of Jews and the consequent repulsiveness of their food to Muslims and Christians, suggesting ambiguities within the history of sensory receptions. When it comes to food, of course, disgusting is relative: readers may now find off-putting some of what Muslims, Christians, and Jews commonly ingested in, say, the tenth century. The salty condiment called *murri* (now forgotten and "surviving" only in recipes) comes to mind here. Made from barley dough that was covered in mold, wrapped in fig leaves, left to rot for several weeks, and then infused in a liquid, it starts to sound somewhat better only when one is told that it may have had a flavor and quality akin to soy sauce or blue cheese![18]

Little details can carry big meanings. The anthropologist Clifford Geertz (1926–2006) noted as much in his landmark study titled *The*

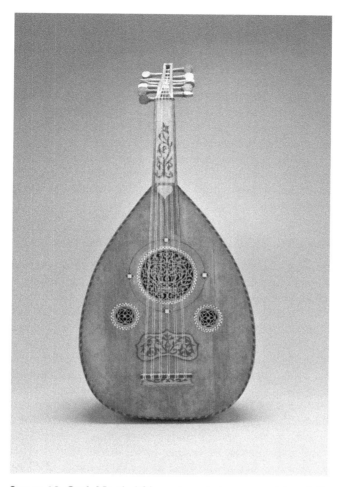

Image 18 Oud, North African, twentieth century (signed Casablanca, 1944, Hassan Ben Bou Chaïb), Yale University Collection of Musical Instruments, Gift of Theodore Woolsey Heermance. Accession No. 4550. Photography credit: Alex Contreras.

Interpretation of Cultures (1973), when he reflected on the significance of an eyelid that rapidly closes and opens. Was that movement a twitch, a wink, or a blink – or was it the winker's parody of someone else's wink? Analyzing the nuances behind this movement could lead to what Geertz approvingly called a "thick description" of culture, with culture itself representing "the webs of significance that [the human animal] himself has spun."[19] By attempting to approach history through the ephemeral and admittedly now muffled evidence of sound, taste, and other sensory experiences, we can get closer to a "thick description" of culture and meaning. For example, consider again the twentieth-century Muslims, Christians, and Jews who converged in adopting industrially produced vegetable oils. These oils were cheap and convenient, and they did not emit much odor when heated. So was it the cheapness and the convenience, or the lack of a stink (or perceived stink), that prompted Jews to abandon sesame oil for these products? The history of something as apparently banal as a cooking fat – in its economic, social, and olfactory dimensions – may carry a multiplicity of eye-opening meanings.

Little People, Little Things, and "Little History"

Attention to sensory experiences like smell, sound, and taste can remind us to broaden our expectations about *where* we can look for history. The sultan's palace, government offices, law courts, and military headquarters (all sites where the state was the primary actor) together with places of worship (the most obvious institutional sites of religion) were not the only places that shaped social circumstances for Muslims, Christians, and Jews. Home kitchens mattered, too. So did public venues like shops, cafés, market squares, parks, *gazino* music clubs, and bath houses. Indeed, at least as far back as the Mamluk era (1250–1517) in Egypt and Syria, and continuing for nearly five more centuries in the Ottoman Middle East, successive edicts required Christians and Jews in bath houses to wear special markers – such as copper, lead, or iron rings around their necks, or strange shoes on their feet (such as one white clog and one black) in order to set them apart from Muslims.[20] Another arrangement was to restrict non-Muslims to bathing on certain days and at certain times of the week.[21] Authorities appeared to worry that naked Muslims, Christians, and Jews would mingle too much when they washed. And maybe people *did* mingle more than state and religious authorities thought appropriate. Recall that in eighteenth-century Istanbul, Muslims frequented the same bars and brothels as Christians and Jews and sometimes ran their own taverns and sex shops, even if the official line was that non-Muslims, and only non-Muslims, operated the "vice trade."[22]

Many places where Muslims, Christians, and Jews mixed were sites of consumption where people bought, sold, swapped, ingested, or otherwise used a wide variety of stuff.[23] Perhaps we can call such places sites of "little history," as a geographic analogue to what French scholars have called the history of the *petites gens* (little people). In contrast to grand narratives associated with sultans and other famous or powerful people, places like kitchens and shops were where ordinary people did ordinary things like eating soup and buying socks. Of course, the soup of, say, the eighteenth and nineteenth centuries was digested long ago, and its eaters are dead. Presumably their socks have decomposed in trash heaps along with most of what people once bought or sold. Faced with gaps and lapses like these, and lacking access to the oral sources from which students of twentieth- and early twenty-first-century history may benefit, scholars are likely to turn, once again, to state and court records and to other manuscript and printed texts (memoirs, travelogues, journals, and the like) – that is, to the words of the relatively powerful in the pre-twentieth-century era of limited literacy. Words on pages have some fixity, after all, despite the fragility of the papyrus, parchment, or paper that holds them and despite the murkiness of their meanings and motives.

Legions of Anglophone doctoral students have read a now-classic article in postcolonial studies called "Can the Subaltern Speak?." Published in 1988 by the comparative literature scholar Gayatri Chakravorty Spivak (b. 1942), this essay reflected on possibilities for, and barriers to, reaching nondominant actors or "subalterns" in history.[24] (She cited in particular the history of widows as it related to *sati* or widow-burning in nineteenth-century northern India, when British colonialists decried the practice and used it to justify their rule in the subcontinent.) What can one do to capture the experiences of, say, peasants, especially when sources are scanty? Are we stuck with recounting versions of history that the ruling classes and the super-literati (including religious authorities like bishops, *qadi*s, and rabbis) passed down? Spivak's article was pessimistic about prospects for reaching subalterns in history and treating them fairly, and yet she still gave a hint of practical advice. If one cannot "hear" certain historical actors loudly or clearly, then try at least to pick up their whispers – perhaps slim references to their lives in other sources. And be ready to acknowledge the limits in doing so.

To collect testimony about the past, we can extend these ideas about subalterns to everyday objects, or to images or descriptions thereof. Can a shoe speak? The answer is yes, as shown by the color-coded history of Ottoman footwear, which had the potential to mark people out as Muslims, Christians, or Jews as they ambled down a street. The same may be true of forks, the spread of which signaled the moments when Ottoman people started imitating the European, *allafranca* custom of eating with cutlery. By listening and looking hard (and maybe by touching if we are allowed), we can glean information about the past and about

Image 19 Bath clogs, wood with velvet and silver metal, nineteenth century. Museum Number 2013,6033.2.a-b. ©The Trustees of the British Museum. The curator's comments in the British Museum's on-line catalogue trace these clogs to an Armenian woman whose family settled in Aleppo, Syria, after 1915 and whose grandmother had received them for her wedding trousseau.

human entanglements from objects that have escaped the trash heap or that have otherwise survived in the landscape.[25]

In a similar vein, the scholar Aviva Muller-Lancet, who helped to develop the Jewish ethnography section at the Israel Museum in Jerusalem, asked herself questions about the religious identity of things when she was collecting materials on Jews in Islamic lands. What made an object sufficiently "Jewish," she asked herself, to warrant inclusion in the museum? She decided that a Singer sewing machine, of the kind that entered Ottoman lands after 1880, passed the test: machines like this one had contributed to the Westernization of clothes that middle-class Jews made at home. Other objects, from the many places where Jews had lived mixed up with Muslims, were harder to assess. Muller-Lancet ultimately decided that if there were no obvious signs (like, say, a Hebrew inscription), then the only way to confirm an object's Jewishness was to ascertain that it had "lived" with a Jewish family. On these grounds, she included a Kurdish rug of the *senneh kelim* type. "[S]old in carpet shops all over the world," she explained, "[it] would never be included in a Jewish collection if it had not been acquired in the home of a Kurdish Jew living on a *moshav* [farming cooperative] in Israel." When she learned that the donor's daughter had woven this rug at home when she was fourteen years old and still living in Persia, the object struck her as doubly Jewish – Jewish-made and Jewish-owned, even though it was identical in style, technique, and material to the carpets that Muslims made in this area.[26]

Working from the premise that life is a "forest of symbols," as the anthropologist Victor Turner (1920–83) declared in a seminal ethnography of the Ndembu of present-day Zambia,[27] one can try to study objects not only as witnesses to the past, but as powerbrokers in their own right. Recall again the history of Ottoman gentlemen's tombstones, which announced the religion and social status of the deceased through carvings of headgear that topped them.[28] Clothing – what people wore on their bodies – made bold statements, too, which is why this book paid such close attention to the history of dress. European diplomats attended to it also: in the sixteenth century, they felt that reading the messages carried by Ottoman court clothing was so important that they studied costume catalogues prepared for this purpose, in order to develop their visual literacy.[29] By examining specimens of clothing if we have them, and descriptions or images if we do not, we can trace the history of Muslim, Christian, and Jewish relations through dress just as effectively – and sometimes *more* effectively – as from the wording of edicts. "Costume is a place," the historian Suraiya Faroqhi asserted. Its changes marked how, when, and where Ottoman state policies and popular social relations shifted on the ground.[30]

Admittedly, the material legacies of clothing have left some gaping silences. Despite the long Islamic history of dress restrictions on Jews, the folklorist Esther Juhasz observed that the Israel Museum in Jerusalem has no specimens of the drab, black clothing that Muslim authorities over many centuries expected Jews, as *dhimmi*s, to wear.[31] Jews appeared more likely to save and take good care of their finest clothes – the ones that Jewish authorities told them to wear behind walls where Muslims could not see them.[32] These were the kinds of clothes, for example, that Yemeni Jews packed to take when they emigrated, leaving textile historians to puzzle over the messages about social status, age, and more that their embroidered leggings were said to convey.[33] Because of this tendency to preserve special-occasion outfits, the Israel Museum has many bridal dresses but not the everyday, out-on-the-streets, self-effacing garb of Jews qua *dhimmi*s.

Everyday lives in the Middle East were about much more than war. In a study of eighteenth-century Damascus, the historian James Grehan added along these lines that, "Over the full range of their affairs, people's lives were simply too complex, improvised, and most of all self-interested to fall in line obediently with ideological schemes of any stripe."[34] Most people were poor – Muslims, Christians, and Jews alike[35] – and they worried about getting enough to eat and having shelter. Men who preened at court in lustrous, multihued silks were not the norm, even if their access to power and the technology of literacy[36] has inflated their place in the past as we see it. Paying attention to material and cultural life – what music people listened to, how they tried to educate their children, what they ate, and how they dressed – has the virtue of restoring a sense of normalcy, and humanity, to the history of the *"petites gens."*[37]

The Limits of Religion

Religion featured prominently in the lives of Middle Eastern people but was not the only basis of their identities. Where they lived, what language they spoke, how much money they had, how they made a living, whether they were male or female: factors like these shaped them, too. So then how and when was religion important in affecting what people did?

Religion was important because it provided the social vasculature through which Muslims, Christians, and Jews coursed in their lives. On the one hand, religion was a creed and devotional system; a model for ethics and upright behavior; and a way of thinking about the afterlife, human suffering, and other questions of existence. On the other hand, and in ways that were critical for Islamic social history in practice, religion was a legal status, interpreted and enforced by judges, state authorities, and ordinary people on the ground. Attitudes toward religion and the law affected whom one could marry, how one could travel (e.g., on donkey or horseback), even in some cases which jobs one could or could not do. For example, apparently influenced by *hadith* that seemed to disapprove of handling gold and other metals, Muslims in western Asia typically ceded Jews a monopoly in working as smiths of gold, silver, copper, and tin, in a pattern that continued into the twentieth century.[38] By providing ways to express or assert differences of social, political, and ethnic kinds, religion could also be a basis for group cohesion – what the great fourteenth-century historian Ibn Khaldun called *'asabiyya* – and later, by the late nineteenth century, a basis for incipient nationalisms. This last point was as true for people living in what remained of the Ottoman Empire as it was for people who broke off. Consider Greece, for example, which enshrined Greek Orthodox Christianity as its religion

Image 20 "Ferblantier juif à Jerusalem" (Jewish tinsmith in Jerusalem),
c. 1876–85, Bonfils Collection, Image Number 165858. Courtesy of
the Penn Museum.

of state, while restricting mosque-building in ways that recalled the history of Ottoman Islamic practice vis-à-vis *dhimmi*s.[39]

But religion has limits as an explanatory framework. Consider, for example, episodes of egregious violence that afflicted Anatolia during the Armenian massacres of the mid-1890s, when some Armenians (adherents of Christianity) on the one hand, and some Turks and Kurds (adherents of Islam) on the other, hacked each other's limbs off and bashed in each other's skulls.[40] No system of ethics and upright behavior can explain these horrors. To understand what happened, one must look to the intersection of economic factors (resentments over wealth), social factors (resentments over health, education, lifestyle), sexual factors (demographic anxiety), and the like, and then see how people invoked religion, in its legal and communal guises, to justify or explain their behavior. The historic privileges that Muslims enjoyed in the legal and political realm did, however, affect what happened – and in this sense religion *did* play a role. That is, in the 1890s, Muslim men were able to marry Christian females, whereas Christian men could not reciprocate. This asymmetry meant that Muslim men could abduct and rape Christian females, and then press them into legally recognized marriages, in a way that Ottoman authorities (representing what was still an Islamic state even after the Tanzimat reforms) would not have abided if Christian men had tried to do the same with Muslim females. Likewise, the historic privileges that Muslim men had enjoyed in bearing arms put them in a more advantageous position relative to Christians in terms of military training and access to weapons – and this helps to explain the acute discrepancies in the death tolls of Armenian (Christian) and Kurdish (Muslim) victims.

With regard to religion, there is also the issue of diversity in religious practice and interpretation. Consider the *jizya*, the special tax that Islamic states historically demanded of Christians and Jews. In the pre-eminent reference work in Islamic studies, the *Encyclopaedia of Islam*, the entry for *jizya* reads like a catalogue of variations from one region and time to another.[41] Who paid the tax? (Only men, but of what ages?) How much did they pay, and did it take account of their means? *How* did they pay it: one by one, or as a group; in a straightforward handover, or in a ritual meant to humiliate? After reading the *Encyclopedia of Islam* article, with its dizzying array of examples, one can only return to the very general statement: again, that there was a tax that Islamic states expected non-Muslims to pay, and it was called the *jizya*. Diversity in application was a feature, similarly, of the Pact of Umar, which purported to be the surrender agreement with Christians in Syria amidst the first Muslim conquests. The Pact of Umar – or rather, what Muslims in different places and times assumed it to be – provided a basis for justifying assertions of hierarchy, but its invocation was selective and spotty, and its content could vary. Not all versions of the pact, for example, mentioned a ban on pig-raising, for pork meat, on the part of Christians.[42] Likewise, in some times and places, Muslims allowed Christians and Jews to build houses of worship, while in others, they forbade new constructions or tore down old ones. On the other hand, some stipulations in the Pact of Umar fell away so quickly and thoroughly that no one bothered to invoke them after a time. The injunction that barred non-Muslims from speaking the language of the Muslim conquerors, Arabic, comes to mind, because Arabic spread deeply and widely. Indeed, Arabic pushed spoken Coptic into extinction in Egypt within a few centuries of the first conquests, while it developed coherent literary and spoken variants that were distinct to Jews, and which linguists now call Judeo-Arabic. Likewise, the Pact of Umar required non-Muslims to wear the *zunnar* belt around their waists, but over time, people forgot what that was. In the absence of *zunnar*-wearing, as the preceding chapters suggested, Muslim rulers over the centuries improvised different rules about clothing instead.[43]

What about diversity in the Muslim population? Across the centuries, the Ottoman state proved extremely successful at maintaining a semblance of continuity and respect for apparently stable traditions of Islamic statehood. This commitment to an ideal of tradition may have figured prominently in the empire's long-term success. Until the end of the empire, the Ottoman state recognized only one Muslim community, one Muslim *millet*, in a manner that harkened back to the early Islamic ideal of the *umma*. By contrast, Ottoman sultans from the time of Mehmet the Conqueror proved amenable to officially recognizing sectarian distinctions among Christians like Greeks and Armenians (and much later, in the nineteenth century, Catholics and Protestants). But in fact, and despite the rhetoric of unitary peoplehood, or *umma*-ness, Muslims in the Ottoman Empire were extremely diverse in how they understood and practiced their Muslim religion. There were Shi'is of assorted kinds, not to mention various 'Alids (to use a vaguer and more neutral term for people who celebrated 'Ali, the Prophet Muhammad's cousin and son-in-law); there were Sufi organizations galore. The sultans themselves often resorted to astrology to make sense of their place in the universe.[44] Meanwhile, "Sunni" at best was an umbrella term, covering a wide array of people and practices. Among the Sunnis, recall, there were even the Dönme, descendants of Jewish converts, whose members asserted their Islam as a matter of public profession while supplementing it in private with an array of beliefs, prayers, and other practices unique to themselves. On a popular level, and in spite of what religious authorities may have taught or maintained, the array of Muslims in nineteenth-century Istanbul also shared with Christians and Jews assumptions about the world of the spirits. These assumptions amounted to "religion," too. For example, people believed in vampires, ghosts, and dream divination, and wore "evil eye" amulets to ward off trouble. The mother of one sultan, convinced that her son was sick from bad magic, even "went as far as having a meaningless prayer read by the preachers during the Friday prayer in various mosques in Istanbul" in an effort to use counter-magic to cure him.[45]

Appreciating the extent of diversity among Muslims is essential for understanding, for instance, how and why the attitudes of Zaydi Muslims toward Jews in late nineteenth-century Yemen diverged from those of Ottoman Muslim authorities and soldiers, with consequences for social policies. Recall that Zaydi Muslims refused to eat with Jews and considered them dirty, but at the same time, and compared to Ottoman authorities, respected Jewish Sabbath and holiday observances more scrupulously. In short, Muslim religion was no monolith. Like Christian and Jewish religion, Islam in practice was always a work in progress among real, and really fallible, people. A history of intercommunal relations in the Middle East must grapple with this complexity.

Looking Forward, Looking Back

In a book about Abdulhamid II and the changing policies and ideologies of his regime, the historian Selim Deringil concluded by describing this history as a "true 'tragedy' in the Greek sense of seeing what is coming, of knowing what to do to avoid it and yet of being unable to resist the march of events."[46] He did not specify what made it tragic, although his book suggested a story like this: There was a paranoid, worry-prone sultan, bent on keeping his throne, who suppressed dissent but allowed some bloodying to occur as a way of keeping his people divided. When he eventually lost control, and events from abroad pressed down, the heaviness of the people's anxieties together with the depth of their mutual resentments guaranteed that the empire would sink.

Following this Greek line of thought with regard to late Ottoman history, recall Cassandra, daughter of Priam (king of Troy). According to myth, the god Apollo fell so deeply in love with this young lady that he gave her the gift of prophecy. But Cassandra did not reciprocate his love. Outraged by her rejection, Apollo cursed her. Henceforth Cassandra continued to see the future and all the catastrophes looming. But she was doomed to issue warnings that no one believed, so disasters continued to fall. Fortunately, because historians look back to the past and not forward in time, they are not cursed quite like Cassandra by being forced to watch, mutely, train wrecks of the future. Perhaps historians *are* cursed like her, however, in knowing what will happen relative to a past moment in time. They can see the Young Turks Revolution of 1908 and know, for example, that the colossal miseries of World War I are "waiting" around the corner, six years ahead. Their awareness of sequenced events – what happened at point Y relative to point X – may be enough to leave the historian *feeling* like Cassandra. No wonder history (in the sense of what happened) often seems like a tragedy.

Illi fat mat – literally, "what's happened is dead" – goes a saying in Egyptian Arabic. It means that the past is over; what is done is done; what is gone is gone. Or is it? The novelist Salman Rushdie asked a similar question in a meditative essay on the city of Bombay where he grew up, and on the experience and lingering guilt of living as an émigré in Britain. Rushdie referred to the wife of Lot who, according to the biblical story in Genesis (19:26), turned into a pillar of salt when she ignored God's warning not to look back as the family fled from the city of Sodom. The Qur'an also notes her inclination to turn around for a glimpse. Looking back is worth it, he concluded after deliberating, even if all we can see are fragments. "There is an obvious parallel here with archaeology," he continued. "The broken pots of antiquity, from which the past can sometimes, but always provisionally, be reconstructed, are exciting to discover, even if they are pieces of the most quotidian objects." Like an archaeologist gluing shards, the historian can assemble pieces of the mundane, and thereby understand something of the past as it once was. Such effort has a deeper purpose, too, Rushdie reasoned, for "redescribing a world is the necessary first step towards changing it," especially for "post-lapsarian" creatures.[47] His allusion to the postlapsarian contained another biblical and koranic reference, to Adam and Eve after their fall, and the idea that all humans are flawed.

Redescribing a world is the necessary first step toward changing it. Why bother combing the past for fragments only to face the struggle of piecing them together – especially if we know that we will never find the whole pot? Why grope to find what happened, and what people thought or perceived, if evidence will always elude us simply because so much – like a thought or a whiff – was fleeting from the start? We should bother because by attempting to redescribe history with a skeptical eye, we can catch glimpses of its warts-and-all form – its marks of beauty and plain, God-forsaken ugliness – and thereby avoid the twin traps of idealizing the past or vilifying it.

This book shows that the sum of Islamic Middle Eastern history, as it applied to Muslims, Christians, and Jews, was neither a golden age nor a dark age, but rather more of a series of people-bumbled-along ages in the plural, interspersed with the very good and the pretty bad in different places and times. The history that happened was complicated. And if we find, upon staring at it, that some policies and practices in the past seemed to work well while others utterly flopped or outlasted their use, then we can use those insights to make choices here and now. Ultimately the lingering historical question that comes out of describing the Middle Eastern past is this one: how much of tradition is worth keeping, and how much is worth chucking aside?

There is an ethical reason, too, for reimagining the past – any past – argued Philip E. Tetlock, Richard Ned Lebow, and Geoffrey Parker in a manifesto for "counterfactual history." They made their comments to introduce essays that questioned the inevitability of the "rise of the

Image 21 Glazed ceramic dish fragment, Islamic, Egypt, c. 700–1299
AD. Object Number 29-140-11. Courtesy of the Penn Museum.

West" in world history. "The primary value of such an exercise" they
wrote, "is humility. The world we inhabit is but one of a vast array
of possible worlds that might have been brought about if some deity
could ... rerun the tape of history over and over." They praised the
authors of the *9/11 Commission Report* (the study that assessed the terrorist attacks of September 11, 2001, in the United States) for beautifully, if
inadvertently, expressing related ideas. "[The] path of what happened is
so brightly lit," the commission observed, "that it places everything else
more deeply into shadow."[48] Psychologists have a name for this perception: they call it "hindsight bias." Once we know how something happened, goes this idea, it is extremely difficult to imagine that it could have
occurred any other way.[49]

Engaging in counterfactual scenario-making may be common in
business schools, military academies, and government agencies, to test
options and mentally and logistically prepare for emergencies, but what
can it do for observers of the past? To answer, think of what we could
counterfactually imagine for late nineteenth-century Ottoman history
alone. We could imagine that pragmatic and idealistic reformers trumped
a paranoid sultan; that a different and better sultan was there to provide

wiser and more caring leadership; that a parliament persisted, giving diverse people a say and a stake in the empire; that military revolutionaries overcame grudges to include and protect people who seemed different from themselves; and that opportunities reached more people, to avert the resentments of haves and have-nots.

NOTES

1 On slavery, see Bernard Lewis, *Race and Slavery in the Middle East: An Historical Enquiry* (Oxford: Oxford University Press, 1990); and Eve Troutt Powell, *Tell This in My Memory: Stories of Enslavement from Egypt, Sudan, and the Ottoman Empire* (Stanford: Stanford University Press, 2012).

2 On the language of "emancipation" see, for example, el Masri, *The Story of the Copts*, p. 507; and Masters, *Christians and Jews in the Ottoman Arab World*, p. 166.

3 The historian Orit Bashkin asserted in the case of Iraq, for example, that, "Zionism did not play a major role in the debates about Iraqi Jewish identity before 1947" – in other words, one year before the emergence of Israel. Bashkin, *New Babylonians*, pp. 5–6.

4 Winock, *La France et les juifs de 1789 à nos jours*, p. 27.

5 Yüksel Sezgin, "The Israeli *Millet* System: Examining Legal Pluralism through Lenses of Nation-Building and Human Rights," *Israel Law Review*, 43:631 (2010), pp. 631–54; Assaf Likhovski, "The Ottoman Legacy of Israeli Law," *Annales de la Faculté de Droit d'Istanbul*, 39 (2007), pp. 71–86.

6 Rogers Brubaker, *Nationalism Reframed: Nationhood and the National Question in the New Europe* (Cambridge: Cambridge University Press, 1996), p. 152.

7 Kasaba, *A Moveable Empire*, pp. 124–25.

8 Elizabeth Deeds Ermarth, Review of *The Future of History*, by Alun Munslow (review 1220), in *Reviews in History*, www.history.ac.uk/reviews/review/1220 (accessed August 11, 2015); and Elizabeth Deeds Ermarth, Review of *Centuries' Ends, Narrative Means*, ed. Robert Newman, in *History and Theory*, 37:1 (1998), pp. 102–10.

9 Edward William Lane, *An Account of the Manners and Customs of the Modern Egyptians*, ed. Edward Stanley Poole, fifth edition (London: John Murray, 1860), p. 553.

10 Sami Zubaida, "National, Communal and Global Dimensions in Middle Eastern Food Cultures," in *Culinary Cultures of the Middle East*, ed. Sami Zubaida and Richard Tapper (London: I.B. Tauris, 1994), p. 38.

11 Benjamin Aldes Wurgaft, "Food Smells and Ethnic Tension," *Gastronomica*, 6:2 (2006) pp. 57–60. See also Jonathan Reinarz, *Past Scents: Historical Perspectives on Smell* (Urbana: University of Illinois Press, 2014), pp. 92–97.

12 Parfitt, *The Road to Redemption*, p. 91.

13 Zubaida, "National, Communal and Global Dimensions in Middle Eastern Food Cultures."

14 Roy Porter, "Foreword," in Alain Corbin, *The Foul and the Fragrant: Order and the French Social Imagination* (Cambridge, MA: Harvard University Press,

1986), cited in Mark S. R. Jenner, "Follow Your Nose? Smell, Smelling, and Their Histories," *American Historical Review*, 116:2 (2011), pp. 335–51.

15 Marcus, *The Middle East on the Eve of Modernity*, p. 33.

16 Zaouali, *Medieval Cuisine of the Islamic World*, pp. x–xi, xxiii; David Waines and Manuela Marín, "Muzawwar: Counterfeit Fare for Fasts and Fevers," in *Patterns of Everyday Life*, ed. David Waines (Aldershot, UK: Ashgate, 2002), pp. 303–15.

17 Lewicka, *Food and Foodways of Medieval Cairenes*, p. 289.

18 Zaouali, *Medieval Cuisine of the Islamic World*, pp. x–xi.

19 Clifford Geertz, "Thick Description: Toward an Interpretive Theory of Culture," in *The Interpretation of Cultures: Selected Essays* (New York: Basic Books, 1973), pp. 3–30.

20 Stilt, *Islamic Law in Action*, pp. 117–19. See also Stillman, *The Jews of Arab Lands*, pp. 70–75; Cohen, *Jewish Life under Islam*, pp. 73, 138, 239 (footnote 2); and Boyar and Fleet, *A Social History of Ottoman Istanbul*, pp. 258–59.

21 Heyberger, *Les Chrétiens du Proche-Orient au temps de la Réforme Catholique*, pp. 51–52.

22 Zarinebaf, *Crime and Punishment in Istanbul*.

23 Daniel Miller, *Stuff* (Cambridge, MA: Polity Press, 2010); Quataert, *Consumption Studies and the History of the Ottoman Empire*.

24 Gayatri Chakravorty Spivak, "Can the Subaltern Speak?," in *Marxism and Interpretation of Culture*, ed. Cary Nelson and Lawrence Grossberg (Urbana: University of Illinois Press, 1988), pp. 271–313.

25 Ian Hodder, *Entangled: An Archaeology of the Relationship between Humans and Things* (Oxford: Wiley-Blackwell, 2012), pp. 1–12.

26 Aviva Muller-Lancet, *Garments with a Message: Ethnography of Jewish Wear in Islamic Lands* (Jerusalem: Ben-Zvi Institute for the Study of Jewish Communities in the East, 2010), pp. 25, 31, 36–37, 46–48.

27 Victor Turner, *The Forest of Symbols: Aspects of Ndembu Ritual* (Ithaca: Cornell University Press, 1970).

28 Eldem, *Death in Istanbul*, p. 52.

29 Scarce, *Women's Costume of the Near and Middle East*, p. 40.

30 Faroqhi, "Introduction, or Why and How One Might Want to Study Ottoman Clothes," p. 39.

31 Esther Juhasz, ed., *The Jewish Wardrobe: From the Collection of the Israel Museum, Jerusalem* (Jerusalem: Israel Museum, 2012), p. 23.

32 Esther Juhasz, "Material Culture," in Simon, Laskier, and Reguer, *The Jews of the Middle East and North Africa in Modern Times*, p. 209.

33 Juhasz, "Material Culture," p. 209.

34 James Grehan, *Everyday Life & Consumer Culture in 18th-Century Damascus* (Seattle: University of Washington Press, 2007), pp. 9–10.

35 See, for example, Lewis, *The Jews of Islam*, which repeatedly mentions the poverty of most Jews.

36 Jack Goody, *The Power of the Written Tradition* (Washington, DC: Smithsonian Institution Press, 2000).

37 For additional arguments on behalf of everyday history, see Faroqhi, *Subjects of the Sultan*; and Mehrdad Kia, *Daily Life in the Ottoman Empire* (Santa Barbara: Greenwood, 2011).

38 Michael Menachem Laskier, "Syria and Lebanon," in Simon, Laskier, and Reguer, *The Jews of the Middle East and North Africa in Modern Times*; and Esther Juhasz, "Material Culture," p. 205.

39 George Th. Mavrogordatos, "Orthodoxy and Nationalism in the Greek Case," *West European Politics*, 26:1 (2003), pp. 117–36.

40 Salt, *Imperialism, Evangelism, and the Ottoman Armenians*, pp. 105, 109.

41 Cl. Cahen and Halil İnalcık, "Djizya" (Parts 1 and 2), in *The Encyclopaedia of Islam*, ed. B. Lewis, Ch. Pellat, and J. Schacht, new edition, Vol. 2 (C–G) (Leiden: E.J. Brill, 1983), pp. 559–66.

42 Fattal, *Le statut légal des non-musulmans en pays d'Islam*, pp. 6–69.

43 "The Pact of Umar," in Lewis, *Islam from the Prophet Muhammad to the Capture of Constantinople*, Vol. 2, pp. 216–23; Stillman, *Arab Dress*.

44 Winter, *The Shiites of Lebanon under Ottoman Rule*, p. 7.

45 Boyar and Fleet, *A Social History of Ottoman Istanbul*, pp. 277–79.

46 Deringil, *The Well-Protected Domains*, p. 176.

47 Rushdie, *Imaginary Homelands*, pp. 10–11, 14.

48 National Commission on Terrorist Attacks upon the United States, *The 9/11 Commission Report* (Washington, DC: Government Printing Office, 2004), p. 339.

49 Philip E. Tetlock, Richard Ned Lebow, and Geoffrey Parker, eds., *Unmaking the West: 'What If?' Scenarios that Rewrite World History* (Ann Arbor: University of Michigan Press, 2006), p. 3.

Bibliography

Abdullah Frères. "Interior of the Imperial Fez Factory," albumen photographic print, Abdul Hamid II Collection, held by the Library of Congress Prints and Photographs Division, Washington, DC www.loc.gov/pictures/item/2003675899/ (accessed February 6, 2015).

Abedin, Syed Z. and Saleha M. Abedin. "Muslim Minorities in Non-Muslim Societies." In *The Oxford Encyclopedia of the Modern Islamic World*, ed. John L. Esposito. Volume 3. New York: Oxford University Press, 1995.

Acehan, Işil. "Outposts of an Empire: Early Turkish Migration to Peabody, Massachusetts," MA thesis, Bilkent University, 2005.

Afifi, Mohammad, Rachida Chih, Brigitte Marino, Nicolas Michel, and Işık Tamdoğan, eds. *Sociétés rurales ottomanes/Ottoman Rural Societies*. Cairo: Institut français d'archéologie orientale, 2005.

Ágoston, Gábor. "Grand Vizier." In *Encyclopedia of the Ottoman Empire*, ed. Gábor Ágoston and Bruce Masters. New York: Facts on File, 2009, pp. 235–36.

Ahmad, Feroz. *The Young Turks: The Committee of Union and Progress in Turkish Politics, 1908–1914*. Oxford: Clarendon Press, 1969.

The Young Turks and the Ottoman Nationalities: Armenians, Greeks, Albanians, Jews, and Arabs, 1908–1918. Salt Lake City: University of Utah Press, 2014.

Ahmed, Leila. *Women and Gender in Islam: Historical Roots of a Modern Debate*. New Haven: Yale University Press, 1992.

Ahroni, Reuben. *Yemenite Jewry: Origins, Culture, and Literature*. Bloomington: Indiana University Press, 1986.

Akçam, Taner. *The Young Turks' Crimes against Humanity: The Armenian Genocide and Ethnic Cleansing in the Ottoman Empire*. Princeton: Princeton University Press, 2012.

Akgönül, Samim. "Les vestiges du système ottoman dans le traitement des minorités en Grèce et en Turquie." In *La perception de l'héritage ottoman dans les Balkans*, ed. Sylvie Gangloff. Paris: L'Harmattan, 2005, pp. 43–61.

Aksakal, Mustafa. *The Ottoman Road to War in 1914: The Ottoman Empire and the First World War*. Cambridge: Cambridge University Press, 2008.

Aksan, Virginia H. "Ottoman Military Recruitment Strategies in the Late Eighteenth Century." In *Arming the State: Military Conscription in the Middle East and Central Asia, 1775–1925*, ed. Erik J. Zürcher. London: I.B. Tauris, 1999, pp. 21–39.

"Ottoman Political Writing, 1768–1808," *International Journal of Middle East Studies*, 25 (1993), pp. 53–69.

al-Qattan, Najwa. "Dhimmis in the Muslim Court: Legal Autonomy and Religious Discrimination," *International Journal of Middle East Studies*, 31:3 (1999).

"When Mothers Ate Their Children: Wartime Memory and the Language of Food in Syria and Lebanon," *International Journal of Middle East Studies*, 46 (2014), pp. 719–36.

Albera, Dionigi and Maria Couroucli, eds. *Sharing Sacred Spaces in the Mediterranean: Christians, Muslims, and Jews at Shrines and Sanctuaries*. Bloomington: Indiana University Press, 2012.

Alfaro-Velcamp, Theresa. *So Far from Allah, So Close to Mexico: Middle Eastern Immigrants in Modern Mexico*. Austin: University of Texas Press, 2007.

Allen, Roger. *The Arabic Literary Heritage: The Development of Its Genres and Criticism*. Cambridge: Cambridge University Press, 1998.

"The Post-Classical Period: Parameters and Preliminaries." In *Arabic Literature in the Post-Classical Period*, ed. Roger Allen and D. S. Richards. Cambridge: Cambridge University Press, 2006, pp. 1–21.

Allouche-Benayoun, Joëlle. "Les enjeux de la naturalisation des Juifs d'Algérie: du dhimmi au citoyen." In *Le choc colonial et l'islam: les politiques religieuses des puissances coloniales en terres d'islam*, ed. Pierre-Jean Luizard. Paris: La Découverte, 2006, pp. 179–95.

Alloula, Malek. *The Colonial Harem*, trans. Myrna Godzich and Wlad Godzich, intro. Barbara Harlow. Minneapolis: University of Minnesota Press, 1986.

Amson, Daniel. *Adolphe Crémieux: L'Oublié de la Gloire*. Paris: Éditions du Seuil, 1988.

Anastassiadou, Meropi and Bernard Heyberger, eds. *Figures anonymes, figures d'élite: pour une anatomie de l'homo ottomanicus*. Istanbul: Isis, 1999.

Anderson, Benedict. *Imagined Communities: Reflections on the Origin and Spread of Nationalism*, revised edition. London: Verso, 1999.

Anderson, Betty S. *The American University of Beirut: Arab Nationalism and Liberal Education*. Austin: University of Texas Press, 2011.

Andrews, Walter G. and Mehmet Kalpakli. *The Age of Beloveds: Love and the Beloved in Early-Modern Ottoman and European Culture and Society*. Durham: Duke University Press, 2005.

Anscombe, Frederick. "Continuities in Ottoman Centre-Periphery Relations, 1878–1915." In *The Frontiers of the Ottoman World*, ed. A. C. S. Peacock. Oxford: Oxford University Press, 2009, pp. 235–51.

Antébi, Élizabeth. *Les Missionaires juifs de la France, 1860–1939*. Paris: Calmann-Lévy, 1999.

Antonius, George. *The Arab Awakening: The Story of the Arab National Movement*. Philadelphia: J.B. Lippincott, 1939.

Arafat, W. N. "New Light on the Story of Banu Qurayza and the Jews of Medina," *Journal of the Royal Asiatic Society of Great Britain and Ireland*, 2 (1976), pp. 100–107.

Arendt, Hannah. *Eichmann in Jerusalem: A Report on the Banality of Evil*. New York: Viking Press, 1963.

Ariel, Ari. *Jewish-Muslim Relations and Migration from Yemen to Palestine in the Late Nineteenth and Twentieth Centuries*. Leiden: E.J. Brill, 2014.

Armanios, Febe. *Coptic Christianity in Ottoman Egypt*. Oxford: Oxford University Press, 2011.

Armenian National Education Committee (United States). "The Congress of Berlin." *Milwaukee Armenian Community*, http://milwaukeearmenians.com/tag/nersess-varjabedian/ (accessed May 20, 2014).

"Armenian Wealth Caused Massacres," *New York Times*, April 25, 1909.

Armstrong, Karen. *A History of God: The 4,000-Year Quest of Judaism, Christianity, and Islam*. New York: A.A. Knopf, 1993.

Artan, Tülay. "Aspects of the Ottoman Elite's Food Consumption: Looking for 'Staples', 'Luxuries', and 'Delicacies' in a Changing Century." In *Consumption Studies and the History of the Ottoman Empire: An Introduction*, ed. Donald Quataert. Albany: State University of New York Press, 2000, pp. 107–200.

Asad, Talal. *Genealogies of Religion*. Baltimore: Johns Hopkins University Press, 1993.

Atiya, Aziz S. *A History of Eastern Christianity*. London: Methuen & Co., 1968.

Ayalon, Ami. "New Practices: Arab Printing, Publishing, and Mass Reading." In *A Global Middle East: Mobility, Materiality, and Culture in the Modern Age, 1880–1940*, ed. Liat Kozma, Cyrus Schayegh, and Avner Wishnitzer. London: I.B. Tauris, 2015, pp. 321–44.

The Press in the Arab Middle East. Oxford: Oxford University Press, 1994.

Reading Palestine: Printing and Literacy, 1900–1948. Austin: University of Texas Press, 2004.

Aydın, Hilmi. *The Sacred Trusts: Pavilion of the Sacred Relics, Topkapı Palace Museum, Istanbul*. Somerset, NJ: Light, 2004.

Ayoub, Mahmoud. "Dhimmah in Qur'an and Hadith." In *Muslims and Others in Early Islamic Society*, ed. Robert Hoyland. Aldershot, UK: Ashgate, 2004, pp. 25–35.

Babinger, Fr. "Kalpak." In *E.J. Brill's First Encyclopaedia of Islam, 1913–1936*, Volume 4, ed. M. Th. Houtsma. Leiden: E.J. Brill, 1993, p. 701.

Badawi, M. M. *A Critical Introduction to Modern Arabic Poetry*. Cambridge: Cambridge University Press, 1975.

Badr, Habib, Suad Abou el Rouss Slim, and Joseph Abou Nohra, eds. *Christianity: A History in the Middle East*. Beirut: Middle East Council of Churches, 2005.

Baer, Marc David. *The Dönme: Jewish Converts, Muslim Revolutionaries, and Secular Turks*. Stanford: Stanford University Press, 2010.

Honored by the Glory of Islam: Conversion and Conquest in Ottoman Europe. New York: Oxford University Press, 2008.

Baer, Marc, Ussama Makdisi, and Andrew Shryock. "Tolerance and Conversion in the Ottoman Empire: A Discussion," *Comparative Studies in Society & History*, 51:4 (2009), pp. 927–40.

Bahloul, Joelle. *The Architecture of Memory: A Jewish-Muslim Household in Colonial Algeria, 1937–1962*, trans. Catherine Du Peloux Ménagé. Cambridge: Cambridge University Press, 1992.

Bahrani, Zainab, Zeynep Çelik, and Edhem Eldem. "Introduction: Archaeology and Empire." In *Scramble for the Past: A Story of Archaeology in the Ottoman Empire, 1753–1914*, ed. Zainab Bahrani, Zeynep Çelik, and Edhem Eldem. Istanbul: SALT, 2011, pp. 1–43.

Ballestriero, R. "Anatomical Models and Wax Venuses: Art Masterpieces or Scientific Art Works?," *Journal of Anatomy*, 216:2 (2010), pp. 223–34.

Bar-Asher, Moshe. *La composante hebraïque du judeo-arabe algerien (communautés de Tlemcen et Aïn-Témouchent)*. Jerusalem: Hebrew University, 1992.

Barakat, Saleh M. "Westernization of Levantine Male Clothing." In *Les Européens vus par les libanais à l'époque ottomane*, ed. Bernard Heyberger and Carsten-Michael Walbiner. Beirut: Orient-Institut, 2002, pp. 203–9.

Bardos, Gordon N. "Jihad in the Balkans," *World Affairs*, 177:3 (2014), pp. 73–79.

Barkey, Karen. "Islam and Toleration: Studying the Ottoman Imperial Model," *International Journal of Politics, Culture, and Society*, 19:1/2 (2005), pp. 5–19.

Baron, Beth. *The Women's Awakening in Egypt: Culture, Society, and the Press*. New Haven: Yale University Press, 1994.

Barrett, Roby Carroll. *The Greater Middle East and the Cold War: U.S. Foreign Policy under Eisenhower and Kennedy*. London: I.B. Tauris, 2007.

Bartlett, John. *Bartlett's Familiar Quotations*, gen. ed. Justin Kaplan, seventeenth edition. Boston: Little, Brown, 2002.

Bartov, Omer and Phyllis Mack, eds. *In God's Name: Genocide and Religion in the Twentieth Century*. New York: Berghahn Books, 2001.

Bashkin, Orit. *New Babylonians: A History of Jews in Modern Iraq*. Stanford: Stanford University Press, 2012.

Bat Ye'or [*sic*]. *The Dhimmi: Jews and Christians under Islam*. Rutherford, NJ: Fairleigh Dickinson University Press, 1985.

Baumgart, Winfried. *The Crimean War, 1853–1856*. London: Arnold, 1999.

Bayhan, Nevzet, ed. *The Family Album of Abdülhamid II*. Istanbul: İstanbul Büyükşehir Belediyesi, 2009.

Beidelman, T. O. *Colonial Evangelism: A Socio-Historical Study of an East African Mission at the Grassroots*. Bloomington: Indiana University Press, 1982.

Beinin, Joel. *The Dispersion of Egyptian Jewry: Culture, Politics, and the Formation of a Modern Diaspora*. Berkeley: University of California Press, 1998.

Beken, Münir Nurretin. "Musicians, Audience, and Power: The Changing Aesthetics in the Music at the Makzim Gazino in Istanbul." PhD diss. (Ethnomusicology), University of Maryland (Baltimore), 1998.

Bellamy, Richard. *Citizenship: A Very Short Introduction*. Oxford: Oxford University Press, 2008.

Ben Naeh [*sic*], Yaron. "The Nasi Family, or the Dream of Tiberias." In *A History of Jewish-Muslim Relations from the Origins to the Present Day*, ed. Abdelwahab Meddeb and Benjamin Stora, trans. Jane Marie Todd and Michael B. Smith. Princeton: Princeton University Press, 2013, pp. 220–21.

Ben Na'eh [*sic*], Yaron. "Hebrew Printing Houses in the Ottoman Empire." In *Jewish Journalism and Printing Houses in the Ottoman Empire*, ed. Gad Nassi. Istanbul: Isis Press, 2001, pp. 73–96.

Ben-Naeh [*sic*], Yaron. "Jews on the Move during the Late Ottoman Period: Trends and Some Problems." In *A Global Middle East: Mobility, Materiality, and Culture in the Modern Age, 1880–1940*, ed. Liat Kozma, Cyrus Schayegh, and Avner Wishnitzer. London: I.B. Tauris, 2015, pp. 134–62.

Berkes, Niyazi. *The Development of Secularism in Turkey*. Montreal: McGill University Press, 1964.

Berkey, Jonathan P. *The Formation of Islam: Religion and Society in the Near East, 600–1800*. Cambridge: Cambridge University Press, 2003.

Bernstein, Fred A. "Ertugrul Osman, Link to Ottoman Dynasty, Dies at 97," *New York Times*, September 24, 2009.

Beşikçi, Mehmet. *The Ottoman Mobilization of Manpower in the First World War: Between Voluntarism and Resistance.* Leiden: E.J. Brill, 2012.

Beydoun, Ahmad. "Movements of the Past and Deadlocks of the Present: Did the Violence of the Nineteenth Century Generate a Society Prone to Civil War?" In *Breaking the Cycle: Civil Wars in Lebanon*, ed. Youssef M. Choueri. London: Stacey International, 2007.

Beyer, Peter. *Religions in Global Society.* Abingdon, UK: Routledge, 2006.

Bilgin, Arif. "Refined Tastes in a Refined Palace: Eating Habits of the Ottoman Palace from the 15th-17th Centuries," *Turkish Cultural Foundation: Turkish Cuisine*, www.turkish-cuisine.org/english/article_details.php?p_id=20&Pages=Articles&PagingIndex=6 (accessed June 1, 2012).

Birge, John Kingsley. *The Bektashi Order of Dervishes.* London: Luzac, 1937.

Bisaha, Nancy. *Creating East and West: Renaissance Humanists and the Ottoman Turks.* Philadelphia: University of Pennsylvania Press, 2004.

Bloxham, Donald. *The Great Game of Genocide: Imperialism, Nationalism, and the Destruction of the Ottoman Armenians.* Oxford: Oxford University Press, 2005.

Bocquet, Jérôme. "Le rôle des missions catholiques dans la fondation d'un nouveau réseau d'institutions éducatives au Moyen-Orient arab." In *Le choc colonial et l'islam: les politiques religieuses des puissances coloniales en terres d'islam*, ed. Pierre-Jean Luizard. Paris: La Découverte, 2006, pp. 327–42.

Bocquet, Jérôme, ed. *L'enseignement français en Méditerranée: les missionaires et l'Alliance Israélite Universelle.* Rennes: Presses universitaires de Rennes, 2010.

van den Boogert, Maurits H. *The Capitulations and the Ottoman Legal System: Qadis, Consuls, and Beratlis in the 18th Century.* Leiden: E.J. Brill, 2005.

"Defining Homo Ottomanicus: How the Ottomans Might Have Done It Themselves," n.d. www.academia.edu/1009873/Defining_Homo_Ottomanicu_How_the_Ottomans_might_have_done_it (accessed April 18, 2013).

"Millets: Past and Present." In *Religious Minorities in the Middle East: Domination, Self-Empowerment, Accommodation*, ed. Anh Nga Longva and Anne Sofie Roald. Leiden: E.J. Brill 2012, pp. 27–45.

Booth, Marilyn. *May Her Likes Be Multiplied: Biography and Gender Politics in Egypt.* Berkeley: University of California Press, 2001.

Bostom, M. D. [*sic*], Andrew G. *The Legacy of Jihad: Islamic Holy War and the Fate of Non-Muslims*, foreword by Ibn Warraq. Amherst, NY: Prometheus Books, 2005.

Bourne, Kenneth and D. Cameron Watt, gen. eds. *British Documents on Foreign Affairs: Reports and Papers from the Foreign Office Confidential Print*, Part 1: From the Mid-Nineteenth Century to the First World War. In David Gillard, ed., Series B: The Near and Middle East, 1856–1914, Volume 1: *The Ottoman Empire in the Balkans, 1856–1875.* Lanham: University Publications of America, 1984.

Boyar, Ebru and Kate Fleet. *A Social History of Ottoman Istanbul.* Cambridge: Cambridge University Press, 2010.

Bozarslan, Hamit. "Alevism and the Myths of Research: The Need for a New Research Agenda." In *Turkey's Alevi Enigma: A Comprehensive Overview*, ed. Paul J. White and Joost Jongerden. Leiden: E.J. Brill, 2003, pp. 3–16.

Braude, Benjamin. "Foundation Myths of the *Millet* System." In *Christians and Jews in the Ottoman Empire*, Volume 1, ed. Benjamin Braude and Bernard Lewis. New York: Holmes and Meier, 1982, pp. 69–88.

Braude, Benjamin, ed. *Christians & Jews in the Ottoman Empire*, abridged edition. Boulder: Lynne Rienner, 2014.

Braude, Benjamin and Bernard Lewis, eds. *Christians and Jews in the Ottoman Empire*, 2 volumes. New York: Holmes and Meier, 1982.

Braudel, Fernand. *The Mediterranean and the Age of Philip II*, 2 volumes. New York: Harper, 1972.

Breyfogle, Nicholas B. *Heretics and Colonizers: Forging Russia's Empire in the South Caucasus*. Ithaca: Cornell University Press, 2005.

Brigham Young University, *Global Mormonism Project: Turkey*, http://globalmormonism.byu.edu/?page_id=169 (accessed July 14, 2014).

British and Foreign Bible Society. *The Gospel in Many Tongues: Specimens of 872 Languages in Which the BFBS Has Published or Circulated Some Portion of the Bible*. London: British and Foreign Bible Society, 1965.

Brown, L. Carl, ed. *Imperial Legacy: The Ottoman Imprint on the Balkans and the Middle East*. New York: Columbia University Press, 1996.

Brubaker, Rogers. *Nationalism Reframed: Nationhood and the National Question in the New Europe*. Cambridge: Cambridge University Press, 1996.

Buch-Andersen, Thomas. "Denmark Row: The Power of Cartoons," BBC News, October 3, 2006.

Bulliet, Richard W. *The Case for Islamo-Christian Civilization*. New York: Columbia University Press, 2006.

Conversion to Islam in the Medieval Period: An Essay in Quantitative History. Cambridge, MA: Harvard University Press, 1979.

Bunton, Martin. "Inventing the Status Quo: Ottoman Land-Law during the Palestine Mandate, 1917–1936," *International History Review*, 21:1 (1999), pp. 28–56.

Butler, Richard Urban. "St. Hugh", *The Catholic Encyclopedia*, Volume 7. New York: Robert Appleton, 1910, www.newadvent.org/cathen/07515b.htm (accessed December 4, 2012).

Cahen, Claude. "Dhimma." In *The Encyclopaedia of Islam*, ed. B. Lewis, Ch. Pellat, and J. Schacht, Volume 2, new edition. Leiden: E.J. Brill, 1983, pp. 227–31.

"Djizya" (Part 1). In *The Encyclopaedia of Islam*, ed. B. Lewis, Ch. Pellat, and J. Schacht, Volume 2, new edition. Leiden: E.J. Brill, 1983, pp. 559–62.

Campos, Michelle U. *Ottoman Brothers: Muslims, Christians, and Jews in Twentieth-Century Palestine*. Stanford: Stanford University Press, 2011.

Cardashian, Vahan. *The Ottoman Empire of the Twentieth Century*. New York: J.B. Lyon, 1908.

Çelik, Zeynep. "Defining Empire's Patrimony: Late Ottoman Perceptions of Antiquities." In *Scramble for the Past: A Story of Archaeology in the Ottoman*

Empire, 1753–1914, ed. Zainab Bahrani, Zeynep Çelik, and Edhem Eldem (Istanbul: SALT, 2011), pp. 443–74.

Empire, Architecture, and the City: French-Ottoman Encounters, 1830–1914. Seattle: University of Washington Press, 2008.

Central Intelligence Agency, *The World Factbook*: "Syria" www.cia.gov/library/publications/the-world-factbook/geos/sy.html (accessed February 29, 2016).

Çetinsaya, Gökhan. "Challenges of a Frontier Region: The Case of Ottoman Iraq in the Nineteenth Century." In *The Frontiers of the Ottoman World*, ed. A. C. S. Peacock. Oxford: Oxford University Press, 2009, pp. 283–85.

Chatty, Dawn. *Displacement and Dispossession in the Modern Middle East.* Cambridge: Cambridge University Press, 2010.

Chen, J. C., A. P. Amar, M. L. Levy, and M. L. Apuzzo. "The Development of Anatomic Art and Sciences: The Ceroplastica Anatomical Models of La Specola," *Neurosurgery*, 45:4 (1999), pp. 883–91.

Chocolaterie d'Aiguebelle. "Massacres d'Armenie" and "Guerre Gréco-Turque," parts of two series of collecting cards issued by the firm, c. 1896–98. Rare Book and Manuscript Library, University of Pennsylvania, Philadelphia.

Choksy, Jamsheed K. *Conflict and Cooperation: Zoroastrian Subalterns and Muslim Elites in Medieval Iranian Society.* New York: Columbia University Press, 1997.

"Zoroastrians in Muslim Iran: Selected Problems of Coexistence and Interaction during the Early Medieval Period," *Iranian Studies*, 20:1 (1987), pp. 17–30.

Chouraqui, Jean-Marc. "Les communautés juives face au processus de l'Émancipation: des stratégies centrifuges (1789) au modèle centralisé (1808)," *Rives Nord-méditerranéennes*, 14 (2003), http://rives.revues.org/407 (accessed November 29, 2012).

Chowers, Eyal. *The Political Philosophy of Zionism: Trading Jewish Words for a Hebraic Land.* Cambridge: Cambridge University Press, 2012.

Çizgen, Gültekin. "Abdülhamid and Photography." In *The Family Album of Abdülhamid II*, ed. Nevzat Bayhan. Istanbul: İstanbul Büyükşehir Belediyesi, 2009, pp. 13–20.

Clancy-Smith, Julia C. *Mediterraneans: North Africa and Europe in an Age of Migration, c. 1800–1900.* Berkeley: University of California Press, 2010.

Clasen, Peter (director). *Camondo Han*, DVD. Istanbul, 2005.

Classen, Constance. *Worlds of Sense: Exploring the Senses in History and Across Cultures.* London: Routledge, 1993.

Clay, Christopher. *Gold for the Sultan: Western Bankers and Ottoman Finance, 1856–1881.* London: I.B. Tauris, 2000.

Cobb, Paul M. *The Race for Paradise: An Islamic History of the Crusades.* New York: Oxford University Press, 2014.

Coffey, Heather. "Between Amulet and Devotion: Islamic Miniature Books in the Lilly Library." In *The Islamic Manuscript Tradition: Ten Centuries of Book Arts in Indiana University Collections*, ed. Christiane Gruber. Bloomington: Indiana University Press, 2010, pp. 79–115.

Cohen, Amnon. *Jewish Life under Islam: Jerusalem in the Sixteenth Century.* Cambridge, MA: Harvard University Press, 1984.

Cohen, David. "Algeria." In *The Jews of the Middle East and North Africa in Modern Times*, ed. Reeva Spector Simon, Michael Menachem Laskier, and Sara Reguer. New York: Columbia University Press, 2003, pp. 458–70.

Cohen, Julia Phillips. *Becoming Ottomans: Sephardi Jews and Imperial Citizenship in the Modern Era*. Oxford: Oxford University Press, 2014.

Cohen, Julia Phillips and Sarah Abreyava Stein. *Sephardi Lives: A Documentary History, 1700–1950*. Stanford: Stanford University Press, 2014.

Cohen, Mark R. *Under Crescent and Cross: The Jews in the Middle Ages*. Princeton: Princeton University Press, 2008.

Cohen, Patricia. "Yale Press Bans Images of Muhammad in New Book," *New York Times*, August 12, 2009.

Coller, Ian. *Arab France: Islam and the Making of Modern Europe, 1798–1831*. Berkeley: University of California Press, 2011.

Corbin, Alain. *The Foul and the Fragrant: Order and the French Social Imagination*. Cambridge, MA: Harvard University Press, 1986.

Council of Europe. *Council of Europe in Brief*, www.coe.int/ (accessed January 27, 2010).

Courbage, Youssef and Philippe Fargues. *Christians and Jews under Islam*, trans. Judy Mabro. London: I.B. Tauris, 1998.

Cowan, Brian. *The Social Life of Coffee: The Emergence of the British Coffeehouse*. New Haven: Yale University Press, 2005.

Custodia Terrae Sanctae (Franciscan Missionaries Serving the Holy Land). "'Opening' of Church of the Holy Sepulchre," www.sepulchre.custodia.org/default.asp?id=4127 (accessed April 27, 2016).

Dale, Stephen Frederic. *The Muslim Empires of the Ottomans, Safavids, and Mughals*. Cambridge: Cambridge University Press, 2010.

Darling, Linda T. "Public Finances: The Role of the Ottoman Centre." In *The Cambridge History of Turkey*, ed. Suraiya Faroqhi, Volume 3. Cambridge: Cambridge University Press, 2006, pp. 118–31.

Revenue-Raising and Legitimacy: Tax Collection and Finance Administration in the Ottoman Empire, 1560–1660. Leiden: E.J. Brill, 1996.

Davidson, Alan. *The Oxford Companion to Food*, ed. Tom Jaine, second edition. Oxford: Oxford University Press, 2006.

Davies, Lizzy. "Pope Francis Completes Contentious Canonisation of Otranto Martyrs," *The Guardian*, May 12, 2013.

Davison, Roderic H. "The Effect of the Electric Telegraph on the Conduct of Ottoman Foreign Relations." In *Nineteenth-Century Ottoman Diplomacy and Reforms*, comp. Nur Bilge Criss. Istanbul: Isis Press, 1999, pp. 371–83.

"The Millets as Agents of Change in the Nineteenth-Century Ottoman Empire." In *Christians & Jews in the Ottoman Empire*, abridged edition, ed. Benjamin Braude. Boulder: Lynne Rienner, 2014, pp. 187–207.

"The *Millet*s as Agents of Change in the Nineteenth-Century Ottoman Empire." In *Nineteenth-Century Ottoman Diplomacy and Reforms*, comp. Nur Bilge Criss. Istanbul: Isis Press, 1999, pp. 319–37.

Reform in the Ottoman Empire, 1856–1876. Princeton: Princeton University Press, 1963.

"Turkish Attitudes concerning Christian-Muslim Equality in the Nineteenth Century," *The American Historical Review*, 59:4 (1954), pp. 844–64.

Dawn, C. Ernest. *From Ottomanism to Arabism: Essays on the Origins of Arab Nationalism.* Urbana: University of Illinois Press, 1973.

Decret, François. *Early Christianity in North Africa,* trans. Edward Smither. Eugene, OR: Cascade Books, 2009.

Deguilhelm, Randi. "The Waqf in the City." In *The City in the Islamic World,* ed. Renata Holod, Attilio Petruccioli, and André Raymond, Volume 2. Leiden: E.J. Brill, 2008, pp. 923–50.

Delpal, Bernard. "Les 'chromos' du chocolat: quand le monastère d'Aiguebelle utilisait la 'réclame' pour ses ventes," *Études Drômoises,* 26 (2006), pp. 28–33.

Demirhan, Aysegül and Oztan Oncel. "Development of the Foundations of Quarantine in Turkey in the Nineteenth Century and Its Place in the Public Health [*sic*]," *Journal of the International Society for the History of Islamic Medicine,* 2:4 (2003), pp. 42–44.

Der Matossian, Bedross. *Shattered Dreams of Revolution: From Liberty to Violence in the late Ottoman Empire.* Stanford: Stanford University Press, 2014.

"From Bloodless Revolution to Bloody Counterrevolution: The Adana Massacres of 1909," *Genocide Studies and Prevention,* 6:2 (2011), pp. 152–73.

Deringil, Selim. "'The Armenian Question is Finally Closed': Mass Conversions of Armenians in Anatolia during the Hamidian Massacres of 1895–1897," *Comparative Studies in Society and History,* 51:2 (2009), pp. 344–71.

"Redefining Identities in the Late Ottoman Empire: Policies of Conversion and Apostasy." In *Imperial Rule,* ed. Alexei Miller and Alfred J. Rieber. New York: Central European University Press, 2004, pp. 107–30.

"'There Is No Compulsion in Religion': On Conversion and Apostasy in the Late Ottoman Empire, 1839–1856." In *The Ottomans, the Turks, and World Power Politics: Collected Studies,* ed. Selim Deringil. Istanbul: Isis Press, 2000, pp. 547–75.

The Well-Protected Domains: Ideology and the Legitimation of Power in the Ottoman Empire, 1876–1909. London: I.B. Tauris, 1999.

al-Dhib, Sami. *Khitan al-dhukur wa al-inath, 'inda al-yahud wa al-masihiyyin wa al-muslimin: al-jadal al-dini,* preface by Nawal al-Sa'dawi. Beirut: Riad El-Rayyes Books, 2000.

Doğan, Mehmet Ali. "From New England into New Lands: The Beginning of a Long Story." In *American Missionaries and the Middle East: Foundational Encounters,* ed. Mehmet Ali Doğan and Heather J. Sharkey. Salt Lake City: University of Utah Press, 2011, pp. 3–32.

"Missionary Schools." In *Encyclopedia of the Ottoman Empire,* ed. Gábor Ágoston and Bruce Masters. New York: Facts on File, 2009, pp. 385–89.

Doğan, Mehmet Ali and Heather J. Sharkey, eds. In *American Missionaries and the Middle East: Foundational Encounters.* Salt Lake City: University of Utah Press, 2011.

Donner, Fred M. *Muhammad and the Believers: At the Origins of Islam.* Cambridge, MA: Harvard University Press, 2010.

Duben, Alan and Cem Behar. *Istanbul Households: Marriage, Family, and Fertility, 1880–1940.* Cambridge: Cambridge University Press, 1991.

Dunn, Geoffrey D. *Tertullian.* London: Routledge, 2004.

Dunn, Ross E. *The Adventures of Ibn Battuta, a Muslim Traveler of the Fourteenth Century.* Berkeley: University of California Press, 1986.

Eldem, Edhem. *Death in Istanbul: Death and Its Rituals in Ottoman-Islamic Culture.* Istanbul: Ottoman Bank Archives and Research Centre, 2005.

Elder, Earl E. *Vindicating a Vision: The Story of the American Mission in Egypt, 1854–1954.* Philadelphia: United Presbyterian Board of Foreign Missions, 1958.

Elliot, Matthew. "Dress Codes in the Ottoman Empire: The Case of the Franks." In *Ottoman Costumes: From Textile to Identity*, ed. Suraiya Faroqhi and Christoph K. Neumann. Istanbul: Eren, 2004, pp. 103–23.

el Masri, Iris Habib. *The Story of the Copts.* n.p. [Beirut]: Middle East Council of Churches, 1978.

Elshakry, Marwa. "The Gospel of Science and American Evangelism in Late Ottoman Beirut." In *American Missionaries and the Middle East: Foundational Encounters*, ed. Mehmet Ali Doğan and Heather J. Sharkey. Salt Lake City: University of Utah Press, 2011, pp. 167–210.

Emrence, Cem. *Remapping the Ottoman Middle East: Modernity, Imperial Bureaucracy, and the Islamic State.* London: I.B. Tauris, 2012.

Eraqi-Klorman, Bat-Zion. "Yemen." In *The Jews of the Middle East and North Africa in Modern Times*, ed. Reeva Spector Simon, Michael Menachem Laskier, and Sara Reguer. New York: Columbia University Press, 2003, pp. 389–408.

Erickson, Edward J. "Template for Destruction: The Congress of Berlin and the Evolution of Ottoman Counterinsurgency Practices." In *War and Diplomacy: The Russo-Turkish War of 1877–1878 and the Treaty of Berlin*, ed. M. Hakan Yavuz with Peter Sluglett. Salt Lake City: University of Utah Press, 2011, pp. 351–81.

Ermarth, Elizabeth Deeds. Review of *Centuries' Ends, Narrative Means*, ed. Robert Newman, *History and Theory*, 37:1 (1998), pp. 102–10.

Review of *The Future of History*, by Alun Munslow (review 1220), in *Reviews in History*, March 2012, www.history.ac.uk/reviews/review/1220 (accessed August 11, 2015).

Esposito, John L. *Unholy War: Terror in the Name of Islam.* New York: Oxford University Press, 2003.

Evans-Pritchard, E. E. *The Sanusi of Cyrenaica.* Oxford: Clarendon Press, 1954.

Exertzoglou, Haris. "The Cultural Uses of Consumption: Negotiating Class, Gender, and Nation in the Ottoman Urban Centers during the 19th Century," *International Journal of Middle East Studies*, 35 (2003), pp. 77–101.

Fahmy, Khaled. *All the Pasha's Men: Mehmed Ali, His Army, and the Making of Modern Egypt.* Cambridge: Cambridge University Press, 1997.

Fahmy, Khalid. "The Nation and Its Deserters: Conscription in Mehmed Ali's Egypt." In *Arming the State: Military Conscription in the Middle East and Central Asia, 1775–1925*, ed. Erik J. Zürcher. London: I.B. Tauris, 1999, pp. 59–77.

Farahani, Ramin (director), *Jews of Iran*, DVD. The Netherlands: NIKmedia, 2005.

Farguès, Philippe. "The Arab Christians of the Middle East: A Demographic Perspective." In *Christian Communities in the Arab Middle East: The Challenge of the Future*, ed. Andrea Pacini. Oxford: Clarendon Press, 1998, pp. 48–66.

Faroqhi, Suraiya, ed. *Animals and People in the Ottoman Empire.* Istanbul: Eren, 2010.

The Cambridge History of Turkey, Volume 3: The Later Ottoman Empire, 1603–1839. Cambridge: Cambridge University Press, 2006.

Faroqhi, Suraiya. "Introduction." In *Animals and People in the Ottoman Empire,* ed. Suraiya Faroqhi. Istanbul: Eren, 2010, pp. 11–54.

"Introduction." In *The Illuminated Table, the Prosperous House: Food and Shelter in Ottoman Material Culture,* ed. Suraiya Faroqhi and Christoph K. Neumann. Würzurg: Ergon Verlag Würzburg, 2003, pp. 9–33.

"Introduction, or Why and How One Might Want to Study Ottoman Clothes." In *Ottoman Costumes: From Textile to Identity,* ed. Suraiya Faroqhi and Christoph K. Neumann. Istanbul: Eren, 2004, pp. 15–48.

"Rural Life." In *The Cambridge History of Turkey, Volume 3: The Later Ottoman Empire, 1603–1839,* ed. Suraiya Faroqhi. Cambridge: Cambridge University Press, 2006, pp. 376–90.

Subjects of the Sultan: Culture and Daily Life in the Ottoman Empire, trans. Martin Bott. London: I.B. Tauris, 2007.

Faroqhi, Suraiya and Christoph K. Neumann, eds. *The Illuminated Table, the Prosperous House: Food and Shelter in Ottoman Material Culture.* Würzurg: Ergon Verlag Würzburg, 2003.

Faroqhi, Suraiya, Bruce McGowan, Donald Quataert, and Şevket Pamuk, eds. *An Economic and Social History of the Ottoman Empire, Volume 2, 1600–1914.* Cambridge: Cambridge University Press, 1994.

Fattal, Antoine. *Le statut légal des non-musulmans en pays d'Islam,* second edition. Beirut: Dar El-Machreq Sarl Éditeurs, 1995.

Fawaz, Leila. "The Beirut-Damascus Road: Connecting the Syrian Coast to the Interior in the 19th Century." In *The Syrian Land: Processes of Integration and Fragmentation (Bilad al-Sham from the 18th to the 20th Century),* ed. Thomas Philipp and Birgit Schaebler. Stuttgart: Franz Steiner Verlag, 1998, pp. 19–27.

Fawaz, Leila Tarazi. *Merchants and Migrants in Nineteenth-Century Beirut.* Cambridge, MA: Harvard University Press, 1983.

An Occasion for War: Civil Conflict in Lebanon and Damascus in 1860. London: I.B. Tauris, 1994.

Feiner, Shmuel. *The Jewish Enlightenment,* trans. Chaya Naor. Philadelphia: University of Pennsylvania Press, 2004.

Feldman, Walter. Liner Notes for Lalezar, *Music of the Sultans, Sufis & Seraglio, Volume 3: Minority Composers.* Compact Disk. New York: Traditional Crossroads, 2001.

Music of the Ottoman Court: Makam, Composition, and the Early Ottoman Instrumental Repertoire. Berlin: Verlag für Wissenschaft und Bildung, 1996.

Fetvaci, Emine. "The Art of Osman Hamdi Bey." In *Osman Hamdi Bey and the Americans,* ed. Renata Holod and Robert Ousterhout. Istanbul: Pera Museum, 2011, pp. 118–36.

"Fifty Thousand Orphans Made So by the Turkish Massacres of Armenians," *New York Times,* December 18, 1896.

Findley, Carter Vaughn. *Bureaucratic Reform in the Ottoman Empire: The Sublime Porte, 1789–1922.* Princeton: Princeton University Press, 1980.

The Turks in World History. Oxford: Oxford University Press, 2005.

Firro, Kais M. "The Attitude of the Druzes and 'Alawis vis-à-vis Islam and Nationalism in Syria and Lebanon." In *Syncretistic Religious Communities in the Near East*, ed. Krisztina Kehl-Bodrogi, Barbara Kellner-Heinkele, and Anke Otter-Beaujean. Leiden: E.J. Brill, 1997, pp. 87–99.

A History of the Druzes. Leiden: E.J. Brill, 1992.

Fisk, Robert. "The Never-Ending Exodus of Christians from the Middle East," *The Independent* (London), January 23, 2010.

Fleischmann, Ellen. "I Only Wish I Had a Home on This Globe: Transnational Biography and Dr. Mary Eddy," *Journal of Women's History*, 21:3 (2009), pp. 108–30.

Fleischmann, Ellen L. "Our Moslem Sisters: Women of Greater Syria in the Eyes of American Protestant Missionary Women," *Islam and Christian-Muslim Relations*, 9:3 (1998), pp. 307–23.

Foda, Omar D. "Grand Plans in Glass Bottles: A Social, Economic, and Technical History of Beer in Egypt, 1880–1970." PhD diss., University of Pennsylvania, 2015.

Fortna, Benjamin C. *Imperial Classroom: Islam, the State, and Education in the Late Ottoman Empire*. Oxford: Oxford University Press, 2002.

"The Reign of Abdülhamid II." In *The Cambridge History of Turkey, Volume 4: Turkey in the Modern World*, ed. Reşat Kasaba. Cambridge: Cambridge University Press, 2008, pp. 38–61.

Frankel, Jonathan. *The Damascus Affair: "Ritual Murder," Politics, and the Jews in 1840*. Cambridge: Cambridge University Press, 1997.

Fraser, Nancy. "Rethinking the Public Sphere: A Contribution to the Critique of Actually Existing Democracy." In *Habermas and the Public Sphere*, ed. Craig Calhoun. Cambridge, MA: MIT Press, 1991, pp. 109–42.

Freidenreich, David M. *Foreigners and Their Food: Constructing Otherness in Jewish, Christian, and Islamic Law*. Berkeley: University of California Press, 2011.

Friedmann, Yohanan. *Tolerance and Coercion in Islam: Interfaith Relations in the Muslim Tradition*. Cambridge: Cambridge University Press, 2003.

Frierson, Elizabeth B. "Cheap and Easy: The Creation of a Consumer Culture in Late Ottoman Society." In *Consumption Studies and the History of the Ottoman Empire: An Introduction*, ed. Donald Quataert. Albany: State University of New York Press, 2000, pp. 243–60.

Fuccaro, Nelida. *The Other Kurds: Yazidis in Colonial Iraq*. London: I.B. Tauris, 1999.

Gangloff, Sylvie, ed. *La perception de l'héritage ottoman dans les Balkans*. Paris: L'Harmattan, 2005.

Gavin, Carney E. S. and the Harvard Semitic Museum. *Imperial Self-Portrait: The Ottoman Empire as Revealed in the Sultan Abdul Hamid II's Photographic Albums*. Cambridge, MA: Harvard University Press, 1988.

Geary, Christraud M. and Virginia-Lee Webb. *Delivering Views: Distant Cultures in Early Postcards*. Washington, DC: Smithsonian Institution Press, 1998.

Geertz, Clifford. "Thick Description: Toward an Interpretive Theory of Culture." In *The Interpretation of Cultures: Selected Essays*. New York: Basic Books, 1973, pp. 3–30.

Gelvin, James L. "The 'Politics of Notables' Forty Years After," *Middle East Studies Association Bulletin*, 40:1 (2006), pp. 19–29.

Gencer, Yasemin. "Ibrahim Müteferrika and the Age of the Printed Manuscript." In *The Islamic Manuscript Tradition: Ten Centuries of Book Arts in Indiana University Collections*, ed. Christiane Gruber. Bloomington: Indiana University Press, 2010, pp. 155–93.

Georgeon, François. *Abdülhamid II: Le sultan calife (1876–1909)*. Paris: Libraire Arthème Fayard, 2003.

"Ottomans and Drinkers: The Consumption of Alcohol in Istanbul in the Nineteenth Century." In *Outside In: On the Margins of the Modern Middle East*, ed. Eugene Rogan. London: I.B. Tauris, 2002, pp. 7–30.

"Le Ramadan à Istanbul de l'Empire à la Republique." In *Vivre dans l'Empire Ottoman: Sociabilités et relations intercommunautaires (XVIIIe-XXe siècles)*, ed. François Georgeon and Paul Dumont. Paris: Editions L'Harmattan, 1997, pp. 31–113.

Georgeon, François and Paul Dumont, eds. "Introduction." In *Vivre dans l'Empire Ottoman: Sociabilités et relations intercommunautaires (XVIIIe-XXe siècles)*, ed. François Georgeon and Paul Dumont. Paris: Editions L'Harmattan, 1997, pp. 1–20.

Vivre dans l'Empire Ottoman: Sociabilités et relations intercommunautaires (XVIIIe-XXe siècles), ed. François Georgeon and Paul Dumont. Paris: Editions L'Harmattan, 1997.

Gerber, Jane S. *Jewish Society in Fez, 1450–1700: Studies in Communal and Economic Life*. Leiden: E.J. Brill, 1980.

Gershoni, Israel and James P. Jankowski. *Egypt, Islam, and the Arabs: The Search for Egyptian Nationhood, 1900–1930*. New York: Oxford University Press, 1986.

Ghosh, Amitav. *In an Antique Land*. New York: A.A. Knopf, 1993.

Gidney, W. T. *The History of the London Society for Promoting Christianity amongst the Jews, from 1809 to 1908*. London: London Society for Promoting Christianity amongst the Jews, 1908.

Ginkel, Jan J. van. "The Perception and Presentation of the Arab Conquest in Syriac Historiography: How Did the Changing Social Position of the Syrian Orthodox Community Influence the Account of their Historiographers?." In *The Encounter of Eastern Christianity with Early Islam*, ed. Emmanouela Grypeou, Mark Swanson, and David Thomas. Leiden: E.J. Brill, 2006, pp. 171–84.

Ginio, Eyal. "Mobilizing the Ottoman Nation during the Balkan Wars (1912–1913): Awakening from the Ottoman Dream," *War in History*, 12:2 (2005), pp. 156–77.

Göçek, Fatma Müge. *Denial of Violence: Ottoman Past, Turkish Present, and Collective Violence against the Armenians, 1789–2009*. Oxford: Oxford University Press, 2015.

Goffman, Carolyn. "From Religious to American Proselytism: Mary Mills Patrick and the 'Sanctification of the Intellect'." In *American Missionaries and the Middle East: Foundational Encounters*, ed. Mehmet Ali Doğan and Heather J. Sharkey. Salt Lake City: University of Utah Press, 2011, pp. 84–121.

Goitein, S. D. "Evidence on the Muslim Poll-Tax from Non-Muslim Sources: A Geniza Study," *Journal of the Economic and Social History of the Orient*, 6: 3 (1963), pp. 278–95.

A Mediterranean Society: The Jewish Communities of the Arab World as Portrayed in the Documents of the Cairo Geniza, 6 volumes. Berkeley: University of California Press, 1967–93.

"Minority Self-rule and Government Control in Islam." In *Muslims and Others in Early Islamic Society*, ed. Robert Hoyland. Aldershot, UK: Ashgate, 2004, pp. 159–74.

"The Rise of the Near Eastern Bourgeoisie in Early Islamic Times," *Cahiers d'Histoire Mondiale*, 3:3 (1957), pp. 583–603.

Goldberg, Harvey E. *Jewish Life in Muslim Libya: Rivals & Relatives*. Chicago: University of Chicago Press, 1990.

Goldberg, Harvey E., ed. and trans. *The Book of Mordechai: A Study of the Jews of Libya*. Philadelphia: Institute for the Study of Human Issues, 1980.

Goldberg, Harvey E., ed. *Sephardi and Middle Eastern Jewries: History & Culture in the Modern Era*. Bloomington: Indiana University Press, 1996.

Goldin, Ian, Geoffrey Cameron, and Meera Balarajan. *Exceptional People: How Migration Shaped Our World and Will Define Our Future*. Princeton: Princeton University Press, 2011.

Gottreich, Emily. *The Mellah of Marrakesh: Jewish and Muslim Space in Morocco's Red City*. Bloomington: Indiana University Press, 2007.

Goodwin, Godfrey. *The Janissaries*. London: Saqi Books, 2006.

Goody, Jack. *The Power of the Written Tradition*. Washington, DC: Smithsonian Institution Press, 2000.

Grabar, Oleg. *The Formation of Islamic Art*, revised and enlarged edition. New Haven: Yale University Press, 1987.

Graetz, Michael. *Les Juifs en France au XIXe Siècle: de la Révolution française à l'Alliance Israélite Universelle*, trans. Salomon Malka. Paris: Éditions Seuil, 1989.

Grafton, David D. "A Critical Investigation into the Manuscripts of the 'So-Called' Van Dyck Bible," *Cairo Journal of Theology*, 2 (2015), pp. 56–64.

Piety, Politics, and Power: Lutherans Encountering Islam in the Middle East. Eugene, OR: Wipf and Stock, 2009.

Gran, Peter. *Islamic Roots of Capitalism: Egypt, 1760–1840*, new edition, intro. Afaf Lutfi al-Sayyid Marsot. Syracuse: Syracuse University Press, 1998.

Greene, Molly. "Beyond the Community: Writing the History of the Greeks under Ottoman Rule," paper presented at the Annenberg Seminar in History, University of Pennsylvania, November 16, 2010.

A Shared World: Christians and Muslims in the Early Modern Mediterranean. Princeton: Princeton University Press, 2000.

Grehan, James. *Everyday Life & Consumer Culture in 18th-Century Damascus*. Seattle: University of Washington Press, 2007.

Griffith, Sidney H. *The Church in the Shadow of the Mosque: Christians and Muslims in the World of Islam*. Princeton: Princeton University Press, 2007.

Gruber, Christiane, ed. *The Islamic Manuscript Tradition: Ten Centuries of Book Arts in Indiana University Collections*. Bloomington: Indiana University Press, 2010.

Gruber, Christiane. "A Pious Cure-All: The Ottoman Illustrated Prayer Manual in the Lilly Library." In *The Islamic Manuscript Tradition: Ten Centuries of Book*

Arts in Indiana University Collections, ed. Christiane Gruber. Bloomington: Indiana University Press, 2010, pp. 117–53.

Grypeou, Emmanouela, Mark Swanson, and David Thomas, eds. *The Encounter of Eastern Christianity with Early Islam*. Leiden: E.J. Brill, 2006.

Güsten, Susanne. "Christians Squeezed Out by Violent Struggle in North Syria," *New York Times*, February 13, 2013.

Haeri, Niloofar. *Sacred Language, Ordinary People: Dilemmas of Culture and Politics in Egypt*. New York: Palgrave Macmillan, 2003.

Halevi, Leo. *Muhammad's Grave: Death Rites and the Making of Islamic Society*. New York: Columbia University Press, 2007.

Hall, Isaac H. "The Arabic Bible of Drs. Eli Smith and Cornelius V.A. Van Dyck," *Journal of the American Oriental Society*, 11 (1882–85), pp. 276–86.

Hamdy Bey [*sic*], Osman and Marie de Launay. *Les costumes populaires de la Turquie en 1873: Ouvrage publié sous le patronage de la Commission impériale ottomane pour l'Exposition universelle de Vienne*. Constantinople: Levant Times & Shipping Gazette, 1873.

Hamilton, Alastair. *The Copts and the West, 1439–1822: The European Discovery of an Egyptian Church*. Oxford: Oxford University Press, 2006.

Hamilton, Robert. *Walid and His Friends: An Umayyad Tragedy*. New York: Oxford University Press, 1988.

Hanioğlu, M. Şükrü. *A Brief History of the Late Ottoman Empire*. Princeton: Princeton University Press, 2008.

"The Second Constitutional Period, 1908–1918." In *The Cambridge History of Turkey*, ed. Reşat Kasaba, Volume 4. Cambridge: Cambridge University Press, 2008, pp. 62–111.

Hanley, Will. "Papers for Going, Papers for Staying: Identification and Subject Formation in the Eastern Mediterranean." In *A Global Middle East: Mobility, Materiality, and Culture in the Modern Age, 1880–1940*, ed. Liat Kozma, Cyrus Schayegh, and Avner Wishnitzer. London: I.B. Tauris, 2015, pp. 177–200.

Hanna, Nelly. *Making Big Money in 1600: The Life and Times of Ismail Abu Taqiyya, Egyptian Merchant*. Syracuse: Syracuse University Press, 1998.

In Praise of Books: A Cultural History of Cairo's Middle Class, Sixteenth to Eighteenth Century. Syracuse: Syracuse University Press, 2003.

Hary, Benjamin H. *Multiglossia in Judeo-Arabic*. Leiden: E.J. Brill, 1992.

Hasan, S. S. *Christians versus Muslims in Modern Egypt: The Century-Long Struggle for Coptic Equality*. Oxford: Oxford University Press, 2003.

Hatch, Nathan O. *The Democratization of American Christianity*. New Haven: Yale University Press, 1989.

Hathaway, Jane. *The Arab Lands under Ottoman Rule, 1516–1800*. Harlow, UK: Pearson Education Limited, 2008.

Hattox, Ralph S. *Coffee and Coffeehouses: The Origins of a Social Beverage in the Medieval Near East*. Seattle: University of Washington Press, 1985.

Healy, Jack. "Exodus from North Signals Iraqi Christians' Slow Decline," *New York Times*, March 10, 2012.

Helou, Anissa. *Mediterranean Street Food*. New York: HarperCollins, 2002.

Heyberger, Bernard. *Les chrétiens au Proche-Orient: De la compassion à la compréhension*. Paris: Éditions Payot & Rivages, 2013.

Les Chrétiens du Proche-Orient au temps de la Réforme Catholique (Syrie, Liban, Palestine, XVIIe–XVIIIe siècles). Rome: École Française de Rome, 1994.

"Individualism and Political Modernity: Devout Catholic Women in Aleppo and Lebanon between the Seventeenth and Nineteenth Centuries." In *Beyond the Exotic: Women's Histories in Islamic Societies*, ed. Amira El-Azhary Sonbol. New York: Syracuse University Press, 2005, pp. 71–85.

"Livres et pratique de la lecture chez les chrétiens (Syrie, Liban), XVIIe – XVIIIe siècles," *Revue des Mondes Musulmans et de la Méditerranée*, 87–88 (1999), pp. 209–23.

"Missions catholiques en Syrie à l'époque modern." In *Missions chrétiennes en terre d'islam (XVIIe–XXe siècles): Anthologie de textes missionnaires*, ed. Chantal Verdeil. Turnhout, Belgium: Brepols, 2013, pp. 61–94.

Heyberger, Bernard and Carsten-Michael Walbiner, eds. *Les Européens vus par les libanais à l'époque ottoman*. Beirut: Orient-Institut, 2002.

Hirschon, Renée, ed. *Crossing the Aegean: An Appraisal of the 1923 Compulsory Population Exchange between Greece and Turkey*. London: Berghahn Books, 2003.

Hobsbawm, Eric and Terence Ranger, eds. *The Invention of Tradition*. Cambridge: Cambridge University Press, 1983.

Hodder, Ian. *Entangled: An Archaeology of the Relationship between Humans and Things*. Oxford: Wiley-Blackwell, 2012.

Hodgson, Marshall G. S. *Rethinking World History: Essays on Europe, Islam, and World History*, ed. Edmund Burke, III. Cambridge: Cambridge University Press, 1993.

The Venture of Islam: Conscience and History in a World Civilization, 3 volumes. Chicago: University of Chicago Press, 1974.

Holod, Renata and Robert Ousterhout. "Osman Hamdi Bey and the Americans." In *Osman Hamdi Bey and the Americans*, ed. Renata Holod and Robert Ousterhout. Istanbul: Pera Museum, 2011, pp. 16–35.

Holod, Renata and Robert Ousterhout, eds. *Osman Hamdi Bey and the Americans*. Istanbul: Pera Museum, 2011.

Hourani, Albert. *Arabic Thought in the Liberal Age, 1798–1939*. Cambridge: Cambridge University Press, 1983.

"Ottoman Reform and the Politics of Notables." In *The Modern Middle East*, ed. Albert Hourani, Philip S. Khoury, and Mary C. Wilson. Berkeley: University of California Press, 1993, pp. 83–109.

Hoyland, Robert, ed. *Muslims and Others in Early Islamic Society*. Aldershot, UK: Ashgate, 2004.

Huart, Clément. *A History of Arabic Literature*. New York: D. Appleton, 1915.

Hughes, Heather and Emily Neumeier. "From Istanbul to Philadelphia: The Journey of 'At the Mosque Door'." In *Osman Hamdi Bey and the Americans*, ed. Renata Holod and Robert Ousterhout. Istanbul: Pera Museum, 2011, pp. 102–17.

Huntington, Samuel P. "The Clash of Civilizations?," *Foreign Affairs*, 72:3 (1993), pp. 22–49.

Human Rights Watch, *World Report 2015*, www.hrw.org/world-report/2015 (accessed April 7, 2015).

"Humanitarianism," *Oxford English Dictionary Online*, July 2012.

Hurewitz, J. C. *Diplomacy in the Near and Middle East: A Documentary Record, 1535–1914,* Volume 1. Princeton: D. van Nostrand, 1956.

Hurvitz, Nimrod. "From Scholarly Circles to Mass Movements: The Formation of Legal Communities in Islamic Societies," *American Historical Review,* 108:4 (2003), pp. 985–1008.

Ibn Khaldun. *The Muqaddimah: An Introduction to History,* trans. Franz Rosenthal, abridged and ed. N.J. Dawood. Princeton: Princeton University Press, 1969.

Ibn Sayyar al-Warraq. *Kitab al-tabikh,* ed. Kaj Öhrnberg and Sahban Mroueh, Studia Orientalia 60. Helsinki: Finnish Oriental Society, 1987.

İhsanoğlu, Ekmeleddin. *A Culture of Peaceful Coexistence: Early Islamic and Ottoman Turkish Examples.* Istanbul: Research Centre for Islamic History, Art, and Culture [IRCICA], 2004.

Imber, Colin. *The Ottoman Empire, 1300–1650: The Structure of Power,* second edition. Houndmills, UK: Palgrave Macmillan, 2009.

İnalcık, Halil. "Foundations of Ottoman-Jewish Cooperation." In *Jews, Turks, Ottomans: A Shared History, Fifteenth through the Twentieth Century,* ed. Avigdor Levy. Syracuse: Syracuse University Press, 2002, pp. 3–12.

The Ottoman Empire: The Classical Age, 1300–1600. London: Phoenix, 2000.

"Djizya" (Part 2: Ottoman). In *The Encyclopaedia of Islam,* ed. B. Lewis, Ch. Pellat and J. Schacht, Volume 2, new edition. Leiden: E.J. Brill, 1983, pp. 562–66.

Institute of Muslim Minority Affairs, "Muslim Minority Communities," www.imma.org.uk/plannedvolume.htm (accessed November 21, 2008).

Iraq Body Count, "Documented Civilian Deaths from Violence," www.iraqbodycount.org/ (accessed February 4, 2010, and April 7, 2016).

al-Isfahani, Abu'l-Faraj. *The Book of Strangers: Medieval Arabic Graffiti on the Theme of Nostalgia,* trans. Patricia Crone and Shmuel Moreh. Princeton: Markus Wiener, 2000.

Issawi, Charles. *An Economic History of the Middle East and North Africa.* New York: Columbia University Press, 1982.

The J. Paul Getty Museum, "A Royal Passion: Queen Victoria and Photography," www.getty.edu/art/exhibitions/victoria/ (accessed June 1, 2014).

al-Jabarti, Abd al-Rahman. *Napoleon in Egypt: al-Jabarti's Chronicle of the First Seven Months,* trans. Shmuel Moreh, intro. Robert L. Tignor. Princeton: Markus Wiener, 1993.

Jackson, Maureen. "The Girl in the Tree: Gender, Istanbul Soundscapes, and Synagogue Song," *Jewish Social Studies,* 17:1 (2010), pp. 31–66.

Jacobs, Joseph and Goodman Lipkind. "Arthur Lumley Davids." In *JewishEncyclopedia.com,* 1906 edition, www.jewishencyclopedia.com/articles/4987-davids-arthur-lumley (accessed July 30, 2015).

Jaffin, Léone. *Algérie Aimée: Mes souvenirs et 222 recettes de là-bas!* Paris: Le Courrier du Livre, 2012.

Jamison, Wallace N. *The United Presbyterian Story: A Centennial Study, 1858–1958.* Pittsburgh: Geneva Press, 1958.

Jarrassé, Dominique. "Synagogues in the Islamic World." In *A History of Jewish-Muslim Relations from the Origins to the Present Day,* ed. Abdelwahab

Meddeb and Benjamin Stora, trans. Jane Marie Todd and Michael B. Smith. Princeton: Princeton University Press, 2013, pp. 911–21.

Jenner, Mark S. R. "Follow Your Nose? Smell, Smelling, and Their Histories," *American Historical Review*, 116:2 (2011), pp. 335–51.

Jennings, Ronald C. "Women in Early 17th Century Ottoman Judicial Records: The Sharia Court of Anatolian Kayseri," *Journal of the Economic and Social History of the Orient*, 18:1 (1975), pp. 53–114.

"Zimmis (Non-Muslims) in Early 17th Century Ottoman Judicial Records: The Sharia Court of Anatolian Kayseri," *Journal of the Economic and Social History of the Orient*, 21:3 (1978), pp. 225–93.

Jirousek, Charlotte. "The Transition to Mass Fashion System Dress in the Later Ottoman Empire." In *Consumption Studies and the History of the Ottoman Empire: An Introduction*, ed. Donald Quataert. Albany: State University of New York Press, 2000, pp. 201–41.

Jones, Jonathan. "Jean-Léon Gérôme: Orientalist Fantasy among the Impressionists," *The Guardian*, July 3, 2012.

Joshi, Sanjay. "Thinking about Modernity from the Margins: The Making of a Middle Class in Colonial India." In *The Making of the Middle Class: Toward a Transnational History*, ed. A. Ricardo López and Barbara Weinstein. Durham: Duke University Press, 2012, pp. 29–44.

Juhasz, Esther, ed. *The Jewish Wardrobe: From the Collection of the Israel Museum, Jerusalem*. Jerusalem: Israel Museum, 2012.

Juhasz, Esther. "Material Culture." In *The Jews of the Middle East and North Africa in Modern Times*, ed. Reeva Spector Simon, Michael Menachem Laskier, and Sara Reguer. New York: Columbia University Press, 2003, pp. 205–23.

Sephardi Jews in the Ottoman Empire: Aspects of Material Culture. Jerusalem: Israel Museum, 1990.

Kadı, Ismail Hakkı. "On the Edges of an Ottoman World: Non-Muslim Ottoman Merchants in Amsterdam." In *The Ottoman World*, ed. Christine Woodhead. London: Routledge, 2012, pp. 276–88.

Kafadar, Cemal. *Between Two Worlds: The Construction of the Ottoman State*. Berkeley: University of California Press, 1995.

Kafescioğlu, Çiğdem. *Constantinopolis/Istanbul: Cultural Encounter, Imperial Vision, and the Construction of the Ottoman Capital*. University Park: Pennsylvania State University Press, 2009.

Kark, Ruth and Joseph B. Glass. "Eretz Israel/Palestine, 1800–1948." In *The Jews of the Middle East and North Africa in Modern Times*, ed. Reeva Spector Simon, Michael Menachem Laskier, and Sara Reguer. New York: Columbia University Press, 2003, pp. 335–46.

Karpat, Kemal H. "The Ottoman Emigration to America, 1860–1914," *International Journal of Middle East Studies*, 17:2 (1985), pp. 175–209.

Ottoman Population, 1830–1914: Demographic and Social Characteristics. Madison: University of Wisconsin Press, 1985.

Kasaba, Reşat. *A Moveable Empire: Ottoman Nomads, Migrants, and Refugees*. Seattle: University of Washington Press, 2009.

The Ottoman Empire in the World Economy: The Nineteenth Century. Albany: State University of New York Press, 1988.

The Cambridge History of Turkey, Volume 4: Turkey in the Modern World. Cambridge: Cambridge University Press, 2008.

Katib Çelebi (a.k.a. Mustafa ibn Abd Allah Haji Khalifa). *The History of the Maritime Wars of the Turks,* trans. James Mitchell, Chapters 1–4. London: Oriental Translation Fund, 1831.

Katz, David S. *Philo-Semitism and the Readmission of the Jews to England, 1603–1655.* Oxford: Clarendon Press, 1982.

Kayali, Hasan. *Arabs and Young Turks: Ottomanism, Arabism, and Islamism in the Ottoman Empire.* Berkeley: University of California Press, 1997.

Keddie, Nikki R. "Afgani, Jamal-al-din," *Encyclopædia Iranica,* 1:5 (1983), pp. 481–86.

An Islamic Response to Imperialism: Political and Religious Writings of Sayyid Jamal al-Din al-Afghani. Berkeley: University of California Press, 1983.

Sayyid Jamal al-Din al-Afghani: A Political Biography. Berkeley: University of California Press, 1972.

Kedourie, Elie. *Afghani and 'Abduh: An Essay on Religious Unbelief and Political Activism in Modern Islam.* New York: Humanities Press, 1966.

Kehl-Bodrogi, Krisztina. "Introduction." In *Syncretistic Religious Communities in the Near East,* ed. Krisztina Kehl-Bodrogi, Barbara Kellner-Heinkele, and Anke Otter-Beaujean. Leiden: E.J. Brill, 1997, pp. xi–xvii.

Kehl-Bodrogi, Krisztina, Barbara Kellner-Heinkele, and Anke Otter-Beaujean, eds. *Syncretistic Religious Communities in the Near East.* Leiden: E.J. Brill, 1997.

Kennedy, Hugh. *The Great Arab Conquests: How the Spread of Islam Changed the World We Live In.* Philadelphia: Da Capo Press, 2007.

Kennedy, Philip F. *Abu Nuwas: A Genius of Poetry.* Oxford: Oneworld, 2005.

Kepel, Gilles. *Jihad: The Trail of Political Islam.* London: I.B. Tauris, 2002.

Kern, Karen M. *Imperial Citizenship: Marriage and Citizenship in the Ottoman Frontier Provinces of Iraq.* Syracuse: Syracuse University Press, 2011.

"'They Are Not Known to Us': The Ottomans, the Mormons, and the Protestants in the Late Ottoman Empire." In *American Missionaries and the Middle East: Foundational Encounters,* ed. Mehmet Ali Doğan and Heather J. Sharkey. Salt Lake City: University of Utah Press, 2011, pp. 122–63.

Kern, Karen M. "Rethinking Ottoman Frontier Policies: Marriage and Citizenship in the Province of Iraq," *Arab Studies Journal,* 25:1 (2007), pp. 8–29.

Kertzer, David I. *The Kidnapping of Edgardo Mortara.* New York: Alfred Knopf, 1997.

Khater, Akram Fouad. *Inventing Home: Emigration, Gender, and the Middle Class in Lebanon, 1870–1920.* Berkeley: University of California Press, 2001.

Khuri-Makdisi, Ilham. *The Eastern Mediterranean and the Making of Global Radicalism, 1860–1914.* Berkeley: University of California Press, 2010.

Kia, Mehrdad. *Daily Life in the Ottoman Empire.* Santa Barbara: Greenwood, 2011.

Kieser, Hans-Lukas. "Missionaires américaines en terre ottomane (Anatolie)." In *Missions chrétiennes en terre d'islam (XVIIe-XXe siècles): Anthologie de textes missionnaires,* ed. Chantal Verdeil. Turnhout, Belgium: Brepols, 2013, pp. 94–126.

Nearest East: American Millennialism and Mission to the Middle East.
Philadelphia: Temple University Press, 2010.

Kister, M. J. "The Massacre of the Banu Qurayza: A Re-Examination of a Tradition," *Jerusalem Studies in Arabic and Islam*, 8 (1986), pp. 61–96.

Klein, Janet. *The Margins of Empire: Kurdish Militias in the Ottoman Tribal Zone.* Stanford: Stanford University Press, 2011.

Kolodziejczyk, Darius. "Polish Embassies in Istanbul, or How to Sponge on Your Host without Losing Your Self-Esteem." In *The Illuminated Table, the Prosperous House: Food and Shelter in Ottoman Material Culture*, ed. Suraiya Faroqhi and Christoph K. Neumann. Würzburg: Ergon Verlag Würzburg, 2003, pp. 51–58.

Kozma, Liat, Cyrus Schayegh, and Avner Wishnitzer, eds. *A Global Middle East: Mobility, Materiality, and Culture in the Modern Age, 1880–1940.* London: I.B. Tauris, 2015.

Klausen, Jytte. *The Cartoons That Shook the World.* New Haven: Yale University Press, 2009.

Krämer, Gudrun. *The Jews in Modern Egypt, 1914–1952.* London: I.B. Tauris, 1989.

"Moving Out of Place: Minorities in Middle Eastern Urban Societies, 1800–1914." In *The Urban Social History of the Middle East, 1750–1950*, ed. Peter Sluglett. Syracuse: Syracuse University Press, 2008, pp. 182–223.

Krstic, Tijana. *Contested Conversions to Islam: Narratives of Religious Change in the Early Modern Ottoman Empire.* Stanford: Stanford University Press, 2011.

Kuklick, Bruce. *Puritans in Babylon: The Ancient Near East and American Intellectual Life, 1880–1930.* Princeton: Princeton University Press, 1996.

Kupferschmidt, Uri M. "On the Diffusion of 'Small' Western Technologies and Consumer Goods in the Middle East during the Era of the First Modern Globalization." In *A Global Middle East: Mobility, Materiality, and Culture in the Modern Age, 1880–1940*, ed. Liat Kozma, Cyrus Schayegh, and Avner Wishnitzer. London: I.B. Tauris, 2015, pp. 229–60.

Kuran, Timur and Scott Lustig. "Judicial Biases in Ottoman Istanbul: Islamic Justice and Its Compatibility with Modern Economic Life," *Journal of Law and Economics*, 55:3 (2012), pp. 631–66.

Lalezar. *Music of the Sultans, Sufis & Seraglio, Volume 3: Minority Composers.* Compact Disk. New York: Traditional Crossroads, 2001.

Lamdan, Ruth. *A Separate People: Jewish Women in Palestine, Syria and Egypt in the Sixteenth Century.* Leiden: E.J. Brill, 2000.

Landau, Jacob M. "Changing Patterns of Community Structures, with Special Reference to Ottoman Egypt." In *Jews, Turks, Ottomans: A Shared History, Fifteenth through the Twentieth Century*, ed. Avigdor Levy. Syracuse: Syracuse University Press, 2002, pp. 77–87.

Landau, Paul. "Islamic 'Reformism' and Jihad: On the Discourse of Tariq Ramadan," *Transatlantic Intelligencer* (2005), www.trans-int.com/wordpress/index.php/islamic-"reformism"-and-jihad-on-the-discourse-of-tariq-ramadan/ (accessed August 12, 2014).

Lane, Edward William. *An Account of the Manners and Customs of the Modern Egyptians*, ed. Edward Stanley Poole, fifth edition. London: John Murray, 1860.

Langner, Joachim. "Religion in Motion and the Essence of Islam: Manifestations of the Global in Muhammad 'Abduh's Response to Farah Antun." In *A Global Middle East: Mobility, Materiality, and Culture in the Modern Age, 1880–1940*, ed. Liat Kozma, Cyrus Schayegh, and Avner Wishnitzer. London: I.B. Tauris, 2015, pp. 356–64.

Lansing, Gulian. *Egypt's Princes: A Narrative of Missionary Labor in the Valley of the Nile*, second edition. Philadelphia: William S. Rentoul, 1864.

Lapidus, Ira M. "The Conversion of Egypt to Islam," *Israel Oriental Studies*, 2 (1972), pp. 248–62.

Laqueur, Walter. *The Changing Face of Antisemitism: From Ancient Times to the Present Day*. Oxford: Oxford University Press, 2006.

Laskier, Michael Menachem. *The Alliance Israélite Universelle and the Jewish Communities of Morocco, 1862–1962*. Albany: State University of New York Press, 1983.

"Syria and Lebanon." In *The Jews of the Middle East and North Africa in Modern Times*, ed. Reeva Spector Simon, Michael Menachem Laskier, and Sara Reguer. New York: Columbia University Press, 2003, pp. 316–34.

Laurens, Henry. "La projection chrétienne de l'Europe industrielle sur les provinces arabes de l'Empire ottoman." In *Le choc colonial et l'islam: les politiques religieuses des puissances coloniales en terres d'islam*, ed. Pierre-Jean Luizard. Paris: La Découverte, 2006, pp. 39–55.

Lauzière, Henri. *The Making of Salafism: Islamic Reform in the Twentieth Century*. New York: Columbia University Press, 2016.

League of Nations. *The Covenant of the League of Nations* (including amendments adopted to December 1924), http://avalon.law.yale.edu/20th_century/leagcov.asp (accessed March 29, 2016).

Leeming, David. *The Oxford Companion to World Mythology*. Oxford: Oxford University Press, 2005.

Lemke, Wolf-Dieter. *Staging the Orient: Fin de Siècle Popular Visions*. Beirut: Éditions Dar An-Nahar, 2004.

Levy, Avigdor, ed. *Jews, Turks, Ottomans: A Shared History, Fifteenth through the Twentieth Century*. Syracuse: Syracuse University Press, 2002.

Levy-Rubin, Milka. *Non-Muslims in the Early Islamic Empire: From Surrender to Coexistence*. Cambridge: Cambridge University Press, 2011.

Lewicka, Paulina B. *Food and Foodways of the Medieval Cairenes: Aspects of Life in an Islamic Metropolis of the Eastern Mediterranean*. Leiden: E.J. Brill, 2011.

Lewis, Bernard. *The Crisis of Islam: Holy war and Unholy Terror*. New York: Modern Library, 2003.

The Emergence of Modern Turkey, third edition. New York: Oxford University Press, 2002.

"Europe and Islam," The Tanner Lectures on Human Values, Delivered at Brasenose College, Oxford University, February 26, March 5, and March 12, 1990, http://tannerlectures.utah.edu/_documents/a-to-z/l/Lewis98.pdf (accessed April 8, 2016).

The Jews of Islam. Princeton: Princeton University Press, 1984.

The Muslim Discovery of Europe. New York: W.W. Norton, 1982.

Race and Slavery in the Middle East: An Historical Enquiry. Oxford: Oxford University Press, 1990.

"The Tanzimat and Social Equality." In *Économie de Sociétés dans l'Empire Ottoman (Fin du XVIIIe – Début du XXe siècle): Actes du colloque de Strasbourg (1er – 5 juillet 1980)*, ed. Jean-Louis Bacqué-Grammont and Paul Dumont. Paris: Éditions du Centre National de la Recherche Scientifique (CNRS), 1983, pp. 47–54.

Lewis, Bernard, ed. and trans. *Islam from the Prophet Muhammad to the Capture of Constantinople*, 2 volumes. New York: Oxford University Press, 1987.

Lia, Brynjar. *The Society of the Muslim Brothers in Egypt: The Rise of an Islamic Mass Movement, 1928–1942*, foreword by Jamal al-Banna. Reading, UK: Ithaca Press, 1998.

Likhovski, Assaf. "The Ottoman Legacy of Israeli Law," *Annales de la Faculté de Droit d'Istanbul*, 39 (2007), pp. 71–86.

Littell, Eliakim, ed. *Littell's Living Age*, Fifth Series, Volume 23, July, August, September 1878. Boston: Littell and Gay, 1878.

Lockman, Zachary. *Contending Visions of the Middle East: The History and Politics of Orientalism.* Cambridge: Cambridge University Press, 2004.

Loeb, Laurence D. "Gender, Marriage, and Social Conflict in Habban." In *Sephardi and Middle Eastern Jewries: History & Culture in the Modern Era*, ed. Harvey E. Goldberg. Bloomington: Indiana University Press, 1996, pp. 259–76.

Longva, Anh Nga. "From the *Dhimma* to the Capitulations: Memory and Experience of Protection in Lebanon." In *Religious Minorities in the Middle East: Domination, Self-Empowerment, Accommodation*, ed. Anh Nga Longva and Anne Sofie Roald. Leiden: E.J. Brill, 2012, pp. 47–69.

López, A. Ricardo and Barbara Weinstein, eds. *The Making of the Middle Class: Toward a Transnational History*. Durham: Duke University Press, 2012.

Lucassen, Jan and Erik Jan Zürcher. "Introduction: Conscription and Resistance: The Historical Context." In *Arming the State: Military Conscription in the Middle East and Central Asia, 1775–1925*, ed. Erik J. Zürcher. London: I.B. Tauris, 1999, pp. 1–20.

Luizard, Pierre-Jean. *Le choc colonial et l'islam: les politiques religieuses des puissances coloniales en terres d'islam*. Paris: La Découverte, 2006.

Maalouf, Amin. *The Crusades through Arab Eyes*, trans. Jon Rothschild. New York: Schocken Books, 1984.

Macdonald, Helen. *Human Remains: Dissection and Its Histories*. New Haven: Yale University Press, 2005.

Mack, Rosamond E. *Bazaar to Piazza: Islamic Trade and Italian Art, 1300–1600*. Berkeley: University of California Press, 2002.

Makdisi, Ussama. "AHR Conversation: Religious Identities and Violence," *American Historical Review*, 112:5 (2007), pp. 1437–38.
  Artillery of Heaven: American Missionaries and the Failed Conversion of the Middle East. Ithaca: Cornell University Press, 2009.
  The Culture of Sectarianism: Community, History, and Violence in Nineteenth-Century Ottoman Lebanon. Berkeley: University of California Press, 2000.

Makdisi, George. *History and Politics in Eleventh-Century Baghdad*. Aldershot, UK: Variorum, 1990.

Makdisi, Ussama. "Ottoman Orientalism," *The American Historical Review*, 107:3 (2002), pp. 768–96.

Mann, Gregory. "What Was the *Indigénat*? The 'Empire of Law' in French West Africa," *Journal of African History*, 50 (2009), pp. 331–53.

Mann, Michael. *The Sources of Social Power, Volume 1: A History of Power from the Beginning to A.D. 1760*. Cambridge: Cambridge University Press, 1986.

Mansel, Philip. *Dressed to Rule: Royal and Court Costume from Louis XIV to Elizabeth II*. New Haven: Yale University Press, 2005.

Ma'oz, Moshe. "Changing Relations between Jews, Muslims, and Christians during the Nineteenth Century, with Special Reference to Ottoman Syria and Palestine." In *Jews, Turks, Ottomans: A Shared History, Fifteenth through the Twentieth Century*, ed. Avigdor Levy. Syracuse: Syracuse University Press, 2002, pp. 108–18.

"Mark Twain Signed Photo by Abdullah Frères in Constantinople," Shapell Manuscript Foundation, www.shapell.org/manuscript.aspx?mark-twain-signed-photo-from-constantinople (accessed June 2, 2014).

Marcus, Abraham. *The Middle East on the Eve of Modernity: Aleppo in the Eighteenth Century*. New York: Columbia University Press, 1989.

"Une Marocaine en burqa se voit refuser la nationalité française," *Le Monde* (Paris), July 11, 2008.

Marten, Michael. *Attempting to Bring the Gospel Home: Scottish Missions to Palestine, 1839–1917*. London: Tauris Academic Studies, 2006.

Marzio, Peter C. *The Democratic Art: Pictures for a 19th-Century America: Chromolithography, 1840–1900*. Boston: D.R. Godine, 1979.

Marzouki, Nadia and Olivier Roy, eds., *Religious Conversions in the Mediterranean World*. Houndmills, UK: Palgrave Macmillan, 2013.

Masters, Bruce. "The 1850 Events in Aleppo: An Aftershock of Syria's Incorporation into the Capitalist World System," *International Journal of Middle East Studies*, 22 (1990), pp. 3–20.

The Arabs of the Ottoman Empire, 1516–1918: A Social and Cultural History. Cambridge: Cambridge University Press, 2013.

Christians and Jews in the Ottoman Arab World: The Roots of Sectarianism. Cambridge: Cambridge University Press, 2001.

"Christians in a Changing World." In *The Cambridge History of Turkey, Volume 3: The Later Ottoman Empire, 1603–1839*, ed. Suraiya N. Faroqhi. Cambridge: Cambridge University Press, 2006, pp. 272–79.

"Missionaries." In *Encyclopedia of the Ottoman Empire*, ed. Gábor Ágoston and Bruce Masters. New York: Facts on File, 2009, pp. 384–85.

Matthee, Rudolph P. *The Politics of Trade in Safavid Iran: Silk for Silver, 1600–1730*. Cambridge: Cambridge University Press, 1999.

Mavrogordatos, George Th. "Orthodoxy and Nationalism in the Greek Case," *West European Politics*, 26:1 (2003), pp. 117–36.

Mayer, Ann Elizabeth. *Islam and Human Rights*, fifth edition. Boulder: Westview Press, 2013.

Mayer, Arno J. "The Perils of Emancipation: Protestants and Jews," *Archives des sciences sociales des religions*, 90 (1995), pp. 5–37.

Mayeur-Jaouen, Catherine. "The Renaissance of Churches at the End of the Ottoman Era (Excluding Egypt) in the 18th and 19th Centuries." In

Christianity: A History in the Middle East, ed. Habib Badr, Suad Abou el Rouss Slim, and Joseph Abou Nohra. Beirut: Middle East Council of Churches, 2005, pp. 757–73.

Mazower, Mark. *Salonica, City of Ghosts: Christians, Muslims, and Jews, 1430–1950*. New York: Alfred A. Knopf, 2005.

McCarthy, Justin. *The Ottoman Peoples and the End of Empire*. New York: Oxford University Press, 2001.

McCullagh, Francis. "What Was Found in the Lair of Abdul Hamid: Amazing Discoveries in the Yildiz Kiosk Following the Fall of Turkey's Sultan Reveal a Condition Surpassing Fiction," *New York Times*, June 6, 1909, Magazine Section, p. SM3.

McLuhan, Marshall. *The Gutenberg Galaxy: The Making of Typographic Man*. Toronto: University of Toronto Press, 1962.

Meddeb, Abdelwahab. "Introduction: Parallel Memories." In *A History of Jewish-Muslim Relations from the Origins to the Present Day*, ed. Abdelwahab Meddeb and Benjamin Stora, trans. Jane Marie Todd and Michael B. Smith. Princeton: Princeton University Press, 2013, pp. 13–14.

Meddeb, Abdelwahab and Benjamin Stora, ed. *A History of Jewish-Muslim Relations from the Origins to the Present Day*. Trans. Jane Marie Todd and Michael B. Smith. Princeton: Princeton University Press, 2013.

Meghnagi, Miriam. *Dialoghi Mediterranei*. Compact Disc. Rome, 2004.

Menocal, María Rosa. *The Ornament of the World: How Muslims, Jews, and Christians Created a Culture of Tolerance in Medieval Spain*. Boston: Little, Brown, 2002.

Micklewright, Nancy. "Womens' Dress in Nineteenth-Century Istanbul: Mirror of a Changing Society," PhD diss., University of Pennsylvania, 1986.

Midhat Bey, Ali Haydar. *The Life of Midhat Pasha: A Record of His Services, Political Reforms, Banishment, and Judicial Murder, Derived from Private Documents and Reminiscences by His Son Ali Haydar Midhat Bey*. London: John Murray, 1903.

Miller, Daniel E. *Stuff*. Cambridge, MA: Polity Press, 2010.

Miller, Donald E. and Lorna Touryan Miller. *Survivors: An Oral History of the Armenian Genocide*. Berkeley: University of California Press, 1993.

Mills, John. "The Coming of the Carpet to the West." In *The Eastern Carpet in the Western World: From the 15th to the 17th Century*, ed. Donald King and David Sylvester. London: Arts Council of Great Britain, 1983, pp. 11–23.

Mitchell, Richard P. *The Society of the Muslim Brothers*. New York: Oxford University Press, 1993.

Modelski, Sylvia. *Port Said Revisited*. Washington, DC: Faros, 2000.

Moreen, Vera B. "The Problems of Conversion among Iranian Jews in the Seventeenth and Eighteenth Centuries," *Iranian Studies*, 19:3/4 (1986), pp. 215–28.

Morony, Michael G. "The Age of Conversions: A Reassessment." In *Conversion and Continuity: Indigenous Christian Communities in Islamic Lands, Eighth to Eighteenth Centuries*, ed. Michael Gervers and Ramzi Jibran Bikhazi. Toronto: University of Toronto Press, 1990, pp. 135–50.

Moulin, Anne Marie. "The Construction of Disease Transmission in Nineteenth-Century Egypt and the Dialectics of Modernity." In *The Development of*

Modern Medicine in Non-Western Countries: Historical Perspectives, ed. Hormoz Ebrahimnejad. London: Routledge, 2009, pp. 42–58.

Muller-Lancet, Aviva. *Garments with a Message: Ethnography of Jewish Wear in Islamic Lands*. Jerusalem: Ben-Zvi Institute for the Study of Jewish Communities in the East, 2010.

Murre-van den Berg, Heleen. "Nineteenth-Century Protestant Missions and Middle Eastern Women: An Overview." In *Gender, Religion and Change in the Middle East: Two Hundred Years of History*, ed. Inger Marie Okkenhaug and Ingvild Flaskerud. Oxford: Berg, 2005, pp. 103–22.

Murre-van den Berg, H. K. *From a Spoken to a Written Language: The Introduction and Development of Literary Urmia Aramaic in the Nineteenth Century*. Leiden: Nederlands Instituut voor het Nabije Oosten, 1999.

Musée d'Histoire d'Art et d'Histoire du Judaisme. *Juifs d'Algérie*. Paris: Skira Flammarion, 2012.

Mustapha, Jennifer. "The Mujahideen in Bosnia: The Foreign Figure as Cosmopolitan Citizen and/or Terrorist," *Citizenship Studies*, 17:6/7 (2013), pp. 742–55.

al-Muwaylihi, Ibrahim. *Spies, Scandals, and Sultans: Istanbul in the Twilight of the Ottoman Empire*, trans. Roger Allen. London: Rowman & Littlefield, 2008.

Nadler, Steven and T. M. Rudavsky, eds. "Introduction." In *The Cambridge History of Jewish Philosophy, Volume 1: From Antiquity through the Seventeenth Century*. Cambridge: Cambridge University Press, 2008, pp. 1–16.

Naguib, Nefissa. "The Fragile Tale of Egyptian Jewish Cuisine: Food Memoirs of Claudia Roden and Colette Rossant," *Food & Foodways*, 14 (2006), pp. 35–53.

Nakash, Yitzhak. *The Shi'is of Iraq*. Princeton: Princeton University Press, 1994.

Nasr, Seyyed Hossein. *Islam: Religion, History, and Civilization*. San Francisco: HarperSanFrancisco, 2003.

Nasrallah, Nawal, ed. and trans. *Annals of the Caliph's Kitchens: Ibn Sayyar al-Warraq's Tenth-Century Baghdadi Cookbook*. Leiden: E.J. Brill, 2007.

Nathan, Joan. "The Legacy of Egyptian Rose, in Time for Passover," *New York Times*, March 20, 2002.

National Commission on Terrorist Attacks upon the United States, *The 9/11 Commission Report*. Washington, DC: Government Printing Office, 2004.

Neumann, Christoph K. "Spices in the Ottoman Palace: Courtly Cookery in the Eighteenth Century." In *The Illuminated Table, the Prosperous House: Food and Shelter in Ottoman Material Culture*, ed. Suraiya Faroqhi and Christoph K. Neumann. Würzurg: Ergon Verlag Würzburg, 2003, pp. 127–60.

New Revised Standard Version Bible. New York: National Council of Churches, 1989.

Nini, Yehuda. *The Jews of the Yemen, 1800–1914*, trans. H. Galai. Chur, Switzerland: Harwood Academic, 1991.

Nongbri, Brent. *Before Religion: A History of a Modern Concept*. New Haven: Yale University Press, 2013.

Oddbjørn, Leirvik. *Human Conscience and Muslim-Christian Relations: Modern Egyptian Thinkers on al-Damir*. London: Routledge, 2007.

Ó Gráda, Cormac. *Eating People Is Wrong, and Other Essays on Famine, Its Past, and Its Future*. Princeton: Princeton University Press, 2015.

Ortaylı, Ilber. "Les groupes hétérodoxes et l'administration ottoman." In *Syncretistic Religious Communities in the Near East*, ed. Krisztina Kehl-Bodrogi, Barbara Kellner-Heinkele, and Anke Otter-Beaujean. Leiden: E.J. Brill, 1997, pp. 205–11.

Orwell, George. *Nineteen Eighty-Four*. London: Secker & Warburg, 1949.

Osman Hamdi Bey and de Launay, Marie. *Les costumes populaires de Turquie en 1873*. Constantinople [*sic*]: Impr. du "Levant Times & Shipping Gazette," 1873.

Özkan, Behlül. *From the Abode of Islam to the Turkish Vatan: The Making of a National Homeland in Turkey*. New Haven: Yale University Press, 2012.

Pagden, Anthony, ed. *The Idea of Europe: From Antiquity to the European Union*. Cambridge: Cambridge University Press, 2002.

Pamuk, Şevket. *The Ottoman Empire and European Capitalism, 1820–1913*. Cambridge: Cambridge University Press, 1987.

Parfitt, Tudor. *The Road to Redemption: The Jews of the Yemen, 1900–1950*. Leiden: E.J. Brill, 1996.

"Partial Transcript of Pakistan President Musharraf's Televised Speech Asking the People of Pakistan to Support His Course of Action," *The Washington Post*, September 19, 2001, www.washingtonpost.com/wp-srv/nation/specials/attacked/transcripts/pakistantext_091901.html (accessed June 1, 2011).

Payaslian, Simon. *The History of Armenia*. New York: Palgrave Macmillan, 2007.

Peacock, A. C. S. "Introduction: The Ottoman Empire and Its Frontiers." In *The Frontiers of the Ottoman World*, ed. A. C. S. Peacock. Oxford: Oxford University Press, 2009, pp. 1–27.

Peacock, A. C. S., ed. *The Frontiers of the Ottoman World*. Proceedings of the British Academy, No. 156. Oxford: Oxford University Press, 2009.

Peirce, Leslie P. *The Imperial Harem: Women and Sovereignty in the Ottoman Empire*. New York: Oxford University Press, 1993.

Penn Archives (University of Pennsylvania) Museum of Archaeology and Anthropology, Photochrome Collection Box S-28.

Peters, Rudolph. *Crime and Punishment in Islamic Law: Theory and Practice from the Sixteenth to the Twenty-First Century*. Cambridge: Cambridge University Press, 2006.

Petersen, Andrew. "The Ottoman Conquest of Arabia and the Syrian Hajj Route." In *The Frontiers of the Ottoman World*, ed. A. C. S. Peacock. Oxford: Oxford University Press, 2009, pp. 81–94.

Philips, H. E. *Blessed Be Egypt My People: Life Studies from the Land of the Nile*. Philadelphia: Judson Press, 1953.

Philipp, Thomas. *Ġurği Zaidan, His Life and Thought*. Wiesbaden: Steiner, 1979.

Philliou, Christine M. *Biography of an Empire: Governing Ottomans in an Age of Revolution*. Berkeley: University of California Press, 2011.

Pinon, Pierre. "The Ottoman Cities of the Balkans." In *The City in the Islamic World*, ed. Salma K. Jayyusi, Renata Holod, Attilio Petruccioli, and André Raymond, Volume 1. Leiden: E.J. Brill, 2008, pp. 143–58.

Pitarakis, Brigitte and Christos Merantzas. *A Treasured Memory: Ecclesiastical Silver from Late Ottoman Istanbul in the Sevgi Gönül Collection*. Istanbul: Sadberk Hanım Museum, 2006.

Bibliography

351

Plunkett, John. *Queen Victoria: First Media Monarch*. New York: Oxford University Press, 2003.

Porter, Roy. "Foreword." In Alain Corbin, *The Foul and the Fragrant: Order and the French Social Imagination*. Cambridge, MA: Harvard University Press, 1986, pp. v–vii.

Powell, Eve Troutt. *Tell This in My Memory: Stories of Enslavement from Egypt, Sudan, and the Ottoman Empire*. Stanford: Stanford University Press, 2012.

Public Broadcasting Service (PBS). "Osama bin Ladin vs. the U.S.: Edicts and Statements," *Frontline*, www.pbs.org/wgbh/pages/frontline/shows/binladen/who/edicts.html (accessed March 11, 2013).

Ramadan, Tariq. *Western Muslims and the Future of Islam*. New York: Oxford University Press, 2004.

Robinson, Ronald and John Gallagher. *Africa and the Victorians: The Climax of Imperialism*. New York: Anchor Books, 1968.

Ryad, Umar. *Islamic Reformism and Christianity: A Critical Reading of the Works of Muhammad Rashid Rida and His Associates (1898–1935)*. Leiden: E.J. Brill, 2009.

Qattan, Najwa al-. See al-Qattan and al-Qattan.

Quartzsite, Arizona, "Hi Jolly Cemetery," http://ci.quartzsite.az.us/index.php/2013-01-08-06-33-10/hi-jolly-cemetary-2 (accessed July 13, 2014).

Quataert, Donald. "The Age of Reforms, 1812–1914." In *An Economic and Social History of the Ottoman Empire, Volume 2: 1600–1914*, ed. Suraiya Faroqhi, Bruce McGowan, Donald Quataert, and Şevket Pamuk. Cambridge: Cambridge University Press, 1994, pp. 759–943.

"Clothing Laws, State, and Society in the Ottoman Empire, 1720–1829," *International Journal of Middle East Studies*, 29 (1997), pp. 403–25.

"Introduction." In *Consumption Studies and the History of the Ottoman Empire: An Introduction*, ed. Donald Quataert. Albany: State University of New York Press, 2000, pp. 1–13.

The Ottoman Empire, 1700–1922. Cambridge: Cambridge University Press, 2000.

Quataert, Donald, ed. *Consumption Studies and the History of the Ottoman Empire: An Introduction*. Albany: State University of New York Press, 2000.

Rafeq, Abdel-Karim. "Public Morality in 18th Century Ottoman Damascus," *Revue du monde musulman et de la Méditerranée*, 55:1 (1990), pp. 180–96.

Rafeq, Abdul-Karim. "Craft Organization, Work Ethics, and the Strain of Change in Ottoman Syria," *Journal of the American Oriental Society*, 111:3 (1991), pp. 495–511.

Raymond, André. "The Management of the City." In *The City in the Islamic World*, ed. Renata Holod, Attilio Petruccioli, and André Raymond, Volume 2. Leiden: E.J. Brill, 2008, pp. 775–93.

Reeves-Ellington, Barbara. "Petko Slaveykov, the Protestant Press, and the Gendered Language of Moral Reform in Bulgarian Nationalism." In *American Missionaries and the Middle East: Foundational Encounters*, ed. Mehmet Ali Doğan and Heather J. Sharkey. Salt Lake City: University of Utah Press, 2011, pp. 211–36.

Reid, Donald Malcolm. *Whose Pharaohs? Archaeology, Museums, and Egyptian National Identity from Napoleon to World War I.* Berkeley: University of California Press, 2002.

Reinarz, Jonathan. *Past Scents: Historical Perspectives on Smell.* Urbana: University of Illinois Press, 2014.

Reinkowski, Maurus. "Hidden Believers, Hidden Apostates: The Phenomenon of Crypto-Jews and Crypto-Christians in the Middle East." In *Converting Cultures: Religion, Ideology and Transformations of Modernity,* ed. Dennis Washburn and A. Kevin Reinhart. Leiden: E.J. Brill, 2007, pp. 409–33.

Renauld, Georges. *Adolphe Crémieux, Homme d'État Français, Juif, et Franc-maçon: Le combat pour le République.* Paris: Detrad, 2002.

Reynolds, Michael A. *Shattering Empires: The Clash and Collapse of the Ottoman and Russian Empires, 1908–1918.* Cambridge: Cambridge University Press, 2011.

Richter, Julius. *A History of Protestant Missions in the Near East.* New York: Fleming H. Revell, 1910.

Ricoeur, Paul. *Memory, History, Forgetting,* trans. Kathleen Blamey and David Pellauer. Chicago: University of Chicago Press, 2004.

Riley-Smith, Jonathan. *The Crusades: A Short History.* London: Athlone Press, 1987.

Robert, Dana L. *Christian Mission: How Christianity Became a World Religion.* Chichester, UK: Wiley-Blackwell, 2009.

Rodogno, Davide. *Against Massacre: Humanitarian Interventions in the Ottoman Empire, 1815–1914: The Emergence of a European Concept and International Practice.* Princeton: Princeton University Press, 2012.

Rodrigue, Aron. *French Jews, Turkish Jews: The Alliance Israélite Universelle and the Politics of Jewish Schooling in Turkey, 1860–1925.* Bloomington: Indiana University Press, 1990.

Roessel, David. *In Byron's Shadow: Modern Greece in the English and American Imagination.* New York: Oxford University Press, 2001.

Rogan, Eugene L. *Frontiers of the State in the Late Ottoman Empire.* Cambridge: Cambridge University Press, 1999.

"Sectarianism and Social Conflict in Damascus: The 1860 Events Reconsidered," *Arabica,* 51:4 (2004), pp. 493–511.

Rosenwein, Barbara H. *A Short History of the Middle Ages,* third edition. Toronto: University of Toronto Press, 2009.

Rozen, Minna. "The Ottoman Jews." In *The Cambridge History of Turkey, Volume 3: The Later Ottoman Empire, 1603–1839,* ed. Suraiya N. Faroqhi. Cambridge: Cambridge University Press, 2006, pp. 256–71.

Rushdie, Salman. *Imaginary Homelands: Essays and Criticism.* London: Granta, 1991.

Sabev, Orlin. *Spiritus Roberti: Shaping New Minds and Robert College in Late Otoman Society (1863–1923).* Istanbul: BÜTEK, 2013.

Said, Edward W. *Orientalism.* New York: Pantheon Books, 1978.

Sajdi, Dana. *The Barber of Damascus: Nouveau Literacy in the Eighteenth-Century Ottoman Levant.* Stanford: Stanford University Press, 2013.

"Decline, Its Discontents and Ottoman Cultural History: By Way of Introduction." In *Ottoman Tulips, Ottoman Coffee: Leisure and Lifestyle in the Eighteenth Century*, ed. Dana Sajdi. London: Tauris Academic Studies, 2007, pp. 1–40.

Salamah ben Musa ben Yitshak. Letter to Judah ben Moses ben Sujmar of Fustat, dated Mazara (Sicily), 1064 CE. Cairo Genizah Collection, Katz Center for Advanced Judaic Studies, University of Pennsylvania, Philadelphia. Halper 389, http://hdl.library.upenn.edu/1017.4/4452-record (accessed April 6, 2016).

Salzmann, Ariel. "The Age of Tulips: Confluence and Conflict in Early Modern Consumer Culture (1550–1730)." In *Consumption Studies and the History of the Ottoman Empire: An Introduction*, ed. Donald Quataert. Albany: State University of New York Press, 2000, pp. 83–106.

Salt, Jeremy. *Imperialism, Evangelism, and the Ottoman Armenians, 1878–1896*. London: Frank Cass, 1993.

Samir [*sic*] (Director). *Forget Baghdad*, DVD. Seattle: Arab Film Production, 2004.

Sarafian, Ara. "The Absorption of Armenian Women and Children into Muslim Households as a Structural Component of the Armenian Genocide." In *In God's Name: Genocide and Religion in the Twentieth Century*, ed. Omer Bartov and Phyllis Mack. New York: Berghahn Books, 2001, pp. 209–21.

Sardar, Marika. "Carpets from the Islamic World," The Metropolitan Museum of Art, www.metmuseum.org/toah/hd/crpt/hd_crpt.htm (accessed March 6, 2016).

Scarce, Jennifer. *Women's Costume of the Near and Middle East*. London: Unwin Hyman, 1987.

Schreier, Joshua. *Arabs of the Jewish Faith: The Civilizing Mission in Colonial Algeria*. New Brunswick: Rutgers University Press, 2010.

Schroeter, Daniel J. "The Changing Relationship between the Jews of the Arab Middle East and the Ottoman State in the Nineteenth Century." In *Jews, Turks, Ottomans: A Shared History, Fifteenth through the Twentieth Century*, ed. Avigdor Levy. Syracuse: Syracuse University Press, 2002, pp. 88–107.

The Sultan's Jew: Morocco and the Sephardi World. Stanford: Stanford University Press, 2002.

Sedgwick, Mark. *Muhammad Abduh*. Oxford: Oneworld, 2010.

Sedra, Paul. *From Mission to Modernity: Evangelicals, Reformers, and Education in Nineteenth-Century Egypt*. London: I.B. Tauris, 2011.

Seib, Philip. *The al-Jazeera Effect: How the New Global Media Are Reshaping World Politics*. Washington, DC: Potomac Books, 2008.

Semerdjian, Elyse. *"Off the Straight Path": Illicit Sex, Law, and Community in Ottoman Aleppo*. Syracuse: Syracuse University Press, 2008.

Şeni, Nora. "Fashion and Women's Clothing in the Satirical Press of Istanbul at the End of the 19th Century." In *Women in Modern Turkish Society: A Reader*, ed. Sirin Tekeli. London: Zed Books, 1995, pp. 25–45.

Sepinwall, Alyssa Goldstein. *The Abbé Grégoire and the French Revolution: The Making of Modern Universalism*. Berkeley: University of California Press, 2005.

Sezgin, Yüksel. "The Israeli *Millet* System: Examining Legal Pluralism through Lenses of Nation-Building and Human Rights," *Israel Law Review*, 43:631 (2010), pp. 631–54.

Shafik, Viola. *Arab Cinema: History and Cultural Identity*. Cairo: American University in Cairo Press, 1998.

Sharkey, Heather J. *American Evangelicals in Egypt: Missionary Encounters in an Age of Empire*. Princeton: Princeton University Press, 2008.

"African Colonial States." In *The Oxford Handbook of Modern African History*, ed. John Parker and Richard Reid. Oxford: Oxford University Press, 2013, pp. 151–70.

"Christianity in the Middle East and North Africa." In *Introducing World Christianity*, ed. Charles Farhadian. Oxford: Wiley-Blackwell, 2012, pp. 7–20.

"Christians among Muslims: The Church Missionary Society in the North Sudan," *Journal of African History*, 43 (2002), pp. 51–75.

"An Egyptian in China: Ahmed Fahmy and the Making of World Christianities," *Church History*, 78:2 (2009), pp. 309–26.

"The Gospel in Arabic Tongues: British Bible Distribution, Evangelical Mission, and Language Politics in North Africa." In *Cultural Conversions: Unexpected Consequences of Christian Missionary Encounters in the Middle East, Africa, and South Asia*, ed. Heather J. Sharkey. Syracuse: Syracuse University Press, 2013, pp. 203–21.

"Muslim Apostasy, Christian Conversion, and Religious Freedom in Egypt: A Study of American Missionaries, Western Imperialism, and Human Rights Agendas." In *Proselytization Revisited: Rights, Free Markets, and Culture Wars*, ed. Rosalind I. J. Hackett. London: Equinox, 2008, pp. 139–66.

"A New Crusade or an Old One?," *ISIM Newsletter*. Leiden: International Institute for the Study of Islam in the Modern World, 12 (June 2003), 48–49.

Cultural Conversions: Unexpected Consequences of Christian Missionary Encounters in the Middle East, Africa, and South Asia. Syracuse: Syracuse University Press, 2013.

Shaw, Stanford A. *History of the Ottoman Empire and Modern Turkey, Volume 1: Empire of the Gazis: The Rise and Decline of the Ottoman Empire, 1280–1808*. Cambridge: Cambridge University Press, 1976.

Shaw, Wendy M. K. *Possessors and Possessed: Museums, Archaeology, and the Visualization of the Ottoman Empire*. Berkeley: University of California Press, 2003.

"From Mausoleum to Museum: Resurrecting Antiquity for Ottoman Modernity." In *Scramble for the Past: A Story of Archaeology in the Ottoman Empire, 1753–1914*, ed. Zainab Bahrani, Zeynep Çelik, and Edhem Eldem. Istanbul: SALT, 2011, pp. 423–31.

Shenfield, Stephen D. "The Circassians: A Forgotten Genocide?." In *The Massacre in History*, ed. Mark Levene and Penny Roberts. New York: Berghahn Books, 1999, pp. 149–83.

Shiloah, Amnon. *The Epistle on Music of the Ikhwan al-Safa (Baghdad, 10th Century)*. Tel Aviv: Tel Aviv University, Faculty of Fine Arts, School of Jewish Studies, 1978.

Music in the World of Islam: A Socio-Cultural Study. Detroit: Wayne State University Press, 1995.

Shohat, Ella. *Israeli Cinema: East/West and the Politics of Representation*, new edition. London: I.B. Tauris, 2010.

Silay, Kemal. *Nedim and the Poetics of the Ottoman Court: Medieval Inheritance and the Need for Change*. Bloomington: Indiana University Turkish Studies, 1994.

Simon, Reeva Spector. "Europe in the Middle East." In *The Jews of the Middle East and North Africa in Modern Times*, ed. Reeva Spector Simon, Michael Menachem Laskier, and Sara Reguer. New York: Columbia University Press, 2003, pp. 19–28.

Simon, Reeva Spector, Laskier, Michael Menachem, and Reguer Sara, eds. *The Jews of the Middle East and North Africa in Modern Times*. New York: Columbia University Press, 2003.

Singer, Amy, ed. *Starting with Food: Culinary Approaches to Ottoman History*. Princeton: Markus Wiener, 2011.

Sinor, Denis. *The Cambridge History of Early Inner Asia*, Volume 1. Cambridge: Cambridge University Press, 1990.

Smith, Charles D. *Palestine and the Arab-Israeli Conflict*, third edition. New York: St. Martin's Press, 1996.

Smith, Eli. Letter to Rev. Dr. Brigham, Bhamdun, Mount Lebanon, October 26, 1848. American Bible Society Library, New York, RG#17.01, Correspondence Files, Levant/Near East Versions. (Note: This archive moved to Philadelphia in 2015.)

Smith, Wilfred Cantwell. *The Meaning and End of Religion: A New Approach to the Religious Traditions of Mankind*. Minneapolis: Fortress, 1991.

Somel, Selçuk Akşin. *The Modernization of Public Education in the Ottoman Empire, 1839–1908: Islamization, Autocracy, and Discipline*. Leiden: E.J. Brill, 2001.

Sommer, Dorothe. *Freemasonry in the Ottoman Empire: A History of the Fraternity and Its Influence in Syria and the Levant*. London: I.B. Tauris, 2015.

Sonbol, Amira El-Azhary. *The New Mamluks: Egyptian Society and Modern Feudalism*, foreword by Robert A. Fernea. Syracuse: Syracuse University Press, 2000.

Sontag, Susan. *On Photography*. New York: Picador, 2001.

Speer, Robert E. *Christianity and the Nations*. New York: Fleming H. Revell, 1910.

Spivak, Gayatri Chakravorty. "Can the Subaltern Speak?." In *Marxism and Interpretation of Culture*, ed. Cary Nelson and Lawrence Grossberg. Urbana: University of Illinois Press, 1988, pp. 271–313.

Stanley, Brian. *The World Missionary Conference, Edinburgh 1910*. Grand Rapids: William B. Eerdmans, 2009.

Starr, Deborah A. *Remembering Cosmopolitan Egypt: Literature, Culture, and Empire*. London: Routledge, 2009.

Stillman, Norman A. *The Jews of Arab Lands: A History and Sourcebook*. Philadelphia: Jewish Publication Society of America, 1979.

"Middle Eastern and North African Jewries Confront Modernity: Orientation, Disorientation, Reorientation." In *Sephardi and Middle Eastern Jewries: History & Culture in the Modern Era*, ed. Harvey E. Goldberg. Bloomington: Indiana University Press, 1996, pp. 59–72.

Stillman, Yedida Kalfon. *Arab Dress: A Short History*, ed. Norman A. Stillman. Leiden: E.J. Brill, 2000.

Stilt, Kristen. *Islamic Law in Action: Authority, Discretion, and Everyday Experiences in Mamluk Egypt*. Oxford: Oxford University Press, 2011.

Stock, Eugene. *The History of the Church Missionary Society: Its Environment, Its Men, and Its Work*, 2 volumes. London: Church Missionary Society, 1899.

Stora, Benjamin. "The Crémieux Decree." In *A History of Jewish-Muslim Relations from the Origins to the Present Day*, ed. Abdelwahab Meddeb and Benjamin Stora, trans. Jane Marie Todd and Michael B. Smith. Princeton: Princeton University Press, 2013, pp. 286–91.

   Les Trois Exils: Juifs d'Algérie. Paris: Stock, 2006.

Stroumsa, Sarah. *Maimonides in His World: Portrait of a Mediterranean Thinker*. Princeton: Princeton University Press, 2009.

   "The Muslim Context." In *The Cambridge History of Jewish Philosophy*, ed. Steven Nadler and T. M. Rudavsky, Volume 1: *From Antiquity through the Seventh Century*. Cambridge: Cambridge University Press, 2008, pp. 39–59.

Suermann, Harald. "Copts and the Islam of the Seventh Century." In *The Encounter of Eastern Christianity with Early Islam*, ed. Emmanouela Grypeou, Mark Swanson, and David Thomas. Leiden: E.J. Brill, 2006, pp. 95–109.

Suny, Ronald Grigor. "Religion, Ethnicity, and Nationalism: Armenians, Turks, and the End of the Ottoman Empire." In *In God's Name: Genocide and Religion in the Twentieth Century*, ed. Omer Bartov and Phyllis Mack. New York: Berghahn Books, 2001, pp. 23–61.

   "They Can Live in the Desert but Nowhere Else": A History of the Armenian Genocide. Princeton: Princeton University Press, 2015.

Tambar, Kabir. *The Reckoning of Pluralism: Political Belonging and the Demands of History in Turkey*. Stanford: Stanford University Press, 2014.

Terzibaşoğlu, Yücel. "Struggles over Land and Population Movements in North-Western Anatolia, 1877–1914." In *Sociétés rurales ottomanes*, ed. Mohammad Afifi et al. Cairo: Institut français d'archéologie orientale, 2005, pp. 297–308.

Tetlock, Philip E., Richard Ned Lebow, and Geoffrey Parker, eds. *Unmaking the West: "What if?" Scenarios that Rewrite World History*. Ann Arbor: University of Michigan Press, 2006.

Tezcan, Baki. "Ethnicity, Race, Religion and Social Class: Ottoman Markers of Difference." In *The Ottoman World*, ed. Christine Woodhead. London: Routledge, 2012, pp. 159–70.

Thomas, David. "Arab Christianity." In *The Blackwell Companion to Eastern Christianity*, ed. Ken Parry. Oxford: Blackwell, 2007, pp. 1–22.

Thomas, David, ed. and trans. *Anti-Christian Polemic in Early Islam: Abu 'Isa al-Warraq's "Against the Trinity."* Cambridge: Cambridge University Press, 1992.

Tibawi, A. L. *American Interests in Syria 1800–1901: A Study of Educational, Literary and Religious Work*. Oxford: Clarendon Press, 1966.

Tomkins, Stephen. *A Short History of Christianity*. Grand Rapids: William B. Eerdmans, 2006.

Turiano, Annalaura. "De la pastorale migratoire à la coopération technique: Missionnaires italiens en Égypte; Les salésiens et l'enseignement professionel (1890–1970)." PhD diss. (History), Aix-Marseille Université, 2015.

"Turkey," *Oxford English Dictionary Online*, December 2011.

"The Turkish Revolution: The Death of Abdel Aziz," *New York Times*, June 19, 1876.

Turner, Victor. *The Forest of Symbols: Aspects of Ndembu Ritual.* Ithaca: Cornell University Press, 1970.

Twain, Mark. *Innocents Abroad, or the New Pilgrim's Progress.* Hartford: American Publishing Company, 1869.

Üngör, Uğur Ümit. *The Making of Modern Turkey: Nation and State in Eastern Anatolia, 1913–1950.* Oxford: Oxford University Press, 2011.

United Nations High Commissioner for Refugees. *Syria Regional Refugee Response,* http://data.unhcr.org/syrianrefugees/regional.php (accessed February 29, 2016).

United Nations Relief and Works Agency for Palestine Refugees in the Near East (UNRWA), "Palestine Refugees," www.unrwa.org/palestine-refugees (accessed February 29, 2016).

University of Pennsylvania Museum of Archaeology and Anthropology, Archives, Bonfils Collection, Image 165914: "Guard turc à la porte de St. Sepulchre," elsewhere listed as "Portiers musulmans du St. Sepulcre [*sic*]," circa 1885–1901.

US Department of State, *2009 Report on International Religious Freedom,* www.state.gov/g/drl/rls/irf/2009/index.htm (accessed January 21, 2010).

International Religious Freedom Report for 2014, www.state.gov/j/drl/rls/irf/religiousfreedom/index.htm?year=2014&dlid=238452#wrapper (accessed February 29, 2016).

van der Veer, Peter. "Communalism." In the *International Encyclopedia of the Social and Behavioral Sciences,* ed. James D. Wright, Volume 4, second edition. Amsterdam: El Sevier, 2015, pp. 263–65.

van der Veer, Peter, ed. *Conversion to Modernities: The Globalization of Christianity.* New York: Routledge, 1996.

van der Veer, Peter. *Religious Nationalism: Hindus and Muslims in India.* Berkeley: University of California Press, 1994.

Verdeil, Chantal. "Introduction." In *Missions chrétiennes en terre d'islam (XVIIe-XXe siècles): Anthologie de textes missionnaires,* ed. Chantal Verdeil. Turnhout, Belgium: Brepols, 2013, pp. 5–59.

Verdeil, Chantal, ed. *Missions chrétiennes en terre d'islam (XVIIe-XXe siècles): Anthologie de textes missionnaires.* Turnhout, Belgium: Brepols, 2013.

Versteegh, Kees. *The Arabic Language.* New York: Columbia University Press, 1997.

Vikør, Knut S. *Sufi and Scholar on the Desert Edge: Muhammad B. 'Ali al-Sanusi and His Brotherhood.* Evanston: Northwestern University Press, 1995.

Voll, John Obert. *Islam: Continuity and Change in the Modern World.* Syracuse: Syracuse University Press, 1982.

Waines, David and Manuela Marín. "Muzawwar: Counterfeit Fare for Fasts and Fevers." In *Patterns of Everyday Life,* ed. David Waines. Aldershot, UK: Ashgate, 2002, pp. 303–15.

Wallerstein, Immanuel. *The Modern World-System.* New York: Academic Press, 1974.

Walters, Keith. "Education for Jewish Girls in Late Nineteenth- and Early Twentieth-Century Tunis and the Spread of French in Tunisia." In *Jewish Culture and Society in North Africa,* ed. Emily Benichou Gottreich and Daniel J. Schroeter. Bloomington: Indiana University Press, 2011, pp. 257–81.

Wasserstrom, Steven M. *Between Muslim and Jew: The Problem of Symbiosis under Early Islam.* Princeton: Princeton University Press, 1995.

Watenpaugh, Keith David. "Being Middle Class and Being Arab: Sectarian Dilemmas and Middle-Class Modernity in the Arab Middle East, 1908–1936." In *The Making of the Middle Class: Toward a Transnational History,* ed. A. Ricardo López and Barbara Weinstein. Durham: Duke University Press, 2012, pp. 267–87.

Being Modern in the Middle East: Revolution, Nationalism, Colonialism, and the Arab Middle Class. Princeton: Princeton University Press, 2006.

Watson, Andrew. *The American Mission in Egypt, 1854 to 1896,* second edition. Pittsburgh: United Presbyterian Board of Publication, 1904.

Weir, Shelagh. *Palestinian Costume.* Austin: University of Texas Press, 1989.

Westbrook, Virginia. "The Role of Trading Cards in Marketing Chocolate during the Late Nineteenth Century." In *Chocolate: History, Culture, and Heritage,* ed. Louis Evan Grivetti and Howard-Yana Shapiro. Hoboken, NJ: Wiley, 2009, pp. 183–92.

Wexler, Arynne. "Clash between Europe and the Ottoman Empire: How Percussive Instruments Set the Beat for Ottoman Influence in the 18th and 19th Centuries," *Journal of International Relations,* 17 (2015), pp. 182–93.

Williams, Brian Glyn. "Hijra and Forced Migration from Nineteenth-Century Russia to the Ottoman Empire: A Critical Analysis of the Great Crimean Tatar Migration of 1860–1861," *Cahiers du Monde russe,* 41:1 (2000), pp. 79–108.

Wilson, Mary C. "The Damascus Affair and the Beginnings of France's Empire in the Middle East." In *Histories of the Modern Middle East: New Directions,* ed. Israel Gershoni, Hakan Erdem, and Ursula Wocöck. Boulder: Lynne Rienner, 2002, pp. 63–74.

Winock, Michel. *La France et les juifs de 1789 à nos jours.* Paris: Éditions du Seuil, 2004.

Winter, Stefan. *The Shiites of Lebanon under Ottoman Rule, 1516–1788.* Cambridge: Cambridge University Press, 2010.

Wishnitzer, Avner. *Reading Clocks, Alla Turca: Time and Society in the Late Ottoman Empire.* Chicago: University of Chicago Press, 2015.

Wissa, Karim. "Freemasonry in Egypt, 1798–1921: A Study in Cultural and Political Encounters," *Bulletin (British Society for Middle Eastern Studies),* 16:2 (1989), pp. 143–61.

Wohl, Anthony S. "'Ben Ju-Ju': Representations of Disraeli's Jewishness in the Victorian Political Cartoon," *Jewish History,* 10:2 (1996), pp. 89–134.

"'Dizzi-ben-Dizzi': Disraeli as an Alien," *Journal of British Studies,* 34:3 (1995), pp. 375–411.

Womack, Deanna Ferree. "Conversion, Controversy & Cultural Production: Syrian Protestants, American Missionaries, and the Arabic Press, 1870–1915," PhD diss., Princeton Theological Seminary, 2015.

Woodhead, Christine. "Ottoman Languages." In *The Ottoman World,* ed. Christine Woodhead. London: Routledge, 2012, pp. 143–58.

Wurgaft, Benjamin Aldes. "Food Smells and Ethnic Tension," *Gastronomica,* 6:2 (2006), pp. 57–60.

Yale University Press. "Statement by John Donatich (Director of Yale University Press)" [about the decision to not print the Danish cartoons of Muhammad],

September 9, 2009, http://yalepress.yale.edu/yupbooks/KlausenStatement
.asp (accessed February 5, 2010).

Yardumian, Aram and Theodore G. Schurr. "Who Are the Anatolian Turks?
A Reappraisal of the Anthropological Genetic Evidence," *Anthropology &
Archeology of Eurasia*, 50:1 (2011), pp. 6–42.

Yavuz, M. Hakan. "The Transformation of 'Empire' through Wars and Reforms:
Integration vs. Oppression." In *War and Diplomacy: The Russo-Turkish War of
1877–87 and the Treaty of Berlin*, ed. M. Hakan Yavuz with Peter Sluglett. Salt
Lake City: University of Utah Press, 2011, pp. 17–55.

Yavuz M. Hakan, with Peter Sluglett, eds. *War and Diplomacy: The Russo-Turkish
War of 1877–1878 and the Treaty of Berlin*. Salt Lake City: University of Utah
Press, 2011.

Yi, Eunjeong. *Guild Dynamics in Seventeenth-Century Istanbul: Fluidity and
Leverage*. Leiden: E.J. Brill, 2004.

Yılmaz, Hale. *Becoming Turkish: Nationalist Reforms and Cultural Negotiations in
Early Republican Turkey, 1923–1945*. Syracuse: Syracuse University Press,
2013.

Yılmaz, Ihsan. "Osman Hamdi's 'Lost' Masterpiece in Action," *Hürriyet Daily
News*, April 28, 2014.

Yosmaoğlu, İpek. *Blood Ties: Religion, Violence, and the Politics of Nationhood in
Ottoman Macedonia, 1878–1908*. Ithaca: Cornell University Press, 2014.

Yücel, Ihsan. *Dolmabahçe Palace*, second edition. Istanbul: TBMM Department
of National Palaces, 1995.

Yuhas, Alan. "Muslim Population in Europe to Reach 10% by 2050, New Study
Shows," *The Guardian*, April 2, 2015.

Zamir, Meir. *The Formation of Modern Lebanon*. London: Croom Helm, 1985.

Zaouali, Lilia. *Medieval Cuisine of the Islamic World: A Concise History
with 174 Recipes*, trans. M. B. DeBevoise, foreword by Charles Perry.
Berkeley: University of California Press, 2007.

Zarcone, Thierry. "Quand la laïcité des francs-maçons du Grand Orient de
France vient aux Jeunes Turcs." In *Le choc colonial et l'islam: les politiques
religieuses des puissances coloniales en terres d'islam*, ed. Pierre-Jean Luizard.
Paris: La Découverte, 2006, pp. 137–58.

Zarinebaf, Fariba. *Crime and Punishment in Istanbul, 1700–1800*. Berkeley:
University of California Press, 2010.

Zayani, Mohamed, ed. *The Al Jazeera Phenomenon: Critical Perspectives on New
Arab Media*. Boulder: Paradigm, 2005.

Zilfi, Madeline C. "The Ottoman *Ulema*." In *The Cambridge History of Turkey,
Volume 3: The Later Ottoman Empire, 1603–1839*, ed. Suraiya Faroqhi.
Cambridge: Cambridge University Press, 2006, pp. 209–25.

"Whose Laws? Gendering the Ottoman Sumptuary Regime." In *Ottoman
Costumes: From Textile to Identity*, ed. Suraiya Faroqhi and Christoph K.
Neumann. Istanbul: Eren, 2004, pp. 125–41.

Zubaida, Sami. "National, Communal and Global Dimensions in Middle Eastern
Food Cultures." In *Culinary Cultures of the Middle East*, ed. Sami Zubaida
and Richard Tapper. London: I.B. Tauris, 1994, pp. 33–45.

Zubaida, Sami and Richard Tapper, eds. *Culinary Cultures of the Middle East*.
London: I.B. Tauris, 1994.

Zürcher, Erik Jan. "The Ottoman Conscription System in Theory and Practice, 1844–1918." In *Arming the State: Military Conscription in the Middle East and Central Asia, 1775–1925*, ed. Erik J. Zürcher. London: I.B. Tauris, 1999, pp. 79–94.

Turkey: A Modern History, second edition. London: I.B. Tauris, 1998.

"The Young Turks: Children of the Borderlands?," *International Journal of Turkish Studies*, 9:1–2 (2003), pp. 275–85.

Arming the State: Military Conscription in the Middle East and Central Asia, 1775–1925. London: I.B. Tauris, 1999.

Zwemer, Samuel M. *Islam: A Challenge to Faith*. New York: Student Volunteer Movement for Foreign Missions, 1907.

Index

Abbasid dynasty
  alcohol consumption during, 42
  differentiation by clothing during, 46
  history of, 31–32
ABCFM (American Board of
      Commissioners for Foreign
      Missions), 138, 201, 221
'Abd al-Halim Pasha, son of Muhammad
      'Ali of Egypt, 254–55
'Abd al-Malik (Umayyad caliph), 53
'Abd al-Qadir al-Jaza'iri, 267
Abduh, Muhammad, 228, 246–47
Abdulaziz (Ottoman sultan), 179–80, 183,
      190, 191, 194, 213, 261
Abdulhamid II (Ottoman sultan)
  censoring under, 189–90
  change in political mood under,
      189–90, 228
  Christian missionaries, 199–204
    in Egypt, 209–10
    and girls/women, 202–3
    inspections of mission
      schools, 211–12
    Jewish/Christian parallel
      experiences, 201–2
    and medicine/public health, 200–1
    Mormons, 199–200
    Muslim audiences, and
      nationalism, 204–12
    numbers of conversions, 210–11
    schools of, 201
    and science debates, 203–4
  conclusions about, 303–4
  continuities during, 227–28
  and end of Tanzimat era, 187–90
    exile of potential challengers, 190
    and increase in bureaucracy, 192
    and Jewish-Ottoman relations, 188
    and military, 192
    and military conscription, 188
    and mixed parliament, 188–89,
      233n52

  and Ottoman constitution, 187–88
  and regulatory functions, 192
  shrinking influence of grand viziers/
      high-level bureaucrats, 190
  as fan of Western culture, 258
  financial crisis under, 183, 189, 228
  imperial revival under, 190–96, 218–23
    and Afghani, 214–17
    and antiquities, 194
    and artwork, 194–96
    becoming more Muslim, 218–27
    and building of schools, 193
    communications, 199
    diplomacy, 196–97
    educational practices, 191
    emigration to Americas, 197–98
      problems from Ottoman state point
        of view, 198
      religious demographics of
        emigrants, 197–98
    influence over residual territories/
      subjects, 190–96
    and Islamic reform
    "new orthodoxy" policy, 223–27
      Alevis' desire for closer connection
        with Protestants, 225
      conscription, 223–24, 225–26
      forced conversion of Yezidis to
        Sunni Islam, 223
      government schools for promoting
        Muslim culture, 225
      influence of Christian
        missionaries, 224–25
      Muslim missionary campaigns,
        224
      reasons for conversions/making
        people more Muslim, 225–27
      Stavriotae, attempted shift
        from Islam to Christianity,
        223–24, 225
    organizational practices, 191
    Ottomans abroad, 196–99

361

Abdulhamid II (Ottoman sultan) (*cont.*)
  overlooking of sectarian distinctions
    among Muslims, 222, 241n214
  and pan-Islamic politics,
    212–18, 228–29
    claim to title of caliph, 213–14
    effect of nationalism on, 228
    effect of Wahhabism on, 228–30
    embracing technology as
      characteristic of, 212–13
    European claims to backwardness
      of, 215
    official respect for tradition as
      characteristic of, 212, 218
  and photography, 182, 193–94,
    243, 257
  and religious diversity, 76
    Alawites (Nusayris), 220–21
    in Albania, 219–20
    Alevis, 220, 221, 225
    in Anatolia and Greater
      Syria, 220–23
    Dönme, 219, 220, 227
    Druze, 220
    and endogamy, 220
    Stavriotae, 219, 220
    Sufism, 220
    Yezidis, 220, 222, 223, 227
  and retrieval of Libya, 191
  scientific practices, 191
  interest in photography, 182
  military exemption tax, 223
  nationalism in, 228
  ordinary Muslims' opinion of, 217–18
  overview of, 179–82
    British/French views on, 180–81
    control over Ottoman Empire, 181–82
    hobbies of, 180
    micromanager and workaholic, 179
    paranoia of, 179–80, 181, 193–94,
      276, 318
    thrift of, 180
  refugee crisis under Abdulhamid II,
    183–84, 185 (*see also muhajir*s)
  Russo-Turkish War of 1877–78
    under, 184–85
  surveillance under, 189–90, 194
  See also Abdulhamid II (Ottoman
    sultan), later years of
Abdulhamid II (Ottoman sultan), later
  years of
  and Armenian massacre, 267–76
  challenges to commerce and natural
    disasters model of social
    relations, 248–53

gazinos, 250
  musicians, 249–50, 257–58
  public venues, 249
  rise of Ottoman middle class,
    250–53, 303
    and cosmopolitanism, 252
    as disproportionately Christian and
      Jewish, 252
    features of, 251
    and literacy, 251
    Muslim members, 252–53
    and women readers and
      writers, 251–52
  contraception and abortion
    rulings, 271
  convergence during, 253–59
    and alcohol consumption, 253
    foreign mission schools, 256–57
    Freemasonry, 254–56
    gazinos, 253
    leisured shopping, 253–54
    picture postcard
      consumption, 253–54
    power of clothes to blur religious
      status, 244–45, 257
    secular spaces, emergence of, 245
    Young Ottomans, 255–56
  conversion to modernities, 246–47
  demographics, 270–71
  dethroning of, 287–88
  divergence during, 245–46
  efforts to keep Arab provinces within
    empire, 283–84
  end of Ottoman Empire, 288–89
  growth of "Turkish"
    consciousness, 284–85
  increasing anxieties
    among social/economically
      beleaguered, 247
    consequences of privileging Islam/
      Muslims, 247–48
    effects Russo-Turkish War, 247
    military, and creation of Hamidiye
      cavalry, 247–48
    Muslim-Jewish relationship, effect
      on, 248
    refusal of Muslim supremacy
      principle, 247
  Jews and Ottoman reforms, 259–66
    in Libya, 265–66
    relationship with Muslims, 266
    status of Jews as *dhimmis*, 266
    in Yemen, 260–63
  Young Turks (*see* Young Turks)
Abdullah Frères, 193

Abdulmajid I (Ottoman sultan)
  attendance of non-Muslim festivities
      by, 124–25
  confirmation of edict of 1839 by, 115
  and edict of 1856, 115–16
abortion rulings, 271
Abougit, Louis, 150
Abougit, Riccadonna, 150
Abrahamic religions, 19
Abu Bakr, 77
Abu Nuwas, 42
Abu Yusuf, 46
acculturation, conversions to Islam
      through, 48
Adana Massacre, 278–79
Aden, 191–92
Afghani, Jamal al-Din al-, 214–17,
      228, 254–55
  Abdulhamid II on, 216–17
  defence/criticism of, 215–16
  in Egypt, 215
  in exile in France, 215
  and Freemasonry, 255
Afghanistan, U.S. and allies launch wars in, 7
Africa
  conversions to Christianity in nineteenth/
      twentieth century, 48–49
  economically motivated migration to
      Middle East from, 2
agriculture
  Armenian innovations, 279
  European-Ottoman exchanges, 70
  Europe/Ottoman Empire exchanges, 70
  moshavot in Palestine, 264
ahl al-dhimma. See dhimmis
Ahmad Mukhtar Pasha, 262
Ahmet III (Ottoman sultan), 100
  pleasure palace of, 101
A'idah, Nasrallah, 97
Akçam, Taner, 286
Aksakal, Mustafa, 286
Alawites, 153, 161
  efforts to convert to Sunni Islam, 224
  exemption from paying jizya, 222
al-Azhar university (Egypt), reforms
      at, 246–47
Albania, nationalism in, 284
alcohol consumption
  by Abdulhamid II, 217, 253
  by Mamluks, 42
  Pact of Umar on, 42
  Qur'an on, 217
Aleppo
  Catholic missionaries in, 97–98
  riot of 1850 in, 141, 146–47

Alevis, 75, 220, 221
Algeria
  'Abd al-Qadir al-Jaza'iri, 267
  Alliance Israélite Universelle in, 159
  French policy toward Jews in, 160–61
  French policy toward Muslims in, 161
  French Christian anti-Semitism
      in, 160–62
'Ali (cousin/son-in-law of Muhammad),
      30, 76, 220, 229
Alliance Israélite Universelle (AIU),
      158–60, 201–2, 261
  expansion of, 159
  and Frenchification of Jewish
      communities, 159
  gender parity at, 159, 252
  reasons for focus on Jews in Islamic
      world, 159–60
Al-Qaeda, worldwide terrorist attacks by, 7
Amara, Ibrahim. See Damascus Affair
American Board of Commissioners for
      Foreign Missions (ABCFM),
      138, 201, 221
American University of Beirut (AUB),
      200, 256
Amis, Kingsley, 306
Amsterdam, and trade, 102
Anatolia
  Christian population, diminution in, 2
  health statistics, 200–1
  migration to Americas from, 197
  Muslim-Christian interrelations in, 117
  Muslim life expectancy in, 201, 267
  Sufism in, 220
  See also Armenian Massacre; Armenians
Anglican missionary schools, 201
Anglo-Jewish Association, 261
Anglo-Turkish Convention, 131
Antioch, Alawites in, 224
anti-Semitism
  in Algeria, 153, 161–62
  and concept of blood libel, 85
  Damascus Affair, 155–58
  and Disraeli, 184
  Dreyfus Affair, 248
  Mortara Affair, 155, 158–60
  in Morocco, 153, 161–62
  persistence of, 155
  and rise of Zionism, 182,
      230–31, 263–64
  and smells, 307
Antonius, George, 205–6, 283
apostasy, and Islam, 139, 141, 209–10
Arab League, founding of, 11
Arab nationalism (nahda), 251, 282–83

Aratin, Butrus, 146–47
archaeology, nineteenth century, 119
architecture
  Baroque, 118
  Gothic, 118
  triumphalist, 118, 166n20
Armenian massacre (1890s), 267–76
  and anti-Armenian violence in
    Sasun, 273
  and Armenian resentments, 272–73
  assimilation through marriage/conversion/
    adoption as genocide, 286
  and attack on Ottoman Bank in
    Istanbul, 273–74
  death tolls from, 267
  and mass conversions of Armenians to
    Islam, 268
  rape and abductions during, 268
  role of Abdulhamid II in,
    268–70, 274–75
  role of improved roads/communications
    in, 276
  role of Muslim resentment against
    Armenians in, 270–72
  violent events of 1890s as pogroms *vs.*
    massacres, 274–75
  See also Armenians
Armenians
  Adana Massacre against, 278–79
  agricultural innovations of, 279
  Bible translations for, 207
  and conscription, 270
  depictions of atrocities by Turkey, 4–6
  dress codes under Ottoman rule, 89–90
  and edict of 1839, 128–29
  elements of Armenophobia, 272
  forced conversions during Safavid
    Empire, 77
  and Hamidiye cavalry, 247–48
  health of, 201
  land ownership by, 270
  nationalism of, 228, 248, 251
  population diminution, 2
  proposed reforms by Britain, France,
    and Russian for, 271–72
  and provision of winter shelter/fodder
    for pastoralist Kurds, 273
  response to wearing kalpak, 131–32
  and World War I, 286–87
  zartonk (renaissance) of, 251
Armenophobia, 272, 287
art
  Baroque/Rococo, 101
  carpet designs, 104–5, 312–13
  Islamic art formation, 53–54
Artan, Tülay, 103

Ashkenazi Jews
  attitude toward "Eastern" Jewish
    others, 265
  and Haskalah or Enlightenment, 154–55
Asia, economic migration to Middle East
  from, 2
Asir, Yusuf al-, 205
assimilation, conversions to Islam
  through, 48
Ataturk, Mustafa Kemal, 134–35
AUB (American University of Beirut),
  200, 256
authoritative power, 52
Ayyubid dynasty, dress distinctions
  during, 54

Babur (Mughal Empire), 78
Baer, Marc D., 227
Baghdad, move of Islamic state to, 31
Balfour Declaration (1917), 288
Bali nightclub attack (2002), 7
Balkans, and Muslim-Christian
  interrelations, 117
Balkan Wars (1912–1913), 285–86
Balkan/Yugoslav Wars (1991–c. 2001), 6
banality of violence, 3
Banna, Hasan al-, 215
Banu Qurayza Jews, massacre of, 33–35
  historical interpretation of, 37–38
Barbarossa (Khayr al-Din), 69
Bashir II, 150
bathhouses, distinguishing Muslims/
  dhimmis at, 56, 90–91, 310
bearing arms and riding mounted
    animals
  and conscription of Christian men, 145
  and conscription of Ottoman
    citizens, 144–45
  exception during Egyptian invasion of
    Syria, 142–43
  exception in remote northern
    Yemen, 142
  exception of Coptic Legion, 142
  Muslim/Christian men asymmetry, 316
  Pact of Umar on, 41, 142
bedouin, 224
Beirut
  Muslim-Christian social tensions
    in, 150
  printing presses in, 251
Belgium, terrorist attacks of 2015 and
    2016 in, 8
Benedict XIV (Pope), 8
ben Gaon, Sa'adiya, 50
Benjamin (patriarch of Coptic Church in
    Egypt), 36

*berat*s (certificates of foreign protection and legal status for translators in Ottoman Empire), 96–97

Berkes, Niyazi, 100, 164, 217, 218, 256, 284–85

Berkey, Jonathan, 50

Bernhardt, Sarah, 228, 258

Beşikçi, Mehmet, 280

Bilu group (Russian Empire), 263–64, 274

bin Laden, Osama, 6, 7

Black Death, 56

Black Sheep Turks, 77

"blood libel" narratives, 156

Bonaparte, Napoleon
  invasion of Egypt by, 13–15, 96, 142
  on Jews, 155

Bonneval, Claude Alexandre Comte de, 74–75, 107n36, 124, 144

Britain. *See* Great Britain

British Museum, 119

Bulgaria
  and Balkan Wars, 285–86
  and nationalism, 206
  tax collection during Ottoman era, 87

Bulgarian Orthodox Church, 99

burials/funerals, Muslim law on, 49–50

Bustani, Butrus al-, 205–6, 282

Byzantine Empire
  defeat by Seljuk Turks, 73
  and Egyptian Copts, 36
  and European Crusades, 55

Cahun, Léon, 285

Cairo Geniza, 44–45, 54

Caliphate Conference of Cairo (1926), 289

Campos, Michele U., 277

Canning, Stratford, 125, 138, 139, 140, 161

Capitulations
  in Ottoman Empire, 95
  on right to appoint translators, 96

Carmona, Behor I., 128

Cassandra (mythological), 318

Catholic Church
  missionary wing of, 14, 100
  printed works in Arabic, 14
  See also Catholic missionaries; Catholics

Catholic missionaries
  in Aleppo, 97–98
  and Christian political allegiances, 95
  and dissimulation or secret Christian belief, 224–25
  and edict of 1856, 138
  in Egypt, 99

at Mount Lebanon, 150
  schools of, 201, 293n65

Catholics
  dragomans, 97
  Melkites, 126–27
  and Damascus massacres, 151–52, 266
  in Ottoman Empire, 83–84, 96

Çelebi, Evliya, 92

cemaats, 82

Cemil Bey, Tanburi, 258

censoring
  under Abdulhamid II, 189–90
  self-censoring by book publishers, 23n33

Central Intelligence Agency (CIA), geopolitical reclassifications by, 10–11

Cevdet, Ahmet Paşa, 285

Charles V (Holy Roman Emperor), 83

Charles VI (France), 154

Charlie Hebdo attacks (2015), 7–8

Chatty, Dawn, 278–79

Chechnya crisis with Russia, 8

cholera, 192, 270

Christian churches
  edict of 1856 on, 136–37
  maintenance of sites in Middle East, 2
  Pact of Umar on, 41, 136, 316
  triumphalist architecture of, 118, 166n20
  Umayyad caliph forbids construction of new, 49

Christian missionaries
  in Egypt, 99, 209–10
  and "new orthodoxy," 224–25
  See also Catholic missionaries; Protestant missionaries

Christians
  in nineteenth/twentieth-century Africa, 48–49
  against conscription, 145
  and Damascus massacres, 151–52
  differences from Shi'is, 77–78
  dress codes under Ottoman rule, 89–90
  and European Crusades, 54–56
  French Christian anti-Semitism
    in Morocco, 161–62
    in Algeria, 160–62
  guilds under Ottoman rule, 94
  individual and communal identities among, 17–18
  internal diversity in religious and doctrines among, 16–17
  maintenance of sites contemporary Middle East, 2

Christians (*cont.*)
  middle class disproportionately as, 252
  nationalism in nineteenth century, 122
  population diminution, contemporary
    Middle East, 2, 20
  reforms, effect on Muslim-Christian
    interrelations, 117
  refusal of principle of Muslim
    supremacy by, 247
  See also Armenians; Catholics; Christian
    churches; Christian missionaries;
    conversion; Coptic Christians;
    Greek Orthodox Christians;
    Protestantism
church bells, ringing of, 41, 118
Church Missionary Society (CMS), 140,
    209, 211
Circassians, 4–6, 184
circumcision, 56
Clarendon (Lord), 139–40
clash of civilizations, 6
Clement XIV (pope), 8
Clot, Antoine Barthélémy, 123
clothing
  changes in nineteenth-century Ottoman
    Empire, 121, 243–44
  consistencies in, 104
  dress codes for *dhimmis*, 89–90, 91–92
  during Fatimid dynasty, 54
  ghiyar (laws of differentiation by
    clothing), 46, 54
  and Jews
    clothing in Fatimid Egypt, 54
    differentiation by clothing in
      Egypt, 306
    dress codes under Ottoman
      rule, 89–90
    European influence on clothing of
      women, 132
  Pact of Umar on, 41, 46
  reform
    clothing choice, 132–35
    expectations of reform by
      rabbis, 133–34
    women's clothing, 134
  restrictions during Ottoman Empire, 66
  as signal of conversion, 74
  under Suleyman the Magnificent, 89–90
  tracing history through study of, 313
  under Umayyad caliph, 49
  and Zoroastrians, 46
  See also footwear; headgear
CMS (Church Missionary Society), 140,
    209, 211
Cohen, Julia Phillips, 118, 278

Cohen, Mark R., 37
Committee of Union and Progress (CUP),
    276–77, 280–81, 286
Congress of Berlin 1878, 185
conscription
  draft as virtual death sentence, 225–26
  and Druze men of Mount
    Lebanon, 142–43
  and Jews, 145, 281
  of Maronites, 142–43
  as reason for emigration, 281
  reasons for failure of universal
    draft, 145–46
  resistance in Egypt, 144
  under Young Turks, 279–81
Constantinople
  conquest/occupation of by Ottomans, 66
  conquest by Mehmet II, 66, 78–79
consumption, emergence of, 102
contraception, rulings on, 271
conversion
  to Christianity
    conversos, 86
    punishment for, 139
  clothing as signal of, 74
  and intercommunal relations, 48
  to Islam
    in Abbasid period, 32, 48
    Armenians, amidst massacre,
      268, 286
    and buildings, 78–79
    forced conversions of Jews, 158
    involuntary, 67–68
    involuntary, in Safavid Empire, 77
    involuntary, of Jews, 77, 158
    involuntary, of slave
      concubines, 67–68
  under Mehmet IV, 78
  through assimilation, 48
  turning Turk, 74–75
conversos, 86
cookery books, 32, 42, 50–51, 308
Coptic Christians
  and ban against building churches, 136
  and Byzantine authorities, 36
  and circumcision, 56
  conversions to Islam, 48, 49–50
  dress codes under Ottoman rule, 89–90
  formation of Coptic Legion by
    Napoleon, 142
  and invasion of Egypt under
    Napoleon, 96
  language of, 42
  reception of Muslim invaders in
    Egypt, 37

problems with historical
  interpretation of, 38
relations with Muslims during
  reforms, 117
See also Christians
counterfactual history, 319–21
courts
  mixed religious, and 1839 edict, 136
  Shari'a, 94–95, 246
Crémieux, Adolphe, 153, 155, 157–58
Crémieux Decree, 160–62
Crete, under Ottoman rule, 83
Crimean War, 137–38
criminal law *(diya)*, 43
Cromwell, Oliver, 154
crosses, displaying in roads or markets, 41
crypto-Christians, 219
crypto-Jews, 219
cultural fermentation, eighteenth century
  and Orthodox Christians, 98–99
  and Protestant missionaries, 99
  and Roman Catholic missionaries,
    95, 97–98
cultural intersections among Muslims,
  Christians, and Jews, 16
Curzon (Lord), 305

D'Aiguebelle chocolate company
  cards, 4–6
Da'ish (ISIS), 8
Damascus
  riot of 1860, 141, 151–52
  shift of Muslim community from
    Arabia to, 30
Damascus Affair, 155–58
Damascus massacres, 151–52, 266–67
Dar al-Hikma (translation institute), 32
Darwin, Charles, 203–4
Davids, Arthur L., 285
Dawn, C. Ernest, 283
Denmark, cartoons lampooning Prophet
  Muhammad in, 7
Deringil, Selim, 116, 196, 223–24, 268
Der Matossian, Bedross, 278
devşirme (tax in young Christian men), 67
dhimmis, 27, 66, 89–95, 302
  classification abandoned under edict of
    1856, 136
  clothing
    consistencies in, 104
    dress/appearance, 37, 46
    dress codes, 89–90, 91–92
  communal geography of, 89
  distinguishing at public bathhouses, 56,
    90–91, 310

guilds, 93–94
intercommunal relations, 39–47
  changing meanings of term
    dhimma, 40
  and conversions, 40, 53–54
  and doctrinaires, 42–44
  and hairstyles/appearance, 41, 46
  and inheritance, 40
  institutionalization of, 40, 56–57
  and Islamic law, 43–44
  and *jizya,* 39 (*see also jizya*)
  and Muslim burials/funerals, 49–50
  and Muslim/non-Muslim
    marriage, 39
  and Pact of Umar, 40–42
    bearing of arms, 41, 142
    on building/repairing of churches/
      synagogues, 136
    exceptions to, 41–42
    on fermented drinks, 42
    historicity of, 40–41
    influences on, 41
    restrictions for Christians under, 41
    restrictions for Jews under, 41
    on riding mounted animals, 41, 142
    on spoken languages, 42
    solidarity among, 47
  and law, Islamic, 43–44
    diya (in cases of wrongful death), 43
    and Shari'a law courts, 94–95
    tax on merchants, 43–44
  prostitution, 92–93, 94–95
  "quarter solidarity," 93, 141
  viability of system of, 20–21
diffused/popular power, 52
Din, Khayr al- (Barbarossa), 69
Din, Nasir al-, 217
disease. *See* public health
Disraeli, Benjamin, 184
diya (in cases of wrongful death), 43
Dome of the Rock, 53
Dönme, 219, 220, 227
  and Sabbatai Sevi, 264, 294n105
Donner, Fred, 34
dragomans (translators), 96–97
dress. *See* clothing
Dreyfus, Albert, 248
Dreyfus Affair, 248, 264
Druze, 147–51
  and assertion of external state
    power, 147–48
  conscription of, 142–43
  and Damascus massacres, 151–52
  demise of feudal order and rise of new
    rich, 148–49

Druze (*cont.*)
  and Maronite Christians, 148–49
  and Maronite-Druze massacres, 150
  and sectarianism, 149
Dung-Gatherers Decree (Latrine or
    Scrapers Edict), 261, 262
dynastic deterioration theory, 108n38

Eastern Europe, Muslim refugees
    from, 185
Eastern Question, 123, 184
eating utensils, 121, 193, 311
Eddy, Mary, 202
edict of 1839, 115–16, 135–36
  administrative changes, 127–28
    translation bureau, 127–28
  ambiguities of reforms, 135–42
    education, 135
    government ministries, 135
    passports, 135, 163
    postal system, 135
  and Armenian Christians,
    128–29, 135–36
  and Greek War of Independence,
    125–28
  and military reform, 128
    abolition of Janissaries, 128–29
      effect on Armenians, 128–29
      effect on bureaucracy, 129
      effect on Jews, 128
  and Muslim workers, 125
  overview of, 115–16
  and urban Muslims, 125
edict of 1856, 115–16, 136–42, 161
  and building of churches and
    synagogues, 136–37
  and Catholic missionaries, 138
  continual recognition of *millets*, 136
  dhimmis classification abandoned, 136
  as expression of *realpolitik*, 137–38
  and Great Britain, 138–40
  and Jews, 141
  and military conscription, 143–46
  and Protestant missionaries, 138–40
  and religious freedom, 136–41, 208
education
  Catholic missionary schools, 201,
    293n65
  Christian missionary schools, 201
  and edict of 1839, 135
  inspections of Christian mission
    schools, 211–12
  medical school human dissections, 135
  Protestant missionary schools, 201,
    293n65

Syrian Protestant College, 200,
    203–4, 256
  See also Alliance Israélite Universelle
    (AIU); literacy
Edward I (England), 154
Egypt
  Afghani in, 215
  al-Azhar university reforms in, 246–47
  Christian missionaries in, 99, 209–10
  Christian reception of Muslim
    invaders in, 37
  conquest by Fatimid dynasty, 54
  conquest by Napoleon, 13–15, 96,
    118, 142
  conquest by Shi'i separatist
    movement, 31–32
  differentiation by clothing of Jews
    in, 306
  dress distinctions during Ayyubid
    dynasty, 54
  effects of European Crusades during
    Malmuk dynasty, 55–56
  freedom of the press in, 251
  Freemasonry in, 254–55
  invasion and occupation by Great
    Britain, 209–10
  languages in, 42
  migration to Americas, from
    British-occupied, 197
  mission schools, effect on literacy rate
    in, 201
  Muhammad Ali (Mehmet Ali)
    in, 122–23
  Muslim Brotherhood in, 212, 240n193
  Muslim-Christian relations during
    reforms, 117
  occupation of Syria by, 142–43
  population diminution, contemporary
    Christians, 2
    Jews, 1
  private land ownership in, 95
  Shari'a law court reform in, 246
  Yemeni Jewish migration to, 263
  See also Coptic Christians
Elgin Marbles, 196
Elizabeth I (England), 210
Emrence, Cem, 259–60
Engels, Friedrich, 273
England. *See* Great Britain
Eniş Pasha, 269
Europe
  Muslim minority in, 20
  tax exemptions for merchants/consular
    officials in, 88
  See also *individual country*

European Crusades, 54–56
European Enlightenment, 70–71
eyeglasses, 251

famine, 97, 263
famine cannibalism, 263
Faroqhi, Suraiya, 313
Fatimid dynasty, 32
  conquest of Egypt, 54
  dress during, 54
Fattal, Antoine, 34
Fawaz, Leila, 276
Feldman, Walter, 250, 258
festivals, religious, convergence
    concerning, 50
fez, 130, 134–35, 243, 257
financial crisis, under Abdulhamid II, 183
Findley, Carter V., 104–5, 107n27
fitna (public disorder), 152
food customs
  in nineteenth-century Ottoman
      Empire, 119
  convergence among, 50–51
  cookery books, 32, 42, 50–51, 308
  eating utensils, 121
  spread of use of forks, 193, 311
footwear, 176n214, 243
  color-coded meanings of, 311
France
  attacks on French newspaper *Charlie
      Hebdo,* 7–8
  cultural influence on Ottoman
      Empire, 101
  exile of Afghani to, 215
  invasion of Egypt under Napoleon,
      13–15, 96
  military advisors to Ottoman
      Empire, 144
  number of Jews at time of French
      Revolution, 154
  proposed reforms for Anatolian
      Armenians, 271–72
  rising Islamophobia in, 7
  support of Catholic missionaries in
      Aleppo, 97–98
  tax exemptions for merchants, 88
  terrorist attacks in Paris, 2015 and
      2016, 8
  views on Abdulhamid II, 180–81
  See also Alliance Israélite Universelle (AIU)
Francis (Pope; Jorge Mario Bergoglio), 8
Franco-Prussian War, 160
Fraser, Nancy, 254
freedom of the press, in Egypt, 251
Freemasonry, 254–56, 267

French Jesuits, 200, 204
French Revolution, 153–54

Gaza, Christian population
    diminution in, 2
gazinos, 250, 253
Geertz, Clifford, 308–10
gender. *See* marriage; women
Genoa, merchant tax exemptions in, 88
Georgeon, François, 181, 258–59
Gérôme, Jean-Léon, 195–96
ghazi (warrior for the faith), 72–73, 77
ghiyar (laws of differentiation by
    clothing), 46, 54
Gladstone, William, 184–85
Goitein, S.D., 44–45, 47, 52
Gökalp, Ziya, 285
Grabar, Oleg, 53
Great Britain
  annexation of Aden, 191–92, 261
  British-Ottoman trade agreement of
      1838, 131
  and edict of 1856 (Hatt-ı
      Hümayun), 138–40
  invasion and occupation of
      Egypt, 209–10
  philo-Semitism in, 154
  proposed reforms for Anatolian
      Armenians, 271–72
  tax exemptions for merchants from, 88
  views on Abdulhamid II, 180–81
Great War (World War I), 286–87
Greece
  and Balkan Wars, 285–86
  reclassification as European by
      CIA, 10
Greek Catholics (Melkites), 126–27
  and Damascus massacres, 151–52, 266
Greek Orthodox Christians, 98–99
  at government school in Syria, 225
  musicians, 250
  and printing presses, 100
  reaction of Arabic-speaking people to
      Greekness of, 126
  Stavriotae, 219, 220
  and trade, 102
Greeks
  depictions of atrocities by Turkey, on
      chocolate cards, 4–6
  and nationalism, 228, 314–15
  perceptions of rampant breeding in
      Ottoman Empire, 271
Greek War of Independence, 125–28
  Ottoman policies under
      Mahmud II, 126

Greek War of Independence (*cont.*)
 reaction of Greek Orthodox patriarch
  to, 126
 reaction of *Rum* Catholics to, 126–27
green tomatoes *(kavata)*, 103
Grégoire, Abbé Henri, 155
Gregory V (Greek Orthodox
  Patriarch), 126
Grehan, James, 314
Gottreich, Emily, 176n214
guest workers, short-term in Middle
  East, 2
guilds, 93–94, 289n6
gypsies. *See* Roma

Habermas, Jürgen, 254
Habsburg Empire, defeat of
  Ottomans by, 96
Ha-Cohen, Mordechai, 265
hairstyles
 European influence on Jewish
  women, 132
 Pact of Umar on, 41, 46
Hajj Ali (Hi Jolly), 197
Hakim, Faris al-, 208–9
Halil, Patrona, 101–2
Hamdi Bey, Osman, 194–96
Hamid al-Din, Yahya Muhammad,
  262–63, 264–65
Hamidiye regiments, 247–48, 267,
  269, 273
Hanioğlu, M. Şükrü, 207
Haskalah (Jewish Enlightenment), 154–55
Hathaway, Jane, 86–87
Hatt-ı Hümayun. *See* edict of 1856
Hattı Şerif of Gülhane. *See* edict of 1839
Hayatizade Mustafa Fevzi Effendi (Moses,
  son of Raphael Abravanel), 74
headgear
 brimmed hat ban, 257
 fez, 130, 134–35, 243, 257
 hotoz, 133–34
 as illustrative of religion/social status,
  289n6, 313
 reform, 129–35
  acceptance by Christian and Jewish
   elites, 130
  Armenian response to wearing
   kalpak, 131–32
  Jewish women's headgear, 133–34
  Mahmud II on dress as social
   engineering tool, 134–35
  resistance by Muslim tradesmen/
   artisans, 130–31
  significance of *reaya* (Raya)
   and, 131–32

 success as leveling device, 130–31
 turban, replacement by fez, 130
 turbans as social markers, 289n6
Henry VIII (England), 210
Herzl, Theodor, 248, 264
Heyberger, Bernard, 166n20, 249
Hibbat Zion (Lovers of Zion), 264
Hijaz Railway, 212–13, 239n180
Hi Jolly (Hajj Ali), 197
Hindu nationalism, 255
history, meanings of term, 305–6
Hodgson, Marshall, 28–29, 35
homeland *(vatan)*, 255, 256, 285
hotoz (headgear), 133–34
Hourani, Albert, 205–6
human dissection, 135
humanitarianism, 121
Hümayun decree (1856) 136
Hunchaks, 273–74
Hungary, tax collection during Ottoman
  era, 87
Huntington, Samuel T., 6
Husayn, Sharif, 288

Ibn Khaldun, 75, 108n38, 314–15
ibn Killis, Ya'qub, 54
ibn Munabbih, Wahb, 53
ibn Nahmias, David, 99–100
ibn Nahmias, Samuel, 99–100
Ibn Sayyar al-Warraq, 42, 51
Ibrahim Pasha, grand vizier to Sultan
  Ahmet III, 100–1
Ibrahim Pasha, son of Muhammad Ali of
  Egypt, and Egyptian invasion of
  Syria, 142–43, 148
Ifraim son of Salomon Lagniado, 97
İnalcık, Halil, 83
India, Muslim minority in, 20
individualism, emergence of, 98
infidels *(kefere)*, 89
intellectual exchange, and convergence, 50
intercommunal relations
 and conversions, 48
 dhimmis (see dhimmis)
 differing views on, 3
 initial Muslim encounters with
  Christians and Jews, 32–38
  conciliation/magnanimity, 35–37
  problems with historical
   interpretation of, 36–38
  war and violence, 33–35
   Banu Qurayza massacres, 33–35
   problems with historical
    interpretation of, 34–35
 and lines of distinction, 49–50
 and points of convergence, 50–52

Iran
  Jewish population diminution in, 1
  marriage ban between Ottoman women/
    Iranian men, 163
  as never conquered by Ottoman
    Empire, 11, 64
  Qajar dynasty, 153, 161
  See also Safavid Empire (Iran);
    Zoroastrians
Iraq
  Christian population diminution in, 2
  move of Islamic state to Baghdad, 31
  U.S. and allies launch wars in, 7
  war to gain area of present-day, 77
Isak, Tanburo, 249–50
Ishaq (translator), 127
ISIS (Islamic State of Iraq and Syria), 8
Islam
  and apostasy, 139, 141, 209–10
  double meaning of, 28
  expansion of state after death of
    Muhammad, 30
  formative period of, 28, 29–32
  Zaydi Islam, 224, 260–63
  See also Muhammad (Prophet);
    Muslims; Qur'an; Shi'i Islam;
    Sunni Islam
Isma'il (Safavid Shah), 149, 218–19
Israel
  population diminution of
    Christians in, 2
  population increase of Jews in, 1–2
  short-term guest workers in, 2
  Yemeni Jewish migration to, 263
Israeli-Palestinian crisis, 8
Isra'ili, Abu Ya'qub Ishaq ibn Sulayman
  al-, 51
Istanbul, 80–81
Italy
  invasion of Libya, 229–30, 266
  Ottoman-Italian War, 285

Janissaries
  abolition of, 128–29
  complaints against convert, 218
  modern, nineteenth-century Ottoman
    reforms and, 121
  and Patrona Halil Revolt, 102
  recruitment of, 144
  and Sufism, 67
Jerusalem, Yemeni Jewish migration to, 263
Jesuits, 200, 204
Jews
  in Alawite Morocco, 154
  in Algeria, 153
  anti-Semitism, mid-nineteenth-century

  Damascus Affair, 155–58
  Mortara Affair, 155, 158–60
  and Banu Qurayza massacres, 33–35
  historical interpretation of, 37–38
  and Black Death, 56
  and circumcision, 56
  communalism despite socio-economic
    diversity, 47
  and conscription, 145, 281
  conversions to, 53–54
  and Crémieux Decree, 160–62
  differences between Shi'is and, 77–78
  and edict of 1856, 141
  European influence on hairstyles/
    clothing of women, 132
  forced conversions to Islam, 77, 158
  in France
    French Revolution, 154
    post-Revolutionary France, 154–55
  and Haskalah or Enlightenment, 154–55
  individual and communal identities
    among, 17–18
  internal diversity in religious practice
    and doctrines among, 16–17
  middle class as disproportionately
    Jewish, 252
  musicians, 249–50
  Ottoman reforms
    effects on Muslim-Jewish
      interrelations, 117–18
    effects on Yemeni Jews, 260–63
  population diminution, contemporary,
    1–2, 20
  refusal of principle of Muslim
    supremacy by, 247
  at Salonica government school, 225
  Sephardic, 86
  taxation, 97
  See also Alliance Israélite Universelle
    (AIU); clothing; *dhimmis*;
    Dönme; headgear; Pact of Umar;
    synagogues; Yemen
Jirousek, Charlotte, 103, 104
jizya, 44–45, 302
  collection of, 86–88
  diversity in application of, 316
  exemption for Alawites, 222
  exemption for Druze, 222
  exemptions for European merchants/
    consular officials, 88
  fairness of, 87–88
  financial burden of, 44–45
  imposed on Yezidis, 222
  psychological burden of, 44
  Qur'an on, 39
  and Zoroastrians, 39

Joan of Arc, 210
John the Baptist, skull fragment of, 109n59
Jordan, 2, 192–93
Juhasz, Esther, 313

Kadizadelis, 89
Kafadar, Cemal, 73–74
Kafescioğlu, Çiğdem 79
kalpak (headgear), 131–32
Karamanli dynasty (Libya), 191, 265
Karbala, mass movement to Shi'ism
    in, 230
kavata (green tomatoes), 103
kefere (infidels), 89
Kemal, Nemik, 285
Kennedy, Hugh, 47–48
Kern, Karen, 163
kişlak (forced provision of winter shelter/
    fodder), 273
Krstic, Tijana, 76
Kurds
    child mortality among, 200–1
    depictions of atrocities by, on chocolate
        cards, 4–6
    in Hamidiye regiments, 247–48, 267,
        269, 273
    forced provision of winter shelter/fodder
        for, 273
    Kurdish Jews, 312–13
    protection racket against
        Armenians, 273
    See also Armenian massacre

land ownership
    by Anatolian Armenians, 270
    private, in Egypt, 95
    and tax liability, 87
Land Reform Law (1858; Ottoman
    Empire), 192, 270
Lane, Edward W., 306
language
    Arabic as language of imperial
        statecraft, 31
    Pact of Umar on, 42, 316–17
    as social marker, 75–76
Law of Nationality (Ottoman Empire), 163
Layard, Henry, 179
Lebanon
    Christian population diminution in, 2
    Muslim-Christian social tensions in, 150
Lebow, Richard Ned, 319–20
Leopold I (Holy Roman Emperor), 96
Lévy, Sam, 225
Levy-Rubin, Milka, 41
Lewis, Bernard, 38, 69, 253

Libya
    conscription of Jews in, 281
    Italian invasion of, 229–30, 266, 285
    Karamanli dynasty in, 191, 265
    migration to Americas, 197
Lincoln, Abraham, 209
literacy
    acceleration during eighteenth
        century, 95, 96
    and Armenians, 270
    effect of mission schools in Egypt on, 201
    printing press, effect on, 14, 99–100
    and rise of Ottoman middle class, 251
literature, Arabic
    during Abbasid period, 32
    Nahda (Arabic literary revival),
        205–6, 255
little history, significance of, 310–14
London Underground attacks (2005), 7
Louis Philippe (France), 157

Macedonia, 87, 277
madhhabs (legal communities/schools of
    law), 31
Madrid subway attacks (2004), 7
Mahan, Alfred T., 10
Mahmud I (Ottoman sultan), military
    advisor to, 74–75, 107n36, 124
Mahmud II (Ottoman sultan), influence of
    European culture on, 119
Maimonides, Moses, 50
Makdisi, Ussama, 196
Malak Tawus (Peacock Angel), 222
Mamluk dynasty, 55–56
Mamluks (Muslim Turk/elite slaves),
    alcohol consumption by, 42
Marcus, Abraham, 97
Maronites
    conscription of, 142–43
    conversion to Protestantism, 208
    and Druze at Mount Lebanon, 147–51
    as nouveau riche, 148–49
marriage
    asymmetry between Muslim/Christian
        men, 245–46, 316
    ban between Ottoman women/Iranian
        men, 163
    conversions to Islam through
        intermarriage, 48
    endogamy under Abdulhamid II, 220
    Qur'an on Muslim/non-Muslim, 39
    between Sunni and Shi'i Muslims, 163
Marx, Karl, 273
Mary Tudor (Bloody Mary), 210
Masters, Bruce, 99, 100, 127, 249, 254

McMahon-Husayn Correspondence (1915 and 1916), 288
Mecca, 33, 191, 229
Medina, 37–38, 191, 229
  Banu Qurayza massacres at, 33–35
Mehmet II (Ottoman sultan)
  and Christian Armenians, 85
  conquering of Constantinople by, 66, 78–79, 302
  and Greek Patriarch, 83
  and Jews, 84–85
  as most powerful Ottoman sultan, 181
  and Orthodox Christianity, 83–84
  repopulation policies of, 80–81
  veneration of relics by, 79
  See also Ottoman Empire
Mehmet IV (Ottoman sultan), 78
Mehmet Ali. *See* Muhammad Ali of Egypt
Melkites (Greek Catholics), 126–27
  and Damascus massacres, 151–52, 266
messianism, 264, 294n106
Mevlevi Sufi Muslims, 250
Miaphysites (Syria), 36
Middle East
  area associated with term, 10–12
  assumptions about Muslims, Jews, and Christians in
    concept of religion/religious, 18
    cultural intersections, 16
    individual/communal identities, 17–18
    intercommunal/intersectional relations as not static, 17
    internal diversity in religious and doctrines, 16–17
  coining of term, 10
  timeframe of "modern," 12–16
    and European imperialism, 14–15
    and Napoleon effect, 13–15
Midhat Pasha, Ahmed Şefik, 187–88, 190, 191
migration
  to Americas from Anatolia, 197
  to Americas from Egypt, 197
  to Americas from Libya, 197
  to Americas from Mount Lebanon, 197
  conscription as reason for, 281
  to Middle East, economically motivated, 2
  of Muslims to United States, 197
  reform, effect on Yemeni Jews, 263–64, 265
military, Ottoman
  exemption tax for, 146
  Hamidiye regiments, 247–48, 267, 269, 273

life of recruits, 144–45
  reform under edict of 1839, 128
  See also bearing arms and riding mounted animals; conscription; Janissaries
millet system, 66, 81–88, 302
  and Christian Armenians, 85
  continual recognition under edict of 1856, 136
  financial lenders, 86
  and Jews, 84–86
  meaning of "*millet* system," 82
  and Orthodox Christians, 83–84
  overview of, 82
  semantics of, 81–82
  See also jizya
millet wars, 127
Misrie, Rose C., 197
missionaries, Mormon, 199–200. *See also* Catholic missionaries; Protestant missionaries
Montenegro, and Balkan Wars, 285–86
Moravian Pietists, 99
Mormon missionaries, 199–200
Morocco
  Alliance Israélite Universelle in, 159, 160
  enclosure policy *(mellahs)*, 137
  French Christian anti-Semitism in, 161–62
  as never conquered by Ottoman Empire, 11, 64
Mortara, Edgardo, 158
Mortara Affair, 155, 158–60
Moses, son of Raphael Abravanel (Hayatizade Mustafa Fevzi Effendi), 74
moshavot in Palestine, 264
mounted animals, Pact of Umar on, 41, 142
Mount Lebanon, migration to Americas from, 197
Mughal Empire, founding of, 78
Muhajirs (Muslim refugees from the Caucasus and Balkans), 2, 267, 271
Muhammad (Prophet)
  and Banu Qurayza massacres, 33–35
  cartoons lampooning, 7–8
  and conquest of Mecca, 33
  relics of, 80
  revelations of, 28, 29
  See also Islam; Muslims; Qur'an

Muhammad Ali (Mehmet Ali) of Egypt
  and occupation of Syria, 142–43
  and recruitment of slaves for the
    military, 173n129
  resistance against military
    conscription in, 144
  and Syria, 157
Muller-Lancet, Aviva, 311
Muqaddasi, Muhammad ibn Ahmad
    Shams al-Din al-, 50
Muqtadir (Abbasid caliph), 46
Murad III (Ottoman sultan), Jewish
    mother of, 68
Murad IV (Ottoman sultan), 255
Musharraf, Pervez, on Banu Qurayza
    massacres, 34
music, convergence concerning, 51–52
Muslim Brotherhood, 212, 240n193
Muslims
  and circumcision, 56
  diversity among, 317–18
  individual and communal identities
    among, 17–18
  internal diversity in religious and
    doctrines among, 16–17
  Kadizadelis, 89
  population in non-Muslim countries,
    contemporary, 20
  sectarian disputes after death of
    Muhammad, 30
  See also Abbasid dynasty; Islam;
    Muhammad (Prophet); Qur'an;
    Umayyad dynasty
Mutawakkil, al- (Abbasid caliph), 46
Müteferrika, Ibrahim, 99, 100
Muwaylihi, Ibrahim al-, 181, 189–90,
    193, 283

Nahda (Arabic literary revival), 205–6, 255
Najaf, mass movement to Shi'ism, 230
Najara, Isaac, 249
Napoleon effect, 13–15
naqus (semantron), 118
Nasi, Gracia, 86
Nasi, Joseph, 86
nationalism
  Albanian, 284
  Arab (nahda), 251, 282–83
  Bulgarian, 206
  Christian, in nineteenth century, 122
  and Christian missionaries, 204–12
  Greek, 228, 314–15
  Hindu, 255
  and pan-Islamic politics, 228
  print culture, role in rise of, 251

Romantic, 119
Serbian, 228
Netherlands, and merchant tax
    exemptions, 88
Nizam-ı Jedid (New Order), 124
North America, Muslim minority in, 20

Operation Magic Carpet, Yemen
    (1949-1950), 265
Orphans Decree, 261, 262, 265
Ortaylı, Ilber, 221
Osman, Ertugrul, 288
Osman Hamdi Bey (see Hamdi Bey,
    Osman)
Osman, family of (the Ottomans), 72
Otranto martyrs, 8, 67
Ottoman Empire
  absorption of converts to Islam within
    ruling class, 73
  agricultural exchanges with Europe, 70
  allegiance to, maintaining, 104
  as Asiatic empire, 69
  biological assimilation of
    Anatolians, 73–74
  Capitulations in, 95
  Christian influences on Islamic practices
    in, 79–80
  class distinctions among Turks, 75–76
  clothing restrictions during (see clothing)
  conversions in (see conversion)
  cultural assimilation of
    Anatolians, 74–75
  culture of consumption in, 102
  decline of, 69–70
  dhimmi society in (see dhimmis)
  distinctions from earlier
    dynasties, 66–69
  diversity in, 64, 80–81
  as European empire, 66–67
  expansion of, 302
  harmony in, differing views on, 65
  historical precedents followed by, 65–66
  and individuality, 70–71
  Islam in (see Islam)
  Istanbul, influence on, 80
  longevity of, 64
  military/diplomatic watershed events, 96
  military in (see conscription; military)
  millet system in (see millet system)
  missionaries in (see missionaries)
  as modern empire, 69–71, 302–3
  and Otranto martyrs, 8, 67
  overview of, 302–5
  population by religious persuasion,
    1876, 20

precursors to, 72–73
public piety displays in, 78
relic veneration in, 79–80
religion, limits to, 314–18
repopulation policies in, 80–81, 271
similarities to earlier dynasties, 65–66
social change, acceleration in eighteenth
    century, 95–102
as Sunni Muslim empire, 76
taxation (*see* taxation)
territories comprising, 11, 64
tomato consumption, as traditional,
    103
translators (dragomans), 96–97
Tulip Period, 101–2
Turkish language, social distinctions
    and, 75–76
urban revolts in, 101–2
See also Abdulhamid II; Ottoman
    Empire, reforms in
Ottoman Empire, reforms in, 303
Alliance Israélite Universelle
    established, 158–60
bearing arms and riding mounted
    animals, 142–46 (*see also*
    conscription)
clothing reform (*see* clothing)
Damascus Affair, 155–58
edict of 1839 (*see* edict of 1839)
edict of 1856 (*see* edict of 1856)
effects on equality, 117
and foreign intervention, 163
headgear reform (*see* headgear)
modern, nineteenth century, 118–25
    archaeology in, 119
    Christian nationalism in, 122
    clothing changes, 121
    cultural developments in, 118–19
    Eastern Question during, 123
    eating utensils, 121, 193, 311
    foodways, 119
    humanitarianism, 121
    influence of Selim III on, 123–25
    Janissary corps, 121
    Muhammad Ali (Mehmet Ali) in
        Egypt, 122–23
    outmigration in, 119–20
    regional politics in, 118
    technology in, 119–20
        telegraph, 120
        transport systems, 119–20
    territorial loss in, 118, 121–22
    tourism in, 119
    trade in, 120–21
Mortara Affair, 155, 158–60

and Muslim-Christian interrelations, 117
and Muslim-Jewish
    interrelations, 117–18
religion, how it mattered during this
    time, 162–65
    in attitudes toward non-Muslims in
        commerce, 162–63
    in cases of law, 163
    in clothing reform, 163–64
    in headgear reform, 163
    in military service, 164
sectarianism, rise of new, 146–52
    Aleppo riot of 1850, 141, 146–47
    Damascus massacres, 141, 151–52
    Druze at Mount Lebanon, 147–51
Young Ottomans on Tazimat reforms, 256
See also Abdulhamid II; Ottoman Empire
Ottoman Enlightenment, 100
Ottoman-Italian War, 285

Pact of Umar, 40–42
diversity in application of, 316–17
on zunnar belt, 41, 46, 317
Palaggi, Hayyim, 133
Palestine, 2, 263–64
pan-Islam, and Abdulhamid II, 180
Parker, Geoffrey, 319–20
passports, 135, 163
Patrona Halil Revolt, 102
Peacock Angel (Malak Tawus), 222
Père Thomas. *See* Damascus Affair
Peter the Great (Russia), 123
Petros the Peloponnesian, 250
photography
    and Abdulhamid II, 182, 193–94,
        243, 257
    as historical source, 134, 164, 203,
        243, 254
    uses of, 10
Pinsker, Leo, 264
Pius IX (Pope), 158, 267
plague, quarantine during, 122–23
poetry, *hilye,* 79
    Ottoman court vs. folk, 75
    wine poetry, 42
population
    Christians in contemporary Middle
        East, 2, 20
    Jews in contemporary Middle East,
        1–2, 20
    Muslims in non-Muslim countries,
        contemporary, 20
    Ottoman Empire, by religious
        persuasion, 1876, 20
    repopulation policies, 80–81, 271

pork, pig-raising for, 316
Porter, Roy, 307
postal system, 135
power
    authoritative, 52
    diffused/popular, 52
Presbyterian Board of Foreign
        Missions, 201
Presbyterians, 200, 209–10
    missionary schools of, 201
printing press, 14, 99–100
Propaganda Fide, 14, 100
Protestantism
    Alevis' desire for closer connection
        with, 225
    conversion of Armenians to, 210–11
    conversion of Maronites to, 208
    Syrian Protestant College, 200,
        203–4, 256
    See also Protestant missionaries
Protestant missionaries
    and eighteenth-century social change, 99
    aids to conversions, 205, 207–12
        foreign advocates, 208–9
    and Bible translations, 205–8
        Bulgarian Bible, 206
        languages used by, 206–7
        Van Dyck Bible, 204–6
    and dissimulation or secret Christian
        belief, 224–25
    and edict of 1856, 138
    at Mount Lebanon, 150
    schools of, 201, 293n65
    women missionaries as fashion
        models, 202–3
public bathhouses, distinguishing
        Muslims/*dhimmis* at, 56,
        90–91, 310
Public Debt Administration (PDA),
        183, 228
public disorder (*fitna*), 152
public health
    under Abdulhamid II, 200–1
    and Armenians, 270
    cholera, 192, 270
    and quarantine, 122–23, 192
    trachoma, 270
    typhus, 184
public piety, 78
publishing industry, self-censoring by,
        23n33

Qajar dynasty (Iran), 153, 161
quarantine, 122–23, 192
Quataert, Donald, 130–31

Qur'an, 29
    on alcohol consumption, 217
    on intermarriage with non-Muslims, 39
    on *jizya,* 39

Ramadan, 217, 219
Rashidun (rightly-guided ones, the early
        caliphs), 30
Ratti-Menton, Comte de, 156, 157
reaya (Raya; flock), 131–32
reforms. *See* Ottoman Empire, reforms in
Refugee Code (Ottoman Empire), 192
refugee crisis, under Abdulhamid II,
        183–84, 185
Reis, Hizir, 69
relic veneration, 79–80
religion
    as basis of group cohesion, 314–15
    as creed and devotional system, 314
    differences in concept of, 18
    diversity in practice and
        interpretation, 316–17
    as legal status, 314–15
    limits to, as explanatory
        framework, 315–18
religious, differences in concept of, 18
religious endowments (*waqfs*), 82
remittances, 270
Renan, Ernest, 215
Reşid Paşa, 133–34
respect toward Muslims, Pact of
        Umar on, 41
Reynolds, Michael, 286
Ricoeur, Paul, 3
Rida, Rashid, 215
Robert College (Istanbul), 256
Robinson, Chase, 41–42
Rodrigue, Aron, 278
Roma, collection of *jizya* from
        Muslim, 87
Roman Catholics. *See* Catholics
Romantic nationalism, 119
Rose Chamber Edict. *See* edict of 1839
Rum/rumi, 126–27, 284
Rushdie, Salman, 3, 21, 318–19
Russell, Alexander, 131
Russia
    crisis with Chechnya, 8
    defeat of Ottoman Empire by, 96
    Muslim refugees from, 185
    proposed reforms for Anatolian
        Armenians, 271–72
Russian Orthodox Church, 96
Russo-Turkish War (1877–78),
        184–85, 247

Sadat, Anwar, on Banu Qurayza
        massacres, 34
Safavid Empire (Iran), 76–78
    differences between Shi'is/non-Muslims
        in, 77–78
    forced conversions in, 77
    founder of, 76–77
    Shi'i Islam (Imami/Twelver
        variety) in, 76
Said, Edward, 196
Said Pasha, Ottoman viceroy of
        Egypt, 208–9
salafism, 215
Salt, Jeremy, 276
Samanids (Iran), 31
Santa Maria, Elia Giacinto di, 220–21
Sanusiya brotherhood, 229–30
Sa'ud, Muhammad ibn, 229
Saudi Arabia, short-term guest
        workers in, 2
Scramble for Africa, 186
sectarianism
    Aleppo riot of 1850, 146–47
    Damascus massacres, 151–52
    disputes after death of Muhammad, 30
    Druze at Mount Lebanon, 147–51
        and assertion of external state
            power, 147–48
        demise of feudal order and rise of new
            rich, 148–49
        and Maronite Christians, 148–49
        and Maronite-Druze massacres, 150
        and sectarianism, 149
    policy under Abdulhamid II, 222,
        241n214
    rise of new, 146–52
self-censoring by book publishers,
        23n33
Selim I (Ottoman sultan), 80
Selim II (Ottoman sultan), Christian
        mother of, 68
Selim III (Ottoman sultan), 123–25,
        250
semantron (naqus), 118
Sephardic Jews, 86
September 11, 2001, terrorist
        attacks, 7, 320
Serbia
    and Balkan Wars, 285–86
    and nationalism, 228
    and Treaty of Bucharest, 125
Serbian Orthodox Church, 99
Sevi, Sabbatai, 219, 264, 294n105
Shafi'i, Abu 'Abd Allah Muhammad ibn
        Idris al-, 49

Shah Isma'il, 149, 218–19
Shah Tahmasp (Safavid shah), 77
Shari'a law courts
    reform in Egypt, 246
    women litigants during Ottoman
        Empire, 94–95
Shaw, Stanford A., 85, 107n27, 124
Sherif Pasha, governor of Syria and
        appointee of Muhammad Ali of
        Egypt, 156–57
Shidyaq, As'ad al-, 208
Shi'i Islam, 76–80, 81
    Imami/Twelver, 76, 149
    mass shift toward under Abdulhamid
        II, 230
Shi'i Muslims
    Abbasid control of Egypt removed
        by, 31–32
    difference from Sunni Muslims, 30
    difference from Zoroastrians,
        77–78
    marriage with Sunni Muslims, 163
    splintering into branches/sects, 31
    and taqiyya (dissimulation),
        77, 216
    Wahhabis' attitude toward, 229
    Zaydis, 224, 260–63
shrines, sharing of, 150
Simon, Reeva S., 265
slave concubinage, and involuntary
        conversion, 67–68
Slaveykov, Petko, 206
smells, and culture
    cooking oil smells, 310
    as marker of identity, 306–10
    stereotypes about, 308
Smith, Eli, 205, 207–8
Sontag, Susan, 6
Sovo, Raphael Asher, 133
Spanish Reconquista, 54, 65
Spivak, Gayatri C., 311
Stavriotae, 219, 220
Stillman, Norman, 41
Stillman, Yedida K., 46
Stock, Eugene, 140
Stora, Benjamin, 161
Stretcher-Bearers' Decree, 262
Suez Canal, 191, 261
Sufism
    in Anatolia and Greater Syria, 220
    Bektashi order, 218
    and Janissaries, 67
    Mevlevi order, 218
    and Turks, 75
    Wahhabis attitude toward, 229

Suleyman the Magnificent (Ottoman
    sultan), 64
  dress codes under, 89–90
  as most powerful sultan, 181
  and siege of Venice, 83
Sunni Islam, 76
  consolidation under Abbasid
    dynasty, 31
  efforts to convert Alawites, 224
  forced conversion of Yezidis to, 223
Sunni Muslims
  difference from Shi-i Muslims, 30
  extremist groups, 6
  marriage with Shi'i Muslims, 163
Sykes-Picot Agreement, 288
synagogues
  edict of 1856 on, 136–37
  monumental, 118
  Pact of Umar on, 41, 136
  Umayyad caliph forbids construction of
    new, 49
Syria
  and Aleppo riot of 1850, 141, 146–47
  Catholic missionaries in, 97–98
  Christian population diminution
    in, 2
  clothing restrictions
    during Mamluk dynasty, 54
    during Ottoman era, 91–92
  convergence to ensure collective
    security, 248–49
  Damascus
    massacres in, 151–52, 266–67
    riot of 1860, 141, 151–52
  shift of Muslim community from
    Arabia to, 30
  Damascus Affair, 155–58
  Egyptian occupation of, 142–43
  languages in, 42
  Miaphysites in, 36
  Muslim-Christian interrelations, 117
  Sufism in, 220
  taxes in Aleppo under Ottoman
    Empire, 97
Syrian Civil War (post-2011), 8
Syrian Protestant College, 200, 203–4,
    256

Tabari, Abu Ja'far Muhammad ibn Jarir
    al-, 48
Tahmasp (Safavid shah), 77
taifes, 82
Tanzimat reforms. See edict of 1839; edict
    of 1856
taqiyya (dissimulation), 77, 216, 220
Tatars, Muslim, 183–84

taxation
  eighteenth century, 97
  based on land ownership, 87
  devşirme (on young Christian
    men), 67
  on dhimmis merchants, 43–44
  exemptions for merchants, 88
  reforms and, 97
  See also jizya
technology, in nineteenth-century
    Ottoman Empire, 119–20, 199
Tedro, Philip, 198
telegraph, 120, 199
terrorist attacks
  Bali nightclub, 2002, 7
  Brussels, 2015 and 2016 , 8
  London Underground, 2005, 7
  Madrid subway, 2004, 7
  Paris, 2015 and 2016, 8
  Tunisia, synagogue, 2002, 7
  United States, September 11,
    2001, 7, 320
Tertullian, 38
Tetlock, Philip E., 319–20
textile industry, 70
thick description, 309–10
Thompson, Anna Y., 216
Tibawi, Abdul Latif, 209
tombstones, as illustrative of religion/social
    status, 130, 313
tourism, nineteenth century, 119
trade
  in nineteenth-century Ottoman
    Empire, 120–21
  British-Ottoman trade agreement of
    1838, 131
translation bureau, 32, 127–28
translators (dragomans), 96–97
Treaty of Balta Liman (1838), 131
Treaty of Berlin (1878), 185
Treaty of Bucharest (1812), 125
Treaty of Karlowitz (1699), 96
Treaty of Kujuk Kaynarca (1774), 96,
    118, 213
Treaty of San Stefano (1878), 185
triumphalist architecture, 118, 166n20
Tunisia
  disappearance of Christians in, 38
  synagogue attack in (2002), 7
turbans
  replacement by fez, 130
  as social markers, 130, 289n6
Turkey
  beginnings of usage of term, 73
  depictions of atrocities by, on chocolate
    cards, 4–6

population diminution, contemporary
Christians, 2
Jews, 1
reclassification as European by CIA, 10
Turkic, meaning of term, 72
Turner, Victor, 313
Turtushi, Abu Bakr Muhammad al-, 40
Twain, Mark, 129–30, 193
Tyndale, William, 210
typhus, 184

'Umar ibn 'Abd al-'Aziz (Umayyad
caliph), 41, 49
'Umar ibn al-Khattab (Rashidun
caliph), 41, 77
Umayyad dynasty
alcohol consumption during, 42
conversions to Islam during, 49
history of, 30–31
umma (Muslim collective), 29
United Arab Emirates, short-term guest
workers in, 2
United States
diplomatic relations with Abdulhamid
II, 196–97
intervention in Ottoman Empire,
163
migration of Muslims to, 197
Muslim minority in, 20
and terrorist attacks of September 11,
2001, 7
and 9/11 Commission Report, 320
Université de Saint-Joseph, 200
Urban II (Pope), 6, 55
'Uthman (Rashidun caliph), 77

Vámbéry, Ármin, 285
Van Dyck, Cornelius, 204–5
Van Dyck Bible, 204–6
van Ginkel, Jan J., 36
Varjabedian, Nerses, 186
vatan (homeland), 255, 256, 285
Venetians, and merchants tax
exemptions, 88
Victoria (Great Britain), 193

Wahhab, Muhammad ibn 'Abd al-,
229
Wahhabism, 228–30
waqfs (religious endowments), 82
Watenpaugh, Keith D., 252–53
Watson, Andrew, 209–10, 216
West Bank, Christian population
diminution in, 2
Western Europe, rising Islamophobia
in, 7–8

Whirling Dervishes, 250
White, Charles, 131–32
White Sheep Turks, 77
Winter, Stefan, 78
women
and education, 159
European influence on hairstyles and
clothing of, 132
French Catholic missions, effect on
behaviors/expectations of, 98
as litigants in Islamic (Shari'a) law
courts, 94–95
as middle class readers/writers in
fin-de-siècle Ottoman
Empire, 251–52
missionaries, effects on, 200, 202–3
rape/abductions during Armenian
massacre, 268
See also marriage
World War I (Great War), 286–87, 304

Yahya (translator), 127
Ya'qub, Mu'allim Hanna, 142
Yaziji, Ibrahim al-, 283
Yaziji, Nasif al-, 205–6
Yellin, Shlomo, 277–78
Yemen
conquest of, under Abdulaziz, 261
exception to Jews bearing arms/riding
animals in, 142
Great Britain in, 191–92
Muslim-Jewish relations in, 259
Ottoman reforms, effects on Jews
in, 260–63
attacks on Jews in Sana'a by
children, 262
British annexation of Aden, 261
Dung-Gatherers Decree, 261
emigration, 263–64, 265
enforcement of jizya, 262, 265
living conditions, 263
Orphans Decree, 261, 262, 265
status as dhimmis, 260, 264–65
work on the Sabbath and
holidays, 262
Zaydis in, 224, 260–63
Yezidis, 18, 220, 222, 223, 227
Young Ottomans, 255–56
Young Turks, 244
and Adana Massacre, 278–79
conscription under, 279–81
feelings of nondominance among Arabs
under, 281–83
initial enthusiasm for, 277–78
as name of leaders of 1908 rebellion
concerning Macedonia, 277

Young Turks (*cont.*)
  secret organization of young
      officers, 276–77, 280–81,
      286
  and wars leading to demise of Ottoman
      Empire, 285–87
Yugoslav Wars (1991–c. 2001), 6

Zaydan, Jurji, 282
Zaydi Islam, 224, 260–63
Zionism, 15, 182, 230–31, 248, 263–64
Zoroastrians, 39, 46, 77–78, 220
Zubaida, Sami, 306–7
zunnar belt, 41, 46, 317
Zürcher, Erik J., 145, 279

For EU product safety concerns, contact us at Calle de José Abascal, 56–1°,
28003 Madrid, Spain or eugpsr@cambridge.org.

www.ingramcontent.com/pod-product-compliance
Ingram Content Group UK Ltd.
Pitfield, Milton Keynes, MK11 3LW, UK
UKHW010248140625
459647UK00013BA/1736